The Works of John Flavel

VOLUME II

The Works of
JOHN FLAVEL

VOLUME II

The Banner of Truth Trust

THE BANNER OF TRUTH TRUST

Head Office
3 Murrayfield Road
Edinburgh, EH12 6EL
UK

North America Office
PO Box 621
Carlisle, PA 17013
USA

banneroftruth.org

First published by W. Baynes and Son, 1820
Reprinted by The Banner of Truth Trust, 1968
Reprinted 1982, 1997, 2015, 2018, 2021

*

ISBN
This volume, print: 978 0 85151 719 3
6-volume set: 978 0 85151 060 6

*

Printed in the USA by
Versa Press Inc.,
East Peoria, IL

Contents

————— ✦⟨✕⟩✦ —————

VI: THE PRESENT AND FUTURE STATE OF
CHRISTLESS SOULS

METHOD OF GRACE

IN THE

GOSPEL-REDEMPTION.

———◦◦◦◦◦———

THE EPISTLE DEDICATORY.

To the Worshipful JOHN UPTON, *of* Lupton, *Esq. and the most accomplished and virtuous* Lady, *his dear* Consort, *the Author wishes Grace, Mercy, and Peace.*

HONOURED AND WORTHY FRIENDS,

IT was a comfortable expression, which Ambrose used in his funeral oration, at the death of Theodosius; " * That though " he were gone, yet he was not wholly gone; for he had left " Honorius, with others of his children, behind him, in whom " Theodosius still lived." Your renowned and worthy *ancestors* are gone, yet (blessed be God) they are not wholly gone; whilst the prudence, piety, and publicness of their spirits, still live and flourish in you, the top branch of a renowned and religious family. It is a great truth, which Philo Judæus recommends to the observation of all posterity, " † That it is not a natural descent " from the most honourable and illustrious progenitors, nor the

---

* *Theodosius tantus imperator recessit a nobis, sed non totus recessit ; reliquit enim nobis liberos suos, in quibus debemus eum agnoscere.* Ambros. in obit. Theod.

* Τοις δε υμνεσι την ευγενειαν ως μεγιστον αγαθον και μεγαλων αγαθων αιτιον, ἃ μετριως επιτιμητεον, ει πρωτον μεν οιονται τας εκ παλαιοπλατων και παλαιανδοξων ευγενεις, μητε των προγονων αφ ων αυχεσι γενεσθαι.—Βαληθεις γαρ ο Θεος δια ημεροτητα και φιλανθρωπιαν και παρ ημιν τεθ ιδρυσασθαι, νεων αξιοπρεπεςερον επι γης εχ ευρε λογισμα κρειτίω ο γαρ νες αγαλμαλοφορει το αγαθον, καν απιςωσι τινες των μη γευσαμενων σοφιας η χειλεσων ακροις. *Philo Judæus* περι Ευγενιας, a book fit for the hands of all gentlemen, translated by *Laurentius Humphredus* in his excellent tract *de Nobilitate.*

" greatest affluence of riches and pleasures that makes a man ei-
" ther honourable or happy; but the habitation of God in his
" soul, as in his temple, tho' (saith he) those that never tasted re-
" ligion, nor have seen its glory, will not credit this assertion."
" The soul which is filled with God, (saith * Plotinus) and brings
" forth the beautiful fruits of righteousness, this is the truly noble
" soul:" Our new birth makes us more honourable than our natural birth, let our birth-right dignities be what they will. The
children of nobles are, by nature, the children of wrath, even
as others: *Omnis Sanguis concolor*, all blood is of one colour : it is
all tainted in Adam, and mingled together in his posterity. " There
" is no king, saith † Seneca, which rose not from a servant; there
" is no *servant* which rose not from a *king :* these things have been
" blended, and jumbled to and fro in a long tissue of changes,
" ever directed by an all-wise Providence."

But though the privileges of natural birth signify nothing as to
eternal salvation, yet in civil and political respects and considerations, those that by birth, education, or estate, possess an higher
station in the world, differ from the vulgar, as stars of greater mag-
nitude and lusture: their interest and influence are great in these
things, and the welfare of kingdoms ‡ greatly depends upon
them.

It is therefore a great design of the enemy of mankind, to corrupt persons of eminent rank and quality both in religion and morality; and by their influence and example, to infect and poison
the whole body politic; and his success herein deserves to be
greatly lamented and bewailed. Persons of eminency are more
especially § obliged to shun base and sordid actions. Hierom professed ‖ he saw nothing desirable in *nobility*, except this, that such
persons are bound by a certain kind of necessity, not to degenerate
from the probity, or stain the glory of their *ancestors*. But alas!

---

* Ψυχη πληρωθεισα θεϗ γεννα το καλλος, γεννα την δικαιοσυνην. *Plotinus.*

† *Neminem regem non ex servis esse oriundum, neminem servum non ex regibus : omnia ista longa varietas miscuit, et sursum deorsum fortuna versavit.* Sen. Ep. 44.

‡ Who manages the reins of government, who is present at, and presides over, both private and public matters, but persons of eminent rank and quality ? Who moderates in the senate, presides in courts, commands at home and abroad ? Chief men and nobles surely. Who command and arrange, act and counteract, manage and canvass all affairs, who make laws and rescind them, who govern the state in the time of peace, and command the forces in time of war, but great men and no-bles ? No wonder that the management of public affairs be committed to him, who both by personal merit and renown of his ancestors hath recommended himself to the good report end esteem of mankind. *Laurent. Humphred on Nobility.*

§ *In maxima fortuna, minima est licentia.* Exalted stations ought to hedge up the way of those who fill them, from every vicious practice. Salust.

‖ *Nihil aliud video in nobilitate appetendum, nisi quod nobiles quadam necessitate con-stringuntur, ne ab anquorum probitate degenerent.* Hieron.

how many in our times have not only exposed Christianity to contempt, but obscured * the glory of their own families, and the
kingdom in which they had their birth and breeding; so that if
you will take right marks of your way to heaven you will have
little direction from those of your own rank. As † mariners take
their direction at sea, by looking up to the heavens, so must you.
In this general corruption it is very hard to escape infection;
many (as Salvian complained) ‡ are compelled to be *evil*, lest they
should be accounted *vile*, and incur the offence of God, to avoid
the slights and censures of men. Although there is no more reason why they should be offended at the rational and religious pleasures you and other pious gentlemen take in the ways of godliness,
than there is, that you should envy the sinful pleasures they take
in the ways of wickedness. It was an excellent apology that Tertullian made for the Christians of his time, against the Gentiles.
" Wherein (saith § he) do we offend you, if we believe there are
" other pleasures? if we will not partake with you in your de-
" lights, it is only for our own injury : we reject your pleasures,
" and you are not delighted with ours."
But by how much the infection spreads and prevails among those
of your order, by so much the more we have reason to value you,
and all those that remain sound and untainted, both in religion and
morality, as persons worthy of singular respect and honour : and
blessed be God there is yet a number of such left.
Sir, It was a special happiness, which Chrysostom earnestly recommended to persons of quality, that they would so order their
conversations, that their parents might rather glory in them, than
they in their parents; " Otherwise (saith ‖ he) it is better to rise

---

* God grant that the end proposed may be obtained, that the ancient and truly
venerable nobility may at length return, who by the honour of prudence and knowledge, and lustre of renowned deeds, may obscure the same progenitors, and quite
remove and wipe off the stain brought on its august name. *Humph. on Nobility.*

† In the same manner, you ought to seek the path of life, as the mariners at
sea seek the designed course of their ships, who, if they observe not some luminary
in the heavens, steer but an uncertain course, but whosoever is resolved to keep in
the right path of life, must not look down to the earth but to heaven ; and (to speak
more plainly) he ought not to follow men but God; therefore if thou wouldest always keep thine eyes fixed on heaven, and observe the sun whence he ariseth, and
take him as thy guide, thy feet of themselves will keep straight in the way. *Lactant.*
lib. 1. *c.* 8.

‡ *Mali esse coguntur, ne viles habeantur.* Salv. de Gubernat.

§ *Quo vos offendimus si alias præsumimus voluptates ? si oblectari nolumus, nostra inju-
ria est ; reprobamus quæ placent vobis, nec vos nostra delectant.* Tertul. Apolog. adv. Gent.

‖ *Melius est de contemptibili fieri clarum, quam de claro genere contemptibilem esse,*
Chrysost. in Mat. 4. *Nec fieri potest quin hunc comitetur ignobilitas etiamsi vel avis, vel
proavis natus sit vita inculpatis, qui ab eorum studiis alienus est, seque longissime tum dictis,
tum factis a nobilitate disjungit.* Nor can aught but ignominy pursue the wretch, who,
though nobly descended, bespatters the escutcheon of his worthy ancestors by his unworthy conduct.

" to honour from a contemptible parent, than to be contemptible
" from an honourable parent;" but blessed be God, you and your
worthy ancestors reflect honour upon each other.

Had God suffered you to degenerate, as many do, it would have
been but a poor consolation to have said, My *progenitors* were men
of honour, the love and delight of their country. This, as * one
excellently expresseth it, would be the same thing, as if one that
is blind himself, should boast what a sharp and piercing sight his
father had; or one that is lame himself, should glory in those
feats of activity his grandfather performed; but God (to whose
bounty therefore you are doubly obliged) hath made you the inhe-
ritor of their virtues, as well as of their lands, and therein fulfilled
many thousand prayers, which have been poured out to God upon
your account. But I must forbear, lest I provoke others to envy,
and draw upon myself the suspicion of flattery. What hath
been already said may serve for a sufficient reason of this dedication. I know the † agreeableness of such discourses to the pious
dispositions of your souls, is of itself sufficient to make it welcome
to you. It is a treatise of Christ, yea, of the *Method of Grace*, in
the application of Christ; than which no subject can be more necessary to study, or sweet to experience. ‡ All goodness is attractive, how powerfully attractive then must Jesus Christ be, who is
the ocean of all goodness, from whom all streams of goodness are
derived, and into whom they all empty themselves? § If Pindarus
could say of the lovely Theoxenus, that whosoever saw that august
and comely face of his, and was not surprised with amazement,
and enflamed with love, must have an heart of adamant or brass;
what then shall we resemble that man's heart unto, that hath
no ferverous affections kindled in it by the incomparable beauty of
Christ! a beauty, which excels in lustre and brightness, that visible
light which so dazzles our eyes ‖, as that light doth darkness itself;
as Plato speaks of the divine light Christ is υπερϐαλλοντως καλος, an

---

* What profit is the sharp-sightedness of ancestors to their offspring, deprived of
sight? What help can it give the man that is dumb, for attaining the power of
speech, that his parents and grandfathers had the voice of orators? In like manner,
just parents cannot help their unjust children; nor the temperate those who are
luxurious: nor at any rate, can the good communicate goodness to the bad. *Philo.*
περι Ευγενειας.

† When the mind of the hearer is good and gracious, it easily assents to speeches of
truth. *Chrysost. Hom.* 26. *in Mat.*

‡ Ουδεν αλλο εςιν ἃ ερωσιν ανθρωποι η τἃ αγαθἃ ανελκει παντα κ̀ ανασπα
ταις οικειαις ελαμψεσιν ως ηλιος. *Plato.*

§ Ακτινας προσωπἃ μαρμαρτιζἃσας δοακεις ος με ποθω κυμαινιται, ως
αδαμαντος.

‖ Το νοητον φως, το αρχετυπον πανλων τοσἃτω τἃ ορατἃ λαμπρωτερον τι κ̀
αυτοειδεςερον ωσπι ρηλιος σκοτἃς.

inexpressible beauty, and all other beauties are but εικον, και σκια an image, nay, a shadow of his beauty. How was holy Ignatius ravished with desires after Christ, when * he cried out, O how I long to be thrown into the jaws of those lions, which I hear roaring for me! and if they will not dispatch me the sooner, και προσ'ιασομαι, I will enforce them to it by violence, that I may enjoy the sight of my blessed Jesus. O my heart, (saith † another) how is it thou art not drawn up by the very root, by thy desires after Christ? The necessity, and the trial of our union with, and interest in, this lovely LORD JESUS, is the main subject of this discourse. Without the personal application of Christ by faith, our hopes of heaven are but deluding dreams, Heb. iii. 11. " I " sware in my wrath, ει εισελευσονται, if they shall enter into my " rest:" What then? Nay, there is all: but it is a dreadful *Aposiopesis* (as one calls it) such a pause as may justly shake every vein of the unbeliever's heart: *If they shall enter:* as if he had said, If ever they come into my glory, then say, I am no God, for I have sworn the contrary.

I will not be tiresome, but conclude all in a few requests to you and to God for you both. That which I request of you is,

(1.) That you will search and try your own hearts by these truths, especially now, when so great trials are like to be made of every man's root and foundation in religion. Account that your first work, which Bellarmine calls " the first error of Protestants," to make sure your interest in Christ; ‡ every thing is as its foundation is: a true *diamond* will endure the smartest stroke of the hammer, but a false one will fly.

(2.) That you be humble under all that dignity and honour, which God hath put upon you; be ye clothed with humility. It was the glory of the primitive Christians, that they § did not speak but live great things: humility will be the lustre of your other excellencies: estates and honours are but appendants and fine trappings, which add not any real worth, yet ‖ how are some vain

---

* Ο εμος ερως εςαυρωται κ, εκ εςιν εν εμοι το πυρ το φιλουλον, αλλ υδωρ αλλομενον, &c. ωναιμην των Θηριων, ινα τε Ιησε Χριςε επιτυχω. *Ignatii Epist.*

† *O cor meum quomodo non te evellis post tantum decorem?* Nieremberg. *Vivere renuo, ut Christo vivam.*

‡ *Primus Hæreticorum error est, posse fideles eam notitiam habere de sua gratia, ut certa fide statuant sibi remissa esse peccata.* The principal heresy of Protestants is, that saints may attain to a certain assurance of their gracious and pardoned estate before God. *Bellarm. de Just. lib. 3. cap. 3.*

§ *Non eloquimur magna, sed vivimus.* Tertul. Apolog.

‖ They report that Bucephalus, without his furniture, would suffer a groom on his back, but when dressed with royal trappings and studded bridles, would suffer none to mount him but the king himself; so it is truly the case with these upstart nobles among us, &c.

minds puffed up with these things! But ye have not so learned Christ.

(3.) That you steadily persevere in those good ways of God, in which you have walked, and beware of heart, or life-apostasy. You expect happiness whilst God is in heaven, and God expects holiness from you whilst you are on earth. It was an excellent truth which Tossanus * recommended to his posterity in his last will and testament, from his own experience : " I beseech you, " (saith he) my dear children and kindred, that you never be " ashamed of the truths of the gospel, either by reason of scan- " dals in the church, or persecutions upon it : truth may labour " for a time, but cannot be conquered; and I have often found " God to be wonderfully present with them that walk before him " in truth, though for a time they may be oppressed with troubles " and calumnies."

(4.) Lastly, that you keep a strict and constant watch over your own hearts, lest they be ensnared by the tempting, charming, and dangerous snares attending a full and easy condition in the world. There are temptations suited to all conditions. Those that are poor and low in estate and reputation, are tempted to cozen, cheat, lie, and flattter, and all to get up to the mount of riches and ho- nours; but those that were born upon that mount, though they be more free from those temptations, yet lie exposed to others no less dangerous, and therefore we find, " Not many mighty, not many " noble are called," 1 Cor. i. 26. Many great and stately ships, which spread much sail, and draw much water, perish in the storms, when small barks creep along the shore under the wind, and get safe into their port. Never aim at an higher station in this world than that you are in † : Some have wished in their dying hour, they had been lower, but no wise man ever wished himself at the top of honour, at the brink of eternity.

I will conclude all with this hearty wish for you, that as God hath set you in a capacity of much service for him in your generation, so your hearts may be enlarged for God accordingly, and that you may be very instrumental for his glory on earth, and may go safe, but late to heaven. That the blessings of heaven may be multiplied

---

* *Obtestor etiam vos liberos, et generos carrisimos ne illius veritatis evangelicæ unquam vos pudeat : potest enim laborare, sed non vinci veritas : et non semel expertus sum Dominum Deum mirabiliter adesse iis qui coram ipso ambulant, et in sua vocatione sedulo et integre versantur ; licet ad tempus, odiis, aut simultatibus, aut calumniis agitentur.* Melch. Adamus, in vita Tossani.

† Hermanus, when dying, bewailed that he had bestowed more time and pains on his palace than on the temple of God, and encouraged the luxury and wickedness of the court, which he ought to have restrained : Thus, with much grief for sin, his hope of mercy from God greatly wavering, by-standers being filled with great horror, and himself doubtful of his state, his soul entered into eternity. *Hist. Bohem.* lib. 11.

upon you both, and your hopeful springing branches: and that you may live to see your children's children, and peace upon Israel. In a word, that God will follow these truths in your hands with the blessing of his Spirit; and that the manifold infirmities of him that ministers them, may be no prejudice or bar to their success with you, or any into whose hands they shall come; which is the hearty desire of

YOUR MOST FAITHFUL FRIEND,

AND SERVANT IN *CHRIST*,

JOHN FLAVFL.

THE EPISTLE TO THE READER.

Every creature, by the instinct of nature, or by the light of reason, strives to avoid danger, and get out of harm's way. The *cattle* in the fields presaging a storm at hand, fly to the hedges and thickets for shelter. The *fowls* of heaven, by the same natural instinct, perceiving the approach of winter, take their timely flight to a warmer *climate*. This *naturalists* * have observed of them, and their observation is confirmed by scripture testimony. Of the *cattle* it is said, Job xxxvii. 6, 7, 8. "He saith to the snow, " Be thou on the earth, likewise the small rain, and the great rain " of his strength ; then the beasts go into dens, and remain in their " places." And of the fowls of the air it is said, Jer. viii. 7. " The stork in the heavens knoweth her appointed times, and the " turtle, and the crane, and the swallow, observe the time of their " coming."

But man being a prudent and prospecting creature hath the advantage of all other creatures in his foreseeing faculty : "For " God hath taught him more than the beasts of the earth, and " made him wiser than the fowls of heaven," Job xxxv. 11. " And a wise man's heart discerneth both time and judgment," Eccl. viii. 5. For as there are natural signs of the change of the weather, Matt. xvi. 3. so there are moral signs of the changes of times and providences ; yet such is the supineness and inexcusable regardlessness of most men, that they will not fear till they feel, nor think any danger very considerable, till it become inevitable.

We of this nation have long enjoyed the light of the glorious gospel among us ; it hath shone in much clearness upon this sinful island, for more than a whole century of happy years : but the longest day hath an end, and we have cause to fear our bright sun is going down upon us ; for the shadows in England are grown greater than the substance, which is one sign of approaching night, Jer. vi. 4. " The beasts of prey creep out of their dens and coverts," which is another sign of night at hand, Psal. civ. 20. " And the " workmen come home apace from their labours, and go to rest," which is as sad a sign as any of the rest, Job vii. 1, 2. Isa. lvii. 1, 2. Happy were it, if, in such a juncture as this, every man would make it his work and business to secure himself in Christ from the storm of God's indignation, which is ready to fall upon these sinful nations. It is said of the Egyptians, when the storm of hail was coming upon the land, Exod. ix. 20. " He that feared the word

---

* Plin, l. 18. c. 35 Virg. Georg. l. 1.

" of the Lord made his servants and cattle flee into the houses."
It is but an odd sight to see the prudence of an Egyptian out-vying
the wisdom and circumspection of a Christian.

God, who provides natural shelter and refuge for all creatures,
hath not left his people unprovided with, and destitute of defence
and security, in the most tempestuous times of national judgments.
It is said, Mic. v. 5. " This man (meaning the man Christ Jesus)
" shall be the peace when the Assyrian shall come into our land,
" and when he shall tread in our palaces." And Isa. xxvi. 20.
" Come, my people, enter thou into thy chambers, and shut thy
" doors about thee; hide thyself as it were for a little moment,
" until the indignation be overpast."

My friends, let me speak as *freely*, as I am sure I speak *seasonably*.
A sound of judgment is in our ears; " The Lord's voice crieth
" unto the city, and the man of wisdom shall see thy name: hear
" ye the rod, and who hath appointed it," Mic. vi. 9. All things
round about us seem to posture themselves for trouble and distress.
Where is the man of wisdom that doth not foresee a shower of
wrath and indignation coming? " We have heard a voice of trem-
" bling, of fear, and not of peace. Ask ye now, and see whether
" a man doth travail with child? Wherefore do I see every man
" with his hands on his loins, as a woman in travail, and all faces
" are turned into paleness? Alas, for that day is great, so that
" none is like it; it is even the day of Jacob's trouble, but he shall
" be delivered out of it," Jer. xxx. 5, 6, 7.

Many eyes are now opened to see the common danger, but some
foresaw it long ago; when they saw the general decay of *godliness*
every where, the *notorious profanity* and *atheism* that overspread
the *nations;* the spirit of enmity and bitterness against the power
of *godliness* wherever it appeared: and though there seemed to be
a present calm, and general quietness, yet those that were wise in
heart could not but discern the distress of nations, with great *per-
plexity*, in these seeds of judgment and calamity : but as the *ephah*
fills more and more, so the determined wrath grows *more* and *more*
visible to every eye ; and it is a fond thing to dream of *tranquillity*
in the midst of so much *iniquity*. Indeed, if these *nations* were
once swept with the *besom* of *reformation*, we might hope God
would not sweep them with the *besom* of *destruction;* but what peace
can be *expected*, whilst the highest *provocations* are *continued*?

It is therefore the great and present concernment of all to provide
themselves of a refuge before the storm overtakes them; for, as
Augustin well observes, *Non facile inveniuntur præsidia in adver-
sitate, quæ non fuerint in pace quæsita.* O take up your lodgings
in the attributes and promises of God before the night overtake you;
view them often by faith, and clear up your interest in them, that

you may be able to go to them in the dark, when the ministers and ordinances of Christ have taken their leave of you, and bid you good night.

Whilst many are hastening on the wrath of God by *profaneness,* and many by smiting their fellow-servants; and multitudes resolve, if trouble come, to fish in the troubled waters for safety and preferment, not doubting, (whensoever the overflowing flood comes) but they shall stand dry.   O that you would be mourning for their sins, and providing better for your own safety.

Reader, it is thy *one thing necessary* to get a cleared interest in Jesus Christ; which being once obtained, thou mayest face the storm with boldness, and say, come troubles and distresses, losses and trials, prisons and death, I am provided for you; do your worst, you can do me no harm : let the winds roar, the lightnings flash, the rains and hail fall never so furiously, I have a good roof over my head, a comfortable lodging provided for me ; " My place " of defence is the munition of rocks, where bread shall be given " me, and my waters shall be sure," Isa. xxxiii. 16.

The design of the ensuing treatise is to assist thee in this great work ; and though it was promised to the world many years past, yet providence hath reserved it for the fittest season, and brought it to thy hand in a time of need.

It contains the method of grace in the *application of the great redemption to the souls of men,* as the former part contains the method of grace in the interpretation thereof by Jesus Christ.   The acceptation God hath given the former part, signified by the desires of many, for the publication of this, hath at last prevailed with me (notwithstanding the secret consciousness of my inequality to so great an undertaking) to adventure this *second part* also upon the ingenuity and candour of the reader.

And I consent the more willingly to the publication of this, because the design I first aimed at, could not be entire and complete without it ; but especially, the quality of the subject matter, which (through the blessing and concurrence of the Spirit) may be useful both to rouse the drowsy consciences of this sleepy generation, and to assist the upright in clearing the work of the Spirit upon their own souls.   These considerations have prevailed with me against all discouragements.

And now, *reader,* it is impossible for me to speak particularly and distinctly to the case of thy soul, which I am ignorant of, except the Lord shall direct my discourse to it in some of the following *suppositions.*

If thou be one that hast sincerely *applied,* and received Jesus Christ by faith, this discourse (through the blessing of the Spirit) may be useful to thee, to clear and confirm thy evidences, to melt thy heart in the sense of thy mercies, and to engage and quicken thee in the way of thy duties. Here thou wilt see what great things the Lord hath done for thy soul, and how these dignities, as thou art his son or daughter, by the double title of *regeneraion* and *adoption*, do oblige thee to yield up thyself to God entirely, and to say from thy heart, Lord, whatever I am, I am for thee, whatever I can do, I will do for thee; and whatever I can suffer, I will suffer for thee; and all that I am, or have, all that I can do or suffer, is nothing to what thou hast done for my soul.

If thou be a stranger to *regeneration* and *faith ;* a person that makest a *powerless profession* of Christ; that hast a name to live, but art dead; here it is *possible* thou mayest meet with something that will convince thee how dangerous a thing it is to be an old creature in the new creature's dress and habit; and what is it that blinds thy judgment, and is likeliest to prove thy ruin; a seasonable and full conviction whereof will be the greatest mercy that can befal thee in this world, if thereby at last God may help thee to put on Christ, as well as the name of Christ.

If thou be in darkness about the state of thy own soul, and willing to have it faithfully and impartially tried by the rule of the word, which will not warp to any man's humour or interest, here thou wilt find some weak assistance offered thee, to clear and disentangle thy doubting thoughts, which, through thy prayer, and the supply of the Spirit of Jesus Christ, may lead thee to a comfortable settlement and inward peace.

If thou be a proud, conceited, presumptuous soul, who hast too little knowledge, and too much pride and self-love, to admit any doubts or scruples of thy state towards God, there are many things in this treatise proper for thy conviction and better information ; for wo to thee, if thou shouldst not *fear,* till thou begin to *feel* thy misery, if thy troubles do not *come on* till all thy hopes are *gone off.*

I know all these things are performed by me with much infirmity ; and that the whole management is quite below the dignity of the subject. But when I consider that the success of sermons and books in the world hath but little relation to the elegancy of language, and accuracy or method, and that many may be *useful,* who cannot be *excellent,* I am willing in all humility and sincerity to commit it to the direction of Providence, and the blessing of the Spirit.

One thing I shall earnestly request of all the people of God, into whose hands this shall fall, that now at last they will be persuaded to end all their unbrotherly quarrels and strifes among themselves, which have wasted so much precious time, and decayed the vital spirits of religion, hindered the conversion of multitudes, and increased and confirmed the atheism of the times, and now at last opened a breach, at which the common enemy is ready to enter and end the quarrel to our cost. O put on, as the *elect of God*, bowels of mercy, and a spirit of charity and forbearance, if not for your own sakes, yet for the church's sake : *Si non vis tibi parcere, parce Carthagini.*

I remember it is noted in our English history as a very remarkable thing, that when the Severn overflowed part of Somersetshire, it was observed that *dogs* and *hares, cats* and *rats*, to avoid the common destruction, would swim to the next rising ground, and abide quietly together in that common danger, without the least discovery of their natural antipathy.

The story *applies* itself, and O that Christians would every where depose their animosities, that the hearts of the fathers might be turned to the children, and the children to the fathers, lest God come and smite the earth with a curse.

O that you would dwell more in your closets, and be more frequently and fervently upon your knees. O that you would search your hearts more narrowly, and sift them more thoroughly than ever, before the day pass as the chaff, and the Lord's fierce anger come upon you : look into your Bibles, then into your *hearts*, and then to *heaven*, for a true discovery of your conditions ; and if this poor mite may contribute any thing to that end, it will be a great reward of the unworthy labours of

THY SERVANT IN CHRIST,

JOHN FLAVEL.

SERMON I.

The general Nature of effectual Application stated.

1 Cor. i. 30.

But of him are ye in Christ Jesus, who of God is made unto us wisdom, and righteousness, and santification, and redemption.

H E that enquires what is the just value and worth of Christ, asks a question which puts all the men on earth, and angels in heaven, to an everlasting non-plus.

The highest attainment of our knowledge in this life, is to know, that himself and his love do pass knowledge, Eph. iii. 19.

But how excellent soever Christ is in himself, what treasures or righteousness soever lie in his blood, and whatever joy, peace, and ravishing comforts, spring up to men out of his *incarnation, humiliation,* and *exaltation,* they all give down their distinct benefits and comforts to them, in the way of *effectual application.*

For never was any wound healed by a prepared, but unapplied plaister. Never any body warmed by the most costly garment made, but not put on: Never any heart refreshed and comforted by the richest cordial compounded, but not received : Nor from the beginning of the world was it ever known, that a poor *deceived, condemned, polluted,* miserable sinner, was actually delivered out of that woful state, until of God, Christ was made unto him, wisdom and righteousness, sanctification and redemption.

For look * as the condemnation of the *first Adam* passeth not to us, except (as by generation) we are his ; so grace and remission pass not from the *second Adam* to us, except (as by regeneration) we are his. Adam's sin hurts none but those that are in him : And Christ's blood profits none but those that are in him : How great a weight therefore doth there hang upon the effectual application of Christ to the souls of men ! And what is there in the whole world so awfully solemn, so greatly important, as this is ! Such is the strong consolation resulting from it, that the apostle, in this context, offers it to the believing Corinthians, as a super-abundant recompence for the despicable meanness, and baseness of their outward condition in this world, of which he had just before

---

* Parisiensis de causis, çur Deus homo, cap. 9. *Quemadmodum non transit Adæ damnatio, nisi per generationem in carnaliter ex eo generatos : sic non transit Christi gratia, et peccatorum remissio, nisi per regenerationem ad spiritualiter per ipsum regeneratos. Sicut delictum Adæ non nocet, nisi suis, in eo quod sui sunt : sic nec gratia Christi prodest, nisi suis, in eo quid sui sunt.*

spoken in ver. 27, 28. telling them, though the world contemned them as vile, foolish, and weak, yet "of God Christ is made " unto them wisdom and righteousness, sanctification and redemp- " tion."

In which words we have an *enumeration* of the chief privileges of believers, and *an account* of the method whereby they come to be invested with them *.

First, Their privileges are enumerated, namely, *wisdom, righteousness, sanctification*, and *redemption*, mercies of inestimable value in themselves, and such as respect a fourfold misery lying upon sinful man, viz. *ignorance, guilt, pollution*, and the whole train of miserable consequences and effects, let in upon the nature of men, yea, the best and holiest of men, by sin.

Lapsed man is not only deep in misery, but grossly ignorant, both that he is so, and how to recover himself from it: Sin hath left him at once senseless of his state, and at a perfect loss about the true remedy.

To cure this, Christ is made to him *wisdom*, not only by *improvement* of those treasures of wisdom that are in himself, for the benefit of such souls as are united to him, as an head, consulting the good of his own members; but also, by *imparting* his wisdom to them by the Spirit of illumination, whereby they come to discern both their sin and danger; as also the true way of their recovery from both, through the application of Christ to their souls by faith.

But alas! simple illumination doth but increase our burden, and exasperate our misery as long as sin in the guilt of it is either imputed to our persons unto condemnation, or reflected by our consciences in a way of accusation.

With design therefore to remedy and heal this sore evil, *Christ* is made of God unto us *righteousness*, complete and perfect righteousness, whereby our obligation to punishment is dissolved, and thereby a solid foundation for a well-settled peace of conscience firmly established.

Yea, but although the removing of guilt from our persons and consciences be an inestimable mercy, yet alone it cannot make us completely happy: For though a man should never be damned for sin, yet what is it less than hell upon earth, to be under the dominion and pollution of every base lust? It is misery enough to be daily defiled by sin, though a man should never be damned for it.

To complete therefore the happiness of the redeemed; Christ is

---

* He ascribes a fourfold commendation of Christ, which comprehends all his virtue, and all the good we receive from him. *Calvin on the place.*

not only made of God unto them *wisdom* and *righteousness*, the one curing our ignorance, the other our guilt; but he is made *sanctification* also, to relieve us against the dominion and pollutions of our corruptions: " He comes both by water and by blood, not by " blood only, but by water also," 1 John v. 6. *purging* as well as *pardoning:* How complete and perfect a cure is Christ !

But yet something is required beyond all this to make our happiness perfect and entire wanting nothing; and that is the removal of those doleful effects and consequences of sin, which (notwithstanding all the fore-mentioned privileges and mercies) still lie upon the souls and bodies of illuminated, justified, and sanctified persons. For even with the best and holiest of men, what swarms of vanity, loads of deadness, and fits of unbelief, do daily appear in, and oppress their souls ! to the imbittering of all the comforts of life to them ? And how many diseases, deformities, and pains oppress their bodies, which daily moulder away by them, till they fall into the grave by death, even as the bodies of other men do, who never received such privileges from Christ as they do ? For if " Christ " be in us (as the apostle speaks, Rom. viii. 10.) the body " is dead, because of sin:" Sanctification exempts us not from mortality.

But from all these, and whatsoever else, the fruits and consequences of sin, Christ is *redemption* to his people also: This seals up the sum of mercies: This so completes the happiness of the saints, that it leaves nothing to desire.

These four, wisdom, righteousness, sanctification and redemption, take in all that is necessary or desirable, to make a soul truly and perfectly blessed.

Secondly, We have here the method and way, by which the elect come to be invested with these excellent privileges: the account whereof, the apostle gives us in these words, " Who of " God is made unto us," in which expression, four things are remarkable.

First, That Christ and his benefits go inseparably and undividedly together: it is Christ himself who is made all this unto us: we can have no saving benefit separate and apart from the person of Christ: many would willingly receive his *privileges,* who will not receive his person; but it cannot be; if we will have one, we must take the other too: Yea, we must accept his person first, and then his benefits: as it is in the marriage covenant, so it is here.

Secondly, That Christ with his benefits must be personally and particularly applied to us, before we can receive any actual, saving privilege by him ; he must be [*made unto us*] i. e. particularly applied to us; as a sum of money becomes, or is made the ransom and liberty of a captive, when it is not only promised, but paid down in his name, and legally applied for that use and end. When Christ died, the ransom was prepared, the sum laid down; but yet the elect continue still in sin and misery, notwithstanding, till by *effectual calling* it be actually *applied* to their persons, and then they are made free, Rom. v. 10, 11. reconciled by Christ's death, by whom " we have now received the atonement."

. *Thirdly,* That this application of Christ is the work of God, and not of man : " Of God he is made unto us :" The same hand that prepared it, must also apply it, or else we perish, notwithstanding all that the Father hath done in contriving, and appointing, and all that the Son hath done in executing, and accomplishing the design thus far. And this actual application is the work of the Spirit, by a singular appropriation.

Fourthly, and *lastly,* This expression imports the suitableness of Christ, to the necessities of sinners; what they want, he is made to them; and indeed, as money answers all things, and is convertible into meat, drink, raiment, physic, or what else our bodily ne-cessities do require; so Christ is virtually, and eminently all that the necessities of our souls require; bread to the hungry, and clothing to the naked soul. In a word, God prepared and furnish-ed him on purpose to answer all our wants, which fully suits the apostle's sense, when he saith, " Who of God is made unto us " wisdom and righteousness, sanctification and redemption." The sum of all is,

Doct. *That the Lord Jesus Christ, with all his precious benefits, becomes ours, by God's special and effectual application.*

There is a twofold application of our redemption, one *primary,* the other *Secondary :* The former is the act of God the *Father,* ap-plying it to Christ our surety, and virtually to us in him : the lat-ter is the act of the *Holy Spirit,* personally and actually applying it to us in the work of conversion : The former hath the respect and relation of an example, model, or pattern to this; and this is pro-duced and wrought by the virtue of that. What was done upon the person of Christ, was not only virtually done upon us, consider-ed in him as a common public representative person, in which sense, we are said to die with him, and live with him, to be cruci-fied with him, and buried with him, but it was also intended for a platform, or idea, of what is to be done by the Spirit, actually upon our souls and bodies, in our single persons. As he died for sin, so the Spirit applying his death to us in the work of *mortification,* causes us to die to sin, by the virtue of his death : And as he was quickened by the Spirit, and raised unto life, so the Spirit applying

unto us the life of Christ, causeth us to live, by spiritual *vivification.*
Now this personal, secondary, and *actual application of redemption*
to us by the Spirit, in his sanctifying work, is that which I am engaged here to discuss and open; which I shall do in these following propositions.

Prop. 1. *The application of Christ to us, is not only comprehen-*
sive of our justification, but of all those works of the Spirit which
are known to us in scripture by the names of regeneration, voca-
tion, sanctification, and conversion.

Though all these terms have some small respective differences
among themselves, yet they are all included in this general, the
applying and *putting* on of Christ, Rom. xiii. 14. " Put ye on the
" Lord Jesus Christ."

Regeneration expresses those supernatural, divine, new qualities,
infused by the Spirit into the soul, which are the principles of all
holy actions.

Vocation expresses the terms from which, and to which, the soul
moves, when the Spirit works savingly upon it, under the gospel-
call.

Sanctification notes an holy dedication of heart and life to God:
Our becoming the temples of the living God, separate from all profane sinful practices, to the Lord's only use and service.

Conversion denotes the great change itself, , which the Spirit
causeth upon the soul, turning it by a sweet irresistible efficacy
from the power of sin and Satan, to God in Christ.

Now all these are imported in, and done by the *application of*
Christ to our souls: for when once the efficacy of Christ's death, and
the virtue of his resurrection, come to take place upon the heart
of any man, he cannot but turn from sin to God, and become a
new creature, living and acting by new principles and rules. So
the apostle observes, 1 Thess. i. 5, 6. speaking of the effect of this
work of the Spirit upon that people, " Our gospel (saith he) came
" not to you in word only, but in power; and in the Holy Ghost :"
There was the effectual application of Christ to them. " And
" you became followers of us, and of the Lord," ver. 6. there was
their effectual call. " And ye turned from dumb idols to serve
" the living and true God, ver. 9. there was their conversion.
" So that ye were ensamples to all that believe," ver. 9. there
was their life of sanctification or dedication to God. So that all
these are comprehended in effectual application.

Prop. 2. *The application of Christ to the souls of men is that*
great project and design of God in this world, for the accomplish-
ment whereof all the ordinances and all the officers of the gospel are
appointed and continued in the world.

This the gospel expressly declared to be its direct end, and the

great business of all its officers, Eph. iv. 11, 12. " And he gave
" some apostles, and some prophets, and some evangelists, and
" some pastors and teachers; till we all come in the unity of the
" faith, and the knowledge of the Son of God; to a perfect man,
" unto the measure of the stature of the fulness of Christ," i. e.
the great aim and scope of all Christ's ordinances and officers, are
to bring men into union with Christ, and so build them up to perfection in him; or to unite them to, and confirm them in Christ:
and when it shall have finished this design, then shall the whole
frame of gospel-ordinances be taken down, and all its officers dis-
banded. " The kingdom (i. e. this present œconomy, manner,
" and form of government) shall be delivered up," 1 Cor. xv. 24.
What are ministers, but the bridegroom's friends, ambassadors
for God, to beseech men to be reconciled? When therefore all
the elect are brought home in a reconciled state in Christ, when
the marriage of the Lamb is come, our work and office expire together.

Prop. 3. *Such is the importance and great concernment of the
personal application of Christ to us by the Spirit, that whatsoever
the Father hath done in the contrivance, or the Son hath done in the
accomplishment of our redemption, is all inavailable and ineffectual
to our salvation without this.*

It is confessedly true, that God's good pleasure appointing us
from eternity to salvation, is, in its kind, a most full and sufficient
impulsive cause of our salvation, and every way able (for so much
as it is concerned) to produce its effect. And Christ's humiliation
and sufferings are a most complete and sufficient *meritorious* cause
of our salvation, to which nothing can be added to make it more
apt, and able to procure our salvation, than it already is: yet
neither the one nor the other can actually save any soul, without the *Spirit's application* of Christ to it; for where there are divers *social causes*, or *concauses*, necessary to produce one effect, there
the effect cannot be produced until the last cause hath wrought.
Thus it is here, the *Father* hath elected, and the *Son* hath redeemed; but until the *Spirit* (who is the last cause) hath wrought his
part also, we cannot be saved. For he comes in the Father's and
in the Son's name and authority, to put the last hand to the work
of our salvation, by bringing all the fruits of election and redemption home to our souls in this work of effectual vocation. Hence
the apostle, 1 Pet. i. 2. noting the order of causes in their operations, for the bringing about of our salvation, thus states it, " Elect,
" according to the foreknowledge of God the Father, through
" sanctification of the Spirit unto obedience, and sprinkling of the
" blood of Jesus Christ." Here you find God's election and
Christ's blood, the two great causes of salvation, and yet neither of

these alone, nor both together can save us: there must be added
the sanctification of the Spirit, by which God's decree is executed;
and the sprinkling (i. e. the personal *application* of Christ's blood)
as well as the shedding of it, before we can have the saving benefit
of either of the former causes.

Prop. 4. *The application of Christ, with his saving benefits, is
exactly of the same extent and latitude with the Father's election,
and the Son's intention in dying, and cannot possibly be extended
to one soul farther.*

" Whom he did predestinate, them he also called," Rom. viii.
30. and Acts xiii. 48. " As many as were ordained to eternal life,
" believed;" 2 Tim. i. 9. " Who hath saved and called us with
" an holy calling, not according to our works, but according to
" his own purpose and grace, which was given us in Jesus Christ,
" before the foundation of the world."

The Father, Son, and Spirit, (betwixt whom was the council
of peace) work out their design in a perfect harmony and consent: as there was no jar in their council, so there can be none
in the execution of it: those whom the Father, before all time,
did chuse; they, and they only, are the persons, whom the Son,
when the fulness of time for the execution of that decree was come,
died for, John xvii. 6. " I have manifested thy name unto the
" men, which thou gavest me out of the world; thine they were,
" and thou gavest them me;" and ver. 19. " For their sakes I
" sanctify myself;" i. e. consecrate, devote, or set myself apart
for a sacrifice for them. And those for whom Christ died, are
the persons to whom the Spirit effectually applies the benefits and
purchases of his blood: he comes in the name of the Father and
Son. " But the world cannot receive him, for it neither sees, nor
" knows him," John xiv. 17. " They that are not of Christ's
" sheep, believe not," John x. 26.

Christ hath indeed a fulness of saving power, but the dispensation thereof is limited by the Father's will; therefore he tells us,
Mat. xx. 23. " It is not mine to give, but it shall be given to them
" for whom it is prepared of my Father." In which words he no
ways denies his authority, to give glory as well as grace; he only
shews that in the dispensation proper to him, as Mediator, he was
limited by his Father's will and counsel.

And thus also are the dispensations of grace by the Spirit, in like
manner, limited, both by the counsel and will of the Father and
Son. For as he proceeds from them, so he acts in the administra-
tion proper to him, by commission from both. John xiv. 26.
" The Holy Ghost whom the Father will send in my name:" and
as he comes forth into the world by this joint commission, so his
dispensations are limited in his commission; for it is said, John xvi.

13. " He shall not speak of himself, but whatsoever he shall hear,
" that shall he speak ?" i. e. He shall in all things act according to
his commission, which the Father and I have given him.

The Son can do nothing of himself, but what he seeth the Father do, John v. 19. And the Spirit can do nothing of himself,
but what he hears from the Father and Son ; and it is impossible it
should be otherwise, considering not only the unity of their nature,
but also of their will and design. So that you see the application
of Christ, and benefits by the Spirit, are commensurable with the
Father's secret counsel, and the Son's design in dying, which are
the rule, model, and pattern of the Spirit's working.

*Prop. 5. The application of Christ to souls, by the regenerating
work of the Spirit, is that which makes the first internal difference
and distinction among men.*

It is very true, that in respect of God's fore-knowledge and purpose, there was a distinction betwixt one man and another, before
any man had a being, one was taken, another left: and with respect to the death of Christ, there is a great difference betwixt one
and another; he laid down his life for the sheep, he prayed for
them, and not for the world; but all this while, as to any *relative
change* of state, or *real change* of temper, they are upon a level with
the rest of the miserable world. The elect themselves are " by
" nature the children of wrath, even as others," Eph. ii. 3. And
to the same purpose the apostle tells the Corinthians, 1 Cor. vi. 11.
(when he had given in that black bill, describing the most lewd,
profligate, abominable wretches in the world, men whose practices
did stink in the very nostrils of nature, and were able to make the
more sober Heathens blush ; after this he tells the Corinthians)
" And such were some of you, but ye are washed," &c. q. d.
look, these were your companions once : as they are, you lately
were.

The work of the Spirit doth not only evidence and manifest that
difference which God's election hath made between man and man,
as the apostle speaks, 1 Thes. i. 4, 5. But it also makes a two-
fold difference itself, namely in *state* and *temper ?* whereby they visibly differ, not only from other men, but also from themselves ;
after this work, though a man be the *who,* yet not the *what* he was.
This work of the Spirit makes us new creatures, namely ; for quality and temper, 2 Cor. v. 17. " If any man be in Christ, he is a
" new creature; old things are past away, behold, all things are
" become new."

*Prop. 6. The application of Christ, by the work of regeneration,
is that which yields unto men all the sensible sweetness and refreshing comforts that they have in Christ, and in all that he hath done,
suffered, or purchased for sinners.*

An unsanctified person may relish the natural sweetness of the creature, as well as he that is sanctified; he may also seem to relish and taste some sweetness in the delicious promises and discoveries of the gospel, by a *misapplication* of them to himself. But this is like the joy of a beggar, dreaming he is a king; but he awakes and finds himself a beggar still: but for the rational, solid, and genuine delights and comforts of religion, no man tastes them, till this work of the Spirit hath first passed upon his soul: it is an enclosed pleasure, a stranger intermeddles not with it. " The white " stone, and the new name," (denoting the pleasant results and fruits of justification and adoption) " no man knows but he that " receives it," Rev. ii. 7. There are all those things wanting in the unsanctified (though elect) soul, that should capacitate and enable it to relish the sweetness of Christ and religion, namely, *propriety*, *evidence*, and suitableness of spirit.

Propriety is the sweetest part of any excellency; therefore Luther was wont to say, that the sweetness of the gospel lay mostly in *pronouns*, as *me, my, thy,* &c. who loved [me] and gave himself for me, Gal. ii. 20. Christ Jesus [my] Lord, Phil. iii. 18. So Matt. ix. 2. Son, be of good cheer, [thy] sins are forgiven. Take away propriety, and you deflower the very gospel of its beauty and deliciousness: and as propriety, so

Evidence is requisite to joy and comfort; yea, so necessary, that even interest and propriety afford no sensible sweetness without it. For as to comfort, it is all one not to appear, and not to be. If I am registered in the book of life, and know it not, what comfort can my name there afford me? Besides, to capacitate a soul for the sweetness and comfort of Christ there is also *an agreeable temper* of spirit required; for how can Christ be sweet to that man's soul, whose thoughts reluctate, decline, or nauseate so holy and pure an object? Now, all these requisites being the proper effects and fruits of the Spirit's sanctifying operations upon us, it is beyond controversy, that the consolations of Christ cannot be tasted, until the application of Christ be first made.

Prop. 7. *The application of Christ to the soul effectually, though it be so far wrought in the first saving work of the Spirit, as truly to unite the soul to Christ, and save it from the danger of perishing; yet it is a work gradually advancing in the believer's soul, whilst it abides on this side heaven and glory.*

It is true, indeed, that Christ is perfectly and completely applied to the soul in the first act for righteousness. " Justification being " a relative change *, properly admits no degrees, but is perfected

---

* *Nullos proprie dictos gradus admittit, sed unico actu simul ac semel existit perfecta, quamvis, quoad manifestationem, sensum, et effecta, varios habeat gradus.* Ames.

" together, and at once, in one only act; though as to its manifesta-
" tion, sense, and effects, it hath various degrees." But the *application* of Christ to us, for wisdom and sanctification, is not perfected
in one single act, but rises by many, and slow degrees to its just
perfection.

And though we are truly said to be come to Christ when we first
believe, John vi. 35. yet the soul after that is still coming to him by
farther acts of faith, 1 Pet. ii. 4. " To whom [coming] as unto a
" living stone;" the *particle* notes a continued motion, by which
the soul gains ground, and still gets nearer and nearer to Christ;
growing still more inwardly acquainted with him. The knowledge
of Christ grows upon the soul as the morning light, from its first
spring to the perfect day, Prov. iv. 18. Every grace of the Spirit
grows, if not sensibly, yet really; for it is in discerning the growth
of sanctification, as it is in discerning the growth of plants, which we
perceive rather *crevisse, quam crescere;* to have grown, rather than
grow. And as it thrives in the soul, by deeper radications of the
habits, and more promptitude and spirituality in the actings; so
Christ, and the soul proportionably, close more and more inwardly
and efficaciously, till at last it is wholly swallowed up in Christ's full
and perfect enjoyment.

Prop. 8. *Lastly, Although the several privileges and benefits be-
forementioned are all truly and really bestowed with Christ upon
believers, yet they are not communicated to them in one and the same
way and manner; but differently and diversly, as their respective
natures do require.*

These four illustrious benefits are conveyed from Christ to us in
three different ways and methods; his righteousness is made ours
by *imputation:* his wisdom and sanctification by *renovation:* his
redemption by our *glorification.*

I know the communication of Christ's righteousness to us by imputation, is not only denied, but * scoffed at by Papists; who own
no righteousness, but what is (at least) confounded with that which
is inherent in us; and for *imputative* (blasphemously stiled by them
putative) righteousness, they flatly deny it, and look upon it as a
most absurd doctrine, every where endeavouring to load it with
these and such like absurdities, That if God imputes Christ's
righteousness to the believer, and accepts what Christ hath performed for him, as if he had performed it himself; then we may
be accounted as righteous as Christ. Then we may be the redeem-
ers of the world. False and groundless consequences; as if a man
should say, my debt is paid by my surety, therefore I am as rich
as he. " When we say the righteousness of Christ is made ours

---

* A phantom sprung of Luther's brain. *Stapleton.*

" by *imputation* *, we think not that it is made ours according to its
" universal value, but according to our particular necessity: not
" to make others righteous, but to make us so: not that we have
" the formal intrinsical righteousness of Christ in us, as it is in him,
" but a relative righteousness, which makes us righteous, even as
" he is righteous; not as to the quantity, but as to the truth of
" it: nor is it imputed to us, as though Christ designed to make
" us the *causes* of salvation to others, but the *subjects* of salvation,
" ourselves;" it is *inhesively* in him, *communicatively* it becomes
ours; by imputation, the sin of the first Adam becomes ours, and
the same way the righteousness of the second Adam becomes ours,
Rom. v. 17. This way the Redeemer became sin for us, and this
way we are made the righteousness of God in him, 2 Cor. v. 21.
This way Abraham the father of believers was justified, therefore
this way all believers, the children of Abraham, must be justified
also, Rom. iv. 22, 23. And thus is Christ's righteousness made ours.

But in conveying and communicating his *wisdom* and *sanctification*, he takes another method, for this is not *imputed*, but really
imparted to us by the illuminating and regenerating work of the
Spirit: these are graces really inherent in us: our righteousness
comes from Christ as a *surety*, but our holiness comes from him as
a quickening *head*, sending vital influences unto all his members.

Now these gracious habits being subjected and seated in the souls
of poor imperfect creatures, whose corruptions abide and work in
the very same faculties where grace hath its residence; it cannot
be, that our sanctification should be so perfect and complete, as our
justification is, which inheres only in Christ. See Gal. v. 17. Thus
are righteousness and sanctification communicated and made ours:
but then,

For *redemption*, that is to say, absolute and plenary deliverance
from all the sad remains, effects, and consequences of sin, both
upon soul and body; this is made ours, (or, to keep to the terms)
Christ is made redemption to us by glorification; then, and not before, are these miserable effects removed; we put off these together
with the body. So that look, as *justification* cures the *guilt* of sin,
and *sanctification*, the *dominion* of sin, so *glorification* removes, together with its *existence* and being, all those *miseries* which it let in
(as at a flood-gate) upon our whole man, Eph. v. 26, 27.

And thus of God, Christ is made unto us † wisdom and righ-

---

* *Non formali intrinsica justitia, sed relativa ; non quoad quantitatem sed veritatem ; fit
enim finita applicatio infinitæ justitiæ ; si aliter, acque justi essemus ut Christus, at non ;
justitia Christi fit nostra, non quoad universalem valorem, sed particularem necessitatem ; et
imputatur nobis, non ut causis salvationis, sed ut subjectis salvandis.* Bradsh. de Justificat.

† But it is said he is made unto us, wisdom, righteousness, sanctification, and
redemption, therefore any worth or merit in us is excluded. Whence it likewise follows, that we were foolish, unrighteous, unholy, and slaves of the devil.

teousness, sanctification and redemption; namely, by imputation, regeneration, and glorification.

I shall next improve the point in some useful inferences.

Inference 1. *Learn from hence, what a naked, destitute, and empty thing, a poor sinner is, in his natural unregenerate state.*

He is one that naturally and inherently hath neither wisdom, nor righteousness, sanctification nor redemption; all these must come from without himself, even from Christ, who is made all this to a sinner, or else he must eternally perish.

As no creature (in respect of external abilities) comes under more natural weakness into the world than man, naked, empty, and more shiftless and helpless than any other creature; so it is with his soul, yea, much more than so: all our excellencies are borrowed excellencies, no reason therefore to be proud of any of them, 1 Cor. iv. 7. " What hast thou that thou hast not received ? Now, if thou " didst receive it, why dost thou glory, as if thou hadst not re- " ceived it ?" *q. d.* What intolerable insolence and vanity would it be for a man that wears the rich and costly robe of Christ's righteousness, in which there is not one thread of his own spinning, but all made by *free-grace*, and not by *free-will*, to jet proudly up and down the world in it, as if himself had made it, and he were beholden to none for it ? O man ! thine excellencies, whatever they are, are borrowed from Christ, they oblige thee to him, but he can be no more obliged to thee, who wearest them, than the sun is obliged to him that borrows its light, or the fountain to him that draws its water for his use and benefit.

And it hath ever been the care of holy men, when they have viewed their own gracious *principles*, or best *performances*, still to disclaim themselves, and own free-grace as the sole author of all. Thus holy Paul, viewing the principles of divine life in himself, (the richest gift bestowed upon man in this world by Jesus Christ) how doth he renounce himself, and deny the least part of the praise and glory as belonging to him, Gal. ii. 20. " Now I live, " yet not I ; but Christ liveth in me :" and so for the best duties that ever he performed for God : (and what mere man ever did more for God ?) Yet when, in a just and necessary defence, he was constrained to mention them, 1 Cor. xv. 10. how carefully is the like [*Yet not I*] presently added ? " I laboured more abundantly " than they all ; yet not I, but the grace of God which was with " me."

Well then, let the sense of your own emptiness by nature humble and oblige you the more to Christ, from whom you receive all you have.

Infer. 2. *Hence we are informed, that none can claim benefit by imputed righteousness, but those only that live in the power of in-*

herent holiness; *to whomsoever Christ is made righteousness, to him he also is made sanctification.*

The gospel hath not the least favour for licentiousness. It is every way as careful to press men to their duties as to instruct them in their privileges, Tit. iii. 8. " This is a faithful saying; and these " things I will that ye affirm constantly; that they which have be-" lieved in God, might be careful to maintain good works." It is a loose principle, divulged by *libertines,* to the reproach of Christ and his gospel, that sanctification is not the evidence of our justification. And Christ is as much wronged by them who separate holiness from righteousness (as if a sensual vile life were consistent with a justified state) as he is in the contrary extreme, by those who confound Christ's righteousness with man's holiness, in the point of justification; or that own no other righteousness, but what is inherent in themselves. The former opinion makes him a *cloak* for sin, the latter a *needless sacrifice* for sin.

It is true, our sanctification cannot justify us before God; but what then, can it not evidence our justification before men? Is there no necessity, or use for holiness, because it hath no hand in our justification? Is the preparation of the soul for heaven, by altering its frame and temper, nothing? Is the glorifying of our Redeemer, by the exercises of grace in the world, nothing? Doth the work of Christ render the work of the Spirit needless? God forbid: " He came not by blood only, but by water also," 1 John v. 6. And when the apostle saith, in Rom. iv. 5. " But unto " him that worketh not, but believeth on him that justifieth the " ungodly, his faith is counted for righteousness:" the scope of it is neither to characterize and describe the justified person, as one that is lazy and slothful, and hath no mind to work, nor the rebellious and refractory, refusing obedience to the commands of God; but to represent him as an humbled sinner, who is convinced of his inability to work out his own righteousness by the law, and sees all his endeavours to obey the law fall short of righteousness, and therefore is said, in a law-sense, *not to work,* because he doth not work so as to answer the purpose and end of the law, which accepts of nothing beneath perfect obedience.

And when (in the same text) the ungodly are said to be justified, that character describes not the temper and frame of their hearts and lives, after their justification, but what it was before; not as it leaves, but as it found them *.

Infer. 3. *How unreasonable, and worse than brutish, is the sin of infidelity, by which the sinner rejects Christ, and with him all those mercies, and benefits, which alone can relieve and cure his misery!*

---

* God justifies the ungodly antecedently not consequently. *Par.*

He is by nature blind and ignorant, and yet refuses Christ, who comes to him with heavenly light and wisdom; he is condemned by the terrible sentence of the law to eternal wrath, and yet rejects Christ, who renders to him complete and perfect righteousness: he is wholly polluted and plunged into original and actual pollutions of nature and practice, yet will have none of Christ, who would become sanctification to him. He is oppressed in soul and body, with the deplorable effects and miseries sin hath brought upon him, and yet is so in love with his bondage, that he will neither accept Christ, nor the redemption he brings with him to sinners.

O! what monsters, what beasts hath sin turned its subjects into! " You will not come to me that ye may have life," John v 40. Sin hath stabbed the sinner to the heart, the wounds are all mortal, eternal death is in his face; Christ hath prepared the only plaister that can cure his wounds, but he will not suffer him to apply it *. He acts like one in love with death, and that judges it sweet to perish. So Christ tells us, Prov. viii. 36. " All they that " hate me, love death :" not in itself but in its causes, with which it is inseparably connected. They are loth to burn, yet willing to sin; though sin kindle those everlasting flames. So that in two things the unbeliever shews himself worse than brutish, he cannot think of damnation, the effect of sin, without horror; and cannot yet think of sin, the cause of damnation, without pleasure; he is loth to perish to all eternity without a remedy, and yet refuses and declines Christ as if he were an enemy, who only can and would deliver him from that eternal perdition.

How do men act therefore, as if they were in love with their own ruin! Many poor wretches now in the way to hell, what an hard shift do they make to cast themselves away! Christ meets them many times in the ordinances, where they studiously shun him: many times checks them in their way by convictions, which they make an hard shift to overcome and conquer. Oh how willing are they to accept a cure, a benefit, a remedy, for any thing but their souls! You see then that sinners cannot, (should they study all their days to do themselves a mischief), take a readier course to undo themselves, than by rejecting Christ in his gracious offers.

Surely the sin of Sodom and Gomorrah is less than this sin.

Mercy itself is exasperated by it, and the damnation of such as reject Christ, (so prepared for them, with whatever they need, and so seriously and frequently offered to them upon the knee of gospel intreaty), is just, inevitable, and will be more intolerable than to any in the world beside them. It is just, for the sinner hath but

---

* Not that any one is so mad, as willingly and knowingly to love death, which we all naturally abhor; but because that is the fruit of despising the wisdom of God, which at length brings death on us. *Lavat. on the place.*

his own option, or choice : he is but come to the end which he was often told his way would bring him to. It is inevitable, for there is no other way to salvation, but that which is rejected. And it will be more intolerable than the damnation of others, because neither heathens nor devils ever aggravated their sins by such an horrid circumstance, as the wilful refusing of such an apt, offered, and only remedy.

Infer. 4. *What a tremendous symptom of wrath, and sad character of death, appears upon that man's soul, to which no effectual application of Christ can be made by the gospel.*

Christ, with his benefits, is frequently tendered to them in the gospel ; they have been beseeched once and again, upon the knee of importunity, to accept him ; those entreaties and persuasions have been urged by the greatest arguments, the command of God, the love of Christ, the inconceivable happiness or misery which unavoidably follow the accepting or rejecting of those offers, and yet nothing will affect them : all their pleas for infidelity have been over and over confuted, their reasons and consciences have stood convinced ; they have been speechless, as well as Christless : not one sound argument is found with them to defend their infidelity : they confess in general, that such courses as theirs are, lead to destruction. They will yield them to be happy souls that are in Christ ; and yet, when it comes to the point, their own closing with him, nothing will do ; all arguments, all entreaties, return to us without success.

Lord! what is the reason of this unaccountable obstinacy? In other things it is not so : If they be sick, they are so far from rejecting a physician that offers himself, that they will send, and pray, and pay him too. If they be arrested for debt, and any one will be a surety, and pay their debts for them, words can hardly express the sense they have of such a kindness : but though Christ would be both a physician and surety, and whatever else their needs require, they will rather perish to eternity, than accept him. What may we fear to be the reason of this, but because they are not of Christ's sheep, John x. 26. The Lord open the eyes of poor sinners, to apprehend not only how great a sin, but how dreadful a sign this is.

Infer. 5. *If Christ, with all his benefits, be made ours, by God's special application, what a day of mercies then is the day of conversion! what multitudes of choice blessings visit the converted soul in that day!*

" This day, (saith Christ to Zaccheus, Luke xix. 9.) is " salvation come to this house." In this day, Christ cometh into the soul, and he comes not empty, but brings with him all his treasures of wisdom and righteousness, sanctification and redemption. Troops of mercies, yea, of the best of mercies,

come with him. It is a day of singular gladness and joy to the
heart of Christ, when he is espoused to, and received by the believing soul: it is a coronation day to a king. So you read, Cant.
iii. 11. " Go forth, O ye daughters of Zion, and behold king
" Solomon with the crown wherewith his mother crowned him in
" the day of his espousals, and in the day of the gladness of his
" heart."

Where, under the type of Solomon in his greatest magnificence
and glory, when the royal diadem was set upon his head, and the
people shouted for joy, so that the earth did ring again, is shadowed out the joy of Christ's heart, when poor souls, by their high
estimation of him, and consent to his government, do, as it were,
crown him with glory and honour, and make his heart glad.

Now, if the day of our espousals to Christ be the day of the
gladness of his heart, and he reckons himself thus honoured and
glorified by us, what a day of joy and gladness should it be to our
hearts, and how should we be transported with joy, to see a King
from heaven, with all his treasures of grace and glory, bestowing
himself freely, and everlastingly upon us, as our portion! No wonder Zaccheus came down joyfully, Luke xix. 6. that the eunuch
went home rejoicing, Acts viii. 39. that the gaoler rejoiced, believing in God with all his household, Acts xvi. 34. that they that
were converted, did eat their meat with gladness, praising God,
Acts ii. 41, 46. that there was great joy among them of Samaria,
when Christ came among them in the preaching of the gospel,
Acts viii, 5, 8. I say, it is no wonder we read of such joy accompanying Christ into the soul, when we consider, that in one day,
so many blessings meet together in it, the least of which is not to
be exchanged for all the kingdoms of this world, and the glory of
them. Eternity itself will but suffice to bless God for the mercies
of this one day.

Infer. 6. *If Christ be made all this to every soul, unto whom he is
effectually applied, what cause then have those souls, that are under
the preparatory work of the Spirit, and are come nigh to Christ and
all his benefits, to stretch out their hands, with vehement desire to
Christ, and give him the most important invitation into their souls!*

The whole world is distinguishable into three classes, or sorts of
persons; such as are *far from Christ*; such as are *not far from
Christ*; and such as are *in Christ*. They that are in Christ have
heartily received him. Such as are far from Christ, will not open
to him; their hearts are fast barred by ignorance, prejudice, and
unbelief against him: But those that are come under the preparatory workings of the Spirit, nigh to Christ, who see their own indispensible necessity of him, and his suitableness to their necessities,
in whom also encouraging hopes begin to dawn, and their souls

are waiting at the foot of God for power to receive him, for an heart to close sincerely and universally with him; O what vehement desires! what strong pleas! what moving arguments should such persons urge, and plead to win Christ, and get possession of him! they are in sight of their only remedy; Christ and salvation are come to their very doors; there wants but a few things to make them blessed for ever. This is the day in which their souls are exercised between hopes and fears: Now they are much alone, and deep in thoughtfulness, they weep and make supplication for a heart to believe, and that against the great discouragements with which they encounter.

Reader, if this be the case of thy soul, it will not be the least piece of service I can do for thee, to suggest such pleas as in this case are proper to be urged for the attainment of thy desires, and the closing of the match between Christ and thee.

First, Plead the absolute necessity which now drives thee to Christ: Tell him thy hope is utterly perished in all other refuges. Thou art come like a starving beggar to the last door of hope. Tell him thou now beginnest to see the absolute necessity of Christ. Thy body hath not so much need of bread, water, or air, as thy soul hath of Christ, and that wisdom and righteousness, sanctification and redemption, that are in him.

Secondly, Plead the Father's gracious design in furnishing and sending him into the world, and his own design in accepting the Father's call. Lord Jesus, wast thou not "anointed to preach "good tidings to the meek, to bind up the broken-hearted, and "to proclaim liberty to the captives, and the opening of the pri- "son to them that are bound?" Isa. lxi. 1, 3. Behold an object suitable to thine office: whilst I was ignorant of my condition, I had a proud rebellious heart, but conviction and self-acquaintance have now melted it: my heart was harder than the nether millstone, and it was as easy to dissolve the obdurate rocks, as to thaw and melt my heart for sin; but now God hath made my heart soft, I sensibly feel the misery of my condition. I once thought myself at perfect liberty, but now I see what I conceited to be perfect liberty, is perfect bondage; and never did a poor prisoner sigh for deliverance more than I. Since then thou hast given me a soul thus qualified, though still unworthy, for the exercise of thine office, and execution of thy commission; Lord Jesus, be, according to thy name, a Jesus unto me.

Thirdly, Plead the unlimited and general invitation made to such souls as you are, to come to Christ freely. Lord, thou hast made open proclamation; "Ho, every one that thirsteth, come ye to "the waters, Isa. lv. 1. and Rev. xxii. 17. "Him that is a-thirst

" come." In obedience to thy call, lo, I come; had I not been
invited, my coming to thee, dear Lord Jesus, had been an act of
presumption, but this makes it an act of duty and obedience.

Fourthly, Plead the unprofitableness of thy blood to God; Lord,
there is no profit in my blood, it will turn to no more advantage
to thee to destroy, than it will to save me: if thou send me to hell,
(as the merit of my sin calls upon thy justice to do,) I shall be
there dishonouring thee to all eternity, and the debt I owe thee
never paid. But, if thou apply thy Christ to me for righteousness,
satisfaction for all that I have done will be laid down in one full, complete sum; indeed, if the honour of thy justice lay as a bar to my
pardon, it would stop my mouth: but when thy justice, as well as
thy mercy, shall both rejoice together, and be glorified and pleased
in the same act, what hinders but that Christ be applied to my
soul, since, in so doing, God can be no loser by it?

Fifthly, and lastly, Plead thy compliance with the terms of the
gospel: tell him, Lord, my will complies fully and heartily to all
thy gracious terms. I can now subscribe a blank: let God offer
his Christ on what terms he will, my heart is ready to comply; I
have no exception against any article of the gospel. And now,
Lord, I wholly refer myself to thy pleasure; do with me what
seemeth good in thine eyes, only give me an interest in Jesus Christ;
as to all other concerns I lie at thy feet, in full resignation of all
to thy pleasure. Never yet did any perish in that posture and
frame; and I hope I shall not be made the first instance and
example.

Inf. 7. Lastly, *If Christ, with all his benefits, be made ours, by
a special application; how contented, thankful, comfortable, and
hopeful, should believers be, in every condition which God casts them
into in this world!*

After such a mercy as this, let them never open their mouths
any more to repine and grudge at the outward inconveniencies of
their condition in this world. What are the things you want,
compared with the things you enjoy? What is a little money,
health, or liberty, to wisdom, righteousness, sanctification, and
redemption? All the crowns and sceptres in the world, sold to
their full value, are no price for the least of these mercies. But I
will not insist here, your duty lies much higher than contentment.

Be thankful, as well as content, in every state. " Blessed be
" God, (saith the apostle) the Father of our Lord Jesus Christ,
" who hath blessed us with all [spiritual blessings] in heavenly
" places in Christ:" O think what are men to angels, that Christ
should pass by them to become a Saviour to men? And what art
thou among men, that thou shouldst be taken, and others left!
And among all the mercies of God, what mercies are comparable

to these conferred upon thee? O bless God in the lowest ebb of outward comforts, for such privileges as these.

And yet you will not come up to your duty in all this, except you be joyful in the Lord, and rejoice evermore, after the receipt of such mercies as these, Phil. iv. 4. "Rejoice in the Lord ye "righteous, and again I say rejoice." For hath not the poor captive reason to rejoice, when he hath recovered his liberty? The debtor to rejoice when all scores are cleared, and he owes nothing? The weary traveller to rejoice, though he be not owner of a shilling, when he is come almost home, where all his wants shall be supplied? Why this is our case, when Christ once becomes yours: you are the Lord's freemen, your debts to justice are all satisfied by Christ; and you are within a little of complete redemption from all the troubles and inconveniences of your present state.

Thanks be to God for Jesus Christ.

———≈◉⋅×⋅◉≈———

SERMON II.

Wherein the Union of the Believer with CHRIST, as a principal Part of effectual Application, is stated and practically improved.

JOHN xvii. 23.

I in them, and Thou in me, that they may be made perfect in one.

THE design and end of the application of Christ to sinners is the communication of his benefits to them; but seeing all communications of benefits necessarily imply communion, and all communion as necessarily presupposes union with his person: I shall therefore, in this place, and from this scripture, treat of the mystical union betwixt Christ and believers; this union being the principal act, wherein the Spirit's application of Christ consists, of which I spake (as to its general nature) in the former sermon.

In this verse (omitting the context) we find a threefold union, one betwixt the Father and Christ, a second betwixt Christ and believers, a third betwixt believers themselves.

First, Thou in me: This is a glorious ineffable union, and is fundamental to the other two. The Father is not only in Christ, in respect of dear affections, as one dear friend is in another, who is as his own soul; nor only essentially, in respect of the identity and sameness of nature and attributes, in which respect Christ is the express image of his person, Heb. i. 3. But he is in Christ also as Mediator, by communicating the fulness of the Godhead, which dwells in him as God-man, in a transcendent and singular manner, so as it never dwelt, nor can dwell in any other, Col. ii. 9.

Secondly, I in them : Here is the mystical union betwixt Christ and the saints, *q. d.* Thou and I are one essentially, they and I are one mystically : and thou and I are one by communication of the Godhead, and singular fulness of the Spirit to me as Mediator ; and they and I are one, by my communication of the Spirit to them in measure.

Thirdly, From hence results a third union betwixt believers themselves ; *that they may be made perfect in one ;* the same Spirit dwelling in them all, and equally uniting them all to me, as living members to their Head of influence, there must needs be a dear and intimate union betwixt themselves, as fellow-members of the same body.

Now my business, at this time, lying in the second branch, namely, the union betwixt Christ and believers, I shall gather up the substance of it into this doctrinal proposition, to which I shall apply this discourse.

> Doct. *That there is a strict and dear union betwixt Christ and all true believers.*

The scriptures have borrowed from the book of nature four elegant and lively metaphors, to help the nature of this mystical union with Christ into our understandings ; namely, that of pieces of timber united by glue ; that of a graff taking hold of its stock, and making one tree ; that of the husband and wife, by the marriage-covenant, becoming one flesh ; and that of the members and head animated by one soul, and so becoming one natural body. Every one of these is more lively and full than the other : and what is defective in one, is supplied in the other ; but yet, neither any of these singly, or all of them jointly, can give us a full and complete account of this mystery.

Not that of two pieces united by glue, 1 Cor. v. 17. "He that " is joined to the Lord is one spirit," κολλαμενος, glued to the Lord. For though this cementeth, and strongly joins them in one, yet this is but a faint and imperfect shadow of our union with Christ ; for though this union by glue be intimate, yet not vital, but so is that of the soul with Christ.

Nor that of the graff and stock, mentioned Rom. vi. 5. for though it be there said, that believers are συμφυτοι, implanted, or ingrafted by way of incision, and this union betwixt it and the stock be vital, for it partakes of the vital sap and juice of it ; yet here also is a remarkable defect, for the graff is of a more excellent kind and nature than the stock, and, upon that account, the tree receives its denomination from it, as from the more noble and excellent part; but Christ, into whom believers are ingrafted, is infinitely more excellent than they, and they are denominated from him.

Nor yet that conjugal union, by marriage-covenant, betwixt a man and his wife; for though this be exceeding dear and intimate, so that a man leaves father and mother, and cleaves to his wife, and they two become one flesh; yet this union is not indissolvable, but may and must be broken by death; and then the relict lives alone without any communion with, or relation to, the person that was once so dear; but this betwixt Christ and the soul can never be dissolved by death, it abides to eternity.

Nor, lastly, that of the head and members united by one vital spirit, and so making one physical body, mentioned Eph. iv. 15, 16. for though one soul actuates every member, yet it doth not knit every member alike near to the head, but some are nearer, and others removed farther from it; but here every member is alike nearly united with Christ the Head; the weak are as near to him as the strong.

Two things are necessary to be opened in the doctrinal part of this point. 1. The reality. 2. The quality of this union.

First, For the reality of it, I shall make it appear, that there is such a union betwixt Christ and believers; it is no *Ens rationis* empty notion, or cunningly devised fable, but a most certain demonstrable truth, which appears,

First, From the communion which is betwixt Christ and believers; in this the apostle is express, 1 John i. 3. " Truly our " fellowship is with the Father, and with his Son Jesus Christ;" κοινωνια. It signifies such fellowship or copartnership, as persons have by a joint interest in one and the same enjoyment, which is in common betwixt them. So Heb. iii. 14. we are μετοχοι, *partakers of Christ.* And Psal. xlv. 7. מחבריך, here the saints are called the companions, consorts or fellows of Christ; " and " that not only in respect of his * assumption of our mortality, and " investing us with his immortality, but it hath a special reference " and respect to the unction of the Holy Ghost, or graces of the " Spirit, of which believers are partakers with him and through " him." Now this communion of the saints with Christ is intirely and necessarily dependent upon their union with him, even as much as the branch's participation of the sap and juice depends upon its union and coalition with the stock: take away union, and

---

* *Ipse venit in sortem nostræ mortalitatis, ut in sortem nos adduceret suæ immortalitis, clarum autem est, hic agi de consortibus unctionis: quales sunt omnes fideles qui unctionis participes fiunt.* Rivet.

there can be no communion, or communications, which is clear
from 1 Cor. iii. 22, 23. "All is yours, and ye are Christ's, and
"Christ is God's." Where you see how all our participation of
Christ's benefits is built upon our union with Christ's person.

Secondly, The reality of the believer's union with Christ, is evident from the imputation of Christ's righteousness to him for his
justification. That a believer is justified before God by a righteousness without himself, is undeniable from Rom. iii. 24. "Being
"justified freely by his grace, through the redemption that is
"in Christ Jesus." And that Christ's righteousness becomes ours
by imputation is as clear from Rom. iv. 23, 24. but it can never
be imputed to us, except we be united to him, and become one
with him: which is also plainly asserted in 1 Cor. i. 30. "But of
"him are ye (in Christ Jesus) who of God is made unto us wis-
"dom and righteousness, sanctification, and redemption." He
communicates his merits unto none but those that are in him.
Hence all those vain cavils of the Papists, disputing against our
justification by the righteousness of Christ, and asserting it to be
by inherent righteousness, are solidly answered.

When they demand, How can we be justified by the righteousness of another? Can I be rich with another man's money, or preferred by another man's honours? Our answer is, Yes, if that
other be my surety or husband. Indeed Peter can not be justified
by the righteousness of Paul; but both may be justified by the
righteousness of Christ imputed to them; they being members,
jointly knit to one common Head. Principal and surety are one
in obligation and construction of law. Head and members are one
body, branch and stock are one tree; and it is no strange thing
to see a graff live by the sap of another stock, when once it is ingrafted into it.

Thirdly, The sympathy that is betwixt Christ and believers,
proves a union betwixt them; Christ and the saints smile and sigh
together. St. Paul in Col. i. 24. tells us, that he did "fill up that
"which was behind," *τα υσερηματα*,——the remainders of the
"sufferings of Christ in his flesh:" not as if Christ's sufferings
were imperfect, ("for by one offering he hath perfected for ever
"them that are sanctified," Heb. x. 14.) but in these two scriptures, Christ is considered in a twofold capacity; he suffered once in
corpore proprio, in his own person, as Mediator; these sufferings
are complete and full, and in that sense he suffers no more: he
suffers also in *corpore mystico*, in his church and members, thus he
still suffers in the sufferings of every saint for his sake; and though
these sufferings in his mystical body are not equal to the other,
either *pondere et mensura*, in their weight and value, nor yet designed *ex officio*, for the same use and purpose, to satisfy by their proper

merit, offended justice; nevertheless they are truly reckoned the sufferings of Christ, because the head suffers when the members do; and without this supposition, that place, Acts ix. 5. is never to be understood, when Christ, the Head in heaven, cries out, " Saul, Saul, why persecutest thou me?" when the foot was trod upon on earth : How doth Christ sensibly feel our sufferings, or we his, if there be not a mystical union betwixt him and us?

Fourthly, and lastly, The way and manner in which the saints shall be raised at the last day, proves this mystical union betwixt Christ and them ; for they are not to be raised as others, by the naked power of God without them, but by the virtue of Christ's resurrection as their Head, sending forth vital, quickening influences into their dead bodies, which are united to him as well as their souls.   For so we find it, Rom. viii. 11.   " But if the Spirit " of him that raised up Jesus from the dead dwell in you, he that " raised up Christ from the dead, shall also quicken your mortal " bodies, by his Spirit that dwelleth in you;" even as it is in our awaking out of natural sleep, first the animal-spirits in the head begin to rouse and play there, and then the senses and members are loosed throughout the whole body.

Now it is impossible the saints should be raised in the last resurrection, by the Spirit of Christ dwelling in them, if that Spirit did not knit and unite them to him, as members to their head. So then by all this, it is proved, that there is a real union of the saints with Christ.

Next, I shall endeavour to open the quality and nature of this union, and shew you what it is, according to the weak apprehensions we have of so sublime a mystery ; and this I shall do in a general and particular account of it.

First, More generally, it is an intimate conjunction of believers to Christ, by the imparting of his Spirit to them, whereby they are enabled to believe and live in him.

All divine and spiritual life is originally in the Father, and cometh not to us, but by and through the Son, John v. 26. to him hath the Father given to have an αυτοζωη,——a quickening, enlivening power in himself; but the Son communicates this life which is in him to none but by and through the Spirit, Rom. viii. 2.   " The Spirit of life which is in Christ Jesus, hath made " me free from the law of sin and death."

The Spirit must therefore first take hold of us, before we can live in Christ ; and when he doth so, then we are enabled to exert that vital act of faith, whereby we receive Christ; all this lies plain in that one scripture, John vi. 57.   " As the living Father " hath sent me, and I live by the Father, so he that eateth me, " (that is by faith applies me) even he shall live by me."   So that these two, namely, the Spirit on Christ's part, and faith, his work on our part, are the two ligaments by which we are knit to Christ.

So that the Spirit's work in uniting or ingrafting a soul in Christ, is like the cutting off the graff from its native stock (which he doth by his illuminations and convictions) and closing it with the living, when it is thus prepared, and so enabling it (by the infusion of faith) to suck and draw the vital sap, and thus it becomes one with him. Or as the many members in the natural body, being all quickened and animated by the same vital spirit, become one body with the head, which is the principal member, Eph. iv. 4. " There is one body and one spirit."

More particularly, we shall consider the properties of this union, that so we may the better understand the nature of it. And here I shall open the nature of it both negatively and affirmatively.

First, Negatively, by removing all false notions and misapprehensions of it. And we say,

First, The saints union with Christ is not a mere mental union only in conceit or notion, but really exists *extra mentem,* whether we conceit it or not. I know the atheistical world censures all these things as fancies and idle imaginations, but believers know the reality of them, John xiv. 20. " At that day you shall know " that I am in my Father, and you in me, and I in you." This doctrine is not fantastical, but scientifical.

Secondly, The saints union with Christ is not a physical union, such as is betwixt the members of a natural body and the head; our nature indeed is assumed into union with the person of Christ, but it is the singular honour of that blessed and holy flesh of Christ, to be so united as to make one person with him; that union is hypostatical, this only mystical.

Thirdly, Nor is it an essential union, or union with the divine nature, so as our beings are thereby swallowed up and lost in the Divine being.

Some there be indeed that talk at that wild rate, of being godded into God, and christed into Christ; and those unwary expressions of Greg. Naz. Θεοποιειν, and Χριϛοποιειν, do but too much countenance those daring spirits; but oh, there is an infinite distance betwixt us and Christ, in respect of nature and excellency, notwithstanding this union.

Fourthly, The union I here speak of, is not a fœderal union, or an union by covenant only: such an union indeed there is betwixt Christ and believers, but that is consequential to and wholly dependent upon this.

Fifthly, and lastly, It is not a mere moral union by love and affection; thus we say, one soul is in two bodies, a friend is another self; the lover is in the person beloved; such an union of hearts and affections there is also betwixt Christ and the saints, but this is of another nature; that we call a moral, this is a mystical union; that only knits our affections, but this our persons to Christ.

Secondly, Positively. And, *First*, Though this union neither makes us one person nor essence with Christ, yet it knits our persons most intimately and nearly to the person of Christ. The church is Christ's body, Col. i. 24. not his natural, but his mystical body; that is to say, his body is a mystery, because it is to him as his natural body. The saints stand to Christ in the same relation that the natural members of the body stand to the head, and he stands in the same relation to them, that the head stands in to the natural members; and consequently they stand related to one another, as the members of a natural body do to each other.

Christ and the saints are not one, as the oak and the ivy that clasps it are one, but as the graff and stock are one; it is not an union by adhesion, but incorporation. Husband and wife are not so near, soul and body are not so near, as Christ and the believing soul are near to each other.

Secondly, The mystical union is wholly supernatural, wrought by the alone power of God. So it is said, 1 Cor. i. 30. "But of " him are ye in Christ Jesus." We can no more unite ourselves to Christ, than a branch can incorporate itself into another stock; it is of him, i. e. of God, his proper and alone work.

There are only two ligaments, or bands of union betwixt Christ and the soul, viz. the Spirit on his part, and faith on ours. But when we say faith is the band of union on our part, the meaning is not, that it is so our own act, as that it springs naturally from us, or is educed from the power of our own wills; no, for the apostle expressly contradicts it, Eph. ii. 8. " It is not of yourselves, " it is the gift of God." But we are the subjects of it, and though the act on that account be ours, yet the power enabling us to believe is God's, Eph. i. 19, 20.

Thirdly, The mystical union is an immediate union; immediate I say, not as excluding means and instruments, for several means and many instruments are employed for the effecting of it; but immediate, as excluding degrees of nearness among the members of Christ's mystical body.

Every member in the natural body stands not as near to the head as another, but so do all the mystical members of Christ's body to him: every member, the smallest as well as the greatest, hath an immediate coalition with Christ, 1 Cor. i. 2. " To the church of God, " which is at Corinth, to them that are sanctified in Christ Jesus,

" called to be saints, with all that in every place call upon the
" name of Jesus Christ our Lord, both theirs and ours."

Among the factions in this church at Corinth, those that said,
I am of Christ, as arrogating Christ to themselves, were as much a
faction, as those that said, *I am of Paul*, 1 Cor. i. 30.   To cure
this he tells them, he is *both theirs and ours*.   Such inclosures are
against law.

Fourthly, The saints mystical union with Christ is a fundamental
union ; it is fundamental by way of sustentation ; all our fruits of
obedience depend upon it, John xv. 4.   " As the branch cannot
" bear fruit except it abide in the vine, no more can ye, except
" ye abide in me."   It is fundamental to all our privileges and
comfortable claims, 1 Cor. iii. 23.   " All is yours, for ye are
" Christ's."   And it is fundamental to all our hopes and expectations of glory ; for it is " Christ in you the hope of glory," Col.
i. 27.   So then, destroy this union, and with it you destroy all our
fruits, privileges, and eternal hopes, at one stroke.

Fifthly, The mystical union is a most efficacious union, for
through this union the divine power flows into our souls, both to
quicken us with the life of Christ, and to conserve and secure that
life in us after it is so infused.

Without the union of the soul to Christ, which is to be conceived efficiently as the Spirit's act, there can be no union formally considered ; and, without these, no communications of life
from Christ to us, Eph. iv. 16.   And as there is that ενεργεια, or
effectual working of the spirit of life in every part, which he there
speaks of, (as though you should say, the first appearances of a new
life, a spiritual vitality diffused through the soul, which ere while
was dead in sin) yet still this union with Christ is as necessary to
the maintaining, as before it was to the producing of it.

For why is it that this life is not again extinguished, and wholly
suffocated in us, by so many deadly wounds as are given it by
temptations and corruptions ?   Surely no reason can be assigned
more satisfying than that which Christ himself gives us, in John
xiv. 19.   " Because I live, ye shall live also :"   q. d. whilst there is
vital sap in me the root, you that are branches in me cannot
wither and die.

Sixthly, The mystical union is an indissoluble union : there is
an everlasting tye betwixt Christ and the believer ; and herein also
it is beyond all other unions in the world ; death dissolves the dear
union betwixt the husband and wife, friend and friend, yea, betwixt soul and body, but not betwixt Christ and the soul, the bands
of this union rot not in the grave.   " What shall separate us from
" the love of Christ ?" saith the apostle, Rom. viii. 35, 38, 39.
He bids defiance to all his enemies, and triumphs in the firmness

of his union over all hazards that seem to threaten it. It is with Christ and us, in respect of the *mystical union*, as it is with Christ himself, in respect of the *hypostatical union ;* that was not dissolved by his death, when the *natural union* betwixt his soul and body was, nor can this mystical union of our souls and bodies with Christ be dissolved, when the union betwixt us and our dearest relations, yea, betwixt the soul and body, is dissolved by death. God calls himself the God of Abraham, long after his body was turned into dust.

Seventhly, It is an *honourable union* *, yea, the highest honour that can be done unto men ; the greatest honour that was ever done to our common nature, was by its assumption into union with the second person *hypostatically*, and the highest honour that was ever done to our single persons, was their union with Christ *mystically.* To be a servant of Christ is a dignity transcendent to the highest advancement among men ; but to be a member of Christ, how matchless and singular is the glory thereof! And yet, such honour have all the saints, Eph. v. 30. " We are members " of his body, of his flesh, and of his bones."

Eighthly, It is a most *comfortable union :* yea, the ground of all solid comfort, both in life and death. Whatever troubles, wants, or distresses befal such, in this is abundant relief and support, Christ is mine, and I am his ; what may not a good soul make out of that ! If I am Christ's, then let him take care for me, and, indeed, in so doing, he doth but take care for his own. He is my head, and to him it belongs to consult the safety and welfare of his own members, Eph. i. 22, 23. He is not only an head to his own, by way of *influence*, but to all things else, by way of *dominion*, for their good. How comfortably may we repose ourselves, under that cheering consideration, upon him at all times and in all difficult cases !

Ninthly, It is a *fruitful union ;* the immediate end of it is fruit, Rom. vii. 4. " We are married to Christ, that we should bring " forth fruit to God." All the fruit we bear before our ingrafture into Christ is worse than none ; till the person be in Christ, the work cannot be evangelically good and acceptable to God : " We are made accepted in the Beloved," Eph. i. 6. Christ is a fruitful root, and makes all the branches that live in him so too, John xv. 8.

Tenthly, and lastly, It is an *enriching union ;* for, by our union with his person, we are immediately interested in all his riches,

---

* Christ is the head, summit, and crown of all dignity, without whom there is nothing (truly) noble in all this sublunary world, who has heaven for his throne, and the earth for his footstool. The earth, I say, with all the persons of high rank and station in it are put under his feet. *Laur. Humphred. on Nobility.*

1 Cor. i. 30. How rich and great a person do the little arms of faith clasp and embrace! " All is yours," 1 Cor. iii. 22. All that Christ hath becomes ours, either by communication to us, or improvement for us: His Father, John xx. 17. His promises, 2 Cor. i. 20. His providences, Rom. viii. 28. His glory, John xvii. 24. It is all ours by virtue of our union with him.

Thus you see briefly what the mystical union is. Next we shall improve it.

Inference 1. *If there be such a union betwixt Christ and believers, Oh then what transcendent dignity hath God put upon believers.*

Well might Constantine prefer the honour of being a member of the church, before that of being head of the empire *; for it is not only above all earthly dignities and honours, but, in some respect, above that honour which God hath put upon the angels of glory.

Great is the dignity of the angelical nature: the angels are the highest and most honourable species of creatures; they also have the honour continually to behold the face of God in heaven, and yet, in this one respect the saints are preferred to them, they have a mystical union with Christ, as their head of influence, by whom they are quickened with spiritual life, which the angels have not.

It is true, there is an αναχεφαλαιωσις, or gathering together of all in heaven and earth under Christ as a common head, Eph. i. 10. He is the Head of *angels* as well as saints, but in different respects. To angels he is an head of *dominion* and government, but to saints he is both an head of dominion, and of vital *influence* too; they are his chief and most honourable subjects, but not his mystical members: they are as the Barons and Nobles in his kingdom, but the saints as the dear Spouse and Wife of his bosom. This dignifies the believer above the greatest angel. And as the nobles of the kingdom think it a preferment and honour to serve the Queen, so the glorious angels think it no degradation or dishonour to them to serve the Saints; for to this honourable office they are appointed, Heb. i. 14. to be ministering or serviceable spirits, for the good of them that shall be heirs of salvation. The chiefest servant disdains not to honour and serve the heir.

Some imperious grandees would frown, should some of these persons but presume to approach their presence; but God sets them before his face with delight, and angels delight to serve them.

Infer. 2. *If there be such a strict and inseparable union betwixt*

---

* If thou wouldst be called a man of power, put on Christ who is the power and wisdom of God, and in all things join thyself to the Lord, that thou mayest be one spirit with him, and then thou shalt become a man of power. *Orig. Hom. in Num.* xxxi.

Christ and believers, then the grace of believers can never totally fail; Immortality is the privilege of grace, because sanctified persons are inseparably united to Christ the Fountain of life: " Your " life is hid with Christ in God," Col. iii. 3. Whilst the sap of life is in the root, the branches live by it. Thus it is betwixt Christ and believers, John xiv. 19. " Because I live, ye shall live also." See how Christ binds up their life in one bundle with his own, plainly intimating, that it is as impossible for them to die, as it is for himself; he cannot live without them.

True it is, the spiritual life of believers is encountered by many strong and fierce oppositions: It is also brought to a low ebb in some, but we are always to remember, that there are some things which pertain to the essence of that life, in which the very being of it lies, and some things that pertain only to its well-being. All those things which belong to the well being of the new-creature, as manifestations, joys, spiritual comforts, &c. may, for a time, fail, yea, and grace itself may suffer great losses and remissions in its degrees, notwithstanding our union with Christ; but still the essence of it is immortal, which is no small relief to gracious souls. When the means of grace fail, as it is threatened, Amos viii. 11. when temporary formal professors drop away from Christ like withered leaves from the trees in a windy day, 2 Tim. ii. 18. and when the natural union of their souls and bodies is suffering a dissolution from each other by death, when that *silver cord* is loosed, this *golden chain* holds firm, 1 Cor. iii. 23.

Inf. 3. *Is the union so intimate betwixt Christ and believers? How great and powerful a motive then is this, to make us open-handed and liberal in relieving the necessities and wants of every gracious person! For in relieving them, we relieve Christ himself.*

Christ *personal* is not the object of our pity and charity, he is at the fountain-head of all the riches in glory, Eph. iv. 10. but Christ *mystical* is exposed to necessities and wants, he feels hunger and thirst, cold and pains, in his body the church *; and he is refreshed, relieved, and comforted, in their refreshments and comforts. Christ the Lord of heaven and earth, in this consideration is sometimes in need of a penny; he tells us his wants and poverty, and how he is relieved, Matt. xxv. 35, 40. A text believed and understood by very few, " I was an hungered, and ye gave me meat: " I was thirsty, and ye gave me drink: I was a stranger, and ye " took me in. Then shall the righteous answer, Lord, when saw " we thee an hungered, &c. And the King shall answer, and say

---

* He who is not moved with the condition of a brother in the church, let him be moved with the contemplation of Christ; and he who does not regard his fellow servant in straits and want, let him regard the Lord, dwelling in that man whom he despises. *Cyprian on Works and Charity.*

" unto them, verily I say unto you, in as much as ye have done
" it unto one of the least of these my brethren, ye have done it
" unto me."

It was the saying of a great divine, that he thought scarce any
man on earth did fully understand and believe this truth, and he
conceives so much hinted in the very text, where the righteous
themselves reply, " Lord, when saw we thee sick," &c. intimating
in the question, that they did not thoroughly understand the nearness, yea, *oneness* of those persons with Christ, for whom they did
these things.   And, indeed, it is incredible that a Christian can be
hard-hearted and close-handed to that necessitous Christian, in refreshing and relieving of whom, he verily believes, that he ministers refreshment to Christ himself.

O think again and again upon this scripture; consider what forcible and mighty arguments are here laid together, to engage relief
to the wants of Christians.

Here you see their near relation to Christ; they are mystically
one person; what you did to them, you did to me.   Here you see
also how kindly Christ takes it at our hands, acknowledging all
those kindnesses that were bestowed upon him, even to a bit of
bread : He is, you see, content to take it as a courtesy, who
might demand it by authority, and bereave you of all immediately
upon refusal.

Yea, here you see one single branch or act of obedience, (our
charity to the saints) is singled out from among all the duties of
obedience, and made the test and evidence of our sincerity in that
great day, and men blessed or cursed according to the love they
have manifested this way to the saints.

O then, let none that understand the relation the saints have to
Christ, as the members to the head, or the relation they have to
each other thereby, as fellow-members of the same body, from henceforth suffer Christ to hunger, if they have bread to relieve him, or
Christ to be thirsty, if they have wherewith to refresh him: this
union betwixt Christ and the saints affords an argument beyond all
other arguments in the world to prevail with us.   Methinks, a little *rhetoric* might persuade a Christian to part with any thing he
hath for Christ, who parted with the glory of heaven, yea, and his
own blood for his sake.

Inf. 4. *Do Christ and believers make but one mystical person ?
How unnatural and absurd then are all those acts of unkindness,
whereby believers wound and grieve Jesus Christ! This is as if
the hand should wound its own head, from which it receives life,
sense, motion, and strength.*

When satan smites Christ by a wicked man, he then wounds him with the hand of an enemy; but when his temptations prevail upon the saints to sin, he wounds him as it were with his own hand: As the *eagle* and *tree* in the *fable* complained, the one that he was wounded by an arrow winged with his own feathers; the other, that it was cleaved asunder by a wedge hewn out of its own limbs.

Now the evil and disingenuity of such sins are to be measured not only by the near relation Christ sustains to believers as their Head; but more particularly from the several benefits they receive from him as such; for in wounding Christ by their sins,

First, They wound their *Head of influence,* through whom they live, and without whom they had still remained in the state of sin and death, Eph. iv. 16. Shall Christ send life to us, and we return that which is death to him! O how absurd, how disingenuous is this!

Secondly, They wound their *Head of government.* Christ is a *guiding,* as well as a *quickening* Head, Col. i. 18. He is your wisdom, he guides you by his counsels to glory: but must he be thus requited for all his faithful conduct! What do you, when you sin, but rebel against his government, refusing to follow his counsels, and obeying, in the mean time, a deceiver, rather than him.

Thirdly, They wound their *consulting Head,* who cares, provides, and projects, for the welfare and safety of the body. Christians, you know your affairs below have not been steered and managed by your own wisdom, but that orders have been given from heaven for your security and supply from day to day. " I know, O Lord, " (saith the prophet) that the way of man is not in himself, neither " is it in him that walks to direct his own steps," Jer. x. 23.

It is true, Christ is out of your sight, and you see him not: but he sees you, and orders every thing that concerns you. And is this a due requital of all that care he hath taken for you? Do you thus requite the Lord for all his benefits? What recompense evil for good! O let shame cover you.

Fourthly, and *lastly,* They wound *their Head of honour.* Christ your Head is the fountain of honour to you: This is your glory that you are related to him as your head: You are, on this account, (as before was noted) exalted above angels.

Now then consider, how vile a thing it is to reflect the least dishonour upon him, from whom you derive all your glory. O consider and bewail it.

Inf. 5. *Is there so strict and intimate a relation and union betwixt Christ and the saints? Then surely they can never want what is good for their souls or bodies.*

Every one naturally cares and provides for his own, especially for his own body: yet we can more easily violate the law of nature, and be cruel to our own flesh, than Christ can be so to his mystical body *. I know it is hard to rest upon, and rejoice in a promise, when necessities pinch, and we see not from whence relief should arise; but O! what sweet satisfaction and comfort might a necessitous believer find in these considerations, would he but keep them upon his heart in such a day of straits.

First, Whatever my distresses are for quality, number, or degree, they are all known even to the least circumstance, by Christ my Head: He looks down from heaven upon all my afflictions, and understands them more fully than I that feel them, Psal. xxxviii. 9. " Lord all my desire is before thee, and my groaning " is not hid from thee."

Secondly, He not only knows them, but feels them as well as knows them ; " We have not an High-priest that cannot be touch- " ed with the feeling of our infirmities," Heb. iv. 15. In all your afflictions he is afflicted ; tender sympathy cannot but flow from such intimate union; therefore in Matt. xxv. 35. he saith, I was an hungered, and I was athirst, and I was naked. For indeed his sympathy and tender compassion gave him as quick a resentment, and as tender a sense of their wants, as if they had been his own. Yea,

Thirdly, He not only knows and feels my wants, but hath enough in his hand, and much more than enough to supply them all; for all things are delivered to him by the Father, Luke x. 22. All the storehouses in heaven and earth are his, Phil. iv. 19.

Fourthly, He bestows all earthly good things, even to superfluity and redundance upon his very enemies, " They have more than " heart can wish," Psal. lxxiii. 7. He is bountiful to strangers; he loads very enemies with these things, and can it be supposed he will in the mean time starve his own, and neglect those whom he loves as his own flesh? It cannot be. Moreover,

Fifthly, Hitherto he hath not suffered me to perish in any former straits; when, and where was it that he forsook me? This is not the first plunge of trouble I have been in; have I not found him a God at hand! How oft have I seen him in the mount of difficulties!

Sixthly, and *lastly*, I have his promise and engagement that he will never leave me nor forsake me, Heb. xiii. 5. and John xiv. 18. a promise which hath never failed since the hour it was first made. If then the Lord Jesus knows and feels all my wants, hath enough, and more than enough to supply them, if he gives even

---

* *Qui misit filium, immisit spiritum, promisit vultum, quid tandem denegabit ?* i. e. He who hath sent his Son, put the Spirit within us, and promised his smiles, What will he deny us ?

to redundance unto his enemies, hath not hitherto forsaken me, and hath promised he never will ? Why then is my soul thus disquieted in me ! Surely there is no cause it should be so.

Inf. 6. *If the saints are so nearly united to Christ, as the members to the head : O then, how great a sin, and full of danger is it for any to wrong and persecute the saints ! For in so doing, they must needs persecute Christ himself.*

" Saul, Saul, (saith Christ) why persecutest thou me?" Acts ix. 4. * The righteous God holds himself obliged to vindicate oppressed innocency, though it be in the persons of wicked men ; how much more when it is in a member of Christ ? " He that toucheth " you toucheth the apple of mine eye," Zech. ii. 8. And is it to be imagined that Christ will sit still, and suffer his enemies to hurt or injure the very apples of his eyes? No, " He hath ordained " his arrows against the persecutors," Psalm vii. 13.

O it were better thine hand should wither, and thine arm fall from thy shoulder, than ever it should be lifted up against Christ, in the poorest of his members. Believe it, sirs, not only your violent actions, but your hard speeches are all set down upon your doom's-day book ; and you shall be brought to an account for them in the great day, Jude 15. Beware what arrows you shoot, and be sure of your mark before you shoot them.

Inf. 7. *If there be such an union betwixt Christ and the saints, as hath been described, upon what comfortable terms then may believers part with their bodies at death ?*

Christ your Head is risen, therefore you cannot be lost : nay, he is not only risen from the dead himself, but is also " become the " first-fruits of them that slept," 1 Cor. xv. 20. Believers are his members, his fulness, he cannot therefore be complete without you : a part of Christ cannot perish in the grave †, much less burn in hell. Remember, when you feel the natural union dissolving, that this mystical union can never be dissolved : the pangs of death cannot break this tye. And as there is a peculiar excellency in the believer's life, so there is a singular support, and peculiar comfort in his death ; " To me to live is Christ, and to die is gain," Phil. i. 21.

---

* Agesilaus was wont to say, That he very much wondered, that those were not reckoned up in the number of sacrilegious persons, who injured those who made supplication to God, or worshipped him : By which he signified, that not only those should be reckoned injurious, who robbed the gods themselves, or their temples, but even these chiefly who affronted their servants or heralds. *Æmyl. Prob.*

† To say that the temple of God, in which the Spirit of the Father dwells, the members of Christ, shall not partake of salvation, but be brought into perdition ? what is it but the greatest blasphemy ? *Iren. lib. 5.*

Inf. 8. If there be such an union betwixt Christ and believers, *How doth it concern every man to try and examine his state, whether he is really united with Christ or not, by the natural and proper effects which always flow from this union?* As,

First, The real communication of Christ's holiness to the soul. We cannot be united with this root, and not partake of the vital sap of sanctification from him; all that are planted into him, are planted into the likeness of his death, and of his resurrection, Rom. vi. 5, 6. viz. by mortification and vivification.

Secondly, They that are so nearly united to him, as members to the head, cannot but love him and value him above their own lives; as we see in nature, the hand and arm will interpose to save the head. The nearer the union, the stronger always is the affection.

Thirdly, The members are subject to the head. Dominion in the head must needs infer subjection in the members, Eph. v. 24. In vain do we claim union with Christ as our head, whilst we are governed by our own wills, and our lusts give us law.

Fourthly, All that are united to Christ do bear fruit to God, Rom. vii. 4. Fruitfulness is the next end of our union; there are no barren branches growing upon this fruitful root.

Inf. 9. *Lastly, How much are believers engaged to walk as the members of Christ, in the visible exercises of all those graces and duties, which the consideration of their near relation to him exacts from them.* As,

First, How contented and well pleased should we be with our outward lot, however providence hath cast it for us in this world? O do not repine, God hath dealt bountifully with you; upon others he hath bestowed the good things of this world; upon you, himself in Christ.

Secondly, How humble and lowly in spirit should you be under your great advancement! It is true, God hath magnified you greatly by this union, but yet do not swell. " You bear not the " root, but the root you," Rom. xi. 18. You shine, but it is as the stars, with a borrowed light.

Thirdly, How zealous should you be to honour Christ, who hath put so much honour upon! Be willing to give glory to Christ, though his glory should rise out of your shame. Never reckon that glory that goes to Christ, to be lost to you: when you lie at his feet, in the most particular heart-breaking confessions of sin, yet let this please you, that therein you have given him glory.

Fourthly, How exact and circumspect should you be in all your ways, remembering whose you are, and whom you represent! Shall it be said, that a member of Christ was convicted of unrighteousness and unholy actions! God forbid. " If we say, we have " fellowship with him, and walk in darkness, we lie," 1 John i. 6.

" And he that saith he abideth in him, ought also himself to walk
" even as he also walked," 1 John ii. 6.

Fifthly, How studious should you be of peace among yourselves,
who are so nearly united to such a Head, and thereby are made
fellow-members of the same body ! The Heathen world was never
acquainted with such an argument as the apostle urges for unity,
in Eph. iv. 3, 4.

Sixthly, and lastly, How joyful and comfortable should you be,
to whom Christ, with all his treasures and benefits, is effectually
applied in this blessed union of your souls with him ! This brings
him into your possession : O how great ! how glorious a person do
these little weak arms of your faith embrace !

Thanks be to God for Jesus Christ.

SERMON III.

Of the Nature and Use of the Gospel-ministry, as an external Mean of applying CHRIST.

2 Cor. v. 20.

*Now then, we are ambassadors for Christ, as though God did be-
seech you by us : we pray you in Christ's stead, be ye reconciled
to God.*

THE effectual application of Christ principally consists in our
union with him ; but, ordinarily, there can be no union without a gospel-tender, and an overture of him to our souls ; for,
" How shall they believe in him, of whom they have not heard ?
" and how shall they hear without a preacher ? and how shall they
" preach, except they be sent ?" Rom. x. 14.

If God be upon a design of espousing poor sinners to his Son,
there must be a treaty in order to it ; that treaty requires interlo-
cution betwixt both the parties concerned in it ; but such is our
frailty, that, should God speak immediately to us himself, it would
confound and overwhelm us : God therefore graciously condescends
and accommodates himself to our infirmity, in treating with us in
order to our union with Christ, by his *ambassadors,* and these not
angels, whose converses we cannot bear, but *men* like ourselves,
who are commissionated for the effecting of this great business betwixt Christ and us. " Now then, we are ambassadors for God,"
&c. In which words you have,

First, Christ's ambassadors commissioned.

Secondly, Their commission opened.

First, Christ's ambassadors commissioned. " Now then, we " are ambassadors for Christ." The Lord Jesus thought it not suf-ficient to print the law of grace and the blessed terms of our union with him in the scriptures, where men may read his willingness to receive them, and see the just and gracious terms and conditions upon which he offers to become theirs; but hath also set up and established a standing office in the church, to expound that law, inculcate the precepts, and urge the promises thereof; to woo and espouse souls to Christ, " I have espoused you to one Husband, " that I may present you as a chaste virgin to Christ," 2 Cor. xi. 20. and this not simply from their own affections and compassions to miserable sinners, but also by virtue of their office and commission, whereby they are authorised and appointed to that work. " We " then are ambassadors for Christ."

Secondly, Their commission opened : Wherein we find,

1. Their work appointed,

2. Their capacity described,

3. And the manner of their acting in that capacity prescribed.

First, The work whereunto the ministers of the gospel are ap-pointed, is to *reconcile the world to God ;* to work these sinful, vain, rebellious hearts, which have a strong aversion from God naturally in them, to close with him according to the articles of peace con-tained in the gospel, that thereby they may be capable to receive the mercies and benefits purchased by the death of Christ, which they cannot receive in the state of enmity and alienation.

Secondly, Their capacity described : They act *in Christ's stead,* as his *vicegerents.* He is no more in this world to treat personally with sinners, as he once did in the days of his flesh; but yet he still continues the treaty with this lower world, by his officers, requiring men to look upon them, and obey them as they would himself, if he were corporeally present, Luke x. 16. " He that " heareth you, heareth me ; and he that despiseth you, despiseth " me."

Thirdly, The manner of their acting in that capacity prescribed ; and that is, by humble, sweet, and condescending entreaties and beseechings. This best suits the meek and lamb-like Saviour whom they represent : thus he dealt with poor sinners himself, when he conversed among them ; he " would not break a bruised reed, nor " quench the smoking flax," Isa. xlii. 3. This is the way to allure and win the souls of sinners to Christ.

From hence the note is,

Doct. *That the preaching of the gospel by Christ's ambassadors, is the mean appointed for the reconciling and bringing home of sinners to Christ.*

This is clear from Rom. x. 14. 1 Cor. i. 21. and many other scriptures.

Here we shall take into consideration these three things.

First, What is implied in Christ's treating with sinners by his ambassadors or ministers.

Secondly, What is the great concernment they are to treat with sinners about.

Thirdly, What, and when is the efficacy of preaching, to bring sinners to Christ.

First, We will open what is implied and imported in Christ's treaty with sinners, by his ambassadors or ministers.

And here we find these six things implied.

1. It necessarily implies the defection and fall of man, from his estate of favour and friendship with God: If no war with heaven, what need of ambassadors of peace? The very office of the ministry is an argument of the fall. Gospel-ordinances and officers came in upon the fall, and expire with the Mediator's dispensatory-kingdom, 1 Cor. xv. 24, 25. " Then shall he deliver up the kingdom " to God, even the Father:" Thenceforth no more ordinances, no more ministers; What use can there be of them, when the treaty is ended? They have done and accomplished all they were ever intended and designed for, when they shall have reconciled to God all the number of his elect, that are dispersed among the lost and miserable posterity of Adam, and have brought them home to Christ in a perfect state, Eph. iv. 12, &c.

2. It implies the singular grace and admirable condescension of God to sinful man. That God will admit any treaty with him at all, is wonderful mercy, it is more than he would do for the angels that fell, Jude, ver. 6. " *They are* reserved in everlasting chains, " under darkness, unto the judgment of the great day." Christ took not on him their nature, but suffered myriads of them to perish, and fills up their vacant places in glory, with a number of sinful men and women, to whom the law awarded the same punishment.

But that God will not only treat, but entreat and beseech sinful men to be reconciled, is yet more wonderful. Barely to propound the terms of peace had been an astonishing mercy; but to woo and beseech stubborn enemies to be at peace, and accept their pardon, oh, how unparalleled was this condescension.

3. It implies the great dignity and honour of the gospel-ministry. *We are ambassadors for Christ*?* Ambassadors represent and personate the prince that sends them; and the honours or contempts

---

* We are ambassadors among those who serve the king of Kings; we represent the person of God and Christ: never any yet despised us with impunity, nay, without being injurious to God and Christ. *Bowles' Præfat. ad Past. Evan.*

done to them, reflect upon, and are reckoned to the person of their master, Luke x. 16. " He that heareth you, heareth me ; " and he that despiseth you, despiseth me."

Neither their persons, nor parts, are the proper ground and reason of our respects to them ; but their office and commission from Jesus Christ.

We are fallen into the dregs of time, wherein a vile contempt is poured, not only upon the persons, but the very office of the ministry ; and I could heartily wish that scripture, Mal. ii. 7, 8, 9. were thoroughly considered by us ; possibly it might inform us of the true cause and reason of this sore judgment : but surely Christ's faithful ministers deserve a better entertainment than they ordinarily find in the world ; and if we did but seriously bethink ourselves, in whose name they come, and in whose stead they stand, we should receive them as the Galatians did Paul, Gal. iv. 14. as angels of God, even as Christ Jesus.

4. Christ's treating with sinners by his ministers, who are his ambassadors, implies the strict obligation they are under to be faithful in their ministerial employment. Christ counts upon their faithfulness whom he puts into the ministry, 1 Tim. i. 12. They are accountable to him for all acts of their office, Heb. xiii. 17. If they be silent, they cannot be innocent : " Necessity is laid " upon them, and woe to them, if they preach not the gospel," 1 Cor. ix. 16.

Yea, necessity is not only laid upon them to preach, but to keep close to their commission in preaching the gospel, 1 Thess. ii. 3, 4, 5. " Our exhortation was not of deceit, nor of uncleanness, nor " in guile, but as we were allowed of God to be put in trust with " the gospel, even so we speak, not as pleasing men, but God who " trieth our hearts:" the word is not to be corrupted to please men, 2 Cor. ii. 17. their business is not to make them their disciples, but Christ's ; not to seek theirs, but them, 2 Cor. xii. 14. to keep close to their instructions, both in the matter, manner, and end of their ministry. So did Christ himself, the treasure of wisdom and knowledge ; yet, being sent by God, he saith, John vii. 16. " My doc- " trine is not mine, but his that sent me." And so he expects and requires that his ambassadors keep close to the commission he hath given them, and be (according to their measure) faithful to their trust, as he was to his. Paul is to deliver to the people, that which he also received from the Lord, 1 Cor. xi. And Timothy must keep that which was committed to him, 2 Tim. i. 14.

5. It implies the removal of the gospel-ministry to be a very great judgment to the people. The remanding of ambassadors presages an ensuing war. If the reconciling of souls to God be the greatest work, then the removal of the means and instruments

thereof, must be the sorest judgment. Some account "the falling "of the salt upon the table," ominous; but surely the falling of them whom Christ calls *the salt of the earth*, is so indeed.

What now are those once famous and renowned places, from whence Christ, (as he threatened) hath removed the candlestick, but *magna latrocinia*, dens of robbers, and mountains of prey!

6. And lastly, It implies both the wisdom and condescension of God to sinful men, in carrying on a treaty of peace with them by such ambassadors, negociating betwixt him and them. Without a treaty, there would be no reconciliation; and no method to carry on such a treaty like this; for had the Lord treated with sinners personally, and immediately, they had been overwhelmed with his awful Majesty. The appearances of God confound the creature, " Let me not hear again the voice of the Lord my God, (saith " Israel) neither let me see this great fire any more, that I die not: " Yea, so terrible was that sight, that Moses said, I exceedingly " fear and quake," Deut. xviii. 16. Heb. xii. 21.

Or, had he commissioned *angels* for this employment, though they stand not at such an infinite distance from us as God doth, yet such is the excellence of their glory (being the highest *species* and order of creatures) that their appearances would be more apt to astonish than persuade us; besides, they being creatures of another rank and kind, and not partaking with us, either in the misery of the fall, or benefit of the recovery by Christ, it is not to be supposed they should speak to us so feelingly and experimentally, as these his ministers do; they can open to you the mysteries of sin, feeling the workings thereof daily in their own hearts; they can discover to you the conflicts of the flesh and Spirit, as being daily exercised in that warfare; and then, being men of the same mould and temper, they can say to you as Elihu did to Job, chap. xxxiii. 6, 7. " Behold, I am according to thy wish, in God's " stead, I also am formed out of the clay; behold, my terror " shall not make thee afraid, neither shall my hand be heavy " upon thee."

So that, in this appointment, much of the Divine wisdom and condescension to sinners is manifested: " We have this treasure " in earthen vessels, that the excellency of the power may be of " God, and not of us," 2 Cor. iv. 7. God's glory and man's advantage are both promoted by this dispensation.

Secondly, Next we are to consider that great concernment about which these *ambassadors* of Christ are to treat with sinners; and that (as the text informs us) is their reconciliation to God.

Now reconciliation with God, is the restoring of men to that former friendship they had with God, which was broken by the fall *, and is still continued by our enmity and aversation whilst we continue in our natural and unregenerate state. Now this is the greatest and most blessed design that ever God had in the world; an astonishing and invaluable mercy to men, as will clearly appear, by considering these particulars following.

First, That God should be reconciled after such a dreadful breach as the fall of man made, is wonderful; no sin, all things considered, was ever like to this sin: other sins, like a single bullet, kill particular persons, but this, like a chain-shot, cuts off multitudes as the sand upon the sea-shore, which no man can number.

If all the posterity of Adam in their several generations, should do nothing else but bewail and lament this sin of his, whilst this world continues, yet would it not be enough lamented; for a man so newly created out of nothing, and admitted the first moment into the highest order, crowned a king over the works of God's hands, Psal. viii. 5. a man perfect and upright, without the least inordinate motion, or sinful inclination: a man whose mind was most clear, bright, and apprehensive of the will of God, whose will was free, and able to have easily put by the strongest temptation: a man in a paradise of delights, where nothing was left to desire for advancing the happiness of soul or body: a man understanding himself to be a public, complexive person, carrying not only his own, but the happiness of the whole world in his hand: so soon, upon so slight a temptation, to violate the law of his God, and involve himself and all his posterity with him, in such a gulf of guilt and misery; all which he might so easily have prevented! O wonderful amazing mercy, that ever God should think of being reconciled, or have any purposes of peace towards so vile an apostate creature as man.

Secondly, That God should be reconciled to *men,* and not to *angels,* a more high and excellent order of creatures, is yet more astonishing; when the angels fell they were lost irrecoverably; no hand of mercy was stretched out to save one of those *myriads* of excellent beings, but chains of darkness were immediately clapped on them, to reserve them to the judgment of the great day, Jude 6.

That the milder attribute should be exercised to the inferior, and the severer attribute to the more excellent creature, is just matter for eternal admiration. Who would cast away vessels of gold, and save earthen potsherds! Some indeed undertake to shew us the reasons, why the wisdom of God made no provision for the recovery of *angels* by a *Mediator* of reconciliation; partly from the

---

* To reconcile is nothing else than to make up that friendship which was broke by some grievous offence, and thus to bring enemies back into their former state of concord. *Dav. on Col.* i. 20.

high degree of the malignity of their sin, who sinned in the light of heaven; partly because it was decent, that the first breach of the Divine law should be punished, to secure obedience for the future. And besides, the angelical nature was not entirely lost, *myriads* of *angels* still continuing in their innocency and glory; when as all mankind was lost in Adam.

But we must remember still the law made no distinction, but awarded the same punishment, and therefore it was mercy alone that made the difference, and mercy for ever is to be admired by men; how astonishing is the grace of God, that moves in a way of reconciliation to us, out of design to fill up the vacant places in heaven, from which angels fell, with such poor worms as we are! Angels excluded, and men received. O stupendous mercy!

Thirdly, That God should be *wholly* and *thoroughly* reconciled to man, so that no fury remains in him against us; according to that scripture, Isa. xxvii. 4. is still matter of further wonder.

The design he sends his *ambassadors* to you about, is not the allaying and mitigating of his wrath, (which yet would be matter of great joy to the damned) but thoroughly to quench all his wrath, so that no degree thereof shall ever be felt by you. O blessed embassy? " Beautiful upon the mountains are the feet of them that " bring such tidings." God offers you a full reconciliation, a plenary remission.

Fourthly, That God should be *freely* reconciled to sinners, and discharge them without any, the least satisfaction to his justice from them is, and for ever will be, marvellous in their eyes.

O what mercy would the damned account it, if after a thousand years torment in hell, God would at last be reconciled to them, and put an end to their misery! But believers are discharged without bearing any part of the curse, not one farthing of that debt is levied upon them.

Object. If you say, how can this be, when God stands upon full satisfaction to his justice before any soul be discharged and restored to favour? freely reconciled, and yet fully satisfied, how can this be?

Solut. Very well, for this mercy comes freely to your hands, how costly soever it proved to Christ; and that free remission, and full satisfaction, are not contradictory and inconsistent things, is plain enough from that scripture, Rom. iii. 24. " Being justified " freely by his grace, through the redemption that is in Christ Je- " sus:" freely, and yet in the way of redemption.

For though Christ, your Surety, hath made satisfaction in your name and stead, yet it was his life, his blood, and not yours, that went for it, and this Surety was of God's own appointment, and providing, without your thoughts or contrivance. O blessed reconciliation ! happy is the people that hear the joyful sound of it.

Fifthly, and lastly, that God should be finally reconciled to sinners, so that never any new breach shall happen betwixt him and them any more, so as to dissolve the league of friendship, is a most ravishing and transporting message.

Two things give confirmation and full security to reconciled ones, viz. the terms of the covenant, and the intercession of the Mediator.

The covenant of grace gives great security to believers, against new breaches betwixt God and them. It is said, Jer. xxxii. 40. " And I will make an everlasting covenant with them, that I will " not turn away from them to do them good, but I will put my " fear in their hearts, that they shall not depart from me." The fear of the Lord is a choice preservative against second revolts, and therefore taken into the covenant. It is no *hinderance,* but a special *guard* to assurance.

There is no doubt of God's faithfulness: that part of the promise is easily believed, that he will not turn away from us to do us good: all the doubt is of the inconstancy of our hearts with God, and against that danger, this promise makes provision.

Moreover, the *intercession* of Christ in heaven secures the saints in their reconciled state, 1 John ii. 1, 2. " If any man sin, we have " an Advocate with the Father, Jesus Christ the righteous, and he " is the Propitiation." He continually appears in heaven before the Father, " as a lamb that had been slain," Rev. v. 6. And as the bow in the clouds, Rev. iv. 3. So that as long as Christ thus appears in the presence of God for us, it is not possible our state of justification and reconciliation can be again dissolved.

And this is that blessed *embassy* gospel-ministers are employed about; he hath committed to them the word of this reconciliation.

In the last place, we are to enquire what, and whence is this efficacy of preaching, to reconcile and bring home sinners to Christ.

That its efficacy is great in convincing, humbling, and changing the hearts of men, is past all debate and question. " The wea-" pons of our warfare (saith the apostle) are not carnal, but migh-" ty through God, to the pulling down of strong holds, cast-" ing down imaginations, and every high thing that exalteth " itself against the knowledge of God, and bringing into captivity " every thought to the obedience of Christ," 2 Cor. x. 4, 5. No heart so hard, no conscience so stupid, but this sword can pierce and wound ; in an instant it can cast down all those vain reasonings and fond imaginations, which the carnal heart hath been building all its life long, and open a fair passage for convictions of sin, and the fears and terrors of wrath to come, into that heart that never was afraid of these things before. So Acts ii. 37. " When " they heard this, they were pricked to the heart, and said unto " Peter, and to the rest of the apostles, Men and brethren, what " shall we do ?"

What shall we do? is the doleful cry of men at their wits end; the voice of one in deepest distress: and such outcries have been no rarities under the preaching of the word; its power hath been felt by persons of all orders and conditions; the great and honourable of the earth, as well as the poor and despicable. The learned and the ignorant, the civil and profane, the young and the old, all have felt the heart-piercing efficacy of the gospel.

If you ask, whence hath the word preached this mighty power? The answer must be, neither from itself nor him that preaches it, but from the Spirit of God whose instrument it is, by whose blessing and concurrence with it, it produceth its blessed effects upon the hearts of men.

First, This efficacy and wonderful power is not from the word itself; take it in an abstract notion, separated from the Spirit, it can do nothing: it is called " the foolishness of preaching," 1 Cor. i. 21. Foolishness, not only because the world so accounts it, but because in itself it is a weak and unsuitable, and therefore a very improbable way to reconcile the world to God; that the stony heart of one man should be broken by the words of another man; that one poor sinful creature should be used to breathe spiritual life into another; this could never be, if this sword were not managed by an omnipotent hand.

And besides, we know what works naturally, works necessarily; if this efficacy were inherent in the word, so that we should suppose it to work as other natural objects do, then it must needs convert all to whom it is at any time preached, except its effect were miraculously hindered, as the fire when it could not burn the three children; but alas, thousands hear it, that never feel the saving power of it, Isa. liii. 1. and 2 Cor. iv. 3, 4.

Secondly, It derives not this efficacy from the *instrument* by which it is ministered: let their gifts and abilities be what they will, it is impossible that ever such effects should be produced from the strength of their natural or gracious abilities, 2 Cor. iv. 7. " We " have this treasure (saith the apostle) in earthen vessels, that the " excellency of the power may be of God, and not of us."

The treasure of the gospel-light is carried εν οςραχινοις σχευεσιν, *in earthen vessels*, as Gideon and his men had their lamps in earthen pitchers, or in *oyster-shells*, for so the word also signifies; the *oyster-*

shell is a base and worthless thing in itself; however, there lies the rich and precious pearl of so great value.   And why is this precious treasure lodged in such weak, worthless vessels?   Surely it is upon no other design but to convince us of the truth I am here to prove, that the excellency of the power is of God, and not of us; as it follows in the next words.   To the same purpose speaks the same apostle, 1 Cor. iii. 7. " So then, neither is he that planteth any " thing, neither he that watereth ; but God that giveth the in-" crease."

Not any thing! What can be more diminutively spoken of the gospel-preachers? But we must not understand these words in a simple and *absolute*, but in a *comparative* and relative sense; not as if they were not necessary and useful in their place, but that how necessary soever they be, and what excellent gifts soever God hath furnished them with; yet it is neither in their power nor choice to make the word they preach effectual to men; if it were, then the damnation of all that hear us must needs lie at our door; then also, many thousands would have been reconciled to God, which are yet in the state of enmity, but the effect of the gospel is not in our power.

Thirdly, But whatever efficacy it hath to reconcile men to God, it derives from the Spirit of God, whose co-operation and blessing (which is arbitrarily dispensed) gives it all the fruit it hath.

Ministers, saith one *, are like trumpets which make no sound, if breath be not breathed into them. Or like Ezekiel's wheels, which move not unless the Spirit move them ; or Elisha's servant, whose presence doth no good except Elisha's spirit be there also. For want of the Spirit of God how many thousands of souls do find the ministry to be nothing to them? If it be something to the purpose to any soul, it is the Lord that makes it so.   This Spirit is not limited by men's gifts or parts; he concurs not only with their labours who have excellent gifts, but oftentimes blesses mean, despicable gifts with far greater success.

Suppose, saith † Austin, there be two conduits in a town, one very plain and homely, the other built of polished marble, and adorned with excellent images, as eagles, lions, angels; the water refreshes as its water, and not as it comes from such or such a conduit.   It is the Spirit that gives the word all that virtue it hath : he is the Lord of all saving influences: he hath dominion over the *word,* over our *souls,* over the *times* and *seasons* of conversion; and if

---

* Mr. Anthony Burgess.

† What is the reason why of two adult ungodly persons, the one is so called as to follow him who calls, the other not? Do not thou judge, if thou wouldst not err : the judgments of God are unsearchable, and he hath mercy on whom he will. *Aug. de bono persec. cap. 8.*

any poor creature attend the ministry without benefit, if he go away
as he came, without fruit, surely we may say in this case, as Martha said to Christ, in reference to her brother Lazarus, Lord, if
thou hadst been here, my brother had not died; so, Lord, if thou
hadst been in this prayer, in this sermon, this poor soul had not
gone dead and carnal from under it.   And what now remains, but
that we apply this truth in those uses that it gives us.

First use of information.

Is the preaching of the gospel by Christ's *ambassadors*, the way
which God takes to reconcile sinners to himself? *Then how inexcusable are all those that continue in their state of enmity, though
the ambassadors of peace have been with them all their lives long,
wooing and beseeching them to be reconciled to God?*

O invincible, obstinate, incurable disease, which is aggravated
by the only proper remedy! Hath God been wooing and beseeching
you by his ambassadors so many years to be reconciled to him, and
will you not yield to any intreaties? Must he be made to speak in
vain, to charm the deaf adder? Well, when the milder attribute
hath done with you, the severer attribute will take you in hand.

The Lord hath kept an account of every year and day of his
patience towards you, Luke xiii. 7. " These three years I came
" seeking fruit on this fig-tree, and find none;" and Jer. xxv. 3.
" These three and twenty years have I spoken unto you, rising
" early and speaking, but you have not hearkened."

Well, be you assured, that God hath both the glass of your time,
and the vials of his wrath, by him? and so much of his abused
patience as runs out of one, so much of his incensed wrath runs
into the other.   There is a time when this treaty of peace will
end, when the Master of the house will rise up, and the doors be
shut, Luke xiii. 25.   Then will you be left without hope, and
without apology.

We read, indeed, of some poor and ineffectual pleas that will
be made by some at the last day; so Matt. vii. 22. " We have
" prophesied in thy name," &c. These pleas will not avail; but
as for you, what will you plead? Possibly many thousand *ideots,* or
poor weak-headed persons, may perish; many young ones that
had little or no time in the world to acquaint themselves with
matters of religion, or understand the way of salvation.   Many
millions of Heathens that never heard the name of Christ, nor
came within the sound of salvation, who will yet perish, and that
justly.

Now whatsoever apologies any of these will make for themselves
in the last day, to be sure you can make none.   God hath given
you a capacity and competent understanding; many of you are

wise and subtle in all your other concernments, and only shew
your folly in the great concernments of your salvation. You cannot plead want of time, some of you are grown grey-headed under
the gospel; you cannot plead want of means and opportunities,
the ordinances and ministers of Christ have been with you all your
life long to this day ; sure if you be Christless now, you must also
be speechless then.

Inf. 2. Hence it also follows, *That the world owes better entertainment than it gives to the ministers of Christ: Christ's ambassadors deserve a better welcome than they find among men.*

Your respects to them is founded upon their office and employment for you, Heb. xiii. 17. and 1 Thes. v. 12. They watch for
your souls, dare any of you watch for their ruin ? They bring glad
tidings, shall they return with sad tidings to him that sent them?
They publish peace, shall they be rewarded with trouble? O ungrateful world! We read in Eph. vi. 20. of an *ambassador in bonds,*
and he no ordinary one neither. We read also of a strange challenge,
made by another at his own death, Acts vii. 52. " Which of all
" the prophets have not your fathers persecuted? And they have
" slain them which shewed before the coming of the just One."
Some that brake the bread of life to you, might want bread to eat,
for any regard you have to them. The office of the ministry
speaks the abundant love of God to you; your contempt and
abuse of it, speaks the abundant stupidity and malignity of your
hearts towards God. What a sad protestation doth Jeremiah make
against his ungrateful people, Jer. xviii, 20. " Shall evil (saith he)
" be recompensed for good? for they have digged a pit for my
" soul; remember that I stood before thee to speak good for them,
" and to turn away thy wrath from them."

God's *mercy* is eminently discovered in the *institution* of, and
Satan's *malice* is eminently discovered in the *opposition* to, the
ministerial office. Satan is a great and jealous prince, and it is no
wonder he should raise all the forces he can to oppose the *ambassadors* of Christ; when, saith * one, the gospel comes into his dominions, it doth, as it were, by sound of trumpet and beat of drum,
proclaim liberty to all his slaves and vassals, if they will quit that
tyrant that hath so long held their souls in bondage, and come
under the sweet and easy government of Christ. And can the devil
endure this, think you? If Christ sends forth *ambassadors*, no
wonder if Satan sends forth *opposers;* he certainly owes them a
spite, that undermine his government in the world.

Infer. 3. Hence it follows, *That it nearly concerns all Christ's*

---

* Mr. Gurnal's Christian Armour.

ambassadors, to see that they be in a state of reconciliation with God themselves.

Shall we stand in Christ's stead by *office*, and yet not be in Christ by union? Shall we entreat men to be reconciled to God, and yet be at enmity with him ourselves? O let us take heed, " Lest after " we have preached to others, we ourselves should be cast-a-ways," 1 Cor. ix. 27. Of all men living we are the most miserable, if we be Christless and graceless: our consciences will make more terrible applications of our doctrine to us in hell, than ever we made to the vilest of sinners on earth. O, it is far easier to study and press a thousand truths upon others, than to feel the power of one truth upon our own hearts; to teach others *facienda quam faciendo:* duties to be done, than duties by doing them.

They are sad *dilemma's* with which a learned * writer poses such graceless ministers; If sin be evil, why do you live in it? If it be not, why do you dissuade men from it? If it be dangerous, how dare you venture on it? If it be not, why do you tell men so? If God's threatenings be true, why do you not fear them? If they be false, why do you trouble men needlessly with them, and put them into such frights without a cause?

Take heed to yourselves, lest you should cry down sin and not overcome it; lest while you seek to bring it down in others, you bow to it, and become its slaves yourselves: it is easier to chide at sin than to overcome it. That is a smart question, Rom. ii. 21. " Thou that teachest another, teachest thou not thyself? A profane minister was converted by reading that text once, but how many have read it as well as he, who never trembled at the consideration of it as he did!

2. Use for conviction.

Is this the method God uses to reconcile men to himself; O, then examine yourselves, whether yet the preaching of the gospel hath reconciled you to God. It is too manifest that many among us are in a state of enmity unto this day. We may say with the prophet, Isa. liii. 1. " Who hath believed our report? and to " whom is the arm of the Lord revealed?" We offer you peace upon gospel-terms and articles, but our peace returns to us again; enemies you were to God, and enemies you still continue. The evidence is undeniable: for,

1. *Evidence.* Many of you were never convinced to this day of your state of enmity against God; and without conviction of this, reconciliation is impossible; without repentance there can be no reconciliation, and without conviction there can be no repentance. When we repent, we lay down our weapons, Isa. xxvii. 4, 5. But

---

* Gildas Salv. p. 15, 16.

how few have been brought to this? Alas! if a few poor, cold, heartless, ineffectual confessions of sin, may pass for a due conviction, and serious repentance, then have we been convinced, then have we repented; but you will find, if ever the Lord intend to reconcile you to himself, your convictions and humiliations for sin, will be other manner of things; and will cost you more than a few cheap words against sin, 2 Cor. vii. 11. " In that ye sorrowed " after a godly sort, what carefulness it wrought in you, yea, what " clearing of yourselves, yea, what indignation, yea, what fear, " yea, what vehement desire, yea, what zeal, yea, what revenge?

2. *Evidence.* Many of us never treated seriously with the Lord about peace, and how then are we reconciled to him? What, a peace without a treaty? Reconciliation without any consideration about it? It can never be. When was the time, and where was the place, that you were found in secret upon your knees, mourning over the sin of your nature, and the evils of your ways? Certainly you must be brought to this; you must with a broken heart bewail your sin and misery.

Friend, that stony heart of thine must feel remorse and anguish for sin, it will cost thee some sad days and sorrowful nights, or ever thou canst have peace with God: it will cost thee many a groan, many a tear, many a hearty cry to heaven. If ever peace be made betwixt God and thee, thou must " take with thee words, and " turn to the Lord, saying, Take away all iniquity and receive " me graciously." O for one smile, one token of love, one hint of favour! The child of peace is not born without pangs and agonies of soul.

3. *Evidence.* Many of us are not reconciled to the duties of religion, and ways of holiness, and how then is it possible we should be reconciled to God? What, reconciled to God, and unreconciled to the ways of God? By reconciliation we are *made nigh :* in duties of communion we *draw nigh ;* and can we be made nigh to God, and have no heart to draw nigh to God? It can never be.

Examine your hearts, and say, Is not the way of strictness a bondage to you? Had you not rather be at liberty to fulfil the desires of the flesh, and of the mind? Could you not wish that the scriptures had not made some things else your sins, and other things your duties: do you delight in the law of God after the inner man, and *esteem his judgments, concerning all things to be right?* Do you love secret prayer, and delight in duties of communion with God: or rather, are they not an ungrateful burden, and irksome imposition? Give conscience leave to speak plain.

4. *Evidence.* Many of us are not enemies to sin, and how then are we reconciled to God? What, friends with God, and our lusts too? It cannot be. Psal. xcvii. 10. " Ye that love the Lord

" hate evil." The same hour our reconciliation is made with God, there is an everlasting breach made with sin: this is one of the articles or conditions of our peace with God, Isa. lv. 7. " Let the wicked " forsake his ways, and the unrighteous man his thoughts, and let " him turn to the Lord, and he will have mercy on him; and to our " God, and he will abundantly pardon."

But it is manifest in many of us, that we are no enemies to sin; we secretly indulge it, what bad names soever we call it. We will commit ten sins to cover one: we cannot endure the most serious, faithful, seasonable, private tender, and necessary reproofs for sin, but our hearts swell and rise at it; sure we are not reconciled to God, whilst we embrace his enemy in our bosoms.

5. *Evidence.* We *love not the children of God*, nor are we reconciled to them that bear his image, and how then can we be reconciled to God? 1 John v. 1. " He that loveth him that begat, " loveth them also that are begotten." What, at peace with the Father, and at war with the children? It cannot be. Do not some that hope they have made their peace with God, hate, revile, and persecute the children of God? Surely, in that day we are reconciled to the Lord, we are reconciled to all his people: we all then love a Christian as a Christian, and by this we may know that we are passed from death to life.

6. *Evidence.* Lastly, How can any man think himself to be reconciled to God, who *never closed heartily with Jesus Christ* by faith, who is the only days-man, and peace-maker: the alone Mediator of reconciliation betwixt God and man.

This is a sure truth, that all whom God accepts into favour, are " made accepted in the beloved," Eph. i. 6. If any man will make peace with God, he must take hold of his strength, accept and close with Christ who is the power of God, or he can never make peace, Isa. xxvii. He must be made " nigh by the blood of " Christ," Eph. ii. 13. But alas! both Christ and faith are strangers to many souls, who yet persuade themselves they are at peace with God: O fatal mistake!

III. *Use of Exhortation.*

Lastly, This point deserves a close, vigorous application in a threefold exhortation.

First, To Christ's ambassadors, who treat with souls in order to their reconciliation with God.

Secondly, To those that are yet in their empty and unreconciled state.

Thirdly, To those that have embraced the terms of peace, and submitted to the gospel-overtures.

First, To the ambassadors of reconciliation. God hath put a great deal of honour upon you in this high and noble employment; great is the dignity of your office;. to some you are " the savour of " death unto death, and to others a savour of life unto life; and " who is sufficient for these things?" 2 Cor. ii. 16. But yet the duty is no less than the dignity. O what manner of men should we be for judgment, seriousness, affections, patience, and examplary holiness, to whom the management of so great a concern betwixt God and man is committed.

First, For judgment and prudence, how necessary are these in so weighty and difficult a business as this! He had need be a man of wisdom that is to inform the ignorant of the nature and necessity of this great work, and win over their hearts to consent to the articles of peace propounded in the gospel; that hath so many subtle temptations to answer, and so many intricate causes of conscience to resolve: there are many strong holds of Satan to be battered, and many stout and obstinate resistances made by the hearts of sinners, which must be overcome; and he had need be no novice in religion, to whom so difficult a province is committed.

Secondly, Let us be serious in our work as well as judicious. Remember, O ye ambassadors of Christ, you bring a message from the God of heaven, of everlasting consequence to the souls of men. The eternal decrees are executed upon them in your ministry: to some you are " the savour of life unto life, and to some the savour of " death unto death," 2 Cor. ii. 16. Heaven and hell are matters of most awful and solemn consideration. O, what an account have we also shortly to give unto him that sent us!

These are matters of such deep concernment, as should swallow up our very spirits; the least they can do, is to compose our hearts unto seriousness in the management of them.

Thirdly, Be filled with tender affections toward the souls of men, with whom you treat for reconciliation: you had need be men of bowels, as well as men of brains* : you see a multitude of poor souls upon the brink of eternal misery, and they know it not, but promise themselves peace, and fill themselves with vain hopes of heaven: and is there a more moving, melting spectacle in the world than this! O think with what bowels of commisseration Moses and Paul were filled, when the one desired rather to be blotted out of God's book, and the other to be accursed from Christ, than that Israel should not be saved, Exod. xxxii. 33. and Rom. ix. 3. Think how the bowels of Christ yearned over Jerusalem, Mat. xxiii. 37. And over the multitude, Mat. ix. 36. " Let the same mind " be in you, which also was in Christ Jesus."

Fourthly, Be patient and long-suffering towards sinners: such is

---

* See Bowle's Pastor, Evang. p. 136.

the value of one soul, that it is worth waiting all our days to save it
at last : " The servant of the Lord must not strive, but be gentle
" unto all men, apt to teach, patient, in meekness instructing them
" that oppose themselves, if God peradventure will give them re-
" pentance," 2 Tim. ii. 24, 25. The Lord waits with patience
upon sinners, and well may you. Consider yourselves, how long
was God treating with you, ere you were won to him ? Be not discouraged, if your success presently answer not your expectation.

Fifthly, and lastly, Be sure to back your exhortations with drawing examples; else you may preach out your last breath before you
gain one soul to God. The devil, and the carnal hearts of your
hearers, will put hindrances enough in the way of your labours;
do not you put the greatest of all yourselves. O study not only to
preach exactly, but to live exactly; let the misplacing of one action in your lives, trouble you more than the misplacing of words
in your discourses; this is the way to succeed in your embassy, and
give up your account with joy.

Secondly, The exhortation speaks to all those that are yet in a
state of enmity and unreconciled to God unto this day. O that
my words might prevail, and that you would now be entreated to be
reconciled to God ! The *ambassadors* of peace are yet with you, the
treaty is not yet ended, the Master of the house is not yet risen up,
nor the door of mercy and hope finally shut : hitherto God hath
waited to be gracious; O that the long-suffering of God might be
your salvation : a day is hasting when God will treat with you no
more, when a *gulph shall be fixed* betwixt him and you for ever,
Luke xvi. 26. O what will you do when the season of mercy,
and all hopes of mercy shall end together ! When God shall become inaccessible, inexorable, and irreconcileable to you for evermore.

O, what wilt thou do, when thou shalt find thyself shut up under
eternal wrath ! when thou shalt feel that misery thou art warned
of ! Is this the place where I must be ! Are these the torments I
must endure ! What, for ever ! yea, for ever : Will not God be
satisfied with the sufferings of a thousand years ? no, nor millions
of years ? Ah, sinners, did you but clearly see the present and future misery of unreconciled ones, and what that wrath of the great
and terrible God is, which is coming as fast as the wings of time
can bring it upon you, it would certainly drive you to Christ, or
drive you out of your wits. O it is a dreadful thing to have God
for your eternal enemy : to have the great and terrible God causing
his infinite power to avenge the abuse of his grace and mercy.

Believe it, friends, it is a fearful thing to fall into the hands of
the living God : knowing the terrors of the Lord we persuade
men : an eternal weight hangs upon an inch of time. O that you

did but know the time of your visitation! that you would not dare
to adventure, and run the hazard of one day more in an unreconciled state.

Thirdly, and lastly, This point speaks to those who have believed our report, who have taken hold of God's strength, and
made peace with him: who had not obtained mercy, but now have
obtained mercy: who once were afar off, but now are made nigh
by the blood of Christ: with you I would leave a few words of exhortation, and I have done.

First, *Admire and stand amazed at this mercy.* " I will praise
" thee, O Lord, (saith the church, Isa. xii. 1.) Though thou wast
" angry with me, thine anger is turned away, and thou comfortest
" me." O how overwhelming a mercy is here before you! God
is at peace, at peace with you that were " enemies in your minds
" by wicked works," Col. i. 21. At peace with you, and at
enmity with millions as good by nature as you; at peace with
you that sought it not: at peace for ever; no dissolving this friendship for evermore. O let this consideration melt your hearts before the Lord, and make you cry, What am I, Lord, that mercy
should take in me, and shut out fallen angels, and millions of men
and women as capable of mercy as myself! O the riches! O the
depths of the mercy and goodness of God!

Secondly, *Beware of new breaches with God:* God will speak
" peace to his people and to his saints, but let them not turn
" again to folly, Psal. lxxxv. 8. What though this state of friendship can never be dissolved, yet it is a dreadful thing to have it
clouded: You may lose the sense of peace, and with it all the joy
of your hearts, and the comforts of your lives in this world.

Thirdly, *Labour to reconcile others to God:* especially those that
are endeared to you by the bonds of natural religion: When Paul
was reconciled to God himself, his heart was full of heaviness for
others that were not reconciled; for his " brethren and kinsmen
" according to the flesh," Rom. ix. 2, 3. When Abraham was
become God's friend himself, then, " O that Ishmael might live
" before thee!" Gen. xvii. 18.

Fourthly, and lastly, " Let your reconciliation with God relieve
" you under all burdens of affliction you shall meet with in your
" way to heaven:" Let them that are at enmity with God droop
under crosses and afflictions; but do not you do so. *Tranquillus
Deus tranquillat omnia*, Rom. v. 1, 2, 3. Let the peace of God
keep your hearts and minds. As nothing can comfort a man that
must go to hell at last; so nothing should deject a man that shall,
through many troubles, at last reach heaven.

SERMON IV.

Concerning the work of the Spirit, as the internal, and most effectual Mean of the Application of CHRIST.

JOHN vi. 44.

No man can come to me, except the Father, which hath sent me, draw him.

OUR last discourse informed you of the usefulness and influence of the preaching of the gospel, in order to the *application* of Christ to the souls of men. There must be (in God's ordinary way) the external ministerial offer of Christ, before men can have union with him.

But yet, all the preaching in the world can never effect this union with Christ in itself, and in its own virtue, except a supernatural and mighty power go forth with it for that end and purpose. Let Boanerges and Barnabas try their strength, let the *angels* of heaven be the preachers; till God draw, the soul cannot come to Christ.

No saving benefit is to be had by Christ, without union with his person, no union with his person without faith, no faith ordinarily wrought without the preaching of the gospel by Christ's *ambassadors*, their preaching hath no saving efficacy without God's drawings, as will evidently appear by considering these words and the occasion of them.

The occasion of these words is found (as learned * Cameron well observes) in the 42d verse, " And they said, is not this Jesus " the son of Joseph, whose father and mother we know?" Christ had been pressing upon them in his ministry, the great and necessary duty of faith; but notwithstanding the *authority* of the preacher; the *holiness* of his life; the miracles by which he confirmed his *doctrine;* they still objected against him, " is not this the carpen- " ter's son?" From whence Christ takes occasion for these words; " No man can come unto me, except my Father which hath sent " me, draw him," q. d. In vain is the authority of my person urged; in vain are all the miracles wrought in your sight, to confirm the doctrine preached to you; till that secret, almighty power of the Spirit be put forth upon your hearts, you will not, you cannot, come unto me.

The words are a negative proposition,

In which the author, and powerful manner of divine operation in working faith, are contained: there must be drawing before

---

* *Cameronis Myrothec.* p. 139.

believing, and that drawing must be the drawing of God : every word hath its weight : we will consider them in the order they lie in the text.

Ουδεις,——*No Man*] not one, let his natural qualifications be what they will, let his external advantages, in respect of means and helps, be never so great : it is not in the power of any man ; all persons, in all ages, need the same power of God, one as well as another ; every man is alike dead, impotent, and averse to faith in his natural capacity. No man, or—not one, among all the sons of men.

Δυναται,——*Can*] or is able : he speaks of impotency to special and saving actions, such as believing in Christ is : no act that is saving can be done without the concurrence of special grace. Other acts that have a remote tendency to it, are performed by a more general concourse and common assistance ; so men may come to the word, and attend to what is spoken, remember and consider what the word tells them ; but as to believing or coming to Christ, that no man can do of himself, or by a general and common assistance. No man can.

Εχθειν προς με,——*Come unto me,*] i. e. believe in me unto salvation. Coming to Christ, and believing in him, are terms *æquipollent*, and are indifferently used to express the nature of saving faith, as is plain, ver. 35. " He that cometh to me shall never hunger, " and he that believeth on me shall never thirst :" it notes the terms from which and to which the soul moves, and the voluntariness of the motion, notwithstanding that divine power by which the will is drawn to Christ.

Εαν μη ο Πατηρ,—*Except my Father*] not excluding the other two Persons ; for every work of God relating to the creatures is common to all the three Persons ; nor only to note that the Father is the first in order of working : but the reason is hinted in the next words.

Ο πεμψας με,—*who hath sent me,*] God hath entered into covenant with the Son, and sent him, stands obliged thereby, to bring the promised seed to him, and that he he doth by drawing them to Christ by faith : so the next words tell us the Father doth,

Ελκυση αυτον.——*Draw him.*] That is, powerfully and effectually incline his will to come to Christ : " * Not by a violent co-action, " but by a benevolent bending of the will which was averse ;" and as it is not in the way of force and compulsion, so neither is it by a simple *moral suasion*, by the bare proposal of an object to the will, and so leaving the sinner to his own election ; but it is such a per-

---

* *Non violenta coactio immediata, sed voluntatis a Deo aversæ benevola flectio.* Glas. Rhet. Sacra. p. 256.

suasion, as hath a mighty overcoming efficacy accompanying it : of which more anon.

The words thus opened, the observation will be this :

Doct. *That it is utterly impossible for any man to come to Jesus Christ, unless he be drawn unto him by the special and mighty power of God.*

No man is compelled to come to Christ against his will, he that cometh, comes willingly, but even that will and desire to come is the effect of grace, Phil. ii. 13. " It is God that worketh in you, " both to will and to do of his own good pleasure."

" If we desire the help and assistance of grace, (saith * Fulgen- " tius) even the desire is of grace ; grace must first be shed forth " upon us, before we can begin to desire it." " By grace are ye " saved through faith, and that not of yourselves, it is the gift of " God," Eph. ii. 8. Suppose the utmost degree of natural ability ; let a man be as much disposed and prepared as nature can dispose or prepare him, and to all this, add the proposal of the greatest arguments and motives to induce him to come ; let all these have the advantage of the fittest season to work upon his heart ; yet no man can come till God draw him : we move as we are moved : as Christ's coming to us, so our coming to him are the pure effects of grace.

Three things require explication in this point before us.

First, *What the drawing of the Father imports.*

Secondly, *In what manner he draws men to Christ.*

Thirdly, *How it appears that none can come till they be so drawn.*

First, What the drawing of the Father imports.

To open this, let it be considered, that drawing is usually distinguished into *physical* and *moral.* The former is either by co-action, force, and compulsion ; or, by a sweet congruous efficacy upon the will. As to violence and compulsion, it is none of God's way and method, it being both against the nature of the will of man, which cannot be forced, and against the will of Jesus Christ, who loves to reign over a free and willing people, Psal. cx. 5. " Thy people shall be willing in the day of thy power." Or, as that word may be rendered, they shall be *voluntarinesses,* as willing as willingness itself. It is not then by a forcible *co-action,* but in a *moral* way of persuasion, that God the Father draws men to Jesus Christ : He draws *with the bands of a man,* as they are called, Hos.

---

* *Ut ergo desideremus adjutorium, hoc quoque est gratiæ ; ipsa namque incipit effundi, ut incipit posci.* Fulgen. Epist. 6. ad Theod.

xi. 14. i. e. in a way of rational conviction of the mind and conscience, and effectual persuasion of the will.

But yet by *moral persuasion*, we must not understand a simple and bare proposal or tender of Christ and grace, leaving it still at the sinner's choice, whether he will comply with it or no.   * For though God does not force the will contrary to its nature, yet there is a real internal efficacy implied in this *drawing*, or an immediate operation of the Spirit upon the heart and will, which, in a way congruous and suitable to its nature, takes away the rebellion and reluctance of it, and of unwilling, makes it willing to come to Christ.   And, in this respect, we own a *physical*, as well as a *moral* influence of the Spirit in this work; and so scripture expresses it, Eph. i. 19, 20. " That we may know what is the exceeding great
" ness of his power towards us who believe, according to the work
" ing of his mighty power, which he wrought in Christ, when he
" raised him from the dead."   Here is much more than a naked proposal made to the will; there is a *power* as well as a *tender ;* greatness of power; and yet more, the exceeding greatness of his power; and this power hath an actual efficacy ascribed to it, he works upon our hearts and wills *according to the working of his mighty power which he wrought in Christ, when he raised him from the dead.*   Thus he fulfils in us all the good pleasure of his will, and the work of faith with power, 2 Thess. i. 11.

And this is that which the schools call *gratia efficax*, effectual grace; and others *victrix delectatio*, an overcoming, conquering delight † : thus the work is carried on with a most efficacious sweetness.   So that the liberty of the will is not infringed, whilst the obstinacy of the will is effectually subdued and over-ruled. For want of this, there are so many *almost Christians* in the world ; hence are all those vanishing and imperfect works which come to nothing, called in scripture, a *morning cloud, an early dew.*   Had this mighty power gone forth with the word, they had never vanished or perished like *embryos* as they do.   So then, God draws not only in a *moral way*, by proposing a suitable object to the will, but also in a *physical way*, or by immediate powerful influence upon the will; not infringing the liberty of it, but yet infallibly and effectually persuading it to come to Christ.

Secondly, Next let us consider the marvellous way and manner in which the Lord draws the souls of poor sinners to Jesus Christ, and you will find he doth it,

---

* We do not see God preaching, writing, and teaching, yet we believe as if we saw these ; for all truth hath a power of inclining the mind to assent; the greater truth, the greater power, and the greatest truth, the greatest power of all.   But why then do not all believe the gospel ? I answer, because all are not drawn by God.   *Baptist. Mantuanus de patientia, lib. 3. cap. 2.*

† A certain heavenly sweetness. *Jansenius Aug. lib. iv. cap. 1.*

1. Gradually,	4. Effectually,
2. Congruously,	and
3. Powerfully,	5. Finally.

First, This blessed work is carried on by the Spirit gradually; bringing the soul step by step in the due method and order of the gospel to Christ; illumination, conviction, compunction, prepare the way to Christ; and then faith unites the soul to him: without humiliation there can be no faith, Matt. xxi. 32. " Ye repented " not, that ye might believe." It is the burdensome sense of sin, that brings the soul to Christ for rest, Matt. xi. 28. " Come unto " me all ye that are weary and heavy laden." But without conviction there can be no compunction, no humiliation; he that is not convinced of his sin and misery, never bewails it, nor mourns for it. Never was there one tear of true repentance seen to drop from the eye of an unconvinced sinner.

And without illumination there can be no conviction; for what is conviction, but the application of the light which is in the understanding, or mind of a man, to his heart and conscience? Acts ii. 37. In this order, therefore, the Spirit (ordinarily) draws souls to Christ, he shines into their minds by illumination; applies that light to their consciences by effectual conviction; breaks and wounds their hearts for sin in compunction; and then moves the will to embrace and close with Christ in the way of faith for life and salvation.

These several steps are more distinctly discerned in some Christians than in others; they are more clearly to be seen in the *adult convert*, than in those that were drawn to Christ in their youth; in such as were drawn to him out of a state of profaneness, than in those that had the advantage of a pious education; but in this order the work is carried on ordinarily in all, however it differ in point of clearness in the one and in the other.

Secondly, He draws sinners to Christ congruously, and very agreeably to the nature and way of man, so he spesks, Hos. xi. 4. " I drew them with the * cords of a man, with bands of love;" Not as beasts are drawn; but as men are inclined and wrought to compliance, by rational conviction of their judgments, and powerful persuasion of their wills: the minds of sinners are naturally blinded by ignorance, 2 Cor. iv. 3, 4. and their affections bewitched to their lusts, Gal. iii. 4. and whilst it is thus, no arguments or entreaties can possibly prevail to bring them off from the ways of sin to Christ.

The way therefore which the Lord takes to win and draw them

---

* *Funibus hominum* (i. e.) *humanis: non quibus trahi ac deduci solent boves.*

to Christ, is by rectifying their false apprehensions, and shewing them infinitely more good in Christ than in the cteature and in their lusts; yea, by satisfying their understandings, that there is goodness enough in Jesus Christ, to whom he is drawing them.

First, Enough to out-bid all temporal good, which is to be denied for his sake.

Secondly, Enough to preponderate all temporal evils, which are to be suffered for his sake.

First, That there is more good in Christ than in all temporal good things, which we are to deny or forsake upon his account. This being once clearly and convincingly discovered to the understanding, the will is thereby prepared to quit all that which entangles and with-holds it from coming to Christ. There is no man that loves money so much, but he will willingly part with it, for that which is more worth to him than the sum he parts with to purchase it, Matth. xiii. 56, 46. " The kingdom of heaven is like " to a merchant-man, seeking goodly pearls, who when he hath " found one pearl of great price, goeth and selleth all that he hath " and buyeth it."

Such an invaluable *pearl* is Jesus Christ; infinitely more worth than all that a poor sinner hath to part with for him; and is a more real good than the creature. These are but vain shadows; Prov. xxiii. 5. Christ is a solid, substantial good: yea, he is, and by conviction appears to be a more suitable good than the creature: The world cannot justify and save, but Christ can. Christ is a more necessary good than the creature, which is only for our temporal conveniency, but he is of eternal necessity. He is a more durable good than any creature comfort is, or can be: " The " fashion of this world passeth away," 1 Cor. vii. 13. But durable riches and righteousness are in him, Prov. viii. 17. Thus Christ appears in the day of conviction, infinitely more excellent than the world; he out-bids all the offers that the world can make; and this greatly forwards the work of drawing a soul to Jesus Christ.

Secondly, And (then to remove every thing out of the way to Christ) God discovers to the soul enough in him to preponderate, and much more than will recompense all the evils and sufferings it can endure for his sake.

It is true, they that close with Christ close with his cross also: they must expect to save no more but their souls by him. He tells us what we must trust to, Luke xiv. 26, 27. " If any man come to " me, and hate not his father and mother, and wife and children, " and brethren and sisters; yea, and his own life also, he cannot " be my disciple." And whosoever doth not bear his cross, and come after me, cannot be my disciple.

To read such a text as this, with such a comment upon it, as

Satan and our flesh can make, is enough to fright a man from Christ for ever. Nor is it possible by all the arguments in the world to draw any soul to Christ upon such terms as these, till the Lord convince it, that there is enough, and much more than enough in Jesus Christ to recompense all these sufferings and losses we endure for him.

But when the soul is satisfied that those sufferings are but *external* upon the vile *body*, but that the benefit which comes by Christ is *internal* in a man's own *soul;* these afflictions are but *temporal*, Rom. viii. 18. But Christ and his benefits are *eternal:* This must needs prevail with the will to come over to Christ, notwithstanding all the evils of suffering that accompany him, when the reality of this is discovered by the Lord, and the power of God goes along with these discoveries. Thus the Lord draws us in our own way, by rational convictions of the understanding, and allurements of the will.

And it is possible this may be the reason why some poor souls mis-judge the working of the Spirit of God upon themselves, thinking they never had that wonderful and mighty power of God in conversion, acting upon their hearts, because they find all that is done upon their hearts that way is done in the ordinary course and method of nature; They consider, compare, are convinced, and then resolved to chuse Christ and his ways; whereas they expect to feel some strange operations, that shall have the visible characters of the immediate power of God upon them, and such a power they might discern, if they would consider it as working in this way and method: but they cannot distinguish God's acts from their own, and that puzzles them.

Thirdly, The drawings of the Father are very *powerful.* " The " arm of the Lord is revealed in this work," Isa. liii. 1. It was a powerful word indeed that made the light at first shine out of darkness, and no less power is required to make it shine into our hearts, 2 Cor. v. 14. That day in which the soul is made willing to come to Christ, is called, " the day of his power," Psal. cx. 3. The scripture expresseth the work of conversion by a threefold *metaphor,* viz.

That of a *resurrection* from the dead, Rom. iv. 4.

That of *creation* Eph. ii. 10. And

That of *victory* or *conquest,* 2 Cor. x. 4, 5. All these set forth the infinite power of God in this work; for no less than Almighty Power is required to each of them, and if you strictly examine the distinct notions, you shall find the power of God more and more illustriously displayed in each of them.

To raise the dead, is the effect of Almighty Power; but then the resurrection supposeth pre-existent matter. In the work of *creation*, there is no pre-existent matter; but then there is no opposition: That which is not, rebels not against the power which gives it being. But *victory* and *conquest* suppose *opposition*, all the power of corrupt nature arming itself, and fighting against God: but yet not able to frustrate his design.

Let the soul whom the Father draws, struggle and reluctate as much as it can, it shall come, yea, and come willingly too, when the drawing power of God is upon it*. O the self-conflicts, the contrary resolves, with which the soul finds itself distracted, and rent asunder! The hopes and fears; the encouragements and discouragements; they will, and they will not: but victorious grace conquers all opposition at last. We find an excellent example of this in blessed † Augustin, who speaks of this very work, the drawing of his soul to Christ, and how he felt in that day two wills in himself, " one old, the other new; one carnal, the other spiritual; " and how in these their contrary motions and conflicts, he was " torn asunder in his own thoughts and resolutions, suffering that " unwillingly which he did willingly." And certainly, if we consider how deep the soul is rooted by natural inclination, and long continued custom in sin, how extremely averse it is to the ways of strict godliness and mortification; how Satan, that invidious enemy, that strong man armed, fortifies the soul to defend his possession against Christ, and intrenches himself in the understanding, will, and affections, by deep-rooted prejudices against Christ and holiness, it is a wonder of wonders to see a soul quitting all its beloved lusts, and fleshly interests and endearments, and coming willingly under Christ's yoke.

Fourthly, the drawings of God are very effectual: There is indeed a common and *ineffectual* work upon hypocrites and apostates, called in scripture a " morning cloud and early dew," Hos. vi. 4. These may believe for a time, and fall away at last, Luke viii. 13. Their wills may be half won, they may be drawn half way to Christ, and return again. So it was with Agrippa, Acts xxvi. 28. εν ολιγω με πειθεις, within a very little thou persuadest me to be a Christian: But in God's elected ones it is effectual: ‡ Their wills are not only *almost*, but *altogether* persuaded to embrace Christ, and quit the ways of sin, how pleasant, gainful, and dear soever they

---

* A sweet moving from the word, and a powerful drawing on God's part. For there is a certain kind of voluntary necessity. *Moulin. Amut. Armin.*

† *Ita duæ voluntates meæ, una vetus, alia nova, illa carnalis, illa spiritualis configebant inter se, atque discordando dissipabant animam meam—ibi enim magis jam non ego, quia, ex magna parte id patiebor invitus, quod faciebam volens.* Aug. confes. lib. 8. cap. 5.

‡ Suasion is the act of one using endeavours: persuasion the act of an efficient cause. He uses suasion, who gives advice; persuasion is the deed of him who determines a man to what he pleases. *Erasmus.*

have been to them. The Lord not only draws, but draws home those souls to Christ, John vi. 37. " All that the Father hath given " me, shall come to me."

It is confessed, that in drawing home of the very elect to Christ, there may be, and frequently are, many pauses, stands, and demurs; they have convictions, affections, and resolutions stirring in them, which, like early blossoms, seem to be nipt and die away again. There is freqûently, (in young ones especially), an hopeful appearance of grace; they make conscience of avoiding sins, and performing duties: they have sometimes great awakenings under the word, they are observed to retire for meditation and prayer; and delight to be in the company of Christians : and after all. this, youthful lusts and vanities are found to stifle and choak these hopeful beginnings, and the work seems to stand, (it may be some years), at a pause; however, at last, the Lord makes it victorious over all opposition, and sets it home with power upon their hearts.

Fifthly, To conclude, those whom the Father draws to Christ, he draws them finally and for ever. " The gifts and calling of " God are without repentance," Rom. xi. 29. they are so, as to God the giver; he never repents, that he hath called his people into the fellowship of his Son Christ Jesus: and they are so on the believer's part; he is never sorry, whatever he afterwards meets with, that he is come to Christ.

There is a time when Christians are drawn to Christ, but there shall never be a time in which they shall be drawn away from Christ, John x. 29. There is no plucking them out of the Father's hand. It was common to a proverb, in the primitive times, when they would express an impossibility, to say, " You may as " soon draw a Christian from Christ, as do it." When Christ asked that question of the disciples, " Will ye also go away ? " Lord, (said Peter, in the name of them all), to whom shall we " go ? Thou hast the words of eternal life," John vi. 68. They who are thus drawn, do with full purpose of heart, cleave unto the Lord. And thus of the manner and quality of effectual drawing.

Thirdly, In the last place, I am to evince the impossibility of coming to Christ without the Father's drawings; and this will evidently appear upon the consideration of these two particulars.

First, The difficulty of this work is above all the power of nature to overcome.

Secondly, That little power and ability that nature hath, it will never employ to such a purpose as this, till the drawing power of God be upon the will of a sinner.

First, If all the power of nature were employed in this design,

yet such are the difficulties of this work, that it surmounts all the
abilities of nature.   This the scripture very plainly affirms, Eph. ii.
8. " By grace are ye saved through faith, and that not of yourselves,
" it is the gift of God."   To think of Christ is easy, but to come to
Christ, is to nature impossible.   To send forth cold and ineffectual
wishes to Christ we may, but to bring Christ and the soul together,
requires the Almighty Power of God, Eph. i. 19.   The grace of
faith by which we come to Christ, is as much the free gift of God,
as Christ himself, who is the object of faith, Phil. i. 29. " To you
" it is freely given to believe."   And this will easily appear to your
understandings, if you do but consider

The $\left\{ \begin{array}{l} \text{Subject,} \\ \text{Act, } and \\ \text{Enemies} \end{array} \right\}$ of this work of faith, or coming to Christ.

First, Consider the subject of faith in which it is wrought; or
what it is that is drawn to Christ: It is the heart of a sinner which
is naturally as indisposed for this work, as the wood which Elijah
laid in order upon the altar was to catch fire, when he had poured
so much water upon it, as did not only wet the wood, but also filled
up the trench round about it, 1 Kings xviii. 33.   For it is naturally
a dark, blind, and ignorant heart, Job xi. 12.   And such an heart
can never believe, till he that commanded the light to shine out of
darkness do shine into it, 2 Cor. iv. 6.

Nor will it avail any thing to say, though man be born in darkness and ignorance, yet afterwards he may acquire knowledge in
the use of means, as we see many natural men do to a very high
degree: For this is not that light that brings the soul to Christ, yea,
this natural unsanctified light blinds the soul, and prejudices it more
against Christ than ever it was before, 1 Cor. i. 21, 26.

As it is a blind, ignorant heart, so it is a selfish heart by nature:
All its designs and aims terminate in self; this is the centre and
weight of the soul; no righteousness but its own is sought after,
that, or none, Rom. x. 3.   Now, for a soul to renounce and deny
self, in all its forms, modes, and interests, as every one doth that
cometh to Christ; to disclaim and deny natural, moral, and religious self, and come to Christ as a poor, miserable, wretched,
empty creature; to live upon his righteousness for ever, is as supernatural and wonderful, as to see the hills and mountains start
from their bases and centres, and fly like wandering atoms in the
air.

Nay, this heart which is to come to Christ, is not only dark and
selfish, but full of pride.   O, it is a desperate proud heart by nature, it cannot submit to come to Christ, as Benhadad's servants
came to the king of Israel, with sackloth on their loins, and
ropes upon their heads.   To take guilt, shame, and confusion

of face to ourselves, and acknowledge the righteousness of God in our eternal damnation; to come to Christ naked and empty, as one that justifies the ungodly. I say, nature left to itself, would as soon be damned as do this; the proud heart can never come to this, till the Lord hath humbled and broken it by his power.

Secondly, Let us take the act of faith into consideration also, as it is here described by the soul's coming to Jesus Christ; and you will find a necessity of the Father's drawings; for this evidently implies, that which is against the stream and current of corrupt nature, and that which is above the sphere and capacity of the most refined and accomplished nature.

First, It is against the stream and current of our corrupt nature to come to Christ. For let us but consider the term from which the soul departs, when it comes to Christ. In that day it leaves all its lusts, and ways of sin, how pleasant, sweet, and profitable soever they have been unto it, Isa. lv. 7. " Let the wicked forsake " his way, and the unrighteous man his thoughts, and let him " return unto the Lord." Way and thoughts, i. e. both the practice of, and delight he had in sin, must be forsaken, and the outward and inward man must be cleansed from it. Now there are in the bosoms of unregenerate men such darling lusts, that have given them so much practical and speculative pleasure, which have brought so much profit to them, which have been born and bred up with them; and which, upon all these accounts, are endeared to their souls to that degree, that it is easier for them to die, than to forsake them; yea, nothing is more common among such men, than to venture eternal damnation, rather than suffer a separation from their sins.

And which is yet more difficult in coming to Christ, the soul forsakes not only its sinful self, but its righteous self, i. e. not only its worst sins, but its best performances, accomplishments, and excellencies. Now this is one of the greatest straits that nature can be put to. Righteousness by works was the first liquor that ever was put into the vessel, and it still retains the tang and savour of it, and will to the end of the world, Rom. x. 3. " For they, being " ignorant of God's righteousness, and going about to establish " their own righteousness, have not submitted themselves unto the " righteousness of God." ઝ υπεταγησαν, they have not submitted. To come naked and empty to Christ, and receive all from him as a free gift, is, to proud corrupt nature, the greatest abasement and submission in the world.

Let the gospel furnish its table with the richest and costliest dainties that ever the blood of Christ purchased, such is the pride of nature, that it disdains to taste them, except it may also pay for the same. If the old hive be removed from the place where it was wont to stand, the bees will come home to the old place, yea, and many of them you shall find will die there, rather than go to the hive, though it stand in a far better place than it did before. Just so stands the case with men. The *hive* is removed, i. e. we are not to expect righteousness as Adam did, by obeying and working, but by believing and coming to Christ; but nature had as soon be damned as do this: It still goes about to establish its own righteousness.

Virtues, duties, and moral excellencies, these are the ornaments of nature ; here is nature set off in its sumptuous attire, and rich embellishments, and now to renounce it, disclaim and contemn it, as dross and dung, in comparison of Christ, as believers do, Phil. iii. 8. this, I say, is against the grain of nature. We reckon it the strange effect of self-denial in Mahomet the Great *, who being so enamoured with his beautiful Irene, would be persuaded, upon reasons of state, with his own hand to strike off her head : and that even when she appeared in all her rich ornaments before him, rather like such a goddess, as the poets in their ecstasies use to feign, than a mortal creature. And yet certainly this is nothing to that self-denial which is exercised in our coming to Christ.

Secondly, And if we look to the other term to which the soul moves, we shall find it acting as much above the sphere and ability of improved nature, as here it acts and moves against the stream and current of corrupted nature : for how wonderful and supernatural an adventure is that, which the soul makes in the day that it comes to Jesus Christ.

Surely, for any poor soul to venture itself for ever upon Jesus Christ whom it never saw, nay, upon Christ, whose very existence its own unbelief calls in question whether he be or no : and that when it is even weighed down to the dust, with the burdensome sense of its own vileness and total unworthiness, feeling nothing in itself but sin and misery, the workings of death and fears of wrath : to go to Christ, of whose pardoning grace and mercy it never had any the least experience, nor can find any ground of hope in itself that it shall be accepted ; this is as much above the power of nature, as it is for a stone to rise from the earth, and fix itself among the stars. Well might the apostle ascribe it to that Almighty Power which raised up Christ from the dead, Eph. i. 19, 20. If the Lord draw not the soul, and that omnipotently, it can never come from itself to Christ. And yet farther,

Thirdly, The natural impossibility of coming to Christ, will more clearly appear, if we consider the enemies to faith, or what blocks are rolled by Satan and his instruments into the way to Christ:

---

* Knolle's History of the Turks.

to mention, in this place, no more but our own carnal reason, as it
is armed and managed by the subtilty of Satan, what a wonder is it
that any soul should come to Christ?

These are the strong holds, (mentioned 2 Cor. x. 4.) out of
which those objections, fears, and discouragements sally, by which
the soul is fiercely assaulted in the way to Christ.

Wilt thou forsake all thy pleasures, merry company, and sensible
comforts, to live a sad, retired, pensive life? Wilt thou beggar
and undo thyself, let go all thy comforts in hand, for an hope of
that which thine eyes never saw, nor hast thou any certainty that it
is any more than a fancy! Wilt thou that hast lived in reputation
and credit all thy life, now become the scorn and contempt of the
world? Thinkest thou thyself able to live such a strict, severe, mortified, and self-denying life, as the word of God requires? And
what if persecution should arise, (as thou mayest expect it will,)
canst thou forsake father and mother, wife and children, yea, and
give up thine own life too, to a cruel and bloody death! be advised
better, before thou resolve in so important a matter. What thinkest thou of thy forefathers, that lived and died in that way thou
art now living? Art thou wiser than they? Do not the generality
of men walk in the same paths thou hast hitherto walked in? If
this way lead to hell, as thou fearest it may, think then how many
millions of men must perish as well as thyself; and is such a supposition consistent with the gracious and merciful nature of God?
Besides, think what sort of people those are, unto whom thou art
about to join thyself in this new way? Are there not to be found
among them many things to discourage thee, and cool thy zeal?
They are generally of the lower and baser sort of men, poor and
despicable: Seest thou not, though their profession be holy, how
earthly, carnal, proud, factious, and hypocritical, many of them
are found to be! And doubtless, the rest are like them, though
their hypocrisy be not yet discovered.

O what stands and demurs, what hesitations and doubts, is the
soul clogged with in its way to Christ! But yet none of these can
withhold and detain the soul when the Father draws: Greater
then is he that is in us, than he that is in the world. And thus
you see the nature, manner, and efficacy of divine drawings, and
how impossible it is for any soul to come to Christ without them.

The inferences and improvements of the point follow.

Inference 1. *How deeply and thoroughly is the nature of man
corrupted, and what an enemy is every man to his own happiness,
that he must be drawn to it?* John v. 40. " You will not come
" unto me, that ye might have life."

Life is desirable in every man's eyes, and eternal life is the most

excellent: yet, in this, the world is rather agreed to die and
perish for ever than come to Christ for life. Had Christ told us
of fields and vineyards, sheep and oxen, gold and silver, honours
and sensual pleasures, who would not have come to him for
these? But to tell of mortification, self-denial, strictness of life, and
sufferings for his sake, and all this for an happiness to be enjoyed
in the world to come, nature will never like such a proposition as
this.

You see where it sticks, not in a simple inability to believe, but
in an inability complicated with enmity; they neither can come,
nor will come to Christ. It is true, all that do come to Christ,
come willingly; but thanks be to the grace of God, that hath
freed and persuaded the will, else they never had been willing to
come. Who ever found his own heart first stir and move towards
Christ? How long may we wait and expect before we shall feel
our hearts naturally burn with desires after, and love to Jesus
Christ?

This aversion of the will and affections from God is one of the
main roots of original sin. No argument can prevail to bring the
soul to Christ, till this be mastered and overpowered by the Father's drawing. In our motions to sin we need restraining, but in
all our motions to Christ we as much need drawing. He that comes
to heaven may say, Lord, if I had had mine own way and will, I
had never come here: if thou hadst not drawn me, I should never
have come to thee. O the riches of the grace of God! Oh unparalleled mercy and goodness! not only to prepare such a glory as
this for an unworthy soul, but to put forth the exceeding greatness of thy power, afterwards to draw an unwilling soul to the
enjoyment of it.

Infer. 2. *What enemies are they to God and the souls of men, that
do all they can to discourage and hinder the conversion of men to
Christ? God draws forward, and these do all that in them lies to
draw backward,* i. e. *to prejudice and discourage them from coming
to Jesus Christ in the way of faith : this is a direct opposition to
God, and a plain confederacy with the devil.*

O how many have been thus discouraged in their way to Christ
by their carnal relations, I cannot say friends! Their greatest enemies have been the men of their own house. These have pleaded
(as if the devil had hired and fee'd them) against the everlasting
welfare of their own flesh. O cruel parents, brethren, and sisters,
that jeer, frown, and threaten, where they should encourage,
assist, and rejoice! Such parents are the devil's children. Satan
chuses such instruments as you are, above all others, for this work :
he knows what influence and authority you have upon them, and
over them; and what fear, love, and dependence they have for

you, and upon you; so that none in all the world are like to manage the design of their damnation so effectually, as you are like to do.

Will you neither come to Christ yourselves, nor suffer your dear relations that would? Had you rather find them in the ale-house than in the closet? Did you instrumentally give them their being, and will you be the instruments of ruining for ever those beings they had from you? Did you so earnestly desire children, so tenderly nurse and provide for them; take such delight in them; and, after all this, do what in you lies to damn and destroy them! If these lines shall fall into any such hands, O that God would set home the conviction and sense of this horrid evil upon their hearts.

And no less guilty of this sin are scandalous and loose professors, who serve to furnish the devil with the greatest arguments he hath to dissuade men from coming to Christ; it is your looseness and hypocrisy by which he hopes to scare others from Christ. It is said, Cant. ii. 7. " I charge you by the roes and hinds of the field, " that ye stir not up, nor awake my beloved till he please."

Roes and hinds, like young converts and comers towards Christ, are shy and timorous creatures, that start at the least sound, or yelp of a dog, and fly away. Take heed what you do in this case, lest you go down to hell under the guilt of damning more souls than your own.

Infer. 3. *Learn hence the true ground and reason of those strange, amazing, and supernatural effects, that you behold and so admire in the world, as often as you see sinners forsaking their pleasant, profitable corruptions and companions, and embracing the ways of Christ, godliness, and mortification.*

It is said, 1 Pet. iv. 4. " They think it strange, that you run " not with them into the same excess of riot." The word is εν ω ξενιζονται, they stand at a gaze, as the hen that hath hatched partridge eggs doth, when she sees them take the wing and fly away from her.

Beloved, it is the world's wonder to see their companions in sin forsake them; those that were once as profane and vain as themselves, it may be more, to forsake their society, retire into their closets, mourn for sin, spend their time in meditation and prayer, embrace the severest duties, and content to run the greatest hazards in the world for Christ; but they see not that Almighty Power that draws them, which is too strong for all the sinful ties and engagements in the world to withhold and detain them.

A man would have wondered to see Elisha leave the oxen, and run after Elijah, saying, " Let me go, I pray thee, and kiss my " father and mother, and then I will follow thee; when Elijah had said nothing to persuade him to follow him only as he passed by him, he cast his mantle on him, 1 Kings x. 19, 20. Surely that soul whom God draws, must needs leave all and follow Christ, for the power of God resteth on it. All carnal ties and engagements to sin break and give way, when the Father draws the soul to Christ in the day of his power.

Infer. 4. *Is this the first spring of spiritual motion after Christ? Learn then from hence, how it comes to pass that so many excellent sermons and powerful persuasions are ineffectual, and cannot draw and win one soul to Christ. Surely it is because ministers draw alone; and the special saving power of God goes not forth at all times alike with their endeavours.*

Paul was a chosen vessel, filled with a greater measure of gifts and graces by the Spirit, than any that went before him or followed after him ; and, as his talents, so his diligence in improving them was beyond any recorded example we read of amongst men ; " He rather flew like a seraphim, than travelled upon his Master's " errand about the world *." Apollos was an eloquent preacher, and mighty in the scriptures, yet Paul is " nothing, and Apollos " nothing; but God that gives the increase," 1 Cor. iii. 7. We are too apt to admire men, yea, and the best are but too apt to go forth in the strength of their own parts and preparations ; but God secures his own glory, and magnifies his own power, frequently, in giving success to weaker endeavours, and men of lower abilities, when he withholds it from men of more raised, refined, and excellent gifts and abilities.

It is our great honour, who are the ministers of the gospel, that we are συνεργοι, *workers together with God,* 1 Cor. iii. 9. in his strength we can prevail; " the weapons of our warfare are mighty " through God," 2 Cor. x. 4. But if his presence, blessing, and assistance be not with us, we are nothing, we can do nothing.

If we prepare diligently, pray heartily, preach zealously, and our hearers go as they came, without any spiritual effects and fruits of our labours, what shall we say, but as Martha said to Christ, " Lord, if thou hadst been here, my brother had not died :" Had the Spirit of God gone forth with his especial efficacy and blessing, with this prayer, or that sermon, these souls had not departed dead and senseless from under it.

Infer. 5. *Doth all success and efficacy depend upon the Father's drawings? Let none then despair of their unregenerate and carnal relations, over whose obstinacy they do, and have cause to mourn.*

What, if they have been as many years under the preaching of the gospel, as the poor man lay at the pool of Bethesda, and hitherto to no purpose? A time may come at last, (as it did for him) when

---

* Ὡς πτηνος την οικουμενην, και ως ασωματος διεδραμε.   Chrysost.

the Spirit of God may move upon the waters; I mean put a quick-ening and converting power into the means, and then the desire of your souls for them shall be fulfilled.

It may be you have poured out many prayers and tears to the Lord for them; you have cried for them as Abraham for his son, " O that Ishmael might live before thee !" O that this poor hus-band, wife, child, brother, or sister, might live in thy sight; and still you see them continue carnal, dead, and senseless : Well, but yet not give up your hopes, nor cease your pious endeavours, the time may come when the Father may draw as well as you, and then you shall see them quit all, and come to Christ; and nothing shall hinder them.   They are now drawn away of their own lusts; they are easily drawn away by their sinful companions; but when God draws, none of these shall withdraw them from the Lord Jesus.   What is their ignorance, obstinacy, and hardness of heart, before that mighty power that subdues all things to itself? Go therefore to the Lord by prayer for them, and say, Lord, I have laboured for my poor relations in vain, I have spent my exhorta-tions to little purpose; the work is too difficult for me, I can carry it no farther, but thou canst: O let thy power go forth; they shall be willing in the day of thy power.

Infer. 6. *If none can come to Christ except the Father draw them, then surely none can be drawn from Christ except the Father leave them : That power which at first drew them to Christ can secure and establish them in Christ to the end.*   John x. 29.   " My Father " which gave them me is greater than all, and no man is able to " pluck them out of my Father's hand."

When the power of God at first draws us out of our natural state to Christ, it finds us not only *impotent* but *obstinate,* not only unable, but unwilling to come; and yet this power of God prevails against all opposition; how much more is it able to pre-serve and secure us, when his fear is put into our inward parts, so that we dare not depart, we have no will to depart from him? Well then if the world say, I will ensnare thee; if the devil say, I will destroy thee; if the flesh say, I will betray thee; yet thou art secure and safe, as long as God hath said, " I will never leave thee " nor forsake thee," Heb. xiii. 5.

Infer. 7. *Let this engage you to a constant attendance upon the ordinances of God, in which this drawing power of God is some-times put forth upon the hearts of men.*

Beloved, there are certain seasons in which the Lord comes nigh to men in the ordinances and duties of his worship; and we know not at what time the Lord cometh forth by his Spirit upon this design: he many times comes in an hour when we think not of him!   " I am found of them that sought me not," Isa. lxv. 1.   It is good therefore to be found in the way of the Spirit. Had that poor man, that lay so long at the pool of Bethesda, reasoned thus with himself, So long have I lain here in vain expecting a cure, it is to no purpose to wait longer, and so had been absent at that very time when the angel came down, he had, in all likelihood, carried his disease to the grave with him.

How dost thou know but this very *sabbath*, this sermon, this prayer, which thou hast no heart to attend, and are tempted to neglect, may be the season and instrument wherein, and by which, the Lord may do that for thy soul which was never done before ?

Infer. 8. *To conclude, How are all the saints engaged to put forth all the power and ability they have for God, who hath put forth his infinite Almighty Power to draw them to Christ ?*

God hath done great things for your souls; he hath drawn you out of the miserable state of sin and wrath; and that when he let others go, by nature as good as you, he hath drawn you into union with Christ, and communion with his glorious privileges. O that you would henceforth employ all the power you have for God in the duties of obedience, and in drawing others to Christ, as much as in you lies, and say continually with the Church, " Draw me, " we will run after thee," Cant. i. 4.

Thanks be to God for Jesus Christ.

SERMON V.

Of the Work of the Spirit more particularly, by which the Soul is enabled to apply Christ.

Eph. ii. 1.

And you hath he quickened who were dead in trespasses and sins.

IN the former sermons we have seen our union with Christ in the general nature of it, and the means by which it is effected, both *external*, by the preaching of the gospel, and *internal*, by the drawing of the Father. We are now to bring our thoughts yet closer to this great mystery, and consider the bands by which Christ and believers are knit together in a blessed union.

And if we heedfully observe the scripture expressions, and ponder the nature of this union, we shall find there are two bands which knit Christ and the soul together, *viz.*

1. The Spirit on Christ's part.
2. Faith on our part.

The *Spirit*, on Christ's part, *quickening* us with spiritual life, whereby Christ first takes hold of us, and *faith* on our part, when thus quickened, whereby we take hold of Christ; accordingly, this union with the Lord Jesus is expressed in scripture sometimes by the one and sometimes by the other of the means or bands by which it is effected.   Christ is sometimes said to be in us; so Col. i. 27. " Christ is in you the hope of glory."   And Rom. viii. 10. " And " if Christ be in you, the body is dead because of sin."   At other times it is expressed by the other band on our part, as 1 John v. 20. " We are in him that is true, even in his Son Christ " Jesus."   And 2 Cor. v. 17. " If any man be in Christ, he is a " new creature."

The difference betwixt both these is thus aptly expressed by a late author *.   Christ is in believers by his *Spirit*, 1 John iv. 13. " The believer is in Christ by *faith*, John i. 12.   Christ is in the " believer by *inhabitation*, Rom. iii. 17.   The believer is in Christ " by *implantation*, Rom. vi. 35.   Christ is in the believer as the " head is in the body, Col. i. 18.   As the root in the branches, " John xv. 5.   Believers are in Christ as the members are in the " head, Eph. i. 23. or as the branches are in the root, John " xv. 1, 7.   Christ in the believer implieth life, and influence " from Christ, Col. iii. 4.   The believer implieth *communion* and " *fellowship* with Christ, 1 Cor. i. 30.   When Christ is said to be " in the believer, we are to understand it in reference to *sanctifi-* " *cation*.   When the believer is said to be in Christ, it is in order " to justification."

Thus we apprehend, being ourselves first apprehended by Jesus Christ, Phil. iii. 12.   We cannot take hold of Christ till first he take hold of us; no vital act of faith can be exercised till a vital principle be first inspired: of both these bands of union we must speak distinctly, and first of " Christ quickening us by his Spirit, " in order to our union with him," of which we have an account in the scripture before us, " You he hath quickened, who were " dead in trespasses and sins:" In which words we find these two things noted, *viz.*

1. The infusion of a vital principle of grace.

2. The total indisposedness of the subject by nature.

First, The infusion of a vital principle of grace, *You hath he quickened*. These words [*hath he quickened*] are a supplement made to clear the sense of the apostle, which else would have been more obscure, by reason of that long parenthesis betwixt the first and fifth verses, " for as the † learned observe, this word υμας, you, is

---

* Mount Pisgah, p. 22, 23.

† *Illud* υμας *regitur a* συνεζωοποιησε, *v. 5. est igitur hoc loco et* hyperbaton *et*

" governed by the verb συνεζωοποιησε, *hath he quickened*, ver. 5. So
" that here the words are transposed from the plain grammatical
" order, by reason of the interjection of a long sentence, there-
" fore, with good warrant our translators have put the verb into
" the first verse, which is repeated, ver. 5. and so keeping faith-
" fully to the scope, have excellently cleared the syntax and order
" of the words." Now this verb συνεζωοποιησε, *hath he quickened*.
imports the first vital act of the Spirit of God, or his first enlivening work upon the soul, in order to its union with Jesus Christ:
For look, as the blood of Christ is the fountain of all merit, so the
Spirit of Christ is the fountain of all spiritual life; and until he
quicken us, i. e. infuse the principle of the divine life into our souls,
we can put forth no hand, or vital act of faith, to lay hold upon
Jesus Christ.

This his quickening work is therefore the first in order of nature
to our union with Christ, and fundamental to all other acts of
grace done and performed by us, from our first closing with Christ
throughout the whole course of our obedience; and this quickening act is said, ver. 5. to be together with Christ. Either noting
(as some expound it) that it is the effect of the same power by
which Christ was raised from the dead, according to Eph. 1. 19.
or rather, to be *quickened together with Christ*, notes that new
spiritual life which is infused into our dead souls in the time of our
union with Christ: " For it is Christ to whom we are conjoined
" and united in our regeneration, out of whom, as a fountain, all
" spiritual benefits flow to us, among which this vivification or
" quickening is one *, and a most sweet and precious one."

Zanchy Bodius, and many others, will have this *quickening* to
comprize both our justification and regeneration, and to stand opposed both to *eternal* and *spiritual* death, and it may well be allowed; but it most properly imports our regeneration, wherein the
Spirit, in an ineffable and mysterious way, makes the soul to live
to God, yea, to live the life of God, which soul was before *dead
in trespasses and sins*. In which words we have,

Secondly, In the next place, the total indisposedness of the subjects by nature: For, as it is well noted by a † learned man, " the
" apostle doth not say of these Ephesians that they were half
" dead, or sick, and infirm, but dead wholly; altogether dead,

---

synobsis et απoχoπη της περιoδ8, *quæ est species* τ8 αναντα πoδoπ8, *cujus quidem ano-
maliæ causa est* επεμϐoλη *interjectio sententiæ prolixioris.* Piscator. Pool's Synop.

* *Ex Christo conjuncto nobiscum, ut capite cum membris, profluunt in nos omnia benefi-
cia, in quorum numero est vivificatio.* Rolloc. in Loc.

† *Non vocat hic semimortuos aut ægrotos ac infirmos, sed prorsus mortuos, omni facul-
tate bene cogitandi aut agendi destituti.* Rolloc. in Loc.

" destitute of any faculty or ability, so much as to think one good
" thought, or perform one good act." You were dead in respect
of *condemnation*, being under the damning sentence of the law, and
you are dead in respect of the privation of spiritual life; dead in
opposition to justification, and dead in opposition to regeneration
and sanctification: And the fatal instrument by which their souls
died is here shewed them ; you were dead in, or by *trespasses* and
sins, this was the sword that killed your souls, and cut them off
from God. Some do curiously distinguish betwixt trespasses and
sins, as if one pointed at *original*, the other at *actual* sins; but I
suppose they are promiscuously used here, and serve to express the
cause of their ruin, or means of their spiritual death and destruction: this was their case when Christ came to quicken them, *dead
in sin ;* and being so, they could not move themselves towards union
with Christ, but as they were moved by the quickening Spirit of
God. Hence the observation will be this,

> Doct. *That those souls which have union with Christ, are quick-
> ened with a supernatural principle of life by the Spirit of God
> in order thereunto.*

The Spirit of God is not only a living Spirit, *formally* considered ;
but he is also the Spirit of life, *effectively* or *casually* considered ;
And without his breathing, or infusing life into our souls, our union
with Christ is impossible.

It is the observation of learned * Camero, " that there must be
" an *unition* before there can be an *union* with Christ. *Unition* is
" to be conceived *efficiently* as the work of God's Spirit, joining
" the believer to Christ, and *union* is to be conceived *formally*, the
" joining itself of the persons together:" We close with Christ by
faith, but that faith being a vital act, pre-supposes a principle of
life communicated to us by the Spirit; therefore it is said, John
xi. 26. " Whosoever liveth and believeth in me, shall never die :"
The vital act and operation of faith springs from this quickening
Spirit: So in Rom. viii. 1, 2. The apostle, having in the first
verse opened the blessed estate of them that are in Christ, shews
us in the second verse how we come to be in him: " The Spirit of
" life (saith he) which is in Christ Jesus, hath made me free from
" the law of sin and death."

There is indeed a quickening work of the Spirit, which is *sub-*

---

* *Observandum est unionem et unitionem inter se differe : unio est rerum actus, qui forma
rationem habet, nempe actus rerum unitarum qua unitæ sunt : unitio autem actus significat
causæ efficientis, &c.* Camero de Eccles. p. 222.

sequent to regeneration, consisting in his exciting, recovering, and actuating of his own graces in us; and from hence is the *liveliness* of a Christian; and there is a quickening act of the Spirit *in our regeneration*, and from hence is the spiritual life of a Christian; of this I am here to speak, and that I may speak profitably to this point, I will in the doctrinal part labour to open these five particulars.

First, What this spiritual life is in its nature and properties.

Secondly, In what manner it is wrought or inspired into the soul.

Thirdly, For what end, or with what design, this life is so inspired.

Fourthly, I shall shew this work to be wholly supernatural.

And then, *Fifthly*, Why this quickening must be antecedent to our actual closing with Christ by faith.

First, We shall enquire into the nature and properties of this life, and discover (as we are able) what it is. And we find it to consist in that *wonderful change which the Spirit of God makes upon the frame and temper of the soul, by his infusing or implanting the principles of grace in all the powers and faculties thereof.*

A change it makes upon the soul, and that a marvellous one, no less than from death to life; for though a man be *physically* a living man, i. e. his natural soul hath union with his body, yet his soul having no union with Christ, he is *theologically* a dead man, Luke xv. 24. and Col. ii. 13. Alas, it deserves not the name of life, to have a soul serving only to season and preserve the body a little while from corruption: to carry it up and down the world, and only enable it to eat, and drink, and talk, and laugh, and then die: Then do we begin to live, when we begin to have union with Christ the Fountain of life, by his Spirit communicated to us: From this time we are to reckon our life * as some have done: There be many changes made upon men besides this, many are changed from profaneness to civility, and from mere civility to formality, and a shadow of religion, who still remain in the state and power of spiritual death, notwithstanding: but when the Spirit of the Lord is poured out upon us, to quicken us with the new spiritual life, this is a wonderful change indeed: It gives us an *esse supernaturale*, a new supernatural being, which is therefore called a *new creature, the new man, the hidden man of the heart*: The natural essence and faculties of the soul remain still, but it is divested of the old qualities, and endowed with new ones, 2 Cor. v. 17. " Old things are passed away, " behold, all things are become new."

And this change is not made by altering and rectifying the disorders of the life only, leaving the temper and frame of the heart

---

* *Hic jacet Similis, cujus ætas multorem annorum fuit, ipse septem duntaxat annos vixit.*

still carnal; but by the infusion of a supernatural permanent principle into the soul, John iv. 14. " It shall be in him a well of water:" principles are to a course of actions, as fountains or springs are to the streams and rivers that flow from them, and are maintained by them : and hence is the evenness and constancy of renewed souls in the course of godliness.

Nor is this principle or habit *acquired* by accustoming ourselves to holy actions, as natural habits are acquired by frequent acts, which beget a *disposition*, and thence grow up to an *habit* or second nature, but it is infused, or implanted in the soul by the Spirit of God. So we read, Ezek. xxxvi. 25, 26. " A new heart also will " I give you, and a new spirit will I put within you :" It grows not up out of our natures, but is put or infused into us: as it is said of the two witnesses, Rev. xi. 11. who lay dead in a *civil sense*, three days and a half, that *the Spirit of life from God entered into them :* so it is here in a *spiritual sense*, the Spirit of life from God enters into the dead, carnal heart : it is all by way of supernatural infusion.

Nor is it limited to this or that faculty of the soul, but grace or life is poured into all the faculties : " Behold, all thing are be- " come new," 2 Cor. v. 17. The *understanding, will, thoughts,* and *affections*, are all renewed by it : the whole inner *man* is changed ; yea, the *tongue* and *hand*, the *discourses* and *actions*, even all the *ways* and *courses* of the outward *man* are renewed by it.

But more particularly, we shall discern the *nature* of this *spiritual life*, by considering the *properties* of it ; among which, these are very *remarkable*.

First, The soul that is joined to Christ is quickened with a *divine life*, so we read in 2 Pet. i. 4. Where believers are said to be *partakers of the divine nature :* a very high expression, and warily to be understood. *Partakers of the divine nature :* not *essentially;* so it is wholly incommunicable to the creature, nor yet *hypostatically,* and personally ; so Christ only was a partaker of it ; but our participation of the divine nature, must be understood in a way proper to believers ; that is to say, we partake of it by the inhabitation of the Spirit of God in us, according to 1 Cor. iii. 16, 17. " Know ye not that ye are the temple of God, and that the Spirit " of God dwelleth in you ?" The Spirit, who is God by nature dwells in, and actuates the soul whom he regenerates, and by sanctifying it, causes it to live a *divine life :* from this life of God the unsanctified are said to be alienated, Eph. iv. 18. but believers are partakers of it.

Secondly, And being divine, it must needs be the most *excellent,* and transcendent life that any creature doth, or can live in this world : it surmounts the natural, rational, and moral life of the unsanctified, as much as the angelical life excels the life of flies and worms of the earth.

Some think it a rare life to live in sensual pleasures; but the scripture will not allow so much as the name of life to them; but tells us, " they are dead whilst they live," 1 Tim. v. 6. certainly it is a wonderful elevation of the nature of man to be quickened with such a life as this. There are two ways wherein the blessed God hath honoured poor man above the very angels of heaven. One was by the hypostatical union of our nature, in Christ, with the divine nature: the other is by uniting our persons mystically to Christ, and thereby communicating spiritual life to us: this latter is a most glorious privilege, and in one respect a more singular mercy than the former; for that honour which is done to our nature by the hypostatical union, is common to all, good and bad, even they that perish have yet that honour; but to be implanted into Christ by regeneration, and live upon him as the branch doth upon the vine, this is a peculiar privilege, a mercy kept from the world that is to perish, and only communicated to God's elect, who are to live eternally with him in heaven.

Thirdly, This life infused by the regenerating Spirit, is a most *pleasant life.* All delights, all pleasures, all joys, which are not fantastic and delusive, have their spring and origin here, Rom. viii. 6. " To be spiritually minded is life and peace," i. e. a most serene, placid life; such a soul becomes, so far as it is influenced and sanctified by the Spirit, the very region of life and peace: when one thing is thus predicated of another, *in casu recto,* (saith a learned man) it speaks their intimate connection: peace is so connatural to this life, that you may either call it a life that hath peace in it, or a peace that hath life in it: yea, it hath its enclosed pleasures in it, " such as a stranger intermeddles not with," Prov. xiv. 10. Regeneration is the term from which all true pleasure commences; you never live a cheerful day, till you begin to live to God: therefore it is said, Luke xv. 24. when the *prodigal son* was returned to his father, and reconciled, then *they began to be merry.*

None can make another, by any words, to understand what that pleasure is which the renewed soul feels diffused through all its faculties and affections, in its communion with the Lord, and in the sealings and witnessings of his Spirit. That is a very apt and well known similitude, which Peter Martyr used, and the Lord blessed to the conversion of that noble marquis Galeacus: if, said he, a man should see a company of people dancing upon the top of a remote hill, he would be apt to conclude they were a company of wild distracted people; but if he draw nearer, and behold the excellent order, and hear the ravishing sweet music that are among them, he will quickly alter his opinion of them, and be for dancing himself with them.

All the *delights* in the sensual *life*, all the pleasure that ever your *lusts* gave you, are but as the putrid, stinking *waters* of a corrupt *pond*, where *toads* lie croaking and spawning, compared to the *crystal streams* of the most pure and pleasant *fountain*.

Fourthly, This life of God, with which the regenerate are quickened in their union with Christ, as it is a *pleasant*, so it is also *a growing increasing life*, John iv. 14. " It shall be in him a well of " water springing up into everlasting life."

It is not in our sanctification, as it is in our justification ; our justification is complete and perfect, no defect is found there ; but the new creature labours under many defects : all believers are equally justified, but not equally sanctified. Therefore you read, 2 Cor. iv. 16. that " the inward man is renewed day by day :" And 2 Pet. iii. 18. Christians are exhorted " to grow in grace, and " in the knowledge of our Lord and Saviour :" if this work were perfect, and finished at once, as justification is, there could be no renewing day by day, nor growth in grace. *Perfectum est cui nihil deest & cui nihil addi potest ;* i. e. that is perfect which wants nothing, and to which nothing can be added. The apostle indeed prays for the Thessalonians, " that God would sanctify them," ολοίελεις,—wholly, perfectly, 1 Thes. v. 23. And this is matter of prayer and hope ; for, at last, it will grow up to perfection ; but this perfect holiness is reserved for the perfect state in the world to come, and none but * deluded, proud spirits boast of it here : but when " that which is perfect is come, then that which is in part " shall be done away," 1 Cor. xiii. 9, 10. And upon the imperfection of the new creature in every faculty, that warfare and daily conflict spoken of, Gal. v. 17. and experienced by every Christian, is grounded ; grace rises gradually in the soul, as the sun doth in the heavens, " which shineth more and more unto a " perfect day," Prov. iv. 18.

Fifthly, To conclude ; This life with which the regenerate are quickened, is an *everlasting life*. " This is the record, that God " hath given to us eternal life, and this life is in his Son," 1 John v. 11. This principle of life, is the seed of God ; and that remains in the soul for ever, 1 John iii. 9. It is no transient, vanishing thing, but a fixed, permanent principle, which abides in the soul for ever ; a man may lose his *gifts*, but grace abides ; the soul may, and must be separated from the body, but grace cannot be separated from the soul : when all forsake us, this will not leave us.

---

* Perfection of sanctification is not found in this life, unless in the dreams of some fanatics. *Ames.*

This infused principle is therefore vastly different, both from the extraordinary gifts of prophecy, wherein the Spirit was sometimes said to come upon men, under the Old Testament, 1 Sam. x. 6, 10. and from the common vanishing effects he sometimes produceth in the unregenerate, of which we have frequent accounts in the New Testament, Heb. vi. 4. and John v. 35. It is one thing for the Spirit to come upon a man in the way of present influence and assistance, and another thing to dwell in a man as in his temple.

And thus of the nature and quality of this blessed work of the Spirit in quickening us.

Secondly, Having seen the nature and properties of the spiritual life, we are concerned in the next place to enquire into the way and manner in which it is wrought and infused by the Spirit, and here we must say,

First of all, that the work is wrought in the soul very *mysteriously*; so Christ tells Nicodemus, John iii. 8. " The wind bloweth " where it listeth, and thou hearest the sound thereof, but canst " not tell whence it cometh, or whither it goeth, so is every one " that is born of the Spirit." There be many opinions among *philosophers* about the original of wind; but we have no certain knowledge of it; we describe it by its effects and properties, but know little of its original: and if the works of God in nature be so obstruse, and unsearchable, how much more so are these sublime, and supernatural works of the Spirit ?

We are not able to solve the *Phænomena* of nature, we can give no account of our own formation in the womb, Eccl. xi. 5. Who can exactly describe how the parts of the body are formed, and the soul infused? " It is curiously wrought in the lowest parts of the " earth," as the Psalmist speaks, Psal. cxxxix. 16. but how, we know not. Basil saith, divers questions may be moved about a *fly*, which may puzzle the greatest *philosopher :* we know little of the forms and essences of natural things, much less of these profound, and abstruse spiritual things.

Secondly, But though we cannot pry into these secrets by the eye of reason, yet God hath revealed this to us in his word, that it is wrought by his own Almighty Power, Eph. i. 19. The *apostle* ascribes this work to *the exceeding greatness* of the power of God ; and this must needs be, if we consider how the Spirit of God expresses it in scripture, by a new creation ; i. e. a giving being to something out of nothing, Eph. ii. 10. In this it differs from all the effects of human power, for man always works upon some preexistent matter, but here is no such matter; all that is in man, the subject of this work, is only a passive capacity, or receptivity, but nothing is found in him to contribute towards this work ; this

supernatural life is not, nor can it be educed out of natural principles; this wholly transcends the sphere of all natural power; but
of this more anon.

Thirdly, This also we may affirm of it, that this divine life is infused into all the natural faculties. and powers of the soul, not one
exempted, 1 Thes. v. 23. The whole soul and spirit is the recipient subject of it; and with respect to this general infusion into
all the faculties and powers of the soul, it is called a new creature,
a new man, having an integral perfection, and fulness of all its
parts and members; it becomes light in the mind, John xvii. 3.
Obedience in the will, 1 Pet. i. 2. In the affections an heavenly
temper and tenderness, Col. iii. 1, 2. And so is variously denominated, even as the sea is from the several shores it washes,
though it be one and the same sea. And here, we must observe,
lies one main difference betwixt a regenerate soul and an hypocrite;
* the one is all of a piece, as I may say, the principle of spiritual
life runs into all, and every faculty and affection, and sanctifies or
renews the whole man; whereas the change upon hypocrites is
but partial and particular; he may have new light, but no new
love; a new tongue, but not a new heart; this or that vice may
be reformed, but the whole course of his life is not altered.

Fourthly, and *lastly,* This infusion of spiritual life is done *instan-
taneously,* as all *creation work* is; hence it is resembled to that *plastic power,* which, in a moment, made the light to shine out of darkness; just so God shines into our hearts, 2 Cor. iv. 6.

It is true, a soul may be a long time under the preparatory
works of the Spirit, he may be under convictions and humiliations,
purposes and resolutions a long time; he may be waiting at the
pool of Bethesda, attending the means and ordinances, but when
the Spirit comes once to quicken the soul, it is done in a moment:
even as it is in the infusion of the rational soul, the body is long
ere it be prepared and moulded, but when once the *embryo* or matter is ready, it is quickened with the spirit of life in an instant: so
it is here; but O what a blessed moment is this! Upon which the
whole weight of our eternal happiness depends; for it is Christ in
us, i. e. Christ formed in us, who is the hope of glory, Col. i. 27.
And our Lord expressly tells us, John iii. 3. That except we be
regenerate and born again, we cannot see the kingdom of God.
And thus of the way and manner of its infusion.

Thirdly, Let the design and end of God, in this his *quickening*

---

* *Ab uno desuper principio quod convenienter voluntati operatur dependent prima, secunda et tertia. Quemadmodum minima pars ferri lapidis magnetis spiritu movetur, per mul-
tos annulos ferreos extensa : ita etiam qui sunt virtute præditi, divino spiritu attracti, cum
prima monsione, conjungantur, deinceps autem alii usque ad postremam.* Clem. Alexand.
Strom. lib. 7.

work, be next considered; for what end and with what design and aim this work is wrought. And if we consult the scriptures in this matter, we shall find this principle of life is infused in order to our glorifying God, in this world, by a *life of obedience*, and our enjoying of God in the world to come.

First, Spiritual life is infused in order to a course of obedience in this world, whereby God is glorified: So we read in Eph. ii. 10. " Created in Christ Jesus unto good works, which God hath be- " fore ordained that we should walk in them:" habits are to ac- tions, as the root is to the fruit, it is for fruit sake that we plant the root, and ingraff the branches. So in Ezek. xxxvi. 26, 27. " A " new spirit will I also put within you, and cause you to walk in " my statutes, and ye shall keep my judgments and do them." This is the next or immediate design and end, not only of the first infusion of the principle of life into the soul, but of all the exciting, actuating, and assisting works of the Spirit afterwards. Now this principle of spiritual life infused, hath a twofold influ- ence into obedience.

First, This makes a sincere and true *obedience*, when it flows from an inward vital principle of grace. The hypocrite is moved by something *ab extra*, from without, as the applause of men, the accommodation of fleshly interests, the force of education: or if there be any thing from within that moves him, it is but self- interest, to quiet a disturbing conscience, and support his vain hopes of heaven; but he never acts from a new principle, a new nature, inclining him to holy actions. Sincerity mainly lies in the harmony and correspondency of actions to their principles: from this infused principle it is, that men hunger and thirst for God, and go to their duties as men do to their meals, when they find an empty craving stomach.

O reader, pause a little upon this ere thou pass on, ask thy heart whether it be so with thee: are holy duties connatural to thee? Doth thy soul move and work after God by a kind of supernatural instinct? This then will be to thee a good evidence of thy in- tegrity.

Secondly, From this infused principle of life results the *excellency of our obedience*, as well as the sincerity of it; for by virtue and reason thereof, it becomes free and voluntary, not forced and constrained, it drops like honey, and of its own accord, out of the comb, Cant. iv. 11. or as waters from the fountain, without forcing, John iv. 14. An unprincipled professor must be pressed hard by some weight of affliction, ere he will yield one tear, or pour out a prayer, Psal. lxxviii. 34. " When he slew them, then " they sought him."

Now the freedom of obedience is the excellency of it, God's eye is much upon that, 1 Cor. ix. 17. yea, and the uniformity of our obedience, which is also a special part of the beauty of it, results from hence : he that acts from a principle acts fluently and uniformly, and there is a proportion betwixt the parts of his conversation ; this is it which makes us holy, εν πασῃ αναϛροφῃ, *in all manner of conversation*, or in every point and turning of our conversations, as the word imports, 1 Pet. i. 15. Whereas he that is moved by this or that external accidental motive, must needs be very uneven, " like the legs of a lame man," as the expression is, Prov. xxvi. 7. " which are not equal." Now a word of God, and then the discourse runs muddy and profane or carnal again ; all that evenness and uniformity that are in the several parts of a Christian's life, are the effect of this infused principle of spiritual life.

Thirdly, Another aim and design of God in the infusion of this principle of life, is thereby to prepare and qualify the soul for the enjoyment of himself in heaven : " Except a man be born again " he cannot see the kingdom of God," John iii. 3. All that shall possess that inheritance must be begotten again to it, as the apostle speaks, 1 Pet. i. 3, 4. This principle of grace is the very seed of that glory ; it is eternal life in the root and principle, John xvii. 3. by this the soul is attempered and qualified for that state and employment. What is the life of glory but the vision of God, and the soul's assimilation to God by that vision ? From both which results that unspeakable joy and delight which passeth understanding : but what vision of God, assimilation to God, or delight in God, can that soul have which was never quickened with the supernatural principle of grace ? The temper of such souls is expressed in that sad character, Zech. xi. 8. " My soul loathed them, and their soul " also abhorred me." For want of this vital principle it is, that the very same duties and ordinances which are the delights and highest pleasures of the saints, are no better than a mere drudgery and bondage to others, Mal. i. 13. Heaven would be no heaven to a dead soul ; this principle of life, in its daily growth and improvement, is our meetness, as well as our evidence, for heaven : these are the main ends of its infusion.

Fourthly, In the next place, according to the method proposed, I am obliged to shew you, *that this quickening work is wholly supernatural ;* it is the sole and proper work of the Spirit of God. So Christ himself expressly asserts it, in John iii. 6, 8. " That which " is born of the flesh is flesh, and that which is born of the Spirit " is spirit : the wind bloweth where it listeth, and thou hearest " the sound thereof, but canst not tell whence it cometh, nor " whither it goeth ; so is every one that is born of the Spirit."

Believers are the birth or offspring of the Spirit, who produceth the new creature in them in an unintelligible manner, even to themselves. So far is it above their own ability to produce, that it is above their capacity to understand the way of its production: as if you should ask, Do you know from whence the wind comes? No: Do you know whither it goes? No: But you hear and feel it when it blows? Yes: Why, so is every one that is born of the Spirit; he feels the efficacy, and discerns the effects of the Spirit on his own soul, but cannot understand or describe the manner of their production. This is not only above the carnal, but above the renewed mind to comprehend; we can contribute nothing, I mean actively, to the production of this principle of life, we may indeed be said to concur passively with the Spirit in it; i. e. there is found in us a capacity, aptness, or receptiveness of this principle of life: our nature is endowed with such faculties and powers as are meet subjects to receive, and instruments to act this spiritual life: God only quickens the rational nature with spiritual life.

It is true also, that in the *progress of sanctification*, a man doth actively concur with the Spirit, but in the first production of this spiritual principle he can do nothing: he can indeed perform those external duties that have a remote tendency to it, but he cannot by the power of nature perform any saving act, or contribute any thing more than a passive capacity to the implantation of a new principle: as will appear by the following arguments.

Arg. 1. He that actively concurs to his own regeneration, makes himself to differ; but this is denied to all regenerate men, 1 Cor. iv. 7. "Who maketh thee to differ from another? And "what hast thou that thou didst not receive?"

Arg. 2. That to which the scripture ascribes both *impotency* and *enmity*, with respect to grace, cannot actively, and of itself, concur to the production of it: but the scripture ascribes both impotency and enmity to nature, with respect to grace. It denies to it a power to do any thing of itself, John xv. 5. And, which is less, it denies to it a power to speak a good word, Mat. xii. 34. And, which is least of all, it denies it power to think a good thought, 2 Cor. iii. 5. This impotency, if there were no more, cuts off all pretence of our active concurrence; but then if we consider that it ascribes enmity to our natures, as well as impotency, how clear is the case! See Rom. viii. 7. "The carnal mind is enmity against God." And Col. i. 21. "And you that were enemies in your minds by wicked "works." So then nature is so far productive of this principle, as impotency and enmity can enable it to be so.

Arg. 3. That which is of natural production, must needs be subject to natural dissolution; that which is born of the flesh is flesh, a perishing thing, for every thing is as its principle is, and there can be no more in the effect, than there is in the cause : but this principle of spiritual life is not subject to dissolution, it is the water that springs up into everlasting life, John iv. 14.   The seed of God, which remaineth in the regenerate soul, 1 John iii. 9. And all this, because it is " born not of corruptible, but of incor- " ruptible seed," 1 Pet. i. 23.

Arg. 4. If our new birth be our resurrection, a new creation, yea, a victory over nature, then we cannot actively contribute to its production ; but under all these notions it is represented to us in the scriptures ; it is our resurrection from the dead, Eph. v. 14. And you know the body is wholly passive in its resurrection : but though it concurs not, yet it gives pre-existent matter : therefore the metaphor is designedly varied, Eph. iv. 24. where it is called a *creation:* in which there is neither active concurrence, nor pre-existent matter ; but though creation excludes pre-existent matter, yet in producing something out of nothing, there is no reluctancy nor opposition : therefore to shew how purely supernatural this principle of life is, it is clothed and presented to us in the notion of a victory, 2 Cor. x. 4.   And so leaves all to grace.

Arg. 5. If nature could produce, or but actively concur to the production of this spiritual life, then the best natures would be soonest quickened with it ; and the worst natures not at all, or at last, and least of all : but contrarily, we find the worst natures often regenerated, and the best left in the state of spiritual death : with how many sweet *homilitical* virtues was the young man adorn-ed ? Mark x. 21. yet graceless : and what a sink of sin was Mary Magdalen, Luke vii. 37. yet sanctified.   Thus beautiful Rachel is barren, while Leah bears children.   And there is scarce any thing that affects and melts the hearts of Christians more than this comparative consideration doth, when they consider vessels of gold cast away, and leaden ones chosen for such noble uses.   So that it is plain enough to all wise and humble souls, that this new life is wholly of supernatural production.

Fifthly, and lastly, I shall briefly represent the necessary ante-cedency of this quickening work of the Spirit, to our first closing with Christ by faith : and this will easily let itself into your under-standings, if you but consider the nature of the vital act of faith ; which is the soul's receiving of Christ, and resting upon him for pardon and salvation : in which two things are necessarily included, viz.

1. The renouncing of all other hopes and dependencies.

2. The opening of the heart fully to Jesus Christ.

First, The renouncing of all other hopes and dependencies what-soever.   Self in all its acceptations, natural, sinful, and moral, is now to be denied and renounced for ever, else Christ can never be

received, Rom. x. 3. not only self in its vilest pollutions, but self
in its richest ornaments and endowments : but this is as impossible
to the unrenewed and natural man, as it is for rocks or mountains
to start from their centre, and fly like wandering atoms in the air :
nature will rather chuse to run the hazard of everlasting damnation, than escape it by a total renunciation of its beloved lusts, or
self-righteousness : this supernatural work necessarily requires a
supernatural principle, Rom. viii. 2.

Secondly, The opening the heart fully to Jesus Christ, without
which Christ can never be received, Rev. iii. 20. but this also is the
effect of the quickening Spirit, the Spirit of life which is in Christ
Jesus. Sooner may we expect to see the flowers and blossoms open
without the influence of the sun, than the heart and will of a sinner
open to receive Christ without a principle of spiritual life first derived from him : and this will be past doubt to all that consider,
not only the impotence, but the ignorance, prejudice, and
aversations of nature, by which the door of the heart is barred,
and chained against Christ, John v. 40. So that nature hath neither ability nor will, power nor desire, to come to Christ : if any
have an heart opened to receive him, it is the Lord that opens it by
his Almighty Power, and that in the way of an infused principle
of life supernatural.

Quest. But here it may be doubted and objected, against this
position. If we cannot believe till we are quickened with spiritual
life, as you say, and cannot be justified till we believe, as all say,
then it will follow, that a regenerate soul may be in the state of condemnation for a time, and consequently perish, if death should
befal him in that juncture.

Sol. To this I return, That when we speak of the priority of this
quickening work of the Spirit to our actual believing, we rather
understand it of the priority of nature, than of time, the nature
and order of the work requiring it to be so : a vital principle must,
in order of nature, be infused before a vital act can be exerted.
First, Make the tree good, and then the fruit good : and admit
we should grant some priority in time also to this quickening principle, before actual faith, yet the absurdity mentioned would be
no way consequent upon that concession ; for as the vital act of
faith quickly follows the regenerating principle, so the soul is
abundantly secured against the danger objected : God never beginning any special work of grace upon the soul, and then leaving
it and the soul with it in hazard, but preserves both to the finishing and completing of his gracious design, Phil. i. 6.

First Use of Information.

Inf. 1. If such be the nature and necessity of this principle of divine life, as you have heard it opened in the foregoing discourse, then hence it follows, *That unregenerate men are no better than dead men.* So the text represents them. " You hath he quickened " who were dead in trespasses and sins:" i. e. spiritually dead, though natually alive ; yea and lively too as any other persons in the world. There is a threefold consideration of objects, viz.

1. Naturally.
2. Politically.
3. Theologically.

First, Naturally, To all those things that are natural, they are alive : they can understand, reason, discourse, project, and con- trive, as well as others ; they can eat, drink, and build, plant, and suck out the natural comfort of these things, as much as any others. So their life is described, Job xxi. 12. " They take the " timbrel and harp, and rejoice at the sound of the organ; they " spend their days in wealth," &c. And James v. 5. " Ye have " lived in pleasure upon earth," as the fish lives in the water its natural element, and yet this natural sensual life is not allowed the name of life, 1 Tim. v. 9. such persons are *dead whilst they live ;* it is a base and ignoble life, to have a soul only to salt the body, or to enable a man for a few years to eat, and drink, and talk, and laugh, and then die.

Secondly, Objects may be considered politically, and with respect to such things, they are alive also : they can buy and sell, and ma- nage all their worldly affairs with as much dexterity, skill, and policy as other men : yea, " the children of this world are wiser in their " generation than the children of light," Luke xvi. 8. The entire * stream of their thoughts, projects, and studies, running in that one channel ; having but one design to manage, they must needs excel in worldly wisdom : But then,

Thirdly, Theologically considered, they are dead ; without life, sense, or motion, towards God, and the things that are above : their understandings are dead, 1 Cor. ii. 14. and cannot receive the things that are of God ; their wills are dead, and cannot move towards Jesus Christ, John vi. 65. Their affections are dead, even to the most excellent and spiritual objects ; and all their duties are dead duties, without life or spirit. This is the sad case of the unre- generate world.

Inf. 2. *This speaks encouragement to ministers and parents, to wait in hopes of success at last, even upon those that yet give them little hope of conversion at the present.*

The work you see is the Lord's ; when the Spirit of life comes upon their dead souls, they shall believe, and be made willing ;

---

* May God free me from him who is a man only of one business. *Bern.*

till then, we do but plough upon the rocks: yet let not our hand slack in duty, pray for them, and plead with them: you know not in which prayer, or exhortation, the Spirit of life may breathe upon them. *Can these dry bones live?* Yes, if the Spirit of life from God breathe upon them, they can, and shall live: what though their dispositions be averse to all things that are spiritual and serious, yet even such have been regenerated, when more sweet and promising natures have been passed by, and left under spiritual death.

It was the observation of Mr. Ward, upon his brother Mr. Daniel Rogers, (who was a man of great gifts and eminent graces, yet of a very bad temper and constitution) Though my brother Rogers, saith he, hath grace enough for two men, yet not half enough for himself.

It may be you have prayed and striven long with your relations and to little purpose, yet be not discouraged. How often was Mr. John Rogers, that famous and successful divine, a grief of heart to his relations in his younger years, proving a wild and lewd young man, to the great discouragement of his pious friends; yet, at last, the Lord graciously changed him, so that Mr. Richard Rogers would say, when he could exercise the utmost degree of charity or hope, for any that at present were vile and naught, *I will never despair of any man for* John Rogers' *sake.*

Inf. 4. *How honourable are Christians by their new birth!* " They are born not of blood, nor of the will of the flesh, nor of the " will of man, but of God," John i. 13. i e. not in an impure, or mere natural way, but in a most spiritual and supernatural manner: they are the offspring of God, the children of the Most High, as well by regeneration as by adoption; which is the greatest advancement of the human nature, next to its hypostatical union with the second person. Oh, what honour is this for a poor sinful creature, to have the very life of God breathed into his soul! All other dignities of nature are trifles compared with this; this makes a Christian a sacred hallowed thing, the living temple of God, 1 Cor. vi. 19. The special object of his delight.

Inf. 4. *How deplorable is the condition of the unregenerate world, in no better case than dead men?* Now to affect our hearts with the misery of such conditions, let us consider and compare it in the following particulars,

First, There is no *beauty* in the dead, all their loveliness goes away at death; there is no spiritual beauty or loveliness in any that are unregenerate: It is true, many of them have excellent moral *homilitical virtues,* which adorn their conversations in the eyes of men; but what are all these, but so many sweet flowers strewed over a dead corpse?

Secondly, The dead have no *pleasure* nor delight; even so the unregenerate are incapable of the delights of the Christian life; " to be spiritually minded is life and peace," Rom. viii. 6. i. e. this is the only serene, placid, and pleasant life: when the *prodigal,* who was once dead, was alive, then he began to be merry, Luke xv. 24. They live in sensual pleasures, but this is to be dead while alive, in scripture-reckoning.

Thirdly, The dead have no *heat,* they are as cold as clay; so are all the unregenerate towards God and things above: their *lusts* are *hot,* but their affections to God *cold* and *frozen :* that which makes a gracious heart *melt,* will not make an unregenerate heart *move.*

Fourthly, The dead must be buried, Gen. xxiii. 4. " Bury my " dead out of my sight:" So must the unregenerate be buried out of God's sight for ever: buried in the lowest hell, in the place of darkness, for ever, John iii. 3. Wo to the unregenerate, good had it been for them had they never been born !

Infer. 5. *How greatly are all men concerned to examine their condition with respect to spiritual life and death !* It is very common for men to * presume upon their union with, and interest in Christ. This privilege is, by common mistake, extended generally to all that profess the Christian religion, and practise the external duties of it, when, in truth, no more are or can be united to Christ, than are quickened by the Spirit of life which is in Christ Jesus, Rom. viii. 1, 2. O try your interest in Christ by this rule, if I am quickened by Christ, I have union with Christ. And,

First, If there be spiritual sense in your souls, there is spiritual life in them: there are αισθητηρια, senses belonging to the spiritual as well as to the animal life, Heb. v. 14. They can feel and sensibly groan under soul pressures and burdens of sin, Rom. vii. 24. The dead feel not, moan not under the burdens of sin, but the living do: they may be sensible indeed of the evil of sin, with respect to themselves, but not as against God; damnation may scare them, but pollution doth not; hell may fright them, but not the offending of God.

Secondly, If there be spiritual *hunger and thirst,* it is a sweet sign of spiritual life; this sign agrees to Christians of a day old, 1 Pet. ii. 2. Even " new born babes desire the sincere milk of the word :" If spiritual life be in you, you know how to expound that scripture, Psal. xlii. 1. without any other interpreter than your own experience: you will feel somewhat like the gnawing of an empty stomach making you restless during the interruption of your daily communion with the Lord.

Thirdly, If there be *spiritual conflicts* with sin, there is spiritual

---

* By presuming they hope, and by hoping they perish. *Ames.*

life in your souls, Gal. v. 17.   Not only a combat betwixt *light* in the higher, and *lust* in the lower faculties; not only opposition to more gross external corruptions, that carry more infamy and horror with them than other sins do: but the same faculty will be the seat of war; and the more inward and secret any lust is, by so much the more will it be opposed and mourned over.

In a word, the weakest Christian may, upon impartial observation, find such signs of spiritual life in himself (if he will allow himself time to reflect upon the bent and frame of his own heart) as desires after God; conscience of duties; fears, cares, and sorrows, about sin; delight in the society of heavenly and spiritual men; and a loathing and burden in the company of vain and carnal persons.

Object. O but I have a very dead heart to spiritual things!

Sol. It is a sign of life that you feel, and are sensible of that deadness; and besides, there is a great deal of difference betwixt *spiritual deadness* and *death;* the one is the state of the unregenerate, the other is the *disease* of regenerate men.

Object. Some signs of spiritual life are clear to me, but I cannot close with others.

Sol. If you can really close with any, it may satisfy you, though you be dark in others; for if a child cannot go, yet if it can suck; but if it cannot suck, yet if it can cry; yea, if it cannot cry, yet if it breathe, it is alive.

SERMON VI.

Of that Act on our Part, by which we do actually and effectually apply Christ to our own Souls.

JOHN i. 12.

But as many as received him, to them gave he power to become the sons of God; even to them that believe on his name.

NO sooner is the soul quickened by the Spirit of God, but it answers, in some measure, the end of God in that work, by its *active reception of Jesus Christ, in the way of believing:* What this vital act of faith is upon which so great a weight depends, as our interest in Christ and everlasting blessedness, this scripture before us will give you the best account of; wherein (omitting the consideration of the coherence and context of the words) we have three things to ponder.

First, The high and glorious privilege conferred, viz. " Power
" to become the sons of God."

Secondly, The subject of this privilege described, " As many as
" received him."

Thirdly, The description explained, by way of opposition, "Even
" as many as believe on his name."-

First, The privilege conferred is a very high and glorious one,
than which no created being is capable of greater; " power to be-
" come the sons of God:" this word εξυσιαν is of large extent and
signification, and is, by some, rendered " *this * right,* by others
" *this dignity,* by others *this prerogative,* this *privilege* or *honour :*"
It implies a title or right to *adoption,* not only with respect to the
present benefits of it in this life, but also to that blessed inheritance
which is laid up in heaven for the sons of God. And so Grotius
rightly expounds it of our *consummate* sonship, consisting in the
actual enjoyment of blessedness, as well as that which is *inchoate :*
not only a right to pardon, favour, and acceptance now, but to
heaven and the full enjoyment of God hereafter. O what an
honour, dignity, and privilege is this!

Secondly, The subjects of this privilege are described; " As many
" as received him." This text describes them by that very grace,
faith, which gives them their title and right to Christ and his benefits; and by that very act of faith, which primarily confers their
right to his person, and secondarily to his benefits, viz. *receiving*
him : there be many graces besides faith, but faith only is the
grace that gives us right to Christ; and there be many acts of faith
besides receiving, but this receiving or embracing of Christ, is the
justifying and saving act: " As many as received him," οσοι δε ελαβον
αυτον,] *as many,* be they of any nation, sex, age, or condition. For
" there is neither Greek nor Jew, circumcision, nor uncircum-
" cision, Barbarian, Scythian, bond or free: but Christ is all, and
" in all," Col. iii. 11.

Nothing but unbelief bars men from Christ and his benefits.
As many as [*received* † *him ;*] the word signifies " to accept, take,"
or, (as we fitly render it), to receive, assume, or take to us; a word
most aptly expressing the nature and office of faith, yea, the very
justifying and saving act; and we are also heedfully to note its
special object, ελαβον αυτον: The text saith not αυτα, *his,* but αυτον,
him, i. e. his person, as he is clothed with his offices, and not

---

* Beza, *hoc jus ;* Piscator, *hanc dignitatem.* Lightfoot, *prærogativam.* Heinsius,
privilegium ; nec multo aliter voce εξυσιας *Hellenistæ usi videntur cum Chaldæorum*
שלטן *expresserunt.*

† Λαμβανειν and παραλαμβανειν, both signify *to receive.*

only his benefits and privileges. These are secondary and consequential things to our *receiving him* *. So that it is a receiving,
assuming, or accepting the Lord Jesus Christ, which must have
respect to the tenders and proposals of the gospel, " for therein is
" the righteousness of God revealed from faith to faith," Rom. i.
17. therein is Jesus Christ revealed, proposed, and offered unto
sinners, as the only way of justification and salvation; which gospel-
offer, as before was opened, is therefore ordinarily necessary to
believing, Rom. x. 11, 12, 13, &c.

Thirdly, This description is yet further explained by this addi-
tional exegetical clause, [*even to them that believe on his name ;*] here
the terms are varied, though the things expressed in both be the
same ; what he called *receiving* there, is called *believing on his name*
here, to shew us that the very essence of saving faith consists in
our receiving of Christ. By *his name*, we are to understand
Christ himself : it is usual to take these two, believing in him, and
believing in his name, as terms convertible, and of the same importance, שמו ושמו ; חוא, הוא—*Ipse est nomen suum, et nomen ejus
ipse est* † : His name is Himself, and Himself is his name. So that
here we have the true nature and precious benefits of saving faith
excellently expressed in this scripture, the sum of which take in
this proposition ;

> Doct. *That the receiving of the Lord Jesus Christ is that saving
> and vital act of faith which gives the soul right both to his
> person and benefits.*

We cannnot act spiritually till we begin to live spiritually : Therefore the spirit of life must first join himself to us, in his quickening work, (as was shewn you in the last sermon), which being
done, we begin to act spiritually, by taking hold upon, or receiving
Jesus Christ, which is the thing designed to be opened in this
sermon.

The soul is the life of the body, faith is the life of the soul, and
Christ is the life of faith. There are several sorts of faith besides
saving faith, and in saving faith there are several acts, besides the
justifying or saving act ; but this receiving act, which is to be our
subject this day, is that upon which both our righteousness and
eternal happiness do depend. " This, as a *form*, differences sa-

---

* The gospel offer is God's act, made by means of the word : acceptance is
man's act ; yet so, as it is also the gift of God ; for a man cannot receive the Mediator, unless faith, which is the instrument of this acceptance, be given him by
God.
† Drusius.

" ving faith from all other kinds or sorts of faith * ;" by this it is that we are justified and saved.   " To as many as received him, " to them gave he power to become the sons of God:" yet it doth not justify and save us by reason of any proper dignity that is found in this act, but by reason of the object it receives or apprehends. The same thing is often expressed in scripture by other terms, as " Coming to Christ," John vi. 35. *Trusting* or *staying* upon Christ, Isa. 1. 10.   But whatever is found in those expressions, it is all comprehended in this, as will appear hereafter.   Now, the method into which I shall cast my discourse on this subject, that I may handle it with as much perspicuity and profit as I can, shall be,

First, To explain and open the nature of this receiving of Christ, and shew you what it includes.

Secondly, To prove that this is the justifying and saving act of faith.

Thirdly, To shew you the excellency of this act of faith.

Fourthly, To remove some mistakes, and give you the true account of the dignity and excellency of this act.

Fifthly, And then bring home all, in a proper and close applica- cation.

First, In the first place then, I will endeavour to explain and open the nature of this receiving of Christ, and shew you what is implied in it.

And, indeed, it involves many deep mysteries, and things of greatest weight. People are generally very ignorant and unac- quainted with the importance of this expression; they have very slight thoughts of faith who never passed under the illuminating, convincing, and humbling work of the Spirit: but we shall find that saving faith is quite another thing, and differs in its whole kind and nature from that traditional faith, and common assent, which is so fatally mistaken for it in the world †.

---

* *Forma vel aliquid formæ analogum ponitur differentiæ loco.*

† There are divers other expressions by which the nature of saving faith is expres- sed in scripture, viz. Eating Christ's flesh, and drinking his blood, John vi. 40. Coming to Christ, Matt. xi. 28. Having the Son, 1 John v. 12. Trusting or de- pending upon him, for which the Hebrew uses three emphatical words, אמן, בטח, and חסה.   The first signifies a firm and stable trust. The second, to lean, or de- pend with security. The third, to betake one's self to a sanctuary for protection. All which is supposed or included in our receiving of the Lord Jesus Christ: In eating and drinking we must receive meat and drink : coming to Christ is neces- sarily supposed in receiving him, for there is no receiving at a distance. Having the Son, and receiving him, are notions of the same importance; and for trusting, relying with security, and betaking ourselves to Christ for refuge, they are all in-

For, *First*, It is evident that no man can receive Jesus Christ in the darkness of natural ignorance: we must understand and discern who and what he is, whom we receive to be *the Lord our righteousness.* If we know not his person, and his offices, we do not take, but mistake Christ. It is a good rule in the civil law, *Non consentit qui non sentit.* A mistake of the person invalidates the match. He that takes Christ for a mere man, or denies the satisfaction of his blood, or divests him of his human nature, or denies any of his most glorious and necessary offices, let them cry up as high as they will, his spirituality, glory, and exemplary life and death, they can never receive Jesus Christ aright. This is such a crack, such a flaw in the very foundation of faith, as undoes and destroys all. *Ignorantis non est consensus:* All saving faith is founded in light and knowledge, and therefore it is called *knowledge,* Isa. liii. 11. and *seeing* is inseparably connected with *believing,* John vi. 40. Men must hear and learn of the Father before they can come to Christ, John vi. 45. The receiving act of faith is directed and guided by knowledge. I will not presume to state the degree of knowledge which is absolutely necessary to the reception of Christ; I know the first actings of faith are, in most Christians, accompanied with much darkness and confusion of understanding: but yet we must say in the general, that wherever faith is, there is so much light as is sufficient to discover to the soul its own sins, dangers and wants, and the all-sufficiency, suitableness, and necessity of Christ, for the supply and remedy of all; and without this, Christ cannot be received. " Come unto me, all ye that labour, and I will give " you rest," Matt. xi. 28.

Secondly, The receiving of Christ, necessarily implies the assent of the understanding to the truths of Christ revealed in the gospel, viz. his person, natures, offices, his incarnation, death, and satisfaction; which assent, though it be not in itself saving faith, yet is it the foundation and ground work of it; it being impossible the soul should receive, and fiducially embrace, what the mind doth not assent unto as true and infallibly certain *. Now, there are three degrees of assent; *conjecture, opinion,* and *belief.* Conjecture is but a slight and weak inclination to assent to the thing propounded, by reason of the weighty objections that lie against it. Opinion is a more steady and fixed assent, when a man is almost certain, though yet some fear of the contrary remains with him. Belief is

---

volved in the receiving act; for as God offers him to us as the only prop of our hearts and hopes, so we receive him to rely upon him. And as he is held forth in the gospel as the only *Asylum,* or city of refuge, so we take or receive him, and accordingly betake ourselves to him for refuge.

* See Dr. Sclater on Rom. iv. 3.

a more full and assured assent to the truth; to which the mind may be brought four ways.

First, By the perfect intelligence of sense, not hindered or deceived. So I believe the truth of these propositions, Fire is hot, water is moist, honey is sweet, gall is bitter.

Secondly, By the native clearness of self-evident principles. So I believe the truth of these propositions, The whole is more than a part; the cause is before the effect.

Thirdly, By discourse, and rational deduction. So I believe the truth of this proposition, Where all the parts of a thing are, th re is the whole.

Fourthly, By infallible testimony, when any thing is witnessed or asserted by one whose truth is unquestionable *. And of this sort is the assent of faith, which is therefore called our receiving the witness of God, 1 John v. 9. our setting to our seal that God is true, John iii. 33. This *prima veritas*, divine verity, is the very formal object of faith: into this we resolve our faith. *Thus saith the Lord*, is that firm foundation upon which our assent is built. And thus we see good reason to believe those profound mysteries of the incarnation of Christ; the hypostatical union of the two natures in his wonderful person; the mystical union of Christ and believers; though we cannot understand these things, by reason of the darkness of our minds. It satisfies the soul to find these mysteries in the written word; upon that foundation it firmly builds its assent: and without such an assent of faith, there can be no embracing of Christ: all acts of faith and religion, without assent, are but as so many arrows shot at random into the open air, they signify nothing for want of a fixed determinate object.

It is therefore the policy of Satan, by injecting or fomenting atheistical thoughts, (with which young converts use to find themselves greatly infested) to undermine and destroy the whole work of faith. But God makes his people victorious over them: yea, and even at that time they do assent to the truths of the word, when they think they do not; as appears by their tenderness and fear of sin, their diligence and care of duty. If I discern these things in a Christian's life, he must excuse me if I believe him not, when he saith he doth not assent to the truths of the gospel.

Thirdly, Our receiving Christ necessarily implies our hearty *approbation*, liking and estimation; yea, the acquiescence of our very

---

* It is not becoming, that God, when he should speak to men, should confirm his words with arguments, as if otherwise he was not to be believed; but, as becomes himself, he speaks as the supreme Judge of all things, whose [prerogative] it is, not to argue, but to pronounce what is truth, &c. *Lactan. de falsa religione, p. (mihi)* 179. Faith fails, where the divine authority of the scripture is wanting.

souls in Jesus Christ, as the most excellent, suitable, and complete remedy for all our wants, sins, and dangers, that ever could be prepared by the wisdom and love of God for us: We must receive him with such a frame of heart, as rests upon, and trusts in him, if ever we receive him aright; "To them that believe he is precious," 1 Pet. ii. 7. This is the only sovereign-plaister in all the world that is large enough, and efficacious enough, to cure our wounds: And therefore as Christ is most highly esteemed, and heartily approved, as the only remedy for our souls; so the sovereign grace and wisdom of God are admired, and the way and method he hath taken to save poor souls, by Jesus Christ, most heartily approved as the most apt and excellent method, both for his glory and our good, that ever could be taken: for it is a plain case, that none will espouse themselves with conjugal affections, to that person whom they esteem not as the best for them that can be chosen: None will forsake and quit all for his sake, except they account him as the spouse did, "The chiefest of ten thousand."

There are two things in Christ, which must gain the greatest approbation in the soul of a poor convinced sinner, and bring it to rest upon Jesus Christ.

First, That it can find nothing in Christ that is distasteful, or unsuitable to it, as it doth experimentally find in the best creatures. In him is no *weakness*, but a fulness of all saving abilities; "Able "to save to the uttermost:" No *pride*, causing him to scorn and contemn the most wretched soul that comes to him: No inconstancy or *levity*, to cause him to cast off the soul whom he hath once received: No *passion* but a Lamb for meekness and patience: There is no spot to be found in him, but "He is altogether lovely," Cant. v. 16.

Secondly, As the believer can find nothing in Christ that is distasteful, so it finds nothing wanting in Christ that is necessary, or desirable: Such is the fulness of wisdom, righteousness, sanctification, and redemption that is in Christ, that nothing is left to desire but the full enjoyment of him. O, saith the soul, how completely happy shall I be, if I can but win Christ! I would not envy the nobles of the earth, were I but in Christ. I am hungry and athirst, and Christ is meat indeed, and drink indeed; this is the best thing in all the world for me, because so necessary and so suitable to the needs of a soul ready to perish. I am a law-condemned and a self-condemned sinner, trembling for fear of the execution of the curse upon me every moment; in Christ is complete righteousness to justify my soul; O there is nothing better for me than Christ. I see myself plunged, both in nature and practice, into the odious pollutions of sin, and in Christ is a fountain opened for sin and for uncleanness: His blood is a fountain of *merit*, his spirit is a fountain

of holiness and purity: None but Christ, none but Christ.   O the
manifold wisdom and unsearchable love of God, to prepare and
furnish such a Christ so fully answering all the needs, all the distresses, all the fears and burdens of a poor sinner! Thus the believing soul approves of Christ as best for it.   And thus in believing,
it gives glory to God, Rom. iv. 21.

Fourthly, Receiving Christ consists in the *consent and choice of
the will*; and this is the opening of the heart and stretching forth of
the soul to receive him : Thy people shall be willing in the day of
" thy power," Psal. cx. 3.

It is the great design and main scope of the gospel, to work over
the wills of poor sinners to this : And this was the great complaint
of Christ against the incredulous Jews, John v. 40. " Ye will not
" come unto me that ye might have life."

It is disputed by some, whether faith can be seated in two distinct faculties, as we seem to place it, when we say it involves both
the *approbation* of the *judgment* and the *consent* of the *will*. I will
not here entangle my discourse with that fruitless dispute.   I am of
the same judgment with those divines, that think faith cannot be
expressed fully by any one single habit, or act of the mind or will
distinctly, for that (as * one well notes) there are such descriptions
given of it in scripture, such things are proposed as the object of it,
and such is the experience of all that sincerely believe, as no one
single act, either of the mind or will, can answer unto : Nor do I
see any thing repugnant to *scripture* or *philosophy* if we place it in
both faculties.   Consent (saith † Vasquez) seems to denote the
concourse of the will with the understanding ; but to leave that,
it is most certain the saving, justifying act of faith lies principally in
the consent of the will, which consent is the effect of the Almighty
Power of God, Eph. i. 19.   He allures and draws the will to
Christ, and he *draws with the cords of a man*, i. e. he prevails with
it by rational arguments : For the soul being prepared by convictions of its lost and miserable estate by sin, and that there is but
one door of hope open to it for an escape from the wrath to come,
and that is Christ ; being also satisfied of the fulness and completeness of his saving ability, and of his willingness to make it over for
our salvation, upon such just and equal terms ; this cannot but
prevail with the will of a poor distressed sinner, to consent and
chuse him.

Fifthly, and *lastly*, The last and principal thing included in our

---

* Dr. Owen in his doctrine of Justification, p. 135.

† Consent seems to denote the concurrence of the will with the understanding, by
relishing the same thing which the understanding doth perceive, 12. Q. 15. a. 1.   Faith
is not a simple act, but consists of divers parts, knowledge, assent, and trust, which do
not all belong to the same faculty.   *Wendel. Theol.* p. 450.

receiving of Christ, is the respect that this act of acceptance hath
unto the terms upon which Christ is tendered to us in the gospel †,
to which it is most agreeable, 1 Cor. xv. 11. " So we preach, and
" so ye believed :" Faith answers the gospel-offer, as the impress
upon the *wax* doth the engraving in the *seal ;* and this is of principal consideration, for there is no receiving Christ upon any other
terms but his own, proposed in the gospel to us ; He will never
come lower, nor make them easier than they are for any man's sake
in the world ; we must either receive him upon these, or part with
him for ever as thousands do, who could not be content to agree
to some articles, but rather chuse to be damned for ever than submit to all : This is the great controversy betwixt Christ and sinners;
upon this, many thousands break off the treaty, and part with
Christ, because he will not come to their terms ; but every true
believer receives him upon his own, i. e. their acceptance of him
by faith, is in all things consentaneous to the overtures made of
him in the written word. So he tenders himself, and so they
receive him ; as will be evident in the following particulars.

First, The gospel offers Christ to us *sincerely* and really, and so
the true believer receives and accepts him, even with a *faith un-
feigned ;* 1 Tim. i. 5. If ever the soul be serious and in earnest in
any thing, it is so in this : Can we suppose the heart of him that
flies for his life to the *refuge city,* to be serious and in earnest to
escape by flight the *avenger of blood* who pursues him ? Then is
the heart of a convinced sinner serious in this matter ; for under
that notion is the work of faith presented to us, Heb. vi. 18.

Secondly, Christ is offered to us in the gospel *entirely* and *undividedly,* as clothed with all his offices, priestly, prophetical, and
regal ; as Christ Jesus the Lord, Acts xvi. 31. and so the true believer receives him ; The *hypocrite,* like the *harlot,* is for dividing,
but the sincere believer finds the need he hath of every office of
Christ, and knows not how to want any thing that is in him.

His ignorance makes him necessary and desirable to him as a
prophet : His guilt makes him necessary as a *priest :* His strong and
powerful lusts and corruptions make him necessary as a *king :* and
in truth, he sees not any thing in Christ that he can spare ; he needs
all that is in Christ, and admires infinite wisdom in nothing more
than the investing Christ with all these offices, which are so suited
to the poor sinner's wants and miseries. Look, as the three offices
are undivided in Christ, so they are in the believer's acceptance ;
and before this trial no hypocrite can stand ; for all hypocrites re-

---

† Rom. iv. 17. υπηκυσατε δε εκ καρδιας εις ον παρεδυθητε τυπον διδαχης. The
will like melted metal, is delivered into the gospel-mould, where it receives the same
form and figure that the mould gives.

ject and quarrel with something in Christ; they like his pardon better than his government. They call him indeed, Lord and Master, but it is but an empty title they bestow upon him; for let them ask their own hearts if Christ be Lord over their *thoughts*, as well as *words;* over their *secret*, as well as *open* actions; over their *darling* lusts, as well as others; let them ask, who will appear to be Lord and Master over them, when Christ and the world come in competition? When the pleasure of sin shall stand upon one side, and sufferings to death, and deepest points of self-denial, upon the other side? Surely it is the greatest affront that can be offered to the Divine Wisdom and Goodness, to separate in our acceptance, what is so united in Christ, for our salvation and happiness. As without any one of these offices, the work of our salvation could not be completed, so without acceptance of Christ in them all, our union with him by faith cannot be completed.

The gospel-offer of Christ includes all his offices, and gospel-faith just so receives him; to submit to him, as well as to be redeemed by him; to imitate him in the holiness of his life, as well as to reap the purchases and fruits of his *death*. It must be an entire receiving of the Lord Jesus Christ *.

Thirdly, Christ is offered to us in the gospel *exclusively*, as the alone and only Saviour of sinners; with whose blood and intercession nothing is to be mixed; but the soul of a sinner is singly to rely and depend on him, and no other, Acts iv. 2. 1 Cor. iii. 11. and so faith receives him, Psal. lxxi. 16. " I will make mention of thy " righteousness, even of thine only." Phil. iii. 9. " And be found " in him, not having mine own righteousness, which is of the law, " but that which is through the faith of Christ." To depend partly upon Christ's righteousness, and partly upon our own, is to set one foot upon a rock, and the other in a quick-sand; either Christ will be to us all in all, or nothing at all, in point of righteousness and salvation; he affects not social honour; as he did the whole *work*, so he expects the sole *praise;* if he be not able to save to the uttermost, why do we depend upon him at all? and if he be, why do we lean upon any beside him?

Fourthly, The gospel offers Christ *freely* to sinners as the *gift*, not the *sale* of God, John iv. 10. Isa. lv. 1. Rev. xxii. 17. and even so faith receives him. The believer comes to Christ with an empty hand, not only as an undeserving, but as an hell-deserving sinner; he comes to Christ as to one that justifies the ungodly, Rom. iv. 5. " Unto him that worketh not, but believeth in him that justifieth

---

* A man may as lawfully join saints or angels in his mediation with Christ, as graces. It is gross idolatry to make the works of God a God, and it is but a more subtle idolatry to make the works of Christ a Christ. *Burgess de Lege.*

" the ungodly, his faith is counted for righteousness." Where by
him that worketh not, he means a convinced, humbled sinner,
who finds himself utterly unable to do the task the law sets him,
i. e. perfectly to obey it; and therefore in a law sense is said not to
work; for it is all one as to the intent and purpose of the law, not
to work, and not to work perfectly. This is he convinced of, and
therefore comes to Christ as one that is in himself ungodly, acknowledging the righteousness, by which alone he can stand before God, is in Christ, and not in himself, in whole, or in part;
and by the way, let this encourage poor souls that are scared and
daunted for want of due qualifications, for closing with and embracing Christ. There is nothing qualifies a man for Christ more
than a sense of his unworthiness of him, and the want of all
excellencies or ornaments, that may commend him to divine acceptance.

Fifthly, The gospel offers Christ *orderly* to sinners, first his *person,* then his *privileges.* God first gives his Son, and then with
him, or as a consequent of that gift, he gives us all things, Rom.
viii. 32. In the same order must our faith receive him. The believer doth not marry the *portion* first, and then the *person,* but to
be found in him is the first and great care of a believer.

I deny not but it is lawful for any to have an eye to the benefits
of Christ. Salvation from wrath is, and lawfully may be intended
and aimed at: " Look unto me, and be saved all ye ends of the
" earth," Isa. xlv. 22. Nor do I deny but there are many poor
souls, who being in deep distress and fear, may, and often do, look
mostly to their own safety at first; and that there is much confusion, as well in the actings of their faith, as in their condition; but
sure I am, it is the proper order in believing, first to accept the person of the Lord Jesus: Heaven is no doubt very desirable, but
Christ is more: " Whom have I in heaven but thee?" Psal. lxxiii.
25. Union with Christ is, in order of nature, antecedent to the
communication of his privileges, therefore so it ought to be in the
order and method of believing.

Sixthly, Christ is *advisedly,* offered in the gospel to sinners, as the
result of God's eternal counsel, a project of grace upon which his
heart and thoughts have been much set, Zech. vi. 13. The counsel
of peace was betwixt the Father and the Son. And so the believer
receives him, most deliberately weighing the matter in his most deep
and serious thoughts; for this is a time of much solicitude and
thoughtfulness. The soul's espousals are acts of judgment, Hos.
ii. 19. on our part, as well as on God's; We are therefore bid to
sit down and count the cost, Luke xiv. 28. Faith, or the actual
receiving of Christ, is the result of many previous debates in the
soul: The matter hath been pondered over and over: The objec-

tions and discouragements, both from the self-denying terms of the gospel, and our own vileness and deep guilt, have been ruminated, and lain upon our hearts day and night, and after all things have been balanced in the most deep consideration, the soul is determined to this conclusion, I must have Christ, be the terms never so hard, be my sins never so great and many, I will yet go to him, and venture my soul upon him ; if I perish, I perish. I have thought out all my thoughts, and this is the result, union with Christ here, or separation from God for ever must be my lot.

And thus doth the Lord open the hearts of his elect, and win the consent of their wills to receive Jesus Christ upon the deepest consideration and debate of the matter in their own most solemn thoughts : They understand and know, that they must deeply deny themselves, take up his cross and follow him, Matt. xvi. 24. renounce not only *sinful* but *religious* self ; these are hard and difficult things, but yet the necessity and excellency of Christ make them appear eligible and rational : by all which you see faith is another thing than what the sound of that word (as it is generally understood) signifies to the understandings of most men. This is that fiducial receiving of Christ here to be opened.

Secondly, Our next work will be to evince this receiving of Christ as hath been opened, to be that special saving faith of God's elect : This is that faith of which such great and glorious things are spoken in the gospel, which, whosoever hath shall be saved, and he that hath it not shall be damned ; and this I shall evidently prove by the following arguments or reasons.

Arg. 1. *First*, That faith which gives the soul right and title to spiritual adoption, with all the privileges and benefits thereof, is true and saving faith.

But such a receiving of Christ as hath been described, gives the soul right and title to spiritual adoption, with all the privileges and benefits thereof.

Therefore such a receiving of Christ as hath been described is true and saving faith.

The major proposition is undeniable, for our right and title to spiritual adoption, and the privileges thereof arise from our union with Jesus Christ ; we being united to the Son of God, are, by virtue of that union, reckoned or accounted sons, Gal. iii. 26. " You are all the children of God by faith in Jesus Christ :" The effect of saving faith is union with Christ's person, the consequent of that union is adoption, or right to the inheritance.

The minor is most plain in the text : " To as many as received " him, to them gave he power or right to become the sons of " God :" A false faith hath no such privilege annexed to it ; no

unbeliever is thus dignified : No stranger entitled to this inheritance.

Arg. 2. Secondly, That only is saving and justifying faith, which
is in all true believers, in none but true believers, and in all true
believers at all times.

But such a receiving of Christ as hath been described, is in all
true believers, in none but true believers, and in all true believers
at all times.

Therefore such a receiving of Christ as hath been described, is
the only saving and justifying faith.

The major is undeniable, that must needs contain the essence of
saving faith, which is proper to every true believer at all times,
and to no other.

The minor will be as clear, for there is no other act of faith, but
this of *fiducial receiving Christ* as he is offered, that doth agree to
all true believers, to none but true believers, and to all true believers at all times.

There be three acts of faith, * *assent, acceptance,* and *assurance:*
The Papists generally give the essence of saving faith to the first,
viz. *assent.* The Lutherans, and some of our own, give it to the
last, viz. *assurance:* But it can be neither way so. *Assent* doth
not agree only to true believers, or justified persons. *Assurance*
agrees to justified persons, and them only, but not to all justified
persons, and that at all times.

Assent is too low to contain the essence of saving faith ; it is
found in the unregenerate as well as the regenerate : yea, in devils
as well as men, James ii. 19. it is supposed and included in justifying faith, but it is not the justifying or saving act. *Assurance* is
as much too high, being found only in some eminent believers :
and in them too but at some times. There is many a true believer to whom the joy and comfort of assurance is denied ; they
may say of their union with Christ, as Paul said of his vision ;
whether in the body or out of the body, I cannot tell ; so they,
whether in Christ or out of Christ, they cannot tell †.

A true believer may " walk in darkness, and see no light," Isa.
l. 10. Nay a man must be a believer before he know himself to be
so ; the *direct act* of *faith* is before the *reflex act :* so that the justifying act of faith lies neither in *assent* nor in *assurance.* *Assent*
saith, I believe that Christ is, and that he is the Saviour of the elect.

---

* The act of faith consists in assent, by which one assents to any proposition revealed by God on the authority of the revealer. *Becan. Theol. Schol. Tom. 3. cap. 8.*
Q. 4.

† Many new born Christians live like the new born babe, *Vivit, et est vitæ nescius ipse
suæ :* The whole stock of many a believer consists in the bare direct acts of faith.

Assurance saith, I believe and am sure that Christ died for me, and that I shall be saved through him. So that *assent widens* the nature of faith too much, and *assurance* upon the other hand *straitens* it too much; but *acceptance*, which saith, I take Christ in all his offices to be mine, this fits it exactly, and belongs to all true believers, and to none but true believers; and to all true believers at all times. This therefore must be the justifying and saving act of faith.

Arg. 3. Thirdly, That and no other is the justifying and saving act of faith, to which the properties and effects of saving faith do belong, or in which they are only found.

But in the fiducial receiving of Christ are the properties and effects of saving faith only found.

This therefore must be the justifying and saving act of faith.

First, By saving faith, Christ is said to " dwell in our hearts," Eph. iii. 17. but it is neither by *assent*, nor *assurance*, but by *acceptance*, and receiving him that he dwells in our hearts; not by *assent*, for then he would dwell in the unregenerate; nor by *assurance*, for he must dwell in our hearts before we can be assured of it: therefore it is by acceptance.

Secondly, By faith we are justified, Rom. v. 1. But neither assent nor assurance, for the reasons above, do justify; therefore it must be by the receiving act, and no other.

Thirdly, The scripture ascribes great difficulties to that faith by which we are saved, as being most cross and opposite to the corrupt nature of man; but of all the acts of faith, none is clogged with like difficulties, or conflicts with greater oppositions than the receiving act doth; this act is attended with the greatest difficulties, fears, and deepest self-denial. In assent, a man's reason is convinced, and yields to the evidence of truth, so that he can do no other but assent to the truth. In assurance there is nothing against a man's will or comfort, but much for it; every one desires it: but it is not so in the acceptance of Christ, upon the self-denying terms of the gospel, as will hereafter be evinced. We conclude therefore, that in this consists the nature and essence of saving faith.

Thirdly, Having seen what the receiving of Jesus Christ is, and that it is the faith by which we are justified and saved, I next come to open the *dignity* and excellency of this faith, whose praises and *encomiums* are in all the scriptures; there you find it renowned by the title of *precious faith,* 2 Pet. i. 7. *enriching faith,* Jam. ii. 5. *the work of God,* John vi. 29. the *great mystery of godliness,* 1 Tim. iii. 16. With many more rich *epithets* throughout the scriptures bestowed upon it.

Now faith may be considered two ways, *viz.* either qualitatively or relatively.

Considered *qualitatively*, as a saving grace, it hath the same excellency that all other precious saving graces have; as it is the fruit of the Spirit, it is more precious than gold, Prov. viii. 11, 19. And so are all other graces as well as faith; in this sense they all shine with equal glory, and that a glory transcending all the glory of this world: but then consider faith *relatively*, as the instrument by which the righteousness of Christ is apprehended and made ours, and in that consideration it excels all other graces.

This is the grace that is singled out from among all other graces, to *receive Christ*, by which office it is dignified above all its fellows: as Moses was honoured above the many thousands of Israel, when God took him up into the *mount*, admitted him nearer to himself than any other of all the tribes might come; for they stood without the *rail*, while Moses was received into the special presence of God, and was admitted to such views as others must not have: so faith is honoured above all its fellow-graces, in being singled out, and solemnly anointed to this high office in our justification: this is that precious eye that looks unto Christ as the stung Israelites did to the brazen serpent, and derives healing virtue from him to the soul. It is the grace which instrumentally saves us, Eph. ii. 8. As it is Christ's glory to be the door of salvation, so it is faith's glory to be the golden key that opens that door.

What shall I say of faith? It is the *bond* of union; the *instrument* of justification; the *spring* of spiritual peace and joy; the *means* of spiritual life and subsistence; and therefore the great *scope* and *drift* of the gospel; which aims at and presseth nothing more than to bring men and women to believe.

First, This is the *bond of our union* with Christ; that union is begun in our vivification, and completed in our actual receiving of Christ; the first is the bond of union on the Spirit's part, the second a bond of union on our part. " Christ dwelleth in our hearts by " faith," Eph. iii. 17. And therein it is a door opened to let in many rich blessings to the soul; for, by uniting us to Christ, it brings us into special favour and acceptation with God, Eph. i. 6. Makes us the special objects of Christ's conjugal love and delight, Eph. v. 29. Draws from his heart sympathy and a tender sense of all our miseries and burdens, Heb. iv. 15.

Secondly, It is the instrument of our justification, Rom. v. 1. Till Christ be received (thus received by us) we are in our sins; under guilt and condemnation; but when faith comes, then comes freedom: " By him all that believe are justified from all things *."

---

* The being found in Christ has a tacit reference to the judgment of God; to us there is no condemnation, because he finds us clothed with a righteousness, such as he requires, i. e. completely perfect, even the righteousness of Christ by faith, imputed to us. *Bern. on the place.*

Acts xiii. 38. Rom. viii. 1.   For it apprehends or receives the pure
and perfect righteousness of the Lord Jesus, wherein the soul, how
guilty and sinful soever it be in itself, stands faultless and spotless
before the presence of God; all obligations to punishment are, upon
believing, immediately dissolved; a full and final pardon sealed.
O precious faith! Who can sufficiently value it!

What respect, reader, wouldst thou hrve to that hand that
should bring thee a pardon when on the ladder or block? Why,
such a pardon, which thou canst not read without tears of joy, is
brought thee by the hand of faith. O inestimable grace! This
clothes the pure righteousness of Jesus upon our defiled souls, and
so causes us to become the "righteousness of God in him," or as it
is 1 John iii. 7. " Righteous as he is righteous:" *Non formali &
intrinsica justitia, sed relativa:* Not with a formal inherent righteousness of our own, but with a relative imputed righteousness from
another.

I know this most excellent and most comfortable doctrine of imputed righteousness, is not only *denied* but *derided* by Papists.
Stapleton calls it *spectrum ccrebri Lutherani:* The monstrous birth
of Luther's brain! But, blessed be God, this comfortable truth is
well secured against all attempts of its adversaries.   Let their blasphemous mouths call it in derision, as they do *putative righteousness,*
i. e. a mere fancied or conceited righteousness: Yet we know assuredly Christ's righteousness is imputed to us, and that in the
way of faith.   If Adam's sin became ours by imputation, then so
doth Christ's righteousness also become ours by imputation, Rom.
v. 17.   If Christ were made a sinner by the imputation of our sins
to him, who had no sin of his own, then we are made righteous
by the imputation of Christ's righteousness to us, who have no
righteousness of our own, according to 1 Cor. v. 21.   This
was the way in which Abraham, the father of them that believe, was justified; and therefore this is the way in which all believers, the children of Abraham, must, in the like manner, be
justified, Rom. iv. 22, 23, 24.   Who can express the worth of
faith in this one respect, were this all it did for our souls?

But, *Thirdly,* It is the *spring* of our spiritual peace and joy: and
that as it is the instrument of our *justification.*   If it be an instrument of our *justification,* it cannot but be the spring of our *consolation,* Rom. v. 1. " Being justified by faith, we have peace with
" God."   In uniting us with Christ, and apprehending and applying his righteousness to us, it becomes the seed or root of all the
peace and joy of a Christian's life.   Joy, the child of faith, therefore bears its name, Phil. 1. 25. " The joy of faith."   So 1 Pet. 1.
8, 9. " Believing we rejoice with joy unspeakable."   We cannot
forbear rejoicing when by faith we are brought to the sight and

knowledge of such a privileged state; when faith hath first given and then cleared our title to Christ, joy is no more under the soul's command; we cannot but rejoice, and that with joy unspeakable.

Fourthly, It is the *means* of our spiritual livelihood and subsistence: all other graces, like birds in the nest, depend upon what faith brings in to them; take away faith, and all the graces languish and die: joy, peace, hope, patience, and all the rest, depend upon faith, as the members of the natural body do upon the vessels by which blood and spirits are conveyed to them. " The life which " I now live (saith the apostle) is by the faith of the Son of God," Gal. ii. 20. It provides our *ordinary food,* and *extraordinary cordials,* Psal. xxvii. 13. " I had fainted, unless I had believed." And seeing it is all this to our souls,

Fifthly, In the last place, it is no wonder that it is the main scope and drift of the gospel, to press and bring souls to believing: it is the gospel's grand design to bring up the hearts of men and women to faith. The urgent *commands* of the gospel aim at this, 1 John iii. 23. Mark i. 14, 15. John xii. 36. Hither also look the great *promises* and encouragements of the *gospel,* John vi. 35, 37. So Mark xvi. 16. And the opposite sin of unbelief is every where fearfully aggravated and *threatened,* John xvi. 8, 9. John iii. 18, 35. And this was the third thing promised, namely, a discovery of the transcendent worth and excellency of saving faith.

Fourthly, But lest we commit a mistake here, to the prejudice of Christ's honour and glory, which must not be given to another, no not to faith itself; I promised you in the fourth place, to shew you upon what account faith is thus dignified and honoured; that so we may give unto *faith* the things that are *faith's,* and to Christ the things that are Christ's.

And I find four opinions about the interest of faith in our justification: some will have it to justify us *formally,* not relatively : i. e. upon the account of his own intrinsical value and worth; and this is the *popish* sense of justification by faith. Some affirm, that though faith be not our perfect legal righteousness, considered as a work of ours, yet the *act* of believing is imputed to us for righteousness, i. e. God graciously accepts it instead of perfect legal righteousness, and so, in his esteem, it is our evangelical righteousness. And this is the Arminian sense of justification by faith.

Some there are also, even among our reformed divines, that contend that faith justifies and saves us, as it is the condition of the new covenant. And lastly, others will have it to justify us as an *instrument* apprehending or receiving the righteousness of Christ; with which opinion I must close. When I consider my text calls it a *receiving of Christ.* Most certain it is,

That, *First*, It doth not justify in the *popish sense*, upon the account of its own proper worth and dignity; for then,

First, Justification should be of debt, not of grace; contrary to Rom. iii. 23, 24.

Secondly, This would frustrate the very scope and end of the death of Christ; for if righteousness come by the law, i. e. by the way of works and desert, then is Christ dead in vain, Gal. ii. 21.

Thirdly, Then the way of our justification by faith would be so far from excluding, that it would establish boasting, expressly contrary to the apostle, Rom. iii. 26, 27.

Fourthly, Then there should be no defects or imperfections in faith, for a defective or imperfect thing can never be the matter of our justification before God: if it justify upon the account of its own worth and proper dignity, it can have no flaw or imperfection in it, contrary to the common sense of all believers. Nay,

Fifthly, Then it is the same thing to be justified by faith, and to be justified by works, which the apostle so carefully distinguisheth and opposeth, Phil. iii. 9. and Rom. iv. 6. So that we conclude it doth not justify in the Popish sense, for any worth or proper excellency that is in itself.

Secondly, And it is as evident, it doth not justify us in the Arminian sense, viz. as the *το credere*, the act of believing is imputed or accepted by God, as our evangelical righteousness, instead of perfect legal righteousness. In the former opinion you have the dregs of Popery, and here you have refined Popery. Let all Arminians know, we have as high an esteem for faith as any men in the world, but yet we will not rob Christ to clothe faith. We cannot embrace their opinion, because,

First, We must then dethrone Christ to exalt faith: we are willing to give it all that is due to it, but we dare not despoil Christ of his glory for faith's sake: " *He is* the Lord our righteousness," Jer. xxiii. We dare not set the servant above the master. We acknowledge no righteousness but what the obedience and satisfaction of Christ yields us. His blood, not our faith; his satisfaction, not our believing it, is the matter of our justification before God.

Secondly, We dare not yield this point, lest we undermine all the comfort of Christians, by setting their pardon and peace upon a weak imperfect work of their own. Oh how tottering and unstable must their station be, that stand upon such a bottom as this! What alterations are there in our faith, what mixtures of unbelief at all times, and prevalency of unbelief at some times; and is this a foundation to build our justification and hope upon? *Debile fundamentum fallit opus*: If we lay the stress here, we build upon very loose ground, and must be at a continual loss both as to safety and comfort.

Thirdly, We dare not wrong the justice and truth of God at that rate, as to affirm that he esteems and imputes our poor weak faith for perfect legal righteousness * We know that the judgment of God is always according to truth; if the justice of God require full payment, sure it will not say, it is fully satisfied by any acts of ours, when all that we can do amounts not to one mite of the vast sum we owe to God. So that we deservedly reject this opinion also.

Thirdly, And for the third opinion, That it justifies as the *condition of the new covenant;* though some of great name and worth among our Protestant divines seem to go that way, yet I cannot see, according to this opinion, any reason why repentance may not as properly be said to justify us as faith, for it is a condition of the new covenant as much as faith; and if faith justify as a condition, then every other grace that is a condition must justify as well as faith. I acknowledge faith to be a condition of the covenant, but cannot allow that it justifies as a condition. And therefore must profess myself best satisfied in the last opinion, which speaks it an instrument in our justification: it is the hand which receives the righteousness of Christ that justifies us, and that gives it its value above all other graces; as when we say a diamond ring is worth one hundred pounds, we mean not the gold that receives, but the stone that is set in it, is worth so much. Faith, considered as an habit, is no more precious than other gracious habits are, but considered as an instrument to receive Christ and his righteousness, so it excels them all; and this instrumentality of faith is noted in these phrases, επι τη πιστει, Rom. iii. 28. and δια της πιστεως, Rom. iii. 22. *By faith, and through faith.* And thus much of the nature and excellency of saving faith.

---

* Because faith receives Christ our righteousness, and ascribes all to the grace of God in him; therefore we are said to be justified by it, only on account of Christ, and not as it is our work. *Confes. Helv.*

SERMON VII.

JOHN i. 12.

*But as many as received him, to them gave he power to become the
sons of God ; even to them that believe on his name.*

THE nature and excellency of saving faith, together with its
relation to justification, as an instrument in receiving Christ and
his righteousness, having been discoursed doctrinally already ;
I now come to make application of it, according to the nature of
this weighty and fruitful point.

And the uses I shall make of it will be for our,

1. Information,	3. Exhortation, and,
2. Examination,	4. Direction.

First Use of Information.

Use 1. And in the first, this point yields us many great and
useful truths for our information : As,

Inference 1. Is the receiving of Christ the vital and saving act
of faith, which gives the soul right to the person and privileges of
Christ ? Then it follows, *That the rejecting of Christ by unbelief,
must needs be the damning and soul-destroying sin, which cuts a
man off from Christ, and all the benefits purchased by his blood.* If
there be life in receiving, there must needs be death in rejecting Christ.

There is no grace more excellent than faith ; no sin more exe-
crable and abominable than unbelief. Faith is the saving grace,
and unbelief the damning sin, Mark xvi. 16. " He that believeth
" not shall be damned." See John iii. 18, 36. and John viii. 24.

And the reason why this sin of unbelief is the damning sin is this,
because, in the justification of a sinner, there must be a co-operation of all the con-causes that have a joint influence on that blessed
effect. As there must be free grace for an impulsive cause, the
blood of Christ as the meritorious cause, so, of necessity, there
must be faith, the instrumental cause, to receive and apply what
the free grace of God designed, and the blood of Christ purchased
for us. For where there are many social causes, or con-causes to
produce one effect, there the effect is not produced till the last
cause be in act.

" To him give all the prophets witness, that through his name,
" whosoever believeth in him shall receive remission of sins," Acts
x. 43. Faith in its place is as necessary as the blood of Christ in
its place : " It is Christ in you the hope of glory," Col. i. 27. Not
Christ in the *womb*, not Christ in the *grave*, nor Christ in *heaven*,
except he be also *Christ in you*.

Though Christ be come in the flesh; though he died and rose again from the dead; yet if you believe not, you must for all that *die in your sins,* John viii. 24.   And what a dreadful thing is this! better die any death whatever than die in your sins.   If you die in your sins, you will also rise in your sins, and stand at the bar of Christ in your sins: you can never receive remission, till first you have received Christ.   O cursed unbelief, which *damns* the soul: *dishonours* God, 1 John v. 10. *slights* Jesus Christ, the wisdom of God, as if that glorious design of redemption by his blood, the triumph and master-piece of divine wisdom, were mere *foolishness,* 1 Cor. i. 23, 24. *frustrates* the great design of the gospel, Gal. iv. 11. and consequently it must be the sin of sins; the worst and most dangerous of all sins; leaving a man under the guilt of all his other sins.

Inf. 2. If such a receiving of Christ, as hath been described, be saving and justifying faith, *then faith is a work of greater difficulty than most men understand it to be, and there are but few sound believers in the world.*

Before Christ can be received, the heart must be emptied and opened: but most men's hearts are full of self-righteousness and vain confidence: this was the case of the Jews, Rom. x. 3. " Being " ignorant of God's righteousness, and going about to establish " their own righteousness, have not submitted themselves to the " righteousness of God."

Man's righteousness was once in himself, and what liquor is first put into the vessel, it ever afterwards savours of it. It is with Adam's posterity as with *bees,* which have been accustomed to go to their own hive, and carry all thither; if the *hive* be removed to another place, they will still fly to the old place, hover up and down about it, and rather die there than go to a new place.   So it is with most men.   God hath removed their righteousness from *doing* to *believing;* from *themselves* to *Christ;* but who shall prevail with them to forsake self? Nature will venture to be damned rather than do it: there is much submission in believing, and great self-denial: a proud self-conceited heart will never stoop to live upon the stock of another's righteousness.

Besides, it is no easy thing to persuade men to receive Christ as their Lord in all things, and submit their necks to his strict and holy precepts, though it be a great truth that " * Christ's yoke " doth not gall, but grace and adorn the neck that bears it ;" that the truest and sweetest liberty is in our freedom from our lusts, not in our fulfilling them ; yet who can persuade the carnal heart to believe this ? And much less will men ever be prevailed withal,

---

* *Jugum Christi non deterit, sed honestat colla.* Bern.

to forsake father, mother, wife, children, inheritance, and life itself, to follow Christ: and all this upon the account of spiritual and
invisible things: and yet this must be done by all that receive the
Lord Jesus Christ upon gospel terms; yea, and before the soul
hath any encouraging experience of its own, to balance the manifold discouragements of sense, and carnal reason, improved by the
utmost craft of Satan to dismay it: for experience is the fruit and
consequent of believing. So that it may well be placed among the
great *mysteries* of godliness, that Christ is believed on in the world,
1 Tim. iii. 16.

Inf. 3. Hence it will follow, *That there may be more true and
sound believers in the world, than know, or dare conclude themselves
to be such.*

For, as many ruin their own souls by placing the essence of
saving faith in naked assent, so some rob themselves of their own
comfort, by placing it in full assurance. Faith, and sense of faith,
are two distinct and separable mercies: you may have truly received Christ, and not receive the knowledge or assurance of it,
Isa. l. 10. Some there be that say, *Thou art our God,* of whom God
never said, *You are my people:* these have no *authority* to be called
the sons of God: others there are, of whom God saith, *These are
my people,* yet dare not call *God their God:* these have authority to
be called the sons of God, but know it not. They have received
Christ, that is their *safety,* but they have not yet received the knowledge and assurance of it; that is their *trouble:* the Father owns
his child in the cradle, who yet knows him not to be his Father.

Now there are two reasons why many believers, who might argue
themselves into peace, do yet live without the comforts of their
faith: and this may come to pass, either from,

First, The inevidence of the *premises.*

Secondly, Or the weighty importance of the *conclusion.*

First, It may come to pass from the inevidence of the premises.
Assurance is a practical *syllogism,* and it proceeds thus:

All that truly have received Christ Jesus, they are the children
of God.

I have truly received Jesus Christ.

Therefore I am the child of God.

The major proposition is found in the scripture, and there can
be no doubt of that. The *assumption* depends upon experience, or
internal sense; *I have truly received Jesus Christ;* here usually is
the stumble: many great objections lie against it, which they cannot clearly answer: As,

Obj. 1. Light and knowledge are necessarily required to the
right receiving of Christ, but I am dark and ignorant; many car-

nal, unregenerate persons know more than I do, and are more able to discourse of the mysteries of religion than I am.

Sol. But you ought to distinguish of the *kinds* and *degrees* of knowledge, and then you would see that your bewailed ignorance is no bar to your interest in Christ. There are two kinds of knowledge:

1. Natural. | 2. Spiritual.

There is a *natural knowledge*, even of spiritual objects, a spark of nature blown up by an advantageous education; and though the objects of this knowledge be spiritual things, yet the light in which they are discerned is but a mere natural light.

And there is a *spiritual knowledge* of spiritual things, the *teaching of the anointing*, as it is called, 1 John ii. 27. i. e. the effect and fruit of the Spirit's sanctifying work upon our souls, when the experience of a man's own heart informs and teacheth his understanding, when by feeling the workings of grace in our own souls, we come to understand its nature; this is spiritual knowledge. Now, a little of this knowledge is a better evidence of a man's interest in Christ, than the most raised and excellent degree of natural knowledge: As the philosopher truly observes; *Præstat paucula de meliori scientia degustasse, quam de ignobilori multa:* One dram of knowledge of the best and most excellent things, is better than much knowledge of common things. So it is here, a little spiritual knowledge of Jesus Christ, that hath life and savour in it, is more than all the natural, sapless knowledge of the unregenerate, which leaves the heart dead, carnal, and barren: it is not the *quantity*, but the *kind*, not the *measure*, but the *savour:* If you know so much of the evil of sin, as renders it the most bitter and burdensome thing in the world to you, and so much of the necessity and excellency of Christ, as renders him the most sweet and desirable thing in the world to you, though you may be defective in many degrees of knowledge, yet this is enough to prove yours to be the fruit of the Spirit: you may have a sanctified heart, though you have an irregular or weak head: many that knew more than you are in *hell:* and some that once knew as little as you, are now in *heaven: In absoluto et facili stat æternitas:* God hath not prepared heaven only for clear and subtle heads. A little sanctified and effectual knowledge of Christ's person, offices, suitableness, and necessity, may bring thee thither, when others, with all their curious speculations and notions, may perish for ever.

Obj. 2. But you tell me, that *assent* to the truths of the gospel is necessarily included in saving faith, which, though it be not the justifying and saving act, yet it is pre-supposed and required to it. Now I have many staggerings and doubtings about the certainty and reality of these things; many horrid atheistical thoughts, which shake the assenting act of faith in the very foundation, and hence I doubt I do not believe.

Sol. There may be, and often is, a true and sincere *assent* found in the soul, that is assaulted with violent atheistical suggestions from Satan; and thereupon questions the truth of it. And this is a very clear evidence of the reality of our assent, that whatever doubts, or contrary suggestions there be, yet we dare not in our practice contradict or slight those truths or duties which we are tempted to disbelieve, *ex. gr.* We are assaulted with atheistical thoughts, and tempted to slight and cast off all fears of sin, and practice of religious duties, yet when it comes to the point of practice, we dare not commit a known sin, the awe of God is upon us; we dare not omit a known duty, the tie of conscience is found strong enough to hold it close to it: in this case, it is plain we do really assent, when we think we do not. A man thinks he doth not love his child, yet carefully provides for him in health, and is full of griefs and fears about him in sickness: why now, so long as I see all fatherly duties performed, and affections to his child's welfare manifested, let him say what he will as to the want of love to him, whilst I see this, he must excuse me if I do not believe him, when he saith he hath no love for him. Just so is it in this case, a man saith I do not assent to the being, necessity, or excellency of Jesus Christ; yet, in the mean time, his soul is filled with cares and fears about securing his interest in him, he is found panting and thirsting for him with vehement desires, there is nothing in all the world would give him such joy, as to be well assured of an interest in him; while it is thus with any man, let him say or think what he will of his assent, it is manifest by this he doth truly and heartily assent, and there can be no better proof of it than these real effects produced by it.

Secondly, But if these, and other objections were never so fully answered for the clearing of the *assumption,* yet it often falls out, that believers are afraid to draw the *conclusion;* and that fear partly arises from,

First, The weighty importance of this matter.

Secondly, The sense of the deceitfulness of their own hearts.

First, The conclusion is of infinite importance to them, it is the everlasting happiness of their souls, than which nothing is, or can be of greater weight upon their spirits: things in which we are most deeply concerned, are not lightly and hastily received by us: it seems so great and so good, that we are still apt (if there be any room for it) to suspect the truth and certainty thereof, as never being sure enough.

Thus when the women that were the first messengers and witnesses of Christ's resurrection, Luke xxiv. 10, 11. came and told the disciples those wonderful and comfortable tidings, it is said, " That their words seemed to them as idle tales, and they be- " lieved them not." They thought it was too good to be true ; too great to be hastily received ; so it is in this case.

Secondly, The sense they have of the deceitfulness of their own hearts, and the daily workings of hypocrisy there, makes them afraid to conclude in so great a point as this is.

They know that very many daily cozen and cheat themselves in this matter ; they know also that their own hearts are full of false- ness and deceit ; they find them so in their daily observations of them ; and what if they should prove so in this ? Why then they are lost for ever ! They also know there is not the like danger in their fears and jealousies, that would be in their vain confidences and presumptions ; by the one, they are only deprived of their present comfort, but by the other, they would be ruined for ever : and therefore chuse rather to dwell with their own fears (though they be uncomfortable companions) than run the danger of so great a mistake, which would be infinitely more fatal. And this being the common case of most Christians, it follows that there must be many more believers in the world than do think, or dare conclude themselves to be such.

Inf. 4. If the right receiving of Jesus Christ, be true, saving, and justifying faith, *then those that have the least, and lowest degree and measure of saving faith, have cause for ever to admire the bounty and riches of the grace of God to them therein.*

If you have received never so little of his bounty by the hand of providence, in the good things of this life, yet if he have given you any measure of true saving faith, he hath dealt bountifully in- deed with you : this mercy alone is enough to balance all other wants and inconveniences of this life, " poor in the world, rich " in faith," James ii. 5. O, let your hearts take in the full sense of this bounty of God to you ; say with the apostle, Eph. i. 3. " Blessed be the God and Father of our Lord Jesus Christ, who " hath blessed us with all spiritual blessings in heavenly places in " Christ Jesus :" and you will in this one mercy, find matter enough of praise and thanksgiving, wonder and admiration to your dying day, yea, to all eternity : for, do but consider,

First, The smallest measure of saving faith which is found in any of the people of God, receives Jesus Christ ; and in receiving him, what mercy is there which the believing soul doth not re- ceive in him, and with him ? Rom. viii. 32.

O believer, though the arms of thy faith be small and weak, yet they embrace a great Christ, and receive the richest gift that ever God bestowed upon the world : no sooner art thou become a be- liever, but Christ is in thee the hope of glory ; and thou hast authority to become a son or daughter of God; thou hast the broad seal of heaven to confirm thy title and claim to the privileges of adoption, for "to as many as received him, to them gave he power "to become the sons of God." [*To as many*] be they strong, or be they weak, provided they really receive Christ by faith; there is authority or power given, so that it is no act of presumption in them to say, God is our Father, heaven is our inheritance. O precious faith! the treasures of ten thousand worlds cannot purchase such privileges as these: all the crowns and sceptres of the earth, sold at full value, are no price for such mercies.

Secondly, The least degree of saving faith brings the soul into a state of perfect and full justification. For if it receives Jesus Christ, it must needs therefore in him, and with him, receive a free, full, and final pardon of sin: the least measure of faith receives remission for the greatest sins. "By him all that believe "are justified from all things," Acts xiii. 39. It unites thy soul with Christ, and then, as the necessary consequent of that union, there is no condemnation, Rom. viii. 1. ϗδεν καταχριμα, not one condemnation, how many soever our sins have been.

Thirdly, The least measure or degree of saving faith, is a greater mercy than God hath bestowed, or ever will bestow upon many that are far above you in outward respects: *All men have not faith:* nay, it is but a remnant among men that believe. Few of the *nobles* and *potentates* of the world have such a gift as this: they have houses and lands, yea, crowns and sceptres, but no faith, no Christ, no pardon; they have authority to rule over men, but no authority to become the sons of God, 1 Cor. i. 26, 27.

Say therefore in thy most debased, straitened, afflicted condition, "Return to thy rest, O my soul, for the Lord hath dealt boun- "tifully with thee."

Fourthly, The least degree of saving faith is more than all the power of nature can produce. There must be a special revelation of the arm of the Lord in that work, Isa. liii. 1. Believers are not "born of the flesh, nor of blood, nor of the will of man, but "of God," John i. 12, 13. All believing motions towards Christ, are the effects of the Father's drawing, John vi. 44. A glorious and irresistible power goes forth from God to produce it, whence it is called "the faith of the operation of God," Col. ii. 12.

So then, let not believers despise the day of small things, or overlook that great and infinite mercy which is wrapt up in the least degree of saving faith.

Infer. 5. *Learn hence the impossibility of their salvation, who neither know the nature, nor enjoy the means of saving faith.*

My soul pities and mourns over the infidel world. Ah! what

will become of the millions of poor unbelievers! there is but one
door of salvation, viz. Christ; and but one key of faith to open that
door: and as that key was never given to the Heathen world: so it
is laid aside, or taken away from the people by their cruel guides, all
over the Popish world; were you among them, you should hear
nothing else pressed as necessary to your salvation but a blind, im-
plicit faith, to believe as the church believes; that is, to believe
they know not what.

To believe as the *pope* believes; that is as an infidel believes,
for so they confess he may be, * and though there be such a thing
as an explict faith sometimes spoken of among them, yet it is very
sparingly discoursed, very falsely described, and exceedingly slighted
by them as the merest trifle in the world.

First, It is but sparingly discoursed of: they love not to accustom the people's ears to such a doctrine; one of themselves
confesses that there is so deep a silence of explicit, particular faith
in the *Romish church,* that you may find many every where, that
believe no more of these things than *Heathen philosophers* †.

Secondly, When it is preached or written of, it is falsely described: for they place the whole nature and essence of justifying
and saving faith in a naked assent, which the devils have as well
as men, James ii. 19. No more than this is pressed upon the people
at any time, as necessary to their salvation.

Thirdly, And even this particular explicit faith, when it is spoken or written of, is exceedingly slighted. I think if the *devil*
himself were in the *pulpit,* he could hardly tell how to bring men
to a more low and slight esteem of faith; to represent it more as
a very trifle, or a quite needless thing, than these his agents have
done. Some ‡ say if a man believe with a particular explicit faith,
i. e. if he actually assent to the scripture-truths once in a year, it
is enough. Yea, and others § think it too much to oblige people
to believe once in twelve months; and, for their ease, tell them,
if they believe once in twelve years it is sufficient; and, lest this
should be too great a task, others ‖ affirm, that if it be done but
once in their whole life, and that at the point of death too, it is
enough, especially for the rude and common people. Good God!
what a doctrine is here! It was a saying long ago of Gregory (as
I remember,) *Malus minister est nisius diaboli:* A wicked minister
is the devil's *gooshawk,* that goes a birding for hell; and O what

---

* For the pope's internal faith is not necessary to the church. *Canus in loc. Theol.*
p. 344.
† Navarr. cap. 11. p. 142.
‡ Petr. a S. Joseph. sum. Art. i. p. 6.
§ Bonacina. Tom. 2. in 1 precept.
‖ Jo. San. Disp. 41. n. 32.

game have these hawks of hell among such numerous flocks of
people ! O, bless God while you live for your deliverance from
popery ; and see that you prize the gospel, and means of grace you
enjoy at an higher rate, lest God bring you once more under that
yoke, which neither you nor your fathers could bear.

Second use for examination.

Doth saving faith consist in a due and right receiving of the
Lord Jesus Christ? Then let me persuade you to examine yourselves in this great point of faith. Reflect solemnly upon the
transactions that have been betwixt Christ and your souls ; think
close on this subject of meditation.

If all you were worth in the world lay in one precious stone, and
that stone were to be tried by the skilful *Lapidary*, whether it were
true or false, whether it would fly or endure under the smart stroke
of his hammer, sure your thoughts could not be unconcerned about
the issue. Why all that you are worth in both worlds depends upon
the truth of your faith which is now to be tried.

O therefore read not these lines with a running, careless eye,
but seriously ponder the matter before you. You would be loth
to put to sea, though it were but to cross the *channel*, in a rotten
leaky bottom : And will you dare to venture into the ocean of
eternity in a false rotten faith ! God forbid. You know the Lord
is coming to try every man's faith as by fire, and that we must
stand or fall for ever with the sincerity or hypocrisy of our faith.
Surely, you can never be too exact and careful about that, on
which your whole estate depends, and that for ever.

Now there are three things upon which we should have a very
tender and watchful eye, for the discovery of the sincerity of our
faith, and they are,

The $\left\{\begin{array}{l}\text{Antecedents}\\\text{Concomitants}\\\text{Consequents}\end{array}\right\}$ of Faith.

As these are, so we must judge and reckon our faith to be. And,
accordingly, they furnish us with three general marks or trials of
faith.

First, If you would discern the sincerity of your faith, examine
whether those *antecedents*, and preparative works of the spirit, were
ever found in your souls, which use to introduce and usher it into
the souls of God's elect : Such are illumination, conviction, self-
despair, and earnest cries to God.

First, *Illumination* is a necessary antecedent to faith : You cannot believe till God hath opened your eyes to see your sin, your
misery by sin, and your remedy in Jesus Christ alone : You find
this act of the Spirit to be the first, in order both of nature and

time, and introductive to all the rest, Acts xxvi. 18. " To turn
" them from darkness to light, and from the power of Satan to
" God." As faith without *works* (which must be a *consequent* to
it) is *dead*, so faith without *light*, which must be an *antecedent* to it,
is *blind :* Faith is the *hand* by which Christ is received, but knowledge is the eye by which that hand is directed.

Well then, hath God opened your eyes to see sin and misery in
another manner than ever you saw them before ? For certainly, if
God hath opened your eyes by saving illumination, you will find as
great a difference betwixt your former and present apprehensions
of sin and danger, as betwixt the painted *lion* upon the wall or a
sign-post, and the real living *lion* that meets you roaring in the
way.

Secondly, *Conviction* is an *antecedent* to believing : Where this
goes not before, no faith can follow after : The Spirit first convinces of sin, then of righteousness, John xvi. 8. So Mark i. 15.
" Repent ye, and believe the gospel :" Believe it, O man ! that
breast of thine must be wounded, that vain and frothy heart of
thine must be pierced and stung with conviction, sense, and sorrow
for sin : Thou must have some sick days, and restless nights for
sin, if ever thou rightly close with Christ by faith. It is true, there
is much difference found in the strength, depth, and continuance
of conviction, and spiritual troubles in converts ; but sure it is, the
child of faith is not ordinarily born without some pangs. Conviction is the application of that light which God makes to shine in
our minds, to our particular case and condition by the conscience ;
and sure, when men come to see their miserable and sad estate by
a true light, it cannot but wound them, and that to the very
heart.

Thirdly, *Self-despair*, or a total and absolute loss in ourselves
about deliverance, and the way of escape, either by ourselves, or
any other mere creature, doth, and must go before faith.

So it was with those believers, Acts ii. 37. " Men and brethren,
" what shall we do ?" They are the words of men at a total loss :
It is the voice of poor distressed souls, that saw themselves in
misery, but knew not, saw not, nor could devise any way of escape
from it, by any thing they could do for themselves, or any other
creature for them : And hence the apostle uses that emphatical
word, Gal. iii. 23. συγκεκλεισμινοι, i. e. *shut up to the faith*, i. e. as
men besieged and distressed in a garrison in a time of storm, when
the enemy pours in upon them through the breaches, and over-
powers them : There is but one *sally-port* or gate, at which they can
escape, and to that they all throng, as despairing of life, if they
take any other course. Just so do men's convictions besiege them,
distress them, beat them off from all their holds and intrench-

ments, and bring them to a pinching distress in themselves, shutting them up to Christ as the only way to escape. Duties cannot save me, reformation cannot save me ; nor angels, nor men can save me ; there is no way but one, *Christ*, or condemnation for ever.

I thought once, that a little repentance, reformation, restitution, and a stricter life, might be a way to escape the wrath to come ; but I find the bed is too short, and the covering too narrow : All is but loss, dung, dross, in comparison with Jesus Christ ; if I trust to those *Egyptian reeds*, they will not only fail me, but pierce and wound me too : I see no hope within the whole *Horizon* of sense.

Fourthly, Hence come *vehement and earnest cries to God* for faith, for Christ, for help from heaven, to transport the soul out of this dangerous condition, to that strong rock of salvation ; to bring it out of this furious, stormy sea of trouble, where it is ready to wreck every moment, into that safe and quiet harbour, Christ.

O when a man shall see his misery and danger, and no way to escape but Christ, and that he hath no ability himself to come to Christ, to open his heart thus to receive him, but that this work of faith is wholly supernatural, the operation of God ; how will the soul return again, and again upon God, with such cries as in Mark ix. 24. " Lord, help my unbelief ?" " Lord, enable me to " come to Christ ; give me Christ or I perish for ever ; What pro- " fit is there in my blood ? Why should I die in the sight and " presence of a Saviour ? O Lord, it is thine own work, a most " glorious work : Reveal thine arm in this work upon my soul, I " pray thee ; give me Christ, if thou deny me bread ? give me " faith, if thou deny me breath. It is more necessary that I be- " lieve, than that I live."

O Reader, reflect upon the days and nights that are past, the places where thou hast been conversant : Where are the bed-sides, or the secret corners where thou hast besieged heaven with such cries ? If God have thus enlightened, convinced, distressed thy soul, and thus set thee a mourning after Christ, it will be one good sign that faith is come into thy soul ; for here are certainly the *harbingers* and forerunners of it, that ordinarily make way for faith into the souls of men.

Secondly, If you would be satisfied of the sincerity and truth of your faith, then examine what *concomitants* it is attended with in your souls. I mean, what frames and tempers your souls were in, at that time when you think you received Christ. For certainly, in those that receive Christ, (excepting those into whose hearts God hath in a more still and insensible way infused faith betimes, by his blessing upon pious education) such concomitant frames of spirit may be remarked as these following.

First, The heart is deeply *serious,* and as much in earnest in this matter, as ever it was, or can be, about any thing in the world. This you see in that example of the gaoler, Acts xvi. 29. "He "came in trembling and astonished:" It is the most solemn and important matter that ever the soul had before it in this world, or ever shall, or can have : How much are the hearts of men affected in their outward straits and distresses, about the concernments of the body? Their hearts are not a little concerned in such questions as these, "What shall I eat? what shall I drink?" wherewithal shall I and mine be fed and cloathed? but certainly the straits that souls are in about salvation, must be allowed to be greater than these ; and such questions as that of the gaoler's, "Sirs! What must I do to be saved?" make deeper impressions upon the heart, than what shall I eat or drink? Some indeed have their thoughts sinking deeper into these things than others : These thoughts lie with different degrees of weight upon men : but all are most solemnly and awfully concerned about their condition : All frothiness and frolics are gone, and the heart settles itself in the deepest earnest about its eternal state.

Secondly, The heart that receives Jesus Christ is in a frame of deep humiliation and self-abasement. O, when a man begins to apprehend the first approaches of grace, pardon, and mercy by Jesus Christ to his soul : When a soul is convinced of its utter unworthiness and desert of hell ; and can scarce expect any thing else from the just and holy God but damnation, how do the first dawnings of mercy melt and humble them ! "O Lord, what am I "that thou shouldst feed me, and preserve me ! that thou "shouldst but for a few years spare me and forbear me ! but that "ever Jesus Christ should love me, and give himself for me; that "such a wretched sinner as I should obtain union with his person, "pardon, peace, and salvation by his blood ! Lord, whence is this "to such a worm as I? and will Christ indeed bestow himself "upon me? shall so great a blessing as Christ ever come within the "arms of such a soul as mine? will God in very deed be recon- "ciled to me in his Son? what, to me ! to such an enemy as I "have been ! shall my sins which are so many, so horrid, so much "aggravated, beyond the sins of most men, be forgiven? O what "am I, vile dust? base wretch, that ever God should do this for "me !" And how is that scripture fulfilled and made good, Ezek. xvi. 63. "That thou mayest remember, and be confounded, and "never open thy mouth any more, because of thy shame, when I "am pacified towards thee for all that thou hast done, saith the "Lord God." Thus, that poor broken-hearted believer stood behind Christ weeping, and washing his feet with tears, as one quite melted down, and overcome with the sense of mercy to such a vile sinner, Luke vii. 38.

Thirdly, The soul that receives Jesus Christ is in a *weary condition,* restless, and full of disquietness, neither able to bear the burden of sin, nor knowing how to be discharged from it, except Christ will give it ease, Mat. xi. 28. " Come unto me," that is, believe in me, " you that are weary and heavy laden:" If they do not look into their own souls, they know there is no *safety,* and if they do, there is no *comfort.*   O ! the burdensome sense of sin overweighs them ; they are ready to fall, to sink under it.

Fourthly, The soul that rightly receives Christ, is not only in a weary, but in a *longing condition :* never did the *hart* pant more earnestly for the water-brooks: never did the *hireling* desire the shadow : never did a *condemned person* long for a pardon more than the soul longs after Jesus Christ.   O, said David, that one would give me of the water of the well of Bethlehem to drink.   O, saith the poor humbled sinner, that one would give me of the opened fountain of the blood of Christ to drink ! O for one drop of that precious blood ! O for one encouraging smile from Christ ! O now were ten thousand worlds at my command, and Christ to be bought, how freely would I lay them all down to purchase him ! but he is the *gift* of God.   O that God would give me Christ, if I should go in rags, and hunger and thirst all my days in this world !

Fifthly, The soul in the time of its closing with, or receiving Christ, is in a *state of conflict :* It hangs between hopes and fears, encouragements and discouragements, which occasions many a sad stand and pause in the way of Christ ; sometimes the number and nature of its sins discourage it, then the riches and freeness of the grace of Christ erects his hopes again : there is little hope, saith unbelief ; nay, it is utterly impossible, saith Satan, that ever such a wretch as thou shouldst find mercy ; now the hands hang down. O but then there is a necessity, an absolute necessity ; I have not the choice of two, but am shut up to one way of deliverance ; others have found mercy, and the invitation is to all that are weary, and to all that are athirst : he saith, him that cometh to him, he will in no wise cast out : now new hopes inspire the soul, and the hands that did hang down are strengthened.

These are the *concomitant frames* that accompany faith.

3. *Mark.* Lastly, Examine the *consequents* and effects of faith, if you would be satisfied of the truth and sincerity of it : And such are,

First, Evangelical meltings, and ingenuous thawings of the heart under the apprehensions of grace and mercy : Zech. xii. 10. " They shall look upon me whom they have pierced, and shall " mourn."

Secondly, Love to Christ, his ways and people, Gal. v. 6. *Faith worketh by love,* i. e. represents the love of God, and then makes use of the sweetness of it by way of argument, to constrain the soul to all acts of obedience, where it may testify the reality of its love to God and Christ.

Thirdly, Heart-*purity,* Acts xv. 9. " Purifying the hearts by " faith :" It doth not only cleanse the *hands* but the *heart.* No principle in man, besides faith, can do this : Morality may hide corruption, but faith only *purifies* the heart from it.

Fourthly, Obedience to the commands of Christ, Rom. xvi. 26. The very name of faith is called upon obedience : for it accepts Christ as Lord, and urges upon the soul the most powerful arguments in the world to draw it to obedience.

In a word, let the poor doubting believer, that questions his faith, reflect upon those things that are unquestionable in his own experience, which being well considered, will greatly tend to his sstisfaction in this point.

It is very doubtful to you whether you believe, but yet in the mean time, it may be past doubt, (being a matter of clear experience) that you have been deeply convinced of sin, struck off from all carnal props and refuges, made willing to accept Jesus Christ upon what terms soever you might enjoy him. You doubt whether Christ be yours, but it is past doubt that you have a most high and precious esteem of Christ, that you heartily long for him, that you prize and love all, whether persons or things, that bear his image : that nothing in the world would please your hearts like a transformation into his likeness : that you had rather your souls should be filled with his Spirit, than your houses with gold and silver. It is doubtful whether Christ be yours, but it is past doubt that one smile from Christ, one token of his love would do you more good than all the honours and smiles of the world ; and nothing so grieves you, as your grieving him by sin doth. You dare not say that you have received him, nor can you deny but that you have had many sick days and nights for him ; that you have gone into many secret places with yearning bowels after him. Whether he be yours or not, you cannot tell ; but that you are resolved to be his, that you can tell. Whether he will save you is but a doubt, but that you resolve to lie at his feet, and wait only on him, and never look to another for salvation, is no doubt.

Well, well ; poor pensive soul, if it be so, arise, lift up thy dejected head, take thine own Christ into thine arms. These are undoubted signs of a real closure with Christ ; thou makest thyself poor, and yet hast great riches : Such things as these are not found in them that despise and reject Christ by unbelief.

3. *Use of Exhortation.*

3. *Use.* This point is likewise very improveable by way of exhortation, and that both to

Unbelievers and Believers.

First, To unbelievers, who from hence must be pressed, as ever
they expect to see the face of God in peace, to receive Jesus Christ
as he is now offered to them in the gospel. This is the very scope
of the gospel; I shall therefore press it by three great considerations, *viz.*

First, What is in Christ whom you are to receive.

Secondly, What is in the offer of Christ by the gospel.

Thirdly, What is in the rejecting of that offer.

First Motive.

First, Consider well what is in Christ, whom I persuade you this
day to receive: Did you know what is in Christ, you would never
neglect or reject him as you do: For,

First, " God is in Christ," 2 Cor. v. 19. the Deity hath chosen
to dwell in his flesh; he is "God manifest in flesh," 1 Tim. iii. 16.
a Godhead dwelling in flesh is the world's wonder; so that in receiving Christ, you receive God himself.

Secondly, The authority of God is in Christ, Exod. xxiii. 21.
" My name is in him: Him hath God the Father sealed," John
vi. 27. he hath the commission, the great seal of heaven to redeem
and save you. All power in heaven and earth is given to him,
Matth. xxviii. 18. he comes in his Father's name to you, as well
as in his own name.

Thirdly, The wisdom of God is in Christ, 1 Cor. i. 24. " Christ
" the wisdom of God," yea, " in him are hid all the treasures of
" wisdom and knowledge," Col. ii. 3. Never did the wisdom of
God display itself before the eyes of angels and men as it hath done
in Christ. The " angels desire to look into it," 1 Pet. i. 12. yet
they are not so much concerned in the project and design of this
wisdom in redemption as you are.

Fourthly, The *fulness of the Spirit* is in Christ; yea, it fills him
so as it never did, nor will fill any creature, John iii. 34. " God
" giveth not the Spirit by measure to him:" all others have their
limits, stints, and measures; some more, some less; but the Spirit
is in Christ without measure. O how lovely and desirable are
those men that have a large measure of the Spirit in them! but
he is anointed with the Spirit of holiness *above all his fellows,* Psal.
xlv. 2, 7. Whatever grace is found in all the saints, which makes
them desirable and lovely, wisdom in one, faith in another, pa-

tience in a third; they all centre in Christ as the rivers do in the sea, *quæ faciunt divisa beatum, in hoc mixta fluunt.*

Fifthly, The righteousness of God is in Christ, by which only a poor guilty sinner can be justified before God, 2 Cor. v. 21. we are "made the righteousness of God in him :" he is יחוה צדקנו " the Lord our righteousness," Jer. xxiii. 6. i. e. " * the author " of our righteousness," or the Lord who justifies us; by that name he will be known, and called by his people, than which none can be sweeter.

Sixthly, The love of God is in Christ; yea, the very yearning bowels of divine love are in him: What is Christ, but the love of God wrapt up in flesh and blood? 1 John iv. 9, 10. " In this was " manifested the love of God towards us :" and herein is love, that God sent his Son; this is the highest flight that ever divine love made; and higher than this it cannot mount. O love, unparalleled and admirable!

Seventhly, The mercies and compassions of God are all in Christ, Jude, ver. 21. Mercy is the thing that poor sinners want, it is that they cry for at the last gasp; it is the only thing that can do them good. O what would they give to find mercy in that great day? Why, if you receive Christ, you shall with him receive mercy; but out of him there is no mercy to be expected from the hands of God; for God will never exercise mercy to the prejudice of his justice; and it is in Christ that justice and mercy meet and embrace each other.

Eighthly, To conclude, The salvation of God is in Christ, Acts iv. 12. " Neither is there salvation in any other." Christ is the *door* of salvation, and faith is the *key* that opens that door to men. If you therefore believe not, i. e. if you so receive not Jesus Christ, as God hath offered him, you exclude yourselves from all hopes of salvation. The devils have as much ground to expect salvation as you. You see what is in Christ to induce you to receive him.

Motive 2.

Next, I beseech you, consider what there is in the offer of Christ to sinners, to induce you to receive him. Consider well to *whom* and *how* Christ is offered in the gospel.

First, To *whom* is he offered; not to the fallen angels, but to you; they lie in chains of darkness, Jude, ver. 6. as he took not their nature, so he designs not their recovery; and therefore will have no treaty at all with them: but he is offered to you, creatures of an inferior rank and order by nature; nor is he offered to the *damned,* the treaty of peace is ended with them: Christ will never

---

* *Autorem justitiæ nostræ.* Calv. in loc.

make them another tender of salvation; nor is he offered to
millions as good as you, now living in the world. The sound
of Christ and salvation is not come to their ears, but he is offered to you by the special favour and bounty of heaven; and will
you not receive him? Oh! then how will the devils, the damned,
and the Heathen upbraid your folly! and say, had we had one
such tender of mercy, of which you have had thousands, we would
never have been now in this place of torments.

Secondly, Consider how Christ is offered to you, and you shall
find that he is offered,

1. Freely, *as the gift of God*, to your souls; you are not to *purchase* him, but only to *receive* him, Isa. lv. i. " Ho, every one
" that thirsteth, come ye to the waters, and he that hath no
" money, let him come," &c.

2. Christ is offered importunately, by repeated intreaties, 2 Cor.
v. 20. " As though God did beseech you, we pray you in Christ's
" stead, be ye reconciled to God." O! what amazing condescension is here in the God of mercy! God now beseeches you,
will you not yield to the intreaties of your God? O then what
wilt thou say for thyself, when God will not hear thee, when thou
shalt intreat and cry for mercy? Which brings us to

Motive 3. Consider the sin and danger that there is in refusing
or neglecting the present offers of Christ in the gospel, and surely
there is much sin in it; the very malignity of sin, and the sum of
all misery lies here; for in refusing Christ,

1. You put the greatest contempt and slight upon all the attributes of God that is possible for a creature to do: God hath
made his justice, his mercy, his wisdom, and all his attributes to
shine in their brightest glory in Christ. Never was there such a
display of the glory of God made to the world in any other way.

O then, what is it to reject and despise Jesus Christ, but to offer
the greatest affront to the glory of God that it is possible for
men to put upon it?

2. You hereby frustrate and evacuate the very design and importance of the gospel to yourselves; you " receive the grace of
" God in vain," 2 Cor. vi. 1. As good, yea, better had it been
for you, that Christ had never come into the world, or, if he had,
that your lot had fallen in the dark places of the earth, where you
had never heard his name; yea, good had it been for that man
if he had never been born.

3. Hereby a man murders his own soul. " I said therefore
" unto you, that you shall die in your sins; for if ye believe not
" that I am he, ye shall die in your sins," John viii. 24. Unbelief is self-murder; you are guilty of the blood of your own souls;
life and salvation were offered you, and you rejected them. Yea,

4. The refusing of Christ by unbelief will aggravate your damnation above all others that perish in ignorance of Christ. O, it will be more tolerable for Heathens than for you; the greatest measures of wrath are reserved to punish the worst of sinners; and among sinners, none will be found worse than unbelievers.

Secondly, To believers, this point is very useful to persuade them to divers excellent duties; among which, I shall single out two principal ones, viz.

1. To bring up their faith of acceptance, to the faith of assurance.

2. To bring up their conversations to the principles and rules of faith.

1. You that have received Jesus Christ truly, give yourselves no rest till you are fully satisfied that you have done so; acceptance brings you to heaven hereafter, but assurance will bring heaven into your souls now. O, what a life of delight and pleasure doth the assured believer live! What pleasure is it to him to look back and consider where he once was, and where he now is? To look forward, and consider where he now is, and where shortly he shall be! I was in my sins, I am now in Christ; I am in Christ now, I shall be with Christ, and that for ever, after a few days. I was upon the brink of hell, I am now upon the very borders of heaven; I shall be in a very little while among the innumerable company of angels and glorified saints, bearing part with them in the song of Moses, and of the Lamb, for evermore.

And why may not you that have received Christ, receive the comfort of your union with him? There be all the grounds and helps of assurance furnished to your hand; there is a real union betwixt Christ and your souls, which is the very ground-work of assurance. * You have the scriptures before you which contain the signs of faith, and the very things within you that answer those signs in the word. So you read, and so, just so, you might feel it in your own hearts, would you attend to your own experience. The Spirit of God is ready to seal you, it is his office and his delight so to do. O therefore, give diligence to this work, attend the study of the scriptures and of your own hearts more, and grieve not the holy Spirit of God, and you may arrive to the very desire of your hearts.

2. Bring up your conversations to the excellent principles and rules of faith; "As you have received Christ Jesus the Lord, so " walk in him," Col. ii. 6. Live as you believe; you received Christ sincerely in your first close with him, O maintain the like seriousness and sincerity in all your ways, to the end of your lives:

---

* The power and constancy of a firm hope reigns in us. *Cypr. Serm. de patientia.*

you received him intirely and *undividedly* at first, let there be no exceptions against any of his commands afterward. You received him *exclusively* to all others, see that you watch against all self-righteousness and self-conceitedness now, and mingle nothing of your own with his blood, whatever gifts or enlargements in duty God shall give you afterwards.

You received him *advisedly* at first, weighing and considering the self-denying terms upon which he was offered to you; O shew that it was real, and that you see no cause to repent the bargain, whatever you shall meet with in the ways of Christ and duty afterwards: convince the world of your constancy and cheerfulness in all your sufferings for Christ, that you are still of the same mind you were, and that Christ, with his cross, Christ, with a prison, Christ, with the greatest afflictions, is worthy of all acceptation: " As ye have received him, so walk ye in him." Let him be as sweet, as lovely, as precious to you now, as he was in the first moment you received him; yea, let your love to him, delights in him, and self-denial for him, increase with your acquaintance with him, day by day.

Use of direction.

Use: Lastly, I will close all with a few words of *direction* to all that are made willing to receive the Lord Jesus Christ; and sure it is but needful that help were given to poor Christians: in this matter, it is a time of trouble, fear, and great temptation; mistakes are easily made of dangerous consequence; attend heedfully, therefore, to a few directions.

Direction 1. First, In your receiving Christ, *Beware you do not mistake the means for the end.* Many do so, but see you do not. Prayer, sermons, reformations, are means to bring you to Christ, but they are not Christ; to close with those duties is one thing, and to close with Christ is another thing. If I go into a *boat*, my design is not to dwell there, but to be carried to the place whereon I desire to be landed: so it must be in this case, all your duties must land you upon Christ; they are means to bring you to Christ.

Direct. 2. Secondly, *See that you receive not Christ for a present help, but for your everlasting portion.* Many do so; they will enquire after Christ, pray for Christ, cast themselves (in their way) upon Christ, and the satisfaction of his blood, when the efficacy and terror of conscience is upon them, and they feel the sting of guilt within them; but as soon as the storm is over, and the rod that conscience shaked over them laid by, there is no more talk of Christ then: alas! it was not Christ, but quietness that they sought; beware of mistaking peace for Christ.

Direct. 3. Thirdly, *In receiving Christ, come empty-handed unto*

him: " believing on him who justifies the ungodly," Rom. iv. 5.
and know that the deepest sense of your own vileness, emptiness,
and unworthiness, is the best frame of heart that can accompany
you to Christ. Many persons stand off from Christ for want of
fit qualifications; they are not prepared for Christ as they should
be, i. e. they would not come naked and empty, but have something to commend them to the Lord Jesus for acceptance. O !
this is the pride of men's hearts, and the snare of the devil. Let
him that hath no money come : You are not to come to Christ
because you are qualified, but that you may be qualified with
whatever you want; and the best qualification you can bring with
you, is a deep sense that you have no worth nor excellency at all in
you.

Direct. 4. Fourthly, *In receiving Christ, beware of dangerous
delays.* O follow on that work till it be finished. You read
of some that are almost persuaded, and of others not far from the
kingdom of God ; O take heed of what the prophet says, Hosea
xiii. 13. Delays here are full of danger, life is uncertain, so are
means of grace too. The man-slayer needed no motives to quicken
his flight to the city of refuge.

Direct. 5. Fifthly, *See that you receive all Christ, with all your
heart.* To receive all Christ, is to receive his person clothed with all
his offices ; and to receive him with all your heart, is to receive him
into your understanding, will, and affections, Acts viii. 37. As there
is nothing in Christ that may be refused, so there is nothing in you
from which he must be excluded.

Direct. 6. Lastly, Understand that the opening of your hearts
to receive the Lord Jesus Christ, is not a work done by any power
of your own, but the arm of the Lord is revealed therein, Isa. liii.
1. It is therefore your duty and interest to be daily at the feet
of God, pouring out your souls to him in secret, for abilities to believe. And so much, as to our actual reception of Christ.

Thanks be to God for Jesus Christ.

SERMON VIII.

Setting forth the Believer's Fellowship with CHRIST, the next End of his Application to them.

PSALM xlv. 7.

Therefore God, thy God, hath anointed thee with the oil of gladness above thy fellows.

THE method of grace in uniting souls with Jesus Christ, hath been opened in the former discourses; thus doth the Spirit, (whose office it is) make application of Christ to God's elect: The result and next fruit whereof is *communion* with Christ in his graces and benefits. Our *mystical union* is the very ground-work and foundation of our sweet, soul-enriching *communion* and participation of spiritual privileges; we are first ingrafted into Christ, and then suck the sap and fatness of the root: first married to the person of Christ, then endowed and instated in the privileges and benefits of Christ. This is my proper work to open at this time, and from this scripture.

" The words read, are a part of that excellent *song of love* *, that " heavenly *Epithalamium*, wherein the spiritual espousals of Christ " and the church are figuratively and very elegantly celebrated " and shadowed. The subject matter of this psalm is the very " same with the whole book of the Canticles;" and in this psalm, under the figure of king Solomon, and the daughter of Egypt, whom he espoused, the spiritual espousals of Christ and the church are set forth and represented to us. Among many rapturous and elegant expressions in praise of this glorious bridegroom, Christ, this is one, which you have before you : " God, thy God, hath anoint- " ed thee with the oil of gladness above thy fellows:" i. e. enriched and filled thee, in a singular and peculiar manner, with the fulness of the Spirit, whereby thou art consecrated to thy office : and by reason whereof thou out-shinest and excellest all the saints, who are thy *fellows* or copartners in these graces. So that in these words you have two parts; viz. *First*, The saints' *dignity*, and *Secondly*, Christ's *pre-eminency :*

First, The saints' *dignity*, which consists in this, that they are Christ's *fellows*. The Hebrew word † is very full and copious,

---

* *Hic Psalmus propheticus est, continetque Epilathamium quo Christi cum ecclesia nuptiæ celebrantur, idemque habet argumentum quod canticum canticorum ejusque videtur esse epitome.* Cocceius in loc.

† מחכריך *Consortes, participes, sodales, socii. Vox Hebræa quodcunque societatis sive communionis genus significat.* Muis.

and is translated " comsorts, companions, copartners, partakers:
or, as ours read it, *fellows*:" i. e. such as are partakers with him
in the anointing of the Spirit, who do, in their measure, receive
the same Spirit, every Christian being anointed, *modo sibi propor-
tionato*, with the same grace, and dignified with the same titles, 1
John ii. 27. Rev. i. 6. Christ and the saints are in common one
with another: Doth the spirit of holiness dwell in him? so it doth
in them too. Is Christ *King* and *Priest?* Why, so are they too by
the grace of union with him. He hath made us kings and priests to
God, and his Father. This is the saints' dignity to be Christ's fellows, consorts, or copartners; so that look, whatever spiritual grace
or excellency is in Christ, it is not appropriated to himself, but
they do share with him: for indeed he was filled with the fulness
of the Spirit, for their sakes and use: as the sun is filled with light,
not to shine to itself, but to others; so is Christ with grace. And
therefore, some translate the text, not *præ consortibus*, above thy
fellows; but *propter consortes*, for thy fellows*. Making Christ the
first receptacle of grace, who first and immediately is filled from
the fountain, the Godhead: but it is for his people, who receive
and derive from him, according to their proportion.

This is a great truth, and the dignity of the saints lies chiefly in
their partnership with Christ, though our translation, *above thy fellows*, suits best, both with the importance of the word, and scope of
the place.

Secondly, But then, whatever *dignity* is ascribed herein to the
saints, there is, and still must be, a *pre-eminency* acknowledged,
and ascribed to Christ: if they are anointed with the Spirit of
grace, much more abundantly is Christ: " God, thy God, hath
" anointed thee with the oil of gladness above thy fellows."

By the *oil of gladness* understand the Spirit of holiness, compared here with oil, of which there was a double use under the
law, viz. a *civil* and a *sacred* use. It had a sacred and a solemn
use, in the inauguration and consecration of the Jewish kings and
high-priests; it had also a civil, and common use, for the anointing their bodies †, to make their limbs more agile, expedite, and
nimble; to make the face shine, for it gave a lustre, freshness,
and liveliness to the countenance. It was also used in lamps, to
feed and maintain the fire, and give them light. These were the
principal uses of oil. Now, upon all these accounts, it excellently

---

* Rivet.

† Oil itself is pure and clear, which supplies and feeds the flame with fuel; hence
the metaphor of anointing with oil used in scripture, frequently signifies the internal illumination of the mind by the Holy Spirit, and the communication of the true knowledge of God, and suitable affections of soul to it. *Moller. on the place.*

expresseth, and figuratively, represents to us the Spirit of grace poured forth upon Christ and his people.   For,

First, By the Spirit poured out upon him, he was prepared for, and consecrated to his offices, he was anointed with the Holy Ghost and with power, Acts x. 38.

Secondly, As this precious oil runs down from Christ, the head, to the borders of his garments, I mean, as it is shed upon believers, so it exceedingly beautifies their faces, and makes them shine with glory.

Thirdly, It renders them apt, expedite, and ready to every good work : *Non tardat uncta rota.*

Fourthly, It kindles and maintains the flame of divine love in their souls, and, like a lamp, enlightens their minds in the knowledge of spiritual things ; the anointing teaches them.

" And this oil is here called *the oil of gladness* *, because it is the " cause of all joy and gladness to them that are anointed with it :" Oil was used (as you heard before) at the instalment of sovereign princes, which was the day of the gladness of their hearts ; and, among the common people, it was liberally used at all their *festivals*, but never upon their days of mourning.   Whence it becomes excellently expressive of the nature and use of the Spirit of grace, who is the cause and author of all joy in believers, John xvii. 13.

And with this oil of gladness is Christ said to be anointed *above his fellows*, i. e. to have a far greater share of the Spirit of grace than they : " For to every one of the saints is given grace accord- " ing to the measure of the gift of Christ," Eph. iv. 7.   But to him the Spirit is not given by measure, John iii. 34.   " It hath " pleased the Father, that in him should all fulness dwell," Col. i. 19. and " of his fulness we all receive grace for grace," John i. 16.   The saints partake with him, and through him in the same Spirit of grace, for which reason they are his fellows ; but all the grace poured out upon believers comes exceeding short of that which God hath poured out upon Jesus Christ.   The words being thus opened, give us this note,

Doct. That all true believers have a real communion or fellowship with the Lord Jesus Christ.

From the saints' union with Christ, there doth naturally and immediately result a most sweet and blessed communion and fellowship with him in graces and spiritual privileges, Eph. i. 3.   " Blessed

---

* Ελαιον αγαλλιασεως *dicitur id quod causam dat summi guadii.* Grot. in Heb. i. 9. Αυτος υμιν αιτιος της δωρεας τ8 πνευματος, και επισπασαμενος καθο εςιν ανθρωπος, το πνευμα και υμιν μεταδ8ς. i. e. He is the cause of the gift of the Spirit to you, and being anointed with the Spirit as he is man, he communicates the Spirit to us also.   O Ecum.

" be the God and Father of our Lord Jesus Christ, who hath
" blessed us with all spiritual blessings in heavenly places (or
" things) in Christ: in giving us his Son, he freely gives us all
" things," Rom. viii. 32. So in 1 Cor. i. 30. " Of him are ye
" in Christ Jesus, who of God is made unto us wisdom, righte-
" ousness, sanctification and redemption." And once more, 1
Cor. iii. 22, 23. " All are yours, and ye are Christ's." What
Christ is and hath is theirs by communication to them, or improvement for them; and this is very evidently implied in all those excellent scripture metaphors, by which our union with Christ is
figured and shadowed out to us; as the *marriage-union* betwixt a
man and his wife, Eph. v. 31, 32. You know that this conjugal
union gives the wife interest in the estate and honours of the husband, be she never so meanly descended in herself*. The *natural
union* betwixt the head and members of the body, by which also
the mystical union of Christ and believers is set forth, 1 Cor. xii.
12. excellently illustrates this fellowship or communion betwixt
them, for from Christ "the whole body fitly joined together,
" and compacted by that which every joint supplieth, according
" to the effectual working in the measure of every part, maketh
" increase of the body," as the apostle speaks, Eph. iv. 16. The
union betwixt the graff and the stock, which is another emblem of
our union with Christ, John xv. 1. imports, in like manner, this
communion or partnership betwixt Christ and the saints; for no
sooner doth the graff take hold of the stock, but the vital sap of
the stock is communicated to the graff, and both live by one and
the same juice.

Now, that the scope of this discourse be not mistaken, let the
reader know that I am not here treating of the saint's communion
or fellowship with God in his duties, as in prayer, hearing, sacraments, *&c.* but of that interest which believers have in the good
things of Christ, by virtue of the mystical union betwixt them
through faith: there is a twofold communion of the saints with
Christ.

The first is an *act.*

The second is a *state.*

There is an actual fellowship or communion the saints have with
Christ in holy duties, wherein Christians let forth their hearts to
God by desires, and God lets forth his comforts and refreshments
again into their hearts; they open their mouths wide, and he fills
them: this communion with God is the joy and comfort of a believer's life, but I am not to speak of that here. It is not any act
of communion, but the state of communion, from which all acts of

---

* *Ubi ego Cajus tu Caja. Uxor clarescit in radiis mariti.*

communion flow, and upon which they all depend, that I am now to treat of; which is nothing else but the joint interest that Christ and the saints have in the same things; as when a ship, an house, or estate, is among many partners, or joint heirs, every one of them hath a right to it, and interest in it, though some of them have a greater, and others a lesser part. So it is betwixt Christ and his people; there is a κοινωνια, i. e. a fellowship or joint interest betwixt them, upon which ground they are called *co-heirs with Christ,* Rom. viii. 17. This communion or participation in Christ's benefits, depends upon the hypostatical union of our nature, and the mystical union of our persons with the Son of God; in the first he partakes with us, in the second we partake with him; the former is the remote, the latter the next cause thereof.

In the explication of this point, I shall speak to these four things:

1. What are those things in which Christ and believers have fellowship.

2. By what means they come to have such a fellowship with Christ.

3. How great a dignity this is to have fellowship with Jesus Christ.

4. And then apply the whole in divers practical inferences.

First, What are those things in which Christ and believers have fellowship, to which I must speak both *negatively* and *positively.*

1. *Negatively,* The saints have no fellowship with Jesus Christ in those things that belong to him as God; such as his consubstantiality, co-equality, and co-eternity with the Father. It is the blasphemy of the wicked *Familists* to talk of being godded into God, and christed into Christ. Neither men nor angels partake in these things; they are the proper and incommunicable glory of the Lord Jesus.

2. The saints have no communion or fellowship in the honour and glory of his mediatory works, viz. his satisfaction to God, or redemption of the elect. It is true, we have the benefit and fruit of his mediation and satisfaction: his righteousness also is imputed to us for our personal justification, but we share not in the least with Christ in the glory of this work; nor have we an inherent righteousness in us as Christ hath; nor can we justify and save others as Christ doth: we have nothing to do with his peculiar honour and praise in these things. Though we have the benefit of being saved, we may not pretend to the honour of being Saviours, as Christ is to ourselves or others. " * Christ's righteousness is

---

* *Justitia Christi fit nostra, non quoad universalem valorem sed particularem necessitatem, et imputatur nobis non ut causis salvationis, sed ut subjectis salvandis.* Bradshaw de Justificatione.

" not made ours as to its universal value, but as to our particular
" necessity; nor is it imputed to us as to so many causes of salva-
" tion to others, but as to so many subjects to be saved by it our-
" selves."

Secondly, But then there are many glorious and excellent things
which are in common betwixt Christ and believers, though in them
all he hath the pre-eminence; he shines in the fulness of them, as
the sun, and we with a borrowed and lesser light, but of the same
kind and nature as the stars. Some of these I shall particularly,
and briefly unfold in the following particulars.

First, Believers have communion with Christ in his *names* and
titles; they are called Christians from Christ, Eph. iii. 15. from him
the whole family in heaven and earth is named: this is that worthy
name the apostle speaks of, James ii. 7. He is the Son of God,
and they also, by their union with him, have power or authority
to become the sons of God, John i. 12. He is the heir of all
things, and they are joint-heirs with him, Rom. viii. 17. He is
both King and Priest, and he hath made them kings and priests,
Rev. i. 6. But they do not only partake in the names and titles,
but this communion consists in things as well as titles. And therefore,

Secondly, They have communion with him in his *righteousness,*
i. e. the righteousness of Christ is made theirs, 2 Cor. v. 21. and
he is " the Lord our righteousness," Jer. xxiii. 6. It is true, the
righteousness of Christ is not inherent in us, as it is in him; but
it is ours by imputation, Rev. iv. 5, 11. and our union with him
is the ground of the imputation of his righteousness to us, 2 Cor.
v. 21. " We are made the righteousness of God in him," Phil. iii.
9. for Christ and believers are considered as one person, in construction of law; as a man and his wife, a *debtor* and *surety*, are
one: and so his payment or satisfaction is in our name, or upon our
account.

Now, this is a most inestimable privilege, the very ground of all
our other blessings and mercies. O, what a benefit is this to a poor
sinner, that owes to God infinitely more than he is ever able to pay,
by doing or suffering; to have such a rich treasure of merit as lies
in the obedience of Christ, to discharge, in one entire payment, all
his debts to the last farthing? " Surely shall one say, in the Lord
" have I righteousness," Isa. xlv. 24. even as a poor woman that
owes more than she is worth, in one moment is discharged of all her
obligations, by her marriage to a wealthy man.

Thirdly, Believers have communion with Christ in his holiness
or sanctification, for of God he is made unto them, not only righteousness, but sanctification also; and as in the former privilege,
they have a stock of merit in the blood of Christ to justify them;

so here, they have the Spirit of Christ to sanctify them, 1 Cor. i.
30. and therefore we are said of his fulness to receive "grace for
grace," John i. 16. i. e. say some, grace upon grace, manifold
graces, or abundance of grace; or grace for grace, that is, grace
answerable to grace: as in the seal and wax, there is line for line,
and cut for cut, exactly answerable to each other; or grace for
grace, that is, say others, the free grace of God in Christ, for the
sanctification or filling of our souls with grace: be it in which sense
it will, it shews the communion believers have with Jesus Christ
in grace and holiness. Now, holiness is the most precious thing
in the world, it is the image of God, and chief excellency of
man: it is our evidence for glory, yea, and the first fruits of glory.
In Christ dwells the fulness of grace, and from him, our head, it
is derived and communicated to us; thus he that sanctifieth, and
they that are sanctified, are all of one, Heb. ii. 11. You would
think it no small privilege to have bags of gold to go to, and enrich
yourselves with, and yet that were but a very trifle in comparison to
have Christ's righteousness and holiness to go to for your justification and sanctification. More particularly,

Fourthly, Believers have communion with Christ *in his death;*
they die with him, Gal. ii. 20. " I am crucified with Christ,"
i. e. the death of Christ hath a real killing and mortifying influence upon the lusts and corruptions of my heart and nature: true
it is, he died for sin one way, and we die to sin another way: he
died to *expiate* it, we die to it, when we *mortify* it: the death of
Christ is the death of sin in believers; and this is a very glorious
privilege; for the death of sin is the life of your souls; if sin do not
die in you by mortification, you must die for sin by eternal damnation. If Christ had not died, the Spirit of God, by which you
now mortify the deeds of the body, could not have been given
unto you: then you must have lived vassals to your sins, and died
at last in your sins; but the fruit, efficacy, and benefit of Christ's
death is yours for the killing those sins in you, which else had
been your ruin.

Fifthly, Believers have communion with Christ in *his life and
resurrection* from the dead; as he rose from the dead, so do they;
and that by the power and influence of his *vivification* and resurrection. It is the Spirit of life which is in Christ Jesus that makes
us free from the law of sin and death, Rom. viii. 2. Our spiritual
life is from Christ, Eph. ii. 1. "And you hath he quickened who
" were dead in trespasses and sins:" and hence Christ is said to
live in the believer, Gal. ii. 20. "Now I live, yet not I, but Christ
" liveth in me:" and it is no small privilege to partake of the very
life of Christ, which is the most excellent life that ever any creature

can live; yet such is the happiness of all the saints, the life of Christ is manifest in them, and such a life as shall never see death.

Sixthly, To conclude, believers have fellowship with Jesus Christ *in his glory,* which they shall enjoy in heaven with him: they " shall be ever with the Lord," 1 Thes. iv. 17. and that is not all, (though, as one saith, it were a kind of heaven but to look through the key-hole, and have but a glimpse of Christ's blessed face) but they shall partake of the glory which the Father hath given him; for so he speaks, John xvii. 22, 24. and more particularly, they shall sit with him in his throne, Rev. iii. 21. and when he comes to judge the world, he will come to be glorified in the saints, 2 Thes. i. 10. So that you may see what glorious and inestimable things are, and will be in common betwixt Christ and the saints. His titles, his righteousness, his holiness, his death, his life, his glory. I do not say that Christ will make any saint equal with him in glory; that is impossible, he will be known from all the saints in heaven, as the sun is distinguished from the stars; but they shall partake of his glory, and be filled with his joy there; and thus you see what those things are that the saints have fellowship with Christ in.

Secondly, Next I would open the way and means by which we come to have fellowship with Jesus Christ in these excellent privileges; and this I shall do briefly in the following positions.

Position 1.

First, No man hath fellowship with Christ in any special saving privilege by nature, howsoever it be cultivated or improved; but only by faith uniting him to the Lord Jesus Christ; It is not the privilege of our first, but second birth. * This is plain from John i. 12, 13. " But to as many as received him, to them gave he power " to become the sons of God, even as many as believe on his name, " who are born not of flesh, nor of blood, nor of the will of man, " but of God." We are by nature children of wrath, Eph. ii. 3. we have fellowship with Satan in sin and misery: the wild branch hath no communication of the sweetness and fatness of a more noble and excellent root until it be ingrafted upon it, and have immediate union and coalition with it, John xv. 1, 2.

Position 2.

Believers themselves have not an equal share one with another, in all the benefits and privileges of their union with Christ, but in some there is an equality, and in others an inequality; according to the measure and gift of Christ, to every one.

In justification they are all equal: the weak and the strong be-

---

* The truly faithful only are members of Christ, not as they are men, but as they are Christians; not by their first, but second birth. *Polan. Syntag. Book* 6. *chap.* 35.

liever are alike justified, because it is one and the same perfect righteousness of Christ, which is applied to the one and to the other, so that there are no different degrees of justification, but all that believe are justified from all things, Acts xiii. 39. and "there "is no condemnation to them that are in Christ Jesus," Rom. viii. 1. be they never so weak in faith, or defective in degrees of grace. But there is apparent difference in the measures of their sanctification, some are strong men, and others are babes in Christ, 1 Cor. iii. 1. The faith of some flourishes and grows exceedingly, 2 Thes. i. 3. the things that are in others are ready to die, Rev. iii. 2. It is a plain case, that there is great variety found in the degrees of grace, and comfort among them that are jointly interested in Christ, and equally justified by him.

Position 3.

The saints have not fellowship and communion with Christ, in the fore-mentioned benefits and privileges by one and the same medium, but by various mediums and ways, according to the nature of the benefits, in which they participate.

For instance, they have partnership and communion with Christ, as hath been said, in his righteousness, holiness, and glory, but they receive these distinct blessings by divers mediums of communion: we have communion with Christ in his righteousness, by the way of imputation; we partake of his holiness, by the way of infusion; and of his glory in heaven, by the beatifical vision. Our justification is a relative change, our sanctification a real change, our glorification a perfect change, by redemption from all the remains both of sin and misery.

Thus hath the Lord appointed several blessings for believers in Christ, and several channels of conveying them from him to us; by imputed righteousness, we are freed from the guilt of sin: by imparted holiness, we are freed from the dominion of sin, and by our glorification with Christ, we are freed from all the relics and remains both of sin and misery let in by sin upon our natures.

Position 4.

That Jesus Christ imparts to all believers, all the spiritual blessings that he is filled with, and withholds none from any that have union with him, be these blessings never so great, or they that receive them never so weak, mean, and contemptible in outward respects, Gal. iii. 27. "Ye are the children of God by faith in Jesus Christ." The salvation that comes by Jesus Christ is stiled the *common salvation,* Jude 3. and heaven the inheritance of the saints in light, Col. i. 12. "There is neither Greek nor Jew, (saith the apostle, circum- "cision, nor uncircumcision, Barbarian, Scythian, bond nor free, "but Christ is all, and in all," Col. iii. 11. He means, there is no privilege in the one to commend them to God, and no want of any thing in the other to debar them from God; let men have or want outward excellencies, as beauty, honour, riches, nobility, gifts of the mind, sweetness of nature, and all such like ornaments, What is that to God? He looks not at these things, but respects them, and communicates his favour to them as they are in Christ: *He is all, and in all.* The gifts and blessings of the Spirit are given to men as they are in Christ, and without respect to any external differences made in this world among men: hence we find excellent treasures of grace in mean and contemptible persons in the world; poor in the world and rich in faith, and heirs of the kingdom; and as all believers, without difference, receive from Christ, so they are not debarred from any blessing that is in Christ: " All is yours, for ye are Christ's, 1 Cor. iii. ult. With Christ God " freely gives us all things," Rom. viii. 32.

Position 5.

The communion believers have with Christ, in spiritual benefits, is a very great mystery, far above the understandings of natural men. There are no footsteps of this thing in all the works of creation; therefore the apostle calls it " The unsearchable riches of Christ," Eph. iii. 8. ανεξιχνιαςον πλατον τε Χϱιςε: The word signifies, that which hath no footsteps to trace it by: yea, it is so deep a mystery, that the angels themselves stoop down to look into it, 1 Pet. i. 12. " Eye hath not seen, nor ear heard, neither have entered " into the heart of man the things which God hath prepared for " them that love him: but God hath revealed them unto us by his " Spirit," 1 Cor. ii. 9, 10.

Thirdly, and lastly, I shall, in a few particulars, open the dignity and excellency of this fruit of our union with Christ, and shew you, that a greater glory and honour cannot be put upon man, than to be thus in fellowship with Jesus Christ, John xvii. 22. " The " glory which thou gavest me, I have given them, that they may " be one, as we are one:" And therefore, more particularly, let it be considered,

First, With whom we are associated, even the Son of God; with him that is *over all, God blessed for ever.* Our association with angels is an high advancement, for angels and saints are fellow-servants in the same family, Rev. xix. 10. and through Christ we are come to an innumerable company of angels, Heb. xii. 22. But what is all this to our fellowship with Jesus Christ himself, and that in another manner than angels have? For though Christ be to them an head of dominion, yet not an head of vital influences, as he is to his mystical body the church; this therefore is to them a great mystery, which they greatly affect to study and pry into.

Secondly, What we are that are dignified with this title, the *fel-*

lows or *co-partners* with Jesus Christ: not only dust by nature, *(Dust thou art)*, but sinful dust; such wretched sinners, as, by nature, and the sentence of the law, ought to be associated with devils, and partakers with them of the wrath of the Almighty God to all eternity.

Thirdly, The benefits we are partakers of, in and with the Lord Jesus Christ; and, indeed, they are wonderful and astonishing things, so far as they do already appear, but yet we see but little of them comparatively, to what we shall see, 1 John iii. 1, 2. " Now are we the sons of God, and it doth not yet appear what " we shall be, but we know that when he shall appear, we shall " be like him, for we shall see him as he is." O, what will that be! to see him as he is, and to be transformed into his likeness!

Fourthly, The way and manner in which we are brought into this fellowship with Christ; which is yet more admirable. The apostle gives us a strange account of it in 2 Cor. viii. 9. " For you " know the grace of our Lord Jesus Christ, that though he was " rich, yet for your sakes he became poor, that ye through his " poverty might be rich:" he empties himself of his glory, that we might be filled; he is made a curse, that we might enjoy the blessing; he submits to be crowned with thorns, that we might be crowned with glory and honour; he puts himself into the number of worms, Psal. xxii. 6. that we might be made equal to the angels. O, the inconceivable grace of Christ!

Fifthly, The reciprocal nature of that communion which is betwixt Christ and believers; we do not only partake of what is his, but he partakes of what is ours: he hath fellowship with us in all our wants, sorrows, miseries and afflictions; and we have communion with him in his righteousness, grace, sonship and glory: he takes part of our misery, and we take part of his blessedness; our sufferings are his sufferings, Col. i. 24. O, what an honour is it to thee, poor wretch, to whom a great many would not turn aside to ask how thou dost; to have a King, yea, the Prince of all the kings of the earth, to pity, relieve, sympathize, groan and bleed with thee, to sit by thee in all thy troubles, and give thee his cordials; to say thy troubles are my troubles, and thy afflictions are my afflictions: whatever toucheth thee, toucheth me also. O what name shall we give unto such grace as this is!

Sixthly, and lastly, Consider the perpetuity of this privilege: Your fellowship with Christ is interminable, and abides for ever. Christ and the saints shall be glorified together, Rom. viii. 17. while he hath any glory they shall partake with him. It is said indeed, 1 Cor. xv. 24. that there shall be a time when Christ will deliver up the kingdom to his Father; but the meaning is not that

ever he will cease to be the Head of his saints, or they from being
his members: No, the relation never ceases; justification, sanctification and adoption, are everlasting things, and we can never
be divested of them.

Inference 1. Are the saints Christ's fellows? *What honourable
persons then are they! and how should they be esteemed and valued
in the world!* If a king, who is the fountain of honour, do but raise a
man by his favour, and dignify him by bestowing some honourable
title upon him, what respect and observance is presently paid him
by all persons? But what are all the vain and empty titles of
honour, to the glorious and substantial privileges with which believers are dignified, and raised above all other men by Jesus
Christ? He is the Son of God, and they are the sons of God
also: he is the Heir of all things, and they are joint-heirs with
Christ: he reigns in glory, and they shall reign with him: he sits
upon the throne, and they shall sit with him in his throne. O that
this vile world did but know the dignity of believers, they would
never slight, hate, abuse, and persecute them as they do! And
O that believers did but understand their own happiness and privileges by Christ, they would never droop and sink under every small
trouble at that rate they do!

*Inf. 2. How abundantly hath God provided for all the necessities
and wants of believers!* Christ is a storehouse filled with blessings
and mercies, and it is all for them: from him they "receive abun-
"dance of grace, and of the gift of righteousness," Rom. v. 17.
"Of his fulness they all receive grace for grace," John i. 16. All
the fulness of Christ is made over to them for the supply of their
wants: "My God shall supply all your needs, (saith the apostle)
"according to his riches in glory by Jesus Christ," Phil. iv. 19.
If all the riches of God can supply your needs, then they shall be
supplied. Say not, Christ is in the possession of consummate glory,
and I am a poor creature, struggling with many difficulties, and
toiling in the midst of many cares and fears in the world; for care
is taken for all thy wants, and orders given from heaven for their
supply: *My God shall supply all your need.* O say with a melting
heart, I have a full Christ, and he is filled for me: I have his
pure and perfect righteousness to justify me, his holiness to sanctify
me, his wisdom to guide me, his comforts to refresh me, his power
to protect me, and his all-sufficiency to supply me. O be cheerful, be thankful, you have all your hearts can wish; and yet be
humble; it is all from free-grace to empty and unworthy creatures.

*Inf. 3. How absurd, disingenuous, and unworthy of a Christian,
is it to deny, or withhold from Christ any thing he hath, or by which
he may be served or honoured?* Doth Christ communicate all he hath
to you, and can you withhold any thing from Christ? On Christ's

part it is not *mine*, and *thine*, but *ours*, or *mine* and *yours;* John xx. 17. " I ascend to my Father, and your Father ; to my God, " and your God." But O this cursed idol *self!* which appropriates all to its own designs and uses. How liberal is Christ ! and how penurious are we to him ! Some will not part with their credit for Christ, when yet Christ abased himself unspeakably for them. Some will not part with a drop of blood for Christ, when Christ spent the whole treasure of his blood freely for us; yea, how loth are we to part with a shilling for Christ, to relieve him in his distressed members, when as yet " we know the grace of our Lord " Jesus Christ, that though he was rich, yet for our sakes he be- " came poor, that we through his poverty might be rich !" O ungrateful return ! O base and disingenuous spirits !" The things Christ gives us are great, and the things we deny to him are small : he parts with the greatest, and yet is denied the least. The things he communicates to us are none of ours, we have no right nor title by nature, or any desert of ours to them ; the things we deny or grudge to Christ are by all titles his own, and he hath the fullest and most unquestionable title to them all ; what he gives to us, he gives to them that never deserved it ; what we withhold from him, we withhold from one that hath deserved that, and infinitely more from us than we have or are.

He interested you freely in all his riches when you were enemies ; you stand upon trifles with him, and yet call him your best and dearest friend : he gave himself and all he hath to you, when you could claim nothing from him ; you deny to part with these things to Christ, who may not only claim them upon the highest title, his own sovereignty, and absolute property, but by your own act, who profess to have given all in covenant to him : what he gives you return no profit to him ; but what you give or part with for him is your greatest advantage. O that the consideration of these things might shame and humble your souls !

Inf. 4. *Then certainly no man is, or can be supposed to be a loser by conversion, seeing from that day, whatever Christ is or hath becomes his.*

O what an inheritance are men possessed of by their new birth ! Some men cry out, Religion will undo you ; but with what eyes do these men see ? Surely, you could never so reckon, except your souls were so incarnated, as to reckon pardon, peace, adoption, holiness, and heaven, for nothing; that invisibles are nonentities, and temporals the only realities. It is true, the converted soul may lose his estate, his liberty, yea, his life for Christ ; but what then ? Are they losers that exchange brass for gold ? or part with their present comforts for an hundred-fold advantage ? Mark x. 29. So that none need be frightened at religion, for the losses that attend it, whilst Christ and heaven are gained by it: they that count religion their loss have their portion in this life.

Inf. 5. How securely is the saints inheritance settled upon them, seeing they are in common with Jesus Christ? Christ and his saints are joint-heirs, and the inheritance cannot be alienated but by his consent; he must lose his interest, if you lose yours. Indeed Adam's inheritance was by a single title, and moreover, it was in his own hand, and so he might, (as indeed he soon did) divest himself and his posterity of it ; but it is not so betwixt Christ and believers ; we are secured in our inheritance by Christ our co-heir, who will never alienate it: and therefore it was truly observed by the father, *Fœlicior Job in sterquilinio, quam Adamus in paradiso:* Job was happier upon the dunghill, than Adam was in paradise. The covenant of grace is certainly the best tenure ; as it hath the best mercies, so it gives the fullest security to enjoy them.

Inf. 6. How rich and full is Jesus Christ, who communicates abundantly to all the saints, and yet hath infinitely still more in himself, than hath ever been received by them all.

Take all the | faith of Abraham, all the meekness of Moses, all the patience of Job, all the wisdom of Solomon, all the zeal of David, all the industry of Paul, and all the tender-heartedness of Josiah ; add to this, all the grace that is poured, (though in lesser meaure,) into all the elect vessels in the world, yet still it is far short of that which remains in Christ; " He is anointed with the " oil of gladness above his fellows :" And in all things he hath, " and must ever have the pre-eminence. There are many thousand stars glittering above your heads, and one star differs from another star in glory, yet there is more light and glory in one sun, than in many thousand stars. Grace beautifies the children of men exceedingly, but still that is true of Christ, Psal. xlv. 2. " Thou art fairer than the children of men, grace is poured into " thy lips." For all grace is secondarily, and derivatively in the saints, but it is primitively and originally in Christ, John v. 16. Grace is imperfect and defective in them, but in him it is in its most absolute perfection and fulness, Col. i. 19. In the saints it is mixed with abundance of corruption, but in Christ it is altogether unmixed, and exclusive of its opposite, Heb. vii. 26. So that as the Heathen said of moral virtue, I may much more say of Christ, That were he to be seen with mortal eyes, he would compel love and admiration from all men, for " he is altogether lovely," Cant. v. 16.

Inf. 7. What delight and singular advantage must needs be in the communion of the saints, who have communion with Jesus Christ in all his graces and benefits.

" That which we have seen and heard, declare we unto you,

" that ye also may have fellowship with us: And truly our fel-
" lowship is with the Father, and with his Son Jesus Christ,"
1 John i. 3.   O it is sweet to have fellowship with those that have
fellowship with God in Jesus Christ.   Christ hath communicated
to the saints varieties of graces, in different measures and degrees;
and as they all receive from Christ the fountain, so it is sweet and
most delightful to be improving themselves by spiritual communion
one with another: Yea, for that end one is furnished with one
grace more eminently than another, that the weak may be assisted
by the strong, as a *modern divine* * well observes.   Athanasius was
prudent and active, Basil of an heavenly, sweet temper, Chrysostom laborious, without affectation, Ambrose resolved and grave,
Luther courageous, and Calvin acute and judicious.   Thus every
one hath his proper gift from Christ, the fountain of gifts and
graces, 1 Cor. vii. 7.   One hath quickness of parts, another soli-
dity of judgment, but not ready and presential; one is zealous, but
ungrounded; another well principled, but timorous; one is wary
and prudent; another open and plain; one is trembling and melting ; another cheerful and joyous ; one must impart his light,
another his heat: The *eye*, the knowing man, cannot say to the
hand, the active man, I have no need of thee.   And O how sweet
would it be, if gifts, graces, and experiences were frequently and
humbly imparted: But idle notions, earthly mindedness, self-inte-
rests, and want of more communion with Christ, have almost
destroyed the comfort of Christian fellowship every where in the
world.

Inf. 8. *In a word, those only have ground to claim interest in
Christ, who do really participate of his graces, and in whom are
found the effects and fruits of their union and communion with him.*

If you have interest in Christ, you have communion in his graces
and benefits; and if you have such communion, it will appear in
your maintaining daily *actual communion with God* in duties;
whereby will be produced,

First, The increase of your sanctification, by fresh-participations
from the fountain; as *cloth* which is often dipt into the *vat* receives
the deeper dye, and livelier tincture; so will your souls by assiduous
communion with God.   It will also be discerned,

Secondly, In your deeper humiliation, and spiritual sense of your
own vileness: The more any man partakes of God, and is acquainted with him, and assimilated to him, the more base and vile in his
own sight he still grows, Job xlii. 5, 6. Isa. vi. 5.

Thirdly, It will appear in your more vehement longings after the
full enjoyment of God in heaven, 1 Pet. i. 8. and Rom. viii. 23.

---

* Mr. Torshel.

You that have the first fruits will groan within yourselves after the full harvest, and satisfying fruition; you will not be so taken with things below, as to be content with the best lot on earth for your everlasting portion. O! if these communicated drops be so sweet, what is there in Christ the fountain?

And thus I have opened the method of grace in bringing home Christ and his benefits to God's elect by union, in order to communion with him.

Thanks be to God for Jesus Christ.

SERMON IX.

Containing the first general Use of Exhortation, inviting all Men to apply JESUS CHRIST.

MATTH. xi. 28.

Come unto me, all ye that labour, and are heavy laden, and I will give you rest.

THE *impetration* of our redemption by Jesus Christ, being finished in the first part, and the way and means by which Christ is *applied* to sinners in the foregoing part of this *treatise;* I am now orderly come to the general *use* of the whole; which in the first place shall be by way of *exhortation,* to invite and persuade all men to come to Christ; who, in all the former sermons, had been represented in his *garments of salvation,* red in his apparel, prepared and offered to sinners as their all-sufficient and only remedy: And in the following sermons, will be represented in his *perfumed garments* coming out of his *ivory palaces,* Psalm xlv. 8. to allure and draw all men unto him.

For a general head to this use, which will be large, I have chosen this scripture, " Come unto me all ye that labour, and are " heavy laden, and I will give you rest."

These words are the voice of our Lord Jesus Christ himself, in which there is a vital, ravishing sound: It is your mercy to have such a joyful sound in your ears this day. And in them I will consider their *dependence, parts,* and *scope.*

As to their dependence, it is manifest they have an immediate relation to the foregoing verse, wherein Christ opens his commission, and declares the fulness of this authority and saving power, and the impossibility of coming to God any other way. " All " things are delivered to me of my Father, and no man knoweth " the Son but the Father: Neither knoweth any man the Father

" save the Son, and he to whomsoever the Son will reveal him," ver. 27.

The 28th verse is brought in proleptically to obviate the discouragements of any poor, convinced, and humbled soul, who might thus object: Lord, I am fully satisfied of the fulness of thy saving power, but greatly doubt whether ever I shall have the benefit thereof; for I see so much sin and guilt in myself, so great vileness and utter unworthiness, that I am over weighed, and even sink under the burden of it: My soul is discouraged because of sin. This objection is prevented in the words of my text, " Come unto " me, all ye that labour, and are heavy laden," q. d. Let not the sense of your sin and misery drive you from your only remedy : Be your sins never so many, and the sense and burden of them never so heavy, yet, for all that, Come unto me : You are the persons whom I invite and call.   I came not to call the righteous, but sinners to repentance.

In the words, three things are especially remarkable.

1. The soul's spiritual distress and burthen: Weary and heavy laden.

2. Its invitation to Christ under that burthen: Come unto me.

3. Its encouragement to that great duty: I will give you rest.

First, The soul's spiritual distress and burthen expressed in two very emphatical words *, οι κοπιωντες και πεφορτισμενοι " Ye that la- " bour and are heavy laden."   The word which we translate labour, signifies a labouring even to faintness and tiring, to the consumption and waste of the spirits; and the other word signifies such a pressure by a burthen that is too heavy to be borne, that we do even sink down under it.

There is some difference among expositors about the quality of this burthen.   Chrysostom, and some others after him, expound it of the burthen of the legal rites and ceremonies, which was a heavy burthen indeed, such as neither they, nor their fathers could bear.   Under the task and burthen of these legal observances, they did sweat and toil to obtain a righteousness to justify them before God, and all in vain : and this is a pious sense : But others expound it of the burthen of sin in general; the corruption of na-

---

* Οι κοπιωντες, i. e. They who labour even to fainting and tiring, for this Greek word το κοπιαν differs by this emphasis from the word πονειν, which signifies only in general to labour. Piscator on the place, explains it thus, Ye who feel the burden of your sins, and yet do not sink under the weight thereof. Chrysostom expounds it of those who are burdened with the legal rites and ceremonies; but we understand it in general, of all those who being pressed with the burden of their sins, and the sense of the malignity of their corrupt natures, do strive with all their might to throw off this depravity, and to obtain righteousness. Musculus on the place.

ture, and evils of practice, which souls are convinced have brought them under the curse, and will bring them to hell, and therefore labour and strive, all that in them lies, by repentance and reformation, to clear themselves from it; but all in vain, whilst they strive in their own strength. Such are they that are here called to come to Christ, which is the second thing; namely,

Secondly, The invitation of burthened souls to Christ: " Come " unto me all ye that labour, and are heavy laden : Come unto " me," i. e. believe in me, lean and rest your burthened souls upon me. I am able to ease all your burthens; in me are that righteousness and peace which you seek in vain in all the legal rites and ceremonies; or in your repentance, reformations, and duties; but it will give you no ease, it will be no benefit to you, except you come unto me. Faith is often expressed under this notion, see John vi. 37. and John vii. 37. and it is to be further noted, that [*all*] burthened souls are invited to come, " All ye that labour." Whatever your sin or guilt have been, whatever your fears or discouragements are, yet come, i. e. believe in me.

Thirdly, Here is the encouragement Christ gives to this duty, *And I will give you rest :* αναπαυσω μας. * I will refresh you, I will give you rest from your labour, your consciences shall be pacified, your hearts at rest and quiet in that pardon, peace and favour of God which I will procure for you by my death. But here it must be heedfully noted, that this promise of rest in Christ is not made to men simply as they are sinners, nor yet as they are burthened and heavy laden sinners, but as they come to Christ, i. e. as they are believers †. For let a man break his heart for sin, let him weep out his eyes, let him mourn as a dove, and shed as many tears for sin (if it were possible) as ever there fell drops of rain upon the ground, yet if he come not to Christ by faith, his repentance shall not save him, nor all his sorrows bring him to true rest. Hence note,

Doct. 1. *That some souls are heavy laden with the burthensome sense of sin.*

Doct. 2. *That all burthened souls are solemnly invited to come to Christ.*

Doct. 3. *That there is rest in Christ for all that come to him under the heavy burthen of sin.*

---

* Why doth thou seek that where thou canst not find it? I am he only that can help thee. *Mus. on the place.*

† The objects of the invitation are sinners, as such, to encourage and warrant them to believe. *Editor.*

Doct. 1. *Some souls are heavy laden with the burthensome sense of sin.*

I do not say all are so, for " fools make a mock at sin," Prov. xiv. 9. It is so far from being burthensome to some, that it is a *sport* to them, Prov. x. 23. But when a man's eyes are opened to see the evil that is in sin, and the eternal misery that follows it, (sin and hell being linked together with such strong chains as nothing but the blood of Christ can loose) then no burden is like that of sin: " A wounded conscience who can bear?" Prov. xviii. 14. For let us but consider the efficacy that the law of God hath upon the consciences of men, when it comes in the spirtuality and power of it, to convince and humble the soul of a sinner. For then,

First, *The memory of sin long since committed, is refreshed and revived, as if it had been but yesterday :* There are fresh recognitions of sin long since acted and forgotten, as if they had never been: What was done in our youth is fetched back *What inward troubles for sin are.* again, and by a new impression of fear and horror set home upon the trembling conscience, Job xiii. 26. " Thou writest bitter things " against me, and makest me to possess the sins of my youth." Conscience can call back the days that are past, and draw up a new charge upon the score of old sins, Gen. xlii. 21. All that ever we did is recorded and entered into the book of conscience, and now is the time to open that book, when the Lord will convince and awaken sinners. We read in Job xiv. 17. of sealing up iniquities in a bag, which is an allusion to the *Clerk of the assizes*, that takes all the indictments that are made against persons at the *assizes*, and seals them up in a bag, in order to a trial. This is the first office and work of conscience; upon which

The *second*, namely, its *accusations*, do depend. These accusations of conscience are terrible things ; who can stand before them? They are full, they are clear, and all of them referring to the approaching judgment of the great and terrible God.

Conscience dives into all sins *, secret as well as open, and into all the circumstances and aggravations of sin, as being committed against light, against mercy, against the strivings, warnings, and regrets of conscience. So that we may say of the efficacy of conscience, as it is said, Psal. xix. 6. of the influence of the *sun*, " nothing is hid from the heat and power thereof." " Come (saith the woman of Samaria) see a man that hath told me all that

---

* This is the first punishment of sin, that no guilty person can be acquitted in his own conscience. *Juv. lib.* 13. *l.* 2.

" ever I did," John iv. 29.   Christ convinced her but of one sin
by his discourse, but conscience, by that one, fetched in, and
charged all the rest upon her.   And as the accusations of conscience are full, so they are clear and undeniable.   A man becomes
self-convinced, and there remains no shift, excuse, or plea, to defend himself.   A thousand witnesses cannot prove any point more
clearly than one testimony of conscience doth.   Mat. xxii. 12.
" The man was speechless, a mute; muzzled (as the word signifies *) by the clear testimony of his own conscience.   These accusations are the second work of conscience, and they make way for
the third, namely,

   Thirdly, The *sentence* and *condemnation* of conscience: And truly
this is an insupportable burthen: The condemnation of conscience
is nothing else but its application of the condemning sentence of
the law to a man's person: The law curseth every one that trans-
gresseth it, Gal. iii. 10.   Conscience applies this curse to the guilty
sinner.   So that it sentences the sinner in God's name and authority, from whence there is no appeal: The voice of conscience is
the voice of God, and what it pronounces in God's name and authority, he will confirm and ratify, 1 John iii. 20.   " If our hearts,
" (*i. e.*) our consciences condemn us, God is greater than our
" hearts, and knoweth all things."   This is that torment which
no man can endure.   See the effects of it in Cain, in Judas,
and in Spira; it is a real foretaste of hell-torments: This is that
worm that never dies, Mark ix. 44.   For look, as a worm in the
body is bred of the corruption that is there, so the accusations and
condemnations of conscience are bred in the soul by the corruption
and guilt that are there.   As the worm in the body preys and bites
upon the tender, sensible, inward parts, so doth conscience touch
the very quick.   This is the third effect, or work, to sentence and
condemn; and this also makes way for a fourth, namely,

   Fourthly, To *upbraid and reproach the sinner under his misery:*
and this makes a man a very *terror to himself:* To be pitied in
misery is some relief, but to be upbraided and reproached, double
our affliction.   You know it was one of the aggravations of Christ's
sufferings to be reproached by the tongues of his enemies, whilst
he hanged in torments upon the cursed tree; but all the scoffs and
reproaches, the bitter jeers and *sarcasms* in the world, are nothing
to those of a man's own conscience, which will cut to the very
bone.

   O! when a man's conscience shall say to him in a day of trouble,
as Reuben to his afflicted brethren, Gen. xliii. 22.   " Spake I not
" unto you, saying, do not sin against the child, and ye would not

---

* Ο δε εφιμωϑη, *et ille capistratus est.*

" hear; therefore behold also his blood is required." So conscience, did I not warn you, threaten you, persuade you in time
against these evils, but you would not hearken to me, therefore
behold now you must suffer to all eternity for it. The wrath of
God is kindled against thy soul for it: This is the fruit of thy own
wilful madness and obstinacy. Now thou shalt know the price
of sinning against God, against light and conscience. O, this is
terrible! Every bite of conscience makes a poor soul to startle, and
in a terrible fright to cry, O the worm! O, the bitter foretaste of
hell! A wounded spirit who can bear?

This is a fourth wound of conscience, and it makes way for a
fifth; for here it is as the pouring out of the vials, and the sounding of those woe-trumpets in Revelations; one woe is past, and
another cometh. After all these deadly blows of conscience upon
the very heart of a sinner, comes another as dreadful as any that
is yet named; and that is,

Fifthly, The fearful expectation of wrath to come, which it begets in the soul of a guilty sinner: Of this you read, Heb. x. 27.
" A fearful looking for of judgment, and fiery indignation." And
this makes the stoutest sinner faint and sink under the burthen of
sin. For the tongue of man cannot declare what it is to lie down
and rise with those fearful expectations. The case of such sinners is
somewhat like that which is described in Deut. xxviii. 65, 66, 67.
" The Lord shall give thee a trembling heart, and failing of eyes,
" and sorrow of mind. And thy life shall hang in doubt before
" thee, and thou shalt fear day and night, and shall have no assu-
" rance of thy life. In the morning thou shalt say, would to God
" it were even: And at even thou shalt say, would to God it were
" morning: For the fear of thine heart, wherewith thou shalt
" fear," &c. Only in this it differs, in this scripture you have the
terror of those described, whose temporal life hangs in doubtful
suspense, but in the persons I am speaking of, it is a trembling
under the apprehensions and expectations of the vengeance of
eternal fire.

Believe it, friends, words cannot express what those poor creatures feel, that lie down, and rise up under these fears, and frights
of conscience. Lord, what will become of me! I am free among
the dead, yea, among the damned. I hang by the frail thread of
a momentary life, which will, and must, break shortly, and may
break the next moment, over the everlasting burnings: No pleasant bread is to be eaten in these days, but what is like the bread
of condemned men.

And thus you see what the burden of sin is, when God makes
it to bear upon the consciences of men, no burden of affliction is

like it : losses of dearest relations, sorrows for an only son, are not so pungent and penetrating as these : For,

First, No creature-enjoyment is pleasant under these inward troubles : In other troubles they may signify something to a man's relief; but here they are nothing; the wound is too deep to be healed by any thing but the blood of Jesus Christ; conscience requires as much to satisfy it, as God requires to satisfy him. When God is at peace with thee, (saith conscience) then will I be at peace with thee too; but, till then, expect no rest nor peace from me. All the pleasures and diversions in the world shall never stop my mouth : go where thou wilt, I will follow thee like thy shadow : be thy portion in the world as sweet as it will, I will drop in gall and wormwood into thy cup, that thou shalt taste no sweetness in any thing, till thou hast got thy pardon.

These inward troubles for sin alienate the mind from all former pleasures and delights; there is no more taste or savour in them, than in the white of an egg. Music is out of tune; all instruments jar and groan. Ornaments have no beauty; what heart hath a poor creature to deck that body, in which dwells such a miserable soul! to feed and pamper that carcase that hath been the soul's inducement to, and instrument in sin, and must be its companion in everlasting misery!

Secondly, These inward troubles for sin put a dread into death, beyond whatever the soul saw in it before. Now it looks like the *King of terrors* indeed. You read in Heb. ii. 15. of some that through fear of death are all their life long subject to bondage. O what a lively comment is a soul in this case able to make upon such a text! They would not scare at the pale horse, nor at him that sits on him, though his name be called *Death,* if it were not for what follows him, Rev. vi. 8. but when they consider that hell follows, they tremble at the very name or thoughts of death.

Thirdly, Such is the nature of these inward troubles of spirit, that they swallow up the sense of all outward troubles. Alas! these are all lost in the deeps of soul-sorrows, as the little rivulets are in the vast sea; he that is wounded at the heart will not cry *Oh,* at the bite of the smallest insect. And surely no greater is the proportion betwixt outward and inward sorrows. A small matter formerly would discompose a man, and put him into a fret; now ten thousand outward troubles are lighter than a feather : For, saith he, " why doth the living man complain?" Am I yet on this side of eternal burnings! O let me not complain then whatever my condition be. Have I losses in the world, or pains upon my body? Alas! these are not to be named with the loss of God, and the feeling of his wrath and indignation for evermore. Thus you see what troubles, inward troubles for sin be.

Secondly, If you ask, in the second place, how it comes to pass that any soul is supported under such strong troubles of spirit, that all that feel them do not sink under them; *How souls are supported under such troubles.* that all that go down into these deep waters of sorrow, are not drowned in them? The answer is,

First, Though this be a very sad time with the soul (much like that of Adam, betwixt the breach of the first covenant, and the first promise of Christ made to him) yet the souls that are thus heavy laden, do not sink, because God hath a most tender care over them, and regard to them; underneath them are the everlasting arms, and thence it is they sink not: were they left to grapple with these troubles in their own strength, they could never stand. But God takes care of these mourners, that their spirits do not fail before him, and the souls that he hath made; I mean those of his elect, whom he is this way preparing for, and bringing unto Christ.

Secondly, The Lord is pleased to nourish still some hope in the soul under the greatest fears and troubles of spirit. Though it have no comfort or joy, yet it hath some *hope,* and that keeps up the heart. The afflicted soul doth, in this case, as the afflicted church, Lam. iii. 29. " He putteth his mouth in the dust, if yet " there may be hope:" He saith, " It is good for a man to hope, " and quietly to wait for the salvation of God." There are usually some glimmerings or dawnings of mercy through Christ, in the midnight darkness of inward troubles; *non dantur puræ tenabræ.* In hell, indeed, there is no hope to enlighten the darkness, but it is not so upon earth.

Thirdly, The experiences of others, who have been in the same deeps of trouble, are also of great use to keep up the soul above water. The experience of another is of great use to prop up a desponding mind, whilst as yet it hath none of its own; and, indeed, for the support of souls in such cases, they were recorded. 1 Tim. i. 16. " For this cause I obtained mercy, that in me first " Jesus Christ might shew forth all long-suffering, for a pattern " to them which should hereafter believe on him to life everlast- " ing." For an encouraging * *Pattern,* an eminent precedent to all poor sinners that were to come after him, that none might absolutely despair of finding mercy through Christ. You know if a man be taken sick, and none can tell what the disease is, none can

---

* The word Ὑποτυπωσις as well as τυπος (which the word rendered **Pattern** in 1 Tim. i. 16.) signifies the first draught of a picture; it is here taken for example, that men might see what they might expect from God : That grace much more abounds, and is more powerful than sin, and that no believer may be diffident of the forgiveness provided for him. *Pol. Synops. on the place.*

say that ever they heard of such a disease before, it is exceeding frightful; but if one and another, it may be twenty, come to the sick man's bed-side, and tell him, sir, be not afraid, I have been in the very same case that you now are in, and so have many more, and all did well at last; why this is half a cure to the sick man. So it is here a great support to hear the experiences of other saints.

Fourthly, As the experiences of others support the soul under these burdens, so the riches of free grace through Jesus Christ uphold it. It is rich and abundant, Psal. cxxx. 7, 8. plenteous redemption; and it is free, and to the worst of sinners, Isa. i. 18. And under these troubles it finds itself in the way and proper method of mercy, for so my text (a text that hath upheld many thousand drooping hearts) states it. All this gives hope and encouragement under trouble.

Fifthly, and *lastly,* Though the state of the soul be sad and sinking, yet Jesus Christ usually makes haste in the extremity of trouble to relieve it by sweet and seasonable discoveries of his grace; *cum duplicantur lateris, venit* Moses *, in the mount of the Lord it shall be seen. It is with Christ as it was with Joseph, whose bowels yearned towards his brethren, and he was in pain till he had told them, " I am Joseph your brother." This is sweetly exhibited to us in that excellent parable of the prodigal, Luke xv. when his father saw him, being yet a great way off, he ran and fell upon his neck, and kissed him. Mercy runs nimbly to help, when souls are ready to fall under the pressure of sin. And thus you see both how they are burdened, and how upheld under the burden.

Why doth God make the burden of sin lie so heavy upon the souls of some sinners?

Thirdly, If it be enquired, in the last place, why God makes the burden of sin press so heavy upon the hearts of poor sinners? It is answered,

First, He doth it to divorce their hearts from sin, by giving them an experimental taste of the bitternesss and evil that is in sin. Men's hearts are naturally glued with delight to their sinful courses; all the persuasions and arguments in the world are too weak to separate them from their beloved lusts. The morsels of sin go down smoothly and sweetly, they roll them with much delectation under their tongues, and it is but need that such bitter potions as these should be administered " to make their " stomachs rise against sin," as that † word used by the apostle in 2 Cor. vii. 11. signifies, *in that ye sorrowed after a godly sort, what indignation it wrought?* It notes the rising of the stomach with rage, a being angry even unto sickness; and this is the way,

---

* When the tale of bricks is doubled, Moses arrives.

† Αγαναχτησις, *indignatio, stomachatio.* Leigh's Critica, in verb.

the best and most effectual way to separate the soul of a sinner from
his lusts; for, in these troubles, conscience saith, as it is in Jer. iv.
18. " Thy way and thy doings have procured these things unto
" thee; this is thy wickedness, because it is great, because it
" reacheth unto thy heart."

Secondly, The Lord doth this to make Jesus Christ most welcome
and desirable to the soul. Christ is not *sweet* till sin be made *bitter*
to us. Matth. ix. 12. " They that be whole need not a physician,
" but they that are sick." If once God wounds the heart of a
sinner, with the stinging sense of sin, then nothing in the world
is so precious, so necessary, so vehemently desired and panted for
as Jesus Christ! O that I had Christ, if I did go in rags, if I did
feed upon no other food all my days, but the bread and water of
affliction! This is the language of a soul filled with the sense of
the evil of sin.

Thirdly, The Lord doth this to advance the riches of his free
grace in the eyes of sinners. Grace never appears grace till sin appear to be sin. The deeper our sense of the evil of sin is, the
deeper our apprehensions of the free grace of God in Christ will be.
The louder our *groans* have been under the burden of sin, the
louder will our *acclamations* and praises be for our salvation from it
by Jesus Christ. " To me (saith Paul) the chiefest of sinners, was
" this grace given," 1 Tim. i. 15. Never doth the grace of a prince
so melt the heart of a traitor, as when trial, sentence, and all preparations for his execution have passed, before his unexpected pardon comes.

Fourthly, The Lord doth this to prevent relapses into sin: " In
" that ye sorrowed after a godly sort, what carefulness it wrought!"
2 Cor. ii. 7. The burnt child dreads the fire, the bird that is delivered out of the *talons* of the *hawk*, trembles afterwards at
the noise of his bells. " After such a deliverance as this, should we
" again break thy commandments?" Ezra ix. 13, 14. Ask a
poor penitent soul, that hath been in the deeps of sorrow for sin,
Will you return to your former course of sin again? And it sounds
in his ears, as if you should ask him, Will you run into the fire?
Will you go to the rack again? O no, it hath cost him dear already *.

Fifthly, Lastly, This the Lord doth, to make them both skilful
and compassionate in relieving others that are under like inward
troubles. None can speak so judiciously, so pertinently, so feelingly to another's case, as he that hath been in the same case himself † ;

---

* *Nolo tanti emere pœnitentiam.* i. e. I will not purchase repentance at so dear a
rate.

† *Haud ignara mali, miseris succurere disco.* Virg.
      Like you, an alien in a land unknown,
      I learn to pity woes, so like mine own. *Dryden.*

this furnishes them with the tongue of the learned, to speak a word
in season to the weary soul; by this means they are able to " com-
" fort others with the same comforts wherewith they themselves
" have been comforted of God," 2 Cor. i. 4.

Thus you have had a brief account, what the burden of sin is,
how souls are supported under that burden, and why the Lord
causes sin to lie so heavy upon the souls of some sinners. The improvement of all will be in a double use, viz.

Of information and direction.

First use for information.

Inference 1. Is there such a load and burden in sin? *What then
was the burden that our Lord Jesus Christ felt and bare for us,
upon whom the whole weight of all the sins of all God's elect lay!*
Isa. liii. 6. " He hath made the iniquities of us all to meet on him."
Our burden is heavy, but nothing to Christ's. O there is a vast
difference betwixt that which Christ bare, and *t*hat which we bear.
We feel but the single weight of our own sins; Christ felt the
whole weight of all our sins. You do not feel the whole weight
that is in any one sin; alas, it would sink you, if God should let
it bear in all its aggravations and effects upon you. Psal. cxxx. 2,
3. " If thou, Lord, shouldst mark iniquity, O Lord, who shall
" stand!" You would sink presently, you can no more stand under
it, than under the weight of a mighty mountain. But Christ
bare all the burden upon himself; his understanding was deep and
large; he knew the extent of its evil, which we do not: we have
many reliefs and helps under our burden, he had none; we have
friends to counsel, comfort, and pity us; all his friends and fami-
liars forsook him, and fled in the day of his trouble: we have
comforts from heaven, he had frowns from heaven: " My
" God, my God, (saith he in that doleful day) why hast thou forsaken me?" There is no comparison betwixt our load and
Christ's.

Inf. 2. If there be such a burden in sin, *then certainly sinners will
pay dear for all the pleasure they find in sin in the days of their
vanity.* " What * one saith of crafty counsels, we may say of all
‘ sins; though they seem pleasant in their first appearance, they
" would be found sad in the event:" they are honey in the mouth,
but the gall of asps in the belly; they tickle the fancy, but rend
the conscience. O sinner, thy mirth will certainly be turned into
mourning, as sure as thou livest; that vain and frothy breast of
thine shall be wounded; thou shalt feel the sting and pain, as well
as relish the sweet and pleasure of sin. O that thou wouldst but

---

* *Consilia callida prima specie læta; tractatu dura; eventu tristia.* Livy.
† Prov. xx. 7. Ibid. xxiii. 31, 32. Job xx. 12, 13, 14. James i. 15. Rom. vi. 21.

give thyself the leisure seriously to ponder those * scriptures in the margin; methinks they should have the same effect that the hand-writing upon the plaister of the wall had upon that jovial king in the height of a frolic, Daniel v. 5. Reason thus with thine own heart, and thou wilt find the conclusion unavoidable ; either I shall repent for sin, or I shall not : If I shall not, then must I howl under the wrath of God for sin, in the lowest hell for evermore. If I shall, then by what I have now read of the throbs and wounds of conscience, I see what this heart of mine, this vain heart of mine, must feel in this world. O how much wiser was the choice that Moses made, Heb. xi. 25. the worst of sufferings rather than the best of sin, the pleasures of sin, which are but for a season !

Inf. 3. Is there such a burden in sin, *then the most tender compassion is a debt due to souls afflicted and heavy laden with sin.* Their condition cries for pity, whatever their tongues do; they seem to call upon you, as Job upon his friends; " Have pity, have pity " upon me, O ye my friends, for the hand of God hath touched " me, Job xix. 21. And O let all that have felt the wounds and anguish of an afflicted conscience themselves, learn from their own experience tenderly to pity and help others. Gal. vi. 1. " You " that are spiritual, restore († or set him in joint again) in the spirit " of meekness, considering thyself."

Israel was commanded to be kind to strangers, for, saith God, you know the heart of a stranger. And surely if any case in the world require help, pity, and all compassionate tenderness, this doth ; and yet how do some slight spiritual troubles upon others ? Parents slight them in their own children, masters in their servants ; the more brutish and wicked they ! O had you but felt yourselves what they feel, you would never treat them as you do. But let this comfort such poor creatures, Christ hath felt them, and will pity and help them ; yea, he therefore would feel them himself, that he might have compassion upon you. If men will not, God will pity you ; if men be so cruel to persecute him whom God hath smitten, God will be so kind to pour balm into the wounds that sin hath made : if they pull away the shoulder from you, and will not be concerned about your troubles, except it be to aggravate them, God will not serve you so : but certainly you that have passed through the same difficulties, you cannot be without compassion to them that are now grappling with them.

Inf. 4. *How inexpressibly dreadful is the state of the damned, who must bear the burden of all their sins upon themselves, without relief, or hope of deliverance!* Mark ix. 44. " where their worm " dieth not, and the fire is not quenched."

---

* Prov. xx. 7. Ibid. xxiii. 31, 32. Job xx. 12, 13, 14. James i. 15. Rom. vi. 21.

† Καταρτίζετε, *luxata membra in suum locum restituere.*

O ! If sin upon the soul that is coming to Christ for deliverance, be so burdensome, what is it upon the soul that is shut out from Christ, and all hopes of deliverance for ever ! For, do but ponder these differences betwixt these two burdens.

First, No soul is so capacious now, to take in the fulness of the evil and misery of sin, as they are who are gone down to the place of torments. Even as the joys of God's face above are as much unknown to them that have the fore-tastes and first fruits of them here by faith, so the misery of the damned is much unknown, even to them that have in their consciences now, the bitterest taste and sense of sin in this world : as we have the visions of heaven, so we have the visions of hell also, but darkly through a glass.

Secondly, No burden of sin presseth so continually upon the soul here as it doth there. Afflicted souls, on earth, have intermissions, and breathing times ; but in hell there are no lucid intervals, the wrath of God there is still flowing ; it is in *fluxu continuo,* Isa. xxx. 33. a stream of brimstone.

Thirdly, No burden of sin lies upon any of God's elect so long as on the damned, who do, and must bear it : our troubles about sin are but short, though they should run parallel with the line of life ; but the troubles of the damned are parallel with the endless line of eternity.

Fourthly, Under these troubles, the soul hath hope, but there, all hope is cut off : all the gospel is full of hope, it breathes nothing but hope to sinners that are moving Christ-ward under their troubles ; but in hell the pangs of desperation rend their consciences for ever. So that, upon all accounts, the state of the damned is inexpressibly dreadful.

Inf. 5. If the burden of sin be so heavy, how sweet then must the pardon of sin be to a sin-burdened soul! Is it a refreshment to a prisoner to have his chains knocked off? A comfort to a debtor to have his debts paid, and obligations cancelled ? What joy must it then be to a sin-burthened soul, to hear the voice of pardon and peace in his trembling conscience ! Is the light of the morning pleasant to a man after a weary, tiresome night ? the spring of the year pleasant after a hard and tedious winter ? They are so indeed ; but nothing so sweet as the favour, peace, and pardon of God, to a soul that hath been long restless, and anxious, under the terrors and fears of conscience. For, though after pardon and peace a man remembers sin still, yet it is as one that remembers the dangerous pits, and deep waters, from which he hath been wonderfully delivered, and had a narrow escape. O the inconceivable sweetness of a pardon ! Who can read it without tears of joy ? Are we glad when the grinding pain of the stone, or racking fits of the cholic are over ? And shall we not be transported, when the accusations and condemnations of conscience are over? Tongue cannot express what these things are; his joy is something that no words can convey to the understanding of another, that never felt the anguish of sin.

Inf. 6. Lastly, *In how sad a case are those that never felt any burden in sin, that never were kept waking and restless one night for sin?*

There is a *burdened* conscience, and there is a *benumbed* conscience. The first is more *painful*, but the last more *dangerous.* O it is a fearful blow of God upon a man's soul, to strike it senseless and stupid, so that though mountains of guilt lie upon it, it feels no pain or pressure: and this is so much more sad, because it incapacitates the soul for Christ, and is a presage and fore-runner of hell. It would grieve the heart of a man, to see a *delirious person* in the rage and height of a fever, to laugh at those that are weeping for him, call them fools, and telling them he is as well as any of them: much so is the case of many thousand souls; the God of mercy pity them.

Second use for counsel.

The only further use I shall make of this point here, shall be to direct and counsel souls that are weary and heavy laden with the burden of sin, in order to their obtaining true rest and peace. And first,

First counsel.

Satisfy not yourselves in fruitless complaints to men. Many do so, but they are never the nearer. I grant it is lawful in spiritual distresses to complain to men, yea, and it is a great mercy if we have any near us in times of trouble that are judicious, tender and faithful, into whose bosoms we may pour out our troubles; but to rest in this, short of Christ, is no better than a snare of the devil to destroy us. Is there not a god to go to in trouble? The best of men, in the neglect of Christ, are but physicians of no value. Be wise and wary in your choice of Christian friends, to whom you open your complaints; some are not clear themselves in the doctrine of Christ and faith, others are of a dark and troubled spirit, as you are, and will but entangle you more. " As for me (saith Job) is " my complaint to man, and if it were so, why should not my " spirit be troubled?" Job xxi. 4. One hour betwixt Christ and thy soul in secret, will do more to thy true relief than all other counsellors and comforters in the world can do.

Second counsel.

Beware of a false peace, which is more dangerous than your trouble for sin can be. Many men are afraid of their troubles, but I think they have more cause to fear their peace a great deal. There is a twofold peace that ruins most men, peace in sin, and peace with sin: O how glad are some persons when their troubles are gone ;

but I dare not rejoice with them. It is like him that rejoices his ague is gone, that it hath left him in a deep consumption. You are got rid of your troubles, but God knows how you have left them; your wounds are skinned over, better they were kept open. Surely they have much to answer for, that help on these delusions, healing the hurt of souls slightly, by crying, Peace, peace, when there is no peace. The false peace you beget in them, will be a real trouble to yourselves in the issue, Jer. vi. 14.

Third counsel.

Let all that are under inward troubles for sin, take heed of drawing desperate conclusions against themselves, and the final state of their own souls. Though your case be sad, it is not desperate; though the night be troublesome and tedious, keep on in the way to Christ, and light will spring up. To mourn for sin is your duty; to conclude there is no hope for you in Christ, is your sin. You have wronged God enough already, do not add a further and greater abuse to all the rest, by an absolute despair of mercy. It was your sin formerly to *presume beyond any promise,* it is your sin now to *despair against many commands.* I would say as the apostle in another case, I would not have you mourn as men that have no hope: your condition is sad as it is, but yet it is much better than once it was. You were once full of sin and void of sense, now you have the sense of sin, which is no small mercy. You were once quite out of the way and method of mercy, now you are in that very path wherein mercy meets the elect of God. Keep hope, therefore, at the bottom of all your troubles.

Fourth counsel.

Observe whether your troubles for sin produce such fruits and effects in your souls as theirs do, which end at last in Christ and everlasting peace.

First, One that is truly burdened with sin, will not allow himself to live in the secret practice of sin; either your trouble will put an end to your course of sinning, or your sinning will put an end to your troubles. Consult 2 Cor. vii. 11.

Secondly, True sorrow for sin, will give you very low and vile thoughts of yourselves; as you were covered with *pride* before, so you will be covered with *shame* after God hath convinced and humbled you, Rom. vi. 21.

Thirdly, A soul really burdened with sin will never stand in his own justification before God, nor extenuate and mince it in his confessions to him, Psal. li. 3, 4.

Fourthly, The burdens of sin will make a man set light by all other burdens of affliction, Lam. iii. 22. Micah vii. 9. The more you feel sin, the less you feel affliction.

Fifthly, A soul truly burdened for sin will take no hearty joy or comfort in any outward enjoyment of this world, till Christ come and seek peace to the soul, Lam. iii. 28. Just so the soul sits alone and keepeth silence; merry company is a burden, and music is but howling to him.

Fifth counsel.

Beware of those things that make your troubles longer than they ought to be. There be several errors and mistakes that hold poor souls much longer in their fears and terrors than else they might be; and such are,

First, Ignorance of the nature of saving faith, and the necessity of it. Till you come to believe, you cannot have peace; and while you mistake the nature, or apprehend not the necessity of faith, you are not like to find that path of peace.

Secondly, Labouring to heal the wounds that the law hath made upon your consciences, by a more strict obedience to it for the future, in the neglect of Christ and his righteousness.

Thirdly, In observance of what God hath already done for you, in these preparatory works of the law, in order to your salvation by Jesus Christ. O! if you would but compare what you now are, with what you lately were, it would give some relief. But the last and principal thing is this:

Sixth counsel.

Hasten to Christ in the way of faith, and you shall find rest; and till then all the world cannot give you rest. The sooner you transact with Christ, in the way of faith, the sooner you shall be at peace and enter into his rest; for those that believe do now enter into rest. You may labour and strive, look this way and that, but all in vain; Christ and peace come together. No sooner do you come to him, and roll your burden on him, receive him as he offers himself, but the soul feels itself eased on a sudden; "being "justified by faith, we have peace with God," Rom. v. 1. And thus in finishing the first, we are brought home to the second observation.

Doct. 2. *That sin-burdened souls are solemnly invited to come to Christ.*

This point sounds sweetly in the ear of a distressed sinner; it is the most joyful voice that ever the soul heard: the voice of blessing from mount Gerizim, the ravishing voice from mount Sion, " Ye are come to Jesus the Mediator." In opening of it I will shew,

1. What it is to come to Christ.
2. How Christ invites men to come to him.
3. Why his invitation is directed to burdened souls..

First, We will enquire what it is to come to Christ, and how many things are included in it.

In general, to come to Christ, is a phrase equipollent, or of the same amount with believing in Christ. It is an expression that carries the nature and necessity of. faith in it, and is reciprocated with believing. John vi. 35. " He that cometh so me shall never " hunger ; and he that believeth in me shall never thirst." Coming to Christ, is believing in Christ ; and believing in Christ, is coming to Christ ; they are *synonyma's,* and import the self same thing. Only in this notion of faith, there are many rich and excellent things hinted to us, which no other word can so aptly convey to our minds. As,

First, It hints this to us, That the souls of convinced and burdened sinners do not only discern the *reality* of Christ, or that he is, but also the necessity of applying Christ, and that their eternal life is in their union with him : for this is most certain, that the object of faith must be determinate and fixed ; the soul must believe that Christ is, or else there can be no emotions of the soul after him : all coming pre-supposes a fixed term to which we come, Heb. xi. 6. " He that cometh to God, must believe that God is." Take away this, and all motions after Christ presently stop. No wonder then that souls, in their first motions to Christ, find themselves clogged with so many atheistical temptations, shaking their assent to the truth of the gospel at the very root and foundation of it ; but they that come to Christ, do see that *he is,* and that their life and happiness lie in their union with him, else they would never come to him upon such terms as they do.

Secondly, Coming to Christ implies the soul's despair of salvation any other way. The way of faith is a supernatural way, and souls will not attempt it until they have tried all natural ways to help and save themselves, and find it all in vain ; therefore the text describes these *comers to Christ* as weary persons, that have been labouring and striving all other ways for rest, but can find none ; and so are forced to relinquish all their fond expectations of salvation in any other way, and come to Christ as their last and only remedy.

Thirdly, Coming to Christ notes a supernatural and almighty power, acting the soul quite above its own natural abilities in this motion. John vi. 44. " No man can come unto me, except my " Father which hath sent me draw him." It is as possible for the ponderous mountains to start from their bases and centres, mount themselves aloft into the air, and there fly like wandering atoms hither and thither, as it is for any man, of himself, i. e. by a pure natural power of his own, to come to Christ. It was not a stranger thing for Peter to come to Christ, walking upon the waves of the sea, than for his, or any man's soul, to come to Christ in the way of faith.

Fourthly, Coming to Christ notes the voluntariness of the soul in its motion to Christ. It is true, there is no coming without the Father's drawing; but that drawing hath nothing of coaction in it; it doth not destroy, but powerfully, and with an overcoming sweetness, persuade the will. It is not forced or driven, *but it comes*; being made "willing in the day of God's power," Psal. cx. 3. Ask a poor distressed sinner in that season, Are you willing to come to Christ? O rather than live! life is not so necessary as Christ is! O! with all my heart, ten thousand worlds for Jesus Christ, if he could be purchased, were nothing answerable to his value in mine eyes! The soul's motion to Christ is free and voluntary, it is *coming*.

Fifthly, It implies this in it, That no duties, or ordinances, (which are but the ways and means by which we come to Christ), are, or ought to be central and terminative to the soul: i. e. the soul of a believer is not to sit down, and rest in them, but to come by them or through them to Jesus Christ, and take up his rest in him only. No duties, no reformations, no ordinances of God, how excellent soever these things are in themselves, and how necessary soever they are in their proper place and use, can give rest to the weary and heavy laden soul: it cannot centre in any of them, and you may see it cannot, because it still gravitates and inclines to another thing, even Christ, and cannot terminate its motion till it be come to him. Christ is the term to which a believer moves; and therefore he cannot sit down by the way, or be as well satisfied as if he were at his journey's end. Ordinances and duties have the nature and use of means to bring us to Christ, but not to be to any man instead of Christ.

Sixthly, * Coming to Christ, implies an hope or expectation from Christ in the coming soul. If he hath no hope, why doth it move forward? As good sit still, and resolve to perish where it is, as to come to Christ, if there is no ground to expect salvation by him. Hope is the spring of motion and industry; if you cut off hope, you hinder faith: it cannot move to Christ, except it be satisfied, at least, of the possibility of mercy and salvation by him. Hence it is, that when comers to Christ are struggling with the doubts and fears of the issue, the Lord is pleased to enliven their faint hopes, by setting home such scriptures as these, John vi. 37. "He that cometh to me, I will in no wise cast out." And Heb. vii. 25. "He is able to save to the uttermost, all that come unto

---

* Come unto me, i. e. with the graces of faith, religious hope, and desire. *Brugensis on the place.*

" God by him." This puts life into hope, and hope puts life into industry and motion.

Seventhly, Coming to Christ for rest implies, that believers have, and lawfully may have an eye to their own happiness, in closing with the Lord Jesus Christ. The poor soul comes for rest; it comes for salvation; its eye and aim are upon it; and this aim of the soul at its own good, is legitimated, and allowed by that expression of Christ, John v. 40. " Ye will not come unto me, that " ye may have life." If Christ blame them for not coming to him, that they might have life, sure he would not blame them, had they come to him for life.

Eighthly, but *Lastly,* and which is the principal thing in this expression; Coming to Christ, notes the all-sufficiency of Christ, to answer all the needs and wants of distressed souls, and their betaking themselves accordingly to him only for relief, being content to come to Christ for whatever they need, and live upon that fulness that is in him. If there were not an all-sufficiency in Christ, no soul would come to him; for this is the very ground upon which men come. Heb. vii. 25. " He is able to save to the ut- " termost, all that come to God by him:" Εις το παντελες, to the uttermost: In the greatest plunges, difficulties, and dangers. He hath a fulness of saving power in him, and this encourages souls to come unto him. One beggar uses not to wait at the door of another, but all at the doors of them they conceive able to relieve them. And as this notes the fulness of Christ as our Saviour, so it must needs note the emptiness and humility of the soul as a comer to him. This is called submission, in Rom. x. 3. Proud nature must be deeply distressed, humbled, and moulded into another temper, before it will be persuaded to live upon those terms, to come to Christ for every thing it wants, to live upon Christ's fulness in the way of grace and favour, and have no stock of its own to live upon. O! this is hard, but it is the way of faith.

Secondly, In the next place, let us see how Christ invites men to come to him, and you shall find the means employed in this work, are either *internal,* and *principal,* namely, the Spirit of God, who is Christ's vicegerent, and comes to us in his name and room, to persuade us to believe, John xv. 26; or *external,* namely, the preaching of the gospel by commissioned ambassadors, who, *in Christ's stead, beseech men to be reconciled to God,* i. e. to come to Christ by faith, in order to their reconciliation and peace with God. But all means and instruments employed in this work of bringing men to Christ, entirely depend upon the blessing and concurrence of the Spirit of God, without whom they signify nothing. How long may ministers preach, before one soul comes to Christ, except the Spirit co-operate in that work! Now as to the manner in which men are persuaded, and their wills wrought upon to come to Christ, I will briefly note several acts of the Spirit, in order thereunto.

First, There is an *illustrating work* of the Spirit upon the minds of sinners, opening their eyes to see their danger and misery; till these be discovered, no man stirs from his place: It is sense of danger that rouzes the secure sinner, that distresses him, and makes him look about for deliverance, crying, *What shall I do to be saved?* And it is the discovery of Christ's ability to save, which is the ground and reason, (as was observed above,) of its motion to Christ. Hence, *seeing the Son,* is joined with believing, or *coming to him,* in John vi. 40.

Secondly, There is the *authoritative call,* or commanding voice of the Spirit in the word; a voice that is full of awful majesty and power. 1 John iii. 23. "This is his commandment, that we " should believe on the name of his Son Jesus Christ." This call of the Spirit to come to Christ, removes one great obstruction, namely, the fear of presumption out of the soul's way to Christ, and, instead of presumption in coming, makes it rebellion, and inexcusable obstinacy, to refuse to come. This answers all pleas against coming to Christ from our unworthiness and deep guilt; and mightily encourages the soul to come to Christ, whatever it hath been, or done.

Thirdly, There are soul-encouraging, *conditional * promises,* to all that do come to Christ in obedience to the command. Such is that in my text, *I will give you rest:* And that in John vi. 37. "Him that cometh to me, I will in no wise cast out." And these breathe life and encouragement into poor souls that fear, and are daunted through their own unworthiness.

Fourthly, There are *dreadful threatenings* denounced by the Spirit in the word, against all that refuse or neglect to come to Christ, which are of great use to engage and quicken souls in their way to Christ. Mark xvi. 16. "He that believes not shall be damned: " Die in his sins," John viii. 14. "The wrath of God shall remain " on him," John iii. ult. Which is as if the Lord had said, Sinners, do not dally with Christ, do not be always treating, and never concluding, or resolving: for if there be justice in heaven, or fire in hell, every soul that comes not to Christ, must, and shall perish to all eternity. Upon your own heads let the blood and destruction of your own souls be for ever, if you will not come unto him.

Fifthly, There are *moving examples* set before souls in the word, to prevail with them to come, alluring and encouraging examples of

---

* Promises which imply the connection of the end with the means. *Editor.*

such as have come to Christ, under the deepest guilt and discouragement, and yet found mercy. 1 Tim. i. 15, 16. " This is a " faithful saying, and worthy of all acceptation, that Jesus Christ " came into the world to save sinners, of whom I am chief: how- " beit, (or nevertheless) for this cause I have obtained mercy, that " in me first Jesus Christ might shew forth all long-suffering, for " a pattern to them which should hereafter believe in him to life " everlasting." Who would not come to Christ after such an example as this? And if this will not prevail, there are dreadful examples recorded in the word, setting before us the miserable condition of all such as refuse the calls of the word to come to Christ. 1 Pet. iii. 19, 20. " By which also he went and preached to the " spirits which are in prison, which sometime were disobedient, " when once the long-suffering of God waited in the days of " Noah." The meaning is, the sinners that lived before the flood, but now are in hell, clapt up in that prison, had the offers of grace made them, but despised them, and now lie for their disobedience in prison, under the wrath of God for it, in the lowest hell.

Sixthly, and *lastly*, There is an effectual *persuading*, overcoming and victorious work of the Spirit upon the hearts and wills of sinners, under which they come to Jesus Christ. Of this I have spoken at large before, in the *fourth sermon*, and therefore shall not add any thing more here. This is the way and manner in which souls are prevailed with to come to Jesus Christ.

Thirdly, In the last place, if you enquire why Christ makes his invitations to weary and heavy laden souls, and to no other, * the answer is briefly this:

First, Because in so doing, he follows the commission which he received from his Father: so you will find it runs, in Isa. lxi. 1. " The Spirit of the Lord is upon me, because the Lord hath " anointed me to preach good tidings to the meek, he hath sent " me to bind up the broken-hearted, to proclaim liberty to the " captives, and the opening of the prison to them that are bound. You see here how Christ's commission directs him: his Father sent him to poor broken-hearted sinners, and he will keep close to his commission. " He came not to call the righteous, but sinners, (i. e. " sensible burdened sinners) to repentance." Matth. ix. 13. " I " am not sent (saith he,) but unto the lost sheep of the house of

---

* Though *weary* and *heavy laden* souls only, and in the issue, will believe; yet sinners, without exception, and as sinners, are the objects of the gospel-proclamation. It is a faithful saying, and worthy of all acceptation, that Christ came into the world TO SAVE SINNERS, 1 Tim. i. 15. God so loved the world, that he gave his only begotten Son, that *whosoever* believeth on him, should not perish, but have everlasting life, John iii. 16. *Editor.*

" Israel." Thus his instructions and commission from the Father
limit him only to sensible and burdened souls, and he will be faithful to his commission.

Secondly, The very order of the Spirit's work in bringing men
to Christ, shews us to whom the invitation and offers of grace in
Christ are to be made.   For none are convinced of righteousness,
i. e. of complete and perfect righteousness, which is in Christ for
their justification, until first they be convinced of sin ; and, consequently, no man will, or can come to Christ by faith, till convictions of sin have awakened and distressed him, John xvi. 8, 9.
This being the due order of the Spirit's operation, the same order
must be observed in gospel-offers and invitations.

Thirdly, It behoves that Christ should provide for his own glory,
as well as for our safety ; and not to expose one to secure the other ;
but save us in that way which will bring him most honour and
praise. And certainly such a way as this, by first convincing, humbling, and burdening the souls of men, and then bringing them
home to rest in himself.

Alas ! let those that never saw, or felt the evil of sin, be told
of rest, peace, and pardon in Christ, they will but despise it as a
thing of no value, Luke v. 31. " The whole need not a physician,
" but those that are sick." Bid a man that thinks himself sound
and whole go to a physician, and he will but laugh at the motion ;
if you offer him the richest composition, he will refuse it, slight it,
and it may be, spill it upon the ground. Ay, but if the same man
did once feel an acute disease, and were made to sweat and groan
under strong pains, if ever he come to know what sick days and
restless nights are, and to apprehend his life to be in imminent
hazard ; then messengers are sent, one after another, in post-haste
to the physician ; then he begs him with tears to do what in him
lies for his relief : he thankfully takes the bitterest potions, and
praises the care and skill of his physician with tears of joy. And
so the patient's safety and the physician's honour are both secured.
So is it in this method of grace. The uses follow.

Infer. 1. If sin-burdened souls are solemnly invited to come to
Christ, *Then it follows, that whatever guilt lies upon the conscience
of a poor humbled sinner, it is no presumption, but his duty to come
to Christ, notwithstanding his own apprehended vileness and great
unworthiness.*

Let it be carefully observed, how happily that universal particle
all, is inserted in Christ's invitation, for the encouragement of sinners ; " Come unto me, [all] ye that labour ;" *q. d.* Let no broken-hearted sinner exclude himself, when he is not by me excluded from mercy : my grace is my own, I may bestow it where
I will, and upon whom I will. It is not I, but Satan that impales
and incloses my mercy from humbled souls that are made willing to

come unto me; he calls that your presumption, which my invitation makes your duty.

Objec. 1. But I doubt my case is excepted by Christ himself, in Mat. xii. 31. where blasphemy against the Holy Ghost is exempted from pardon, and I have had many horrid blasphemous thoughts injected into my soul.

Sol. Art thou a burdened and heavy laden soul? If so, thy case is not in that, or any other scripture exempted from mercy; for the unpardonable sin is always found in an impenitent heart: as that sin finds no pardon with God, so neither is it followed with contrition and sorrow in the soul that commits it.

Objec. 2. But if I am not guilty of that sin, I am certainly guilty of many great and heinous abominations of another kind, too great for me to expect mercy for; and therefore I dare not go to Christ.

Sol. The greater your sins have been, the more need you have to go to Jesus Christ. Let not a *motive* to go to Christ be made an *obstacle* in your way to him. Great sinners are expressly called, Isa. i. 18. great sinners have come to Christ and found mercy, 1 Cor. vi. 7. and to conclude, it is an high reproach and dishonour to the blood of Christ, and mercy of God, which flows so freely through him, to object the greatness of sin to either of them. Certainly you have not sinned beyond the *extent of mercy*, or beyond the *efficacy of the blood of Christ*: but pardon and peace may be had, if you will thus come to Christ for it.

Objec. 3. Oh! but it is now too late; I have had many thousand calls by the gospel, and refused them; many purposes in my heart to go to Christ, and quenched them; my time therefore is past, and now it is to no purpose.

Sol. If the time of grace be past, and God intends no mercy for thee, how comes it to pass thy soul is now filled with trouble and distress for sin? Is this the frame of a man's heart that is past hope. Do such signs as these appear in men that are hopeless? Beside, the time of grace is a *secret* hid in the breast of God; but coming to Christ is a *duty* plainly revealed in the *text:* And why will you object a thing that is secret and uncertain, against a duty that is so plain and evident? Nor do you yourselves believe what you object; for at the same time that you say your seasons are over, it is too late, you are, notwithstanding, found repenting, mourning, praying, and striving to come to Christ. Certainly, if you knew it were too late, you would not be found labouring in the use of means. Go on, therefore, and the Lord be with you. It is not presumption, but obedience, to come when Christ calls, as he here doth, "Come unto me, all ye that labour, and are "heavy laden."

Infer. 2. Hence it follows, *That none have cause to be troubled, when God makes the souls of their friends or relations sick with the sense of sin.* It was the saying (as I remember) of Hieron to Sabinian, Nothing (said he) makes my heart sadder, than that nothing can make my heart sad. It is matter of joy to all that rightly understand the matter, when God smites the heart of any man with the painful sense of sin; of such sickness it may be said, " This sick-" ness is not unto death, but for the glory of God." Yet how do many carnal relations lament and bewail this as a misery, as an undoing to their friends and acquaintances; as if then they must be reckoned lost, and never till then, that Christ is finding and saving them. O! if your hearts were spiritual and wise, their groans for sin would be as music in your ears. When they go alone to bewail their sin, you would go alone also to bless God for such a mercy, that ever you should live to such a happy day: You would say, Now is my friend in the blessed pangs of the new birth; now is he in the very way of mercy; never in so hopeful a condition as now. I had rather he should groan now at the feet of Christ, than groan hereafter under the wrath of God for ever. O! parents, beware, as you love the souls of your children, that you do not damp and discourage them, tempt or threaten them, divert or hinder them in such cases as this, lest you bring the *blood* of their *souls* upon your own heads.

Inf. 3. It also follows from hence, *That those to whom sin was never any burthen, are not yet come to Christ, nor have any interest in him.* We may as well suppose a child to be born without any pangs, as a soul to be born again, and united to Christ, without any sense or sorrow for sin. I know many have great *frights of conscience*, that never were made duly sensible of the evil of sin; many are afraid of *burning*, that never were afraid of *sinning*. Slight and transient troubles some have had, but they vanished like an early cloud, or morning dew. Few men are without checks and throbs of conscience at one time or other; but instead of going to the closet, they run to the *alehouse* or *tavern* for cure. If their sorrow for sin had been right, nothing but the sprinkling of the blood of Christ could have appeased their consciences, Heb. x. 22. How cold should the consideration of this thing strike to the hearts of such persons! Methinks, reader, if this be thy case, it should send thee away with an aking heart; thou hast not yet tasted the bitterness of sin, and if thou do not, thou shalt never taste the sweetness of Christ, his pardons and peace.

Inf. 4. *How great a mercy is it for sin-burthened souls to be within the sound and call of Christ in the gospel!*

There be many thousands in the Pagan and Popish parts of the world, that labour under distresses of conscience as well as we, but have no such reliefs, no such means of peace and comfort as we have that live within the joyful sound of the gospel. If the conscience of a Papist be burdened with guilt, all the relief he hath, is to afflict his body to quiet his soul; a penance, or pilgrimage, is all the relief they have. If a Pagan be in trouble for sin, he hath no knowledge of Christ, nor notion of a satisfaction made by him; the voice of nature is, Shall I give my *first-born* for my *transgression*, the *fruit* of my *body* for the sin of my soul? The damned endure the terrible blows and wounds of conscience for sin, they roar under that terrible lash, but no voice of peace or pardon is heard among them. It is not, " Come unto me, ye that labour, and are heavy " laden," but " depart from me, ye cursed."

Blessed are your ears, for you hear the voice of peace; you are come to Jesus the Mediator, and to the blood of sprinkling. O, you can never set a due value upon this privilege.

Inf. 5. How sweet and unspeakably relieving is the closing of a burthened soul with Jesus Christ, by faith! It is rest to the weary soul.

Soul-troubles are spending, wasting troubles; the pains of a distressed conscience are the most acute pains. A poor soul would fain be at rest, but knows not where; he tries this duty and that, but finds none. At last, in a way of believing, he casts himself, with his burden of guilt and fear, upon Christ, and there is the rest his soul desired. Christ and rest come together; till faith bring you to the bosom of Jesus, you can find no true rest: The soul is rolling and tossing, sick and weary, upon the billows of its own guilt and fears. Now the soul is come like a ship tossed with storms and tempests, out of a raging ocean into the quiet harbour! or like a *lost sheep* that hath been wandering in weariness, hunger, and danger, into the fold. Is a soft bed in a quiet chamber sweet to one that is spent and tired with travel? Is the sight of a shore sweet to the *shipwrecked mariner*, who looked for nothing but death? Much more sweet is Christ to a soul that comes to him pressed in conscience, and broken in spirit under the sinking weight of sin.

How did the Italians rejoice, after a long and dangerous voyage, to see Italy again! crying, with loud and united voices which made the very heavens ring again, * Italy! Italy! But no shore is so sweet to the weather-beaten passenger, as Christ is to a brokenhearted sinner: This brings the soul to a sweet repose. Heb. iv. 3. " We, which have believed, do enter into rest." And this endears the way of faith to their souls ever after.

Inf. 6. Learn hence the usefulness of the law to bring souls to Jesus Christ. It is utterly useless, as a *covenant*, to *justify* us; but exceeding useful to convince and humble us; it cannot relieve nor ease

---

* *Italiam, Italiam, læto clamore salutant.* Virg.

us, but it can and doth awaken and rouse us. It is a fair glass to shew us the face of sin, and till we have seen that we cannot see the face of Jesus Christ.

The law, like the *fiery serpent*, smites, stings, and torments the conscience; this drives us to the Lord Jesus, lifted up in the gospel, like the *brazen serpent* in the wilderness, to heal us. The use of the law is to make us feel our *sickness;* this makes us look out for a *Physician:* " I was alive once, without the law, (saith Paul) " but when the commandment came, sin revived, and I died," Rom. vii. 9. The hard, vain, proud hearts of men require such an hammer to break them to pieces.

Inf. 7. It is the immediate duty of weary and heavy-laden sinners to come to Christ by faith, and not stand off from Christ, or delay to accept him upon any terms whatsoever.

Christ invites and commands such to come unto him; it is therefore your sin to neglect, draw back, or defer whatever seeming reasons and pretences there may be to the contrary. When the *gaoler* was brought (where I suppose thee now to be) to a pinching distress, that made him cry, " Sirs, what must I do to be saved?" The very next counsel the apostles gave him was, " Believe on the Lord Jesus " Christ, and thou shalt be saved," Acts xvi. 30, 31. And, for your encouragement, know, that he who calleth you to come, knows your burden, what your sins have been and troubles are, yet he calls you: if your sin hinder not Christ from *calling,* neither should it hinder you from *coming.* He that calls you, is able to ease you, " to " save to the uttermost, all that come to God by him," Heb. vii. 25. Whatever fulness of sin be in you, there is a greater fulness of saving power in Christ. Moreover, he that calls you to come, never yet rejected any poor burdened soul that came to him; and hath said he never will. John vi. 37. " Him that cometh unto me, I will in " no wise cast out." Fear not, therefore, he will not begin with thee, or make thee the first instance and example of the feared rejection.

And, *Lastly,* Bethink thyself, what wilt thou do, and whither wilt thou go, in this case, if not to Jesus Christ? Nothing shall ease or relieve thee till thou dost come to him. Thou art under an happy necessity to go to him; with him only is found rest for the weary soul; which brings us to the third and last observation,

Doct. 3. *That there is rest in Christ, for all that come unto him, under the heavy burden of sin.*

Rest is a sweet word to a weary soul; all seek it, but none but believers find it. *We which have believed,* (saith the apostle) * *do*

---

* *Non dicit* εισηλθομεν, *ingressi sumus, sed* εισερχομεθα, *ingredimur, significans, initia quietis fideles nunc habere; plenam quietem suo tempore consecuturos.* Pareus in loc.

enter into rest, Heb. iv. 3. " He doth not say, they *shall,* but they
" do enter into rest; noting their spiritual rest to be already begun
" by faith on earth in the tranquillity of conscience, and shall be
" consummated in heaven, in the full enjoyment of God." There
is a sweet calm upon the troubled soul after believing, an ease, or
rest of the mind, which is an unspeakable mercy to a poor weary
soul.   Christ is to it as the ark was to the dove, when she wandered
over the watery world, and found no place to rest the sole of her
foot.   Faith centres the unquiet spirit of man in Christ, brings it to
repose itself and its burden on him.   It is the soul's dropping anchor
in a storm, which stays and settles it.

The great debate which cost so many anxious thoughts is now
issued into this resolution; I will venture my all upon Christ, let
him do with me as seemeth him good.   It was impossible for the
soul to find rest, whilst it knew not where to bestow itself, or how
to be secured from the wrath to come; but when all is embarked
in Christ for eternity, and the soul fully resolved to lean upon
him, and to trust to him, now it feels the very *initials* of eternal rest in itself: it finds an heavy burden unloaded from its
shoulders; it is come, as it were, into a new world; the case is
strangely altered.   The word *rest,* in this place, notes *, (and is so
rendered by some) a *recreation;* it is restored, renewed, and re-
created, as it were, by that sweet repose it hath upon Christ.
Believers, know that faith is the sweetest recreation you can take.
Others seek to divert and lose their troubles, by sinful recreations,
vain company, and the like; but they little know what the recreation and sweet restoring rest that faith gives the soul is.   You
find, in Christ, what they seek in vain among the creatures.   Believing is the highest recreation known in this world.   But to prevent mistakes, three *Cautions* need to be premised, lest we do, *in
ipso limine impingere,* stumble at the threshold, and so lose our way
all along afterward.

Caution 1.

*You are not to conceive, that all the soul's fears, troubles and sor-
rows are presently over and at an end, as soon as it is come to Christ
by faith.* † They will have many troubles in the world after that,
it may be, more than ever they had in their lives: " Our flesh
" (saith Paul) had no rest," 2 Cor. vii. 5.   They will be infested
with many temptations after that; that, it may be, the assaults of
Satan may be more violent upon their souls than ever. *Horribilia*

---

* I will give you recreation from weariness, troubles and burdens. *Vatab. et
Erasm.*

 † Luther, upon his conversion, was so buffeted by Satan, that neither heat, blood,
sensation, or speech remained.

de Deo, terribilia de fide: injections that make the very bones to
quake, and the belly to tremble.   They will not be wholly freed
from sin; that rest remains for the people of God; nor from inward trouble and grief of soul about sin.   These things are not to
be expected presently.

Caution 2.

We may not think all believers do immediately enter into the full,
actual sense of rest and comfort, but they presently enter into the
state of rest.   " Being justified by faith, we have peace with God,"
Rom. v. 1. i. e. we enter into the state of peace immediately.   " Peace
" is sown for the righteous, and gladness for the upright in heart,"
Psal. cxvii. 11.   And he is a rich man that hath a thousand acres
of corn in the ground, as well as he that hath so much in his barn,
or the money in his purse.   They have rest and peace in the seed
of it, when they have it not in the fruit; they have rest in the
promise, when they have it not in possession; and he is a rich man
that hath good bonds and bills for a great sum of money, if he
have not twelve-pence in his pocket.   All believers have the promise, have rest and peace granted them under God's own hand,
in many promises which faith brings them under; and we know
that the truth and faithfulness of God stands engaged to make
good every line and word of the promise to them.   So that though
they have not a full and clear actual sense and feeling of rest, they
are, nevertheless by faith come into the state of rest.

Caution 3.

We may not conceive that faith itself is the soul's rest, but the
means and instruments of it only.   We cannot find rest in any
work or duty of our own, but we may find it in Christ, whom faith
apprehends for justification and salvation.

Having thus guarded the point against misapprehensions, by
these needful cautions, I shall next shew you how our coming to
Christ by faith brings us to rest in him.   And here let it be considered what those things are that burden, grieve and disquiet the
soul before its coming to Christ; and how it is relieved and eased
in all those respects, by its coming to the Lord Jesus; and you
shall find,

First, That one principal ground of trouble is the guilt of sin
upon the conscience, of which I spake in the former point.   The
curse of the law lies heavy upon the soul, so heavy that nothing is
found in all the world able to relieve it under that burden; as you
see in a condemned man, spread a table in prison with the greatest dainties, and send for the rarest musicians, all will not charm
his sorrow: but if you can produce an authentic pardon, you ease
him presently.   Just so it is here, faith plucks the thorn out of

the conscience, which so grieved it, unites the soul with Christ, and then that ground of trouble is removed: for " there is no condem- " nation to them that are in Christ Jesus," Rom. viii. 1. The same moment the soul comes to Christ, it hath passed from death to life, is no more under the law, but grace. If a man's debt be paid by his surety, he need not fear to shew his face boldly abroad; he may freely meet the serjeant at the prison-door.

Secondly, The soul of a convinced sinner is exceedingly burden- ed with the uncleanness and filthiness wherewith sin hath defiled and polluted it. Conviction discovers the universal pollution of heart and life, so that a man loathes and abhors himself by reason thereof: if he do not look into his own corruptions, he cannot be safe; and if he do, he cannot bear the sight of them; he hath no quiet; nothing can give rest, but what gives relief against this evil; and this only is done by faith uniting the soul with Jesus Christ. For though it be true that the pollution of sin be not presently and perfectly taken away by coming to Christ, yet the burden thereof is exceedingly eased; for, upon our believing, there is an heart- purifying principle planted in the soul, which doth, by degrees, cleanse that fountain of corruption, and will at last perfectly free the soul from it. Acts xv. 9. " Purifying their hearts by faith;" and being once in Christ, he is concerned for the soul as a member now of his own mystical body, to purify and cleanse it, that at last he may present it perfect to the Father, without spot or wrinkle, or any such thing, Eph. v. 26. The reigning power of it is gone immediately upon believing, and the very existence and being of it shall at last be destroyed. O, what rest must this give under those troubles for sin:

Thirdly, It was an intolerable burden to the soul to be under the continual fears, alarms, and frights of death and damnation; its life hath been a life of bondage, upon this account, ever since the Lord opened his eyes to see his condition. Poor souls lie down with tremblings, for fear what a night may bring forth. It is a sad life indeed to live in continual bondage of such fears; but faith sweetly relieves the trembling conscience, by removing the guilt which breeds its fears. The sting of death is sin. When guilt is removed, fears vanquish. " Smite, Lord, smite, said Luther, " for my sins are forgiven *." Now, if sickness come, it is another thing than it was wont to be. Isa. xxxiii. 24. " The inhabitant " shall not say, I am sick, the people that dwell therein shall be " forgiven their iniquities." A man scarce feels his sickness, in comparison to what he did, whilst he was without Christ and hope of pardon.

---

* *Feri, Domine, feri, nam a peccatis meis absolutus sum.* Luther.

Fourthly, A convinced sinner, out of Christ, sees every thing against him ; nothing yields any comfort, yea, every thing increases and aggravates his burden, when he looks to things past, present, or to come. If he reflect upon things past, his soul is filled with anguish, to remember the sins committed and the seasons neglected, and the precious mercies that have been abused ; if he look upon things present, the case is doleful and miserable ; nothing but trouble and danger, Christless and comfortless ; and if he look forward to things to come, that gives him a deeper cut to the heart than any thing else ; for though it be sad and miserable for the present, yet he fears it will be much worse hereafter ; all these are but the beginning of sorrows. And thus the poor, awakened sinner becomes a *Magor Missabib ;* fear round about.

But, upon his coming to Christ, all things are marvellously al tered ; a quite contrary face of things appears to him ; every thing gives him hope and comfort, which way soever he looks. So speaks the apostle, 1 Cor. iii. 22, 23. " All things are yours, (saith he) " whether life or death, or things present, or things to come ; all " is yours, and ye are Christ's, and Christ is God's :" They are ours, i. e. for our advantage, benefit, and comfort. More particularly upon our coming to Christ,

First, Things past are ours, they conduce to our advantage and comfort. Now the soul can begin to read the gracious end and design of God, in all its preservations and deliverances ; whereby it hath been reserved for such a day as this. O ! it melts his heart to consider his companions in sin and vanity are cut off, and he spared ; and that for a day of such mercy, as the day of his espousals with Christ is. Now all his past sorrows, and deep troubles of spirit, which God hath exercised him with, begin to appear the greatest mercies that ever he received ; being all necessary and introductive to this blessed union with Christ.

Secondly, Things present are ours, though it be not yet with us as we would have it ; Christ is not sure enough, the heart is not pure enough ; sin is too strong, and grace is too weak ; many things are yet out of order ; yet can the soul bless God for this, with tears of joy and praise, being full of admiration and holy astonishment, that it is as it is ; and that he is where he is, though he be not yet where he would be. O ! it is a blessed life to live as a poor recumbent, by acts of trust and affiance, though, as yet, he have but little evidence ; that he is resolved to trust all with Christ, though he be not yet certain of the issue. O this it a comfortable station, a sweet condition to what it was, either when the soul wallowed in sin, in the days before conviction, or was swallowed up in fears and troubles for sin after conviction ; now it hath hope, though it want assurance : and hope is sweet to a soul coming out of such deep distresses. Now it sees the remedy, and is applying it; whereas before the wound seemed desperate. Now all hesitations and debates are at an end in the soul; it is no longer unresolved what to do; all things have been deeply considered, and after consideration, issued into this resolve, or decree of the will: I will go to Christ; I will venture all upon his command and call; I will embark my eternal interests in that bottom; here I fix, and here I resolve to live and die. O! how much better is this than that floating life it lived before, rolling upon the billows of inward fears and troubles, not able to drop anchor any where, nor knowing where to find an harbour?

Thirdly, *Things to come are ours;* and this is the best and sweetest of all: Man is a prospecting creature, his eye is much upon things to come, and it will not satisfy him that it is well at present, except he have a prospect that it shall be so hereafter. But now the soul hath committed itself and all its concernments to Christ for eternity, and this being done, it is greatly relieved against evils to come.

I cannot (saith the believer) think all my troubles over, and that I shall never meet any more afflictions; it were a fond vanity to dream of that: but I leave all these things where I have left my soul: he that hath supported me under inward, will carry me through outward troubles also. I cannot think all my *temptations* to sin past; O! I may yet meet with sore assaults from Satan, yet it is infinitely better to be watching, praying, and striving against sin, than it was when I was obeying it in the lusts of it. God, that hath delivered me from the love of sin, will, I trust, preserve me from ruin by sin. I know also death is to come; I must feel the pangs and agonies of it: but yet the aspect of death is much more pleasant than it was. I come, Lord Jesus to thee, who art the death of death, whose death hath disarmed death of its sting: for I fear not its dart if I feel not its sting. And thus you see briefly, how by faith believers enter into rest; how Christ gives rest, even at present, to them that come to him, and all this but as a beginning of their everlasting rest.

Inference 1. Is there rest in Christ for weary souls that come unto him? *Then, certainly it is a design of Satan against the peace and welfare of men's souls, to discourage them from coming to Christ in the way of faith.*

He is a restless spirit himself, and would make us so too; it is an excellent note of * Minutius Felix, " Those desperate and rest-" less spirits (saith he) have no other peace but in bringing us to " the same misery themselves are in:" He goeth about as a roar-

---

* *Ad solamen calamitatis suæ, non desinunt perditi perdere.*   Minut. Felix.

ing lion, seeking whom he may devour. It frets and grates his proud and envious mind, to see others find rest when he can find none; an effectual plaister applied to heal our wound, when his own must bleed to eternity: And he obtains his end fully, if he can but keep off souls from Christ.   Look therefore, upon all those objections and discouragements raised in your hearts against coming to Christ, as so many artifices and cunning devices of the devil, to destroy and ruin your souls.   It is true they have a very specious and colourable appearance; they are gilded over with pretences of the justice of God, the heinous nature of sin, the want of due and befitting qualifications for so holy and pure a God, the lapsing of the season of mercy, and an hundred others of like nature: but I beseech you, lay down this as a sure conclusion, and hold it fast; that whatever it be that discourages and hinders you from coming to Christ, is directly against the interest of your souls, and the hand of the devil is certainly in it.

Infer. 2. Hence also it follows, *that unbelief is the true reason of all that disquietness and trouble, by which the minds of poor sinners are so racked and tortured.*

If you will not believe, you cannot be established; till you come to Christ, peace cannot come to you: Christ and peace are undivided.   Good souls, consider this; you have tried all other ways, you have tried duties, and no rest comes; you have tried reformation, restitution, and a stricter course of life; yet your wounds are still open, and fresh bleeding: these things, I grant, are in their places both good and necessary; but, of themselves, without Christ, utterly insufficient to give what you expect from them: why will you not try the way of faith? Why will you not carry your burthen to Christ? O! that you would be persuaded to it, how soon would you find what so long you have been seeking in vain! How long will you thus oppose your own good? How long will you keep yourselves upon the rack of conscience? Is it easy to go under the throbs and wounds of an accusing and condemning conscience? You know it is not: you look for peace, but no good comes; for a time of healing, and behold trouble.   Alas! it must and will be so still, until you are in the way of faith, which is the true and only method to obtain rest.

Inf. 3. *What cause have we all to admire the goodness of God, in providing for us a Christ, in whom we may find rest to our souls!*

How hath the Lord filled and furnished Jesus Christ with all that is suitable to a believer's wants! Doth the guilt of sin terrify his conscience? Lo, in him is perfect righteousness to remove that guilt, so that it shall neither be imputed to his person, nor reflected by his conscience, in the way of condemnation as it was before. In him also is a fountain opened, for washing and for cleansing the filth of sin from our souls; in him is the fulness both of *merit,* and of *spirit,* two sweet springs of peace to the souls of men: well might the apostle say, " Christ the wisdom of God," 1 Cor. i. 30. and well might the Church say, " He is altogether lovely," Cant. v. 16. Had not God provided Jesus Christ for us, we had never known one hour's rest to all eternity.

Inf 4. *How unreasonable, and wholly inexcusable, in believers, is the sin of backsliding from Christ!* Have you found rest in him, when you could not find it in any other! Did he receive, and ease your souls, when all other persons and things were *physicians of no value?* And will you, after this, backslide from him again? O what madness is this! " Will a man leave the snow of Lebanon, which " cometh from the rock of the field? Or shall the cold, flowing " waters, that come from another place, be forsaken?" No man that is in his wits would leave the pure, cold, refreshing stream of a crystal fountain, to go to a filthy puddle, lake, or an empty cistern; such the best enjoyments of this world are, in comparison with Jesus Christ.

That was a melting expostulation of Christ's with the disciples, John vi. 67, 68. when some had forsaken him, " Will ye also " go away?" And it was a very suitable return they made, Lord, whither away from thee should we go! q. d. From thee, Lord! No, where can we mend ourselves? be sure of it, whenever you go from Christ, you go from rest to trouble. Had Judas rest? Had Spira rest? and do you think you shall have rest? No, no, "The " backslider in heart shall be filled with his own ways," Prov. xiv. 14. " Cursed be the man that departeth from him, he shall be as the " heath in the desert, that seeth not when good cometh, and shall " inhabit the parched places of the wilderness," Jer. xvii. 5. If fear of sufferings, and worldly temptations, ever draw you off from Christ, you may come to those straits and terrors of conscience that will make you wish yourselves back again with Christ in a prison, with Christ at a stake.

Infer. 5. *Let all that come to Christ learn to improve him to the rest and peace of their own souls, in the midst of all the troubles and outward distresses they meet with in the world.*

Surely rest may be found in Christ in any condition; he is able to give you peace in the midst of all your troubles here. So he tells you in John xvi. 33. " These things have I spoken to you, that in " me you might have peace; in the world ye shall have tribula- " tion." By peace he means not a deliverance from troubles, by taking off affliction from them, or taking them away by death from all afflictions; but it is something they enjoy from Christ in the very midst of troubles, and amidst all their afflictions, that quiets and gives them rest, so that troubles cannot hurt them. Certainly,

believers, you have peace in Christ, when there is little in your
own hearts; and your hearts might be filled with peace too, if
you would exercise faith upon Christ for that end.   It is your own
fault if you be without rest in any condition in this world.   Set
yourselves to study the *fulness* of Christ, and to clear your *interest*
in him; believe what the scriptures reveal of him, and live as you
believe, and you will quickly find the peace of God filling your
hearts and minds.

Blessed be God for Jesus Christ.

SERMON X.

Wherein the general Exhortation is enforced by one Motive drawn from the first Title of CHRIST.

MATTH. ix. 12.

*But when Jesus heard that, he said unto them, They that be whole
need not a physician, but they that are sick.*

HAVING opened, in the former discourses, the *nature* and
method of the *application* of Christ to sinners; it remains now that
I press it upon every soul, as it expects peace and pardon from God,
to *apply* and *put on Jesus Christ*, i. e. to get union with him by
faith, whilst he is yet held forth in the free and gracious tenders of
the gospel.   To which purpose I shall now labour in this general
use of exhortation, in which my last subject engaged me; wherein
divers arguments will be further urged, both from
    1. The titles, and
    2. The privileges of Jesus Christ.
    The titles of Christ are so many motives or arguments fitted to
persuade men to come unto him.   Amongst which, *Christ, as the
Physician of souls*, comes under our first consideration, in the text
before us.
    The occasion of these words of Christ, was the call of Matthew
the publican, who, having first opened his heart, next opened his
house to Christ, and entertains him there.   This strange and unexpected change, wrought upon Matthew, quickly brings in all
the neighbourhood, and many publicans and sinners resorted
thither; at which the stomachs of the proud Pharisees began to
swell.   From this occasion they took offence at Christ, and, in this
verse, Christ takes off the offence, by such an answer as was fitted
both for their *conviction* and his own *vindication*.   But when Jesus

heard that, he said unto them, "The whole have no need of a
"physician, but they that are sick."

He gives it, saith one, as a reason why he conversed so much with
Publicans and sinners, and so little among the Pharisees, because
there was more work for him; Christ came to be a physician to
sick souls; Pharisees were so well in their own conceit, that Christ
saw that they would have little to do with him, and so he applied
himself to those who were more sensible of their sickness.

In the words, we have an account of the *temper* and *state* both
of,

1. The secure and unconvinced sinner,
2. The humbled and convinced sinner. And,
3. Of the carriage of Christ, and his different respect to both.

First, The secure sinner is here described, both with respect to
his own apprehensions of himself, as one that is *whole,* and also by
his low value and esteem for Christ, he sees no need of him;
"The whole have no need of a physician."

Secondly, The convinced and humbled sinner is here also described, and that both by his state and condition, he is *sick;* and
by his valuation of Jesus Christ, he greatly needs him: they that
are sick need the *physician.*

Thirdly, We have here Christ's carriage, and different respect
to both; the former he rejects and passeth by, as those with whom
he hath no concernment; the latter he converseth with in order to
their cure.

The words thus opened, are fruitful in observations. I shall
neither note nor insist upon any beside this one, which suits the
scope of my discourse, viz.

Doct. *That the Lord Jesus Christ is the only physician for sick
souls.*

The world is a great *hospital,* full of sick and dying souls, all
wounded by one and the same mortal weapon, sin. Some are senseless of their misery, feel not their pains, value not a physician;
others are full of sense, as well as danger: mourn under the apprehension of their condition, and sadly bewail it. The merciful
God hath, in his abundant compassion to the perishing world, sent
a physician from heaven, and given him his orders under the great
seal of heaven, for his office, Isa. lxi. 1, 2. which he opened and
read in the audience of the people, Luke iv. 18. "The Spirit of
"the Lord is upon me, because he hath anointed me to preach
"good tidings unto the meek, he hath sent me to bind up the
"broken-hearted," &c. He is the tree of life, whose leaves are
for the healing of the nations: he is *Jehovah Rophe,* the Lord that

healeth us; and that as he is *Jehovah Tzidkenu*, the Lord our righteousness. The *brazen serpent* that healed the Israelites in the wilderness, was an excellent type of our great physician, Christ, and is expressly applied to him, John iii. 14. He rejects none that come, and heals all whom he undertakes; but more particularly, I will,

First, Point at those diseases which Christ heals in sick souls, and by what means he heals them.

Secondly, The excellency of this physician above all others: there is none like Christ, he is the only physician for wounded souls.

First, We will enquire into the diseases which Christ the physician cures, and they are reducible to two heads, viz.

1. Sin, and,
2. Sorrow.

First, The disease of sin ; in which three things are found exceeding burdensome to sick souls.

1. The guilt,
2. The dominion,
3. The inherence of sin; all cured by this physician, and how.

First, The guilt of sin; this is a mortal wound, a stab in the very heart of a poor sinner. It is a fond and groundless distinction that Papists make of sins *mortal* and *venial ;* all sin, in its own nature is mortal, Rom. vi. 23. " The wages of sin is death." Yet though it be so in its own nature, Christ can and doth cure it by the sovereign balsam of his own precious blood, Eph. i. 7. " In " whom we have redemption through his blood, the forgiveness " of sins, according to the riches of his grace." This is the deepest and deadliest wound the soul of man feels in this world. What is guilt but the obligation of the soul to everlasting punishment and misery? It puts the soul under the sentence of God to eternal wrath ; the condemning sentence of the great and terrible God; than which, nothing is found more dreadful and insupportable : put all pains, all poverty, all afflictions, all miseries, in one scale, and God's condemnation in the other, and you weigh but so many feathers against a talent of lead.

This disease, our great physician, Christ, cures, by remission, which is the dissolving of the obligation to punishment ; the loosing of the soul that was bound over to the wrath and condemnation of God, Col. i. 13, 14. Heb. vi. 12. Micah vii. 17, 18, 19. This remission being made, the soul is immediately cleared from all its obligations to punishment. Rom. viii. 1. " There is no condemnation." All bonds are cancelled, the guilt of all sins is healed or removed, original and actual, great and small. This cure is performed upon souls *by the blood of Christ :* nothing is found in

heaven or earth, besides his blood that is able to heal this disease.
Heb. ix. 22. "Without shedding of blood there is no remission;"
nor is it any blood that will do it, but that only which dropped from
the wounds of Christ. Isa. liii. 5. "By his stripes we are healed."
His blood only is innocent and precious blood, 1 Pet. i. 19. blood
of infinite worth and value; blood of God, Acts xx. 18. blood
prepared for this very purpose, Heb. x. 5. This is the blood that
performs the cure; and how great a cure is it! for this cure, the
souls of believers shall be praising and magnifying their great Physician in heaven to all eternity, Rev. i. 5, 6. "To him that loved
"us, and washed us from our sins in his own blood, &c. to him
"be glory and dominion, for ever and ever."

Secondly, The next evil in sin cured by Christ, is the dominion
of it over the souls of poor sinners. Where sin is in dominion, the
soul is in a very sad condition; for it darkens the understanding,
depraves the conscience, stiffens the will, hardens the heart, mis-
places and disorders all the affections; and thus every faculty is
wounded by the power and dominion of sin over the soul. How
difficult is the cure of this disease! It passes the skill of angels or
men to heal it; but Christ undertakes it, and makes a perfect cure
of it at last, and this he doth by his Spirit. As he cures the guilt
of sin by pouring out his blood for us; so he cures the dominion
of sin by pouring out his Spirit upon us. Justification is the cure
of guilt, sanctification the cure of the dominion of sin. For,

First, As the dominion of sin darkens the *understanding*, 1 Cor.
ii. 14. so the Spirit of holiness which Christ sheds upon his
people, cures the darkness and blindness of that noble faculty, and
restores it again, Eph. v. 8. They that were darkness are hereby
light in the Lord; the anointing of the Spirit teacheth them all
things, 1 John ii. 27.

Secondly, As the dominion of sin depraved and defiled the conscience, Tit. i. 15. wounded it to that degree, as to disable it to
the performance of all its offices and functions; so that it was neither able to apply, convince, or tremble at the word: So, when
the Spirit of holiness is shed forth, O what a tender sense fills the
renewed conscience! For what small things will it check, smite,
and rebuke! How strongly will it bind to duty, and bar against
sin.

Thirdly, As the dominion of sin stiffened the will and made it
stubborn and rebellious, so Christ, by sanctifying it, brings it to
be pliant and obedient to the will of God. "Lord, (saith the sin-
"ner) what wilt thou have me to do!" Acts ix. 6.

Fourthly, As the power of sin hardeneth the heart so that nothing could affect it, or make any impression upon it; when sanctification comes upon the soul, it thaws and breaks it, as hard as

it was, and makes it to dissolve in the breast of a sinner in godly sorrow, Ezek. xxxvi. 26. " I will take away the heart of stone out " of your flesh, and I will give you an heart of flesh." It will now melt ingenuously under the threatenings of the word, 2 Kings xxii. 19. or the strokes of the rod, Jer. xxxi. 18. or the manifestations of grace and mercy, Luke vii. 38.·

Fifthly, As the power of sin misplaced and disordered all the affections, so sanctification reduces them again and sets them right, Psal. iv. 6, 7. And thus you see how sanctification becomes the rectitude, health, and due temper of the soul, so far as it prevails, curing the diseases that sin in its dominion filled the soul with. True it is, this cure is not perfected in this life ; there are still some remains of the old diseases in the holiest souls, notwithstanding sin be dethroned from its dominion over them : but the cure is begun, and daily advances towards perfection, and at last will be complete, as will appear in the cure of the next evil of sin ; namely,

Thirdly, The *inherence* of sin in the soul : this is a sore disease, the very core and root of all our other complaints and ailes. This made the holy apostle bemoan himself and wail so bitterly, Rom. vii. 17. because of " sin that dwelt in him." And the same misery is bewailed by all sanctified persons all the world over.

It is a wonderful mercy to have the guilt and dominion of sin cured, but we shall never be perfectly sound and well, till the existence or in-dwelling of sin in our natures be cured too : when once that is done, then we shall feel no more pain nor sorrows for sin : and this our great *Physician* will at last perform for us and upon us. But as the cure of guilt was by our *justification*, the cure of the dominion of sin by our *sanctification :* so the third and last, which perfects the whole cure, will be by our *glorification :* and till then, it is not to be expected. For it is a clear case, that sin like ivy in the old walls, will never be gotten out till the walls be pulled down, and then it is pulled up by the roots. This cure Christ will perform in a moment, upon our dissolution. For it is plain,

First, That none but perfected souls, freed from all sin, are admitted into heaven, Eph. v. 27. Heb. xii. 23. Rev. xxi. 27.

Secondly, It is as plain, that no such personal perfection and freedom is found in any man on this side death and the grave, 1 John i. 8. 1 Kings viii. 46. Phil. iii. 12. a truth sealed by the sad experience of all the saints on earth.

Thirdly, If such freedom and perfection must be before we can be perfectly happy, and no such thing be done in this life, it remains that it must be done immediately upon their *dissolution*, and at the very time of their glorification. As sin came in at the time

of the union of their souls and bodies in the womb, so it will go
out at the time of their separation by death; then will Christ put
the last hand to this glorious work, and perfect that cure which
hath been so long under his hand, in this world; and thenceforth
sin shall have no power upon them, it shall never tempt them
more, it shall never defile them more, it shall never grieve and
sadden their hearts any more: henceforth it shall never cloud their
evidences, darken their understandings, or give the least interruption to their communion with God. When sin is gone, all
these, its mischievous effects, are gone with it. So that I may
speak it to the comfort of all gracious hearts, according to what
the Lord told the Israelites, in Deut. xii. 8, 9. (to which I allude
for illustration of this most comfortable truth) "Ye shall not do
" after all the things that ye do here this day, every man whatso-
" ever is right in his own eyes, for ye are not as yet come to the
" rest, and to the inheritance which the Lord your God giveth
" you." Whilst you are under Christ's cure upon earth, but not
perfectly healed, your understandings mistake, your thoughts
wander, your affections are dead, and your communion with God
is daily interrupted; but it shall not be so in heaven, where the
cure is perfect: you shall not there know, love, or delight in God
in the manner you do this day; for you are not as yet come to the
rest, and to the inheritance which the Lord your God giveth you.
And so much as to the diseases of sin, and Christ's method of
curing them.

Secondly, As sin is the disease of the *saints,* so also is *sorrow;*
the best *saints* must pass through the valley of *Bacha,* to heaven.
How many tears fall from the eyes of the *saints,* upon the account
of outward as well as inward troubles, even after their reconciliation
with God? Through much tribulation we must enter into the
" kingdom of God," Acts xiv. 22. It would be too great a di-
gression in this place, to note but the more general heads under
which almost infinite particulars of troubles and afflictions are
found; it shall suffice only to shew, that whatever distress or
trouble any poor soul is in, upon any account whatsoever, if that
soul belongs to Jesus Christ, he will take care of it *for the present,*
and deliver it at last by a complete cure.

First, Christ cures troubles, by *sanctifying* them to the souls of
his that are under affliction, and makes their very troubles *medici-
nal* and healing to them. Trouble is a *scorpion,* and hath a deadly
sting, but Christ is a wise *physician,* and extracts a sovereign oil
out of this *scorpion,* that heals the wound it makes. By afflictions,
our wise Physician purges our corruptions, and so prevents or
cures greater troubles by lesser; inward sorrows by outward ones.

Isa. xxvii. 9. " By this therefore shall the iniquity of Jacob be " purged, and this is all the fruit to take away his sin."

Secondly, Christ cures outward *troubles* by inward *consolations*, which are made to rise in the inner man as high as the waters of affliction do upon the outward man, 2 Cor. i. 5. One drop of spiritual comfort is sufficient to sweeten a whole ocean of outward trouble. It was an high expression of an afflicted father, whom God comforted, just upon the death of his dear and only son*, with some clearer manifestations of his love than was usual : " O, " (said he) might I but have such consolations as these, I could " be willing (were it possible) to lay an only son into the grave " every day I have to live in this world." Thus all the troubles of the world are cured by Christ. John xvi. 33. " In the world " ye shall have trouble, but in me ye shall have peace."

Thirdly, Christ cures all outward sorrows and troubles in his people *by death*, which is their removal from the place of sorrows to peace and rest for evermore. Now God wipes all tears from their eyes, and the days of their mourning are at an end ; they then put off the garments and spirit of mourning, and enter into peace, Isa. lvii. 2. They come to that place and state where tears and sighs are things unknown to the inhabitants ; one step beyond the state of this mortality, brings us quite out of the sight and hearing of all troubles and lamentations. These are the diseases of souls ; *sin*, and *sorrow* ; and thus they are cured by Christ, the *Physician*.

Secondly, Next I shall shew you that Jesus Christ is the only *Physician* of souls, none like him for a sick *sinner* ; and this will be evident in divers respects.

First, None so *wise* and judicious as Jesus Christ, to understand and comprehend the nature, depth and danger of soul-diseases. O how ignorant and unacquainted are men with the state and case of afflicted souls ! But " Christ hath the tongue of the learned, " that he should know how to speak a word in season to him that " is weary," Isa. l. 4. He only understands the weight of sin, and depth of inward troubles of sin.

Secondly, None so able to cure and heal the wounds of afflicted souls as Christ is ; he only hath those medicines that can cure a sick soul. The blood of Christ, and nothing else, in heaven or earth, is able to cure the mortal wounds which guilt inflicts upon a trembling conscience ; let men try all other receipts, and costly experience shall convince them of their insufficiency. Conscience may be benumbed by stupefactive medicines, prepared by the devil,

---

* *Nihil corpus sentit in nervo, cum anima sit in cælo*, i. e. The body has no feeling when the soul is in heaven.

for that end; but pacified it can never be but by the blood of Christ, Heb. xvi. 22.

Thirdly, None so tender-hearted and sympathizing with sick souls as Jesus Christ; he is full of bowels and tender compassions to afflicted souls; he is one that can have compassion, because he hath had experience, Heb. v. 2. If I must come unto the surgeon's hands with broken bones, give me such an one to chuse whose own bones have been broken, who hath felt the anguish in himself. Christ knows what it is by experience, having felt the anguish of inward troubles, the weight of God's wrath, and the terrors of a forsaking God, more than any or all the sons of men: this makes him tender over distressed souls. Isa. xlii. 3. "A " bruised reed he will not break, and smoking flax he will not " quench."

Fourthly, None cures in so wonderful a method as Christ doth; he heals us by his stripes, Isa. liii. 5. The Physician dies that the patient may live: his wounds must bleed, that ours may be cured; he feels the smart and pain, that we might have ease and comfort. No physician but Christ will cure others at this rate.

Fifthly, None so ready to relieve a sick soul as Christ; he is within the call of a distressed soul at all times. Art thou sick for sin, weary of sin, and made truly willing to part with sin? lift up but thy sincere cry to the Lord Jesus for help, and he will quickly be with thee. When the prodigal, the emblem of a convinced, humbled sinner, said, in himself, I will return to my father, the father ran to meet him, Luke xv. 20. He can be with thee in a moment.

Sixthly, None so willing to receive and undertake all distressed and afflicted souls as Jesus Christ is; he refuses none that come to him. John vi. 37. "He that cometh unto me, I will in no wise " cast out." Whatever their sins have been, or their sorrows are; however they have wounded their own souls with the deepest gashes of guilt; how desperate and helpless soever their case appears in their own or others eyes, he never puts them off, or discourages them, if they be but willing to come, Isa. i. 18, 19.

Seventhly, None so happy and successful as Christ; he never fails of performing a perfect cure upon those he undertakes; never was it known that any soul miscarried in his hands, John iii. 15, 16. Other physicians, by mistakes, by ignorance, or carelessness, fill church-yards, and cast away the lives of men; but Christ suffers none to perish that commit themselves to him.

Eighthly, None so free and generous as Christ; he doth all *gratis;* he sells not his medicines, though they be of infinite value; but freely gives them; Isa. lv. 1. "He that hath no money, let him " come." If any be sent away, it is the rich, Luke i. 53. not the poor and needy : those that will not accept the remedy as a free gift, but will needs purchase it at a price.

Ninthly, and *lastly,* None rejoice in the recovery of souls more than Christ doth. O ! it is unspeakably delightful to him to see the efficacy of his blood upon our souls; Isa. liii. 11. " Hé shall see " the travail of his soul, (i. e. the success of his death and suffer- " ings) and shall be satisfied." When he foresaw the success of the gospel upon the world, it is said, Luke x. 21. " In that hour " Jesus rejoiced in Spirit." And thus you see there is no physician like Christ for sick souls.

The uses of this point are,

For information and direction.

First, From whence we are informed of many great and neces- sary truths deducible from this : As,

Inference 1. *How inexpressible is the grace of God, in providing such a physician as Christ, for the sick and dying souls of sinners!* O blessed be God that there is a *balm in Gilead, and a Physician there !* that their case is not desperate, forlorn and remediless, as that the devils and damned is. There is but one case exempted from cure, and that, such as is not incident to any sensible, afflicted soul, Matth. xii. 31. and this only excepted, all manner of sins and dis- eases are capable of a cure. Though there be such a disease as is incurable, yet take this for thy comfort, never any soul was sick, i. e. sensibly burdened with it, and willing to come to Jesus Christ for healing; for under that sin the will is so wounded, that they have no desire to Christ. O inestimable mercy ! that the sickest sinner is capable of a perfect cure ! There be thousands, and ten thousands now in heaven and earth, who said once, Never was any case like theirs; so dangerous, so hopeless. The greatest of sinners have been perfectly recovered by Christ, 1 Tim. i. 15. 1 Cor. vi. 11. O mercy, never to be duly estimated !

Infer. 2. *What a powerful restraint from sin is the very method ordained by God for the cure of it!* Isa. liii. 5. " By his stripes we " are healed." The Physician must die, that the patient might live; no other thing but the blood, the precious blood of Christ, is found in heaven or earth able to heal us, Heb. ix. 22, 26. This blood of Christ must be freshly applied to every new wound sin makes upon our souls, 1 John ii. 1, 2. every new sin wounds him afresh, opens the wounds of Christ anew. O think of this again and again, you that so easily yield to the solicitations of Satan. Is it so easy and so cheap to sin as you seem to make it ? Doth the cure of souls cost nothing ? True, it is free to us, but was it so to Christ ? No, it was not; he knows the price of it, though you do not. Hath Christ healed you by his stripes, and can you put him under fresh sufferings for you so easily ? Have you forgot also your own sick days and nights for sin, that you are careless in resisting and preventing it? Sure it is not easy for saints to wound Christ, and their own souls, at one stroke. If you renew your sins, you must also renew your sorrows and repentance, Psal. li. title. 2 Sam. xii. 13. you must feel the anguish and pain of a troubled spirit again, things with which the saints are not unacquainted; of which they may say, as the church, " Remembering my affliction, the worm- " wood and the gall, my soul hath them still in remembrance," Lam. iii. 19. Yea, and if you will be remiss in your watch, and so easily incur new guilt, though a pardon in the blood of Christ may heal your souls, yet some rod or other, in the hand of a dis- pleased father, shall afflict your bodies, or smite you in your out- ward comforts, Psal. lxxxix. 23.

Inf. 3. If Christ be the only physician of sick souls, what sin and folly is it for men to take Christ's work out of his hands, and at- tempt to be their own physician.

Thus do those that superstitiously endeavour to heal their souls by afflicting their bodies; not Christ's blood, but their own, must be the plaister: and as blind Papists, so many carnal and ignorant Protestants strive, by confession, restitution, reformation, and stricter course of life, to heal those wounds that sin hath made upon their souls, without any respect to the blood of Christ: but this course shall not profit them at all. It may, for a time divert, but can never heal them: the wounds so skinned over, will open and bleed again. God grant it be not when our souls shall be out of the reach of the true and only remedy.

Inf. 4. How sad is the case of those souls, to whom Christ hath not yet been been a physician? They are mortally wounded by sin, and are like to die of their sickness; no saving, healing applications have hitherto been made unto their souls: and this is the case of the greatest part of mankind, yea, of them that live under the discoveries of Christ in the gospel. Which appears by these sad symptoms.

First, In that their eyes have not yet been opened, to see their sin and misery; in which illumination the cure of souls begin, Acts xxvi. 18. To this day he hath not given them eyes to see, Deut. xxix. 4. but that terrible stroke of God which blinds and hardens them, is too visibly upon them, mentioned in Isa. vi. 9, 10. No hope of healing, till the sinner's eyes be opened to see his sin and misery.

Secondly, In that nothing will divorce and separate them from their lusts; a sure sign they are not under Christ's cure, nor were ever made sick of sin. O if ever Christ be a physician to thy soul, he will make thee loathe what now thou lovest, and say to thy most pleasant and most profitable lusts, *Get ye hence,* Isa. xxx. 22.

Till then, there is no ground to think that Christ is a physician to you.

Thirdly, In that they have no sensible and pressing need of Christ, nor make any earnest enquiry after him, as most certainly you would do, if you were in the way of healing and recovery. These, and many other sad symptoms, do too plainly discover the disease of sin, to be in its full strength upon your souls; and if it so continue, how dreadful will the issue be? See Isa. vi. 9, 10.

Inf. 5. *What cause have they to be glad, that are under the hand and care of Christ, in order to a cure, and who do find, or may, upon due examination, find their souls are in a very hopeful way of recovery!* Can we rejoice when the strength of a natural disease is broken, and nature begins to recover ease and vigour again? And shall we not much more rejoice, when our souls begin to mend, and recover sensibly, and all comfortable signs of health and life appear upon them? particularly, when the understanding, which was ignorant and dark, hath the light of life beginning to dawn into it; such is that in 1 John ii. 27. When the will which was rebellious and inflexible to the will of God, is brought to comply with that holy will, saying, " Lord, what wilt thou " have me to do?" Acts ix. 6. When the heart, which was harder than an adamant, is now brought to contrition for sin, and can mourn as heartily over it, as ever a father did for a dead son, a beloved and only son; when its aversations from God are gone, at least have no such power as once they had; but the thoughts are now fixed much upon God, and spiritual things begin to grow pleasant to the soul; when times of duty come to be longed for, and the soul never better pleased than in such seasons: when the hypocrisy of the heart is purged out, so that we begin to do all that we do heartily, as unto the Lord, and not unto men, Col. iii. 23. 1 Thess. ii. 4. when we begin to make conscience of secret sins, Psal. cxix. 113. and of secret duties, Matth. vi. 5, 6. when we have an equal respect to all God's commandments, Psal. cxix. 8. and our hearts are under the holy and awful eye of God, which doth indeed over-awe our souls, Gen. xvii. 1. O what sweet signs of a recovering soul are these! Surely such are in the skilful hand of the great Physician, who will perfect what yet remains to be done.

Second use for direction.

In the last place, this point yields matter of advice and direction to poor souls that are under the disease of sin; and they are of two sorts, which I will distinctly speak to: viz. *First,* Such as are under their first sickness of spiritual sorrow for sin, and know not what course to take: or, *Secondly,* Such as have been longer in the hands of Christ the Physician, but are troubled to see the cure advance so slowly upon them, and fear the issue.

First, As to those that are in their first troubles for sin, and know not what course to take for ease and safety; I would address to them these following counsels.

First, Shut your ears against the dangerous counsels of carnal persons, or relations; for as they themselves are unacquainted with these troubles, so also are they with all proper remedies: and it is very usual with the devil to convey his temptations to distressed souls, by such hands; because, by them, he can do it with least suspicion. It was Augustine's complaint, that his own father took little care for his soul; and many parents act, in this case, as if they were employed by Satan.

Secondly, Be not too eager to get out of trouble, but be content to take God's way, and wait his time. No woman that is wise, would desire to have her travail hastened one day before the due time; nor will it be your interest to hasten too soon out of trouble. It is true, times of trouble are apt to seem tedious; but a false peace will endanger you more than a long trouble: a man may lengthen his own troubles to the loss of his own peace, and may shorten them to the hazard of his own soul.

Thirdly, Open your case to wise, judicious, and experienced Christians, and especially the ministers of Christ, whose office it is to counsel and direct you in these difficulties; and let not your troubles lie, like a secret, smothering fire, always in your own breasts. I know men are more ashamed to open their sins under convictions, than they were to commit them before conviction: but this is your interest, and the true way to your rest and peace. If there be with you, or near you, an interpreter, one of a thousand, to shew you your righteousness, and remedy, as it lies in Christ; neglect not your own souls, in a sinful concealment of your case: it will be the joy of their hearts to be employed in such work as this.

Fourthly, Be much with God in secret, open your hearts to him, and pour out your complaints into his bosom. The cii. Psalm bears a title very suitable to your case and duty; yea, you will find if your troubles work kindly, and God intend a cure upon your souls, that nothing will be able to keep God and your souls asunder: whatever your incumbrances in the world be, some time will be daily redeemed, to be spent betwixt God and you.

Fifthly, Plead hard with God in prayer for help and healing. " Heal my soul, (saith David) for I have sinned against thee," Psal. xli. 4. Tell him Christ hath his commission sealed for such as you are: he was sent to " bind up the broken-hearted," Isa. lxi. 1. Tell him he came into the world, " to seek and save that which

" was lost," and so are you now, in your own account and apprehensions. Lord, what profit is there in my blood? Wilt thou pursue a dried leaf? And why is my heart wounded with the sense of sin, and mine eyes open to see my danger and misery; Are not these the first dawnings of mercy upon sinners? O let it appear, that the time of mercy, even the set time, is now come.

Sixthly, Understand your peace to be in Christ only, and faith to be the only way to Christ and rest; let the great enquiry of your souls be after Christ and faith; study the nature and necessity of these, and cry to God day and night for strength to carry you to Christ in the way of faith.

Secondly, As to those that have been longer under the hands of Christ, and yet are still in troubles, and cannot obtain peace, but their wounds bleed still, and all they hear in sermons, or do in the way of duty, will not bring them to rest; to such I only add two or three words for a close.

First, Consider whether you have rightly closed with Christ since your first awakening, and whether there be not some way of sin, in which you still live: if so, no wonder your wounds are kept open, and your souls are strangers to peace.

Secondly, If you be conscious of no such flaw in the foundation, consider how much of this trouble may arise from your constitution and natural temper, which being melancholy, will be doubtful and suspicious; you may find it so in other cases of less moment, and be sure Satan will not be wanting to improve it.

Thirdly, Acquaint yourselves more with the nature of true justifying faith; a mistake in that hath prolonged the troubles of many; if you look for it in no other act but assurance, you may easily overlook it as it lies, in the mean time, in your affiance or acceptance. A true and proper conception of saving faith would go far in the cure of many troubled souls.

Fourthly, Be more thankful to shun sin, than to get yourselves clear of trouble: it is sad to walk in darkness, but worse to lie under guilt. Say, Lord, I would rather be grieved myself, than be a grief to thy Spirit. O keep me from sin, how long soever thou keep me under sorrow. Wait on God in the way of faith, and in a tender spirit towards sin, and thy wounds shall be healed at last by thy great Physician.

Thanks be to God for Jesus Christ.

SERMON XI.

Containing the Second Motive to enforce the general Exhortation, from a second Title of CHRIST.

LUKE i. 72.

To perform the mercy promised to our fathers, and remember his holy covenant.

THIS scripture is part of Zechariah's prophecy, at the rising of that bright star, John, the harbinger and fore-runner of Christ: They are some of the first words he spake after God had loosed his tongue, which, for a time, was struck dumb for his unbelief. His tongue is now unbound, and at liberty to proclaim to all the world, the unspeakable riches of mercy through Jesus Christ, in a song of praise. Wherein note,

The mercy celebrated, viz. redemption by Christ, ver. 68.

The description of Christ by place and property, ver. 69.

The faithfulness of God in our redemption this way, ver. 70.

The benefit of being so redeemed by Christ, ver. 71.

The exact accomplishment of all the promises made to the *fathers* in sending Christ, the mercy promised, into the world, ver. 72. " To perform the mercy promised to our fathers," &c. In these words we find two parts, viz.

1. A mercy freely promised.

2. The promised mercy faithfully performed.

First, You have a mercy freely promised, viz. by God the Father, from the beginning of the world, and often repeated and confirmed in several succeeding ages, to the fathers, in his covenant-transactions.

This mercy is Jesus Christ, of whom he speaks in this prophecy: the same which he stiles " An horn of salvation in the house of " David," ver. 69.

The mercy of God in scripture, is put either for,

1. His free favour to the creature. Or,

2. The effects and fruits of that favour.

It is put for the free and undeserved favour of God to the creature, and this favour of God may respect the creature two ways, either as *undeserving,* or as *ill-deserving.*

It respected innocent man, as *undeserving,* for Adam could put no obligation upon his benefactor. It respecteth fallen man, as *ill-deserving.* Innocent man could not merit favour, and fallen man did merit wrath: the favour or mercy of God to both is every way free; and that is the first acceptation of the word *mercy:*

but then it is also taken for the effects and fruits of God's favour, and they are either,

1. Principal and primary: or,
2. Subordinate and secondary.

Of secondary and subordinate mercies, there are multitudes, both temporal, respecting the body, and spiritual, respecting the soul; but the principal and primary mercy is but one, and that is Christ, the first-born of mercy; the capital mercy, the comprehensive root-mercy, from whom are all other mercies; and therefore called by a singular emphasis in my text, *The mercy;* i. e. the mercy of all mercies; without whom no drop of saving mercy can flow to any of the sons of men; and in whom are all the tender bowels of divine mercy yearning upon poor sinners. *The mercy,* and *the mercy promised.* The first promise of Christ was made to Adam, Gen. iii. 15. and was frequently renewed afterwards to Abraham, to David, and as the text speaks, *unto the fathers,* in their respective generations.

Secondly, We find here also the promised mercy faithfully performed; " To perform the mercy promised." What mercy soever the love of God engaged him to promise, the faithfulness of God stands engaged for the performance thereof. Christ, the promised mercy, is not only performed *truly,* but he is also performed according to the promise in all the circumstances thereof, *exactly.* So he was promised to the fathers, and just so performed to us their children: Hence the note is,

Doct. *That Jesus Christ, the mercy of mercies, was graciously promised and faithfully performed by God to his people.*

Three things are here to be opened.
First, Why Christ is stiled *the mercy.*
Secondly, What kind of mercy Christ is to his people.
Thirdly, How this mercy was performed.

First, Christ is the mercy, *emphatically* so called: the peerless, invaluable, and matchless mercy: Because he is the prime fruit of the mercy of God to sinners. The mercies of God are infinite; mercy gave the world and us our being; all our protection, provision, and comforts in this world are the fruits of mercy, the free gifts of divine favour: but Christ is the first and chief; all other mercies, compared with him, are but fruits from that root, and streams from that fountain of mercy; the very bowels of divine mercy are in Christ, as in ver. 78. according to the tender mercies, or as the Greek, the yearning bowels of the mercy of God.

Secondly, Christ is the *mercy,* because all the mercy of God to

sinners is dispensed and conveyed through Christ to them, John i.
16. Col. ii. 3. Eph. iv. 7.   Christ is the *medium* of all divine communications, the *channel* of grace, through him are both the *de-
cursus et recursus gratiarum;* the flows of mercy from God to us,
and the returns of praise from us to God.   Fond and vain therefore
are all the expectations of mercy out of Christ; no drop of saving
mercy runs beside this channel.

Thirdly, Christ is the *mercy,* because all inferior mercies derive
both their *nature, value, sweetness,* and *duration* from Christ, the
fountain-mercy of all other-mercies.

First, They derive their *nature* from Christ; for out of him,
those things which men call mercies, are rather traps and snares,
than mercies to them, Prov. i. 32.   The time will come when the
rich that are christless, will wish, O that we had been poor ! And
nobles, that are now ennobled by the new birth, O that we had been
among the low rank of men !   All these things that pass for valuable
mercies, like *cyphers,* signify much when such an important figure as
Christ stands before them, else they signify nothing to any man's
comfort or benefit.

Secondly, They derive their *value* as well as nature from Christ:
For how little, I pray you, doth it signify to any man to be rich,
honourable, politic, and successful in all his designs in this world,
if after all he must lie down in hell?

Thirdly, All other mercies derive their *sweetness* from Christ, and
are but insipid things without him.   There is a twofold sweetness
in things; one *natural,* another *spiritual:* Those that are out of
Christ can relish the first, believers only relish both.   They have
the natural sweetness that is in mercy itself, and a sweetness supernatural from Christ and the covenant, the way in which they receive them.   Hence it is, that some men taste more spiritual sweetness in their *daily bread,* than others do in the *Lord's supper;* and
the same mercy, by this means, becomes a feast to soul and body at
once.

Fourthly, All mercies have their *duration* and perpetuity from
Christ; all christless persons hold their mercies upon the greatest
contingencies and terms of uncertainty; if they be continued during this life, that is all: there is not one drop of mercy after
death.   But the mercies of the saints are continued to eternity;
the end of their mercies on earth, is the beginning of their better
mercies in heaven.   There is a twofold end of mercies, one *per-
fective,* another *destructive;* the death of the saints perfects and
completes their mercies ; the death of the wicked destroys and
cuts off their mercies.   For these reasons, Christ is called the
mercy.

Secondly, In the next place, let us enquire what kind of mercy

Christ is; and we shall find many lovely and transcendent properties to commend him to our souls.

First, He is *free* and undeserved mercy, called upon that account, *The gift of God*, John iv. 10.   And to shew how freè this
gift was, God gave him to us when we were enemies, Rom. v. 8.
Needs must that mercy be free, which is given, not only to the undeserving, but to the ill-deserving; the benevolence of God was
the sole, impulsive cause of this gift, John iii. 16.

Secondly, Christ is a *full* mercy, replenished with all that answers
to the *wishes*, or *wants* of sinners; in him alone is found whatever
the justice of an angry God requires for satisfaction, or the necessities of souls require for their supply.   Christ is full of mercy, both
extensively, and *intensively*; in him are all kinds and sorts of mercies; and in him are the highest and most perfect degrees of
mercy; " For it pleased the Father, that in him should all fulness
" dwell," Col. i. 19.

Thirdly, Christ is the *seasonable* mercy, given by the Father to
us in due time, Rom. v. 6.   In the fulness of time, Gal. iv. 4. a
seasonable mercy in his *exhibition* to the world in *general*, and a
seasonable mercy in his *application* to the soul in *particular*; the
wisdom of God pitched upon the best time for his incarnation,
and it takes the very properest for its application.   When a poor
soul is distressed, lost, at its wits end, and ready to perish, then
comes Christ.   All God's works are done in season, but none more
seasonable than this great work of salvation by Christ.

Fourthly, Christ is the *necessary mercy*, there is an absolute necessity of Jesus Christ; hence in scripture he is called the " bread
of life," John vi. 41. he is bread to the hungry; he is the " water
of life," John vii. 37. as cold water to the thirsty soul.   He is a
ransom for captives, Mat. xx. 28. a garment to the naked, Rom.
xiii. *ult.*   Bread is not so necessary to the hungry, nor water to the
thirsty, nor a ransom to the captive, nor a garment to the naked,
as Christ is to the soul of a sinner: The breath of our nostrils, the
life of our souls is in Jesus Christ.

Fifthly, Christ is a *fountain-mercy*, and all other mercies flow
from him: A believer may say with Christ, " All my springs are
" in thee ;" from his merit, and from his spirit, flow our redemption, justification, sanctification, peace, joy in the Holy Ghost, and
blessedness in the world to come: " In that day shall there be a
" fountain opened," Zech. xiii. 1.

Sixthly, Christ is a *satisfying mercy*; he that is full of Christ, can
feel the want of nothing.   " I desire to know nothing but Jesus
" Christ, and him crucified," 1 Cor. ii. 2.   Christ bounds and
terminates the vast desires of the soul: He is the very sabbath of
the soul.   How hungry, empty, and straitened on every side is the

soul of man in the abundance and fulness of all outward things, till it come to Christ? the weary motions of a restless soul, like those of a river, cannot be at rest till they pour themselves into Christ, the ocean of blessedness.

Seventhly, Christ is a *peculiar mercy,* intended for, and applied to a remnant among men; some would extend redemption as large as the world, but the gospel limits it to those only that believe; and those believers are upon that account called a *peculiar people,* 1 Pet. ii. 9. The offers of Christ indeed are large and general, but the application of Christ is but to few, Isa. liii. 1. The greater cause have they to whom Christ comes, to lie with their mouths in the dust, astonished and overwhelmed with the sense of so peculiar and distinguished a mercy.

Eighthly, Jesus Christ is a *suitable mercy,* suited in every respect to all our needs and wants, 1 Cor. i. 20. wherein the admirable wisdom of God is illustriously displayed; " Ye are complete in " him," (saith the apostle) Col. ii. 20. Are we enemies? He is *reconciliation:* Are we sold to sin and Satan? He is *redemption:* Are we condemned by the law? He is the Lord our righteousness: Hath sin polluted us? He is a *fountain opened* for sin, and for uncleanness: Are we lost by departing from God? He is the *way* to the Father. Rest is not so suitable to the weary, nor bread to the hungry, as Christ is to the sensible sinner.

Ninthly, Christ is an *astonishing and wonderful mercy;* his Name is called *wonderful,* Isa. ix. 6. and as his name is, so is he; a wonderful Christ: His Person is a wonder, 1 Tim. iii. 16. " Great is " the mystery of godliness, God manifested in the flesh."

His abasement is wonderful, Phil. ii. 6. His love is a wonderful love; his redemption full of wonders; angels desire to look into it. He is, and will be admired by *angels* and *saints* to all eternity.

Tenthly, Jesus Christ is *an incomparable and matchless mercy;* " as the apple-tree among the trees of the wood, so is my beloved " among the sons," (saith the enamoured spouse) Cant. ii. 3. Draw the comparison how you will betwixt Christ and all other enjoyments, you will find none in heaven nor on earth to equal him: He is more than all *externals,* as the light of the *sun* is more than that of a *candle:* Nay, even the worst of Christ is better than the best of the world; his reproaches are better than the world's pleasures, Heb. xi. 25. He is more than all *spirituals,* as the *fountain* is more than the *stream.* He is more than justification, as the *cause* is more than the *effect*; more than sanctification, as the *person* himself is more than the image or *picture.* He is more than all peace, all comfort, all joy, as the *tree* is more than the *fruit.* Nay, draw the comparison betwixt Christ and things eternal, and you will find him better than they; for what is in heaven without Christ, Psal. lxxiii. 25. " Whom have I in heaven but thee?" If Christ should say to the saints, take heaven among you, but as for me I will withdraw myself from ycu; the saints would weep, even in heaven itself, and say, Lord, heaven will be no more heaven to us, except thou be there, who art by far the better half of heaven.

Eleventhly, Christ is an *unsearchable mercy;* who can fully express his wonderful name? Prov. xxx. 4. Who can tell over his *unsearchable riches?* Eph. iii. 8. Hence it is that souls never tire in the study or love of Christ, because new wonders are eternally rising out of him. He is a deep which no line of any created understanding, angelical or human, can fathom.

Twelfthly, and *lastly,* Christ is an *everlasting mercy;* " the same " yesterday, to day, and for ever," Heb. xiii. 8. All other enjoyments are perishable, time-eaten things; time, like a moth, will fret them out; but the riches of Christ are durable riches, Prov. viii. 18. The graces of Christ are durable graces, John iv. 14. All the creatures are flowers, that appear and fade in their month; but this Rose of Sharon, this Lily of the Valley never withers. Thus you see the mercy performed with its desirable properties.

Thirdly, The last thing to be opened is the manner of God's performing his mercy to his people; which the Lord did,

1. Really and truly, as he had promised him.

2. Exactly agreeable to the promises and predictions of him.

First, Really and truly; as he had promised, so he made good the promise. Acts ii. 36. " Let all the house of Israel know assu- " redly, that God hath made that same Jesus, whom ye crucified, " both Lord and Christ."

The manifestation of Christ in the flesh was no phantasm or delusion, but a most evident and palpable truth. 1 John i. 1. " That which we have heard, which we have seen with our eyes, " which we have looked upon, and our hands have handled." A truth so certain, that the assertors of it appealed to the very enemies of Christ for the certainty thereof, Acts ii. 22. Yea, not only the sacred, but profane writers, witness to it; not only the *evangelists* and *apostles,* but even the *heathen* writers of those times, both *Roman* and *Jewish,* as Suetonius, Tacitus, Plinius the younger, and Josephus the *Jewish antiquary,* do all acknwledge it.

Secondly, As God did really and truly perform Christ the promised mercy, so he performed this promised mercy *exactly* agreeable to the promises, types, and predictions made of him to the fathers, even the most minute circumstances thereof. This is a great truth for our faith to be etablished in: let us, therefore, cast our eyes both upon the *promises* and *performances* of God, with respect to Christ, the mercy of mercies.   See how he was represented to the fathers long before his manifestation in the flesh ; and what an one he appeared to be when he was really exhibited in the flesh.

First, As to his person and qualifications, as it was *foretold,* so it was *fulfilled.*   His original was said to be unsearchable and eternal, Micah v. 2. and so he affirmed himself to be, Rev. i. 11.   " I am " Alpha and Omega, the first and the last." John vi. 31, 32. " Before Abraham was, I am."   His two natures, united into one person, were plainly foretold, Zech. xiii. 7.   *The man my Fellow ;* and such a one God performed, Rom. ix. 5.   His immaculate purity and holiness were foretold, Dan. ix. 24.   " To anoint the " most Holy ;" some render it, *the great Saint,* the Prince of Saints ; and such an one he was indeed, when he lived in this world.   John viii. 46.   " Which of you convinceth me of sin ?" His Offices were foretold, the prophetical Office predicted, Deut. xviii. 15. and fulfilled in him, John i. 18.   His priestly Office foretold, Psal. cx. 4. fulfilled, Heb. ix. 14. his kingly Office foretold, Micah v. 2. and in him fulfilled ; his very enemies being judges, Matth. xxvii. 37.

Secondly, As to his birth, the time, place, and manner thereof were foretold to the fathers, and exactly performed to a tittle.

First, The time prefixed, more generally in *Jacob's prophecy,* Gen. xliv. 10.   When the sceptre should depart from Judah, as, indeed, it did in Herod the Idumean : More particularly in Daniel's seventy weeks, from the decree of Darius, Dan. ix. 24. answering exactly to the time of his birth ; so cogent and full of proof, that Porphyry, the great enemy of Christians, had no other evasion, but that this prophecy was devised after the event : Which yet the Jews (as bitter enemies to Christ as himself) will by no means allow to be true.   And, lastly, the time of his birth was exactly pointed at in Haggai's prophecy, Hag. ii. 7, 9. compared with Mal. iii. 1.   He must come while the second temple stood ; at that time was a general expectation of him, John i. 19. and at that very time he came, Luke ii. 38.

Secondly, The place of his birth was foretold to be Bethlehem Ephrata, Micah v. 2. and so it was, Matth. ii. 5, 6. to be brought up in Nazareth, Zech. vi. 12.   " Behold the man whose name is " the Branch."   The word is *Netzer,* whence is the word Nazarite.   And there indeed was our Lord brought up, Mat. ii. 23.

Thirdly, His parent was to be a *virgin,* Isa. vii. 14. punctually fulfilled, Matth. i. 20, 21, 22, 23.

Fourthly, His stock, or tribe, was foretold to be Judah, Gen.

xlix. 10. and it is evident, saith the apostle, " that our Lord sprang
" out of Judah," Heb. vii. 14.

Fifthly, His *harbinger,* or forerunner was foretold, Mal. iv. 5,
6. fulfilled in John the Baptist, Luke i. 16, 17.

Sixthly, The obscurity and meanness of his birth were predicted, Isa. liii. 2. Zech. ix. 9. to which the event answered, Luke
ii. 12.

Thirdly, His doctrine and miracles were foretold, Isa. xvi. 1, 2.
xxxv. 4, 5. the accomplishment whereof in Christ is evident in the
history of all the *evangelists.*

Fourthly, His death for us was foretold by the prophets, Dan.
ix. 26. " The Messiah shall be cut off, but not for himself:" Isa.
liii. 5. " He was wounded for our transgressions." And so he was,
John xi. 50. The very kind and manner of his death was pre-
figured in the brazen serpent, his type; and answered in his death
upon the cross, John iii. 14.

Fifthly, His burial in the *tomb* of a rich man was foretold, Isa.
liii. 9. and accomplished most exactly, Matth. xxvii. 59, 60.

Sixthly, His resurrection from the dead was typed out in Jonah,
and fulfilled in Christ's abode three days and nights in the grave,
Matth. xii. 49.

Seventhly, The wonderful spreading of the gospel in the world,
even to the Isles of the Gentiles, was prophesied of, Isa. xlix. 6.
to the truth whereof we are not only the witnesses, but the happy
instances and examples of it. Thus the promised mercy was performed.

Inference 1. *If Christ be the mercy of mercies, the medium of
conveying all other mercies from God to men; then in vain do men
expect and hope for mercy of God out of Jesus Christ.*

I know many poor sinners comfort themselves with this, when
they come upon a bed of sickness; I am sinful, but God is merciful: and it is very true God is merciful; plenteous in mercy; his
mercy is great above the heavens; mercy pleaseth him; and all
this they that are in Christ shall find experimentally, to their comfort and salvation. But what is all this to thee, if thou art Christless? There is not one drop of saving mercy that comes in any
other channel than Christ to the soul of any man.

But must I then expect no mercy out of Christ? This is a hard
case, very uncomfortable doctrine. Yes, thou mayest be a Christless, and covenantless soul, and yet have variety of temporal mercies, as Ishmael had, Gen. xvii. 20, 21. God may give thee the
fatness of the earth, riches, honours, pleasures, a numerous and
prosperous posterity; will that content thee? Yes, yes, if I may
have heaven too: No, neither heaven, nor pardon, nor any other
spiritual or eternal mercy may be expected out of Christ, Jude,

ver. 21. O deceive not yourselves in this point; there are two bars betwixt you and all spiritual mercies, viz. the guilt of sin, and the filth of sin; and nothing but your own union with Christ can remove these, and so open the passage for spiritual mercies to your souls.

Why, but I will repent of sin, strive to obey the commands of God, make restitution for the wrongs I have done, cry to God for mercy, bind my soul with vows and strong resolutions against sin for time to come: will not all this lay a ground-work for hope of mercy to my soul? No, this will not, this cannot do.

First, All your *sorrows,* tears and mournings for sin cannot obtain mercy; could you shed as many tears for any sin that ever you committed, as all the children of Adam have shed upon any account whatsoever, since the creation of the world; they will not purchase the pardon of that one sin; for the law accepts no short payment; it requires plenary satisfaction, and will not discharge any soul without it; nor can it acknowledge or own your souls to be such. The repentance of a soul finds, through Christ, acceptance with God, but out of him it is nothing.

Secondly, All your *strivings* to obey the commands of God, and live more strictly for time to come, will not obtain mercy. Matth. v. 20. " Except your righteousness shall exceed the righteousness " of the Scribes and Pharisees, ye shall in no case enter into the " kingdom of heaven."

Thirdly, Your *restitution,* and reparation of wrongs you have done, cannot obtain mercy. Judas restored, and yet was damned. Man is repaired, but God is not. Remission is the act of God, it is he must loose your consciences from the bond of guilt, or they can never be loosed.

Fourthly, All your *cries* to God for mercy will not prevail for mercy, if you be out of Christ, Matth. vii. 22. Job xxvii. 29. A righteous judge will not reverse the just sentence of the law, though the prisoner at the bar fall upon his knees, and cry, Mercy, mercy.

Fifthly, Your *vows* and engagements to God for time to come cannot obtain mercy; for they being made in your own strength, it is impossible you should keep them; and if you could, yet it is impossible they should obtain remission and mercy: should you never sin more for time to come, yet how shall God be satisfied for sins past? Justice must have satisfaction, or you can never have remission, Rom. iii. 25, 26. and no work wrought by man can satisfy divine justice; nor is the satisfaction of Christ made over to any for their discharge, but to such only as are in him: therefore never expect mercy out of Christ.

Inf. 2. Is Christ, the mercy of mercies, greater, better, and more necessary than all other mercies : then let no inferior mercy satisfy you for your portion.

God hath mercies of all sorts to give, but Christ is the chief, the prime mercy of all mercies ; O be not satisfied without that mercy. When * Luther had a rich present sent him, "he protested God " should not put him off so :" and David was of the same mind, Psal. xvii. 14.   If the Lord should give any of you the desires of your hearts in the good things of this life, let not that satisfy you, whilst you are Christless.   For,

First, What is there in these earthly enjoyments, whereof the vilest men have not a greater fulness than you ? Job xxi. 7, 8, 9, 10, 11. Psal. xvii. 10. and lxxiii. 3, 12.

Secondly, What comfort can all these things give to a soul already condemned as thou art ; John iii. 18.

Thirdly, What sweetness can be in them, whilst they are all unsanctified things to you ? enjoyments and sanctification are two distinct things, Psal. xxxvii. 16. Prov. x. 22.   Thousands of unsanctified enjoyments will not yield your souls one drop of solid spiritual comfort.

Fourthly, What pleasure can you take in these things, of which death must shortly strip you naked ? You must die, you must die ; and whose then shall all those things be, for which you have laboured ? Be not so fond, to think of leaving a great name behind you : it is but a poor felicity (as Chrysostom well observes) to be tormented where thou art, and praised where thou art not † : the sweeter your portion hath been on earth, the more intolerable will your condition be in hell ; yea, these earthly delights do not only increase the torments of the damned, but also prepare (as they are instruments of sin) the souls of men for damnation, Prov. i. 32. " Surely the prosperity of fools shall destroy them."   Be restless, therefore, till Christ, the mercy of mercies, be the root and fountain, yielding and sanctifying all other mercies to you.

Inf. 3. Is Christ, the mercy of mercies, infinitely better than all other mercies ? then let all that be in Christ be content, and well satisfied, whatever other inferior mercies the wisdom of God sees fit to deny them.   You have a Benjamin's portion, a plentiful inheritance in Christ ; will you yet complain ? Others have houses, splendid and magnificent upon earth ; but you have " an house made without hands, eternal in the heavens," 2 Cor. v. 1.   Others are clothed with rich and costly apparel, your souls are clothed with the white, pure robes of Christ's righteousness.   Isa. lxi. 10. " I will greatly re-

---

* *Valde protestatus sum, me nolle sic ab eo satiari.* Luth.
† For then the devouring flame burns up those whom carnal pleasure pollutes.

" joice in the Lord, my soul shall be joyful in my God : for he
" hath clothed me with the garment of salvation, he hath covered
" me with the robe of righteousness, as a bridegroom decketh him-
" self with ornaments, and as a bride adorneth herself with jewels."
Let those that have full tables, heavy purses, rich lands, but no
Christ, be rather objects of your pity, than envy : it is better, like
store-cattle, to be kept lean and hungry, than with the fatted ox, to
tumble in flowry meadows, thence to be lead away to the shambles.
God hath not a better mercy to give than Christ, thy portion ; in
him all necessary mercies are secured to thee, and thy wants and
straits sanctified to thy good.   O ! therefore, never open thy mouth
to complain against the bountiful God.

  Inf. 4. Is Christ *the mercy*, i. e. he in whom all the tender mercies of God towards poor sinners are ; *then let none be discouraged
in going to Christ, by reason of the sin and unworthiness that are
in them :* his very name is *mercy,* and as his name is, so is he. Poor
drooping sinner, encourage thyself in the way of faith ; the Christ
to whom thou art going, is mercy itself to broken hearted sinners
moving towards him in the way of faith ; doubt not that mercy
will repulse thee ; it is against both its name and nature so to do.
Jesus Christ is so merciful to poor souls that come to him, that he
hath received and pardoned the chiefest of sinners ; men that
stood as remote from mercy as any in the world, 1 Tim. i. 15.
1 Cor. vi. 11.   Those that shed the blood of Christ, have yet
been washed in that blood from their sin, Acts ii. 36, 37.   Mercy receives sinners, without exception of great and heinous ones.
John vii. 37. " If any man thirst, let him come to me and drink."
Gospel invitations run, in general terms, to all sinners that are
heavy laden, Mat. xi. 28.   When Mr. Bilney the martyr heard a
minister preaching at this rate, O thou old sinner, who hast been
serving the devil these fifty or sixty years ; dost thou think that
Christ will receive thee now ? O ! said he, what a preaching of
Christ is here ? Had Christ been thus preached to me in the day
of my trouble for sin, what had become of me ? But, blessed be
God there is a sufficiency both of merit and mercy in Jesus Christ
for all sinners, for the vilest among sinners, whose hearts shall be
made willing to come unto him.   So merciful is the Lord Jesus
Christ, that he moves first, Isa. lxii. 1, 2. so merciful, that he up-
braids none, Ezek. xviii. 22. so merciful, that he will not despise
the weakest, if sincere, desires of souls, Isa. xlii. 3. so merciful,
that nothing more grieves him than our unwillingness to come
unto him for mercy, John v. 40. so merciful, that he waiteth to the
last upon sinners to shew them mercy, Rom. x. 21. Mat. xxiii. 37.
in a word, so merciful, that it is his greatest joy when sinners come
unto him, that he may shew them mercy, Luke xv. 5, 22.

Object. But yet it cannot enter into my thoughts that I should obtain mercy.

Sol. First, You measure God by yourselves, 1 Sam. xxiv. 19. " If a man find his enemy, will he let him go well away ?" Man will not, but the merciful God will, upon the submission of the enemies to him.

Secondly, You are discouraged, because you have not tried. Go to Jesus Christ, poor distressed sinners ; try him, and then report what a Christ thou findest him to be.

Object. But I have neglected the time of mercy, and now it is too late.

Sol. How know you that? Have you seen the book of life, or turned over the records of eternity ? Or do you not unwarrantably intrude into the secrets of God, which belong not to you ? Besides, if the treaty were at an end, how is it that thy heart is now distressed for sin, and solicitous after deliverance from it ?

Object. But I have waited long, and yet see no mercy for me.

Sol. May not mercy be coming, and you not see it ? Or have you not waited at the wrong door ? If you wait for the mercy of God through Christ, in the way of humiliation and faith, and continue waiting, assuredly mercy shall come at last.

Inf. 5. *Hath God performed the mercy promised to the Fathers, the great mercy, the capital mercy, Jesus Christ ; then let no man distrust God for the performance of lesser mercies contained in any other promises of the scripture.* The performance of this mercy secures the performance of all other mercies to us. For,

First, Christ is a greater mercy than any other which yet remains to be performed, Rom. viii. 32.

Secondly, This mercy virtually comprehends all other mercies, 1 Cor. iii. 21, 22, 23.

Thirdly, The promises that contain all other mercies, are ratified and confirmed to believers in Christ, 2 Cor. i. 20.

Fourthly, It was much more improbable that God would bestow his own Son upon the world, than that he should bestow any other mercy upon it. Wait, therefore, in a comfortable expectation of the fulfilling of all the rest of the promises in their seasons. Hath he given thee Christ? He will give thee bread to eat, raiment to put on, support in troubles, and whatsoever else thy soul or body stands in need of : The blessings contained in all other promises are fully secured by the performance of this great promise ; thy pardon, peace, acceptance with God now, and enjoyment of him for ever shall be fulfilled : The great mercy, Christ, makes way for all other mercies to the souls of believers.

Inf. 6. Lastly, *How mad are they that part with Christ, the best of mercies, to secure and preserve any temporal lesser mercies to*

themselves! Thus Demas and Judas gave up Christ to gain a little of the world; O soul-undoing bargain! How dear do they pay for the world, that purchase it with the loss of Christ, and their own peace for ever!

Blessed be God for Jesus Christ, the Mercy of mercies.

SERMON XII.

Containing a third Motive to enliven the general Exhortation from a third Title of CHRIST.

CANT. v. Part of Verse 16.

Yea, He is altogether lovely.

At the ninth verse of this chapter, you have a query propounded to the *spouse*, by the *daughters of Jerusalem*, "What is thy beloved more than another beloved?" To this question the spouse returns her answers in the following verses, wherein she asserts his excellency in general. Ver. 10. "He is the chiefest among ten thousands;" confirms that general assertion, by an enumeration of his particular excellencies, to ver. 16. where she closes up her *character* and *encomium* of her beloved, with an elegant *epiphonema*, in the words that I have read: "Yea, he is altogether lovely."

The words, you see, are an affirmative proposition, setting forth the transcendent loveliness of the Lord Jesus Christ; and naturally resolve themselves into three parts, viz.

1. The subject.
2. The predicate.
3. The manner of predication.

First, The *subject*, *He*, viz. the Lord Jesus Christ, after whom she had been seeking, for whom she was sick of love; concerning whom these daughters of Jerusalem had enquired: whom she had endeavoured so *graphically* to describe in his particular excellencies. This is the great and excellent *subject* of whom she here speaks.

Secondly, The *predicate*, or what she affirmeth or saith of him, viz. That he is a *lovely one, Machamaddim*, desires; according to the import of the * original, "which signifies earnestly to desire, covet, "or long after that which is most pleasant, grateful, delectable, "and admirable." The original word is both in the *abstract*, and

---

* *Significat appetere, expetere quod jocundum, gratum, voluptuosum, utile et amabile est.* Pag.

of the *plural number*, which speaks Christ to be the very essence of all delights and pleasures, the very soul and substance of them. As all the rivers are gathered into the ocean, which is the congregation or meeting-place of all the waters in the world : so Christ is that ocean in which all true delights and pleasures meet.

Thirdly, The *manner of predication;* He is [*altogether*] *lovely, Totus, totus desiderabilis;* lovely in all, and in every part; as if she had said, Look on him in what respect or particular you will; cast your eye upon this lovely object, and view him any way; turn him in your serious thoughts which way you will; consider his person, his offices, his works, or any other thing belonging to him; you will find him *altogether lovely,* There is nothing ungrateful in him, there is nothing lovely without him.   Hence note,

> Doct. *That Jesus Christ is the loveliest person souls can set their eyes upon,* Psal. xlv. 2. " Thou art fairer than the children " of men."

That is said of Jesus Christ, which cannot be said of any crea-ture ; that he is " altogether lovely."   In opening this lovely point I shall,

1. Weigh the importance of this phrase " altogether lovely."
2. Shew you in what respect Christ is so.

First, Let us weigh this excellent expression, and particularly consider what is contained in it, and you shall find this expression " altogether lovely."

First, That it excludes all unloveliness and distastefulness from Jesus Christ.   So * Vatablus; " There is nothing in him which is "not amiable."   The excellencies of Jesus Christ are perfectly ex-clusives of all their opposites; there is nothing of a contrary nature or quality found in him to alloy or debase his excellency.   And in this respect Christ infinitely transcends the most excellent and love-liest creatures.   For whatsoever loveliness is found in them, it is not without a distasteful tang; the fairest pictures must have their *shadows :* The most orient and transplendent stones must have their *foils* to set off their beauty ; the best creature is but a bitter sweet at best : If there be somewhat pleasing, there is also somewhat dis-tasting ; if there be gracious and natural excellencies in the same person to delight us, yet there is also some natural corruption in-termixed with it to distaste us : But it is not so in our altogether lovely Christ ; his excellencies are pure and unmixed ; he is a sea of sweetness without one drop of gall.

---

* *Nihil in eo quod non est amabile.*

Secondly, * *Altogether lovely,* i. e. as there is nothing unlovely found in him, so all that is in him is wholly lovely; as every ray of God is precious, so every thing that is in Christ is precious: Who can weigh Christ in a pair of balances, and tell you what his worth is? " His price is above rubies, and all that thou canst desire " is not to be compared with him," Prov. viii. 11.

Thirdly, Altogether lovely, i. e. He is comprehensive of all things that are lovely: he seals up the sum of all loveliness: *Quæ faciunt divisa beatum, in hoc mixta fluunt:* Things that shine as single stars with a particular glory, all meet in Christ as a glorious constellation. Col. i. 19. " It pleased the Father that in him should all fulness " dwell." Cast your eyes among all created beings, survey the universe, observe strength in one, beauty in a second, faithfulness in a third, wisdom in a fourth; but you shall find none excelling in them all as Christ doth. Bread hath one quality, water another, raiment another, physic another; but none hath all in itself as Christ hath: He is bread to the hungry, water to the thirsty, a garment to the naked, healing to the wounded; and whatever a soul can desire is found in him, 1 Cor. i. 30.

Fourthly, Altogether lovely, i. e. Nothing is lovely in *opposition* to him, or in separation from him. If he be altogether lovely, then whatsoever is opposite to, or separate from him can have no loveliness in it; take away Christ, and where is the loveliness of any enjoyment? The best creature-comfort out of Christ, is but a broken cistern; it cannot hold one drop of true comfort, Psal. lxxiii. 26. It is with the creature, the sweetest and loveliest creature, as with a beautiful image in the glass: turn away the face and where is the image? Riches, honours, and comfortable relations are sweet when the face of Christ smiles upon us through them; but without him, what empty trifles are they all?

Fifthly, Altogether lovely, i. e. Transcending all created excellencies in beauty and loveliness; so much it speaks. If you compare Christ and other things, be they never so lovely, never so excellent and desirable; Christ carries away all loveliness from them; " He is (saith the apostle) before all things," Col. i. 17. Not only before all things in time, nature, and order; but before all things in dignity, glory, and true excellency: In all things he must have the pre-eminence. For let us but compare Christ's excellency with the creature's in a few particulars, and how evidently will the transcendent loveliness of Jesus Christ appear! For,

First, All other loveliness is *derivative* and secondary; but the loveliness of Christ *original* and *primary.* Angels and men, the

---

* The more excellent he is, the more he is to be sought after, by earnest prayer and desires. *Brightman.*

world and all the desirables in it, receive what excellency they
have from him; they are streams from the fountain. But as the
waters in the fountain itself are more abundant, so more pure and
pleasant * than in the streams. And the farther any thing departs,
and is removed from its fountain and original, the less excellency
there is in it.

Secondly, The loveliness and excellency of all other things, is
but *relative* and *respective*, consisting in its reference to Christ, and
subserviency to his glory; but Christ is lovely, considered *absolutely* in himself: He is desirable for himself, other things are so
for him.

Thirdly, The beauty and loveliness of all other things is fading
and perishing; but the loveliness of Christ is fresh to all eternity:
the sweetness of the best creatures is a fading flower; if not before, yet certainly at death it must fade away. Job iv. 21. " Doth
" not their excellency, which is in them, go away?" Yes, yes,
whether natural excellencies of the body, or acquired endowments
of the mind, lovely features, amiable qualities, attracting excellencies; all these like pleasant flowers are withered, faded, and destroyed by death; "but Christ is still the same, yesterday, to day,
" and for ever," Heb. xiii. 8.

Fourthly, The beauty and holiness of creatures are *ensnaring*
and dangerous; a man may make an *idol* thereof, and dote beyond the bounds of moderation upon them, but there is no danger
of excess in the love of Christ. The soul is then in the healthiest
frame and temper when it is most sick of love to Christ, Cant.
v. 8.

Fifthly, The loveliness of every creature is of a *cloying* and glut-
ting nature; our estimation of it abates and sinks by our nearer
approach to it, or longer enjoyment of it: creatures, like pictures,
are fairest at a due distance, but it is not so with Christ; the nearer
the soul approacheth him, and the longer it lives in the enjoyment
of him, still the more sweet and desirable is he.

Sixthly, and *lastly,* All other loveliness is *unsatisfying* and strait-
ening to the soul of man; there is not room enough in any one,
or in all the creatures for the soul of man to dilate and expatiate
itself; but it still feels itself confined and narrowed within those
strait limits †: And this comes to pass from the inadequateness and
unsuitableness of the creature, to the nobler and more excellent

---

* *Dulcius ex ipso fonte bibuntur aquæ.*   Waters drink more pleasantly from the fountain itself.

† *Unus Pellæo juveni non sufficit orbis;*
   Æstuat infœlix angusto in limite mundi.
The world is not sufficient for the Macedonian youth (*viz.* Alexander;) he frets at
being confined within the narrow boundary of the world

soul of man, which like a ship in a narrow river hath not room to turn; and besides, is ever and anon striking ground and foundering in those shallows. But Jesus Christ is every way adequate to the vast desires of the soul; in him it hath sea-room enough; there it may spread all its sails, no fear of touching the bottom. And thus you see what is the importance of this phrase, *Altogether lovely.*

Secondly, Next I promised to shew you in what respects Jesus Christ is altogether lovely. And,

First, He is altogether lovely in his person: a Deity dwelling in flesh, John i. 14. The wonderful union and perfection of the divine and human nature in Christ, render him an object of admiration and adoration to angels and men, 1 Tim. iii. 16. God never presented to the world such a vision of glory before: And then consider how the human nature of our Lord Jesus Christ is replenished with all the graces of the Spirit, so as never any of all the saints was filled; O how lovely doth this render him! John iii. 34. " God giveth not the Spirit by measure unto him." This makes him fairer than the children of men, grace being poured into his lips, Psal. xlv. 2. If a small measure of grace in the saints make them such sweet and desirable companions, what must the riches and fulness of the Spirit of grace filling Jesus Christ without measure, make him in the eyes of believers? O what a glory and lustre must it stamp upon him!

Secondly, He is altogether lovely in his offices: for let us but consider the suitableness, fulness, and comfortableness of them.

First, The *suitableness* of the offices of Christ to the miseries and wants of men; and we cannot but adore the infinite wisdom of God in his investiture with them; we are, by nature, blind and ignorant, at best but groping in the dim light of nature after God, Acts xvii. 27. Jesus Christ is a light to lighten the Gentiles, Isa. xlix. 6. When this great prophet came into the world, then did the day-spring from on high visit us, Luke i. 78. The state of nature is a state of alienation from, and enmity against God; Christ comes into the world an atoning sacrifice, making peace by the blood of his cross, Col. i. 20. All the world, by nature, are in bondage and captivity to Satan, a lamentable thraldom; Christ comes with kingly power, to rescue sinners, as a prey from the mouth of the terrible one.

Secondly, Let the *fulness* of his offices be also considered, by reason whereof he is able "to save to the uttermost, all that come to " God by him," Heb. vii. 25. The three offices, comprising in them all that our souls do need, become an universal relief to all our wants; and therefore,

Thirdly, Unspeakably *comfortable* must the offices of Christ be to the souls of sinners. If light be pleasant to our eyes, how pleasant is that light of life springing from the Sun of righteousness! Mal. iv. 2. If a pardon be sweet to a condemned malefactor, how sweet must the sprinkling the blood of Jesus be to the trembling conscience of a law-condemned sinner? If a rescue from a cruel tyrant be sweet to a poor captive, how sweet must it be to the ears of enslaved sinners, to hear the voice of liberty and deliverance proclaimed by Jesus Christ? Out of the several offices of Christ, as out of so many fountains, all the promises of the new covenant flow, as so many soul-refreshing streams of peace and joy: all the promises of illumination, counsel and direction flow out of the *prophetical office ;* all the promises of reconciliation, peace, pardon, and acceptation flow out of the *priestly office*, with the sweet streams of joy, and spiritual comforts depending thereupon; all the promises of converting, increasing, defending, directing, and supplying grace, flow out of the *kingly office* of Christ; indeed, all promises may be reduced to the three offices: so that Jesus Christ must needs be *altogether lovely* in his offices.

Thirdly, Jesus Christ is altogether *lovely* in his relations.

First, He is a lovely *Redeemer*, Isa. lxi. 1. He came to open the prison-doors to them that are bound. Needs must this Redeemer be a lovely one, if we consider the *depth of misery* from which he redeemed us, even "from the wrath to come," 1 Thess. i. 10. How lovely was Titus, in the eyes of the poor enthralled Greeks, whom he delivered from their bondage! this endeared him to them to that degree, that when their liberty was proclaimed, they even trod one another to death to see the herald that proclaimed it; and all the night following, with instruments of music, danced about his tent, crying with united voices, " a Saviour, a Saviour." Or, whether we consider the *numbers redeemed*, and the *means* of their redemption. Rev. v. 9. And they sang a new song, saying, " Thou art worthy to take the book, and to open the seals there-
" of: for thou wast slain, and hast redeemed us to God by thy
" blood, out of every kindred and tongue, and people, and na-
" tion." He redeemed us not with silver and gold, but with his own precious blood, by way of price, 1 Pet. i. 18, 19. with his out-stretched and glorious arm, by way of *power*, Col. i. 13. he redeemed us *freely*, Eph. i. 7. *fully*, Rom. viii. 1. *seasonably*, Gal. iv. 4. and out of special and peculiar *love*, John xvii. 9. In a word, he hath redeemed us for ever, never more to come into bondage, 1 Pet. i. 5. John x. 28. O how lovely is Jesus Christ in the relation of a Redeemer to God's elect!

Secondly, He is a lovely bridegroom to all that he espouses to himself. How doth the church glory in him, in the words following my text; " this is my Beloved, and this is my Friend,

" O ye daughters of Jerusalem !" q. d. Heaven and earth cannot
shew such another : which needs no fuller proof than the following particulars.

First, That he espouses to himself, in mercy and in loving-kind-
ness, such deformed, defiled, and altogether unworthy souls as we
are ; who have no beauty, no excellency to make us desirable in
his eyes ; all the springs of his love to us are in his own breast,
Deut. vii. 7. he chuseth us, not because we were, but that he might
make us lovely, Eph. v. 27. he passed by us when we lay in our
blood, and said unto us, Live; and that was the time of love,
Ezek. xvi. 5.

Secondly, He expects nothing with us, and yet bestows himself,
and all that he hath, upon us. Our poverty cannot enrich him,
but he made himself poor to enrich us, 2 Cor. viii. 9. 1 Cor.
iii. 22.

Thirdly, No husband loves the wife of his bosom, as Christ
loved his people, Eph. v. 25. He loved the church and gave himself for it.

Fourthly, None bears with weaknesses and provocations as
Christ doth ; the church is stiled " the Lamb's wife," Rev.
xix. 9.

Fifthly, No husband is so immortal and everlasting a husband
as Christ is ; death separates all other relations, but the soul's
union with Christ is not dissolved in the grave ; yea, the day of a
believer's death, is his marriage day, the day of his fullest enjoyment
of Christ. No husband can say to his wife, what Christ saith to
the believer, " I will never leave thee, nor forsake thee," Heb.
xiii. 5.

Sixthly, No bridegroom advanceth his bride to such honours by
marriage, as Christ doth ; he relates them to God as their father,
and from that day the mighty and glorious angels think it no dishonour to be their servants, Heb. i. 14. they are brought in admiring the beauty and glory of the spouse of Christ, Rev. xxi. 9.

Seventhly, and lastly, No marriage was ever consummated with
such triumphal solemnity, as the marriage of Christ and believers shall be in heaven, Psal. xlv. 14, 15. " She shall be brought to
" the king in raiment of needle-work, the virgins, her compani-
" ons that follow her, shall be brought unto thee ; with gladness
" and rejoicing shall they be brought; they shall enter into the
" king's palace." Among the Jews the marriage-house was called
Bethillula, the house of praise ; there was joy upon all hands, but
none like the joy that will be in heaven, when believers, the spouse
of Christ, shall be brought thither : *God the Father* will rejoice, to
behold the blessed accomplishment and confirmation of those glorious designs of his love. *Jesus Christ, the Bridegroom,* will rejoice

to see the travail of his soul, the blessed birth and issue of all his bitter pangs and agonies, Isa. liii. 11. *The Holy Spirit* will rejoice to see the completion and perfection of that sanctifying design which was committed to his hand, 2 Cor. v. 5. to see those souls whom he once found as rough stones, now to shine as the bright, polished stones of the spiritual temple. *Angels* will rejoice : great was the joy when the foundation of this design was laid, in the incarnation of Christ, Luke ii. 13. great therefore must their joy be, when the top-stone is set up with shouting, crying, Grace, grace, The *saints* themselves shall rejoice unspeakably, when they shall enter into the King's palace, and be for ever with the Lord, 1 Thes. iv. 17. Indeed there will be joy on all hands, except among the devils and damned, who shall gnash their teeth with envy at the everlasting advancement aud glory of believers.

Thus Christ is altogether lovely, in the relation of a Bridegroom.

Thirdly, Christ is altogether lovely, in the relation of an Advocate. 1 John ii. 1. " If any man sin, we have an advocate with " the Father, Jesus Christ the righteous, and he is the Propitia- " tion ;" it is he that pleads the cause of believers in heaven; appears for them in the presence of God, to prevent all new breaches, and continues the state of friendship and peace betwixt God and us. In this relation Christ is altogether lovely. For,

First, He makes our cause his own, and acts for us in heaven, as for himself, Heb. iv. 15. He is touched with the tender sense of our troubles and dangers, and is not only one with us, by way of representation, but also one with us in respect of sympathy and affection.

Secondly, Christ our Advocate, follows our suit and business in heaven, as his great and main design and business; therefore, in Heb. vii. 25. he is said to " live for ever to make intercession for " us ;" as if our concernments were so minded by him there, as to give up himself wholly to that work, as if all the glory and honour which is paid him in heaven would not satisfy him, or divert him one moment from our business.

Thirdly, He pleads the cause of believers by his blood ; it satisfies him not, as other advocates, to be at the expence of words and oratory, which is a cheaper way of pleading ; but he pleads for us by the voice of his own blood, Heb. xii. 24. where we are said to be come " to the blood of sprinkling, that speaketh better things " than that of Abel :" Every wound he received for us on earth, is a mouth opened to plead with God on our behalf in heaven ; *Quot vulnera, tot ora.* And hence it is, that in Rev. v. 6. he is represented standing before God, *as a lamb that had been slain ;* as it were, exhibiting and opening in heaven those deadly wounds received on earth, from the justice of God, on our account. Other advocates spend their breath, Christ his blood.

Fourthly, He pleads the cause of believers freely. Other advocates plead for reward, and exhaust the purses, while they plead the causes of their clients.

Fifthly, In a word, he obtaineth for us all the mercies for which he pleads ; no cause miscarries in his hand, which he undertakes, Rom. viii. 33, 34. O what a lovely Advocate is Christ for believers !

Fourthly, Christ is altogether lovely in the relation of a *friend*, for in this relation he is pleased to own his people, Luke xii. 4, 5. There are certain things in which one friend manifests his affection and friendship to another, but none like Christ. For,

First, No friend is so *open-hearted* to his friend as Christ is to his people : he reveals the very counsels and secrets of his heart to them. John xv. 15. " Henceforth I call you not servants, for the servant " knoweth not what his Lord doth ; but I have called you friends ; " for all things that I have heard of my Father, I have made " known unto you."

Secondly, No friend in the world is so *generous and bountiful* to his friend, as Jesus Christ is to believers ; John xv. 13. he parts with his very blood for them ; " Greater love (saith he) hath no " man than this, that a man lay down his life for his friends." He hath exhausted the precious treasures of his invaluable blood to pay our debts. O what a lovely friend is Jesus Christ to believers !

Thirdly, No friend *sympathizes* so tenderly with his friend in affliction, as Jesus Christ doth with his friends : " In all our afflic- " tions he is afflicted," Heb. iv. 15. He feels all our sorrows, wants and burdens as his own. Whence it is that the sufferings of believers are called the sufferings of Christ, Col. i. 24.

Fourthly, No friend in the world takes that *complacency* in his friend, as Jesus Christ doth in believers. Cant. iv. 9. " Thou " hast ravished my heart, (saith he to the spouse) thou hast ravish- " ed my heart with one of thine eyes, with one chain of thy neck." The Hebrew, here rendered *ravished*, signifies to puff up, or to make one proud : how is the Lord Jesus pleased to glory in his people ! how is he taken and delighted with those gracious ornaments which himself bestows upon them ! No friend so lovely as Christ.

Fifthly, No friend in the world loves his friend with so fervent and strong *affection* as Jesus Christ loves believers. Jacob loved Rachel, and endured for her sake the parching heat of summer and cold of winter ; but Christ endured the storms of the wrath of God, the heat of his indignation, for our sakes. David manifested

his love to Absalom, in wishing, " O that I had died for thee !"
Christ manifested his love to us, not in wishes that he had died,
but in death itself, in our stead, and for our sakes.

Sixthly, No friend in the world is so *constant* and *unchangeable*
in friendship as Christ is, John xiii. 1. " Having loved his own
" which were in the world, he loved them unto the end." He
bears with millions of provocations and injuries, and yet will not
break friendship with his people. Peter denied him, yet he will
not disown him ; but after his resurrection he saith, " Go, tell the
" disciples, and tell Peter," *q. d.* Let him not think he hath forfeited, by that sin of his, his interest in me ; though he have denied me, I will not disown him, Mark xvi. 7. O how lovely is
Christ in the relation of a friend ! I might farther shew you the
loveliness of Christ in his ordinances and in his providences, in
his communion with us and communications to us, but there is
no end of the account of Christ's loveliness : I will rather chuse to
press believers to their duties towards this altogether lovely Christ,
which I shall briefly dispatch in a few words.

Use. First, Is Jesus Christ altogether lovely, then I beseech you
set your souls upon this lovely Jesus. Methinks such an object as
hath been here represented, should compel love from the coldest
breast and hardest heart. Away with those empty nothings, away
with this vain deceitful world, which deserves not the thousandth
part of the love you give it ; let all stand aside and give way to
Christ. O did you but know his worth and excellency, what he is
in himself, what he hath done for, and deserved from you, you
would need no arguments of mine to persuade you to love him.

*Secondly, Esteem nothing lovely but as it is enjoyed in Christ, or
improved for Christ.* Affect nothing for itself, love nothing separate from Jesus Christ. In two things we all sin in love of creatures,
viz. in the *excess* of our affections, loving them above the rate and
value of creatures ; and in the *inordinacy* of our affections, i. e. in
loving them out of their proper places.

*Thirdly, Let us all be humbled for the baseness of our hearts, that
are so free of their affections to vanities and trifles, and so hard to
be persuaded to the love of Christ, who is altogether lovely.* O how
many pour out streams of love and delight upon the vain and empty
creature ; whilst no arguments can draw forth one drop of love
from their obdurate and unbelieving hearts to Jesus Christ ! I
have read of one Joannes Mollius, who was observed to go often
alone, and weep bitterly ; and being pressed by a friend to know
the cause of his troubles ; O ! said he, it grieves me that I cannot
bring this heart of mine to love Jesus Christ more fervently.

Fourthly, Represent Christ, as he is, to the world, by your car-

riage towards him. Is he altogether lovely; let all the world see
and know that he is so, by your delights in him and communion
with him; zeal for him, and readiness to part with any other lovely
thing upon his account; proclaim his excellencies to the world, as
the spouse here did; convince them how much your beloved is
better than any other beloved; display his glorious excellencies in
your heavenly conversations; hold him forth to others, as he is in
himself, altogether lovely. See that you " walk worthy of him
" unto all well-pleasing," Col. i. 10. " Shew forth the praises of
" Christ," 1 Pet. ii. 19. Let not that " worthy name be blas-
" phemed through you," James ii. 7. He is glorious in himself,
and will put glory upon you; take heed ye put not shame and dishonour upon him; he hath committed his honour to you, do not
betray that trust.

First, Never be ashamed to own Christ: he is altogether lovely;
he can never be a shame to you; it will be your great sin to be
ashamed of him. Some men glory in their shame; be not you
ashamed of your glory: if you be *ashamed of Christ now, he will
be ashamed of you when he shall appear in his own glory, and the
glory of all his holy angels.* Be ashamed of nothing but sin; and
among other sins, be ashamed especially for this sin, that you have
no more love for him who is *altogether lovely.*

*Sixthly, Be willing to leave every thing that is lovely upon earth,
that you may be with the altogether lovely Lord Jesus Christ in heaven.* Lift up your voices with the spouse, Rev. xx. 20. " Come
" Lord Jesus, come quickly." It is true, you must pass through
the pangs of death into his bosom and enjoyment; but sure it is
worth suffering much more than that to be with this lovely Jesus.
" The Lord direct your hearts into the love of God, and the pa-
" tient waiting for Jesus Christ," 2 Thes. iii. 5.

*Seventhly, Strive to be Christ-like, as ever you would be lovely
in the eyes of God and man.* Certainly, my brethren, it is the Spirit of Christ within you, and the beauty of Christ upon you, which
only can make you lovely persons; the more you resemble him in
holiness, the more will you discover of true excellency and loveliness; and the more frequent and spiritual your converse and communion with Christ is, the more of the beauty and loveliness of
Christ will be stamped upon your spirits, changing you into the
same image, from glory to glory.

Eighthly, Let the loveliness of Christ draw all men to him. Is
loveliness in the creature so attractive? And can the transcendent
loveliness of Christ draw none? O the blindness of man! If you
see no beauty in Christ why you should desire him, it is because
the god of this world hath blinded your minds.

SERMON XIII.

Alluring the Hearts of Men to come to CHRIST, by a fourth Motive contained in another Title of CHRIST.

HAGGAI ii. 7.

—— *And the desire of all nations shall come.*

THE former chapter is mainly spent, in reproving the negligence of the Jews, who, being discouraged from time to time, had delayed the rebuilding the *temple :* and, in the mean time, employed their care and cost in building and adorning their own houses : but, at last, being persuaded to set about the work, they met with this discouragement, that such was the poverty of the present time, that the second structure would no way answer the magnificence and splendor of the first. In Solomon's days the nation was wealthy, now drained ; so that there would be no proportion betwixt the second and the first. To this grand discouragement the prophet applies this relief ; that whatsoever should be wanting in external pomp and glory, should be more than recompensed by the presence of Jesus Christ in this *second temple.* For Christ, "the desire of all nations," saith he, shall come into it. Which, by the way, may give us this useful note : That the presence of Jesus Christ gives a more real and excellent glory to the places of his worship, than any external beauty or outward ornaments whatsoever can bestow upon them. Our eyes, like the disciples, are apt to be dazzled with the goodly stones of the temple, and, in the mean time, to neglect and overlook that which gives it the greatest honour and beauty.

But to return. In these words we have both the description of Christ, and an *index* pointing at the time of his incarnation : he is called "the desire of all nations ;" and the time of his coming in the flesh, is plainly intimated to be whilst the second *temple* should be standing. Where, by the way, we find just cause to admire at and bemoan the blindness that is happened to the Jews, who, owning the truth of this prophecy, and not able to deny the destruction of the second temple, many hundred years past, will not yet be brought to acknowledge the incarnation of the true Messiah notwithstanding.

But to the point. The character, or description of Christ, stiled *the desire of all nations,* who was to come into the world in the time of the second temple, Mal. iii. 12. and that, after grievous concussions and shakings of the world, which were to make way for

his coming; for so our prophet here speaks, " I will shake all na-
" tions, and the desire of all nations shall come," to which the
apostle alludes, in Heb. xii. 26. applying this prophecy to Jesus
Christ, here called the " desire of all nations:" putting the act
for the object, desire for the thing desired : as in Ezek. xxiv. 16.
" The desire of thine eyes," i. e. the desirable wife of thy bosom;
so here, the " desire of all nations," i. e. Christ, the object of the
desires of God's elect, in all nations of the world : a Saviour infinitely desirable in himself, and actually desired by all the people of
God, dispersed among all kindreds, tongues, and nations of the
world.   From whence this note is,

Doct. *That the desires of God's elect in all kingdoms, and among*
all people of the earth, are, and shall be drawn out after, and
fixed upon the Lord Jesus Christ.

The merciful God beholding the universal ruins of the world
by sin, hath provided an universal remedy for his own elect, in
every part of the earth.   Christ is not impropriated to any one
kingdom or nation in the world ; but intended to be God's salvation to the ends of the earth ; and accordingly speaks the apostle,
Col. ii. 11. " There is neither Greek, nor Jew, Barbarian, Scy-
" thian, bond nor free ; but Christ is all and in all." In the explication of this point two things must be enquired into.
    1. Why Christ is called the desire of all nations.
    2. Upon what account the people of God, in all nations, desire
him.
    First, Why he is called the desire of all nations, and what that
phrase may import ; and there are divers things that are supposed,
or included in it.
    First, That God the Father hath appointed him as a common
remedy for the sins and miseries of his people, in all parts and
quarters of the world.   So in the covenant of redemption, betwixt
the Father and the Son, the Lord expresseth himself, Isa. xlix. 6.
and he said, " It is a light thing that thou shouldest be my servant,
" to raise up the tribes of Jacob, and to restore the preserved of
" Israel : I will also give thee for a light to the Gentiles, that thou
" mayest be my salvation unto the end of the earth." Suitable
whereunto is that prophecy, Isa. lii. 15. " He shall sprinkle many
" nations." If God had not appointed him for, he could not be
desired by all nations.
    And, indeed, herein the grace of God doth admirably shine
forth in the freeness of it, that even the most barbarous nations
are not excluded from the benefits of redemption by Christ.   This
is what the apostle admires, that Christ should be *preached to the*

Gentiles, 1 Tim. iii. 16. a people that seemed to be lost in the darkness of idolatry; yet even for them Christ was given by the Father, "Ask of me (saith he) and I will give thee the Heathen for "thine inheritance, and the uttermost parts of the earth for thy "possession."

Secondly, Christ, *the desire of all nations*, plainly notes the sufficiency that is in him, to supply the wants of the whole world; as the sun in the heavens suffices all nations for light and influence, so doth the Sun of righteousness suffice for the redemption, justification, sanctification and salvation of the people of God all over the world; Isa. xlv. 22. "Look unto me, and be ye saved, all ye "ends of the earth."

Thirdly, It implies the *reality that is in godliness*. It shews you that religion is no fancy, as the atheistical world would persuade us; and this evidently appears in the uniform effects of it upon the hearts of all men, in all nations of the world, that are truly religious: all their desires, like so many needles touched by one and the same loadstone, move towards Jesus Christ, and all meet together in one and the same blessed object, Christ. Were it possible for the people of God to come out of all nations, kindreds and languages in the world, into one place, and there confer and compare the desires and workings of their hearts, though they never saw each other's faces, nor heard of each other's names, yet, as face answers to face in a glass, so would their desires after Christ answer to each other. All hearts work after him in the same manner; what one saith, all say: These are my troubles and burdens, these my wants and miseries; the same things my desires and fears: one and the same Spirit works in all believers throughout the world; which could never be if religion were but a fancy, as some call it; or a combination or confederacy, as others call it: fancies are as various as faces; and confederacies presuppose mutual acquaintance and conference.

Fourthly, Christ, the desire of all nations, implies the vast extent his kingdom hath, and shall have in the world; out of every nation under heaven some shall be brought to Christ, and to heaven by him; and though the number of God's elect, compared with the multitudes of the ungodly in all nations, is but a remnant, a little flock; and, in that comparative sense, there are few that shall be saved; yet considered absolutely, and in themselves, they are a vast number, which no man can number, Matth. viii. 11. "Many "shall come from the east, and from the west, and shall sit "down with Abraham, and Isaac, and Jacob, in the kingdom "of heaven." In order whereunto, the gospel, like the sun in the heavens, circuits the world. It arose in the east, and takes its course towards the *western world*; rising, by degrees, upon the

remote, idolatrous nations of the earth: out of all which a number is to be saved, even " Ethiopia shall stretch out her hands to
" God," Psal. lxviii. 31. And this consideration should move us
to pray earnestly for the poor Heathens, who yet sit in darkness,
and the shadow of death; there is yet hope for them.

Fi, thly, It holds forth this, that when God opens the eyes of
men to see their sin and danger by it, nothing but Christ can give
them satisfaction: it is not the amenity, fertility, riches and pleasures, the inhabitants of any kingdom of the world do enjoy, that
can satisfy the desires of their souls: when once God touches their
hearts with the sense of sin and misery, then Christ, and none
but Christ is desirable and necessary, in the eyes of such persons.
Many kingdoms of the world abound with riches and pleasures;
the providence of God hath carved liberal portions of the good
things of this life to many of them, and scarce left any thing to
their desires that the world can afford. Yet all this can give no
satisfaction without Jesus Christ, the desire of all nations, the one
thing necessary, when once they come to see the necessity and excellency of him: then take the world who will, so they may have
Christ, the desire of their souls. Thus we see upon what grounds
and reasons Christ is stiled the desire of all nations.

Object. But there lies one great objection against this truth,
which must be solved; viz. if Christ be the de ire of all nations,
how comes it to pass, that Jesus Christ finds no entertainment in so
many nations of the world among whom Christianity is hissed at,
and Christians not tolerated to live among them? Who see no
beauty in him that they should desire him.

Sol. First, We must remember the nations of the world have
their times and seasons of conversion; those that once embraced
Christ, have now lost him, and idols are now set up in the places
where he once was sweetly worshipped. The sun of the gospel is
gone down upon them, and now shines in another *Hemisphere;*
and so the nations of the world are to have their distinct days and
seasons of illumination. The gospel, like the sea, gaineth in one
place what it loseth in another; and in the times and seasons appointed by the Father, they come successively to be enlightened in
the knowledge of Christ; and then shall the promise be fulfilled,
Isa. xlix. 7. " Thus saith the Lord, the Redeemer of Israel, and his
" holy One, To him whom man despiseth, to him whom the na-
" tion abhorreth, to a servant of rulers; kings shall see and arise,
" princes also shall worship, because of the Lord that is faithful."

Secondly, Let it also be remembered, that although Christ be
rejected by the rulers and body of many nations; yet he is the
desire of all the elect of God dispersed and scattered among those
nations.

In the next place, *Secondly*, we are to enquire upon what account Christ becomes the desire of all nations, i. e. of all those in all the nations of the world, that belong to the election of grace. And the true ground and reason thereof is, because Christ only hath that in himself which relieves their wants, and answers to all their need. As.

First, They are all, by nature, under condemnation, Rom. v. 16, 18. under the curse of the law; against which, nothing is found in heaven or earth, able to relieve their consciences, but the blood of sprinkling, the pure and perfect righteousness of the Lord Jesus: and hence it is, that Christ becomes so desirable in the eyes of poor sinners, all the world over. If any thing in nature could be found to pacify and purge the consciences of men from guilt and fear, Christ would never be desirable in their eyes; but finding no other remedy but the blood of Jesus, to him, therefore, shall all the ends of the earth look for righteousness, and for peace.

Secondly, All nations of the world are polluted with the filth of sin, both in nature and practice, which they shall see, and bitterly bewail, when the light of the gospel shall shine amongst them; and the same light, by which this shall be discovered, will also discover the only remedy of this evil to lie in the spirit of Christ, the only fountain opened to all nations for sanctification and cleansing: and this will make the Lord Jesus incomparably desirous in their eyes. O how welcome will he be that cometh unto them, not by blood only, but by water also, John i. 5, 6.

Thirdly, When the light of the gospel shall shine upon the nations, they shall then see, that by reason of the guilt and filth of sin, they are all barred out of heaven; those doors are chained up against them, and that none but Christ can open an entrance for them into that kingdom of God! that "no man cometh to the " Father but by him," John xiv. 6. " Neither is there any name " under heaven given among men, whereby they must be saved, " but the name of Christ," Acts iv. 12. Hence the hearts of sinners shall pant after him, as a hart panteth for the water-brooks. And thus you see upon what grounds Christ becomes the *desire of all nations*. The improvement of all followeth, in five several uses of the point; viz.

1. For information.
2. For examination.
3. For consolation.
4. For exhortation.
5. For direction.

First use for information.

First, Is Christ the desire of all nations? *how vile a sin is it then in any nation, upon whom the light of the gospel hath shined, to reject*

Jesus Christ? And say, as those in Job xxi. 14. "Depart from us,
"we desire not the knowledge of thy ways." To thrust away his
worship, government, and servants from amongst them; and in
effect to say, as it is Luke xix. 14. "We will not have this man
"to reign over us." Thus did the Jews, Acts xiii. 46. they put
away Christ from among them, and thereby judged themselves
unworthy of eternal life. This is at once a fearful *sin*, and a dreadful *sign*. How soon did vengeance overtake them like the overthrow of Sodom? O, let it be for a warning to all nations to the
end of the world. He would have gathered the children of Israel
under his wings as a *hen* doth her brood, even when the *Roman
Eagle* was hovering over them, but they would not; therefore
their houses were left unto them desolate, their city and temple
made an heap.

Secondly, If Jesus Christ be the desire of all nations, *how incomparably happy then must that nation be, that enjoys Christ in the
power and purity of his gospel-ordinances!* If Christ, under a vail
made Canaan a glorious land, (as it is called) Dan. xi. 41. what a
glorious place must that nation be, that beholds him with open
face in the bright sun-shine of the gospel! O England, know thy
happiness and the day of thy visitation: what others desire, thou
enjoyest: provoke not the Lord Jesus to depart from thee, by cor-
rupting his worship, longing after idolatry, abusing his messengers,
and oppressing his people, lest his soul depart from thee.

Second use for examination.

If Christ be the desire of all nations, examine whether he be the
desire of your souls in particular; else you shall have no benefit by
him. Are your desires after Christ true spiritual desires? Reflect,
I beseech you, upon the frames and tempers of your heart. Can
you say of your desires after Christ, as Peter did of his love to
Christ? Lord, thou knowest all things; thou knowest that I desire thee. Try your desires as to their sincerity by the following
characters:

First, Are they vehement and ardent? Hath Christ the supreme
place in your desires? Do you esteem all things to be but dross and
dung in comparison of the excellencies of Jesus Christ your Lord?
Phil. iii. 8. Is he to you as the refuge-city to the man-slayer?
Heb. vi. 18, 19. As a spring of water in a dry place, as the shadow of a great rock in a weary land? Isa. xxxii. 2. Such vehement desires are true desires.

Secondly, Are your desires after Christ universal; i. e. is every
thing in Christ desirable in your eyes? The *hypocrite,* like the *harlot,* is for a divided Christ; they would be called by his name, but
live upon their own stock, Isa. iv. 1. If his holiness and govern-

ment, his cross and sufferings be desirable for his sake : such universal desires are right desires.

Thirdly, Are your desires after Christ industrious desires, using all the means of accomplishing what you desire ! You say you desire Christ, but what will you do to obtain your desires ? If you seek him carefully and incessantly in all the ways of duty ; if you will strive in prayer, labour to believe, cut off right hands, and pluck out right eyes, i. e. be content to part with the most profitable and pleasant ways of sin that you may enjoy Christ, the desire of your souls; then are your desires right desires.

Fourthly, Are your desires after Christ permanent desires, or only a sudden motion or fit which goes off again without effect ? If your desires after Christ abide upon your hearts, if your longings be after him at all times, though not in the same height and degree, then are your desires right desires. Christ always dwells in the desires of his people ; they can feel him in their desires, when they cannot discern him in their love or delight.

Fifthly, Will your desires after Christ admit no satisfaction, nor find rest any where but in the enjoyment of Christ ? then are your desires right desires. The soul that desires Christ, can never be at rest till it come home to Christ, 2 Cor. v. 2, 6. Phil. i. 23. The devil can satisfy others with the riches and pleasure of this world, as children are quieted with rattles; but if nothing but Christ can rest and terminate your desires, surely such restless desires are right desires.

Sixthly, Do your desires after Christ spring from a deep sense of your need and want of Christ ? Hath conviction opened your eyes to see your misery, to feel your burthens, and to make you sensible that your remedy lies only in the Lord Jesus ? then are your desires right desires. Bread and water are made necessary and desirable by hunger and thirst; by these things try the truth of your desires after Christ.

Third use for consolation.

Do you indeed, upon serious trial, find such desires after Christ as were described above ? O, bless the Lord for that day wherein Christ, the desire of all nations, became the desire of your souls; and for your comfort, know that you are happy and blessed souls at present.

First, Blessed in this, that your eyes have been opened to see both the want and worth of Christ. Had not Christ applied his precious eye-salve to the eyes of your mind, you could never have desired him ; you would have said with them in Isa. liii. 2, 3. " He hath no form nor comeliness, and when we shall see him, " there is no beauty that we should desire him :" Or, as they to the spouse, Cant. v. 9. " What is thy beloved more than another " beloved ?" O, blessed souls, enlightened of the Lord, to see those things that are hid from them that perish !

Secondly, You are blessed in this, that your desires after Christ are a sure evidence that the desire of Christ is towards you : had he not first desired you, you could never have desired him. We may say of desires, as it is said of love, we desire him because he first desired us : your desires after Christ are inflamed from the desires of Christ after you.

Thirdly, Blessed in this, that your desires shall surely be satisfied, Matt. v. 6. " Blessed are they that hunger and thirst after " righteousness, for they shall be filled." Prov. x. 24. " The de- " sires of the righteous shall be granted." God never raised such desires as these in the souls of his people, to be a torment to them for ever.

Fourthly, Blessed in this, that God hath guided your desires to make the best choice that ever was made in the world ; whilst the desires of others are hunting after riches, pleasure, and honour in the world ; toiling themselves like children in pursuit of a painted butter-fly, which when they have caught, doth but daub their fingers : God, meanwhile, hath directed your desires to Christ, the most excellent object in heaven or earth. Any good will satisfy some men ; O, happy soul, if none but Christ can satisfy thee ! Psal. iv. 6.

Fifthly, Blessed in this, that there is a work of grace certainly wrought upon thy soul ; and these very desires after Christ are a part thereof.

Sixthly, Blessed in this, that these desires after Christ keep thy soul active and working after him continually in the ways of duty, Psal. xxvii. 4. " One thing have I desired, that will I seek after." Desire will be a continual spring to diligence and industry in the ways of duty ; the desire of the end quickeneth to the use of means, Prov. xviii. 1. Others may fall asleep and cast off duty, but it will be hard for you to do so, whose souls burn with desire after Christ.

Seventhly, Blessed in this, that your desires after Christ will make death much the sweeter and easier to you, Phil. i. 23. " I de- " sire to be dissolved, and to be with Christ, which is far better." When a Christian was once asked, Whether he was willing to die ? He returned this answer *, " Let him be unwilling to die, who is " unwilling to go to Christ." And much like it, was that of another, *Vivere renuo, ut Christo vivam :* I refuse this life, to live with Christ.

---

* *Illius est nolle mori, cujus nolle ire ad Christum.*

Fourth use for exhortation.

In the fourth place, let me exhort and persuade all to make Jesus Christ the desire and choice of their souls. And here I fall in with the main scope and design of the gospel. And O that I could effectually press home this exhortation upon your hearts; let me offer some moving considerations to you, and may the Lord accompany them to your hearts.

First, Every creature naturally desires its own preservation; do not you desire the preservation of your precious and immortal soul! If you do, then make Christ your desire and choice, without whom they can never be preserved, Jude, ver. 1.

Secondly, Do not your souls earnestly desire the bodies they live in? How tender are they over them, how careful to provide for them? though they pay a dear rent for those tenements they live in. And is not union with Christ infinitely more desirable than the union of soul and body? O covet union with him! then shall your souls be happy, when your bodies drop off from them at death, 2 Cor. v. 1, 3. yea, soul and body shall be happy in him, and with him for evermore.

Thirdly, How do the men of this world desire the enjoyments of it? They pant after the dust of the earth; they rise early, sit up late, eat the bread of carefulness; and all this for very vanity: Shall a worldling do more for earth, than you for heaven? Shall the creature be so earnestly desired, and Christ neglected?

Fourthly, What do all your desires in this world benefit you, if you go christless? Suppose you had the desire of your hearts in these things, how long should you have comfort in them, if you miss Christ?

Fifthly, Doth Christ desire you, who have nothing lovely or desirable in you? And have you no desires after Christ, the most lovely and desirable one in both worlds? " His desires are towards " you," Prov. viii. 31. O make him the desire and choice of your souls.

Sixthly, How absolutely necessary is Jesus Christ to your souls? Bread and water, breath and life, are not so necessary as Christ is; " One thing is necessary," Luke x. 42. and that one thing is Christ. If you miss your desires in other things, you may yet be happy; but if you miss Christ you are undone for ever.

Seventhly, How suitable a good is Christ to your souls! comprising whatsoever they want, 1 Cor. i. 30. Set your hearts where you will, none will be found to match and suit them, as Christ doth.

Eighthly, How great are the benefits that will redound to you by Jesus Christ! In him you shall have a rich inheritance settled upon you: all things shall be yours, when you are Christ's, 1 Cor. iii. 22. And is not such a Christ worth desiring?

Ninthly, All your well-grounded hopes of glory are built upon your union with Christ, 1 Cor. i. 21. If you miss Christ, you must die without hope. Will not this draw your desires to him;

Tenthly, Suppose you were at the judgment-seat of God, where you must shortly stand, and saw the terrors of the Lord in that day; the sheep divided from the goats; the sentences of absolution and condemnation passed, by the great and awful Judge, upon the righteous and wicked: would not Christ be then desirable in your eyes? As ever you expect to stand with comfort at that bar, let Christ be the desire and choice of your souls now.

Fifth use for direction.

Do these, or any other considerations, put thee upon this enquiry; how shall I get my desires kindled and enflamed towards Christ? Alas! my heart is cold and dead, not a serious desire stirring in it after Christ. To such I shall offer the following directions.

Direct. 1. Redeem some time every day for meditation; get out of the noise and clamour of the world, Psal. iv. 4. and seriously bethink yourselves how the present state of your soul stands, and how it is like to go with you for ever: here all sound conversion begins, Psal. lxix. 59.

Direct. 2. Consider seriously of that lamentable state, in which you came into the world; children of wrath by nature, under the curse and condemnation of the law: so that either your state must be changed, or you inevitably damned, John iii. 3.

Direct. 3. Consider the way and course you have taken since you came into the world, proceeding from iniquity to iniquity. What command of God have you not violated a thousand times over? What sin is committed in the world, that you are not one way or other guilty of before God? How many secret sins upon your score, unknown to the most intimate friend you have in the world? Either this guilt must be separated from your souls, or your souls from God to all eternity.

Direct. 4. Think upon the severe wrath of God due to every sin; "The wages of sin is death," Rom. vi. 23. And how intolerable the fulness of that wrath must be when a few drops sprinkled upon the conscience in this world, are so insupportable, that hath made some to chuse strangling rather than life; and yet this wrath must abide for ever upon you, if you get not interest in Jesus Christ, John iii. 36.

Direct. 5. Ponder well the happy state and condition they are in who have obtained pardon and peace by Jesus Christ, Psal. xxxii. 12. And seeing the grace of God is free, and you are set under the means thereof; why may not you be as capable thereof as others ?

Direct. 6. Seriously consider the great uncertainty of your time, and preciousness of the opportunities of salvation, never to be recovered, when they are once past, John ix. 4. let this provoke you to lay hold upon those golden seasons whilst they are yet with you ; that you may not bewail your folly and madness, when they are out of your reach.

Direct. 7. Associate yourselves with serious Christians; get into their acquaintance, and beg their assistance ; beseech them to pray for you; and see that you rest not here, but be frequently upon your knees, begging of the Lord a new heart, and a new state.

In conclusion of the whole, let me beseech and beg all the people of God, as upon my knees, to take heed, and beware, lest by the carelessness and scandal of their lives they quench the weak desires beginning to kindle in the hearts of others. You know what the law of God awards for striking a woman with child, so that her fruit go from her, Exod. xxi. 22, 23. O shed not soul-blood, by stifling the hopeful desires of any after Christ.

Blessed be God for Jesus Christ, the desire of all nations.

———— ·∶•◦◦•✦•◦◦•∶· ————

SERMON XIV.

Containing the fifth Motive to apply CHRIST, drawn from another excellent Title of CHRIST.

1 Cor. ii. 8.

Which none of the princes of this world have known, for had they known him, they would not have crucified the Lord of glory.

IN this chapter the apostle discourses to the Corinthians, of the excellency of his ministry, both to obviate the contempt which some cast upon it for want of human ornaments, and to give the greater authority unto it among all : and whereas the spiritual simplicity of his ministry laid it under the contempt of some, he removes that several ways, by shewing them,

First, That it was not suitable to the design and end of his ministry, his aim being " to know nothing among them, save Jesus " Christ, and him crucified," ver. 1, 2.

Secondly, Neither was it for the advantage of their souls; it might indeed tickle their fancies, but could be no solid foundation to their faith and comfort, ver. 4, 5.

Thirdly, Though his discourses seemed jejune and dry to carnal hearers, yet they had a depth and excellency in them, which spiritual and judicious Christians saw and acknowledged, ver. 6, 7.

Fourthly, Therefore this excellent wisdom which he preached far transcended all the natural wisdom of this world ; yea, the most raised and improved understandings of those that were most renowned and admired in that age for wisdom, ver. 8. " which none " of the princes of this world knew."

In which words we have,

1. A negative proposition.

2. The proof of the proposition.

First, A negative proposition : None of the princes of this world knew that spiritual wisdom which he taught. By *princes of this world,* or rather, *principes seculi,* the princes of that age, he means, as Cameron well notes, the learned Rabbies, Scribes, and Pharisees, renowned for wisdom and learning among them ; and honoured upon that account as so many princes : but he adds a diminutive term, which darkens all their glory : They are but the *princes of this world,* utterly unacquainted with the wisdom of the other world. To which he adds,

Secondly, A clear and full proof ; " For had they known it, they " would not have crucified the Lord of glory." In which words we find one of Christ's glorious and royal titles, *The Lord of glory :* upon which title will be my present discourse. The words being fitly rendered, and nothing of ambiguity in them, they give us this observation,

Doct. *That Christ crucified is the Lord of glory.*

Great and excellent is the glory of Jesus Christ, the scriptures every where proclaim his glory : yea, we may observe a notable *climax,* or gradation, in those scriptures that speak of his glory. The prophet Isaiah, speaking of him, calls him *glorious ;* Isa. iv. 2. " In that day shall the branch of the Lord be beautiful and glo- " rious." John, speaking of his glory, rises a step higher, and ascribeth to him a " glory as of the only begotten Son of the " Father," John i. 14. i. e. a glory meet for, and becoming the Son of God : proper to him, and incommunicable to any other. The apostle James rises yet higher, and doth not only call him glorious, or glorious as the only begotten of the Father, but *the glory,* James ii. 1. glory in the abstract ; " My brethren, (saith he) " have not the faith of our Lord Jesus Christ, the glory, with " respect of persons ;" For the word *Lord,* which is in our translation, is a supplement ; Christ is glory itself, yea, the glory emphatically so stiled ; the glory of heaven ; the glory of Sion ; the glory of our souls for ever. The author to the Hebrews goes yet higher, and calls him not simply the glory, but "the brightness "of the Father's glory *," Heb. i. 3. as though he should say, the radiancy, sparkling, or beaming forth of his Father's glory; the very splendor or refulgency of divine glory. O what a glorious Lord is our Lord Jesus Christ! the bright, sparkling diamond of heaven; who shines in glory there, above the glory of angels and saints, as the glory of the sun excels the lesser, twinkling stars. When he appeared to Paul, Acts xxvi. 13. "I saw (saith he) a "light from heaven above the brightness of the sun, shining "round about me:" Needs must the glory of Christ be unspeakable, who reflects glory upon all that are with him, John xvii. 24. and stamps glory upon all that belong to him. His works on earth were *glorious works*, Luke xiii. 17. the purchased liberty of his people, a glorious liberty, Rom. viii. 21. the church his mystical body, a glorious church, Eph. v. 27. the gospel which reveals him is a glorious gospel, 1 Tim. i. 11.

But more particularly let us consider the glory of Christ, as it is distinguished into his either,

1. Essential, or,
2. Mediatorial glory.

First, The essential glory of Christ, which he hath as God from everlasting; which is unspeakable and inconceivable glory: For (saith the apostle, Phil. ii. 6.) "He being in the form of God, "thought it no robbery to be equal with God," i. e. he has a peerage or equality with his Father in glory; John x. 30. "I and "my Father are one." And again, John xvi. 15. "All things "that the Father hath are mine:" the same name, the same nature, the same essential properties, the same will, and the same glory.

Secondly, The mediatorial glory of Christ is exceeding great. This is proper to him, as the head of the church, which he hath purchased with his own blood. Of this glory the apostle speaks, Phil. ii. 9, 10. "Wherefore God also hath exalted him, and given "him a name, which is above every name, *&c.* υπερυψωσε, exalted above all exaltation. Now the mediatorial glory of our Lord Jesus Christ consisteth either,

1. In the fulness of grace inherent in him; or,
2. In the dignity and authority put upon him.

First, In the fulness of grace inherent in him: The humanity of Christ is filled with grace, as the sun with light: John i. 14. "Full of grace and truth." Never any creature was filled by the Spirit of grace, as the man Christ Jesus is filled; for "God gives

---

* Απαυγασμα της δοξης.

" not the Spirit to him by measure," John iii. 34. By reason of
this fulness of grace inherent in him, he is " fairer than the chil-
" dren of men," Psal. xlv. 2. excelling all the saints in spiritual
lustre and gracious excellencies.

Secondly, In the dignity and authority put upon him. He is
crowned King in Sion ; all power in heaven and earth is given unto
him, Matth. xxviii. 18. he is a law-giver to the church, James iv.
12. all acts of worship are to be performed in his name ; prayer,
preaching, censures, sacraments, all to be administered in his
name. Church officers are commissioned by him, Eph. iv. 11.
The judgment of the world in the great day will be administered
by him ; Matth. xxv. 31. " Then shall he sit upon the throne of
" his glory."

To conclude, Jesus Christ shall have glory and honour ascribed
to him for evermore, by angels and saints, upon the account of his
mediatorial work ; this some divines call his passive glory, the
glory which he is said to receive from his redeemed ones. Rev.
v. 8, 9, 10. " And when he had taken the book, the four beasts,
" and the four and twenty elders, fell down before the Lamb,
" having every one of them harps, and golden vials full of
" odours, which are the prayers of the saints ; and they sung a
" new song, saying, Thou art worthy to take the book, and to
" open the seals thereof; for thou wast slain, and hast redeemed
" us to God by thy blood, out of every kindred, and tongue, and
" people, and nation," &c. And thus you see that our Lord
Jesus Christ is upon all accounts the *Lord of glory.* The uses
follow.

Inference 1. *How wonderful was the love of Christ, the Lord of
glory, to be so abased and humbled, as he was for us, vile and sinful dust ?* It is astonishing to conceive that ever Jesus Christ should
strip himself of his robes of glory, to clothe himself with the mean
garment of our flesh : O what a stoop did he make in his incarnation for us ! If the most magnificent monarch upon earth had
been degraded into a toad ; if the sun in the heavens had been
turned into a wandering atom ; if the most glorious angel in heaven had been transformed even into a fly ; it had been nothing to
the abasement of the Lord of glory. This act is every where celebrated in scripture as the great mystery, the astonishing wonder of
the whole world, 2 Tim. iii. 16. Phil. ii. 8. Rom. viii. 3. The
Lord of glory looked not like himself, when he came in the habit
of a man ; Isa. liii. 3. " We hid, as it were our faces from him :"
Nay, rather like a worm than a man ; Psal. xxii. 6. " A reproach
" of men, and despised of the people." The birds of the air and
beasts of the earth were here provided of better accommodations
than the Lord of glory, Matth. viii. 20. O stupendous abase-

ment! O love unspeakable! "Though he was rich, yet for our
"sakes he became poor, that we through his poverty might be
"rich," 2 Cor. viii. 9.   He put off the crown of glory to put on
the crown of thorns; *Quanto pro me vilior, tanto mihi charior,*
said Bernard; The lower he humbled himself for me, the dearer he
shall be to me.

   *Inf. 2. How transcendently glorious is the advancement of be-
lievers, by their union with the Lord of glory?* This also is an admirable and astonishing mystery; it is the highest dignity of which
our *nature* is capable, to be *hypostatically* united; and the greatest
glory of which our *persons* are capable is to be *mystically* united to
this Lord of glory; to be bone of his bone, and flesh of his flesh.
O what is this! Christian, dost thou know and believe all this, and
thy heart not burn within thee in love to Christ? O! then, what a
heart hast thou? What art thou, by nature, but sinful dust, a
loathsome sinner, viler than the vilest creature, cast out to the loathing of thy person in the day of thy nativity! O that ever the Lord
of glory should unite himself to such a lump of vileness! take such
a wretch into his very bosom! Be astonished, O heavens and earth,
at this! this is the great mystery which the angels stooped down to
look into: Such an honour as this could never have entered into
the heart of man.   It would have seemed a rude blasphemy in us,
once to have thought or spoken of such a thing, had not Christ
made first the motion thereof; yet how long didst thou make this
Lord of glory wait upon thy undetermined will, before he gained
thy consent? Might he not justly have spurned thee into hell,
upon thy first refusal, and never have made thee such another
offer? Wilt thou not say, Lord, what am I, and what is my father's house, that so great a King should stoop so far beneath himself, to such a worm as I am! That strength should unite itself to
weakness, infinite glory to such baseness! O grace, grace, for ever
to be admired!

   Inf. 3. Is Jesus Christ the Lord of glory? *Then let no man count
himself dishonoured by suffering the vilest indignities for his sake:*
The Lord of glory puts glory upon the very suffering you undergo in this world for him.   "Moses esteemed the reproaches of
"Christ greater riches than the treasures of Egypt," Heb. xi. 26.
he cast a kingdom at his heels, to be crowned with reproaches, for
the name of Christ.   The *diadem* of Egypt was not half so glorious
as self-denial for Christ.   This Lord of glory freely degraded himself for thee; wilt thou stand hesitating with him upon terms? It
is certainly your honour to be dishonoured for Christ, Acts v. 41.
to you it is given, in behalf of Christ, not only to believe, but also
to suffer for his sake, Phil. i. 29.   The gift of suffering is there

matched with the gift of faith; it is given as an *honorarium,* a badge of honour to suffer for the Lord of glory. As all have not the honour to wear the crown of glory in heaven, so few have the honour to wear the chain of Christ upon earth.   * Thanus reports of Ludovicus Marsacus, a knight of France, that being led to suffer with other martyrs, who were bound, and he unbound, because a person of honour; he cried out, "Why don't you honour "me with a chain too, and create me a knight of that noble "order?" My brethren count it all joy when ye fall into divers temptations, James i. 2. i. e. trials by sufferings. David thought it an honour to be vile for God, and that is a true observation that disgrace itself is glorious when endured for the Lord of glory.

Inf. 4. Is Christ the Lord of glory? *How glorious then shall the saints one day be, when they shall be made like this glorious Lord, and partake of his glory in heaven?* John xvii. 22. "The glory "which thou gavest me, I have given them:" Yea, the vile bodies of believers shall be made like to the glorious body of Christ, Phil. iii. 21. What glory then will be communicated to their souls? True, his essential glory is incommunicable; but there is a glory which Christ will communicate to his people. "When he comes "to judge the world, he will come to be glorified in his saints, and "to be admired in all them that believe," 2 Thes. i. 10. Thus he seemeth to account his social glory, which shall result from his saints, a great part of his own glory: As we have now fellowship with him in his sufferings, so we shall have a fellowship or communion with him in his glory: When he shall appear, then shall we also appear with him in glory; then the poorest believer shall be more glorious than Solomon in all his royalty. It was a pious saying of Luther, that he had rather be *Christianus rusticus, quam Ethnicus Alexander;* a Christian *clown,* than a Pagan *emperor.* The righteous is more excellent than his neighbour, though he live next door to a graceless nobleman: But it doth not yet appear what they shall be. The day will come, it certainly will come, for the Lord hath spoken it, when they shall shine forth as the sun in the king dom of their Father.

Inf. 5. *How hath the devil blindfolded, and deluded them that are frighted off from Christ, by the fears of being dishonoured by him?* Many persons have half a mind to religion, but when they consider the generality of its professors to be persons of the lowest and meanest rank in the world, and that reproaches and sufferings attend that way; they shrink back as men ashamed, and as Salvian saith, *Mali esse coguntur, ne viles habeantur;* they chuse rather to remain wicked, than to be esteemed vile: But to them that believe, Christ is

---

* *Cur me non quoque donas, et insignis hujus ordinis militem creas ?*   Thuanus.

an honour; as the word which we translate *precious* might be rendered, 1 Pet. ii. 7. Till God open men's eyes thus, they will
put evil for good, and good for evil. But O dear bought honours,
for which men stake their souls and everlasting happiness! Paul
was not of your mind: for birth he was an Hebrew of the
Hebrews; for dignity and esteem, a Pharisee; for moral accomplishments, touching the law, blameless: Yet all this he trampled
under his feet, counting it all but dross and dung in comparison of
Jesus Christ. Moses had more honour to lay down for Christ than
you; yet it was no temptation to him to conceal or deny the faith
of Christ. Noble Galeacius would not be withheld from Christ
by the splendor and glory of Italy; but O, how doth the glory of
this world dazzle and blind the eyes of many: " How can ye be-
" lieve (saith Christ) who receive honour one of another?" John
v. 44. Saints and sinners, upon this account, are wonders one
to the other. It is the wonder of the world to see Christians glo-
rying in reproaches; they wonder that the saints run not with them
into the same excess of riot; and it is a wonder to believers, how
such poor toys and empty titles (rather than titles of honour) should
keep the world as it doth from Jesus Christ, and their everlasting
happiness in him.

Inf. 6. If Christ be the Lord of glory, *how careful should all be
who profess him, that they do not dishonour Jesus Christ, whose
name is called upon by them?* Christ is a glory to you, be not you
a shame and dishonour to him. How careful had Christians need to
be, to draw every line and action of their lives exactly: The more
glorious Christ is, the more circumspect and watchful ye had need
to be. How lovely would Jesus Christ appear to the world, if the
lives of Christians did adorn the doctrine of God their Saviour, in
all things! Remember, you represent the Lord of glory to the
world; it is not your honour only, but the honour of Christ which
is engaged and concerned in your actions. O let not the carelessness or scandal of your life, make Jesus Christ ashamed to be
called your Lord. When Israel had grievously revolted from God,
he bids Moses rise and get down from thence; for (saith he) *thy
people,* which thou hast brought forth out of Egypt, have corrupted themselves, Deut. ix. 12. as if the Lord were ashamed to own
them for his people any longer. It was a cutting question, James
ii. 7. apt to startle the consciences of these loose professors; " Do
" they not blaspheme that worthy name by which ye are called?"
Your duty is to adorn the gospel by your conversations, Titus ii.
10. The words signify to deck, trim, or adorn the gospel, to make
it trim, neat, and lovely, to the eyes of beholders. When there
is such a beautiful harmony, and lovely proportion betwixt Christ's
doctrine and your practices, as there is in the works of creation,

wherein the comeliness and elegancy of the world much consists, (for to this the apostle's word here alludes) then do we walk suitably to the Lord of glory.

Inf. 7. What delight should Christians take in their daily converse with Jesus Christ in the way of duty? * Your converses in prayer, hearing, and meditation, are with the Lord of glory: The greatest peers in the kingdom count it more honour to be in the presence of a king, bare-headed, or upon the knee at *court*, than to have thousands standing bare to them in the country. When you are called to the duties of communion with Christ, you are called to the greatest honour, dignified with the noblest privilege creatures are capable of in this world: Had you but a sense of that honour God puts upon you by this means, you would not need so much pressing and striving, to bring a dead and backward heart into the special presence of Jesus Christ. When he saith, Seek ye my face, your hearts would echo to his calls; Thy face, Lord, will we seek. But alas! the glory of Christ is much hid and veiled by ignorance and unbelief, from the eyes of his own people; it is but seldom the best of saints, by the eye of faith, do see the King in his glory.

Inf. 8. If Christ be so glorious, *how should believers long to be with him, and behold him in his glory above?* Most men need patience to *die*, a believer should need patience to *live*. Paul thought it well worth enduring the pangs of death, to get a sight of Jesus Christ in his glory, Phil. i. 23. " The Lord direct your hearts into " the love of God, and into the patient waiting for Christ," (saith the apostle) 2 Thess. iii. 5. intimating that the saints have great need of patience, to enable them to endure the state of distance and separation from Christ, so long as they must endure it in this world. *The spirit and the bride say, come, and let him that heareth say, come, and let him that is a-thirst come: even so, come Lord Jesus, and be thou as a swift roe upon the mountains of* separation.

Blessed be God for Jesus Christ, the Lord of glory.

---

* Suppose (saith Mr. Rutherford) there were no letter of command, yet there is a suitableness betwixt the law engraven on the heart, and the spiritual matter commanded. There is an heaven in the bosom of prayer, though there were not a granting of the suit. *Rutherford's Treatise of the Covenant,* p. 71.

SERMON XV.

Opening the sixth Motive to come to CHRIST, contained in
the sixth and last Title of CHRIST.

LUKE ii. 25.

——Waiting for the [Consolation] of Israel.

SEVERAL glorious titles of Christ have been already spoken to,
out of each of which much comfort flows to believers: It is comfortable to a wounded soul to eye him as a *Physician;* comfortable to
a condemned and unworthy soul to look upon him under the notion
of *mercy:* The loveliness, the desirableness, and the glory of Christ,
are all so many springs of consolation.   But now I am to shew you,
from this scripture, that the saints have not only much consolation
from Christ, but that Christ himself is the *very consolation* of believers: He is pure comfort wrapped up in flesh and blood.

In this context, you have an account of Simeon's prophecy concerning Christ; and in this text, a description of the person and
quality of Simeon himself, who is described two ways.

1. By his *practice.*
2. By his *principle.*

His practice was heavenly and holy; he was a *just and devout
man:* The principle from which his righteousness and holiness did
flow, was his faith in Christ; " he waited for the consolation of
" Israel."   In which words, by way of *periphrasis,* we have,

1. A description of Christ, the consolation of Israel.
2. The description of a believer, one that waited for Christ.

First, That *the consolation of Israel* is a phrase descriptive of
Jesus Christ, is beyond all doubt, if you consult ver. 26. where he,
i. e. Simeon is satisfied by receiving Christ into his arms, *the consolation* for which he had so long waited.

Secondly, * And that waiting for Christ is a phrase describing the
believers of those times that preceded the incarnation of Christ is
past doubt; they all waited for that blessed day: But it was Simeon's lot to fall just upon that happy point of time, wherein the
prophecies and promises of his incarnation were fulfilled.   Simeon
and others that waited with him, were sensible that the time of the
promise was come, which could not but raise (as indeed it did) a
general expectation of him, John ix. 19.   But Simeon's faith was

---

* It was a phrase common and well known among the Jews at that time, by which
the coming of Christ was signified.   *Ludov. Capell.*

confirmed by a particular revelation, ver. 26. That he should see
Christ before he saw death, which could not but greatly encourage
and raise his expectation to look out for him, whose coming would
be the greatest consolation to the whole *Israel* of God. *The consolation* παραχλησις. The Spirit is frequently called in scripture,
παραχλητης, *the Comforter:* But Christ in this place is called παραχλησις,
comfort, or *consolation itself:* The reason of both is given in John
xvi. 14. " He shall take of mine and shew it unto you:" Where
Christ is said to be the matter, and the Spirit, the applier of true
comfort to the people of God. Now this consolation is here expressed both with a singular *emphasis* [*the consolation*] intimating
that there is nothing of consolation in any thing besides him; all
other comforts compared with this, are not worth naming. And as
it is emphatically expressed, so it is also limited and bounded within
the compass of God's *Israel,* i. e. true believers, stiled the *Israel
of God,* whether Jews or Gentiles, Gal. vi. 16. From whence the
point of doctrine is,

Doct. *That Jesus Christ is the only consolation of believers, and
of none besides them.*

So speaks the apostle, Phil. iii. 3. " For we are the circumci-
" sion, which worship God in the Spirit, and rejoice in Christ
" Jesus, and have no confidence in the flesh." Those that *worship
God in the Spirit* are sincere believers; to such sincere believers,
Christ is consolation, *our rejoicing is in Christ Jesus :* And they
have no consolation in any thing beside him; nothing in the world
can give them comfort without Christ, *We have no confidence in the
flesh.* The gospel is glad tidings of great joy; but that which
makes it to be so is Jesus Christ, whom it imparts and reveals to
us, Luke ii. 10, 11. In the opening of this comfortable point, four
things must be spoken to, for the right stating the method of our
discourse, viz.

1. What is meant by consolation.
2. That Christ, and he only, is consolation to believers.
3. That believers only have consolation in Christ.
4. How it comes to pass that any believer should be dejected,
since Christ is consolation to all believers.

The first thing to be opened, is the nature of consolation, which
is nothing else but *the cheerfulness of a man's spirit, whereby he is
upheld, and fortified against all evils felt, or feared.* Consolation,
is to the soul what health is to the body after wasting sickness; or
the reviving spring to the earth after a long and hard winter. And
there are three sorts of consolation, or comfort, suitable to the disposition and temper of the mind, *viz.*

Natural,
Sinful, and
Spiritual.

Natural comfort is the refreshment of our natural spirits by the good creatures of God, Acts xiv. 17. " Filling their hearts with " food and gladness." *Sinful comfort* is the satisfaction and pleasure men take in the fulfilling of their lusts, by the abuse of the creatures of God, James v. 5. " Ye have lived in pleasure upon " earth," i. e. your life hath been a life of sensuality and sin.

Spiritual comfort is the refreshment, peace, and joy, gracious souls have in Christ, by the exercise of faith, hope, and other graces, Rom. v. 2. And this only deserves the name of true solid consolation: To which four things are required.

First, That the matter thereof be some *spiritual*, eminent, and durable good; else our consolation in it will be but as the crackling of thorns under a pot, a sudden blaze, quickly extinct with the failing matter of it. Christ only gives the matter of solid, durable consolation; the righteousness of Christ, the pardon of sin, the favour of God, the hopes of glory, are the substantial materials of a believer's consolation, Rom. v. 2. Mat. ix. 2. Psal. iv. 6, 7. 2 Pet. i. 8. Things are as their foundations be.

Secondly, Interest and propriety in these comfortable things, are requisite to our consolation by them, Luke i. 47. " My spirit re" joiceth in God my Saviour." It is no consolation to him that is hungry to see a feast; to him that is poor to see a treasure; if the one may not taste, or the other partake thereof.

Thirdly, Knowledge, and evidence of interest, in some degree is requisite to actual consolation, though without it a man may be in the state of consolation; for that which appears not, is (in point of actual comfort) as if it were not.

Fourthly, In order hereunto, the work of the Spirit upon our hearts is requisite, both to give, and clear our interest in Christ and the promises: And both these ways he is the Comforter, " The fruit of the Spirit is joy," Gal. v. 22. And thus briefly of the nature of consolation.

Secondly, Next I will shew you that Christ, and he only, is matter of consolation to believers: which will demonstratively appear by this argument.

First, He that brings to their souls all that is comfortable, and removes from their souls all that is uncomfortable, must needs be the only consolation of believers.

But Jesus Christ brings to their souls all that is comfortable, and removes from their souls all that is uncomfortable.

Therefore Christ only is the consolation of believers.

First, Jesus Christ brings whatsoever is comfortable to the souls of believers. Is pardon comfortable to a person condemned? Nothing can be matter of greater comfort in this world. Why, this Christ brings to all believers, Jer. xxiii. 6. " And this is the name " whereby he shall be called the Lord our righteousness." This cannot but give strong consolation ; righteousness is the foundation of peace, and joy in the Holy Ghost, Rom. xiv. 17. " The work " of righteousness shall be peace ; and the effect of righteousness, " quietness and assurance for ever," Isa. xxxii. 17. Come to a dejected soul, labouring under the burden of guilt, and say, cheer up, I bring you good tidings, there is such an estate befallen you, or such a troublesome business comfortably ended for you; alas! this will not reach the heart: If you can bring me (saith he) good news from heaven, that my sins are forgiven, and God reconciled, how soon should I be comforted! And therefore (as one well observes) this was the usual receipt with which Christ cured the souls of men and women, when he was here on earth ; Son or daughter, " be of good cheer, thy sins be forgiven thee." And, indeed, it is as easy to separate light and warmth from the beams of the sun, as cheerfulness and comfort from the voice of pardon.

Are the hopes and expectations of heaven and glory comfortable! Yes sure, nothing is comfortable if this be not, Rom. v. 2. " We " rejoice in hope of the glory of God." Now, Christ brings to the souls of men all the solid grounds and foundations upon which they build their expectations of glory, Col. i. 27. " Which is " Christ, in you, the hope of glory." Name any thing else that is solid matter of comfort to the souls of men, and the grounds thereof will be found in Christ, and in none but Christ; as might easily be demonstrated by the enumeration of multitudes of particular instances, which I cannot now insist upon.

Secondly, Jesus Christ removes from believers whatever is uncomfortable; therein relieving them against all the matters of their affliction and sorrow. As namely,

First, Is sin a burden and matter of trouble to believers? Christ, and none but Christ, removes that burden, Rom. vii. 24, 25. " O wretched man that I am! (saith sin-burdened Paul) who will " deliver me from the body of this death? I thank God through " Jesus Christ our Lord." The satisfaction of his blood, Eph. v. 2. The sanctification of his Spirit, John i. 5, 6. His perfect deliverance of his people from the very being of sin at last, Eph. v. 26, 27. This relieves at present, and removes at last the matter and ground of all their troubles and sorrows for sin.

Secondly, Do the temptations of Satan burden believers? O yes, by reason of temptations, they go in trouble and heaviness of spirit. Temptation is an enemy under the walls; temptation greatly endangers, and therefore cannot but greatly afflict the souls of believers; but Christ brings the only matter of relief against temptations. The intercession of Christ is a singular relief at present, Luke xxii. 32. " But I have prayed for thee that thy faith fail " not." And the promises of Christ are a full relief for the future; " The God of peace shall shortly tread Satan under your feet," Rom. xvi. 20.

Thirdly, Is spiritual *desertion,* and the hiding of God's face, matter of affliction and casting down to believers? Yes, yes, it distresses their hearts, nothing can comfort them; " Thou hidest thy " face, and I was troubled," Psal. xxx. 7. Outward afflictions do but break the *skin,* this touches the *quick;* they like rain fall only upon the tiles, this soaks into the house; but Christ brings to believers substantial matter of consolation against the troubles of desertion : He himself was deserted of God for a time, that they might not be deserted for ever. In him also the relieving promises are made to believers, that notwithstanding God may desert them for a time, yet the union betwixt him and them shall never be dissolved, Heb. xiii. 4. Jer. xxxii. 40. Though he forsake them for a moment, in respect of evidenced favour, yet he will return again and comfort them, Isa. liv. 7. Though Satan pull hard, yet he will never " be able to pluck them out of his Father's hand," John x. 20. O, what relief is this! What consolation is Christ to a deserted believer.

Fourthly, Are outward afflictions matter of dejection and trouble? Alas, who finds them not to be so? How do our hearts fail and our spirits sink under the many smarting rods of God upon us? But our relief and consolation under them all is in Christ Jesus; for the rod that afflicts us is in the hand of Christ that loveth us, Rev. iii. 29. " Whom I love, I rebuke and chasten." His design in affliction is our profit, Heb. xii. 10. That design of his for our good shall certainly be accomplished, Rom. viii. 28. And after that no more afflictions for ever. Rev. xxi. 3, 4. " God shall wipe " away all tears from their eyes." So that upon the whole, two things are most evident.

First, Nothing can comfort the soul without Christ! he is the soul that animates all comforts; they would be dead things without him. Temporal enjoyments, riches, honours, health, relations yield not a drop of true comfort without Christ. Spiritual enjoyments, ministers, ordinances, promises, are fountains sealed and springs shut up; till Christ open them, a man may go comfortless in the midst of them all.

Secondly, No troubles, sorrows, or afflictions can deject or sink the soul that Christ comforteth, 2 Cor. vi. 20. " As sorrowful, " yet always rejoicing." A believer may walk with a heart full of comfort amidst all the troubles of this world: Christ makes the darkness and troubles to be light round about his people. So that the conclusion stands firm, and never to be shaken, that Christ, and Christ only, is the consolation of believers; which was the thing to be proved.

In the third place, I am to shew you that believers, and none but believers, can have consolation in Christ; which will convincingly appear from the consideration of those things which we laid down before as the requisites to all true spiritual consolation. For,

First, No unbeliever hath the *materials,* out of which spiritual comfort is made, which (as I there told you) must be some solid, spiritual, and eternal good, as Christ and the covenant are: what do unregenerate men rejoice in but trifles and mere vanities, in a thing of nought? Amos vi. 13. See how their mirth is described in Job xxi. 12. " They take their timbrel and harp, and rejoice at " the sound of the organ." He doth not say, they take the Bible, turn to the promises, and rejoice in Christ and the covenant; it is not the melody of a good conscience, the joy of the Holy Ghost; no, no, they have no acquaintance with such music as that; but the rejoicing of believers is in those things, 2 Cor. i. 12. and this is well built consolation, which reaches the heart.

Secondly, I told you that propriety and interest in Christ and the promises are required to all spiritual consolation: but no unbeliever hath any title or interest in Christ and the promises, and so they can signify nothing to him in point of comfort. It is not another man's money, but my own, that must feed, clothe and comfort me; nor is it another man's Christ, but my own Christ, that must justify, save, and comfort my soul.

Thirdly, You were told, that evidence of a man's peace and reconciliation with God, is necessary to his actual consolation, which no unbeliever can possibly have; he hath neither grace within him to make him a qualified subject of any special promise, nor any witness or seal of the Spirit, to confirm and clear his propriety in Christ; for he never seals, but where he first sanctifies. So that it is beyond all contradiction, that believers, and none but believers are partakers of the consolations that are in Christ Jesus.

Fourthly and *lastly,* There is one inquiry remains to be satisfied; namely, seeing Jesus Christ is consolation to believers, how it comes to pass, that so many believers in the world should walk so dejectedly as they do, without any spiritual consolation?

First, This need not be wondered at, if we consider that the consolations of Christ are of two sorts; *seminal* and in preparation, or *actual* in present possession. Every *believer* in the world hath the root and seed of comfort planted and sown for him, Psal. xcvii. 11. " Light is sown for the righteous, and gladness for the upright in

" heart." They have Christ and the promises, which are the seeds of consolation, and will bring forth joy at last, though at present they have no actual consolation; the seed of all joy is sown, and in due time they shall reap the full ripe fruit thereof.

Secondly, It must be remembered, that *interest* and *evidence* are distinct blessings, every *believer* hath interest in Christ: but every *believer* hath not the evidence thereof, Isa. l. 10. " Who is among " you, that feareth the Lord, and obeyeth the voice of his servant; " that walketh in darkness, and hath no light?" Every child of God is not of sufficient age to know his Father, or take comfort in that blessed inheritance whereunto he is begotten again, 1 Pet. i. 3, 4.

Thirdly, Every believer doth not walk with like strictness, and exact holiness: all do not exercise faith in a like degree. Among Christians some are strong in grace, rich in faith, strict in obedience, tender of sin to an eminent degree; these usually are owners of much consolation: but others are weak in grace, poor in faith, comparatively careless of their hearts and ways, frequently grieving the good Spirit of God, and wounding their own consciences (the vessel into which spiritual consolation is poured;) and these are usually denied the joy and comfort which others abound withal.

Fourthly, The consolations of Christ are arbitrarily dispensed by the Spirit, who is the Comforter, and giveth to every man in such proportions, and at such seasons, as pleaseth him: whence it comes to pass, that he that is rich in comfort to-day, may be poor to-morrow; and, contrarily, the heart that is quite full of sorrow one hour, is filled with peace and joy in believing in the next. Things that are necessary to *the being* of a Christian, are fixed and stable; but things belonging only to the well-being of a Christian, come and go, according to the good pleasure and appointment of the Spirit. The use of all follows.

Inf. 1. Hence it follows, *That the state of unbelievers is the most sad and uncomfortable state in the world, having no interest in Christ, the consolation of Israel.* It is true, they abound in creature-comforts; they live in pleasure upon earth; joy displays its colours in their faces; but for all this, there is not the least drop of true consolation in any of their hearts; they have some comfort in the creature, but none in Christ: that little they gather from the creature now, is all their portion of joy, Luke vi. 24. " Ye have received " your consolation:" as this is all they have, so they shall enjoy it but a little while, Job xxi. 13, 17. And while they do enjoy it, it is mixed with many gripes of conscience, Job xiv. 13. " Even in laughter " the heart is sorrowful, and the end of that mirth is heaviness." Whatever consolation any unbeliever speaks of besides this, is but by rote; for when the day of his distress cometh, and the terrors of conscience shall awake him out of his pleasant dreams, all his sensual joys will vanish from him, and the doors of true consolation will be shut against him. Let him go to Jesus Christ, knock at that door, and say, Lord Jesus, thy name is consolation : my heart is ready to burst within me ; hast thou no consolation for me ? O Lord, for one drop of spiritual comfort now ; but alas there is none, no not in Christ himself, for any unbeliever. It is children's bread, the saints privilege ; comfort and grace are undivided. Let him return into himself, search his own conscience for comfort, and say, O conscience ! thou art more than a thousand witnesses, and thousands have been comforted by thee ; where thou speakest comfort, none can speak trouble ; hast thou no consolation for me in my deepest distress ? Alas, no ; if God condemn thee, where- withal shall I comfort thee ? I can speak neither more nor less than the scriptures put into my mouth, and I find not one word in all the book of God warranting me to be thy comforter. Be- lieve it is an undoubted truth (though the sense of the bewitched world over-rules it) that the state of unbelievers, even at the best, is a sad and dismal state.

Inf. 2. Let all believers fetch all their comfort out of Christ, who is the consolation of his people : " We rejoice (saith the apostle) in Christ Jesus, and have no confidence in the flesh." That is the true temper of a believing soul : take heed you live not partly upon Christ and partly upon the creature for your comfort ; much rather beware that you forsake not Christ, the fountain of living waters, and hew out cisterns for yourselves which can hold no water, Jer. ii. 13. If you make any creature the spring and fountain of your comfort, as- suredly God will dry up that spring. If your souls draw their com- fort from any creature, you know they must out-live that creature, and what then will you do for comfort ? Besides, as your comforts are, so are you. The food of every creature is suitable to its na- ture. You see divers creatures feeding upon several parts of the same herb, the bee upon the flower, the bird upon the seeds, the sheep upon the stalk, and the swine upon the root, according to their nature so is their food. Sensual men feed upon sensual things, spiritual men upon spiritual things ; as your food is, so are you. If carnal comforts can content thy heart, sure thy heart must then be a very carnal heart. Yea, and let Christians themselves take heed, that they fetch not their consolations out of themselves in- stead of Christ. Your graces and duties are excellent means and instruments, but not the ground-work and foundation of your comfort, they are useful buckets to draw, but not the well itself in which the springs of consolation rise. If you put your duties in the room of Christ, Christ will put your comforts out of the reach of your duties.

Inf. 3. If Christ be the consolation of believers, what a comfort-able life should all believers live in the world? Certainly, if the fault be not your own, you might live the happiest and comfortablest lives of all men in the world. If you would not be a discomfort to Christ, he would be a comfort to you every day, and in every condition, to the end of your lives. Your condition abounds with all the helps and advantages of consolation. You have the command of Christ to warrant your comforts, Phil. iv. 4. You have the Spirit of Christ for a spring of comfort; you have the scriptures of Christ for the rules of comfort; you have the duties of religion for the means of comfort. Why is it then that you go comfortless? If your afflictions be many in the world, yet your encouragements are more in Christ. Your troubles in the world have been turned into joy, but your comforts in Christ can never be turned into trouble. Why should troubles obstruct your comfort, when the blessing of Christ upon your troubles makes them subservient to promote your happiness? Rom. viii. 28. Shake off despondency then, and live up to the principles of religion. Your dejected life is uncomfortable to yourselves, and of very ill use to others.

Inf. 4. If Christ be the consolation of believers, then let all that desire comfort in this world, or in that to come, embrace Jesus Christ, and get real union with him. The same hour you shall be in Christ, you shall also be at the fountain-head of all consolations: thy soul shall be then a pardoned soul, and a pardoned soul hath all reason in the world to be a joyful soul: in that day the conscience shall be sprinkled with the blood of Christ; and a sprinkled conscience hath all the reason in the world to be a comforting conscience: in that day you become the children of your Father in heaven, and he that hath a Father in heaven, hath all reason to be the joyfullest man upon earth; in that day you are delivered from the sting and hurt of death; and he that is delivered from the sting of death, hath the best reason to take in the comfort of life. O come to Christ! come to Christ! till you come to Christ, no true comfort can come to you.

SERMON XVI.

Enforcing the general Exhortation, by a seventh Motive drawn from the first Benefit purchased by CHRIST.

EPH. i. 7.

In whom we have redemption through his blood, the forgiveness of sins according to the riches of his grace.

SIX great motives have been presented already from the titles of Christ, to draw the hearts of sinners to him; more are now to be offered from the benefits redounding to believers by Christ; essaying, by all means, to win the hearts of men to Christ. To this end I shall in the first place, open that glorious *privilege of gospel-remission*, freely and fully conferred upon all that come to Christ by faith, "in whom we have redemption by faith," &c.

In which words we have, *first*, a singular benefit, or choice mercy bestowed, viz. *redemption*, interpreted by way of *opposition, the remission of sins:* this is a privilege of the first rank, a mercy by itself; none sweeter, none more desirable among all the benefits that come by Christ. And therefore,

Secondly, You have the price of this mercy, an account what it cost, even the *blood of Christ*, in whom we have redemption [through his blood :] precious things are of great price ; the blood of Christ is the *meritorious cause* of remission.

Thirdly, You have here also the *impulsive cause,* moving God to grant pardons at this rate to sinners, and that is said to be the *riches of his grace:* where, by the way, you see that the freeness of the grace of God, and the fulness of the satisfaction of Christ, meet together without the least jar in the remission of sin, contrary to the vain cavil of the Socinian adversaries: "In whom we have "redemption, even the remission of sins, according to the riches of "his grace."

Fourthly, You have the *qualified subjects* of this blessed privilege, viz. Believers, in whose name he here speaks, [*we*] *have remission*, i. e. We the saints and faithful in Christ Jesus, ver. 1. We whom he hath chosen in Christ before the foundation of the world, and predestinated unto the adoption of children, ver. 4, 5. We that are made accepted in the beloved, ver. 6. It is *we*, and *we* only, who have redemption through his blood. Hence observe,

Doct. *That all believers, and none but believers, receive the re-mission of their sins through the riches of grace, by the blood of Jesus Christ.*

In the explication of this point three things must be spoken to.
1. That all that are in Christ are in a pardoned state.
2. That their pardon is the purchase of the blood of Christ.
3. That the riches of grace are manifested in remission.

First, That all that are in Christ are in a pardoned state : where I will first shew you what pardon or remission of sin is.

Secondly, That this is the privilege of none but believers.

First, Now remission of sin is the gracious act of God, in and through Christ, discharging a believing sinner from all the guilt and punishment of his sin, both temporal and eternal.

It is the act of God; he is the author of remission; none can for-give sins but God only, Mark ii. 7.   Against him only, i. e. prin-cipally and especially, the offence is committed, Psal. li. 4.   To his judgment guilt binds over the soul; and who can remit the debt but the creditor ? Matth. vi. 12.

It is an act of God, discharging the sinner; it is God's loosing of one that stood bound, the cancelling of his bond or obligation, called therefore remission or releasing in the text; the blotting out of our iniquities, or the removing of our sins from us, as it is called in other scriptures; see Psal. ciii. 11. Micah vii. 18, 19.

It is a gracious act of God, the effect of pure grace, done for his own name's sake, Isa. xliii. 25. discharging us without any satis-faction at all by us : there is much grace in that; and providing a surety for us every way able to pay our debt, there is more grace in that.

It is the gracious act of God in and through Christ : the satis-faction of Christ is the procuring cause of our remission, and so God declares himself just in the remission of our sin, Rom. iii. 25. " Gracious is the Lord and righteous," Psal. cxvi. 5.   Justice and mercy meet here, and embrace each other ; " in whom (saith the " text) we have remission :" no other price could purchase this privilege, Micah vi. 6, 7. not rivers of oil, or of human blood.

And this gracious act of God discharges the pardoned soul both from guilt and punishment.   Guilt is nothing else but the force and power that is in sin, to oblige the sinner to undergo the pen-alty due to sin ; therefore sinners are said to be *guilty of hell-fire.* Matth. v. 22.   *Guilty of eternal judgment,* Mark iii. 29.   To be under the judgment of God, Rom. iii. 19.   Remission takes away both guilt and punishment together ; it takes away all guilt, Acts xiii. 38, 39. and all punishment.   And so much of the first thing to be opened, namely, what the remission of sin is.

Secondly, Now that this remission of sin is the privilege of believers, is most apparent, for all the causes of remission are in conjunction to procure it for them; the love of God, which is the
impulsive cause of pardon; the blood of Christ, which is the meritorious cause of pardon; and saving faith, which is the instrumental cause of pardon, do all co-operate for their remission, as is
plain in the text.

Besides, all the promises of pardon are made to them, Jer. xxxi.
34. Micah vii. 18. And, lastly, all the signs of pardon are found
in them, and in them only, that love God, Luke vii. 47. Merci-
fulness to others, Matth. vi. 14. A blessed calmness and peace in
the conscience, Rom. v. 1. So that it is a truth beyond controversy, that all that are in Christ are in a pardoned state.

Secondly, Next I will shew you, that the pardon of believers is
the purchase of the blood of Christ: nothing but the blood of Christ
is a price equivalent to the remission of sin, for this blood was innocent and untainted blood, 1 Pet. i. 19. the blood of a Lamb
without spot; this blood was precious blood, blood of infinite
worth and value, the blood of God, Acts xx. 28. It was prepared
blood for this very purpose, Heb. x. 5. Prepared by God's eternal
appointment; prepared by Christ's miraculous and extraordinary
production by the operation of the Spirit; prepared by his voluntary sequestration, or sanctification of himself to this very use and
purpose.

The blood of Jesus is not only innocent, precious, and prepared
blood, but it is also blood actually shed and sacrificed to the justice
of God, for the expiation of guilt, and procurement of our discharge, Isa. liii. 5. To conclude, the severe justice of God could
put in no exception against the blood of Christ; it is unexceptionable blood, being, (as before was noted,) untainted by sin, and
dignified above all estimation by the person whose blood it was.
Justice required no less, and could demand no more; and this is
the price at which our pardons are purchased, and without which
no sin could be pardoned; for " without shedding of blood, (such
" blood as this) there is no remission," Heb. ix. 22.

Thirdly, The last thing to be opened is, That God hath manifested the riches of his grace, in the remission of our sins. So
speaks the apostle, Rom. v. 20. " Where sin abounded, grace did
" much more abound: And, 1 Tim. i. 14. " The grace of our
" Lord (viz. in the pardon of sin) was exceeding abundant."
Which will appear, if we bring our thoughts close to the matter,
in several particulars.

First, From the nature of the mercy, which is the richest of all
mercies, except Christ the purchaser of it: No mercy sweeter
than a pardon to a condemned sinner; no pardon like God's par-

don to a man condemned at his bar; all the goodness of God is
made to pass before our eyes in his pardoning acts of grace, Exod.
xxxiii. 19.

Secondly, The very riches of grace must needs be in the pardon
of sin, if we consider the method in which pardons are dispensed,
which is, as the text speaks, "through his blood." Herein
"God commends his love to us," Rom. v. 8. He commends it
more than if he had pardoned sin without such a sacrifice; for
then he had only displayed his mercy, but not caused mercy and
justice to meet and triumph together.

Thirdly, The riches of his grace shine forth in the peculiarity of
the mercy. Remission is no common favour; it is never extended
to the fallen angels, nor to the greater part of the children of men,
but only to a little flock, a small remnant of mankind, Luke xii. 32.
John xvii. 9.

Fourthly, The riches of grace are manifested in remission, if we
consider the subjects of this privilege, who are not only equally
plunged into sin and misery with others by nature, Eph. ii. 3. but
many of the Lord's pardoned ones have been actually guilty of a
deeper-dyed abomination than many unpardoned ones, in the ci-
vilized world, are defiled with. " To me, (saith Paul), the great-
" est of sinners, one that was before a blasphemer, a persecutor,
" &c. yet to me is this grace given; I obtained mercy," 1 Tim.
i. 15. "And such were some of you, but ye are justified," 1 Cor.
vi. 11. Yea, God singles out the most base, despised, poor, and
contemptible ones among men, to be the subjects of this glorious
privilege, 2 Cor. i. 26. "You see your calling, brethren," &c.

Fifthly, More of the riches of grace still appear, if we view the
latitude and extent of this act of grace. O how innumerable are
our transgressions ! "Who can understand his errors?" Psal. xix.
12. " Yet the blood of Christ cleanseth us from all sin," 1 John
i. 7. Small and great sins, open and secret sins, old and new sins,
all pardoned without exception. O the riches of grace ! O the
unsearchable goodness of God ! "With the Lord there is mercy,
" and with him there is plenteous redemption; and he shall re-
" deem Israel from all his iniquities," Psal. cxxx. 7, 8.

Sixthly, and *lastly,* The riches of grace shine forth in the irre-
vocableness and perpetuity of remission. As grace pardons all sins
without exception, so the pardons it bestows are without revoca-
tion: The pardoned soul shall "never come into condemnation,"
John v. 24. " As far as the east is from the west, so far hath he
" removed our transgressions from us," Psal. ciii. 10. The *east*
and *west* are the two opposite points of heaven, which can never
come together; neither shall the pardoned soul and its sins ever

meet any more. " Thou hast cast, (saith Hezekiah) all my sins
" behind thy back." The penitent believer sets his sins before his
face, but the merciful God casts them all behind his back, never
to behold them more, so as to charge them upon his pardoned
people. And thus you see what the pardon of sin is, what the
price that purchaseth pardon is, and what riches of grace God
manifesteth in the remission of a believer's sins; which were the
things to be explained and opened in the doctrinal part. The improvement of the whole you will have in the following uses.

Inference 1. If this be so, that all believers, and none but believers,
receive the remission of their sins through the riches of grace, by
the blood of Christ; *What a happy condition then are believers in !*
Those that never felt the load of sin may make light of a pardon;
but so cannot you, that have been in the deeps of trouble and fear
about it; those that have been upon the rack of an accusing and
condemning conscience, as David, Heman, and many of the saints
have been, can never sufficiently value a pardon. "Blessed is the
" man whose transgression is forgiven, whose sin is covered; bles-
" sed is the man unto whom the Lord imputeth not iniquity,"
Psal. xxxii. 1, 2. or, O the blessedness and felicities of the pardoned man ! as in the Hebrew *. Remission cannot but appear
the wonder of mercies, if we consider through what difficulties
the grace of God makes way for it to our souls; what strong bars
the love of God breaks asunder, to open our way to this privilege;
for there can be no pardon without a Mediator; no other Mediator but the Son of God: the Son of God cannot discharge our
debts, but by taking them upon himself as our surety, and making
full payment, by bearing the wrath of God for us; and when all
this is done, there can be no actual pardon, except the Spirit of
grace open our blind eyes, break our hard hearts, and draw them
to Christ in the way of believing. And as the mercy of remission
comes to us through wonderful difficulties, so it is in itself a complete
and perfect mercy: God would not be at such vast expence of the
riches of his grace; Christ would not lay out the invaluable treasures of his precious blood to procure a cheap and common blessing for us. Rejoice then, ye pardoned souls, God hath done
great things for you, for which you have cause to be glad.

Inf. 2. Hence it follows, *That interest in Christ by faith, brings
the conscience of a believer into a state of rest and peace,* Rom. v. 1.
" Being justified by faith, we have peace with God." I say not
that every believer is presently brought into actual peace and tranquillity of conscience; there may be many fears, and much trouble
even in a pardoned soul; but this is an undoubted truth, that

---

* אשרי חיש   *O viri beatitudines !*

faith brings the pardoned soul into that condition and state, where he may find perfect rest in his conscience, with respect to the guilt and danger of sin. The blood of Christ sprinkles us from an evil (that is, an accusing, condemning) conscience. We are apt to fear, that this or that special sin, which has most terrified and affrighted our conscience, is not forgiven : but if there be riches enough in the grace of God, and efficacy enough in the blood of Christ, then the sins of believers, all their sins, great as well as small, one as well as another, without limitation or exception, are pardoned.

For let us but consider, If Christ remits no sin to any man, but with respect to the blood of Christ, then all sins are pardoned, as well as any one sin ; because the dignity and desert of that blood is infinite, and as much deserves an universal pardon for all sins, as the particular pardon of any, even the least sin : moreover, remission is an act of God's fatherly love in Christ ; and if it be so, then certainly no sin of any believer can be retained or excluded from pardon ; for then the same soul should be in the favour of God, so far as it is pardoned, and out of favour with God, so far as it is unpardoned, and all this at one and the same instant of time : which is a thing both repugnant to itself, and to the whole strain of the gospel.

To conclude : What is the design and end of remission, but the saving of the pardoned soul ? But if any sin be retained or excluded from pardon, the retaining of that sin must needs make void the pardon of all other sins ; and so the acts of God must cross and contradict each other, and the design and end of God miscarry and be lost ; which can never be. So then we conclude, faith brings the believing soul into a state of rest and peace.

Inf. Hence it also follows, *That no remission is to be expected by any soul, without an interest by faith in Jesus Christ : no Christ, no pardon ; no faith, no Christ.* Yet how apt are many poor deluded souls to expect pardon in that way, where never any soul yet did, or ever can meet it. Some look for pardon from the absolute mercy of God, without any regard to the blood of Christ, or their interest therein : we have sinned, but God is merciful ! Some expect remission of sin by virtue of their own duties, not Christ's merits : I have sinned, but I will repent, restore, reform, and God will pardon ! But little do such men know how they therein diminish the evil of sin, undervalue the justice of God, slight the blood of Christ, and put an undoing cheat upon their own souls for ever. To expect pardon from absolute mercy, or our own duties, is to knock at the wrong door, which God hath shut up to all the world, Rom. iii. 20. Whilst these two principles abide firm, that the price of pardon is only in the blood of Christ, and the benefit of pardon, only by the application of his blood to us ; this must remain a sure conclusion, that no remission is to be expected by any soul, without an interest by faith in Jesus Christ. Repentance, restitution, and reformation are excellent duties in their kind, and in their proper places, but they were never meant for saviours, or satisfaction to God for sin.

Inf. 4. If the riches of grace be thus manifested in the pardon of sin, *How vile an abuse is it of the grace of God, to take the more liberty to sin, because grace abounds in the pardon of it !*

" Shall we continue in sin, that grace may abound ? God for- " bid !" Rom. vi. 1, 2. Will nothing cheaper than the grace of God serve to make a cloak for sin ? O vile abuse of the most excellent thing in the whole world ? Did Christ shed his blood to expiate our guilt, and dare we make that a plea to extenuate our guilt ? God forbid !

If it be intolerable ingratitude among men, to requite good with evil, sure that sin must want a name bad enough to express it, which puts the greatest dishonour upon God for the greatest mercy that ever was given by God to the world. " There is mercy " with thee, (saith the Psalmist,) that thou mayest be feared," not that thou mayest be the more abused, Psal. cxxx. 4. Nay, let me say, the devils never sinned at this rate ; they cannot abuse the pardoning grace of God, because such grace was never offered unto them. And certainly, if the abuse of the common mercies of God, as meat and drink, by gluttony and drunkenness, be an heinous sin, and highly provoking to God ; then the abuse of the riches of his grace, and the precious blood of his Son, must be out of measure sinful, and the greatest affront we can put upon the God of mercy.

Inf. 5. To conclude : *If this be so, as ever you expect pardon and mercy from God, come to Christ in the way of faith ; receive and embrace him now in the tenders of the gospel.*

To drive home this great exhortation, I beseech you, as in the bowels of Christ Jesus, and by all the regard and value you have for your souls, let these following considerations sink down in your hearts.

First, That all christless persons are actually under the condemnation of God, John iii. 18. " He that believeth not is condemned " already :" and it must needs be so, for every soul is concluded under the curse of the law, till Christ make him free, John viii. 36. Till we are in Christ, we are dead by law ; and when we believe unto justification, then we *pass from death to life.* A blind mistaken conscience may possibly acquit you, but assure yourselves God condemns you.

Secondly, Consider what a terrible thing it is to lie under the condemnation of God; the most terrible things in nature cannot shadow forth the misery of such a state; put all sicknesses, all poverty, all reproaches, the torments invented by all tyrants into one scale, and the condemnation of God into the other, and they will be all found lighter than a feather. Condemnation is the sentence of God, the great and terrible God; it is a sentence shutting you up to everlasting wrath: it is a sentence never to be reversed, but by the application of Christ in the season thereof. O souls! you cannot bear the wrath of God; you do not understand it, if you think it tolerable: One drop of it upon your consciences now, is enough to distract you in the midst of all the pleasures and comforts of this world: yet all that are out of Christ, are sentenced to the fulness of God's wrath for ever.

Thirdly, There is yet a possibility of escaping the wrath to come; a door of hope opened to the worst of sinners; a day of grace is offered to the children of men, Heb. iii. 15. God declares himself unwilling that any should perish, 2 Pet. iii. 9. O what a mercy is this! Who, that is on this side heaven or hell, fully understands the worth of it?

Fourthly, The door of mercy will be shortly shut, Luke xii. 25. God hath many ways to shut it: he sometimes shuts it by withdrawing the means of grace, and removing the *candlesticks;* a judgment at this time to be greatly feared. Sometimes he shuts it by withdrawing the Spirit and blessing from the means, whereby all ordinances lose their efficacy, 1 Cor. iii. 7. But if he shut it not by removing the means of grace from you, certain it is, it will be shortly shut by your removal from all the means and opportunities of salvation by death.

Fifthly, When once the door of mercy is shut, you are gone beyond all the possibilities of pardon and salvation for evermore. The night is then come, in which no man can work, John ix. 4. All the golden seasons you now enjoy, will be irrecoverably gone out of your reach.

Sixthly, Pardons are now daily granted to others: some (and they once as far from mercy as you now are,) are at this day reading their pardons with tears of joy dropping from them. The world is full of the examples and instances of the riches of pardoning grace. And whatever is needful for you to do in the way of repentance and faith to obtain your pardon, how easily shall it be done, if once the day of God's power come upon you? Psal. cx. 3. O therefore, lift up your cries to heaven, give the Lord no rest, take no denial till he open the blind eye, break the stony heart, open and bow the stubborn will, effectually draw thy soul to Christ, and deliver thy pardon signed in his blood.

SERMON XVII.

Opening the eighth Motive to come to CHRIST, drawn from the sixth Benefit purchased by CHRIST for Believers.

EPH. i. 6.

To the praise of the glory of his grace, wherein he hath made us accepted in the Beloved.

IN our last discourse we opened to you the blessed privilege of remission of sin, from the following verse; in this verse lies another glorious privilege, viz. the *acceptation* that believers have with God through Jesus Christ; both which comprise (as the two main branches) our justification before God. In the words read, (to omit many things that might be profitably observed from the method and dependence of the apostle's discourse) three things are observable, viz.

1. The privilege itself,
2. The meritorious cause,
3. The ultimate end thereof.

First, The privilege itself, which is exceeding rich and sweet in its own nature; "he hath made us accepted;" the word is εχαριτωσεν ημας, he hath ingratiated us, or brought us into the grace, favour and acceptance of God the Father; endeared us to him, so that we find grace in his sight.

Secondly, The meritorious cause, purchasing and procuring this benefit for us, noted in the words, εν τω ηγαπημενω, *in the Beloved;* which words are a *periphrasis* of Christ, who is here emphatically stiled *the Beloved,* the great favourite of heaven, the delight of God's soul, the prime object of his love: it is he that obtaineth this benefit for believers: he is accepted for his own sake, and we for his.

Thirdly, The ultimate end and aim of conferring this benefit upon believers; "To the praise of the glory of his grace;" or, to the end that his grace might be made glorious in praises: there are riches of grace in this act of God; and the work and business of believers, both in this world and in that to come, is to search and admire, acknowledge and magnify God for his abundant grace herein. Hence the note is,

Doct. *That Jesus Christ hath purchased and procured special favour and acceptation with God for all that are in him.*

This point lies plain in scripture, Eph. ii. 13. "But now in

" Jesus Christ, ye who sometimes were afar off, are made nigh by
" the blood of Christ," εγγυς εγενηθητε, made nigh, a term of endearedness: nothing is taken into the very bosom and embraces
but what is very dear, precious and acceptable; and in Rev. ii. 5,
6. believers are said to be made by Jesus Christ " kings and priests
" unto God, and his Father," i. e. dignified favourites, upon
whom the special marks of honour are set by God.

In opening of this point three things must be doctrinally discussed
and opened, viz.

1. What the acceptation of our persons with God is?
2. How it appears that believers are so accepted with God?
3. How Christ the Beloved procures this benefit for believers?

First, What the acceptation of our persons with God is? To
open which, it may be proper to remember, that there is a two-
fold acceptance of persons mentioned in scripture.

1. One is the sinful act of corrupt man.
2. The other the gracious act of a merciful God.

First, Accepting of persons is noted in scripture as the sinful act
of a corrupt man; a thing which God abhors, being the corruption and abuse of that power and authority which men have in
judgment; overlooking the merit of the cause through sinful respect to the quality of the person whose cause it is; so that the
cause doth not commend the person, but the person the cause.
This God every where brands in men, as a vile perverting of judgment, and utterly disclaims it himself, Gal. ii. 6. " God accepteth
" no man's person;" Rom. ii. 11. " There is no respect of persons
with God."

Secondly, There is also an accepting of persons, which is the gracious act of a merciful God; whereby he receives both the persons
and duties of believers into special grace and favour for Christ's
sake; and of this my text speaks. In which act of favour three
things are supposed or included.

First, It supposes an estate of alienation and enmity; those only
are accepted into favour that were out of favour; and indeed so
stood the case with us, Eph. ii. 12, 13. " Ye were aliens and
" strangers, but now in Christ Jesus, ye who sometimes were afar
" off, are made nigh by the blood of Christ:" So the apostle
Peter, in 1 Pet. ii. 10. " Which in time past were not a people, but
" now are the people of God; which had not obtained mercy,
" but now have obtained mercy." The fall made a fearful breach
betwixt God and man. Sin, like a thick cloud, intercepted all
the beams of divine favour from us; the satisfaction of Christ dissolves that cloud, Isa. xliv. 22. " I have blotted out, as a thick
" cloud, thy transgressions, and, as a cloud, thy sins." This dark
cloud thus dissolved, the face of God shines forth again with cheer-

ful beams of favour and love upon all, who, by faith, are interested in Jesus Christ.

Secondly, It includes the removing of guilt from the persons of believers, by the imputation of Christ's righteousness to them, Rom. v. 1, 2. " Being justified by faith, we have peace with God, " through our Lord Jesus Christ: by whom also we have access " by faith into this grace wherein we stand:" for the face of God cannot shine upon the wicked ; the person must be first made righteous, before he can be made accepted.

Thirdly, It includes the offering up, or tendering of our persons and duties to God by Jesus Christ. Accepting implies presenting or tendering : believers indeed do present themselves to God, Rom. xii. 1. But Christ's presenting them makes their tender of themselves acceptable to the Lord ; Col. i. 22. " In the body of his " flesh through death to present you holy, and unblameable, and " unreproveable, in his sight." Christ leads every believer, as it were, by the hand, into the gracious presence of God ; after this manner bespeaking acceptance for him : " Father, here is a poor " soul that was born in sin, hath lived in rebellion against thee all " his days ; he hath broken all thy laws, and deserved all thy " wrath ; yet he is one of that number which thou gavest me be- " fore the world was. I have made full payment by my blood for " all his sins : I have opened his eyes to see the sinfulness and " misery of his condition : broken his heart for his rebellions " against thee ; bowed his will in obedience unto thy will ; united " him to myself by faith, as a living member of my body : and " now, Lord, since he is become mine by regeneration, let him " be thine also by special acceptation : let the same love with " which thou lovest me embrace him also, who is now become " mine." And so much for the first particular, viz. What acceptation with God is.

Secondly, In the next place I must shew you how it appears that believers are thus ingratiated, or brought into the special favour of God by Jesus Christ. And this will be evinced divers ways.

First, By the *titles* of love and endearedness, with which the Lord graceth and honoureth believers, who are sometimes called *the household of God*, Eph. ii. 19. the *friends of God*, James ii. 23. the *dear children of God*, Eph. v. 1. the *peculiar people of God*, 1 Pet. ii. 9. *a crown of glory*, and a *royal diadem* in the hand of their God, Isa. lxii. 3. The object of his *delight* and *pleasure*, Psal. cxlvii. 10, 11. O what terms of endearedness doth God use towards his people ! Doth not all this speak them to be in special favour with him ? Which of all these alone doth not signify a person highly in favour with God.

Secondly, The gracious manner in which he treats them upon

the throne of grace, to which he allows them to come with boldness, Heb. iv. 16.   This also speaks them in the special favour of
God; he allows them to come to him in prayer, with the liberty,
confidence and filial boldness of children to a father; Gal. iv. 6.
" Because ye are sons, God hath sent forth the Spirit of his Son
" into your hearts, crying Abba, Father;" the familiar voice of
a dear child: yea, which is a wonderful condescension of the great
God to poor worms of the earth, he saith, Isa. xlv. 11. " Thus
" saith the Lord, the holy One of Israel, and his Maker, Ask me
" of things to come concerning my sons; and concerning the work
" of my hands command ye me:" an expression so full of grace
and special favour to believers, that it needs great caution in reading and understanding such an high and astonishing expression:
the meaning is, that God hath, as it were, subjected the works of
his hands to the prayers of his saints; and it is as if he had said,
if my glory, and your necessity shall require it, do but ask me in
prayer, and whatever my Almighty Power can do, I will do it for
you.   However, let no favourite of heaven forget the infinite distance betwixt himself and God.   Abraham was a great favourite
of heaven, and was called *the friend of God*; yet see with what humility of spirit and reverential awe he addresseth God, Gen. xviii.
27. " Behold now I have taken upon me to speak unto the Lord,
" which am but dust and ashes."   So that you see the titles of favour above-mentioned are no empty titles.

Thirdly, God's readiness to grant, as well as their liberty to ask,
speaks them the special favourites of God.   The heart of God is
so propense, and ready to grant the desires of believers, that it is
but ask and have, Matth. vii. 7.   The door of grace is opened by
the key of prayer.   That is a favourite indeed, to whom the king
gives a blank to insert what request he will: " If ye abide in me,
" and my words abide in you, ye shall ask what ye will, and it
" shall be done unto you," John xv. 7.   O blessed liberty of the
sons of God!   David did but say, " Lord, turn the counsel of
" Ahithophel into foolishness," and it was done as soon as asked,
2 Sam. xv. 31.   Joshua did but say, " Thou sun stand still in
" Gibeon," and a miraculous stop was presently put to its swift
motion in the heavens; nay, which is wonderful to consider, a
prayer, yet unborn, I mean conceived in the heart, and not yet
uttered by the lips of believers, is often anticipated by the propen-
siveness of free grace, Isa. lxv. 24. " And it shall come to pass,
" that before they call I will answer, and whilst they are yet
" speaking I will hear."   The prayers of others are rejected as an
abomination, Prov. xv. 8.   God casts them back into their faces,
Mal. ii. 3.   But free grace signs the petitions of the saints more

readily than they are presented; we have not that freedom to ask
that God hath to give: it is true, the answer of a believer's prayers may be a long time suspended from his sense and knowledge;
but every prayer, according to the will of God, is presently granted in heaven, though, for wise and holy ends, they may be held
in a doubtful suspense about them upon earth.

Fourthly, The free discoveries of the secrets of God's heart to
believers, speak them to be his special favourites: men open not
the counsels and secrets of their own hearts to enemies or strangers
but to their most inward and intimate friends: " The secret of the
" Lord is with them that fear him, and he will shew them his
" covenant," Psal. xxv. 14. When God was about to destroy Sodom, he would do nothing in that work of judgment until he had
acquainted Abraham his friend, with his purpose therein, Gen.
xviii. 17. " And the Lord said, Shall I hide from Abraham that
" thing which I do? For I know him," &c. So when a *king* was to
be elected for Israel, and the person whom God had chosen was
yet unknown to the people, God, as it were, whispered that secret
unto Samuel the day before, 1 Sam. ix. 15. " Now the Lord had
" told Samuel in his ear a day before Saul came:" according to
the manner of princes with some special favourite.

Fifthly, The Lord's receiving every small thing that comes from
them with grace and favour, when he rejects the greatest things
offered by others, doth certainly bespeak believers the special favourites of God. There was but one good word in a whole sentence from Sarah, and that very word is noted and commended
by God, 1 Pet. iii. 6. " She called him Lord." There were but
some small beginnings or buddings of grace in young Abijah, and
the Lord took special notice thereof, 1 Kings xiv. 13. " Because
" in him there is found some good thing toward the Lord God of
" Israel, in the house of Jeroboam." Let this be an encouragement to young ones, in whom there are found any breathing desires after Christ; God will not reject them if any sincerity be
found in them; a secret groan, uttered to God in sincerity, shall
not be despised, Rom. viii. 26. The very bent of a believer's will,
when he had no more to offer unto God, is an acceptable present,
2 Cor. viii. 11. The very intent and purpose that lie secretly in
the heart of a believer, not yet executed, are accepted with him,
1 Kings viii. 18. " Whereas it was in thine heart to build an house
" to my name, thou didst well that it was in thine heart." Thus
small things offered to God by believers find acceptance with him,
whilst the greatest presents, even solemn assemblies, sabbaths, and
prayers from others are rejected: " They are a trouble unto me;
" (saith God) I am weary to bear them," Isa. i. 14, 15. " Incense
" from Sheba, the sweet cane from a far country" are not accept-

able, nor sacrifices sweet from other hands, Jer. vi. 20. From all which it appears beyond doubt, that the persons and duties of believers are accepted in the special favour of God by Jesus Christ ; which was the second thing to be spoken to, and brings us to the third general, *viz.*

Thirdly, How Christ, the beloved, procures this benefit for believers ? And this he doth four ways.

First, By *the satisfaction of his blood,* Rom. v. 10. " When we " were enemies, we were reconciled to God by the death of his " Son." No friendship without reconciliation, no reconciliation but by the blood of Christ : therefore the new and living way, by which believers come unto God with acceptance, is said to be consecrated for us through the veil of Christ's flesh ; and hence believers have boldness to enter into the holiest by the blood of Jesus, Heb. x. 19, 20.

Secondly, The favour of God is procured for believers, *by their mystical union with Christ,* whereby they are made " members of his " body, of his flesh, and of his bones, Eph. v. 30. So that as Adam's posterity stood upon the same terms that he their natural head did, so believers, Christ's mystical members, stand in the favour of God, by the favour which Christ their spiritual head hath, John xvii. 33. " I in them, and thou in me, that they may " be made perfect in one, and that the world may know that thou " hast sent me, and hast loved them as thou hast loved me."

Thirdly, Believers are brought into favour with God *by Christ's becoming their altar,* upon which their persons and duties are all offered up to God : *The altar* sanctifies the gift, Heb. xiii. 10. And this was typified by the legal rite mentioned Luke i. 9, 10. Christ is that golden altar from whence all the prayers of the saints ascend to the throne of God, perfumed with the odours and incense of his merits, Rev. viii. 34. " And another angel came and stood " at the altar, having a golden censer, and there was given unto " him much incense that he should offer it, with the prayers of " all the saints upon the golden altar which was before the throne ; " and the smoke of the incense which came with the prayers of " the saints ascended up before God out of the angel's hand." And thus you see how the persons and duties of believers are brought into favour and acceptance with God by Jesus Christ. The uses follow.

Inf. 1. *If all believers be in favour with God, how great a mercy is it to have the prayers of such engaged on our behalf ?* Would we have our business speed in heaven, let us get into the favour of God ourselves, and engage the prayers of his people, the favourites of heaven for us. *Vis unita fortior,* one believer can do much, many can do more : When Daniel designed to get the knowledge of that secret, hinted in the obscure dream of the king, which none but the God of heaven could make known, it is said, Dan. ii. 17. " Then Daniel went to his house, and made the thing known un- " to Hananiah, Mishael, and Azariah, his companions; that they " would desire mercies of the God of heaven concerning this " secret." The benefit of such assistance in prayer by the help of other favourites with God, is plainly intimated by Jesus Christ to us, Mat. xviii. 19. " If two of you shall agree on earth as touching " any thing that they shall ask, it shall be done for them of my " Father which is in heaven." God sometimes stands upon a number of voices, for the carrying of some public mercy, because he delighteth in the harmony of many praying souls; and also loves to oblige and gratify many in the answer and return of the same prayer. I know this usage is grown too formal and comple- mental among professors; but certainly it is a great advantage to be sincere with them who are so with God. St. Bernard, prescribing rules for effectual prayer, closes them up with this wish, *et cum talis fueris, momento mei*, when thy heart is in this frame, then remem- ber me.

Inf. 2. If believers be such favourites in heaven, in what a desper- ate condition is that cause and those persons, against whom the gen- erality of believers are daily engaged in prayers and cries to heaven?

Certainly Rome shall feel the dint and force of the many mil- lions of prayers that are gone up to heaven from the saints for many generations; the cries of the blood of the martyrs of Jesus, joined with the cries of thousands of believers, will bring down vengeance at last upon the man of sin. It is said, Rev. viii. 4, 5, 6. " That the smoke of the incense which came with the prayers " of the saints, ascended up before God out of the angel's " hand:" And immediately it is added, ver. 5. " And the angel " took the censer and filled it with fire of the altar, and cast it " into the earth, and there were voices, and thunderings, and " lightnings, and earthquakes; and the seven angels, which had " the seven trumpets, prepared themselves to sound." The prayer of a single saint is sometimes followed with wonderful effects, Psal. xviii. 6, 7. " In my distress I called upon the Lord, and I " cried unto my God: he heard my voice out of his temple, " and my cry came before him, even into his ears: then the earth " shook and trembled; the foundation also of the hills moved and " were shaken, because he was wroth:" what then can a thunder- ing legion of such praying souls do? It was said of Luther, *Iste vir potuit cum Deo quicquid voluit*, that man could have of God what he would; his enemies felt the weight of his prayers, and the church of God reaped the benefit thereof. The *queen of Scots* professed she was more afraid of the prayers of Mr. Knox *, than of an army of ten thousand men: these were mighty wrestlers with God, however contemned and vilified among their enemies. There will a time come, when God will hear the prayers of his people, who are continually crying in his ears, *How long? Lord, how long?*

Inf. 3. *Let no believer be dejected at the contempts and slightings of men, so long as they stand in the grace and favour of God.* It is the lot of the best men to have the worst usage in the world: those of whom the world was not worthy, were not thought worthy to live in the world, Heb. xi. 38. Paul and his companions were men of choice and excellent spirits; yet, saith he, 1 Cor. iv. 12. " Being defamed, we intreat; we are made as the filth of the " world, and are the offscouring of all things unto this day." They are words signifying the basest, most contemptible, and ab-horred things among men. How are heaven and earth divided in their judgments and estimations of the saints? Those whom men call filth and dirt, God calls a peculiar treasure, a crown of glory, a royal diadem. But trouble not thyself, believer, for the unjust censures of the blind world; they speak evil of the things they know not: " He that is spiritual judgeth all things, yet he himself " is judged of no man," 1 Cor. ii. 14. You can discern the earthliness and baseness of their spirits: they want a faculty to dis-cern the excellency and choiceness of your spirits: he that carries a dark lantern in the night can discern him that comes against him, and yet is not discerned by him. A courtier regards not a slight in the country, so long as he hath the ear and favour of his prince.

Inf. 4. *Never let believers fear the want of any good thing ne-cessary for them in this world.* The favour of God is the fountain of all blessings, provisions, protections, even of all that you need. He hath promised that he will withhold no good thing from them that walk uprightly, Psal. lxxxiv. 11. He that is bountiful to his ene-mies will not withhold what is good from his friends. The favour of God will not only supply your needs, but protect your persons, Psal. v. 12. " Thou wilt bless the righteous, with favour wilt thou " compass him as with a shield."

Inf. 5. Hence also it follows, *that the sins of believers are very piercing things to the heart of God.* The unkindness of those whom he hath received into his very bosom, upon whom he hath set his special favour and delight, who are more obliged to him than all the people of the earth beside, O this wounds the very heart of God. What a melting expostulation was that which the Lord

---

* Jacobus Songius, the Sorbonne doctor, who wrote the lives of Luther, Knox, and Calvin, speaks as if the devil had hired his pen to abuse those precious servants of Christ.

used with David, 2 Sam. xii. 7, 8. " I anointed thee king over
" Israel, and I delivered thee out of the hand of Saul, and I gave
" thee thy master's house, and thy master's wives into thy bosom,
" and gave thee the house of Israel and Judah, and if that had
" been too little, I would moreover have given unto thee such and
" such things: wherefore hast thou despised the commandment of the
" Lord?"   But reader, if thou be a reconciled person, a favourite
with God, and hast grieved him by any eminent transgression,
how should it melt thy heart to hear the Lord thus expostulating
with thee: I delivered thee out of the hand of Satan; I gave thee
into the bosom of Christ; I have pardoned unto thee millions of
sins; I have bestowed upon thee the riches of mercy; my favour
hath made thee great: and, as if all this were too little, I have
prepared heaven for thee: for which of all these favours dost thou
thus requite me?

*Inf. 6. How precious should Jesus Christ be to believers, by whose
blood they are ingratiated with God, and by whose intercession they
are, and shall for ever be continued in his favour?* When the apostle mentions the believer's translation, from the sad state of nature
to the blessed privileged state of grace, see what a title he bestows
upon Jesus Christ, the purchaser of that privilege, calling him the
dear Son, Col. i. 13.   Not only dear to God, but exceeding dear
to believers also.   Christ is the favourite in heaven, to him you owe
all the preferment there: Take away Christ, and you have no
ground on which to stand one minute in the favour of God.   O
then let Jesus Christ, the fountain of your honour, be also the
object of your love and praise.

*Inf. 7. Estimate by this the state and condition of a deserted saint,
upon whom the favour of God is eclipsed.* If the favour of God be
better than life, the hiding of it from a gracious soul must be more
bitter than death: Deserted saints have reason to take the first
place among all the mourners in the world: The darkness before
conversion had indeed more danger, but this hath more of trouble.   Darkness after light is dismal darkness.   Since therefore the
case is so sad, let your preventing care be the more; grieve not the
good Spirit of God; you prepare but for your own grief in so
doing.

*Inf. 8. Lastly, Let this persuade all men to accept Jesus Christ,
as ever they expect to be accepted with the Lord themselves.*   It is a
fearful case, for a man's person and duties to be rejected of God; to
cry and not be heard: And much more terrible to be denied audience in the great and terrible day.   Yea, as sure as the scriptures
are the sealed and faithful sayings of God, this is no more than
what every christless person must expect in that day, Mat. vii. 22.
Luke xiii. 26. trace the history of all times, even as high as Abel,

and you shall find that none but * believers did ever find acceptance with God; all experience confirms this great truth, that *they that are in the flesh cannot please God.* Reader, if this be thy condition, let me beg thee to ponder the misery of it in a few sad thoughts.

Consider how sad it is to be rejected of God, and forsaken by all creatures at once; what a day of straits thy dying day is like to be, when heaven and earth shall cast thee out together. Be assured whatever thy vain hopes for the present quiet thee withal, this must be thy case, the door of mercy will be shut against thee; no man cometh to the Father but by Christ. Sad was the case of Saul, when he told Samuel, " the Philistines make war against " me, and God is departed from me," 1 Sam. xxviii. 15. The saints will have boldness in the day of judgment, 1 John iv. 17. But thou wilt be a confounded man; there is yet, blessed be the God of mercy, a capacity and opportunity for reconciliation, 2 Cor. v. 19. Isa. xxvii. 5. But this can be of no long continuance. O therefore, by all the regard and love you have for the everlasting welfare of your own souls, come to Christ; embrace Christ in the offers of the gospel, that you may be made accepted in the beloved.

SERMON XVIII.

The Liberty of Believers opened and stated.

JOHN viii. 36.

If the Son therefore shall make you free, ye shall be free indeed.

FROM the 30th verse of this chapter unto my text, you have an account of the different effects which the words of Christ had upon the hearts of his hearers: Some believed, ver. 30. These he encourageth to continue in his word, ver. 31. giving them this encouragement, ver. 32. " Ye shall know the truth, and the truth " shall make you free." Hereat the unbelieving Jews take offence, and commence a quarrel with him, ver. 33. " We be Abra- " ham's seed, and were never in bondage to any man." We are of no slavish extraction; the blood of Abraham runs in our veins. This scornful boast of the proud Jews, Christ confutes, ver. 34. where he distinguisheth on a two-fold bondage; one to men, ano-

---

* If any one desires to know the will of God, let him be a friend of God. *Aug.*

ther to sin; one civil, another spiritual : Whosoever committeth sin is the servant of sin, then tells them, ver. 36. " The servant " abideth not in the house for ever, but the Son abideth for ever." Wherein he intimateth two great truths, viz. That the servants and slaves of sin may for a time enjoy the external privileges of the house or church of God; but it would not be long before the master of the house would turn them out of doors : But if they were once the adopted children of God, then they should abide in the house for ever. And this privilege is only to be had by their believing in, and union with the natural Son of God, Jesus Christ : which brings us fairly to the text; " If the Son therefore shall " make you free, ye shall be free indeed." In which words we have two parts; viz.

  1. A supposition.
  2. A concession.

First, A *supposition*, " If the Son therefore shall make you free," q. d. The womb of nature cast you forth into the world in a state of bondage ! in that state you have lived all your days; servants to sin; slaves to your lusts; yet freedom is to be obtained : And this freedom is the prerogative belonging to the Son of God to bestow : " If the Son shall make you free."

Secondly, Christ's concession upon this supposition, " Then shall " ye be free indeed," i. e. you shall have a real freedom, an excellent and everlasting freedom : No conceit only, as that which you now boast of is : If ever therefore you will be free men indeed, belive in me. Hence note,

  Doct. *That interest in Christ sets the soul at liberty from all that bondage whereunto it was subjected in its natural state.*

Believers are the children of the new covenant, the denizens of Jerusalem which is above, which is free, and the mother of them all, Gal. iv. 26. The glorious liberty, viz. that which is spiritual and eternal, is the liberty of the children of God, Rom. viii. 21. Christ, and none but Christ, delivers his people out of the hand of their enemies, Luke i. 74.

In the doctrinal part of this point, I must shew you,

First, What believers are not freed from by Jesus Christ in this world.

Secondly, What that bondage is from which every believer is freed by Christ.

Thirdly, What kind of freedom that is which commences upon believing.

Fourthly, Open the excellency of this state of spiritual freedom.

First, What those things are from which believers are not made free in this world: We must not think that our spiritual liberty by Christ, presently brings us into an absolute liberty, in all respects, For,

First, Christ doth not free believers from obedience to the moral law : It is true we are no more under it as a *covenant* for our *justification ;* but we are, and must still be under it, as a *rule* for our *direction.* The matter of the moral law is unchangeable, as the nature of good and evil is, and cannot be abolished except that distinction could be destroyed, Mat. v. 17, 18. The precepts of the law are still urged under the gospel to enforce duties upon us, Eph. vi. 12. It is therefore a vain distinction, invented by Libertines, to say it binds us as *creatures,* not as Christians; or that it binds the unregenerate part, but not the regenerate : but this is a sure truth, that they who are freed from its *penalties* are still under its *precepts.* Though believers are no more under its *curse,* yet they are still under its *conduct :* The law sends us to Christ to be *justified,* and Christ sends us to the law to be *regulated.* Let the heart of every Christian join therefore with David's in that holy wish, Psal. cxix. 4, 5. " Thou hast commanded us to keep thy precepts diligently ; " O that my heart were directed to keep thy statutes." It is excellent when Christians begin to obey the law *from* life, which others obey *for* life; because they *are* justified, not that they *may be* justified. It is also excellent when duties are done in the strength, and for the honour of Christ, which is evangelical ; and not in our own strength, and for our own ends, which is servile and legal obedience : Had Christ freed us from obedience, such a liberty had been to our loss.

Secondly, Christ hath not freed believers, in this world, from the temptations and assaults of Satan : even those that are freed from his *dominion,* are not free from his *molestation.* It is said indeed, Rom. xvi. 20. " God shall shortly bruise Satan under your feet :" But mean time he hath power to bruise and buffet us by his injections, 2 Cor. xii. 7. He now bruiseth Christ's heel, Gen. iii. 15. i. e. bruiseth him in his tempted and afflicted members : Though he cannot kill them, yet he can and doth afflict and fright them, by shooting his fiery darts of temptation among them, Eph. vi. 16. It is true, when the saints are got safe into heaven they are out of gunshot ; there is perfect freedom from all temptation. A believer may then say, O thou enemy, temptations are come to a perpetual end. I am now arrived there, where none of thy fiery darts can reach me : But this freedom is not yet.

Thirdly, Christ hath not yet freed believers, in this world, from the motions of indwelling sin ; these are continually acting, and infesting the holiest of men, Rom. vii. 21, 23, 24.   Corruptions, like Canaanites, are still left in the land to be thorns in your eyes, and goads in your sides.   Those that boast most of freedom from the motions of sin, have most cause to suspect themselves still under the dominion of sin.   All Christ's freemen are troubled with the same complaint : who among them complains not as the apostle did, Rom. vii. 24.   "Oh wretched man that I am! who shall de-"liver me from the body of this death?"

Fourthly, Jesus Christ doth not free believers, in this world, from inward troubles and exercises of soul, upon the account of sin. God may let loose Satan, and conscience too, in the way of terrible accusations, which may greatly distress the soul of a believer, and woefully eclipse the light of God's countenance, and break the peace of their souls.   Job, Heman, and David were all made free by Christ, yet each of them hath left upon record his bitter complaint upon this account, Job vii. 19, 20. Psal. lxxxviii. 14, 15, 16. Psal. xxxviii. unto ver. 11.

Fifthly, Christ hath not freed believers, in this world, from the rods of affliction.   God, in giving us our liberty, doth not abridge his own liberty, Psal. lxxxix. 32.   All the children of God are made free, yet what son is there whom the father chasteneth not? Heb. xii. 8.   Exemption from affliction is so far from being the mark of a free man, that the apostle there makes it the mark of a slave. Bastards, not sons, want the discipline and blessing of the rod : To be free from affliction would be no benefit to believers, who receive so many benefits by it.

Sixthly, No believer is freed by Christ from the *stroke* of death, though they are all freed from the *sting* of death, Rom. viii. 10. The bodies of believers are under the same law of mortality with other men, Heb. ix. 27.   We must come to the grave as well as others; yea, we must come to it through the same agonies, pangs, and dolours that other men do : The foot of death treads as heavy upon the bodies of the redeemed, as of other men.   Believers, indeed, are distinguished by mercy from others, but the distinguishing mercy lies not here.   Thus you see what believers are not freed from in this world : If you shall now say, what advantage then hath a believer, or what profit is there in regeneration? I answer,

Secondly, That believers are freed from many great and sad miseries and evils by Jesus Christ, notwithstanding all that hath been said.   For,

First, All believers are freed from the *rigour* and *curse* of the law : The rigorous yoke of the law is broken off from their necks, and the sweet and easy yoke of Jesus Christ put on, Matth. ix. 28. The law required perfect working, under the pain of a curse, Gal.

iii. 10. accepted of no short endeavours; admitted no repentance; gave no strength: It is not so now; proportionable strength is given, Phil. iv. 13. Evangelical sincerity is reckoned perfection, Job i. 1. Transgression brings not under condemnation, Rom. viii. 1. O blessed freedom! when duty becomes light, and failings hinder not acceptance! This is one part of the blessed freedom of believers.

Secondly, All believers are freed from the guilt of sin; it may *trouble,* but it cannot *condemn* them, Rom. viii. 33. The hand-writing which was against us is cancelled by Christ, nailed to his cross, Col. ii. 14. When the seal and hand-writing are torn off from the bond, the debtor is made free thereby: Believers are totally freed, Acts xiii. 39. " Justified from all things:" And finally freed, John v. 24. " They shall never come into condemnation." O blessed freedom! How sweet is it to lie down in our beds, yea, in our graves, when guilt shall neither be our bed-fellow, nor grave-fellow!

Thirdly, Jesus Christ frees all believers from the *dominion* as well as the guilt of sin. " Sin shall not have dominion over you, for " ye are not under the law, but under grace," Rom. vi. 14. " The law of the Spirit of life which is in Christ Jesus, hath made " me free from the law of sin and death," Rom. viii. 2. Now, who can estimate such a liberty as this? What slavery, what an intolerable drudgery is the service of divers lusts, from all which believers are freed by Christ; not from the *residence,* but from the *reign* of sin. It is with sin in believers as it was with those beasts mentioned Dan. vii. 12. " They had their dominion taken away, " yet their lives were prolonged for a season and a time."

Fourthly, Jesus Christ sets all believers free from the power of Satan, in whose right they were by nature, Col. i. 13. they are translated from the power of darkness into the kingdom of Christ. Satan had the possession of them, as a man of his own goods; but Christ dispossesseth that strong man armed, alters the property, and recovers them out of his hand, Luke xi. 21, 22. There are two ways by which Christ frees believers out of Satan's power and possession; namely,

1. By price.
2. By power.

First, By *price.* The blood of Christ purchaseth believers out of the hands of justice, by satisfying the law for them, which being done, Satan's authority over them falls of course, as the power of a gaoler over the prisoner doth, when he hath a legal discharge, Heb. ii. 14. " Forasmuch then as the children are partakers of flesh and blood; " he also himself took part of the same, that through death he " might destroy him that had the power of death, that is, the devil." The cruel tyrant beats and burdens the poor captive no more after the ransom is once paid, and he actually freed; and therefore Christ delivers his,

Secondly, By *power*.   Satan is exceeding unwilling to let go his prey: He is a strong and malicious enemy; every rescue and deliverance out of his hand is a glorious effect of the Almighty Power of Christ, Acts xxvi. 18. 2 Cor. x. 5.   How did our Lord Jesus Christ grapple with Satan at his death, and triumph over him, Col. ii. 15.   O glorious salvation! blessed liberty of the children of God!

Fifthly, Christ frees believers from the poisonous sting and hurt of death: Kill us it can, but hurt us it cannot, 1 Cor. xv. 55, 56. " O death! where is thy sting? O grave! where is thy victory? " The sting of death is sin, and the strength of sin is the law: But " thanks be to God which giveth us the victory through our Lord " Jesus Christ."   If there be no hurt, there should be no horror in death: It is guilt that arms death, both with its hurting and terrifying power.   To die in our sins, John viii. 24.   To have our bones full of the sins of our youth, which shall lie down with us in the dust, Job xx. 11.   To have death, like a dragon, pulling a poor guilty creature as a prey into its dreadful den, Psal. xlix. 14. In this lies the danger and horror of death: But from death, as a curse, and from the grave, as a prison, Christ hath set believers at liberty, by submitting to death in their room; and by his victorious resurrection from the grave, as the first-born of the dead, death is disarmed of its hurting power.   The death of believers is but a sleep in Jesus.

Thirdly, The next thing to be briefly spoken to, is the kind and nature of that freedom and liberty purchased and procured by Christ for believers.

Now liberty may be considered two ways; *viz.*

1. As civil.

2. As sacred.

As to civil freedom, or liberty, it belongs not to our present business: Believers, as to their civil capacity, are not freed from the duties they owe to their superiors.   Servants, though believers, are still to be subject to their masters, according to the flesh, with fear and trembling, Eph. vi. 5. nor from obedience to lawful magistrates, whom we are to obey in the Lord, Rom. xii. 1, 4.   Religion dissolves not the bonds of civil relations; nor is it to be used as an occasion to the flesh, 1 Pet. ii. 16.   It is not a carnal, but a spiritual freedom Christ hath purchased for us: And this spiritual freedom is again to be considered, either as,

1. Inchoate.

2. Consummate.

The liberty believers have at present is but a beginning liberty;

they are freed but in part from their spiritual enemies; but it is a growing liberty every day, and will be consummate and complete at last.

To conclude, Christian liberty is either,

1. Privative, or,

2. Positive.

The liberty believers are invested with is of both kinds: They are not only freed from many miseries, burdens and dangers, but also invested by Jesus Christ with many royal privileges and invaluable immunities.

Fourthly, And this brings us to the fourth and last thing; namely, the properties of this blessed freedom which the saints enjoy by Jesus Christ; and, if we consider it duly, it will be found to be,

First, A wonderful liberty, never enough to be admired. How could it be imagined that ever those who owed unto God more than ever they could pay by their own eternal sufferings; those that were under the dreadful curse and condemnation of the law, in the power and possession of Satan the strong man armed; those that were bound with so many chains in their spiritual prison; their understanding bound with ignorance, their wills with obstinacy, their hearts with impenetrable hardness, their affections with a thousand betwitching vanities, that slight their state of slavery so much, as industriously to oppose all instruments and means of deliverance; for such persons to be set at liberty, notwithstanding all this, is the wonder of wonders, and will be deservedly marvellous in the eyes of believers for ever.

Secondly, The freedom of believers is a peculiar freedom; a liberty which few obtain; the generality abiding still in bondage to Satan, who, from the multitude of his subjects, is stiled *the god of this world,* 2 Cor. iv. 4. Believers in scripture are often called a remnant, which is but a small part of the whole piece: The more cause have the people of God to admire distinguishing mercy. How many nobles and great ones of the world are but royal slaves to Satan, and their own lusts!

Thirdly, The liberty of believers is a liberty dearly purchased by the blood of Christ. What that captain said, Acts xxii. 28. " With a great sum obtained I this freedom," may be much more said of the believers' freedom: It was not silver or gold, but the precious blood of Christ that purchased it, 1 Pet. i. 18.

Fourthly, The freedom and liberty of believers is a growing and increasing liberty; they get more and more out of the power of sin, and nearer still to their complete salvation every day, Rom. xiii. 11. The body of sin dieth daily in them: they are said to be crucified with Christ: the strength of sin abates continually in them, after the manner of crucified persons, who die a slow, but sure death : And look in what degree the power of sin abates, proportionably their spiritual liberty increases upon them.

Fifthly, The freedom of believers is a comfortable freedom : the apostle comforts Christians of the lowest rank, poor servants, with this consideration, 1 Cor. vii. 22. " He that is called in the " Lord, being a servant, is the Lord's freeman," q. d. Let not the meanness of your outward condition, which is a state of subjection and dependence, a state of poverty and contempt, at all trouble you : you are the Lord's freemen, of precious account in his eyes. O it is a comfortable liberty !

Sixthly, and *Lastly,* It is a perpetual and final freedom; they that are once freed by Christ, have their manumission and final discharge from that state of bondage they were in before : sin shall never have dominion over them any more : it may tempt them and trouble them, but shall never more rule and govern them, Acts xxvi. 18. And thus you see what a glorious liberty the liberty of believers is.

The improvement whereof will be in the following inferences.

Inf. 1. *How rational is the joy of Christians, above the joy of all others in the world?* Shall not the captive rejoice in his recovered liberty ? the very birds of the air (as one observes) had rather be at liberty in the woods, though lean and hungry, than in a golden cage with the richest fare : every creature naturally prizes it; none more than believers, who have felt the burden and bondage of corruption, who in the days of their first illumination and conviction have poured out many groans and tears for this mercy. What was said of the captive people of God in Babylon, excellently shadows forth the state of God's people under spiritual bondage, with the way and manner of their deliverance from it, Zech. ix. 11. " By the blood of the covenant I have sent forth thy prisoners " out of the pit, wherein is no water." Believers are delivered by the blood of Christ, out of a worse pit than that of Babylon; and look, as the tribes in their return from thence were overwhelmed with joy and astonishment, Psal. cxxvi. 1, 2. " When the " Lord turned again the captivity of Sion, we are like them that " dream : Then was our mouth filled with laughter, and our " tongue with singing."

They were overwhelmed with the sense of the mercy : So should it be with the people of God. It is said, Luke xv. 24. when the prodigal son (there made the emblem of a returning, converting sinner) was returned again to his father's house, that there was heard music and dancing, mirth and feasting in that house. The angels in heaven rejoice when a soul is recovered out of the power of Satan : And shall not the recovered soul, immediately concerned in the mercy, greatly rejoice ? Yea, let them rejoice in the Lord, and let no earthly trouble or affliction ever have power to interrupt their joy for a moment, after such a deliverance as this.

Inf. 2. *How unreasonable and wholly inexcusable is the sin of apostasy from Jesus Christ?* What is it but for a delivered captive to put his feet again into the shackles; his hands into the manacles; his neck into the iron yoke, from which he hath been delivered? It is said, Mat. xii. 44, 45. "When the unclean spirit is gone out of a " man, he walketh through dry places, seeking rest and findeth none: " Then he saith, I will return into mine house from whence I came " out; and when he is come, he findeth it empty, swept, and " garnished; then goeth he, and taketh with him seven other " spirits more wicked than himself, and they enter in and dwell " there, and the last state of that man is worse than the first." Even as a prisoner that hath escaped, and is again recovered, is loaded with double irons. Let the people of God be content to run any hazard, endure any difficulties in the way of religion, rather than return again into their former bondage, to sin and Satan. O Christian! if ever God gave thee a sight and a sense of the misery and danger of thy natural state, if ever thou hast felt the pangs of labouring and distressed conscience, and, after all this, tasted the unspeakable sweetness of the peace and rest that are in Christ, thou wilt rather chuse to die ten thousand deaths, than to forsake Christ, and go back again into that sad condition.

Inf. 3. *How suitable and well-becoming is a free spirit in believers to their state of liberty and freedom?* Christ hath made your condition free, O let the temper and frame of your hearts be free also; do all that you do for God with a spirit of freedom; not by constraint, but willingly. Methinks, Christians, the new nature that is in you should stand for a command, and be instead of all arguments that use to work upon the hopes and fears of other men. See how all creatures work according to the principle of their natures. You need not command a mother to draw forth her breasts to a sucking child; nature itself teaches and prompts to that. You need not bid the sea ebb and flow at the stated hours. O Christian! why should thy heart need any other argument, than its own spiritual inclination, to keep its stated times and seasons of communion with God? Let none of God's commandments be grievous to you: let not thine heart need dragging and forcing to its own benefit and advantage. Whatever you do for God, do it cheerfully; and whatever you suffer for God suffer it cheerfully. It was a brave spirit which actuated holy Paul, "I am ready " saith he) not only to be bound, but also to die at Jerusalem for " the name of the Lord Jesus," Acts xxi. 13.

Inf. 4. *Let no man wonder at the enmity and opposition of Satan to*

the preaching of the gospel: for by the gospel it is that souls are recovered out of his power, Acts xxvi. 18. It is the express work of
ministers "to turn men from darkness to light, and from the
" power of Satan unto God." Satan (as one saith) is a great and
jealous prince: he will never endure to have liberty proclaimed by
the ministers of Christ within his dominions. And, indeed, what
is it less, when the gospel is preached in power, but as it were by
beat of drum, and sound of trumpet, to proclaim liberty, spiritual,
sweet, and everlasting liberty, to every soul sensible of the bondage
of corruption and the cruel servitude of Satan, and will now come
over to Jesus Christ? And O what numbers and multitudes of
prisoners have broken loose from Satan at one proclamation of
Christ, Acts ii. 41. But Satan owes the servants of Christ a spite
for this, and will be sure to pay them if ever they come within his
reach; persecution is the evil genius of the gospel, and follows it as
the shadow doth the body.

Inf. 5. How careful should Christians be to maintain their
spiritual liberty in all and every point thereof! "stand fast (saith
" Paul) in the liberty wherewith Christ hath made us free, and
" be not again entangled in the yoke of bondage," Gal. v. 1.
And again, " Ye are bought with a price, be not ye the servants
" of men." It is Christ's prerogative to prescribe the rules of his
own house; he hath given no man dominion over your faith,
2 Cor. i. 24. One man is no rule to another, but the word of
Christ is a rule to all: follow not the holiest of men one step farther than they follow Christ, 1 Cor. xi. 4. Man is an ambitious
creature, naturally affecting dominion; and dominion over the
mind rather than over the body. To give law to others, feeds
pride in himself; so far as any man brings the word of Christ to
warrant his injunctions, so far we are to obey, and no farther;
Christ is your Lord and Lawgiver.

Inf. 6. *Lastly,* Let this encourage and persuade sinners to come
to Christ; for with him is sweet liberty to poor captives. Oh
that you did but know what a blessed state Jesus Christ would
bring you into! " Come unto me (saith he) ye that labour and are
" heavy laden:" and what encouragement doth he give to comers?
Why this, " My yoke is easy, and my burden is light." The
devil persuades you, that the ways of obedience and strict godliness
are a perfect bondage; but if ever God regenerate you, you will
find his ways, " ways of pleasantness, and all his paths peace: you
" will rejoice in the way of his commandments as much as in all
" riches:" you will find the worst work Christ puts you about,
even suffering work, sweeter than all the pleasures that ever you
found in sin. O therefore open your hearts at the call of the gospel: Come unto Christ, *then shall you be free indeed.*

SERMON XIX.

The Saints coming home to GOD by Reconciliation and Glorification, opened and applied.

1 PET. iii. 18.

For Christ hath once suffered for sins, the just for the unjust, that he might bring us to God.

THE scope of the apostle in this place is to prepare and fortify Christians for a day of suffering. In order to their cheerful sustaining whereof, he prescribeth two excellent rules of mighty use for all suffering Christians.

First, To get a good conscience within them, ver. 16, 17. *hic murus aheneus esto.*

Secondly, To set the example of Christ's sufferings before them, ver. 18. " For Christ hath once suffered for sinners;" the sufferings of Christ for us, is the great motive engaging Christians to suffer cheerfully for him.

In the words before us we have,

First, The sufficiency and fulness of Christ's sufferings intimated in that particle [once] ; Christ needs to suffer no more, having finished and completed that whole work at once.

Secondly, The meritorious cause of the sufferings of Christ, and that is sin, *Christ once suffered for sins ;* not his own sins, but ours ; as it follows in the next clause, which is the third thing here observable, viz.

Thirdly, The admirable grace and unexampled love of Christ to us sinners, *the just for the unjust ;* in which words the substitution of Christ in the room and place of sinners, the vicegerence of his death is plainly expressed. Christ died not only *nostro bono,* for our good, but also *nostro loco,* in our stead.

Fourthly, Here is also the final cause or design and scope of the sufferings of Christ, which was *to bring us to God.*

Fifthly, Here is also the issue of the sufferings of Christ, which was the death of Christ in the flesh, and the quickening of Christ after death by the Spirit. Many excellent observations are lodged in the bosom of this scripture ; all which I must pass over in silence at this time, 'and confine my discourse to the final cause of the sufferings of Christ, namely, *that he might bring us to God:* where the observation will be plainly and briefly this.

Doct. *That the end of Christ's cursed death, and bitter sufferings, was to bring all those for whom he died unto God.*

In the explication and preparation of this point for use, two things must be spoken unto, viz.

1. What Christ's bringing us to God imports?

2. What influence the death of Christ hath upon this design of bringing us to God?

First, What Christ's bringing us to God imports? And certainly there be many great and excellent things contained in this expression: more generally it notes our state of reconciliation, and our state of glorification. By reconciliation we are brought nigh to God, Eph. ii. 13. " Ye are made nigh," i. e. reconciled, " by the blood of Christ," Heb. xii. 22, 23. we are said " to come " to God the Judge of all." By reconciliation we are brought nigh unto God now; by glorification we shall be brought home to God hereafter, 1 Thes. iv. 17. " We shall be ever with the Lord." But more particularly this phrase, " that he might bring us to " God," imports,

First, That the chief happiness of man consisteth in the enjoyment of God: that the creature hath as necessary dependence upon God for happiness, as the stream hath upon the fountain, or the image in the glass upon the face of him that looks into it. For as the sum of the creature's misery lies in this, *depart from me ;* separation from God being the principal part of damnation; so, on the contrary, the chief happiness of the creature consisteth in the enjoyment and blessed vision of God, 1 John iii. 2. Psal. xvii. 15. " I shall be satisfied when I awake with thy likeness."

Secondly, It implies man's revolt and apostasy from God, Eph. ii. 12. " But now in Christ Jesus, ye who were some time afar off, " are made nigh by the blood of Christ." Those whom Christ bringeth unto God were before afar off from him, both in state and condition, and in temper and disposition: we were lost creatures, and had no desire to return to God *. The prodigal was said to go into a far country, Luke xv. 30.

Thirdly, Christ's bringing us to God, implies our inability to return to God of ourselves; we must be brought back by Christ, or perish for ever in a state of separation from God: the lost sheep is made the emblem of the lost sinner, Luke xv. 5. The sheep returns not to the fold of itself, but the shepherd seeks it, finds it, and carries it back upon his shoulders. And the apostle plainly tells us, Rom. v. 6. That when *we were without strength,* i. e. any

---

* Although the faculties of the soul were not extinguished by the fall, yet their inclination to spiritual objects was wholly lost. *Zeæm on the image of God.*

ability to recover, help, or save ourselves, *in due time Christ died for the ungodly.*

Fourthly, Christ bringing us to God evidently implies this, that God's unsatisfied justice was once the great bar betwixt him and man. Man can have no access to God but by Christ: Christ brings us to God by no other way but the way of satisfaction by his blood: " He hath suffered for sins, the just for the unjust, that " he might bring us to God." Better ten thousand worlds should perish for ever, than that God should lose the honour of his justice. This great *obex*, or bar to our enjoyment of God, is effectually removed by the death of Christ, whereby God's justice is not only fully satisfied, but highly honoured and glorified, Rom. iii. 24. And so the way by which we are brought to God is again opened (to the wonder and joy of all believers) by the blood and sufferings of Christ.

Fifthly, and *lastly,* It shews us the peculiar happiness and privilege of believers above all people in the world: these only are they which shall be brought to God by Jesus Christ in a reconciled state: others, indeed, shall be brought to God as a Judge, to be condemned by him: believers only are brought to God in the Mediator's hand, as a reconciled Father, to be made blessed for ever in the enjoyment of him: every believer is brought singly to God at his death, Luke xvi. 22. And all believers shall be jointly and solemnly presented to God in the great day, Col. i. 22. Jude, ver. 24. They shall be all presented faultless before the presence of his glory with exceeding joy. Now the privilege of believers in that day will lie in divers things.

First, That they shall be all brought to God together. This will be the general assembly mentioned, Heb. xii. 22. There shall be a collection of all believers, in all ages of the world, into one blessed assembly; they shall come from the *east,* and *west,* and *north,* and *south,* and shall sit down in the kingdom of God, Luke xiii. 29. O what a glorious train will be seen following the Redeemer in that day !

Secondly, As all the saints shall be collected into one body ; so they shall be all brought or presented unto God, faultless and without blemish, Jude, ver. 24. " A glorious church, without spot or " wrinkle, or any such thing," Eph. v. 27. For this is the general assembly of the spirits of just men that are made perfect, Heb. xii. 23. All sin was perfectly separated from them when death had separated their souls and bodies.

Thirdly, In this lies the privilege of believers, that as they shall be all brought together, and that in a state of absolute purity, and perfection, so they shall be all brought to God: they shall see his face, in the vision whereof is " fulness of joy, and at whose right-

" hand are pleasures for evermore," Psal. xvi. 11.   The objective blessedness of the saints consisteth in their fruition of God, Psal. lxxii. 25.   To see God in his word and works, is the happiness of the saints on earth ; but to see him face to face, will be the fulness of their blessedness in heaven, 1 John iii. 2.   This is that intuitive, transforming, and sanctifying vision, of which the scriptures frequently speaks, Psal. xvii. 15. 1 Cor. xv. 28. Rev. vii. 17.

Fourthly, To be brought unto God, must needs imply a state of perfect joy and highest delight.   So speaks the apostle, Jude 14. Christ shall present, or bring them to God with exceeding joy. And more fully the joy of this day is expressed, Psal. xlv. 15. " With joy and rejoicing shall they be brought ; they shall enter " into the king's palace."   It will be a day of universal joy, when all the saints are brought home to God in a perfected state.   For,

1. God the Father will rejoice when Christ brings home that precious number of his elect, whom he redeemed by his blood : he rejoiceth in them now, though imperfect, and under many distasteful corruptions and weaknesses, Zeph. iii. 17.   How much more will he rejoice in them when Christ presents them without spot or wrinkle to him, Eph. v. 27.

2. Jesus Christ will exceedingly rejoice ; it will be the day of the gladness and satisfaction of his heart ; for now, and not till now, he receives his mystical fulness, Col. i. 24. beholds all the blessed issues of his death, which cannot but give him unspeakable contentment, Isa. liii. 11. " He shall see of the travail of his soul, and " shall be satisfied."

3. The day in which believers are brought home to God, will be a day of unspeakable joy to the Holy Spirit of God himself. For unto this all his sanctifying designs in this world had respect : to this day he sealed them : towards this day he stirred up desires, and groanings in their hearts that cannot be uttered, Eph. iv. 30. Rom. viii. 26. Thus the great and blessed persons, Father, Son, and Spirit, will rejoice in the bringing home of the elect to God. For as it is the greatest joy to a man to see the designs which his heart hath been long projecting, and intently set upon, by an orderly conduct, at last brought to the happy issue he first aimed at ; much more will it be so here ; the counsel and hand of each person being deeply concerned in this blessed design.

4. The angels of God will rejoice at the bringing home of believers to him : the spirits of just men made perfect, will be united in one general assembly, with an innumerable company of angels, Heb. ii. 22.   Great is the affection and love of angels to redeemed ones ; they greatly rejoiced at the incarnation of Christ for them, Luke ii. 13.   They greatly delighted to pry into the mystery of their redemption, 1 Pet. i. 12.   They were marvellously delighted at

their conversion, which was the day of their espousals to Christ, Luke xv. 10. They have been tender and careful over them, and very serviceable to them in this world, Heb. i. 14. and therefore cannot but rejoice exceedingly, to see them all brought home in safety to their father's house.

5. To conclude, Christ's bringing home all believers unto God, will be matter of unspeakable joy to themselves; for, whatever knowledge and acquaintance they had with God here, whatever sights of faith they had of heaven and the glory to come in this world, yet the sight of God and Christ the Redeemer will be an unspeakable surprise to them in that day. This will be the day of relieving all their wants, the day of satisfaction to all their desires; for now they are come where they would be, arrived at the very desires of their souls.

Secondly, In the last place, let it be considered, what influence the death of Christ hath upon this design, and you shall find it much every way. In two things especially, the death of Christ hath a blessed casualty and influence in this matter, *viz.*

1. It effectually removes all obstacles to it.

2. It purchaseth (as a price) their title to it.

First, The death of Christ removes all obstacles out of the way of this mercy : such were the bars hindering our access to God as nothing but the death of Christ could remove, and thereby open a way for believers to come to God. The guilt of sin barred us from his gracious presence, Rom. i. 2, 3. Hos. xiv. 2. The filth of sin excluded us from God, Hab. i. 23. Heb. xii. 14. The enmity of our nature perfectly stopped up our way to God, Col. i. 21. Rom. viii. 7. by reason hereof fallen man hath no desire to come unto God, Job xxi. 14. The justice of God, like a flaming sword, turning every way, kept all men from access to God. And *Lastly,* Satan, that malicious and armed adversary, lay as a lion in the way to God, 2 Pet. v. 8. O, with what strong bars were the gates of heaven shut against our souls ! The way of God was chained up with such difficulties, as none but Christ was able to remove; and he by death hath effectually removed them all : The way is now open, even the new and the living way, consecrated for us by his blood. The death of Christ effectually removes the guilt of sin, 1 Pet. ii. 24. washes off the filth of sin, 1 John v. 6. takes away the enmity of nature, Col. i. 20, 21. satisfies all the demands of justice, Rom. iii. 25, 26. hath broken all the power of Satan, Col. ii. 15. Heb. ii. 14. and consequently the way to God is effectually and fully opened to believers by the blood of Jesus, Heb. x. 20.

Secondly, The blood of Christ purchased for believers their right and title to this privilege, Gal. iv. 4, 5. " But when the fulness of " time was come, God sent forth his Son, made of a woman,

" made under the law ; to redeem them that were under the law,
" that we might receive the adoption of sons," i. e. both the relation and inheritance of sons.   There was value and worth enough
in the precious blood of Christ, not only to pay all our debts to
justice, but over and above the payment of our debts, to purchase
for us this invaluable privilege.   We must put this unspeakable
mercy of being brought to God, as my text puts it, upon the account, and to the score of the death of Christ: no believer had
ever tasted the sweetness of such a mercy, if Christ had not tasted
the bitterness of death for him.   The use of all you will have in
the following deductions of truth.

Deduction 1. *Great is the preciousness and worth of souls, that the
life of Christ should be given to redeem and recover them to God.*   As
God laid out his thoughts and counsel from eternity, upon them,
to project the way and method of their salvation, so the Lord
Jesus, in pursuance of that blessed design, came from the bosom of
the Father, and spilt his invaluable blood to bring them to God.
No wise man expends vast sums to bring home trifling commodities:
how cheap soever our souls are in our estimation, it is evident by
this they are of precious esteem in the eyes of Christ.

Deduct. 2. *Redeemed souls must expect no rest or satisfaction on
this side heaven, and the full enjoyment of God.*   The life of a believer in this world, is a life of motion and expectation : they are now
coming to God, 1 Pet. ii. 4.   God, you see, is the centre and rest
of their souls, Heb. iv. 9.   As the rivers cannot rest till they pour
themselves into the bosom of the sea, so neither can renewed souls
find rest till they come into the bosom of God *.   There are four
things which do and will break the rest, and disturb the souls of
believers in this world ; afflictions, temptations, corruptions, and
absence from God.   If the three former causes of disquietness were
totally removed, so that a believer were placed in such a condition
upon earth, where no affliction could disturb him, no temptation
trouble him, no corruption defile or grieve him, yet his very absence from God must still keep him restless and unsatisfied, 2 Cor.
v. 6.   " Whilst we are at home in the body, we are absent from
" the Lord."

Deduct. 3. *What sweet and pleasant thoughts should all believers
have of death !*   When they die, and never till they die, shall they
be fully brought home to God.   Death to the saints, is the door
by which they enter into the enjoyment of God : the dying Christian is almost at home, yet a few pangs and agonies more, and
then he is come to God, in whose presence is the fulness of joy.

---

* Thou hast made us for thyself, and our hearts are unsatisfied till they rest in thee.
Aug. Confes. lib. 1. *c.* 1.

" I desire (saith Paul) to depart, and to be with Christ, which is
" far better," Phil. i. 23.   It should not affright us to be brought
to death, the king of terrors, so long as it is the office of death to
bring us to God.   That dreaming opinion of the soul sleeping
after death, is as ungrounded, as it is uncomfortable : the same day
we loose from this shore, we shall be landed upon the blessed
shore, where we shall see and enjoy God for ever.   O, if the friends
of dead believers did but understand where, and with whom their
souls are, whilst they are mourning over their bodies, certainly a
few believing thoughts of this would quickly dry up their tears.
and fill the house of mourning with voices of praise and thanksgiving !

*Deduct. 4. How comfortable and sweet should the converses and
communication of Christians be one with another, in this world !*
Christ is bringing them all to God through this vale of tears : they
are now in the way to him ; all bound for heaven ; going home to
God, their everlasting rest in glory : every day, every hour, every
duty brings them nearer and nearer to their journey's end, Rom. xiii.
11.   " Now (saith the apostle) is our salvation nearer than when
" we believed."   O, what manner of heavenly communications
and ravishing discourses should believers have with each other as
they walk by the way !   O, what pleasant and delightful converse
should they have with one another about the place and state
whither Christ is bringing them, and where they shall shortly be !
What ravishing, transporting, transforming visions they shall have
that day they are brought home to God !   How surprizingly glorious to them the sight of Jesus Christ will be, who died for them
to bring them unto God !   how should such discourses as these,
shorten and sweeten their passage through this world, strengthen
and encourage the dejected and feeble-minded, and exceedingly
honour and adorn their profession ?   Thus lived the believers of
old, Heb. xi. 9, 10.   " By faith he sojourned in the land of pro-
" mise, as in a strange country, dwelling in tabernacles with Isaac
" and Jacob, the heirs with him of the same promise ; for he
" looked for a city which hath foundations, whose builder and
" maker is God."   But, alas ! most Christians are either so entangled
in the cares and troubles, or so ensnared by the delights and pleasures which almost continually divert and take up their thoughts
by the way, that there is but little room for any discourses of Christ
and heaven, among many of them : but certainly this would be as
much your interest as your duty.   When the apostle had entertained the Thessalonians with a lovely discourse of their meeting
the Lord in the air, and being ever with the Lord, he charges it
upon them as their great duty, to comfort one another with these
words, 1 Thes. iv. 17, 18.

Deduct. 5. *How unreasonable are the dejections of believers upon the account of those troubles which they meet with in this world!* It is true, afflictions of all kinds do attend believers in their way to God; through many tribulations we must enter into that kingdom. But what then? must we despond and droop under them as other men? Surely no; If afflictions be the way through which you must come to God, then never be discouraged at affliction; troubles and afflictions are of excellent use, under the blessings of the Spirit, to further Christ's great design in bringing you to God. How often would you turn out of that way which leads to God, if he did not hedge up your way with thorns, Hos. ii. 6. Doubtless when you come home to God, you shall find you have been much beholden (it may be a great deal more) to your troubles than to your comforts, for bringing you thither: however, the sweetness of the end will infinitely more than recompense the sorrows and troubles of the way: nor are they worthy to be compared with the glory that shall be revealed in you, Rom. viii. 18.

Deduct. 6. *How much are all believers obliged, in point of interest, to follow Jesus Christ whithersoever he goes!* Thus are the saints described, Rev. xiv. 4. " These are they which follow the Lamb " whithersoever he goeth: these were redeemed from among " men, being the first-fruits unto God, and to the Lamb." If it be the design of Christ to bring us to God, then certainly it is our duty to follow Christ in all the paths of active and passive obedience through which he now leads us, as ever we expect to be brought home to God at last: " We are made partakers of Christ, " if we hold the beginning of our confidence stedfast unto the " end," Heb. iii. 14. If we have followed him through many sufferings and troubles, and shall turn away from him at last, we lose all that we have wrought and suffered in religion, and shall never reach home to God at last. The crown of life belongs only to them who are faithful to the death.

Deduct. 7. *Let all that desire, or expect to come to God hereafter, come to Christ by faith now.* There is no other way to the Father, but by Christ; no other way to Christ but faith. How vain therefore are the hopes and expectations of all unbelievers? Be assured of this great truth, Death shall bring you to God as an avenging Judge, if Christ do not bring you now to God as a reconciled Father: without holiness no man shall see God: the door of hope is shut against all christless persons, John xiv. 6. " No man cometh " unto the Father but by me." O what a sweet voice cometh down from heaven to your souls this day, saying, As ever you expect or hope to come to God, and enjoy the blessing that is here, come unto Christ, obey his calls, give up yourselves to his conduct and government, and you shall certainly be brought to God! As sure as you shall now be brought to Jesus Christ by spiritual union, so sure shall you be brought to God in full fruition.

Blessed be God for Jesus Christ, the new and living way to the Father.

And thus I have finished the motives drawn from the titles and benefits of Christ, serving to enforce and quicken the great gospel-exhortation of coming to, and effectually applying the Lord Jesus Christ in the way of faith. O that the blessings of the Spirit might follow these calls, and fix these considerations as nails in sure places ! But seeing the great hindrance and obstruction to faith is the false opinion and persuasion of most unregenerate men, that they are already in Christ ; my next work therefore shall be, in a second use of conviction, to undeceive men in that matter ; and that, by shewing them the undoubted certainty of these two things :

First, That there is no coming ordinarily to Christ without the application of the law to our consciences, in a way of effectual con-viction.

Secondly, Nor by that neither, without the teachings of God, in the way of spiritual illumination. The first of these will be fully confirmed and opened in the following sermon.

SERMON XX.

The great usefulness of the Law or Word of GOD, in order to the Application of CHRIST.

ROM. vii. 9.

For I was alive without the law once, but when the commandment came, sin revived, and I died.

THE scope of the apostle in this epistle, and more particularly in this chapter, is to state the due use and excellency of the law, which he doth accordingly.

First, By denying to it a power to justify us, which is the pecu-liar honour of Christ.

Secondly, By ascribing to it a power to convince us, and so pre-pare us for Christ *.

Neither attributing to it more honour than belongeth to it, nor yet detracting from it that honour and usefulness which God hath given it. It cannot make us righteous, but it can convince us that

---

* The author means that it shews us our need of Christ. *Editor.*

we are unrighteous; it cannot heal, but it can open and discover
the wounds that sin hath given us; which he proves in this place
by an argument drawn from his own experience, confirmed also
by the general experience of believers, in whose persons and names
we must here understand him to speak; " For I was alive without
" the law once; but when the commandment came, sin revived,
" and I died." Wherein three particulars are very observable.

First, The opinion Paul had, and all unregenerate men have of
themselves before conversion: *I was alive once.* By *life,* understand here liveliness, cheerfulness, and confidence of his good
estate and condition: he was full of vain hope, false joy, and presumptuous confidence; a very brisk and jovial man.

Secondly, The sense and opinion he had, and all others will have
of themselves, if ever they come under the regenerating work of the
Spirit in his ordinary method of working: *I died.* The death he
here speaks of, stands opposed to that life before mentioned; and
signifies the sorrows, fears, and tremblings that seized upon his
soul, when his state and temper were upon the change: the apprehensions he then had of his condition struck him home to the
heart, and damped all his carnal mirth: *I died.*

Thirdly, The ground and reason of this wonderful alteration and
change of his judgment, and apprehension of his own condition;
the commandment came, and sin revived: The commandment came,
i. e. it came home to my conscience, it was fixed with a divine and
mighty efficacy upon my heart: the commandment was come before by way of promulgation, and the literal knowledge of it; but
it never came till now in its spiritual sense and convincing power
to his soul; though he had often read, and heard the law before,
yet he never clearly understood the meaning and extent, he never
felt the mighty efficacy thereof upon his heart before; it so came
at this time, as it never came before. From hence the observations are,

Doct. 1. *That unregenerate persons are generally full of groundless confidence and cheerfulness, though their condition be sad
and miserable.*

Doct. 2. *That there is a mighty efficacy in the word or law of
God, to kill vain confidence, and quench carnal mirth in the
hearts of men, when God sets it home upon their consciences.*

We shall take both these points under consideration, and improve
them to the design in hand.

Doct. 1. *That unregenerate persons are generally full of ground-*

*less confidence and cheerfulness, though their condition be sad
and miserable ;* Rev. iii. 17. Because thou sayest I am rich,
and increased with goods, and have need of nothing ; and
knowest not that thou art wretched, and miserable, and poor,
and blind, and naked ; *This is the very life that unregenerate men do live.*

In opening whereof, I shall shew you,
1. What is the life of the unregenerate.
2. What maintains that life.
3. How it appears that this is the life the generality of the world
do live.
4. The danger of living such a life as this : and then apply it.
First, What is the life of the unregenerate, and wherein it consists ? Now there being, among others, three things in which the
life of the unregenerate doth principally consist, viz.

> Carnal security,
> Presumptuous hope, and
> False joy,

Of these briefly in their order.
First, There is in unregenerate men a great deal of carnal security ; they dread no danger ; Luke xi. 21. " When a strong man
" armed keepeth his palace, his goods are at peace :" There is
generally a great stillness and silence in the consciences of such men ;
when others, in a better condition, are watching and trembling,
they sleep securely : so they live, and so oftimes they die, Psal.
lxxiii. 4. " They have no bonds in their death," [Hebrew, on
knots], no difficulties that puzzle them. It is true, the consciences
of few men are so perfectly stupified, but that some time or other
they twang and gird them ; but it seldom works to that height,
or continues with them so long as to give any considerable interruption to their carnal peace and quietness.
Secondly, The life of the unregenerate consisteth in presumptuous
hope : this is the very foundation of their carnal security. So
Christ tells the Jews, John viii. 54, 55. " Of whom ye say that
" he is your God, and yet ye have not known him." The world
is full of hope without a promise, which is but as a spider's web,
when a stress comes to be laid upon it, John xxvii. 8. Unregenerate men are said indeed to be without hope, Ephes. ii. 12. but the
meaning is, they are without any solid, well-grounded hope ; for in
scripture-account, vain hope is no hope, except it be a lively hope,
1 Pet. i. 3. A hope flowing from union with Christ, Col. i. 27.
A hope nourished by experience, Rom. v. 4. A hope for which
a man can give a reason, 1 Pet. iii. 15. a hope that puts men upon
heart-purifying endeavours, 1 John iii. 3. It is in the account

of God a cypher, a vanity, not deserving the name of hope; and yet such a groundless, dead, christless, irrational, idle hope is that which the unregenerate live upon.

Thirdly, The life of the unregenerate consisteth in false joy, the immediate offspring of ungrounded hope, Mat. xiii. 28. The stony ground receive the word with joy.

There are two sorts of joy upon which the unregenerate live, viz.

1. A sensitive joy in things carnal.
2. A delusive joy in things spiritual.

They rejoice in corn, wine, and oil, in their estates and children, in the pleasant fruitions of the creature; yea, and they rejoice also in Christ and the promises, in heaven and in glory: with all which they have just such a kind of communion as a man hath in a dream with a full feast and curious music; and just so their joy will vanish when they awake. Now these three, *security, hope,* and *joy,* make up the livelihood of the carnal world.

Secondly, Next it concerns us to enquire what are the things that maintain and support this security, hope and joy in the hearts of unregenerate men; and if we consider duly, we shall find that church-privileges, natural ignorance, false evidences of the love of God, slight workings of the gospel, self-love, comparing themselves with the more profane, and Satan's policy managing all these in order to their eternal ruin, are so many springs to feed and maintain this life of delusion in the unregenerate.

1. *First,* Church privileges lay the foundation to this strong delusion. Thus the Jews deceived themselves, saying in their hearts, " We have Abraham for our father," Mat. iii. 9. This propt up the vain hopes that Abraham's blood ran in their veins, though Abraham's faith and obedience never wrought in their hearts.

2. *Secondly,* Natural ignorance; this keeps all in peace: they that see not, fear not. There are but two ways to quiet the hearts of men about their spiritual and eternal concernments, viz. *the way of assurance* and faith, or *the way of ignorance* and self-deceit; by the one we are put beyond danger, by the other beyond fear, though the danger be greater. Satan could never quiet men, if he did not first blind them.

3. *Thirdly,* False evidences of the love of God is another spring feeding this security, vain hope, and false joy in the hearts of men: see the power of it to hush and still the conscience, Mat. vii. 22. " Many will say to me in that day, Lord, Lord, have we " not prophesied in thy name?" &c. The things upon which they built their evidence and confidence, were external things in religion; yet they had a quieting power upon them, as if they had been the best evidences in the world.

4. *Fourthly*, Slight workings of the gospel; such are transient motions of the affections under the word, Heb. vi. 8. the working of their desires about spiritual objects, John vi. 34. Math. xxv. 8. the external change and reformation of their ways, Mat. xii. 43. all which serve to nourish the vain hopes of the unregenerate.

5. *Fifthly*, Self-love is an apparent reason and ground of security and false hope, Mat. vii. 3. It makes a man to overlook great evils in himself, whilst he is sharp-sighted to discover and censure lesser evils in others : self-love takes away the sight of sin, by bringing it too near the eye.

6. *Sixthly*, Mens comparing themselves with those that are more profane and grossly wicked than themselves, serves notably to quiet and hush the conscience asleep; " God, I thank thee, (said the " Pharisee), I am not as other men, or as this publican." O what a saint did he seem to himself, when he stood by those that were externally more wicked.

7. *Seventhly*, and *lastly*, The policy of Satan to manage all these things to the blinding and ruining of the souls of men, is another great reason they live so securely and pleasantly as they do, in a state of so much danger and misery, 2 Cor. iv. 3, 4. " The god of this " world hath blinded the minds of them that believe not."

Thirdly, You have seen what the life of the unregenerate is, and what maintains that life. In the next place, I shall give you evidence that this is the life the generality of the world do live; a life of carnal security, vain hope, and false joy; this will evidently appear, if we consider,

First, The activity and liveliness of men's spirits in pursuit of the world. O how lively and vigorous are their hearts in the management of earthly designs! Psal. vi. 4. " Who will shew us any " good ?" The world eats up their hearts, time, and strength. Now this could never be, if their eyes were but opened to see the danger and misery their souls are in. How few designs for the world run in the thoughts of a condemned man? O if God had ever made the light of conviction to shine into their consciences, certainly the temptations would lie the quite contrary way, even in too great a neglect of things of this life ! But this briskness and liveliness plainly shew the great security which is upon most men.

Secondly, The marvellous quietness and stillness that is in the thoughts and consciences of men, about their everlasting concernments, plainly shews this to be the life of the unregenerate : How few scruples, doubts, or fears shall you hear from them ? How many years may a man live in carnal families, before he shall hear such a question as this seriously propounded, " What shall I do to " be saved ?" There are no questions in their lips, because no fear or sense of danger in their hearts.

Thirdly, The general contentedness, and professed willingness of carnal men to die, give clear evidence that such a life of security and vain hope is the life they live; " Like sheep they are laid in " the grave," Psal. xlix. 14. O how quiet and still are their consciences, when there are but a few breaths more between them and everlasting burnings! Had God opened their eyes to apprehend the consequences of death, and what follows the *pale horse,* Rev. vi. 8. it were impossible but that every unregenerate man should make that bed on which he dies shake and tremble under him.

Fourthly, and *lastly,* The low esteem men have for Christ, and the total neglect of, at least the mere trifling with, those duties in which he is to be found, plainly discover this stupid secure life to be the life that the generality of the world do live; for were men sensible of the disease of sin, there could be no quieting them without " Christ the physician," Phil. iii. 8. All the business they have to do in this world could never keep them from their knees, or make them strangers to their closets; all which, and much more that might be said of the like nature, gives too full and clear proof of this sad assertion, that this is the life the ungenerate world generally lives.

Fourthly, In the last place, I would speak a few words to discover the danger of such a life as hath been described; to which purpose let the following brief hints be seriously minded.

First, By these things souls are inevitably betrayed into hell and eternal ruin; this blinding is in order to damning, 2 Cor. iv. 3, 4. " If our gospel be hid, it is hid to them that are lost; whose " eyes the god of this world hath blinded." Those that are turned over into eternal death are thus generally hoodwinked and blinded in order thereunto, Isa. vi. 9, 10. " And he said go and " tell this people, hear ye indeed, but understand not: and see " ye indeed, but perceive not. Make the hearts of this people " fat, and make their ears heavy, and shut their eyes; lest they " see with their eyes, and hear with their ears, and understand " with their hearts, and convert, and be healed."

Secondly, As damning is the event of blinding, so nothing makes hell a more terrible surprize to the soul than this doth : By this means the wrath of God is felt before its danger be apprehended; a man is past all hope, before he begins to have any fear: his eternal ruin, like a breach ready to fall, swelling out in a high wall, cometh suddenly at an instant, Isa. xxx. 13. and as it damns surely and surprizingly, so,

Thirdly, Nothing more aggravates a man's damnation than to sink suddenly into it, from amidst so many hopes, and high confidence of safety : For a man to find himself in hell, when he thought and concluded himself within a step of heaven, O what a hell will it be to such men! The higher vain hopes lifted them up, the more dreadful must their fall be, Matth. vii. 22. And as it damns surely, surprizingly, and with highest aggravations, so,

Fourthly, This life of security and vain hope frustrates all the means of recovery and salvation, in the only season wherein they can be useful and beneficial to us : ·By reason of these things the word hath no power to convince men's consciences, nothing can bring them to a sight and sense of their condition : Therefore Christ told the self-confident and blind Jews, Matth. xxi. 21. " That the publicans and harlots go into the kingdom of God be-" fore them :" And the reason is, because their hearts lie more open and fair to the strokes of conviction and compunction for sin than those do, who are blinded by vain hopes and confidences.

Inference 1. *Is this the life that the unregenerate world lives ? Then it is not to be wondered at that the preaching of the gospel hath so little success :* " Who hath believed our report ? (saith the " prophet) and to whom is the arm of the Lord revealed ?" Isa. liii. 1. Ministers study for truths apt to awaken and convince the consciences of them that hear them, but their words return again to them : They turn to God, and mourn over the matter ; we have laboured in vain, and spent our strength for nought : And this security is the cause of all ; vain hopes bar fast the doors of men's hearts against all the convictions and persuasions of the word. The greater cause have they to admire the grace of God, who have found, or shall find the convictions of the word sharper than any two-edged sword, piercing to the dividing asunder of the soul and spirit ; to whose hearts God brings home the commandment by an effectual application.

Inf. 2. *If this be the life of the unregenerate world, what deadly enemies are they that nourish and strengthen the groundless confidences and vain hopes of salvation in men ?* This the scripture calls the healing of the hurt of souls slightly, by crying, " Peace, " peace, when there is no peace," Jer. vi. 14. The sewing of pillows under their arm-holes, Ezek. xiii. 18. That they may lie soft and easy under the ministry ; and this is the doctrine which the people love : but oh, what will the end of these things be ! And what an account have those men to give to God for the blood of those souls by them betrayed to the everlasting burnings ! Such flattery is the greatest cruelty : Those whom you bless upon earth, will curse you in hell, and the day in which they trusted their souls to your conduct.

Inf. 3. *How great a mercy is it to be awakened out of that general sleep and security which is fallen upon the world !* You cannot estimate the value of that mercy, for it is a peculiar mercy. O that ever the Spirit of the Lord should touch thy soul under the ministry of the word, startle, and rouse thy conscience, whilst others are left in the dead sleep of security round about thee! When the Lord dealt with thy soul much after the same manner he did with Paul in the way to Damascus, who not only saw a light shining from heaven, which those that travelled with him saw as well as he, but heard that voice from heaven which did the work upon his heart, though his companions heard it not. Besides, it is not only a peculiar mercy, but it is a leading, introductive mercy, to all other spiritual mercies that follow it to all eternity. If God had not done this for thee, thou hadst never been brought to faith, to Christ, or heaven. From this act of the Spirit all other saving acts take their rise; so that you have cause for ever to admire the goodness of God in such a favour as this is.

Inf. 4. Lastly, *Hence it follows that the generality of the world are in the direct way to eternal ruin; and whatever their vain confidences are, they cannot be saved.* "Narrow is the way, and strait " is the gate that leadeth unto life, and few there be that find it." Hear me all you that live this dangerous life of carnal security and vain hope, whatever your persuasions and confidences are, except you give them up, and get better grounds for your hope, you cannot be saved. For,

First, Such hopes and confidences as yours are directly contradictory to the established order of the gospel, which requires repentance, Acts v. 31. faith, Acts xiii. 39. and regeneration, John iii. 3. in all that shall be saved. And this order shall never be altered for any man's sake.

Secondly, If such as you be saved, all the threatenings in scripture must be reversed, which lie in full opposition to your vain hopes, Mark xvi. 16. John iii. 16. Rom. iii. 8, 9. Either the truth of God, in these threatenings must fail, or your vain hopes must fail.

Thirdly, If ever such as you be saved, new conditions must be set to all the promises; for there is no condition of any special promise found in any unregenerate person *. Compare your hearts with these scriptures, Matth. v. 3, 4, 5, 6. Psal. xxiv. 4. Psal. lxxxiv. 11. Gen. xvii. 1, 2.

Fourthly, If ever such a hope as yours bring you to heaven, then the saving hope of God's elect is not rightly described to us in the scriptures. Scripture-hope is the effect of regeneration, 1 Pet. i. 3. And purity of heart is the effect of that hope, 1 John iii. 3. Nay,

Fifthly, The very nature of heaven is mistaken in scripture, if such as you be subjects qualified for its enjoyment: For assimilation, or the conformity of the soul to God in holiness, is, in the

---

* The author by *condition* must be understood here, as meaning *evidence* of interest in these promises. *Editor.*

scripture account, a principal ingredient of that blessedness : By all which it manifestly appears that the hopes of most men are in vain, and will never bring them to heaven.

SERMON XXI.

Rom. vii. 9.

For I was alive without the law once : But when the commandment came, sin revived, and I died.

Doct. 2. THAT there is a mighty efficacy in the word or law of God, to kill vain confidence, and quench carnal mirth in the hearts of men, when God sets it home upon their consciences. " The weapons of the word are not carnal, but mighty through " God ; to the pulling down of strong holds, casting down imagina- " tions, and every thing that exalteth itself against the knowledge " of God, and bringing into captivity every thought to the obedi- " ence of Christ," 2 Cor. x. 4, 5.

In the opening of this point I shall,

1. Demonstrate the efficacy of the word or law of God.
2. Shew wherein the efficacy thereof lies.
3. From whence it hath all this mighty power and efficacy.

First, I shall give you some demonstrations of the mighty power and efficacy that there are in the word or law of God ; which will appear with the fullest evidence,

First, From the various *subjects* upon whom it works : The hearts and consciences of men of all orders and qualities, have been reached and wounded to the quick by the two-edged sword of God's law.   Some, among the *great* and *honourable* of the earth, (though indeed the fewest of that rank) have been made to stoop and tremble under the word, Acts xxiv. 16. Mark vi. 20. 1 Sam. xv. 24.   The wise and learned of the world have felt its power, and been brought over to embrace the humbling and self-denying ways of Christ, Acts xvii. 34.   Thus Origen, Hierom, Tertullian, Bradwardine, and many more, came into Canaan laden with the Egyptian gold, as one speaks, i. e. they came into the church of God abundantly enriched and furnished with the learned arts and sciences, devoting them all to the service of Christ.   Yea, and which is as strange, *the most simple, weak, and illiterate* have been wonderfully changed, and wrought upon by the power of the word : " The testimonies of the Lord make wise the simple :" Men of weak understandings, in all other matters, have been made wise to salvation by the power of the word, Matth. xi. 25. 1 Cor. i. 27. Nay the most malicious and obstinate enemies of Christ have been wounded and converted by the word, 1 Tim. i. 13. Acts xvi. 25. Those that have been under the prejudice of the worst and most *idolatrous education,* have been the subjects of its mighty power, Acts xix. 26. To conclude, men of the most profligate and debauched lives have been wonderfully changed and altered by the power of the word, 1 Cor. vi. 10, 11.

Secondly, The mighty efficacy of the law of God appears in the *manner of its operation ;* it works suddenly ; strikes like a dart through the hearts and consciences of men, Acts ii. 37. A wonderful change is made in a short time : And, as it works quickly and suddenly, so it works irresistibly, with an uncontrouled power upon the spirits of men, 1 Thes. i. 5. Rom. i. 16. Let the soul be armed against conviction with the thickest ignorance, strongest prejudice, or most obstinate resolution, the word of God will wound the breast even of such a man, when God sends it forth in his authority and power.

Thirdly, The wonderful power of the law or word of God is evidently seen in the strange effects which are produced by it in the hearts and lives of men. For,

First, It changes and alters the frame and temper of the mind : It moulds a man into a quite contrary temper, Gal. i. 23. " He " which persecuted us in times past, now preacheth the faith, " which once he destroyed :" Thus a tyger is transformed into a lamb, by the power of the word of God.

Secondly, It makes the soul, upon which it works, to forego and quit the dearest interests it hath in this world for Jesus Christ, Phil. iii. 7, 8, 9. Riches, honours, self-righteousness, dearest relations, are denied and forsaken. Reproach, poverty, and death itself, are willingly embraced for Christ's sake, when once the efficacy of the word hath been upon the hearts of men, 1 Thes. i. 6. Those that were their companions in sin, are declined, renounced, and cast off with abhorrence, 1 Pet. iv. 3, 4. In such things as these the mighty power of the word discovers itself.

Secondly, Next, let us see wherein the efficacy of the word upon the souls of men principally consisteth : and we find in scripture it exerteth its power in five distinct acts upon the soul ; by all which it strikes at the life, and kills the very heart of vain hopes. For,

First, It hath an awakening efficacy upon secure and sleepy sinners : It rouses the conscience, and brings a man to a sense and feeling apprehension, Eph. v. 13, 14. The first effectual touch of the word startles the drowsy conscience. A poor sinner lies in his sins, as Peter did in his chains, fast asleep, though a warrant was signed for his execution the next day : but the Spirit in the word awakens him as the angel did Peter : And this awakening power of the word is in order, both of time and nature, antecedent to all its operations and effects.

Secondly, The law of God hath an enlightening efficacy upon the minds of men : It is eye-salve to the blinded eye, Rev. iii. 18. A light shining in a dark place, 2 Pet. i. 19. A light shining into the very heart of man, 2 Cor. iv. 6. When the word comes in power, all things appear with another face : The sins that were hid from our eyes, and the danger which was concealed by the policy of Satan from our souls, now lie clear and open before us, Eph. v. 8.

Thirdly, The word of God hath a convincing efficacy : It sets sin in order before the soul, Psal. l. 21. As an army is drawn up in an exact order, so are the sins of nature and practice, the sins of youth and age, even a great and terrible army is drawn up before the eye of the conscience ; the convictions of the word are clear and full, 1 Cor. xiv. 24, 25. The very secrets of a sinner's heart are made manifest ; his mouth is stopped ; his pleas are silenced ; his conscience yields to the charge of guilt, and to the equity of the sentence of the law, so that the soul stands mute, and self-condemned at the bar of conscience : It hath got nothing to say why the wrath of God should not come upon it to the uttermost, Rom. iii. 19.

Fourthly, The law of God hath a soul-wounding, an heart-cutting efficacy : It pierces into the very soul and spirit of man, Acts ii. 37. " When they heard this, they were pricked at their hearts, " and said unto Peter, and to the rest of the apostles ; men and " brethren, what shall we do ?" A dreadful sound is in the sinner's ears ; his soul is in deep distress ; he knows not which way to turn for ease ; no plaister but the blood of Christ can heal these wounds which the word makes : No outward trouble, affliction, disgrace, or loss, ever touched the quick as the word of God doth.

Fifthly, The word hath a heart-turning, a soul converting efficacy in it : It is a regenerating, as well as a convincing word, 1 Pet. i. 23. 1 Thes. i. 9. The law wounds, the gospel cures ; the law discovers the evil that is in sin, and the misery that follows it ; and the Spirit of God, working in fellowship with the word, effectually turns the heart from sin. And thus we see in what glorious acts the efficacy of the word discovers itself upon the hearts of men ; and all these acts lie in order to each other : For, until the soul be awakened, it cannot be enlightened, Eph. v. 14. Till it be enlightened, it cannot be convinced, Eph. v. 13. Conviction being nothing else but the application of the light that shines in

the mind to the conscience of a sinner : Till it be convinced, it cannot be wounded for sin, Acts ii. 37. And until it be wounded for
sin, it will never be converted from sin, and brought effectually to
Jesus Christ. And thus you see what the power of the word is.

Thirdly, In the last place, it will concern us to enquire whence
the word of God hath all this power? And it is most certain, that
it is not a power inherent in itself, nor derived from the instrument by which it is managed, but from the Spirit of the Lord,
who communicates to it all that power and efficacy which it hath
upon our souls.

1. Its power is not in, or from itself : It works not in a *physical
way*, as natural agents do ; for then the effect would always follow,
except it were miraculously hindered : But this spiritual efficacy is
in the word, as the healing virtue was in the waters of Bethesda,
John v. 4. " An angel went down at a certain season into the pool,
" and troubled the water : Whosoever then first, after the troub-
" ling of the water, stept in, was made whole of whatsoever disease
" he had." It is not a power naturally inherent in it at all times,
but communicated to it at some special seasons. How often is the
word preached, and no man awaked or convinced by it !

2. The power of the word is not communicated to it by the instrument that manageth it, 1 Cor. iii. 7. "Neither is he that
" planteth any thing, neither he that watereth." Ministers are
nothing to such an effect and purpose as this is ; he doth not mean
that they are useless and altogether unnecessary, but insufficient of
themselves to produce such mighty effects : It works not as it is
the word of man, 2 Thess. ii. 13. Ministers may say of the ordinary, as Peter said of the extraordinary effects of the Spirit, Acts
iii. 12. " Ye men of Israel, why marvel ye at this? or why look
" ye so earnestly on us, as though by our own power or holiness
" we had made this man to walk?" If the effects of the word
were in the power, and at the command of him that preacheth it,
then the blood of all the souls that perish under our ministry must
lie at our door, as was formerly noted.

3. If you say, whence then hath the word all this power? Our
answer is, It derives it all from the Spirit of God *, 1 Thes. ii. 13.
" For this cause thank we God without ceasing, because when ye
" received the word of God which ye heard of us, ye received it
" not as the word of man, but (as it is in truth) the word of God,
" which effectually worketh also in you that believe." It is a successful instrument only when it is in the hand of the Spirit, without whose influence it never did, nor can convince, convert, or save

---

* What is commanded by the word, is given by the Spirit. *Aug. Ep.* 157.

any soul. Now, the Spirit of God hath a sovereignty over three things in order to the conversion of sinners.

1. Over the word which works.
2. Over the soul wrought upon.
3. Over the time and season of working.

First, The Spirit hath a glorious sovereignty over the word itself whose instrument it is to make it successful or not, as it pleaseth him, Isa. lv. 10, 11. " For as the rain cometh down, and the snow " from heaven, &c. so shall my word be that goeth out of my " mouth :" as the clouds, so the word is carried and directed by divine pleasure. It is the Lord that makes them both give down their blessings, or to pass away fruitless and empty : yea, it is from the Spirit that this part of the word works, and not another. Those things upon which ministers bestow greatest labour in their preparation, and from which accordingly they have the greatest expectation ; these do nothing, when, mean time, something that dropped occasionally from them, like a chosen shaft, strikes the mark and doth the work.

Secondly, The Spirit of the Lord hath a glorious sovereignty over the souls wrought upon : it is his peculiar work " to take away the " stony heart out of our flesh, and to give us an heart of flesh," Ezek. xxxvi. 26. We may reason, exhort, and reprove, but nothing will abide till the Lord set it home. The Lord opened the heart of Lydia under Paul's ministry : he opens every heart that is effectually opened to receive Christ in the word : if the word can get no entrance, if your hearts remain dead under it still, we may say concerning such souls, as Martha did concerning her brother Lazarus ; " Lord, if thou hadst been here, my brother had not " died." So, Lord, if thou hadst been in this sermon, in this prayer, or in that counsel, these souls had not remained dead under them.

Thirdly, The Spirit hath dominion over the times and seasons of conviction and conversion. Therefore the day in which souls are wrought upon is called " the day of his power," Psal. cx. 3. That shall work at one time, which had no efficacy at all at another time ; because this, and not that, was the time appointed. And thus you see whence the word derives that mighty power it hath.

Now this word of God, when it is set home by the Spirit, is mighty to convince, humble, and break the hearts of sinners, John xvi. 9. " The Spirit when it cometh shall convince the world of " sin." The word signifies conviction by such clear demonstration as compelleth assent : it not only convinces men in general that they are sinners, but it convinceth men particularly of their own sins, and the aggravations of them. So in the text, *Sin revived,* that is, the Lord revived his sins, the very circumstances and aggravations with which they were committed : and so it will be

with us when the commandment comes; sins that we had forgotten, committed so far back as our youth or childhood; sins that
lay slighted in our consciences, shall now be roused up as so many
sleepy lions to affright and terrify us: for now the soul hears the
voice of God in the word, as Adam heard it in the cool of the
day and was afraid, and hides itself; but all will not do, for the
Lord is come in the word; sin is held up before the eyes of the
conscience in its dreadful aggravations and fearful consequences, as
committed against the holy law, clear light, warnings of conscience,
manifold mercies, God's long-suffering, Christ's precious blood,
many warnings of judgment, the wages and demerit whereof, by the
verdict of a man's own conscience, is death, eternal death, Rom. vi.
23. Rom. i. 32. Rom. ii. 9. Thus the commandment comes, sin
revives, and vain hope gives up the ghost.

Inf. 1. *Is there such a mighty power in the word?* then certainly
the word is of divine authority. There cannot be a more clear and
satisfying proof that it is no human invention, than the common
sense that all believers have of the Almighty power in which it works
upon their hearts. So speaks the apostle, 1 Thes. ii. 13. " When
" ye received the word of God which ye heard of us, ye received
" it not as the word of man, but (as it is in truth) the word of
" God, which effectually worketh also in you that believe." Can the
power of any creature, the word of a mere man, so convince the
conscience, so terrify the heart, so discover the very secret thoughts
of the soul, as to put a man into such tremblings? No, a greater
than man must needs be here; none but a God can so open the
eyes of the blind, so open the graves of the dead, so quicken and
enliven the conscience that was seared, so bind over the soul of a
sinner to the judgment to come, so change and alter the frame and
temper of a man's spirit, or so powerfully raise, refresh and comfort a drooping dying soul; certainly the power of God is in all
this; and, if there were no more, yet this alone were sufficient to
make full proof of the divine authority of the scriptures.

Inf. 2. *Judge from hence what an invaluable mercy the preaching
of the word is to the world:* It is a blessing far above our estimation
of it; little do we know what a treasure God committeth to us in
the ordinances, Acts xiii. 25. " To you is the word of this salva-
" tion sent." It is the very power of God to salvation, Rom. i.
16. And salvation is ordinarily denied to whom the preaching of
the word is denied, Rom. x. 14. It is called *the word of life*, Phil.
ii. 16. and deserves to be valued by every one of us as our life.
The eternal decree of God's election is executed by it upon our
souls; as many as he ordained to eternal life shall believe by the
preaching of it. Great is the ingratitude of this generation, which
so slights and undervalues this invaluable treasure; which is a sad

presage of the most terrible judgment, even in the removing our candlestick out of its place, except we repent.

Inf. 3. How sore and terrible a judgment lies upon the souls of those men to whom no word of God is made powerful enough to convince and awaken them! Yet so stands the case with thousands, who constantly sit under the preaching of the word; many arrows are shot at their consciences, but none goes home to the mark, all fall short of the end; the commandment hath come unto them many thousand times, by way of *promulgation* and ministerial *inculcation*, but yet never came home to their souls by the Spirit's effectual *application.* O friends! you have often heard the voice of man, but you never yet heard the voice of God; your understandings have been *instructed*, but your consciences to this day were never thoroughly *convinced.* "We have mourned unto you, but ye have not " lamented," Matth. xi. 17. "Who hath believed our report? " And unto whom is the arm of the Lord revealed?" Alas! we have laboured in vain, we have spent our strength for nought; our word returns unto us empty; but O what a stupendous judgment is here! Heb. vi. 7, 8. " The earth which drinketh in the " rain that cometh oft upon it, and bringeth forth herbs meet for " them by whom it is dressed, receiveth blessing from God; but " that which beareth thorns and briars is rejected, and is nigh " unto cursing, whose end is to be burned." What a sore judgment and sign of God's displeasure would you account it, if your fields were cursed; if you should manure, dress, plow, and sow them, but never reap the fruit of your labour; the increase being still blasted? And yet this were nothing, compared with the blasting of the word to your souls: that which is a savour of life unto life unto some, becomes the savour of death unto death to others, 2 Cor. ii. 16. The Lord affect our hearts with the terrible strokes of God upon the souls of men!

Use of Exhortation.

I shall conclude this point with a few words of exhortation to three sorts of men, *viz.*

1. To those that never felt the power of the word.
2. To those that have only felt some slight and common effects thereof.
3. To those unto whose very hearts the commandment is come, in its effectual and saving power.

First, You that never felt any power in the word at all, I beg you in the name of him that made you, and by all the regard and value you have for those precious souls within you, that now at last such considerations as these may find place in your souls, and that you will bethink yourselves.

Consideration 1.

Whose word is that which cannot gain entrance into your hearts? Is it not the word of God which you despise and slight? " Thou " casteth my word behind thy back," Psal. l. 17. O what an affront and provocation to God is this! You despise not man, but God; the great and terrible God, in whose hand your breath and soul are: This contempt runs higher than you imagine.

Consideration 2.

Consider, that however the word hath no power upon you, the commandment cannot come home to your hearts; yet it doth work, and comes home with power to the hearts of others: Whilst you are hardened, others are melted under it; whilst you sleep, others tremble; whilst your hearts are fast locked up, others are opened. How can you choose but reflect with fear and trembling upon these contrary effects of the word; especially when you consider that the eternal decrees, both of election and reprobation, are now executed upon the souls of men, by the preaching of the word; some believe, and others are hardened.

Consideration 3.

That no judgment of God, on this side hell, is greater than a hard heart and stupid conscience under the word; it were much better that the providence of God should blast thy estate, take away thy children, or destroy thy health, than harden thy heart, and sear thy conscience under the word: So much as thy soul is better than thy body, so much as eternity is more valuable than time, so much is this spiritual judgment more dreadful than all temporal ones. God doth not inflict a more terrible stroke than this upon any man in this world.

O therefore, as you love your own souls, and are loth to ruin them to all eternity, attend upon every opportunity that God affords you; for you know not in which of them the Lord may work upon your hearts. Lay aside your prejudices against the word or the weaknesses and infirmities of them that preach it; for the word works not as it is the word of man, as it is thus neat and elegant, but as it is the word of God. Pray for the blessing of God upon the word; for except his word of blessing go forth with it, it can never come home to thy soul. Meditate upon what you hear; for, without meditation, it is not like to have any effectual operation upon you. Search your souls by it, and consider whether that be not your very case and state which it describes; your very danger whereof it gives warning. Take heed, lest after you have heard it, the cares of the world choke what you have heard, and cause those budding convictions which begin to put forth, to blast and wither. Carefully attend to all those *items* and *memorandums* your consciences give you under the word, and conclude that the Lord is then come nigh unto you.

Secondly, Let this be matter of serious consideration and caution to all such as have only felt some slight, transient, and ineffectual operations of the gospel upon their souls: The Lord hath come nigh to some of our souls; we have felt a strange power in the ordinances, sometimes terrifying, and sometimes transporting our hearts; but, alas! it proves but a morning-dew, or an early cloud, Hos. vi. 4. We rejoice in the word, but it is but for a season, John iii. 25. Gal. iv. 14, 15. They are vanishing motions, and come to nothing. Look, as in nature there are many *abortives*, as well as perfect children, so it is in religion; yea, where the new creature is perfectly formed in one soul, there be many abortives and miscarriages in others; and there may be three reasons assigned for it, *viz.*

First, The subtilty and deep policy of Satan, who never more effectually deceives and destroys the souls of men, than in such a method, and by such an artifice as this; for when men have once felt their consciences terrified under the word, and their hearts at other times ravished with the joys and comforts of it, they now seem to have attained all that is necessary to conversion, and constitutive of the new creature; these things look so well like the regenerating effects of the Spirit, that many are easily deceived by them. The devil beguiles the hearts of the unwary by such false appearances: for it is not every man that can distinguish betwixt the natural and spiritual motions of the affections under the word: It is very frequently seen that even carnal and unrenewed hearts have their meltings and transports, as well as spiritual hearts. The subject-matter upon which the word treats, are the weighty things of the world to come; heaven and hell are very awful and affecting things, and an unrenewed heart is apt to thaw and melt at them: Now here is the cheat of Satan, to persuade a man that these must needs be spiritual affections, because the objects about which they are conversant are spiritual; whereas it is certain the objects of the affections may be very spiritual and heavenly, and yet the workings of man's affections about them may be in a mere natural way.

Secondly, The dampening efficacy of the world is a true and proper cause of these abortions and miscarriages under the word, Luke viii. 12, 13, 14. There are hopeful and promising beginnings and buddings of affections in some persons, especially in their youth; but when once they come to be engaged in the world, how soon are they damped and quenched! As the cares of a family grow on, so does the care of salvation wear off. It is not as it was wont to be, What shall I do to be saved? How shall I get interest in Christ?

But what shall I eat, and drink, and wherewith shall I, and mine, be maintained? Thus earth justles out heaven, and the present world drowns all thoughts of that to come. Good had it been for many men, they had never been engaged so deep in the world as they are; their life is but a constant hurry of business, and a perpetual diversion from Christ, and things that are eternal.

Thirdly, and *lastly*, The deceitfulness and treachery of the heart, which too easily gives way to the designs of Satan, suffers itself to be imposed upon by him, is not the least cause why so many hopeful beginnings come to nothing, and the effects of the word vanish. Pride and self-love are very apt to over-rule every little good, and slight or undervalue every ill that is in us; and so quickly choke those convictions that begin to work in our souls.

But oh! that such men would consider, that the dying away of their convictions is that which threatens the life of their souls for ever; now is the bud withered, the blossom blasted: and what expectation is there of fruit after this, except the Lord revive them again? The Lord open men's eyes to discern the danger of such things as these are! Jude 12. Heb. x. 58. Yet I deny not but there are many stands and pauses in the work of conversion; it seems to die away, and then revives again; and revive it must, or we are lost. But how many are there who never recover it more! This is a sore judgment of a most terrible consequence to the souls of men!

Thirdly, In the last place, let it be a word of counsel and advice to them, upon whom the word works effectually and powerfully; to whose hearts the commandment is come home to revive sin, and kill their vain hopes; and these are of two sorts.

1. Embryos under the first workings of the Spirit.
2. Complete births of the Spirit, regenerated souls.

First, Embryos that are under the first workings of the Spirit in the word. O let it not seem a misery, or unhappiness to you, that the commandment is come, and sin revived, and your former hopes overthrown. It must be thus, if ever God intend mercy for you. Had you gone on in that dangerous security you were in before, you had certainly been lost for ever: God hath stopt you in that path that leads down to hell, and none that go in there do ever return again, or take hold of the paths of life. O! it is better to weep, tremble, and be distressed now, than to mourn without hope for ever. Let it not trouble you that sin hath found you out; you could never have found out the remedy in Christ, if you had not found out the disease and danger, by the coming of the commandment. And I beseech you carefully to observe, whether the effects and operations of the word upon your hearts be deeper and more powerful than they are found to be in such souls as miscarry under it: the commandment comes to them, and shews them this or that more gross and startling sin.   Doth it come to you, and shew you not only this or that particular sin, but all the evils of your heart and life; the corruption of your natures, as well as the transgressions of your lives? If so, it promises well, and looks hopefully and comfortably to you.   The commandment comes to others, and startles them with the fears of damnation for their sin: it puts them into a grievous fright at hell, and the everlasting burnings: but doth it come to thee and discover the infinite evil that is in thy sin, as it is committed against the great, holy, righteous, and good God, and so melts thy heart into tears for the wrong that thou hast done him, as well as the danger into which thou hast brought thyself? This is a hopeful work, and may encourage thee. It comes to others, and greatly shakes, but never destroys and razes the foundation of their vain hopes: if it so revive sin as to kill all vain hopes in thee, and send thee to Christ alone, as thy only door of hope, fear not; these troubles will prove the greatest mercies that ever befel thee in this world, if thus they work, and continue to work upon thy soul.

Secondly, Others there are upon whom the word hath had its full effect as to conversion. O bless God for ever for this mercy; you cannot sufficiently value it! God hath not only made it a convincing and wounding, but a converting and healing word to your souls; he hath not only revived your sins, and killed your vain hopes, but begotten you again to a lively hope; see that you be thankful for this mercy. How many have sate under the same word, but never felt such effects of it? As Christ said in another case, there were many widows in Israel in the time of Elijah, but unto none of them was the prophet sent, save unto Sarepta, a city of Sidon, to a certain widow there, Luke iv. 46. So I may say, in this case, there were many souls in the same congregation, at the same time, but unto none of them was the word sent with a commission to convince and save, but such a one as thyself; one as improbable to be wrought upon as any soul there. O let this beget thankfulness in your souls; and let it make you love the word as long as you live: " I will never forget thy precepts, for by them " thou hast quickened me," Psal. cxix. 93.

But above all, I beseech you make it appear that the commandment hath come home to your hearts, with power to convince you of the evil of sin, by your tenderness and care to shun it as long as you live.   If ever you have seen the face of sin, in the glass of the law of God; if your hearts have been humbled and broken for it in the days of your trouble and distress, certainly you will choose the worst affliction rather than sin: It would be the greatest folly in the world to return again to iniquity, Psal. lxxxv. 8. You that have seen so much of the evil that is in it, and the danger that follows it; you that have had such inward terrors and fears of spirit about it, when that terrible representation was made you, will be loth to feel those gripes and distresses of conscience again, for the best enjoyment in this world.

Blessed be God if any word has been brought home to our hearts, which hath been instrumental to bring us to Christ!

------◦◦◦◦◦------

SERMON XXII.

The Teachings of God opened, in their Nature and Necessity.

JOHN vi. 45.

It is written in the prophets, And they shall be all taught of God. Every man therefore that hath heard, and hath learned of the Father, cometh unto me.

HOW necessary to our union with Jesus Christ, the application of the law, or coming home of the commandment to the heart of a sinner is, we have heard in the last discourse; and how impossible it is, either for the commandment to come to us, or for us to come to Christ without illumination and instruction from above, you shall hear in this.

This scripture hath much of the mind of God in it; and he that is to open it, had need himself to be taught of God. In the foregoing verses, Christ offers himself as the bread of life unto the souls of men: against this doctrine they oppose their carnal reason, ver. 41, 42. Christ strikes at the root of all their cavils and objections in his reply, ver. 43, 44. "Murmur not among yourselves: "no man can come to me, except the Father which hath sent me "draw him;" q. d. you slight me because you do not know me; you do not know me because you are not taught of God; of these divine teachings, the prophets of old have spoken, and what they foretold is at this day fulfilled in our sight; so many as are taught of God, and no more, come unto me in the way of faith: it is impossible to come without the teachings of God, ver. 44. It is as impossible not to come, or to miscarry in their coming unto me, under the influence of these divine teachings, ver. 45.

The words read, consist of two parts, viz.

1. An allegation out of the prophets.

2. The application thereof made by Christ.

First, An allegation out of the prophets: "It is written in the "prophets, And they shall be all taught of God." The places in the prophets to which Christ seems here to refer, are, Isa. liv. 13. " And all thy children shall be taught of the Lord ;" and, Jer. xxxi. 34. " And they shall teach no more every man his neigh- " bour, and every man his brother, saying, know the Lord ; for " they shall all know me, from the least of them unto the greatest " of them, saith the Lord." These promises contain the great blessings of the new covenant, viz. Divine instruction and heavenly illumination, without which no man can obtain an interest in the new covenant.

Secondly, We have here the application of these testimonies out of the prophets, made by Christ himself; " Every man therefore " that hath heard, and learned of the Father, come unto me."

In which words we have both the necessity and the efficacy of these divine teachings ; without them no man can come, and under them no man can miscarry. The words being fitly rendered, and the sense obvious,

The notes are,

Doct. 1. *That the teachings of God are absolutely necessary to every man that cometh unto Christ, in the way of faith.*

Doct. 2. *No man can miss of Christ, or miscarry in the way of faith, that is under the special instructions and teachings of the Father.*

Doct. 1. *That the teachings of God are absolutely necessary to every man that cometh unto Christ, in the way of faith.*

Of the necessity of divine teaching, in order to believing, the apos- tle speaks, in Eph. iv. 20, 21. " But ye have not so learned Christ ; " if so be that you have heard him, and been taught by him, as " the truth is in Jesus ;" i. e. Your faith must needs be effectual, both to the reformation of your lives, and your perseverance in the ways of holiness, if it be such a faith as is begotten and intro- duced into your hearts by divine teachings*. Now, in the explica- tion of this point, I shall speak distinctly to the following enqui- ries.

1. How doth God teach men, or what is imported in our being taught of God ?

2. What those special lessons are, which all believers do hear, and are taught of God ?

---

* They who believe, by means of the preacher speaking to them outwardly, hear and learn inwardly of the Father ; they who believe not, hear outwardly, but not inwardly. *Aug. on Predest. chap.* 8.

3. In what manner doth God teach these things to men in the day of their conversion to Christ?

4. What influence God's teaching hath upon our believing?

5. Why it is impossible for any man to believe, or come to Christ without the Father's teachings.

First, How doth God teach men, or what is imported in our being taught of God? To this I will speak both negatively and positively, for your clearer apprehension of the sense and meaning of the Spirit of God in this phrase.

First, The teaching of God, and our hearing and learning of him, is not to be understood of any extraordinary visional appearances, or oraculous and immediate voice of God to men: God indeed hath so appeared unto some, Numb. xii. 8. Such voices have been heard from heaven, but now these extraordinary ways are ceased, Heb. i. 1, 2. and we are no more to expect them; we may sooner meet with satanical delusions than divine illuminations in this way. I remember, the learned Gerson tells us that the devil once appeared to an holy man in prayer, personating Christ, and saying, I am come in person to visit thee, for thou art worthy. But he with both hands shut his eyes, saying, *Nolo hic Christum videre, satis est ipsum in gloria videre;* i. e. I will not see Christ here; it is enough for me to see him in glory. We are now to attend only to the voice of the Spirit in the scriptures: this is a more sure word than any voice from heaven, 2 Pet. i. 19.

Secondly, The teachings of God are not to be understood as opposite unto, or exclusive of the teachings of men. Divine teachings do not render ministerial teachings in vain or useless. Paul was taught of God, Gal. i. 12. and his conversion had something extraordinary in it, yet the ministry of Ananias was used and honoured in that work, Acts ix. 4, 17. compared. Divine teachings do indeed excel, but not exclude human teachings. I know that scripture, Jer. xxxi. 24. to which Christ here refers, is objected against the necessity of a standing ministry in the church, " They " shall teach no more every man his neighbour, and every man " his brother," &c. But if those words should be understood absolutely, they would not only overthrow all public ordinances of God's own institution, 1 Cor. xii. 28. and deprive us of a principal fruit of Christ's ascension, Eph. iv. 11. 12. but, for the same reason, would destroy all private instructions and fraternal admonitions also. Such a sense would make the prophet to contradict the apostle, and spoil the consent and harmony of the scriptures: the sense thereof cannot be negative, but comparative; it shews the excellency of divine, but doth not destroy the usefulness of human teachings; *Subordinata non pugnant.* The teachings of men are made effectual by the teachings of the Spirit; and the Spirit in his teachings will use and honour the ministry of man.

Thirdly, But to speak positively, the teachings of God are nothing else but that spiritual and heavenly light, by which the Spirit of God shineth into the hearts of men, to give them " the light " of the knowledge of the glory of God in the face of Jesus " Christ," as the apostle speaks, 2 Cor. iv. 6. And though this be the proper work of the Spirit, yet it is called the teachings of the Father, because the Spirit who enlightens us is commissioned and sent by the Father so to do, John xiv. 26. Now these teachings of the Spirit of God, consist in two things, *viz.* in his,

1. Sanctifying impressions.
2. Gracious assistances.

First, In his sanctifying impressions or regenerating work upon the soul, by virtue whereof it receives marvellous light and insight into spiritual things; and that not only as illumination is the first act of the Spirit in our conversion, Col. iii. 10. but as his whole work of sanctification is illuminative and instructive to the converted soul, 1 John ii. 27. " The anointing which you have received " of him abideth in you, and ye need not that any man teach " you, but as the same anointing teacheth you." The meaning is that sanctification gives the soul experience of those mysterious things which are contained in the scriptures, and that experience is the most excellent key to unlock and open those deep scripture-mysteries; no knowledge is so distinct, so clear, so sweet, as that which the heart communicates to the head, John vii. 17. " If any " man do his will, he shall know of the doctrine." A man that never read the nature of love in books of philosophy, nor the transports and extasies thereof in history, may yet truly describe and express it by the sensible motions of that passion in his own soul; yea, he that hath felt, much better understands, than he that hath only read or heard. O what a light doth spiritual sense and experience cast upon a great part of the scriptures! for indeed sanctification is the very copy or transcript of the word of God upon the heart of man; Jer. xxxi. 33. " I will write my law in their " hearts:" so that the scriptures and the experiences of believers, by this means answer to each other, as the lines and letters in the press answer to the impressions made upon the paper; or the figures in the wax, to the engravings in the seal. When a sanctified man reads David's psalms, or Paul's epistles, how is he surprized with wonder to find the very workings of his own heart so exactly decyphered and fully expressed there! O, saith he, this is my very case, these holy men speak what my heart hath felt.

Secondly, The Spirit of God teacheth us, as by his sanctifying impressions, so by his gracious assistances, which he gives us *pro re*

nata, as our need requires, Mat. x. 19. " It shall be given you in
" that same hour what ye shall speak, John xiv. 26. " He shall
" bring all things to your remembrance : he assisteth both the understanding in due apprehensions of truth, and the heart in the
spiritual improvements of truth. And so much briefly of the first
particular.

Secondly, In the next place we are to enquire what those special
truths are which believers hear and learn of the Father, when they
come to Christ.

And there are divers great and necessary truths, wherein the
Spirit enlightens men in that day. I cannot say they are all taught
every believer in the same degree and order; but it is certain they
are taught of God such lessons as these are, which they never so
understood before.

Lesson 1. *First*, They are taught of God *that there is abundantly
more evil in their sinful natures and actions, than ever they discerned or understood before:* " the Spirit when he cometh shall
" convince the world of sin," John xvi. 8, 9. Men had a general
notion of sin before; so had Paul, when a Pharisee: but how vastly
different were his apprehensions of sin, from all that ever he had in
his natural state, when God brought home the commandment to his
very heart ? There is a threefold knowledge of sin, viz. *traditional,
discursive*, and *intuitive*. The first is the more rude and illiterate
multitude. The second is more rational and knowing men. The
third is only found in those that are enlightened and taught of
God. And there is as great a difference betwixt this intuitive knowledge of sin, whereby God makes a soul to discern the nature and
evil of it in a spiritual light, and the two former, as there is betwixt the sight of a *painted lion* upon the wall, and the sight of a
living lion that meets us roaring in the way. The intuitive sight of
sin is another thing than men imagine it to be : it is such a sight as
wounds a man to the very heart, Acts ii. 37. for God doth not
only shew a man this or that particular sin, but in the day of
conviction, he sets all his sins in order before him, Psal. l. 21.
yea, the Lord shews him the sinfulness of his nature as well as
practice. Conviction digs to the root, shews and lays open that
original corruption, from whence the innumerable evils of the life
do spring, James i. 14, 15. and which is yet more, the Lord
shews the man whom he is bringing to Christ the sinful and miserable estate which he is in by reason of both, John xvi. 9. And
now all excuses, pleas and defences of sin are gone, he shews him
" how their iniquities have exceeded," Job xxxvi. 8, 9. exceeded
in number, and in aggravations of sinfulness; exceeding many,
and exceeding vile; no such sinner in the world as I ; can such
sins as mine be pardoned ? The greatness of God greatens my

sin; the holiness of God makes it beyond measure vile; the goodness of God puts unconceivable weight into my guilt. O, can there
be mercy for such a wretch as I ! If there be, then there will not
be a greater example of the riches of free grace in all the world
than I am. Thus God teacheth the evil of sin.

Lesson 2. Secondly, *God teacheth the soul whom he is bringing to
Christ, what that wrath and misery are which hang over it in the
threatenings because of sin.*   Scripture-threatenings were formerly
slighted, now the soul trembles at them : They once apprehended
themselves safe enough, Isa. xxviii. 15. Psal. l. 21.   They thought,
because they heard no more of their sins after the commission of them,
that therefore they should never hear more; that the effect had
been as transient a thing as the act of sin was; or if trouble must
follow sin, they should speed no worse than others, the generality
of the world being in the same case; and besides, they hoped to
find God more merciful than sour and precise preachers represented him.   But when a light from God enters into the soul, to
discover the nature of God, and of sin, then it sees that whatever
wrath is treasured up for sinners in the dreadful threatenings of the
law, is but the just demerit of sin, the recompence that is meet:
" The wages of sin is death," Rom. vi. 23.   The *penal* evil of
damnation is but equal to the *moral* evil of sin : So that in the
whole ocean of God's eternal wrath, there is not one drop of in-
justice; yea, the soul doth not only see the justice of God in its
eternal damnation, but the wonderful mercy of God in the suspension thereof so long. O, what is it that hath withheld God from
damning me all this while ! How is it that I am not in hell ! Now
do the fears and awful apprehensions of eternity seize the soul, and
the worst of sensitive creatures is supposed to be in a better condition than such a soul. Never do men tremble at the threatenings
of God, nor rightly apprehend the danger of their condition, until
sin, and wrath, and the wages of sin be discovered to them by a
light from heaven.

Lesson 3. Thirdly, *God teaches the soul whom he brings to Christ
that deliverance from sin, and wrath to come, is the greatest and
most important business it hath to do in this world.* Acts xvi. 30.
" What must I do to be saved ?" *q. d.* O direct me to some effectual way (if there be any) to secure my poor wretched soul from
the wrath of God. Sin, and the wrath that follows it, are things
that swallow up the souls, and drink up the very spirits of men :
Their thoughts never conversed with things of more confessed truth
and awful solemnity : These things float not upon their fancies as
matters of mere speculation, but settle upon their hearts day and
night, as the deepest concernment in all the world : They now

know much better than any mere scholar, the deep sense of that text, Matth. xvi. 26. " What is a man profited, if he should gain " the whole world, and lose his own soul? or what shall a man " give in exchange for his soul?"

Five things shew how weighty the thoughts and cares of salvation are upon their hearts.

First, Their continual thoughtfulness and solicitude about these things: if earthly affairs divert them for a while, yet they are still returning again to this solemn business.

Secondly, Their careful redeeming of time, and saving the very moments thereof to employ about this work: Those that were prodigal of hours and days before, look upon every moment of time as a precious and valuable thing now.

Thirdly, Their fears and tremblings lest they should miscarry, and come short at last, shew how much their hearts are set upon this work.

Fourthly, Their inquisitiveness and readiness to embrace all the help and assistance that they can get from others, evidently discover this to be their great design.

Fifthly, and *lastly,* The little notice they take of all other troubles and afflictions, tells you their hearts are taken up about greater things. This is the third lesson they are taught of God.

Lesson 4. Fourthly, *The Lord teaches the soul that is coming to Christ, that though it be their duty to strive to the uttermost for salvation; yet all strivings, in their own strength, are insufficient to obtain it.* This work is quite above the power of nature: " It is " not of him that willeth, nor of him that runneth, but of God " that sheweth mercy." The soul is brought to a full conviction of this, by the discovery of the heinous nature of sin, and of the rigour and severity of the law of God. No repentance nor reformation can possibly amount unto a just satisfaction, nor are they within the compass and power of our will. It was a saying that Dr. Hill often used to his friends, speaking about the power of man's will; he would lay his hand upon his breast, and say, " Every man hath something here to confute the Arminian doc- " trine." This fully takes off the soul from all expectations of deliverance that way; it cannot but strive, that is its duty; but to expect deliverance, as the purchase of its own strivings, that would be its sin.

Lesson 5. Fifthly, *The soul that is coming to Christ by faith, is taught of God, that though the case it is in be sad, yet it is not desperate and remediless:* There is a door of hope, a way of escape for poor sinners, how black and fearful soever their own thoughts and apprehensions are; there is usually at this time a dawning light of hope in the soul that is under the Father's teachings; and this commonly arises from the general and indefinite encouragements and promises of the gospel, which, though they do not presently secure the soul from danger, yet they prop and mightily support it against despair : For though they be not certain that deliverance shall be the event of their trouble ; yet the possibilities, and much more the probabilities of deliverance are a great stay to a sinking soul. The troubled soul cannot but acknowledge itself to be in a far better case than the damned are, whose hopes are perished from the Lord, and a death-pang of despair hath seized their consciences. And herein the merciful and compassionate nature of God is eminently discovered, in hasting to open the door of hope, almost as soon as the evil of sin is opened. It was not long after Adam's eyes were opened to see his misery, that God opened Christ, his remedy, in that first promise, Gen. iii. 15. And the same method of grace is still continued to his elect offspring, Gal. iii. 21, 22. Rom. iii. 21, 22. These supporting hopes the Lord sees necessary to encourage industry in the use of means ; it is hope that sets all the world awork ; if all hope were cut off, every soul would sit down in a sullen despair, yielding itself for hell.

Lesson 6. Sixthly, *The Lord teaches those that come to Christ, that there is a fulness of saving power in him, whereby any soul that duly receives him, may be perfectly delivered from all its sin and misery*, Heb. vii. 25. Col. i. 19. Matth. xxviii. 18. This is a great and necessary point for every believer to learn and hear from the Father ; for unless the soul be satisfied of the fulness of Christ's saving power, it will never move forward towards him ; and herein also the goodness of God is most sweetly and seasonably manifested ; for, at this time, it is the great design of Satan to fill the soul with despairing thoughts of a pardon ; but all those black and heart-sinking thoughts vanish before the discovery of Christ's all-sufficiency. Now the sin-sick soul saith with that woman, Matth. ix. 21. " If I may but touch the hem of his garment, I shall be " healed." How deep soever the guilt and stain of sin be, yet the soul which acknowledges the infinite dignity of the blood of Christ, the offering it up to God in our room, and God's declared satisfaction in it, must needs be satisfied that Christ is " able to save, " to the uttermost, all that come unto God by him ;" which is the sixth lesson believers are taught of God.

Lesson 7. Seventhly, *Every man that cometh to Christ is taught of God, that he can never reap any benefit by the blood of Christ, except he have union with the person of Christ*, 1 John v. 12. Eph. iv. 16. Time was when men fondly thought nothing was necessary to their salvation but the death of Christ ; but now the Lord shews them that their union with Christ by faith is as necessary, in the place of an *applying cause*, as the death of Christ is, in the place of a *meritorious cause* : The *purchase* of salvation is an act of Christ *without us*, whilst we are yet sinners ; the *application* thereof is by a work wrought *within us*, when we are believers, Col. i. 27. In the purchase all the elect are redeemed together by way of price ; in the application they are actually redeemed, each person, by way of power. Look, as the sin of the first Adam could never hurt us, unless he had been our head by way of generation ; so the righteousness of Christ can never benefit us, unless he be our head by way of regeneration. In teaching this lesson, the Lord, in mercy, unteaches and blots out that dangerous principle, by which the greatest part of the christianized world do perish, viz. that the death of Christ is, in itself, effectual to salvation, though a man be never regenerated or united to him by saving faith.

Lesson 8. Eighthly, *God teaches the soul, whom he is bringing to Christ, that whatever is necessary to be wrought in us, or done by us, in order to our union with Christ, is to be obtained from him in the way of prayer*, Ezek. xxxvi. 37. And it is observable, that the soul no sooner comes under the effectual teachings of God, but the Spirit of prayer begins to breathe in it, Acts ix. 8. " Behold, he pray-
" eth." Those that were taught to pray by men before, are now taught of the Lord to pray : To pray did I say ? yea, and to pray fervently too, as men concerned for their eternal happiness ; to pray not only with others, but to pour out our souls before the Lord in secret ; for their hearts are as bottles full of new wine, which must vent or break. Now the soul returns upon its God often in the same day ; now it can express its burdens and wants, in words and groans which the Spirit teacheth. They pray, and will not give over praying, till Christ come with complete salvation.

Lesson 9. Ninthly, *All that come to Christ are taught of God to abandon their former ways and companions in sin, as ever they expect to be received unto mercy*, Isa. lv. 7. 2 Cor. v. 17. Sins that were profitable and pleasant, that were as the right hand, and right eye, must now be cut off. Companions in sin, who were once the delight of their lives, must now be cast off. Christ saith to the soul concerning these, as he said in another case, John xviii. 8. " If
" therefore ye seek me, let these go their way." And the soul saith unto Christ, as it is, Psal. cxix. 115. " Depart from me, ye
" evil-doers, for I will keep the commandments of my God."
And now pleasant sins and companions in sin, become the very burden and shame of a man's soul. Objects of delight are become objects of pity and compassion : No endearments, no union of blood, no earthly interests whatsoever, are found strong enough to hold the soul any longer from Christ : Nothing but the effectual teachings of God are found sufficient to dissolve such bonds of iniquity as these.

Lesson 10. Tenthly, *All that come unto Christ are taught of God, that there is such a beauty and excellency in the ways and people of God, as is not to be equalled in the whole world,* Psal. xvi. 3. When the eyes of strangers to Christ begin to be opened, and enlightened in his knowledge, you may see what a change of judgment is wrought in them, with respect to the people of God: and towards them especially, whom God hath any way made instrumental for the good of their souls, Cant. v. 9. they then call the spouse of Christ, *the fairest among women.* The convincing holiness of the bride then began to enamour and affect them, with a desire of nearer conjunction and communion: *We will seek him with thee; with thee* that hast *so charged us,* that hast taken so much pains for the good of our souls; now, and never before, the righteous appeareth more excellent than his neighbour. Change of heart is always accompanied with change of judgment, with respect to the people of God: thus the gaoler, Acts xvi. 33. washed the apostle's stripes, to whom he had been so cruel before. The godly now seem to be the glory of the places where they live; and the glory of any place seems to be darkened by their removal; as one said of holy Mr. Barrington, " Methinks the town is not at home when " Mr. Barrington is out of town." They esteem it a choice mercy to be in their company and acquaintance; Zech. viii. 23. " We " will go with you, for we have heard that God is with you." No people like the people of God now; as one said, when he heard of two faithful friends, *Utinam tertius essem!* O that I might make the third! Whatever vile or low thoughts they had of the people of God before, to be sure now they are the excellent of the earth, in whom is all their delight: The holiness of the saints might have some interest in their consciences before, but they never had such an interest in their estimation and affections, till this lesson was taught them by the Father.

Lesson 11. Eleventhly, *All that come to Christ are taught of God, that whatever difficulties they apprehend in religion, yet they must not, upon pain of damnation, be discouraged thereby, or return again to sin,* Luke ix. 62. " No man having put his hand to the " plough, and looking back, is fit for the kingdom of God." Ploughing-work is hard work; a strong and steady hand is required for it: he that ploughs must keep on, and make no balks of the hardest and toughest ground he meets with. Religion also is the running of a race, 1 Cor. ix. 24. there is no standing still, much less turning back, if ever we hope to win the prize.

The devil, indeed, labours every way to discourage and daunt the soul, by representing the insuperable difficulties of religion to it; and young beginners are but too apt to be discouraged, and fall under despondency; but the teachings of the Father are encouraging teachings; they are carried on from strength to strength against all the oppositions they meet with from without them, and the many discouragements they find within them. To this conclusion they are brought by the teaching of God, *We must have Christ, we must get a pardon, we must strive for salvation, let the difficulties, troubles, and sufferings in the way be never so great or many.* As he said, *Necesse est ut eam, non ut vivam*; it is necessary that I go on, it is not necessary that I live: So saith the soul that is taught of God; it is easier for me to dispense with ease, honour, relations, yea, with life itself, than to part with Christ, and the hopes of eternal life.

Lesson 12. Twelfthly, *They that come to Christ, are taught of God, that whatever guilt and unworthiness they discover in themselves, and whatever fears and doubts are upon their hearts, as to pardon and acceptance; yet as the case stands, it is their wisdom and great interest to venture themselves in the way of faith, upon Jesus Christ, whatever the issue thereof be.*

Three great discouragements are usually found upon the hearts of those that come to Christ in the way of faith.

First, The sensible greatness of guilt and sin. How can I go to Christ that am in such a case, that have been so vile a wretch? And here measuring the grace and mercy of Christ, by what it finds in itself, or in other creatures, 1 Sam. xxiv. 19. the soul is ready to sink under the weight of its own discouraging and misgiving thoughts.

Secondly, The sense they have of their own weakness and inability to do what God requires, and must of necessity be done, if ever they be saved. My heart is harder than adamant, how can I break it? My will is stubborn, and exceeding obstinate, I am no way able to bow it; the frame and temper of my spirit is altogether carnal, and earthly; and it is not in the power of my hand to alter and change it; alas! I cannot subdue any one corruption, nor perform one spiritual duty, nor bear one of those sufferings and burdens which religion lays upon all that follow Christ: this also proves a great discouragement in the way of faith.

Thirdly, And, which is more than all, the soul that is coming to Jesus Christ, hath no assurance of acceptance with him, if it should adventure itself upon him: it is a great hazard, a great adventure; it is much more probable, if I look to myself, that Christ will shut the door of mercy against me.

But under all these discouragements the soul learns this lesson from God, That, as ungodly as it is, nevertheless it is every way its great duty and concernment to go on in the way of faith, and make that great adventure of itself upon Jesus Christ: and of this the Lord convinceth the soul by two things, viz.

1. From the absolute necessity of coming.

2. From the encouraging probabilities of speeding.

First, The soul seeth an absolute necessity of coming : necessity is laid upon it, there is no other way, Acts iv. 12. God hath shut it up by a blessed necessity to this only door of escape, Gal. iii. 23. Damnation lies in the neglect of Christ, Heb. ii. 3. The soul hath no choice in this case ; angels, ministers, duties, repentance, reformation cannot save me ; Christ, and none but Christ can deliver me from present guilt, and the wrath to come. Why do I dispute, demur, delay, when certain ruin must inevitably follow the neglect or refusal of gospel-offers ?

Secondly, The Lord sheweth those that are under his teaching, the probabilities of mercy, for their encouragement in the way of believing. And these probabilities the soul is enabled to gather from the general and free invitations of the gospel, Isa. lv. 1, 7. Rev. xxii. 17. from the conditional promises of the gospel, John vi. 37. Mat. xi. 28. Isa. i. 18. from the vast extent of grace, beyond all the thoughts and hopes of the creatures, Isa. lv. 8, 9. Heb. vii. 25. from the encouraging examples of other sinners, who have found mercy in as bad a condition as they, 1 Tim. i. 13. 2 Chron. xxxiii. 3. 2 Cor. vi. 10, 11. from the command of God, which warrants the action, and answers all the objections of unworthiness and presumption in them that come to Christ, 1 John iii. 23. and lastly, from the sensible changes already made upon the temper and frame of the heart. Time was, when I had no sense of sin, nor sorrow for sin ; no desire after Christ, no heart to duties. But it is not so with me now ; I now see the evil of sin, so as I never saw it before ; my heart is now broken in the sense of that evil ; my desires begin to be enflamed after Jesus Christ ; I am not at rest, nor where I would be, till I am in secret mourning after the Lord Jesus ; surely these are the dawnings of the day of mercy ; let me go on in this way. It saith, as the lepers at the siege of Samaria, 2 Kings vii. 3, 4. "If I stay here, I perish :" If I go to Christ I can but perish. Hence believers bear up against all objected discouragements, *certum exitium commutemus incerto ;* it is the dictate of wisdom, the vote of reason, to exchange a certain for an uncertain ruin. And thus you have here what those excellent lessons are, which all that come to Christ are taught by the Father.

SERMON XXIII

JOHN vi. 45.

*It is written in the Prophets, And they shall be all taught of God.
Every man therefore that hath heard, and hath learned of the
Father, cometh unto me.*

IN the former sermon, you have been taught this great truth;

> Doct. *That the teachings of God are absolutely neccesary to every
> soul that cometh unto Christ, in the way of faith.*

What the teachings of God import, hath been formerly opened;
and what those special lessons are, which all believers hear and learn
of the Father, was the last thing discoursed: that which remains to
be further cleared about this subject, before I come to the application of the whole, will be to shew you,

1. What are the properties of divine teachings.
2. What influence they have in bringing souls to Christ.
3. Why it is impossible for any man to come to Christ without
these teachings of the Father.

First, What are the properties of divine teachings? Concerning
the teachings of God, we affirm in general, that, though they exclude not, yet they vastly differ from all human teachings: as the
power of God in effecting transcends all human power, so the wisdom of God in teaching transcends all human wisdom.   For,

1. God teacheth powerfully; he speaketh to the soul with a
strong hand; when the word cometh accompanied with the Spirit,
it is "mighty through God, to cast down all imaginations," 2 Cor.
x. 4.   Now the gospel "comes not in word only, (as it was wont
to do,) but in power," 1 Thes. i. 4, 5. a power that makes the
soul fall down before it, and acknowledge that God is in that word,
1 Cor. xiv. 25.

2. The teachings of God are sweet teachings.   Men never relish
the sweetness of a truth, till they learn it from God, Cant. i. 3.
" His name is as ointment poured forth."   Cant. v. 16. " His
" mouth is most sweet."   O how powerfully and how sweetly
doth the voice of God slide into the hearts of poor melting sinners!
how jejune, dry, and tasteless are the discourses of men, compared
with the teachings of the Father!

3. God teacheth plainly and clearly: He not only opens truths
to the understanding, but he openeth the understanding also to
perceive them, 2 Cor. iii. 16.   In that day the vail is taken away

from the heart; a light shineth into the soul; a clear beam from heaven is darted into the mind, Luke xxiv. 45. Divine teachings are fully satisfying; the soul doubts no more, staggers and hesitates no more, but acquiesces in that which God teaches; it is so satisfied, that it can venture all upon the truth of what it hath learned from God; as that martyr said, *I cannot dispute, but I can die for Christ.* See Prov. viii. 8, 9.

Fourthly, The teachings of God are *infallible teaching's.* The wisest and holiest of men may mistake, and lead others into the same mistakes with themselves; but it is not so in the teachings of God. If we can be sure that God teacheth us, we may be as sure of the truth of what he teacheth; for his Spirit *guideth us into all truth,* John xvi. 3. and into nothing but truth.

Fifthly, The teachings of God are *abiding teachings;* they make everlasting impressions upon the soul, Psal. cxix. 98. *they are ever with it:* The words of men vanish from us; but the words of God abide by us: what God teacheth, he writeth upon the heart, Jer. xxxi. 33. and that will abide; *litera scripta manet.* It is usual with souls, whose understandings have been opened by the Lord, many years afterward to say, I shall never forget such a scripture that once convinced, such a promise that once encouraged me.

Sixthly, The teachings of God are *saving teachings;* they make the soul wise unto salvation, 2 Tim. iii. 15. There is a great deal of other knowledge that goes to hell with men: The pavement of hell (as one speaks) is pitched with the skulls of many great *scholars,* but eternal life is the teachings of God, John xvii. 3. " This is the eternal life, to know thee the only true God, and " Jesus Christ, whom thou hast sent." This is deservedly stiled the light of this life, John viii. 12. " In this light we shall see light," Psal. xxxvi. 9.

Seventhly, The teachings of God make their own way into the dullest and weakest capacities, Isa. xxxii. 4. " The heart also of " the rash shall understand knowledge, and the tongue of the " stammerers shall be ready to speak plainly." Upon this account Christ said, Matth. xi. 25. " I thank thee, O Father, Lord of " heaven and earth, because thou hast hid these things from the " wise and prudent, and hast revealed them unto babes." It is admirable to see what clear illuminations some poor illiterate Christians have in the mysteries of Christ and salvation, which others, of great abilities, deep and searching heads, can never discover with all their learning and study.

Eighthly, To conclude, The teachings of God are *transforming teachings;* 2 Cor. iii. 18. they change the soul into the same image; God casts them, whom he teacheth, into the very mould of those

truths which they learn of him, Rom. vi. 17. These are the teachings of God, and thus he instructeth those that come to Christ.

Secondly, Next let us see what influence divine teachings have
upon souls, in bringing them to Christ; and we shall find a threefold influence in them.

1. They have an influence upon the external *means*, by which
they come to Christ.

2. They have an influence upon the mind, to remove what hindered it from Christ.

3. They have an influence upon the will, to allure and draw it
to Christ.

First, They have an influence upon the *means* by which we come
to Christ; the best ordinances are but a dead letter except the
Spirit, the teaching and quickening Spirit of God, work in fellowship with them, 2 Cor. iii. 6. The best ministers, like the disciples, cast forth the net, but take nothing, win not one soul to
God, till God teach as well as they. Paul is nothing, and Apollos
nothing, but God that giveth the increase, 1 Cor. iii. 7. Let the
most learned, eloquent, and powerful orator be in the pulpit, yet
no man's heart is persuaded till it hear the voice of God ; *Cathe-
dram in cœlis habet, qui corda docet.*

Secondly, They have influence upon the mind, to remove what
hindered it from Christ. Except the minds of men be first un-
taught those errors, by which they are prejudiced against Christ,
they will never be persuaded to come unto him ; and nothing but
the Father's teachings can unteach those errors, and cure those
evils of the mind. The natural mind of man slights the truths of
God, until God teach them ; and then they tremble with an awful reverence of them. Sin is but a trifle, till God shews us the
face of it in the glass of the law, and then it appears *exceeding sinful*, Rom. vii. 13. We think God to be such a one as
ourselves, Psal. l. 21. until he discover himself unto us in his infinite greatness, awful holiness, and severe justice ; and then we
cry, who can stand before this great and dreadful God ! We
thought it was time enough hereafter, to mind the concernments
of another world, until the Lord open our eyes, to see in what
danger we stand upon the very brink of eternity ; and then nothing alarms us more, than the fears that our time will be finished
before the great work of salvation be finished. We thought ourselves in a converted state before, till God made us to see the necessity of another manner of conversion, upon pain of eternal damnation. We readily caught hold upon the promises before, when
we had no right to them ; but the teachings of God make the presumptuous sinner let go his hold, that he may take a better and
surer hold of them in Christ. We once thought that the death

of Christ, in itself, had been enough to secure our salvation; but, under the teachings of God, we discern plainly the necessity of a change of heart and state; or else the blood of Christ can never profit us. Thus the teachings of God remove the errors of the mind, by which men are withheld from Christ.

Thirdly, The teachings of God powerfully attract and allure the will of a sinner to Christ, Hos. ii. 14. But of these drawings of the Father I have largely spoken before, and therefore shall say no more of them in this place, but hasten to the last thing propounded, viz.

Thirdly, Why it is impossible for any man to come to Christ without the Father's teachings; and the impossibilities hereof will appear three ways.

1. From the power of sin.
2. From the indisposition of man.
3. From the nature of faith.

By all which, the last point designed to be spoken to from this scripture, will be fully cleared, and the whole prepared for application.

First, The impossibility of coming to Christ without the teachings of the Father, will appear from the power of sin, which hath so strong an holdfast upon the hearts and affections of all unregenerate men, that no human arguments or persuasions whatsoever can divorce or separate them; for,

First, Sin is connatural with the soul, it is born and bred with a man; Psal. li. 4. Isa. xlviii. 8. It is as natural for fallen man to sin, as it is to breathe.

Secondly, The power of sin hath been strengthening itself from the beginning, by long continued custom, which gives it the force of a second nature, and makes regeneration and mortification naturally impossible, Jer. xv. 23. " Can the Ethiopian change his " skin, or the leopard his spots ? Then may he also do good that " is accustomed to do evil."

Thirdly, Sin is the delight of a sinner: " It is sport to a fool " to do mischief," Prov. x. 23. Carnal men have no other pleasure in this world, but what arises from their lusts; to cut off their corruptions by mortification, were at once to deprive them of all the pleasure of their lives.

Fourthly, Sin being connatural, customary, and delightful, doth therefore bewitch their affections and inchant their hearts, to that degree of madness and fascination, that they rather chuse damnation by God, than separation from sin : " Their hearts are fully " set in them to do evil," Eccles. viii. 11. they rush into sin, as the " horse rusheth into the battle," Jer. viii. 6. And now, what think you can separate a man from his beloved lust, except the powerful and effectual teachings of God ? Nothing but a light from heaven can rectify and reduce the inchanted mind; no power, but that of God, can change and alter the sinful bent and inclination of the will; it is a task above all the power of the creature.

Secondly, The impossibility of coming to Christ, without the Father's teachings, evidently appears from the *indisposedness* of man, the subject of this change; "The natural man receives not "the things which are of God," 1 Cor. ii. 14. Three things must be wrought upon man, before he can come to Christ: His blind understanding must be enlightened; his hard and rocky heart must be broken and melted; his stiff, fixed, and obstinate will must be conquered and subdued: but all these are effects of a supernatural power. The illumination of the mind is the peculiar work of God, 2 Cor. iv. 6. Rev. iii. 17. Eph. v. 8. The breaking and melting of the heart is the Lord's own work; it is he that giveth repentance, Acts v. 31. It is the Lord that "takes away the heart "of stone, and giveth an heart of flesh, Ezek. xxxvi. 26. It is he that poureth out the spirit of contrition upon man, Zech. xii. 10. The changing of the natural bent and inclination of the will, is the Lord's sole prerogative, Phil. ii. 13. All these things are effectually done in the soul of man, when God teacheth it, and never till then.

Thirdly, The nature of faith, by which we come to Christ, plainly shews the impossibility of coming without the Father's teaching. Every thing in faith is supernatural; the implantation of the habit of faith is so, Eph. ii. 8. It is not of ourselves, but the gift of God; it is not an habit *acquired* by industry, but *infused* by grace, Phil. i. 29. The *light* of faith, by which spiritual things are discerned, is supernatural, Heb. xi. 1, 27. It seeth things that are invisible. The *adventures* of faith are supernatural; for "against hope, a man *believeth* in hope, giving glory to God," Rom. iv. 18. By faith a man goeth unto Christ, against all the dictates and discouragements of natural sense and reason. The *self-denial* of faith is supernatural; the cutting off the right-hand, and plucking out of right-eye sins, must needs be so, Matt. v. 29. The *victories* and conquests of faith do all speak it to be supernatural; it overcomes the strongest oppositions from without, Heb. xi. 33, 34. It subdueth and purgeth the most obstinate and deeprooted corruptions within, Acts xv. 9. It overcometh all the blandishments and charming allurements of the bewitching world, 1 John v. 4. All which considered, how evident is the conclusion, that none can come to Christ without the Father's teachings? The uses follow.

First use for information.

Inference 1. *How notoriously false and absurd is that doctrine which asserteth the possibility of believing without the efficacy of supernatural grace?* The desire of self-sufficiency was the ruin of Adam, and the conceit of self-sufficiency is the ruin of multitudes of his posterity. This doctrine is not only contradictory to the current stream of scripture, Phil. ii. 13. 1 John i. 13. with many other scriptures; but it is also contradictory to the common sense and experience of believers; yet the pride of nature will strive to maintain what scripture and experience plainly contradict and overthrow.

Inf. 2. Hence we may also inform ourselves, how it cometh to pass that so many rational, wise and learned men miss Christ, whilst the simple and illiterate, even babes in natural knowledge, obtain interest in him, and salvation by him. The reason hereof is plainly given us by Christ, in Matth. xiii. 11. " To you it is given to know the " mysteries of the kingdom of heaven, but to them it is not given." It is the dropping and dews of divine teaching upon one, and not upon another, that dryeth up the green tree, and maketh the dry tree to flourish. Many natural men have very fine brains, searching wits, solid judgments, nimble fancies, tenacious memories; they can search out the mysteries of nature, solve the *phænomena*, satisfy the enquiries of the most curious; they can measure the earth, discover the motions of the heavens; but after all take up their place in hell, when, in the mean time, *the statutes of the Lord* (by the help of his teachings) *make wise the simple*, Psal. xix. 17. It is no matter how dull and incapable the scholar be, if God undertake to be the teacher. I remember, Austin speaks of one who was commonly reputed a fool, and yet he could not but judge him to be truly godly, and that by two signs of grace which appeared in him; one was, his seriousness when he heard any discourses of Christ; the other was, his indignation manifested against sin. It was truly said by those two Cardinals, (who, riding to the council of Constance, overheard a poor shepherd in the fields with tears bewailing his sins) *Surgent indocti et rapient cœlum;* The unlearned will rise and take heaven, whilst we with all our learning shall descend into hell.

Inf. 3. This also informs us of the true reason of the strange and various successes of the gospel upon the souls of men. Here we see why the ministry of one man becomes fruitful, and another's barren; yea why the labours of the same poor man prosper exceedingly at one time, and not at another; these things are according as the teachings of God do accompany our teachings. We often see a weaker and plainer discourse blessed with success, whilst that which is more artificial, neat and laboured, comes to nothing. St. Austin hath a pretty similitude to illustrate this; Suppose, saith he, two *conduits*, the one very plain, the other curiously carved and adorned with images of lions, eagles, &c. the water doth not refresh and nourish as it cometh from such a curious *conduit*, but as it is water. Where we find most of man, we frequently find least of God. I speak not this to encourage carelessness and laziness, but to provoke the dispensers of the gospel to more earnestness and frequent prayer for the assistance and blessing of the Spirit upon their labours, and to make men less fond of their own gifts and abilities; blear-eyed Leah may bear children, when beautiful Rachel proves barren.

Inf. 4. Learn hence the transcendent excellency of saving, spiritual knowledge, above that which is merely literal and natural. One drop of knowledge taught by God, is more excellent than the whole ocean of human knowledge and acquired gifts, Phil. iii. 8. John xvii. 3. 1 Cor. ii. 2. Let no man therefore be dejected at the want of those gifts with which unsanctified men are adorned. If God have taught thee the evil of sin, the worth of Christ, the necessity of regeneration, the mystery of faith, the way of communion with God in duties; trouble not thyself because of thine ignorance in natural or moral things : thou hast that, reader, which will bring thee to heaven; and he is a truly wise man that knows the way of salvation, though he be ignorant and unskilful in other things : thou knowest those things which all the learned doctors and libraries in the world could never teach thee, but God hath revealed them to thee; others have more *science,* thou hast more *savour* and sweetness; bless God, and be not discouraged.

Second use for examination.

If there be no coming to Christ without the teachings of the Father : then it greatly concerns us to examine our own hearts, whether ever we have been under the saving teachings of God, during the many years we have sat under the preaching of the gospel. Let not the question be mistaken; I do not ask what books you have read, what ministers you have heard, what stock of natural or speculative knowledge you have acquired; but the question is, whether ever God spake to your hearts, and hath effectually taught you such lessons, as were mentioned in our last discourse? O there is a vast difference betwixt that notional, speculative, and traditional knowledge which man learneth from men, and that spiritual, operative, and transforming knowledge which a man learneth from God. If you ask how the teachings of God may be discerned from all other mere human teachings; I answer, they may be discerned, and distinguished by these six signs.

Sign 1. *The teachings of God are very humbling to the soul that is taught.* Human knowledge puffeth up, 1 Cor. viii. 1. but the teachings of God do greatly abase the soul, Job xlii. 5. " I have " heard of thee by the hearing of the ear, but now mine eye seeth " thee; wherefore I abhor myself, and repent in dust and ashes :"

the same light which discovers to us the holiness, justice, greatness, and goodness of God, discovereth also the vileness, baseness, emptiness, and total unworthiness of men; yea, of the best and holiest of men, Isa. vi. 5.

Sign 2. *The teachings of God are deeply affecting and impressive teachings;* they fully reach the heart of man, Hos. ii. 14. " I will " allure her, and bring her into the wilderness, and speak com- " fortably unto her;" or, as it is in the Hebrew, I will speak to her heart. When God sheweth unto man the evil of sin, he so convinceth the soul, that no creature-comforts have any pleasure or sweetness in them; and when he sheweth unto man his righteousness, pardon, and peace in Christ, he so comforteth and refresheth the heart, that no outward afflictions have any weight or bitterness in them: one drop of consolation from heaven, sweetens a sea of trouble upon earth, Psal. xciv. 19. " In the multitude of my " thoughts within me, thy comforts delight my soul."

Sign 3. *The teachings of God are sanctifying and renewing teachings;* they reform and change the heart, Eph. iv. 21, 22, 23. " If so be that you have heard him, and been taught by him, as the " truth is in Jesus; that ye put off concerning the former conver- " sation the old man, which is corrupt, according to the deceitful " lusts: and be renewed in the spirit of your mind," &c. See here what holiness and purity are the effect of divine teaching! Holiness, both external and internal, negative and positive: holiness of every kind follows the Father's teachings: all the discoveries God makes to us of himself in Christ, have an assimilating quality, and change the soul into their own likeness, 2 Cor. iii. 18.

Sign 4. *All God's teachings are practical, producing obedience.* Idle notions and useless speculations are not learned from God. As God's creating words, so his teaching words are with effect: as when he said, " Let there be light, and there was light:" so when he saith to the soul, Be comforted, be humbled; it is effectually comforted, Isa. lxvi. 13. it is humbled, Job xl. 4, 5. As God hath in nature made no creature in vain, so he speaks no word in vain: every thing which men hear, or learn from the Father, is for use, practice, and benefit to the soul.

Sign 5. *All teachings of God are agreeable with the written word:* The Spirit of God, and the word of God do never jar, John xiv. 26. " He shall take of mine, and shew it unto you." When God speaketh unto the heart of man, whether in a way of conviction, consolation, or instruction in duty, he always either maketh use of the express words of scripture, or speaks to the heart in language every way consentaneous and agreeable to scripture: So that the written word becomes the *standard* to weigh and try all divine teachings, Isa. viii. 20. " To the law, and to the testimony: If

" they speak not according to this word, it is because there is no
" light (or morning) in them." Whatever is disagreeing or jarring
with the scripture must not pass for an inspiration of God, but a
deluding sophism, and insinuation of Satan.

Sign 6. *The teachings of God are very satisfying teachings to the
soul of man:* The understanding faculty, like a *dial*, is enlightened
with the beams of divine truth shining upon it: this no man's teachings can do: Men can only teach *objectively*, by propounding truth
to the understanding; but they cannot enlighten the faculty itself,
as God doth, 1 John v. 20. He giveth man understanding as well as
instructions, to be understood; he opens the eyes of the understanding, as well as propoundeth the object, Eph. i. 18. And thus
we may discern and distinguish the teachings of God from all
other teachings.

Third use of exhortation.

The last use I shall make of this point, shall be a word of *exhortation*, both to them that never were yet effectually taught of God,
and to them also that have heard his voice, and are come to
Christ.

First, To those that never yet heard the voice of God speaking
to their hearts; and truly this is the general case of most men and
women, in the professing world: They have heard the sound of
the gospel, but it hath been a confused, empty, and ineffectual
sound in their ears; they have heard the voice of man, but have
never yet heard the voice of God. The gifts and abilities of preachers have, in a notional and mere human way, improved their understandings, and sometimes slightly touched their affections: All
this is but the effect of man upon man. O that you would look
for something which is beyond all this: satisfy not yourselves with
what is merely natural and human in ordinances; come to the
word with higher ends and more spiritual designs, than to get some
notions of truth which you had not before, or to judge the gifts
and abilities of the speaker: If God speak not to your hearts, all
the ordinances in the world can do you no good, 1 Cor. iii. 7. O
remember what a solemn and awful thing it is to come to those
ordinances, and attend upon that ministration, in and by which the
eternal decrees of heaven are to be executed upon your souls,
which must be to you the " savour of life unto life, or of death
" unto death;" Wrestle with God by prayer for a blessing upon the
ordinances. Say, Lord, speak thyself to my heart, let me hear
" thy voice, and feel thy power in this prayer, or in this sermon:
" Others have heard thy voice, cause me to hear it: It had been
" much better for me if I had never heard the voice of preachers,
" except I hear thy voice in them."

Secondly, Let all those that have heard the voice of God, and

are come to Christ in the virtue of his teachings, admire the wonderful condescension of God to them.   O that God should speak
to thy soul, and be silent to others! There be many thousands
living at this day under ordinances, to whom the Lord hath not
given an ear to hear, nor an heart to obey, Deut. xxix. 4. "To you
" it is given to know the mysteries of the kingdom of heaven, but
" to them it is not given," Mat. xiii. 11.   And I beseech you, walk
as men and women that have been taught of God.   When Satan
and your corruptions tempt you to sin, and to walk in the ways of
the carnal and careless world; remember then that scripture, Eph.
iv. 20, 21. " But ye have not so learned Christ, if so be that you
" have heard him, and have been taught by him, as the truth is in
" Jesus."   To conclude, see that you be exceeding humble, and
lowly in spirit.   Humility qualifies you for divine teachings, Psal.
xxv. 9. *The meek he will teach;* and the more ye are taught of
God, the more humble you will still be.

And thus you see, that no man can come to Christ without the
application of the law, and *the teachings of the Father;* which being
considered, may be very useful to convince us, (which indeed is the
design of it) that among the multitudes of men and women, living
under the ordinances of God, and the general profession of religion,
there are but few, very few to be found, who have effectually received the Lord Jesus Christ by saving faith.

And now, reader, I suppose by this time thou art desirous to
know by what signs and evidences thy union with Christ by faith
may be cleared up, and made evident to thee; and how that great
question, whether thou hast yet effectually applied Christ to thy
soul or no, may be clearly decided; which brings me to the third
general use of the whole, viz.

The examination of our interest in Christ, by

1. The donation of the Spirit, from 1 John iii. 24.
2. The new creation, from 2 Cor. v. 17.
3. The mortification of sin, from Gal. v. 24.
4. The imitation of Christ, from 1 John ii. 6.

Of each of these trials of our interest in Christ I shall speak in
their order: And, first, of the donation of the Spirit.

SERMON XXIV.

Of the Manner and Importance of the SPIRIT's Indwelling.

1 JOHN iii. 24.

——*And hereby we know that he abideth in us, by the Spirit which he hath given us.*

THE apostle in this chapter is engaged in a very trying discourse; his scope is to discriminate the spirits and states of sincere believers, from merely nominal and pretended Christians; which he attempts not to do by any thing that is external, but by the internal effects and operations of the Spirit of God upon their hearts. His enquiry is not into those things which men profess, or about the duties which they perform, but about the frames and tempers of their hearts, and the principles by which they are acted in religion. According to this test, he puts believers upon the search and study of their own hearts; calls them to reflect upon the effects and operations of the Spirit of God, wrought within their own souls, assuring them, that these gracious effects, and the fruits of the Spirit in their hearts, will be a solid evidence unto them of their union with Jesus Christ, amounting to much more than a general, conjectural ground of hope, under which it is possible there may *subesse falsum*, lurk a dangerous and fatal mistake: But the gracious effects of the Spirit of God within them, are a foundation upon which they may build the certainty and assurance of their union with Christ: *Hereby we know that he abideth in us, by the Spirit which he hath given us.* In which words we have three things to consider, viz.

1. The thing to be tried, our union with Christ.
2. The trial of it, by the giving of his Spirit to us.
3. The certainty of the trial this way: *Hereby we know,*

First, The thing to be tried; which is indeed the greatest and weightiest matter that can be brought to trial in this world, or in that to come, namely, our union with Christ, expressed here by *his abiding in us;* a phrase clearly expressing the difference betwixt those who, by profession and common estimation, pass for Christians among men, though they have no other union with Christ, but by an *external adhesion* to him in the external duties of religion, and those whose union with Christ is real, vital, and permanent, by the indwelling of the Spirit of Christ in their souls. John xv. 5, 6. opens the force and importance of this phrase, " I am the " vine, ye are the branches; he that abideth in me and I in him,

" the same bringeth forth much fruit: If a man abide not in me, he
" is cast forth as a branch, and is withered." The thing then
to be tried is, Whether we stand in Christ as dead branches in a
living stock, which are only bound to it by external ligatures or
bonds that hold them for a while together; or whether our souls
have a vital union and coalition with Christ, by the participation of
the living sap of that blessed root?

Secondly, The trial of this union, which is by the *giving of the
Spirit to us:* The Spirit of Christ is the very bond of union betwixt
him and our souls. I mean not that the very person of the Spirit
dwelleth in us, imparting his *essential properties* to us; it were a rude
blasphemy so to speak; but his saving influences are communicated
to us in the way of sanctifying operations; as the sun is said to
come into the house, when his beams and comforting influence
come there. Nor yet must we think that the graces or influences
of the Spirit abide in us in the self-same measure and manner they
do in Christ; " for God giveth not the Spirit to him by measure;"
in him all fulness dwells. He is anointed with the Spirit above
his fellows; but there are measures and proportions of grace differently communicated to believers by the same Spirit; and these
communicated graces, and real operations of the Spirit of grace in
our hearts, do undoubtedly prove the reality of our union with
Christ; as the communication of the self-same vital juice or sap of
the stock, to the branch whereby it lives, and brings forth fruit
of the same kind, certainly proves it to be a real part or a member
of the same tree.

Thirdly, Which brings us to a third thing; namely, the certainty of the trial this way, εν τϗτω γινωσκομεν, in this, or by *this we
know:* We so know that we cannot be deceived. To clear this,
let us consider two things in grace, viz.

1. Somewhat *constitutive,* }
2. Somewhat *manifestative,* } of its being.

There is something in grace which is essential, and *constitutive* of
its being; and somewhat that flows from grace, and is *manifestative*
of such a being: We cannot immediately and intuitively discern
the essence of grace, as it is in its simple nature. So God only
discerns it, who is the author of it; but we may discern it *mediately*
and *secondarily,* by the effects and operations of it. Could we see
the simple essence of grace, or intuitively discern our union with
Christ, our knowledge would be *demonstrative, a priori ad posterius,*
by seeing effects, as they are lodged in the cause: But we come to
know the being of grace, and the reality of our union with Christ,
a posteriori, by ascending in our knowledge from the effects and
operations, to their true cause and being.

And, accordingly, God hath furnished us with a power of self-intuition and reflection; whereby we are able to turn it upon our own hearts, and make a judgment upon ourselves, and upon our own acts.   The soul hath not only power to *project*, but a power also to *reflect* upon its own actions; not only to put forth a *direct act* of faith upon Jesus Christ, but to judge and discern that act also, 2 Tim. i. 12. *I know whom I have believed:* And this is the way in which believers attain their certainty and knowledge of their union with Christ: from hence the observation will be,

Doct. *That interest in Christ may be certainly gathered and concluded from the gift of the Spirit to us:* " No man (saith the apostle) " hath seen God at any time; if we love one another, God dwelleth " in us, and his love is perfected in us: Hereby know we that we " dwell in him, and he in us, because he hath given us of his " Spirit," 1 John iv. 12, 13.   The being of God is invisible, but the operations of his Spirit in believers, are sensible and discernable.   The soul's union with Christ is a supernatural mystery, yet it is discoverable by the effects thereof, which are very perceptible in and by believers.

Two things require explication and confirmation in the doctrinal part of this point.

1. What the giving of the Spirit imports and signifies.

2. How it evidences the soul's interest in Jesus Christ.

First, As to the import of this phrase, we are to enquire what is meant by the Spirit, and what by the giving of the Spirit.

Now the Spirit is taken in scripture two ways, viz.

Essentially, or personally.

In the first sense it is put for the Godhead, 1 Tim. iii. 16. *Justified in the Spirit,* i. e. By the power of his divine nature, which raised him from the dead.   In the second sense it denotes the third person, or subsistence in the glorious and blessed Trinity; and to him this word *Spirit* is attributed, sometimes *properly* in the sense before-mentioned, as denoting his *personality;* at other times *metonymically,* and then it is put for the effects, fruits, graces, and gifts of the Spirit communicated by him unto men, Eph. v. 11. *Be ye filled with the Spirit.*   Now the fruits or gifts of the Spirit are either,

1. Common and assisting gifts: Or,

2. Special and sanctifying gifts.

In the last sense and signification, it must be taken in this place; for, as to the common assisting and ministering gifts of the Spirit, they are bestowed promiscuously upon one as well as another; such gifts in an excellent degree and a large measure, are found in the unregenerate, and therefore can never amount to a solid evidence of the soul's union with Christ: but his special sanctifying gifts, being the proper effect and consequent of that union, must needs strongly prove and confirm it.   In this sense therefore we are to understand *the Spirit* in this place; and by *giving the Spirit to us*, we are to understand more than the *coming of the Spirit upon us :* The Spirit of God is said to come upon men in a transient way, for their present assistance in some particular service, though in themselves they be unsanctified persons: Thus *the Spirit of God came upon Balaam*, Num. xxiv. 2. enabling him to prophesy of things to come: And, although those extraordinary gifts of the Spirit be now ceased, yet the Spirit ceaseth not to give his ordinary assistances unto men, both regenerate and unregenerate, 1 Cor. xii. 8, 9, 10, 31. compared: But, whatever gifts he gives to others, he is said to *be given, to dwell,* and *to abide* only in believers, 1 Cor. iii. 6. " Know ye not that ye are the temple of " God, and that the Spirit of God dwelleth in you?" An expression denoting both his special property in them, and gracious familiarity with them.   There is a great difference betwixt the *assisting* and the *indwelling* of the Spirit; the one is *transient*, the other *permanent.*   That is a good rule the schoolmen give us, *Illa tantum dicuntur inesse, quæ insunt per modum quietis :* those things are only said to be in a man, which were in him by way of rest and permanency, and so the Spirit is in believers: Therefore they are said *to live in the Spirit*, Gal. v. 25. to be *led by the Spirit,* ver. 18. to be in the Spirit, and the Spirit to dwell in them, Rom. viii. 9.   And so much of the first thing to be opened, viz. What we are to understand by the giving of the Spirit.

Secondly, In the next place we are to enquire and satisfy ourselves, how this giving of the Spirit evidently proves and strongly concludes that soul's interest in Christ unto whom he is given: and this will evidently appear by the consideration of these five particulars.

1. The Spirit of God in believers is the very bond by which they are united unto Christ: If therefore we find in ourselves the bond of union, we may warrantably conclude, that we have union with Jesus Christ: This is evidently held forth in those words of Christ, John xvii. 22, 23. " The glory which thou gavest me, " have I given them, that they may be one, even as we are one. " I in them and thou in me, that they may be made perfect in " one, and that the world may know that thou hast sent me, and " hast loved them as thou hast loved me." It is the glory of Christ's human nature to be united to the Godhead: " This " (said Christ) thou gavest me, and the glory thou gavest me, I " have given them," i. e. By me they are united unto thee. And how this is done, he sheweth us more particularly, *I in them ;* there is Christ in us, viz. *mystically :* And *thou in me ;* there is God in Christ, viz. *hypostatically :* So that in Christ, God and be-

lievers meet in a blessed union: It is Christ's glory to be one with God; it is our glory to be one with Christ, and with God by him: But how is this done? Certainly no other way but by the giving of his Spirit unto us; for so much the phrase, *I in them*, must needs import: Christ is in us by the sanctifying Spirit, which is the bond of our union with him.

Secondly, The scripture every where makes this giving, or indwelling of the Spirit, the great mark and trial of our interest in Christ; concluding from the presence of it in us, *positively*, as in the text; and from the absence of it, *negatively*, as in Rom. viii. 9. " Now if any man have not the Spirit of Christ, the same is none " of his," Jude, ver. 19. " Sensual, not having the Spirit." This mark therefore agreeing to all believers, and to none but believers, and that always, and at all times, it must needs clearly infer the soul's union with Christ, in whomsoever it is found.

Thirdly, That which is a certain mark of our freedom from the covenant of works, and our title to the privileges of the covenant of grace, must needs also infer our union with Christ, and special interest in him; but the giving or indwelling of the sanctifying Spirit in us, is a certain mark of our freedom from the *first covenant*, under which all Christless persons still stand, and our title to the special privileges of the *second covenant*, in which none but the members are interested; and, consequently, it fully proves our union with the Lord Jesus. This is plain from the *apostle's* reasoning, Gal. iv. 6, 7. " And because ye are sons, God hath sent forth the " spirit of his Son into your hearts, crying, Abba Father: Where- " fore thou art no more a servant, but a son: and if a son, then " an heir of God, through Christ." The spirit of the first covenant was a servile spirit, a spirit of fear and bondage, and they that were under that covenant were not *sons*, but *servants;* but the spirit of the new covenant is a free, ingenuous spirit, acting in the strength of God, and those that do so, are the children of God; and children inherit the blessed privileges and royal immunities contained in that great charter, the covenant of grace: they are *heirs of God,* and the evidence of this their inheritance, by virtue of the second covenant, and of freedom from the servitude and bondage of the first covenant, is *the Spirit of Christ in their hearts, crying, Abba Father;* So Gal. v. 18. " If ye be led by the Spirit, " ye are not under the law."

Fourthly, If the eternal decree of God's electing love be executed, and the virtues and benefits of the death of Christ applied by the Spirit, unto every soul in whom he dwelleth, as a spirit of sanctification; then such a giving of the Spirit unto us must needs be a certain mark and proof of our special interest in Christ; but the decree of God's electing love is executed, and the benefits of the blood

of Christ are applied to every soul in whom he dwelleth, as a spirit of sanctification. This is plain from 1 Pet. i. 2. " Elect accord-
" ing to the foreknowledge of God the Father, through sanctifica-
" tion of the Spirit unto obedience, and sprinkling of the blood of
" Jesus Christ:" Where you see both God's election executed,
and the blood of Jesus sprinkled or applied unto us by the Spirit,
which is given to us as a Spirit of sanctification. There is a blessed order of working observed as proper to each person in the Godhead; the Father electeth, the Son redeemeth, the Spirit sanctifieth. The Spirit is the last efficient in the work of our salvation;
what the Father decreed, and the Son purchased, that the Spirit
applieth; and so puts the last hand to the complete salvation of
believers. And this some divines give as the reason why the sin
against the Spirit is unpardonable, because he being the last agent,
in order of working, if the heart of a man be filled with enmity against the Spirit, there can be no remedy for such a sin;
there is no looking back to the death of Christ, or to the love of
God for remedy. This sin against the Spirit is that *obex infernalis*,
the deadly stop and bar to the whole work of salvation; Oppositely,
where the Spirit is received, obeyed, and dwelleth in the way of
sanctification; into that soul the eternal love of God, the inestimable benefits of the blood of Christ run freely, without any interruption; and, consequently, the interest of such a soul in Jesus
Christ is beyond all dispute.

Fifthly, The giving of the Spirit to us, or his residing in us, as
a sanctifying Spirit, is every where in scripture made the pledge
and earnest of eternal salvation, and consequently must abundantly
confirm and prove the soul's interest in Christ, Eph. i. 13, 14.
" In whom also after that ye believed, ye were sealed with that
" holy Spirit of promise; which is the earnest of our inheritance,"
&c. So, 2 Cor. i. 22. " who hath also sealed us, and given the
" earnest of the Spirit in our hearts." And thus you have the
point opened and confirmed. The use of all followeth:

Use. Now the only use I make of this point shall be that which
lieth directly, both in the view of the text, and of the design for
which it was chosen; namely, by it to try and examine the truth
of our interest in, and the validity of our claim to Jesus Christ. In
pursuance of which design, I shall first lay down some general rules,
and then propose some particular trials.

First, I shall lay down some general rules for the due information of our minds in this point, upon which so much depends.

Rule 1. *Though the Spirit of God be given to us, and worketh in
us, yet he worketh not as a natural and necessary, but as a free and
arbitrary agent:* He neither assists, nor sanctifies, as the fire burn-
eth, *ad ultimum sui posse,* as much as he can assist or sanctify, but as

much as he pleaseth : dividing to every man severally as he will," 1 Cor. xii. 11.   Bestowing greater measures of gifts and graces upon some than upon others ; and assisting the same person more at one season than another ; and all this variety of operation floweth from his own good pleasure.   His grace is his own, he may give it as he pleaseth.

Rule 2. There is a great difference in the manner of the Spirit's working before and after the work of regeneration.   Whilst we are unregenerate, he works upon us as upon dead creatures that work not at all with him ; and what motion there is in our souls, is a counter-motion to the Spirit ; but after regeneration it is not so, he then works upon a complying and willing mind ; we work, and he assists, Rom. viii. 26.   Our conscience witnesseth, and he beareth witness with it, Rom. viii. 16.   It is therefore an error of dangerous consequence to think that sanctified persons are not bound to stir and strive in the way of duty, without a sensible impulse, or preventing motion of the Spirit, Isa. lxiv. 7.

Rule 3. Though the Spirit of God be given to believers, and worketh in them, yet believers themselves may do or omit such things as may obstruct the working, and obscure the very being of the Spirit of God in them.   Ita notis tractat, ut a nobis tractatur : He dealeth with us in his evidencing and comforting work, as we deal with him in point of tenderness and obedience to his dictates ; there is a grieving, yea, there is a quenching of the Spirit by the lusts and corruptions of those hearts in which he dwelleth ; and though he will not forsake his habitation, as a Spirit of sanctification, yet he may for a time desert it as a Spirit of consolation, Psal. li. 11.

Rule 4. Those things which discover the indwelling of the Spirit in believers are not so much the matter of their duties, or substance of their actions, as the more secret springs, holy aims, and spiritual manner of their doing or performing of them.   It is not so much the matter of a prayer, the neat and orderly expressions in which it is uttered, as the inward sense and spiritual design of the soul ; it is not the choice of elegant words, whereby our conceptions are clothed, or the copiousness of the matter with which we are furnished, for even a poor stammering tongue, and broken language, may have much of the Spirit of God in it.   This made Luther say, he saw more excellency in the duty of a plain rustic Christian, than in all the triumphs of Cæsar and Alexander.   The beauty and excellency of spiritual duties is an inward hidden thing.

Rule 5. All the motions and operations of the Spirit are always harmonious, and suitable to the written word, Isa. viii. 20.   " To the " law and to the testimony, if they speak not according to this word, " it is because there is no light in them."   The scriptures are by the inspiration of the Spirit, therefore this inspiration into the hearts of believers must either substantially agree with the scriptures, or the inspiration of the Spirit be self-repugnant, and contradictory to itself. It is very observable, that the works of grace wrought by the Spirit in the hearts of believers, are represented to us in scripture, as a transcript, or copy of the written word, Jer. xxxi. 33. " I will write my law in their hearts." Now, as a true copy answers the original, word for word, letter for letter, point for point; so do the works of the Spirit in our souls harmonize with the dictates of the Spirit in the scriptures; whatsoever motion therefore shall be found repugnant thereto, must not be fathered upon the Spirit of God, but laid at the door of its proper parents, the spirit of error and corrupt nature.

Rule 6. *Although the works of the Spirit, in all sanctified persons, do substantially agree, both with the written word, and with one another, (as ten thousand copies, penned from one original, must needs agree within themselves;) yet as to the manner of infusion and operation, there are found many circumstantial differences.* The Spirit of God doth not hold one and the same method of working upon all hearts: The work of grace is introduced into some souls with more terror and trouble for sin, than it is in others; he wrought upon Paul one way, upon Lydia in another way; he holds some much longer under terrors and troubles than he doth others; inveterate and more profane sinners find stronger troubles for sin, and are held longer under them, than those are, into whose heart grace is more early and insensibly infused by the Spirit's blessing upon religious education; but as these have less trouble than the other at first, so commonly they have less clearness, and more doubts and fears about the work of the Spirit afterwards.

Rule 7. *There is a great difference found betwixt the sanctifying and the comforting influences of the Spirit upon believers, in respect of constancy and permanency.* His sanctifying influences abide for ever in the soul, they never depart; but his comforting influences come and go, and abide not long upon the hearts of believers. Sanctification belongs to the being of a Christian, consolation only to his well-being: The first is fixed and abiding, the latter various and inconstant. Sanctification brings us to heaven hereafter, consolation brings heaven unto us here; our safety lies in the former, our cheerfulness only in the latter. There are times and seasons, in the lives of believers, wherein the Spirit of God doth more signally and eminently seal their spirits, and ravish their hearts with joy unspeakable. But what Bernard speaketh is certainly true in the experience of Christians: " * It is a sweet hour, and it is but

---

* *Rara hora, brevis mora; sapit quidem suavissime, sed gustatur rarissime.* Bern.

" an hour ; a thing of short continuance : the relish of it is exceed-
" ing sweet, but it is not often that Christians taste it." And so
much may suffice for the general rules about the inbeing and workings of the Spirit in believers, for the better information of our
understandings, and prevention of mistakes in this matter : I shall
next, according to promise, lay down the particular marks and
trials by which we may discern whether God hath given us his
Spirit or no, by which grown Christians, when they are in a due
composed frame, may, by the assistance of the Spirit of God, (for
which therefore they are bound to pray), discern his indwelling and
working in themselves.

 Evidence 1. *In whomsoever the Spirit of Christ is a Spirit of
sanctification, to that man or woman he hath been, more or less, a
Spirit of conviction and humiliation.* This is the order which the
Spirit constantly observes in adult or grown converts, John xvi. 8,
9. " And when he is come, he will reprove the world of sin, and of
" righteousness, and of judgment : of sin because they believe not
" on me." This, you see, is the method he observes all the world
over ; he shall reprove or convince the world of sin. Conviction of
sin hath the same respect unto sanctification, as the blossoms of trees
have to the fruits that follow them : A blossom is but *fructus imperfectus, et ordinabilis ;* an imperfect fruit in itself, and in order to a
more perfect and noble fruit. Where there are no blossoms, we can
expect no fruit ; and where we see no conviction of sin, we can expect no conversion to Christ. Hath then the Spirit of God been a
Spirit of conviction to thee ? Hath he more particularly convinced
thee of sin, because thou hast not believed on him ? i. e. hath he
shewn thee thy sin and misery, as an unbeliever ? Not only terrified and affrighted thy conscience with this or that more notorious
act of sin, but fully convinced thee of the state of sin that thou art
in by reason of thy unbelief, which, holding thee from Christ,
must needs also hold thee under the guilt of all thy other sins.
This gives, at least, a strong probability that God hath given thee
his Spirit, especially when this conviction remains day and night
upon thy soul, so that nothing but Christ can give it rest, and
consequently the great enquiry of thy soul is after Christ, and none
but Christ.

 Evidence 2. *As the Spirit of God hath been a convincing, so he is
a quickening Spirit, to all those to whom he is given ;* Rom. viii. 2.
" The law of the Spirit of life in Christ Jesus hath made me free
" from the law of sin and death :" He is the Spirit of life, i. e. the
principle of spiritual life in the souls whom he inhabiteth ; for,
uniting them to Christ, he unites them to the fountain of life ; and
this spiritual life, in believers, manifests itself as the natural life
doth in vital actions and operations. When the Spirit of God

comes into the soul of a man that was dead and senseless under sin,
" O (saith he) now I begin to feel the weight and load of sin,
" Rom. vii. 24. now I begin to hunger and thirst after Christ
" and his ordinances, 1 Pet. ii. 2. now I begin to breathe after
" God in spiritual prayer," Acts ix. 11. Spiritual life hath its
spiritual senses, and suitable operations. O think upon this you
that cannot feel any burden in sin, you that have no hungerings
or thirstings after Christ; how can the Spirit of God be in you?
I do not deny but there may, at some times, be much deadness
and senselessness upon the hearts of Christians, but this is their
disease, not their nature; it is but at some times, not always, and
when it is so with them, they are burdened with it, and complain
of it as their greatest affliction in this world; their spirits are not
easy and at rest, in such a condition as yours are; their spirits are
as a bone out of joint, an arm dislocated, which cannot move
any way without pain.

Evidence 3. *Those to whom God giveth his Spirit have a tender
sympathy with all the interests and concernments of Christ.* This
must needs be so, if the same Spirit which is in Christ dwelleth also
in thy heart; if thou be a partaker of his Spirit, then what he loves,
thou lovest, and what he hateth, thou hatest. This is a very plain
case; even in nature itself, we find that the many members of the
same natural body being animated by one and the same spirit of
life, " whether one member suffer, all the members suffer with
" it; or one member be honoured, all the members rejoice with
" it: Now ye are the body of Christ, and members in particular,"
1 Cor. xii. 26, 27. For look, as Christ, the head of that body is
touched with a tender sense and feeling of the miseries and troubles
of his people, he is persecuted when they are persecuted, Acts ix.
4. so they that have the Spirit of Christ in them, cannot be without a deep and tender sense of the reproach and dishonours that
are done to Christ: This is " as it were a sword in their bones,"
Psal. xlii. 3. If his public worship cease, or the assemblies of his
people are scattered; it cannot but go to the hearts of all, in
whom the Spirit of Christ is: " They will be sorrowful for the so-
" lemn assemblies; the reproach of them will be a burden," Zeph.
iii. 18. Those that have the Spirit of Christ do not more earnestly
long after any one thing in this world, than the advancement of
Christ's interest by conversion and reformation in the kingdoms of
the earth, Psal. xlv. 3, 4. Paul could rejoice that Christ was
preached, though his own afflictions were increased, Phil. i. 16,
18. and John could rejoice that Christ increased, though he himself decreased; yet therein was his joy fulfilled, John iii. 29. So
certainly the concernments of Christ must and will touch that heart
which is the habitation of his Spirit. I cannot deny, but even a

good Baruch may be under a temptation to seek great things for himself, and be too much swallowed up in his own concernments, when God is plucking up and breaking down, Jer. xlv. 4, 5. But this is only the influence of a temptation: the true temper and spirit of a believer inclines him to sorrow and mourning, when things are in this sad posture: Ezek. ix. 4. " Go through the midst of " the city, through the midst of Jerusalem, and set a mark upon " the foreheads of the men that sigh, and that cry for all the " abominations that be done in the midst thereof."

O reader, lay thine hand upon thine heart: Is it thus with thee? Dost thou sympathize with the affairs and concernments of Christ in the world? or, carest thou not which way things go with the people of God, and gospel of Christ, so long as thine own affairs prosper, and all things are well with thee?

Evidence 4. *Wherever the Spirit of God dwelleth, he doth in some degree, mortify and subdue the evils and corruptions of the soul in which he resides.* This Spirit lusteth against the flesh, Gal. v. 7. and believers, " through the Spirit, do mortify the deeds of the body," Rom. viii. 13. This is one special part of his sanctifying work. I do not say he kills and subdues sin in believers, as that it shall never trouble or defile them any more: No; that freedom belongs to the perfect state in heaven, but its dominion is taken away, though its life be prolonged for a season. It lives in believers still, but not upon the provision they willingly make to fulfil the lust of it, Rom. xiii. 27. The design of every true believer, is co-incident with the design of the Spirit, to destroy and mortify corruption: They long after the extirpation of it, and are daily in the use of all sanctified means and instruments, to subdue and destroy it; the workings of their corruption are the afflictions of their souls, Rom. vii. 24. " O wretched man that I am, who shall deliver me " from the body of this death?" And there is no one thing that sweetens the thoughts of death to believers (except the sight and full enjoyment of God) more than their expected deliverance from sin doth.

Evidence 5. *Wherever the spirit of God dwelleth in the way of sanctification, in all such he is the Spirit of prayer and supplication,* Rom. viii. 26. " Likewise the Spirit also helpeth our infirmities, " for we know not what we should pray for as we ought, but the " Spirit itself maketh intercession for us, with groanings which " cannot be uttered:" Wherever he is poured out as the Spirit of *grace,* he is also poured out as the Spirit of *supplication,* Zech. xii. 10. His praying and his sanctifying influences are undivided. There is a threefold assistance that the Spirit gives unto sanctified persons in prayer. He helps them before they pray, by setting an edge upon their desires and affections: He helps them in prayer, by supplying matters of request to them, teaching them what they should ask of God: He assisteth them in the manner of prayer, supplying them with suitable affections, and helping them to be sincere in all their desires to God. It is he that humbles the pride of their hearts, dissolves, and breaks the hardness of their hearts; Out of deadness makes them lively; out of weakness makes them strong. He assisteth the spirits of believers after prayer, helping them to faith and patience, to believe, and wait for the returns and answers of their prayers. O reader, reflect upon thy duties, consider what spirituality, sincerity, humility, broken-heartedness, and melting affections after God, are to be found in thy duties: Is it so with thee? Or dost thou hurry over thy duties as an interruption to thy business and pleasures? Are they an ungrateful task, imposed upon thee by God, and thy own conscience? Are there no hungerings and thirstings after God in thy soul? Or, if there be any pleasure arising to thee out of prayer, is it not from the ostentation of thy gifts? If it be so, reflect sadly upon the carnal state of thy heart; these things do not speak the Spirit of grace and supplication to be given thee.

Evidence 6. *Wherever the Spirit of grace inhabits, there is an heavenly, spiritual frame of mind accompanying, and evidencing the indwelling of the Spirit,* Rom. viii. 5, 6. " For they that are after " the flesh, do mind the things of the flesh; but they that are after " the Spirit, the things of the Spirit: for to be carnally minded " is death: but to be spiritually minded is life and peace." **By** the mind, understand the musings, reasonings, yea, and the cares, fears, delights and pleasures of the soul, which follow the workings and meditations of the mind. As these are, so are we; if these be ordinarily and habitually taken up, and exercised about earthly things, then is the frame and state of the man carnal, and earthly: The workings of every creature follow the being and nature of it. If God, Christ, heaven, and the world to come, engage the thoughts and affections of the soul, and the temper of such a soul is spiritual, and the Spirit of God dwelleth there; this is the life of the regenerate, Phil. iii. 20. " Our conversation is in " heaven ;" and such a frame of heart is *life* and *peace :* A serene, placid, and most comfortable life. No pleasures upon earth, no gratifications of the senses, do relish and savour, as spiritual things do. Consider, therefore, which way thy heart ordinarily works, especially in thy solitudes and hours of retirement. These things will be a great evidence for, or against thy soul. David could say, "How precious are thy thoughts unto me, O God! " How great is the sum of them: if I should count them, they " are more in number than the sand ; when I awake, I am still " with thee," Psal. cxxxix. 17, 18. Yet it must be acknowledged, for the relief of weaker Christians, that there is a great difference and variety found in this matter, among the people of God: For the strength, steadiness, and constancy of a spiritual mind, result from the depth and improvement of sanotification: The more grace, still the more evenness, spirituality, and constancy there is in the motions of the heart after God. The minds of weak Christians are more easily entangled in earthly vanities, and more frequently diverted by inward corruptions; yet still there is a spiritual *Pondus*, inclination and bent of their hearts towards God; and the vanity and corruption which hinders their communion with him are their greatest grief and burthen under which they groan in this world.

Evidence 7. *Those to whom the Spirit of grace is given, are led by the Spirit*, Rom. viii. 14. "As many as are led by the Spirit of " God, they are the sons of God:" Sanctified souls give themselves up to the government and conduct of the Spirit; they obey his voice, beg his direction, follow his motions, deny the solicitations of flesh and blood, in obedience to him, Gal. i. 16. And they that do so, they are the sons of God. It is the office of the Spirit to guide us into all truth; and it is our great duty to follow his guidance. Hence it is, that in all enterprises and undertakings, the people of God so earnestly beg direction and counsel from him. " Lead me, O Lord, in thy righteousness, (saith David) make " thy way straight before my face," Psal. v. 8. They dare not, in doubtful cases, lean to their own understandings; yea, in points of duty, and in points of sin, they dare not neglect the one, or commit the other, against the convictions and persuasions of their own consciences; though troubles and sufferings be unavoidable in that path of duty, when they have balanced duties with sufferings, in their most serious thoughts, the conclusion and result will still be, it is better to obey God, than man, the dictates of the Spirit, rather than the counsels of flesh and blood.

But, before I leave this point, I reckon myself a debtor unto weak Christians, and shall endeavour to give satisfaction to some special doubts and fears, with which their minds are ordinarily entangled in this matter; for it is a very plain case, that many souls have the presence and sanctification of the Spirit without the evidence and comfort thereof. Divers thing are found in believers, which are so many fountains of fears and doubts to them. And,

Objection 1. First, I greatly doubt the Spirit of God is not in me, (saith a poor Christian) because of the great darkness and ignorance which clouds my soul; for I read, 1 John ii. 27. that he enlighteneth the soul which he inhabiteth. "The anointing which " ye have received of him abideth in you, and ye need not that

" any man teach you, but as the same anointing teacheth you of
" all things," &c. but alas, my understanding is weak and cloudy,
I have need to learn of the meanest of God's people : This only I
know, that I know nothing as I ought to know.

Sol. Two things are to be regarded in spiritual knowledge ; viz.
the quantity, and the efficacy thereof. Your condition doth not
so much depend upon the measures of knowledge ; for, haply, you
are under many natural disadvantages, and want those helps and
means of increasing knowledge, which others plentifully enjoy.
It may be you have wanted the helps of education, or have been
incumbered by the necessities and cares of the world, which have
allowed you but little leisure for the improvement of your minds :
But if that which you do know, be turned into practice and obedience, Col. i. 9, 10. If it have influence upon your hearts, and
transform your affections into a spiritual frame and temper, 2 Cor.
iii. 17, 18. If your ignorance humble you, and drive you to God
daily for the increase of knowledge, one drop of such knowledge
of Christ, and yourselves as this, is more worth than a sea of human, moral, unsanctified, and speculative knowledge.   Though
you know but little, yet that little, being sanctified, is of great
value : Though you know but little, time was when you knew
nothing of Jesus Christ, or the state of your own souls. In a word,
though you know but little, that little you do know will be still
increasing, " like the morning light, which shineth more and more
" unto the perfect day," Prov. iv. 18.   If thou knowest so much
as brings thee to Christ, thou shalt shortly be where thy knowledge
shall be as the light at noon-day.

Object. 2. I sometimes find my heart raised, and my affections
melted in duties, but I doubt it is in a natural way, and not from
the Spirit of God : could I be assured those motions of my heart
were from the Spirit of grace, and not merely a natural thing, it
would be a singular comfort and satisfaction to me.

Sol. First, Consider whether this be not the ground of your fear
and doubting, because you are fain to take pains in the way of
meditation, prayer, and other duties, to bring your hearts to relish
and savour the things of God ; whereas, it may be, you expect
your spiritual enlargements and comforts should flow in upon you
spontaneously, and drop from heaven immediately of their own
accord, without any pains or industry of yours.   Here may be,
(and probably is) a great mistake in this matter ; for the Spirit of
God works in the natural method, wherein affections use to be
raised, and makes use of such duties as meditation and prayer, as
instruments to do that work by, Ezek. xxxvi. 37.   So David was
forced to reason with, and chide his own heart, Psal. xlii. 5.   Thy

comfort and enlargement may nevertheless be the fruit of the Spirit, because God makes it spring up, and grow upon thy duties.

Secondly, Take this as a sure rule, Whatsoever rises from self, always aims at, and terminates in self. This stream cannot be carried higher than the fountain; if therefore thy aim, and end in striving for affections and enlargements in duty, be only to win applause from men, and appear to be what in reality thou art not, this, indeed, is the fruit of nature, and a very corrupt and hypocritical nature; but if thy heart be melted, or desire to be melted in the sense of the evil of sin, in order to the further mortification of it; and, under the apprehensions of the free grace and mercy of God in the pardon of sin, in order to the engaging of thy soul more firmly to him; if these, or such like, be thy ends and designs, or be promoted and furthered by thine enlargements and spiritual comforts, never reject them as the mere fruits of nature: A carnal root cannot bring forth such fruits as these.

Object. 3. Upon the contrary, spiritual deadness, and indisposedness to duties, and to those especially which are more secret, spiritual, and self-denying than others, is the ground upon which many spiritual souls, who are yet truly gracious, do doubt the indwelling of the Spirit in them. O, saith such a soul, if the Spirit of God be in me, Why is it thus? Could my heart be so dead, so backward and averse to spiritual duties? No; these things would be my meat and my drink, the delights and pleasures of my life.

Sol. First, These things indeed are very sad, and argue thy heart to be out of frame, as the body is, when it cannot relish the most desirable meats or drinks: But the question will be, how thy soul behaves itself in such a condition as this is? whether this be easy or burdensome to be borne by thee? * and if thou complain under it as a burden; then what pains thou takest to ease thyself, and get rid of it?

Secondly, Know also, that there is a great difference betwixt spiritual death, and spiritual deadness; the former is the state of the unregenerate, the latter is the disease and complaint of many thousand regenerate souls: If David had not felt it as well as thee, he would never have cried out nine times in the compass of one Psalm, *Quicken me, quicken me.* Besides,

Thirdly, Though it be *often,* it is not so *always* with thee; there are seasons wherein the Lord breaks in upon thy heart, enlarges thy affections, and sets thy soul at liberty; to which times thou wilt do well to have an eye, in these dark and cloudy days.

Object. 4. But the Spirit of God is the *comforter,* as well as a

---

* He who inclines to that which is good, and is averse to that which is evil, has a desire of pleasing God, though sometimes, being seduced by evil concupiscence, through infirmity he may commit that which is displeasing to God. *Daven.*

sanctifier: He doth not only enable men to believe, but after they
believe, he also seals them, Eph. i. 13. But I walk in darkness, and
am a stranger to the sealing and comforting work of the Spirit :
How therefore can I imagine the Spirit of God should dwell in me,
who go from day to day in the bitterness of my soul, mourning as
without the sun ?

Sol. There is a twofold sealing, and a two-fold comfort : The
Spirit sealeth both *objectively,* in the work of sanctification ; and
formally, in giving clear evidence of that work. Thou mayest be
sealed in the first, whilst thou art not yet sealed in the second sense :
If so, thy condition is safe, although it be at present uncomfortable. And, as to comfort, that also is of two sorts, .viz. *seminal,* or
actual: in the root, or in the fruit ; *Light is sown for the righteous,*
Psal. xcvii. 11. though the harvest to reap and gather in that joy
and comfort be not yet come. And there are many other ways
beside that of joy and comfort, whereby the indwelling of the Spirit may evidence itself in thy soul : If he do not enable thee to rejoice, yet if he enable thee sincerely to mourn for sin ; if he do not
enlarge thy heart in comfort, yet if he humble and purge thy heart
by sorrows : if he deny thee the *assurance of faith,* and yet give thee
the *dependence of faith,* thou hast no reason to call in question, or
deny the indwelling of the Spirit in thee for that cause.

Object. 5. But the apostle saith, " They that walk in the Spirit,
" do not fulfil the lusts of the flesh," Gal. v. 16. but I find myself
entangled, and frequently overcome by them : Therefore I doubt
the Spirit of God is not in me.

Sol. It is possible the ground of your doubting may be your mistake of the true sense and meaning of that scripture : It is not the
apostle's meaning in that place, that sin in believers doth not work,
tempt, and oftentimes overcome, and captivate them ; for then he
would contradict himself in Rom. vii. 23. where he thus complains, " But I see another law in my members, warring against
" the law of my mind, and bringing me into captivity to the law
" of sin which is in my members." But two things are meant by
that expression, " Ye shall not fulfil the lusts of the flesh."

First, That the principle of grace will give a check to sin in its
first motions, and cause it to miscarry in the womb, like an untimely birth, before it come to its full maturity ; it shall never be
able to gain the full consent of the will, as it doth in the unregenerate.

Secondly, If, notwithstanding all the opposition grace makes to
hinder the birth or commission of it, it doth yet prevail, and break
forth into act ; yet such acts of sin, as they are not committed
without *regret,* so they are followed with *shame, sorrow,* and true

repentance : And those very surprisals, and captivities of sin at one time, are made cautions and warnings to prevent it at another time If it be so with thee, thou dost not fulfil the lusts of the flesh.

And now, reader, upon the whole, if upon examination of thy heart by these rules, the Lord shall help thee to discern the saving work of the Spirit upon thy soul, and thereby thine interest in Christ, What a happy man or woman art thou! what pleasure will arise to thy soul from such a discovery! Look upon the frame of thine heart *absolutely* as it is in itself at present, or *comparatively,* with what once it was, and others still are, and thou wilt find enough to transport and melt thy heart within thee: Certainly this is the most glorious piece of workmanship that ever God wrought in the world upon any man, Eph. ii. 10. The Spirit of God is come down from heaven, and hath hallowed thy soul to be a temple for himself to dwell in; as he hath said, " I will dwell in them, and walk " in them, and I will be their God, and they shall be my people," 2 Cor. vii. 16. Moreover, this gift of the Spirit is a sure pledge and earnest of thy future glory: Time was, when there was no such work upon thy soul. And, considering the frame and temper of it, the total aversation, strong opposition, and rooted enmity that was in it; it is the wonder of wonders, that ever such a work as this should be wrought upon such a heart as thine: that ever the Spirit of God, whose nature is pure and perfect holiness, should chuse such an unclean, polluted, abominable heart to frame an habitation for himself there to dwell in; to say of thy soul (now his spiritual *temple)* as he once said of the material temple at Jerusalem, Psal. cxxxii. 13, 14. " The Lord hath chosen it, he hath de-" sired it for his habitation. This is my rest for ever: Here will " I dwell; for I have desired it." O what hath God done for thy soul!

Think, reader, and think again: Are there not many thousands in the world of more ingenuous, sweet, and amiable dispositions than thyself, whom yet the Spirit of God passeth by, and leaveth them as tabernacles for Satan to dwell in? Such a one thou lately wast, and hadst still remained, if God had not wrought for thee, beyond all the expectations and desires of thine own heart. O bless God that you have received not the spirit of the world, but the Spirit which is of God; that ye might know the things which are freely given unto you of God.

SERMON XXV.

Of the Nature and Necessity of the New Creature.

2 Cor. v. 17.

Therefore if any man be in Christ, he is a new creature : old things are passed away ; behold, all things are become new.

YOU have seen one trial of an interest in Christ, in our last discourse, namely, by the donation of the Spirit. We have here another trial of the same matter, from one of the greatest, and most noble effects of the Spirit upon our souls; namely, his work of renovation, or *new creation :* " If any man be in Christ, he is a new " creature." The apostle's scope in the immediate context, is to dissuade Christians from a carnal, sinful partiality, in their respects to men: Not to despise them after the manner of the world, according to the external differences, but the real internal worth and excellency that is in men. This the apostle presses by two arguments; one drawn from the end of Christ's death, ver. 15. which was to take off from these selfish designs and carnal ends by which the whole world is swayed. *Secondly,* From the *new spirit,* by which believers are actuated : they that are in Christ are to judge and measure all things by a new rule : " If any man be in Christ, " he is a new creature: Old things are passed away ;" q. d. we have done with that low, selfish spirit of the world, which was wholly governed by carnal interest ; we are now to judge by a new rule, to be actuated from a new principle, aim at a new and more noble end ; " Behold, all things are become new." In these words we have three general parts, to be distinctly considered, viz.

1. The great question to be determined, " If any man be in " Christ ?"

2. The rule by which it may be determined, viz. " he· is a new " creature."

3. This general rule more particularly explained, " Old things " are passed away ; behold, all things are become new."

First, We have here the great question to be determined, Whether a man be in Christ ? A question upon the determination whereof, we must stand, or fall for ever. By [*being in Christ*] the apostle doth not here mean the general profession of Christianity, which gives a man the *reputation* of an interest in him ; but by being in Christ, he means an interest in him, by *vital union* with his person, and real participation of his benefits. Now this is the question to be determined, the matter to be tried ; than which, nothing can be more solemn and important in the whole world.

Secondly, The rule by which this great question may be determined, viz. *The new creation;* " If any man be in Christ, he is a new " creature." By this rule all the titles and claims made to Christ in the professing world, are to be examined. [*If any man*] be he what he will, high or low, great or small, learned or illiterate, young or old, if he pretend interest in Christ, this is the standard by which he must be tried : if he be in Christ, he is *a new creature ;* and if he be not *a new creature,* he is not in Christ, let his endowments, gifts, confidence, and reputation be what they will : [*A new creature*] not new physically, he is the same person he was ; but a new creature, that is, a creature renewed by gracious principles, newly infused into him from above, which sway him and guide him in another manner, and to another end than ever he acted before ; and these gracious principles not being educed out of any thing which was pre-existent in man, but infused *de novo,* from above, are therefore called, in this place, a new creature : This is the rule by which our claim to Christ must be determined.

Thirdly, This general rule is here more particularly explained ; " Old things are passed away ; behold, all things are become " new." He satisfies not himself to lay down this rule concisely, or express it in general terms, by telling us, the man in Christ must be a new creature ; but more particularly, he shews us what this new creature is, and what the parts thereof are, viz. Both

1. The privative part ; " Old things are passed away."
2. The positive part thereof ; " All things are become new."

By old things, he means all those carnal principles, self-ends, and fleshly lusts belonging to the carnal state, or the old man: all these are *passed away ;* " * not simply, and perfectly, but only in " part at present, and wholly in hope and expectation hereafter." So much briefly of the privative part of the new creature, " Old " things are passed away." A word or two must be spoken of the *positive* part ; " All things are become new." He means not that the old faculties of the soul are abolished, and new ones created in their room ; but as our bodies may be said to be new bodies, by reason of their new endowments and qualities super-induced, and bestowed upon them in their resurrection, so our souls are now renewed by the infusion of new gracious principles into them, in the work of regeneration. These two parts, viz. the *privative* part, the passing away of old things ; and the *positive* part, the renewing of all things, do, betwixt them, comprize the whole nature of sanctification, which, in other scriptures, is expressed by equivalent phrases ; sometimes by putting off the old, and putting on

---

* *Non simpliciter, et perfecte, sed partim spe.* Estius in loc.

the new man, Eph. iv. 24. sometimes by dying unto sin, and living unto righteousness, Rom. vi. 11. which is the self-same thing
the apostle here intends, by the passing away of old things, and
making all things new. And because this is the most excellent,
glorious, and admirable work of the Spirit, which is, or can be
wrought upon man in this world; therefore the apostle asserts it
with an *ecce*, a note of special remark and observation, " Behold,
" all things are become new;" *q. d.* Behold and admire this sur-
prizing, marvellous change which God hath made upon men; they
are come out of darkness into his marvellous light, 1 Pet. ii. 9.
out of the old, as it were, into a new world; " Behold, all things
" are become new." Hence note,

Doct. *That God's creating of a new supernatural work of grace
in the soul of any man, is that man's sure, and infallible evidence of a saving interest in Jesus Christ.*

Suitable hereunto are those words of the apostle, Eph. iv. 20,
21, 22, 23, 24. " But ye have not so learned Christ; if so be that
" ye have heard him, and have been taught by him, as the truth
" is in Jesus: That ye put off, concerning the former conversation,
" the old man, which is corrupt, according to the deceitful lusts:
" and be renewed in the Spirit of your mind: and that ye put on
" the new man, which after God is created in righteousness and
" true holiness." Where we have, in other words of the same
importance, the very self-same description of the man that is in
Christ, which the apostle gives us in this text. Now, for the
opening and stating of this point, it will be necessary that I shew
you,

1. Why the regenerating work of the Spirit is called a new
creation.

2. In what respect every soul that is in Christ is renewed, or
made a new creature.

3. What are the remarkable properties and qualities of this
new creature.

4. The necessity of this new creation to all that are in Christ.

5. How this new creation evidences our interest in Christ.

6. And then apply the whole in the proper uses of it.

First, Why the regenerating work of the Spirit is called a new
creation. This must be our first enquiry. And, doubtless, the
reason of this appellation is the analogy, proportion, and similitude which is found betwixt the work of regeneration, and God's
work in the first creation. And their agreement and proportion
will be found in the following particulars.

First, The same almighty Author who created the world,

createth also this work of grace in the soul of man, 2 Cor. iv. 6. " God, who commanded the light to shine out of darkness, hath " shined into our hearts, to give the light of the knowledge of " the glory of God in the face of Jesus Christ." The same powerful word which created the natural, createth also the spiritual light. * It is equally absurd for any man to say, I make myself to repent, or to believe, as it is to say, I made myself to exist, and be.

Secondly, The first thing that God created in the natural world, was light, Gen. i. 3. and the first thing which God createth in the new creation, is the light of spiritual knowledge, Col. iii. 10. " And have put on the new man, which is renewed in knowledge " after the image of him that created him."

Thirdly, Creation is out of nothing; it requires no pre-existent matter; it doth not bring one thing out of another, but something out of nothing; it gives a being to that which before had no being: So it is also in the new creation, 1 Pet. ii. 9, 10. " Who hath " called you out of darkness into his marvellous light; which in " time past were not a people, but are now the people of God; " which had not obtained mercy, but now have obtained mercy." The work of grace is not educed out of the power and principles of nature, but it is a pure work of creation. The Heathen philosophers could neither understand, nor acknowledge the creation of the world, because that notion was repugnant to this maxim of reason, *ex nihilo nihil fit,* out of nothing, nothing can be made. Thus did they *insanire cum ratione,* befool themselves with their own reasonings; and after the same manner some great pretenders to reason among us, voting it an absurdity to affirm, that the work of grace is not virtually and potentially contained in nature, the new creation in the old.

Fourthly, It was the virtue and efficacy of the Spirit of God, which gave the natural world its being by creation; Gen. i. 2. the Spirit of God moved upon the face of the waters; it hovered over the *chaos,* as the wings of a bird do over her eggs, as the same word is rendered, Deut. xxxii. 11. cherishing, as it were by incubation, that rude mass by a secret quickening influence, by which it drew all creatures into their several forms, and particular natures: So it is in the new creation; a quickening influence must come from the Spirit of God, or else the new creation can never be formed in us; John iii. 8. " So is every one that is born of the " Spirit." And ver. 6. " That which is born of the Spirit, is " spirit."

---

* *Minus est, te fecisse hominem, quam sanctum,* i. e. We may sooner make ourselves men, than saints.

Fifthly, The word of God was the instrument of the first creation; Psal. xxxiii. 6, 9. "By the word of the Lord were the "heavens made, and all the host of them by the breath of his "mouth: For he spake, and it was done; he commanded, and "it stood fast." The word of God is also the instrument of the new creation, or work of grace in man; 1 Pet. i. 23. "Being "born again, not of corruptible seed, but of incorruptible; by "the word of God, which liveth, and abideth for ever." So James i. 18. "Of his own will begat he us, with the word of "truth." *Of his own will;* that was the impulsive cause; with the *word of truth;* that was the instrumental cause. Great respect and honour, love, and delight, is due to the word upon this account, that it is the instrument of our regeneration, or new creation.

Sixthly, The same power which created the world, still underprops and supports it in its being: the world owes its conservation, as well as its existence, to the power of God, without which it could not subsist one moment. Just so it is with the new creation, which entirely depends upon the preserving power, which first formed it; Jude ver. 1. "Preserved in Christ Jesus," and 1 Pet. i. 5. "Who are kept by the power of God, through faith, unto "salvation." As in a natural way "we live, move, and have our "being in God," Acts xvii. 28. so in a spiritual way, we continue believing, repenting, loving, and delighting in God; without whose continued influence upon our souls, we could do neither.

Seventhly, In a word, God surveyed the first creation with complacence and great delight; he beheld the works of his hands, and approved them as very good, Gen. i. 31. So this also in the second creation; nothing pleaseth and delights God more than the works of grace in the souls of his people. It is not an outward privilege of nature, or gift of providence, which commends any man to God; "Circumcision is nothing, and uncircumcision is nothing, but a new "creature," Gal. vi. 15. And thus you see upon what grounds the work of regeneration in man is stiled a new creature; which was the first thing to be opened.

Secondly, Next we must enquire, in what respects every soul that is in Christ is renewed, or made a new creature: and here we shall find a threefold renovation of every man that is in Christ, viz.

1. In his state and condition.
2. In his frame and constitution.
3. In his practice and conversation.

First, He is renewed in his state and condition: for he passeth from death to life in his justification, 1 John iii. 14. He was condemned by the law, he is now justified freely by grace, through the redemption which is in Christ: he was under the curse of the first covenant; he is under the blessing of the new covenant: he was afar off, but is now made nigh unto God; an alien, a stranger once, now of the household of God, Eph. ii. 12, 13. O blessed change, from a sad to a sweet and comfortable condition! " There " is therefore no condemnation to them which are in Christ Jesus," Rom. viii. 1.

Secondly, Every man in Christ is renewed in his frame and constitution; all the faculties and affections of his soul are renewed by regeneration: his understanding was dark, but now is light in the Lord, Eph. v. 8. his conscience was dead and secure, or full of guilt and horror, but is now become tender, watchful, and full of peace, Heb. ix. 14. his will was rebellious, stubborn, and inflexible; but is now made obedient and complying with the will of God, Psal. cx. 2. his desires did once pant and spend themselves in the pursuit of vanities, now they are set upon God, Isa. xxvi. 8. his love did fondly dote upon ensnaring earthly objects, now it is swallowed up in the infinite excellencies of God and Christ, Psal. cxix. 97. his joy was once in trifles and things of nought, now his rejoicing is in Christ Jesus, Phil. iii. 3. his fears once were about noxious creatures, now God is the object of the fear of reverence, Acts ix. 31. and sin the object of the fear of caution, 2 Cor. vii. 11. his hopes and expectations were only from the world present, but now from that to come, Heb. vi. 19. Thus the soul in its faculties and affections is renewed; which being done, the members and senses of the body must needs be destinated and employed by it in new services; no more to be the weapons of unrighteousness, but instruments of service to Jesus Christ, Rom. vi. 19. And thus all that are in Christ are renewed in their frame and constitution.

Thirdly, The man in Christ is renewed in his practice and conversation: the manner of operation always follows the nature of beings. Now the regenerate not being what they were, cannot walk and act as once they did; Eph. ii. 1, 2, 3. " And you hath " he quickened, who were once dead in trespasses and sins; " wherein ye walked according to the course of this world." They were carried away, like water by the strength of the tide, by the influence of their own corrupt natures, and the customs and examples of the world; but the case is now altered. So in 1 Cor. vi. 11. the apostle shews believers their old companions in sin, and tells them, " Such were some of you, but ye are washed, but ye " are sanctified," &c. q. d. the world is now well altered with you, thanks be to the grace of God for it. This wonderful change of practice, which is so universal and remarkable in all the regenerate, and immediately consequent upon their conversion, sets the world a wondering at them; 1 Pet. iv. 4. Wherein they think it

strange, that you run not " with them into the same excess of riot,
" speaking evil of you.   They think it strange:" * The word signifies to stand and gaze, as the hen doth which hath brooded,
and hatched partridge eggs, when she seeth the chickens which she
hath brought forth, take the wing and fly away from her.   Thus
do the men of the world stand amazed to see their old companions
in sin, whose language once was vain and earthly, it may be, profane and filthy, now to be praying, speaking of God, heaven, and
things spiritual, having no more to do with them, as to sin, except
by way of reprehension and admonition : this amazes the world,
and makes them look with a strange admiring eye upon the people
of God.

   Thirdly, In the next place let us enquire into the properties and
qualities of this new creature, and shew you, as we are able, what
they are; yet, reader, expect not here an exact and accurate account of that which is so great a mystery ; for if questions may be
moved about a silly fly, which may puzzle the greatest philosopher
to resolve them ; how much more may we conceive this great and
marvellous work of God, the most mysterious and admirable of all
his works, to surmount the understandings of the most illuminated
Christians ? O how little do we know of the nature, properties,
and operations of this new creature ! So far as God hath revealed
it to our weak understandings, we may speak of it.   And,

   First, The scripture speaks of it as a thing of great difficulty to
be conceived by man, John iii. 8. " The wind bloweth where it
" listeth, and thou hearest the sound thereof, but canst not tell
" whence it cometh and whither it goeth : So is every one that is
" born of the Spirit." The original of winds is a question of great
difficulty in philosophy : We hear the voice of the wind, feel its
mighty force, and behold its strange effects; but neither know
whence it comes, or whither it goes.   Ask a man, Do you hear
the wind blow ? Yes.   Do you feel it blow ? Yes, very sensibly.
Do you see the effects of it, rending and overturning the trees ?
Yes, very plainly.   But can you describe its nature, or declare its
original ? No, that is a mystery which I do not understand.   Why
just so it is with him that is born of the Spirit.   The holy Spirit of
God, whose nature and operations we understand but little of,
comes from heaven, quickens and influences our souls, beats down
and mortifies our lusts by his Almighty Power : These effects of
the Spirit in us we experimentally feel, and sensibly discern : But

---

   * Εν ω ξενιζονlαι, i. e. Then stand amazed, as at the sight of an uncommon thing.
Bern.   Ils se trouvent tous nouveaux, et comme en un autre monde, i. e. They find themselves all new, and as in another world.

how the Spirit of God first entered into, and quickened our souls, and produced this new creature in them, we understand little more of it than how the bones do grow in the womb of her that is with child, Eccles. xi. 5. Therefore is the life of the new creature called a hidden life, Col. iii. 3. The nature of that life is not only hidden totally from all carnal men, but in a very great measure it is an hidden and unknown life unto spiritual men, though themselves be the subjects of it.

Secondly, But though this life of the new creature be a great mystery, and secret in some respects; yet so far as it is known, and appears unto us, the new creature is the most *beautiful* and lovely creature that ever God made; for the beauty of the Lord himself is upon it: " The new man is created after God," Eph. iv. 24. As the picture is drawn after the man, it is a draught of God himself delineated by the Spirit, that admirable Artist, upon the soul of man. Holiness is the beauty and glory of God; and in holiness the new creature is created after God's own image, Col. iii. 10. The regenerate soul hereby becomes holy, 1 John iii. 3. not *essentially* holy, as God is, nor yet *efficiently* holy; for the regenerate soul can neither make itself, nor others holy: But the life of the new creature may be said to resemble the life of God in this, that as God lives to himself, so the new creature wholly lives to God; as God loves holiness, and hates the contrary, so doth the new creature; it is in these things formed *after the image of God that created it.* When God creates this creature in the soul of man, we are said then to be " partakers of the divine nature," 2 Pet. i. 4. So that there can be nothing communicated unto men which beautifies and adorns their souls as this new creation doth: Men do not resemble God as they are noble, and as they are rich, but as they are holy: no gift, no endowment of nature embellishes the soul as this new creature doth: An awful Majesty sits upon the brow of the new creature, commanding the greatest and worst of men to do homage to it, Mark vi. 20. Yea, such is the beauty of the new creature, that Christ, its *author,* is also its *admirer,* Cant. iv. 2. " Thou hast ravished mine heart with one of thine eyes."

Thirdly, This new creature is created in man, upon the highest design that ever any work of God was wrought: the end of its creation and infusion is high and noble: salvation to the soul in which it is wrought; this is both the *finis operis,* and the *finis operantis :* It is the design both of the work and of the workman that wrought it. When we receive the end of our faith, we receive the salvation of our souls; salvation is the end of faith: as death is the end of sin, so life eternal is the end of grace. The new creature doth, by the instinct and steady direction of its own nature, take its course as directly to God, and to heaven, the place of its full enjoyment, as the rivers do to the ocean; it declares itself to be made for God, by its restless workings after him; and as salvation is the end of the new creature, so it is the express design and end of him that created it. 2 Cor. v. 5. " Now he that hath " wrought us for the self-same thing, is God;" by this workmanship of his upon our souls, he is now polishing, preparing, and " making them meet to be partakers of the inheritance of the saints " in light," Col. i. 12.

Fourthly, This new creation is the most necessary work that ever God wrought upon the soul of man : the eternal well-being of his soul depends upon it; and without it no man shall see God, Heb. xii. 14. and John i. 3, 5. " Except ye be regenerate, and " born again, you cannot see the kingdom of God." Can you be saved without Christ? You know you cannot. Can you have interest in Christ without the new creature? My text expressly tells you it can never be; for, " If any man be in Christ, he is a " new creature." O reader, whatever slight thoughts of this matter, and with what a careless and unconcerned eye soever thou readest these lines; yet know thou must either be a new creature, or a miserable and damned creature for ever. If civility without the new creature could save thee, why are not the *moral Heathens* saved also? If strictness of life without the new creature could save thee, why did it not save the Scribes and Pharisees also? If an high profession of religion without the new creature can save thee, why did it not save Judas, Hymenæus and Philetus also? Nothing is more evident than this, that no repentance, obedience, self-denial, prayers, tears, reformations or ordinances, without the new creation, avail any thing to the salvation of thy soul: The very blood of Christ himself, without the new creature, never did, and never will save any man. Oh how necessary a work is the new creation! " Circumcision avails nothing, and uncircumcision nothing: but a " new creature."

Fifthly, The new creature is a marvellous and wonderful creature : there are many wonders in the first creation, " The works " of the Lord are great, sought out of all them that have plea- " sure therein," Psal. cxi. 2. But there are no wonders in nature, like those in grace. Is it not the greatest wonder that ever was seen in the world, (except the incarnation of the Son of God) to see the nature and temper of man so altered and changed as it is by grace? to see *lascivious Corinthians,* and *idolatrous Ephesians,* become mortified and heavenly Christians? to see a fierce and cruel *persecutor,* become a glorious *confessor* and sufferer for Christ? Gal. i. 23. to see the carnal mind of man, which was lately fully set in a strong bent to the world, to be wholly taken off from its lusts, and set upon things that are spiritual and heavenly? Certainly it was not a greater miracle to see dead Lazarus come out of his *sepulchre*, than it is to see the dead and carnal mind coming out of its lusts to embrace Jesus Christ; it was not a greater wonder to see the dead and dry bones in the valley to move and come together, than it is to see a dead soul moving after God, and moving to Christ in the way of faith.

Sixthly, The new creature is an *immortal creature*, a creature that shall never see death, John iv. 14. it is in the soul of man, a well of water, springing up unto eternal life. I will not adventure to say, it is immortal in its own nature, for it is but a creature, as my text calls it; and we know, that essential interminability is the incommunicable property of God: The new creature hath both a beginning and succession; and therefore might also have an end, as to any thing in itself, or its own nature. Experience also shews us, that it is capable both of increasing and decreasing, and may be brought nigh unto death, Rev. iii. 2. The work of the Spirit in believers, *may be ready to die;* but though its perpetuity flow not out of its own nature, it flows out of God's covenant and promises, which make it an immortal creature: when all other excellencies in man go away, as at death they will, Job iv. 21. this excellency only remains: our gifts may leave us, our friends leave us, our estates leave us, but our graces will never leave us; they ascend with the soul (in which they inhere) into glory, when the stroke of death separates it from the body.

Seventhly, The new creature is an *heavenly creature;* " It is not " born of flesh, nor of blood, nor of the will of man, but of " God," John i. 13. its descent and original is heavenly, it is spirit born of spirit, John iii. 6. its centre is heaven, and thither are all its tendencies, Psal. lxiii. 8. its proper food, on which it lives, are heavenly things, Psal. iv. 6, 7. It cannot feed, as other creatures do, upon earthly things; the object of all its delight and love is in heaven, Psal. lxxiii. 26. " Whom have I in heaven but thee ?" The hopes and expectations of the new creature are all from heaven; it looks for little in this world, but waits for the coming of the Lord. The life of the new creature upon earth, is a life of patient waiting for Christ; his desires and longings are after heaven, Phil. i. 93. The flesh indeed lingers, and would delay, but the new creature hastens, and would fain be gone, 2 Cor. v. 2. It is not at home whilst it is here; it came from heaven, and cannot be quiet, nor suffer the soul, in which it dwells, to be so, until it comes thither again.

Eighthly, The new creature is an active and laborious creature; no sooner is it born, but it is acting in the soul. Acts ix. 6. *Behold he prayeth!* Activity is its very nature. Gal. v. 25. " If we " live in the Spirit, let us walk in the Spirit." Nor is it to be admired, that it should be always active and stirring in the soul, seeing activity in obedience was the very end for which it was created. " For we are his workmanship, created in Christ Jesus " unto good works," Eph. ii. 10. and he that is acted in the duties of religion, by this principle of the new creature, or nature, will (so far as that principle acts him) delight to do the will of God; rejoice in the way of his commandment, and find the sweetest pleasure in the paths of duty.

Ninthly, The new creature is a *thriving creature,* growing from strength to strength, 1 Pet. ii. 2. and changing the soul in which it is subjected, from glory unto glory, 2 Cor. iii. 18. The vigorous tendencies, and constant striving of this new creature, are to attain its just perfection and maturity, Phil. iii. 11. It can endure no stints and limits to its desire, short of perfection; every degree of strength it attains, doth but whet and sharpen its desires after higher degrees: Upon this account, it greatly delights in the ordinances of God, duties of religion, and society of the saints; as they are helps and improvements to it, in order to its great design.

Tenthly, The new creature, is *a creature of wonderful preservations**: There are many wonders of divine providence in the preservation of our natural lives, but none like those whereby the life of the new creature is preserved in our souls: There are critical times of temptation and desertion, in which it is ready to die, Rev. iii. 2. the degrees of its strength and liveliness, are sometimes sadly abated, and its sweet and comfortable workings intermitted, Rev. ii. 4. the evidences by which its being in us was wont to be discovered, may be, and often are darkened, 2 Pet. i. 9. and the soul in which it is may draw very sad conclusions about the issue and event; concluding its life not only to be hazarded, but quite extinguished, Psal. li. 10, 11, 12. but though it be ready to die, God wonderfully preserves it from death; it hath as well its reviving, as its fainting seasons. And thus you see, what are the lovely and eximious properties of the new creature. In the next place,

Fourthly, We will demonstrate the necessity of this new creation to all that are in Christ, and by him expect to attain salvation; and the necessity of the new creature will appear divers ways.

First, From the positive and express will of God, revealed in

---

* Grace indeed cannot be totally intermitted, nor finally lost, but there may be an omission of the act, though not an omission of the habit; the act may be perverted, though faith cannot be subverted; it may be shaken, though not shaken out; its fruits may fall, but its sap lies hid in the root; the effect of justification may be suspended, but the state of the justified cannot be dissolved, *Suffrag. Brit.*

scripture, touching this matter: Search the scriptures, and you shall find God hath laid the whole stress and weight of your eternal happiness, by Jesus Christ, upon this work of the Spirit in your souls. So our Saviour tells Nicodemus, John iii. 5. " Ve- " rily, verily, I say unto thee, except a man be born of water, " and of the Spirit, he cannot enter into the kingdom of God." Agreeable whereunto are those words of the apostle, Heb. xii. 14. " Without holiness no man shall see the Lord." And whereas some may think, that their birth-right privileges, enjoyment of ordinances, and profession of religion, may commend them to God's acceptance, without this new creation; he shews them how fond and ungrounded all such hopes are. Gal. vi. 15. " For in Christ " Jesus neither circumcision availeth any thing, nor uncircum- " cision, but a new creature." Christ and heaven are the gifts of God, and he is at liberty to bestow them, upon what terms and conditions he pleaseth: and this is the way, the only way, and stated method in which he will bring men, by Christ, unto glory. Men may raze out the impressions of these things from their own hearts, but they can never alter the settled course and method of salvation. Either we must be new creatures, as the precept of the word command us, or lost, and damned creatures, as the threatenings of the word plainly tell us.

Secondly, This new creation, is the inchoative part of that great salvation which we expect through Christ, and therefore, without this, all hopes and expectations of salvation must vanish. Salvation, and renovation, are inseparably connected. Our glory in heaven, if we rightly understand its nature, consisteth in two things; namely, our assimilation to God, and our fruition of God: and both these take their beginning and rise from our renovation in this world. Here we begin to be changed into his image, in some degree, 2 Cor. iii. 18. for the new man is created *after God*, as was opened above. In the work of grace, God is said *to begin that good work*, which is to be *finished*, or consummated, in the day of Christ, Phil. i. 6. Now nothing can be more irrational, than to imagine that ever that design, or work should be finished or perfected, which never had a beginning.

Thirdly, So necessary is the new creation to all that expect salvation by Christ, that without this, heaven would be no heaven, and the glory thereof no glory to us, by reason of the unsuitableness and aversion of our carnal minds thereunto; " The carnal " mind is enmity against God," Rom. viii. 7. and enmity is exclusive of all complacency and delight. There is a necessity of a suitable and agreeable frame of heart to God, in order to that complacential rest of our souls in him: And this agreeable temper is wrought by our new creation, 2 Cor. v. 5. " He that hath

" wrought us for the self-same thing, is God." Renovation, you see, is the working or moulding of a man's spirit into an agreeable temper, or as it is in Col. i. 12. the making of us meet for the inheritance of the saints in light.

From all which, it follows, that seeing there can be no complacence, or delight in God, without suitableness and conformity to him, as it is plain, from 1 John iii. 2. as well as from the reason and nature of the thing itself; either God must become like us, suitable to our sinful, corrupt and vain hearts, which were but a rude blasphemy once to imagine; or else we must be made agreeable and suitable to God, which is the very thing I am now proving the necessity of.

Fourthly, There is an absolute necessity of the new creature to all that expect interest in Christ, and the glory to come, since all the characters, marks, and signs of such an interest, are constantly taken from the new creature wrought in us. Look over all the marks and signs of interest in Christ, or salvation by him, which are dispersed through the scriptures, and you shall still find purity of heart, Mat. v. 8. Holiness both in principle and practice, Heb. xii. 14. Mortification of sin, Rom. viii. 13. Longing for Christ's appearance, 2 Tim. iv. 8. with multitudes more of the same nature, to be constantly made the marks and signs of our salvation by Christ. So that either we must have a *new bible*, or a *new heart;* for if these scriptures be the true and faithful words of God, no unrenewed creature can see his face; which was the fourth thing to be opened.

Fifthly, The last thing to be opened is, how the new creation is an infallible proof and evidence of the soul's interest in Christ; and this will appear divers ways.

First, Where all the saving graces of the Spirit are, there interest in Christ must needs be certain; and where the new creature is, there all the saving graces of the Spirit are: For what is the new creature but the frame or system of all special saving graces? It is not this or that particular grace, as faith, or hope, or love to God, which constitutes the new creature; for these are but as so many particular limbs or branches of it; but the new creature is comprehensive of all the graces of the Spirit, Gal. v. 22, 23. " The fruit " of the Spirit is love, peace, joy, long-suffering, gentleness, good- " ness, faith, meekness, temperance," &c. Any one of the saving, special graces of the Spirit gives proof of our interest in Christ: how much more, then, the new creature, which is the complex frame or system of all the graces together?

Secondly, To conclude; Where all the causes of an interest in Christ are found, and all the effects and fruits of an interest in Christ do appear; there, undoubtedly, a real interest in Christ is found : but wherever you find a new creature, you find all the causes and all the effects of an interest in Christ: For there you shall find,

First, The impulsive cause, viz. The electing love of God, from which the new creature is inseparable, 1 Pet. i. 2. with the new creature also, the meritorious, efficient, and final causes of interest in Christ, and union with him, are ever found, Eph. ii. 10. chap. i. 4, 5, 6.

Secondly, All the effects and fruits of interest in Christ are found in the new creature; there are all the fruits of obedience, for we are created in Christ Jesus unto good works, Eph. ii. 10. Rom. vii. 4. there is true spiritual opposition to sin. 1 John v. 18. " He that is begotten of God, keepeth himself, and that wicked " one toucheth him not." There is love to the people of God ; 1 John iv. 7. " Every one that loveth is born of God." There is a conscientious respect to the duties of both tables ; for the new creature is created after God in righteousness and true holiness, Eph. iv. 25. There is perseverance in the ways of God to the very end, and victory over all temptations ; for whosoever is born of God, overcometh the world, 1 John v. 4. It were easy to run over all other particular fruits of our union with Christ, and shew you every one of them in the new creature. And thus much of the doctrinal part of this point.

SERMON XXVI.

2 Cor. v. 17.

Therefore if any man be in Christ, he is a new creature : old things are passed away ; behold, all things are become new.

AFTER the explication of the sense of this scripture, we observed,

> Doct. *That God's creating of a new supernatural work of grace in the soul of any man, is that man's sure and infallible evidence of a saving interest in Jesus Christ.*

You have heard why the regenerating work of the Spirit is called a new creation; in what respect every soul in Christ is renewed; what the eximious properties of this new creature are; the indispensibleness and necessity thereof have been also proved; and how it evidences our interest in Christ, was cleared in the doctrinal part:

Which we now come to improve, in the several uses serving for our

1. Information.
2. Conviction.
3. Examination.
4. Exhortation.
5. Consolation.

First use, for information.

Is the new creature the sure and infallible evidence of our saving interest in Christ? From hence then we are informed,

Inference 1. *How miserable and deplorable an estate all unrenewed souls are in;* who can lay no claim to Christ during that state, and therefore are under an impossibility of salvation. O reader! if this be the state of thy soul, better had it been for thee not to have been God's natural workmanship as a man, except thou be his spiritual workmanship also, as a new man. I know the schoolmen determine otherwise, and say, that damnation is rather to be chosen than annihilation: a miserable being is better than no being: and it is very true, with respect to the glory of God, whose justice shall triumph for ever in the damnation of the unregenerate; but, with respect to us, it is much better never to have been his creatures, in the way of generation, than not to be his new creatures, in the way of *regeneration.* So Christ speaks of Judas, that son of perdition, Mark xiv. 21. " Good had it been for that man if he had never been born:" For what is a being without the comfort of it? What is life without the joy and pleasure of it? A damned being is a being without comfort; no glimpse of light shines into that darkness; they shall, indeed, see and understand the felicity, light, and joy of the saints in glory; but not partake, in the least measure, of the comfort, Luke xiii. 28. " They shall see Abraham, and Isaac, " and Jacob, in the kingdom of God, but they themselves shut out:" Such a sight is so far from giving any comfort, that it will be the aggravation and increase of torment. O it is better to have no being at all, than to have a being only to capacitate a man for misery; to desire death, while death flies from him, Rev. iv. 6. The opinion of the schoolmen will never pass for sound doctrine among the damned. Think on it, reader, and lay it to thine heart, better thou hadst died from the womb, better the knees had prevented thee, and the breasts which thou hast sucked, than that thou shouldst live and die a stranger to the new birth, or that thy mother should bring thee forth only to increase, and fill up the number of the damned.

Inf. 2. And, on the contrary, we may hence learn, *what cause regenerate souls have to bless God, for the day wherein they were born.*

O what a privileged state doth the new birth bring men into! It is possible, for the present, they understand it not; for many believers are like a great *heir* lying in the *cradle*, that knows not to what an estate and honour he is born: nevertheless, on the same day wherein we become new creatures by regeneration, we have a firm title and solid claim to all the privileges of the sons of God, John i. 12, 13. God becomes our Father by a triple title, not only the Father of our *beings* by nature, which was all the relation we had to him before, but our Father by *adoption*, and by *regeneration:* which is a much sweeter, and more comfortable relation. In that day the image of God is restored, Eph. iv. 24. this is both the health and beauty of the soul. In that day we are begotten again to a lively hope, 1 Pet. i. 3. a hope more worth than ten thousand worlds, in the *troubles of life*, and in the *straits of death:* this is a creature which lives for ever, and will make thy life happy for ever. Some have kept their birth-day as a *festival*, a day of rejoicing; but none have more cause to rejoice that ever they were born, than those that are new-born.

Inf. 3. *Learn from hence, that the work of grace is wholly supernatural; it is a creation, and a creation-work is above the power of the creature.* No power but that which gave being to the world, can give a being to the new creature: Almighty Power goes forth to give being to the new creature. This creature is not born of flesh, or of blood, nor of the will of man, but of God, John i. 13. The nature of this new creature speaks its original to be above the power of nature; the very notion of a new creation spoils the proud boasts of the great asserters of the power and ability of the will of man. When God, therefore, puts the question, who maketh thee to differ? And what hast thou that thou hast not received? Let thy soul, reader, answer it with all humility and thankfulness. It is thou, Lord, thou only, that madest me to differ from another; and what I have received, I have received from thy free grace.

Inf. 4. *If the work of grace be a new creation, let not the parents, and friends of the unregenerate utterly despair of the conversion of their relations, how great soever their present discouragements are.* If it had been possible for a man to have seen the rude and indigested *chaos* before the Spirit of God moved upon it, would he not have said, Can such a beautiful order of beings, such a pleasant variety of creatures, spring out of this dark lump? Surely it would have been very hard for a man to have imagined it. It may be, you see no dispositions or hopeful inclinations in your friends towards God and spiritual things; nay, possibly they are totally opposite, and filled with enmity against them; they deride and jeer all serious piety wherever they behold it; this, indeed, is very sad; but yet remember the work of grace is creation-work : though there be no disposition at all in their wills, no tenderness in their consciences, no light or knowledge in their minds ; yet God, that commanded the light to shine out of darkness, can shine into their hearts, to give them the light of the knowledge of the glory of God in the face of Jesus Christ : he can say to the dry bones, live ; to the proud and stubborn heart, come down and yield thyself to the will of God ; and if he command, the work is done. God can make thee yet to rejoice over thy most uncomfortable relations ; to say with the father of the prodigal, Luke xv. 24. " This my son was dead, " and is alive again ; he was lost and is found ; and they began to be merry." Difficulties are for men, but not for God : he works, in conversion, by a power which is able to subdue all things unto itself.

Inf. 5. *If none but new creatures be in Christ, how small a remnant among men belong to Christ in this world !* Among the multitude of rational creatures inhabiting this world, how few, how very few, are new creatures ? It is the observation of the learned Mr. Brerewood, that if the world be divided into thirty parts, nineteen parts are heathenish Idolaters ; six parts Mahometans, and only five out of thirty which may be, in a large sense, called Christians ; of which the far greater part is overspread with Popish darkness : separate from the remainder, the multitudes of profane, merely civil, and hypocritical professors of religion ; and how few will remain for Jesus Christ in this world ? Look over the *cities, towns,* and *parishes* in this populous *kingdom,* and how few shall you find that speak the language or do the works of new creatures ? How few have ever had any awakening convictions on them ? And how many of those that have been convinced have miscarried, and never come to the new-birth ? The more cause have they, whom God hath indeed regenerated, to admire the riches of God's distinguishing mercy to them.

Inf. 6. *If the change by grace be a new creation, how universal and marvellous a change doth regeneration make upon men !* The new creation speaks a marvellous and universal alteration, both upon the state and tempers of men ; they come out of darkness, gross, hellish darkness, into light, a marvellous and heavenly light, 1 Pet. ii. 9. Eph. v. 8. their condition, disposition, and conversation, (as you have heard) are all new ; and yet this marvellous change, as great and universal as it is, is not alike evident, and clearly discernible in all new creatures : and the reasons are,

First, Because the work of grace is wrought in divers methods and manners in the people of God. Some are changed from a state of notorious profaneness unto serious godliness ; there the change is conspicuous and very evident ; all the neighbourhood rings of it: but in others it is more insensibly distilled in their tender years, by the blessing of God, upon religious education, and there it is more indiscernible.

Secondly, Though a great change be wrought, yet much natural corruption still remains for their humiliation and daily exercise; and this is a ground of fear and doubting; they see not how such corruptions are consistent with the new creature.

Thirdly, In some, the new creature shews itself mostly in the affectionate part, in desires and breathings after God; and but little in the clearness of their understandings, and strength of their judgments; for want of which they are entangled and kept in darkness most of their days.

Fourthly, Some Christians are more tried, and exercised by temptation from Satan than others are; and these clouds darken the work of grace in them.

Fifthly, There is great difference and variety found in the natural tempers and constitutions of the regenerate; some are of a more melancholy, fearful, and suspicious temper than others are; and are therefore much longer held under doubtings and trouble of spirit; nevertheless, what differences soever these things make, the change made by grace is a marvellous change.

Inf. 7. Lastly, *How incongruous are carnal ways and courses to the spirit of Christians! who being new creatures, can never delight or find pleasure in their former sinful companions and practices.* Alas! those things are now most unsuitable, loathsome and detestable, how pleasant soever they once were; that which they counted their liberty, would now be reckoned their greatest bondage; that which was their glory, is now their shame; Rom. vi. 21. " What " fruit had ye then in those things, whereof ye are now ashamed; " for the end of those things is death:" they need not be pressed by others, but will freely confess of themselves, what fools and mad-men they once were. None can censure their former conversation more freely than themselves do, 1 Tim. 13, 14.

Second use, for conviction.

If none be in Christ but new creatures, and the new creation makes such a change, as hath been described; this may convince us, how many of us deceive ourselves, and run into dangerous and fatal mistakes, in the greatest concernment we have in this world. But before I urge this use, I desire none may make a perverse and ill use of it; let not the wicked conclude, from hence, that there is no such thing as true religion in the world, or that all who do profess it, are but hypocrites; neither let the godly injure themselves by that which is designed for their benefit: let none conclude, that seeing there are so many mistakes committed about this new creature, that therefore assurance must needs be impossible,

as the Papists affirm it to be.   The proper use that should be made
of this doctrine, is, to undeceive false pretenders, and to awaken
all to a more deep and thorough search of their own conditions;
which being precautioned, let all men be convinced of the following truths :

First, That the change made by civility, upon such as were lewd
and profane, is, in its whole kind and nature, a different thing
from the new creature ; the power and efficacy of moral virtue is
one thing, the influence of the regenerating Spirit is quite another
thing, however some have studied to comfort them.   The Heathens excelled in moral and homolitical virtues : Plato, Aristides,
Seneca, and multitudes more, have outvied many professed Christians, in justice, temperance, patience, &c. yet were perfect strangers to the new creation.   A man may be very strict and temperate,
free from the pollutions of the world, and yet a perfect stranger to
regeneration all the while, John iii. 10.

Secondly, That many strong convictions and troubles for sin may
be found where the new creature is never formed.   Conviction, indeed, is an antecedent unto, and preparative for the new creature,
as the blossoms of the tree are to the fruit that follows them ; but
as fruit doth not always follow where those blossoms and flowers
appear, so neither doth the new creature follow all convictions and
troubles for sin.   Conviction is a common work of the Spirit both
upon the elect and reprobate ; but the new creature is formed
only in God's elect.   Convictions may be blasted, and vanish away,
and the man that was under troubles for sin, may return again,
with " the dog to his vomit, and the sow that was washed, to her
" wallowing in the mire," 2 Pet. ii. 22. but the new creature
never perishes, nor can consist with such a return to sin.

Thirdly, That excellent gifts and abilities, fitting men for service in the church of God, may be where the new creature is not ;
for these are promiscuously dispensed by the Spirit both to the regenerate and unregenerate : Matth. vii. 22.   " Many will say unto
" me, in that day, Lord, Lord, have we not prophesied in thy
" name ?" Gifts are attainable by study ; prayer and preaching are
reduced to an art ; but regeneration is wholly supernatural.   Sin, in
dominion, is consistent with excellent gifts, but wholly incompatible
with the new creature.   In a word, these things are so different in
nature from the new creature, that they oft-times prove the greatest bars and obstacles in the world to the regenerating work of the
Spirit.   Let no man, therefore, trust to things whereby multitudes
deceive and destroy their own souls.   Reader, it may cost thee
many an aking head to attain gifts, but thou wilt find an aking
heart for sin if ever God make thee a new creature.

Fourthly, Be convinced that multitudes of religious duties may be performed by men, in whom the new creature was never form-ed. Though all new creatures perform the duties of religion, yet all that perform the duties of religion, are not new creatures; re-generation is not the only root from which the duties of religion spring, Isa. lviii. 2. " Yet they seek me daily, and delight to know " my ways, as a nation that did righteousness, and forsook not the " ordinances of their God, they ask of me the ordinances of justice, " they take delight in approaching to God." These are but weak and slippery foundations for men to build their confidence and hopes upon.

The third use, for examination.

Next, therefore, let me persuade every man to try the state of his own heart in this matter, and closely consider and weigh this great question : Am I really and indeed a new creature ? or am I an old creature still, in a new creature's dress and habit ? Some light may be given for the discovery hereof, from the considera-tion of the

1. Antecedents,
2. Concomitants, } of the new creation.
3. Consequents,

First, Weigh and consider well the *antecedents* of the new crea-ture ; have those things passed upon your souls, which ordinarily make way for the new creature, in whomsoever the Lord forms it ?

1. Hath the Lord opened the eyes of your understanding in the knowledge of sin and of Christ ? Hath he shewed you both your disease and remedy, by a new light shining from heaven into your souls ! Thus the Lord doth wherever he forms the new crea-ture, Acts xxvi. 18.

2. Hath he brought home the word with mighty power and efficacy upon your hearts to convince and humble them ? This is the method in which the new creature is produced, Rom. vii. 9. 1 Thes. i. 5.

3. Have these convictions over-turned your vain confidences, and brought you to a great concern and inward distress of soul, making you to cry, *What shall we do to be saved ?* These are the ways of the Spirit, in the formation of the new creature, Acts xvi. 29. Acts ii. 37. If no such antecedent works of the Spirit have passed upon your hearts, you have no ground for your confidence, that the new creature is formed in you.

Secondly, Consider the *concomitant* frames and workings of spirit' which ordinarily attend the production of the new creature, and judge impartially betwixt God and your own souls, whether they have been the very frames and workings of your hearts.

1. Have your vain spirits been composed to the greatest serious-

ness, and most solemn consideration of things eternal, as the
hearts of all those are whom God regenerates? When the Lord
is about this great work upon the soul of man, whatever vanity,
levity, and sinful jollity was there before, it is banished from the
heart at this time; for now heaven and hell, life and death, are
before a man's eyes, and these are the most awful and solemn things
that ever our thoughts conversed with in this world.   Now a man
of the most airy and pleasant constitution, when brought to the
sight and sense of those things, saith of " laughter, It is mad; and
" of mirth, What doth it?" Eccl. ii. 2.

2. A lowly, meek, and humble frame of heart accompanies the
new creation; the soul is weary and heavy laden, Mat xi. 28.
Convictions of sin have plucked down the pride and loftiness of
the spirit of man, emptied him of his vain conceits; those that
were of lofty, proud, and blustering humours before, are meek-
ened and brought down to the very dust now : it is with them (to
speak allusively) as it was with Jerusalem, that lofty city, Isa. xxix.
1, 4. " Wo to Ariel, to Ariel, the city where David dwelt; thou
" shalt be brought down, and shalt speak out of the ground, and
" thy speech shall be low out of the dust." Ariel signifies the
Lion of God: so Jerusalem in her prosperity was; other cities
trembled at her voice; but when God brought her down, by
humbling judgments, then she whispered out of the dust. So it
is in this case.

3. A longing, thirsting frame of spirit accompanies the new
creation; the desires of the soul are ardent after Christ; never did
the hireling long for the shadow, as the weary soul doth for Christ,
and rest in him : if no such frames have accompanied that which
you take for your new birth, you have the greatest reason in the
world to suspect yourselves under a delusion.

Thirdly, Weigh well the effects and *consequents* of the new creature, and consider whether such fruits as these are found in your
hearts and lives.

1. Wherever the new creature is formed, there a man's course
and conversation is changed : Eph. iv. 22. " That ye put off, con-
" cerning the former conversation, the old man, which is cor-
" rupt, according to the deceitful lusts; and be renewed in the
" spirit of your mind :" the new creature cannot but blush and be
ashamed of the old creature's conversation, Rom. vi. 21.

2. The new creature continually opposes and conflicts with the
motions of sin in the heart; Gal. v. 17. " The spirit lusteth
" against the flesh." Grace can no more incorporate with sin,
than oil with water: contraries cannot consist in the same subject
longer than they are fighting with each other; if there be no conflict with sin in thy soul, or if that conflict be only betwixt the

conscience and affections, light in the one, struggling with lust in the other; thou wantest that fruit which should evidence thee to be a new creature.

3. The mind and affections of the new creature are set upon heavenly and spiritual things, Col. iii. 1, 2. Eph. iv. 23. Rom. viii. 5. If, therefore, thy heart and affections be habitually earthly and wholly intent upon things below, driving eagerly after the world, as the great business and end of thy life, deceive not thyself, this is not the fruit of the new creature, nor consistent with it.

5. The new creature is a praying creature, living by its daily communion with God, which is its livelihood and subsistence, Zech. xii. 10. Acts ix. 11. If, therefore, thou be a prayerless soul, or if, in all thy prayers, thou art a stranger to communion with God; if there be no brokenness of heart for sin in thy confessions, no melting affections for Christ and holiness in thy supplications; surely Satan doth but baffle and delude thy over-credulous soul, in persuading thee that thou art a new creature.

Fifthly, The new creature is restless, after falls into sin, until it have recovered peace and pardon; it cannot endure itself in a state of defilement and pollution, Psal. li. 8, 9, 10, 11, 12. It is with the conscience of a new creature, under sin, as it is with the eye, when any thing offends it; it cannot leave twinkling and watering till it have wept it out: and in the very same restless state it is, under the hiding of God's face and divine withdrawments, Cant. v. 2, 3, 4, 5, 6, 7, 8. If, therefore, thou canst sin and sin again without such a burdensome sense of sin, or restlessness, or solicitude how to recover purity and peace, with the light of God's countenance shining, as in days past, upon thy soul; delude not thyself, thou hast not the signs of a new creature in thee.

Fourth use, of exhortation.

If the new creation be a sound evidence of our interest in Christ, then hence let me persuade all that are in Christ, to evidence themselves to be so, by walking as it becomes new creatures.

The new creature is *born from above*, all its tendencies are heavenward; accordingly, set your affections on things that are above, and let your conversation be in heaven: if you live earthly and sensual lives, as others do, you must cross your new nature therein; and can those acts be pleasant unto you which are done with so much regret? wherein you must put a force upon your own spirits, and offer a kind of violence to your own hearts. Earthly delights and sorrows are suitable enough to the unregenerate and sensual men inthe world, but exceedingly contrary unto that Spirit by which you are renovated. If ever you will act becoming the principles and nature of new creatures, then seek earthly things with submission, enjoy them with fear and caution, resign them with cheerfulness and readiness; and thus "let your moderation " be known unto all men," Phil. iv. 5. Let your hearts daily meditate, and your tongues discourse about heavenly things; be exceeding tender of sin, strict and punctual in every duty; and hereby convince the world that you are men and women of another spirit.

Fifth use, for consolation.

Let every new creature be cheerful and thankful: if God hath renewed your natures, and thus altered the frame and temper of your hearts, he hath bestowed the richest mercy upon you that heaven or earth affords. This is a work of the greatest rarity; a new creature, may be called, One among a thousand : it is also an everlasting work, never to be destroyed, as all other natural works of God (how excellent soever) must be : it is a work carried on by Almighty Power, through unspeakable difficulties and mighty oppositions, Eph. i. 12. The exceeding greatness of God's power goes forth to produce it; and indeed no less is required to enlighten the blind mind, break the rocky heart, and bow the stubborn will of man; and the same Almighty Power which at first created it, is necessary to be continued every moment to preserve and continue it, 1 Pet. i. 5. The new creature is a mercy which draws a train of innumerable and invaluable mercies after it, Eph. ii. 13, 14. 1 Cor. iii. 20. When God hath given us a new nature, then he dignifies us with a *new name*, Rev. ii. 17. brings us into a *new covenant*, Jer. xxxi. 33. begets us again to a *new hope*, 1 Pet. i. 3. intitles us to a *new inheritance*, John i. 12, 13. It is the new creature which through Christ makes our persons and duties acceptable with God, Gal. vi. 15. In a word, it is the wonderful work of God, of which we may say, " This is the Lord's doing, and " it is marvellous in our eyes." There are unsearchable wonders in its *generation*, in its *operation*, and in its *preservation*. Let all therefore, whom the Lord hath thus renewed, fall down at the feet of God, in an humble admiration of the unsearchable riches of free grace, and never open their mouths to complain under any adverse or bitter providences of God.

SERMON XXVII.

Of the Nature, Principle, and Necessity of Mortification.

GAL. v. 24.

And they that are Christ's, have crucified the flesh, with the affections and lusts.

TWO great trials of our interest in Christ are finished; we now proceed to the third, namely, *The mortification of sin:* "They that " are Christ's have crucified the flesh." The scope of the apostle in this context is, to heal the unchristian breaches among the Galatians, prevailing, by the instigation of Satan, to the breach of brotherly love. To cure this, he urges four weighty arguments.

First, From the great commandment, to *love one another;* upon which the whole law, i. e. all the duties of the second table do depend, ver. 15.

Secondly, He powerfully dissuades them from the consideration of the sad events of their bitter contests, calumnies, and detractions, viz. mutual ruin, and destruction, ver. 15.

Thirdly, He dissuades them from the consideration of the contrariety of these practices unto the Spirit of God, by whom they all profess themselves to be governed, from ver. 17. to ver. 23.

Fourthly, He powerfully dissuades them from these animosities, from the inconsistency of these, or any other lusts of the flesh, with an interest in Christ: "They that are Christ's, have crucified the " flesh," &c. q. d. You all profess yourselves to be members of Christ, to be followers of him; but how incongruous are these practices to such a profession? Is this the fruit of the dove-like Spirit of Christ? Are these the fruits of your faith and professed mortification? Shall the sheep of Christ snarl and fight like rabid and furious beasts of prey? *Tantæne animis cælestibus iræ?* So *much rage in heavenly souls?* O how repugnant are these practices with the study of mortification *, which is the great study and endeavour of all that are in Christ! "They that are Christ's have crucified the flesh, with the affections and lusts." So much for the order of the words; the words themselves are a *proposition* wherein we have to consider, both

  1. The subject.
  2. The predicate.

---

* ———*Non secus ac*
Cum duo conversis inimica, in prælia tauri,
Frontibus incurrunt———
Shall Christians one another wound and push,
Like furious bulls, when they together rush?

First, The *subject* of the proposition, they that are Christ's, *viz.*
" * True Christians, real members of Christ; such as truly belong
" to Christ, such as have given themselves up to be governed by
" him," and are indeed acted by his Spirit; such, all such persons (for the indefinite is equipollent to an universal) all such, and
none but such.

Secondly, The predicate; " They have crucified the flesh, with
" the affections and lusts." By flesh we are here to understand
carnal concupiscence, the workings and motions of corrupt nature;
and by the affections we are to understand, not the natural, but the
inordinate affections; for Christ doth not abolish and destroy, but
correct and regulate the affections of those that are in him: And
by crucifying the flesh, we are not to understand the total extinc-
tion or perfect subduing of corrupt nature, but only the deposing
of corruption from its regency and dominion in the soul; its dominion is taken away, though its life be prolonged for a season; but
yet, as death surely, though slowly, follows crucifixion, (the life
of crucified persons gradually departing from them, with their
blood) it is just so in the mortification of sin; and therefore what
the apostle in this place calls crucifying, he calls in Rom. viii. 13.
mortifying. " If ye, through the Spirit, do mortify," Θανατɛτɛ;
if ye put to death the deeds of the body: But he chuses, in this
place, to call it crucifying, to shew not only the conformity there
is betwixt the death of Christ and the death of sin, in respect of
shame, pain, and lingering slowness; but to denote also the principal means and instruments of mortification, *viz.* the death, or
cross of Jesus Christ, in the virtue whereof believers do mortify the
corruptions of their flesh; the great arguments and persuasives to
mortification being drawn from the sufferings of Christ for sin. In
a word, he doth not say, They that believe Christ was crucified for
sin, are Christ's; but they, and they only, are his, who *feel* as
well as *profess* the power and efficacy of the sufferings of Christ, in
the mortification and subduing of their lusts and sinful affections.
And so much, briefly, of the parts and sense of the words.

The observation followeth.

Doct. *That a saving interest in Christ may be regularly and
strongly inferred and concluded from the mortification of the
flesh, with its affections and lusts.*

This point . is fully confirmed by those words of the apostle,
Rom. vi. 5, 6, 7, 8. " For if we have been planted together in the
" likeness of his death, we shall be also in the likeness of his re-

---

* *Vere Christiani qui ad Christum pertinent, qui se ei dedere regendos.*   Pol. Synop.

" surrection, knowing this, that our old man is crucified with him,
" that the body of sin might be destroyed, that henceforth we
" should not serve sin : for he that is dead is free from sin : Now
" if we be dead with Christ, we believe that we shall also live with
" him."

Mark the force of the apostle's reasoning ; if we have been planted into the likeness of his death, viz. by the mortification of sin, which resembles, or hath a likeness to the kind and manner of Christ's death (as was noted above) then we shall be also in the likeness of his resurrection ; and why so, but because the mortification of sin is an undoubted evidence of the union of such a soul with Christ, which is the very ground-work and principle of that blessed and glorious resurrection : And therefore he saith, ver. 11. " Reckon ye also yourselves to be dead indeed unto sin, but alive " unto God, through Jesus Christ our Lord ;" q. d. Reason thus with yourselves, these mortifying influences of the death of Christ are unquestionable presages of your future blessedness, God never taking this course with any but those who are in Christ, and are designed to be glorified with him. The death of your sin is as evidential as any thing in the world can be of your spiritual life for the present, and of your eternal life with God hereafter. Mortification is the fruit and evidence of your union, and that union is the firm ground-work and certain pledge of your glorification ; and so you ought to reckon or reason the case with yourselves, as the word λογιζεσθε there signifies. Now for the stating and explicating of this point, I shall, in the doctrinal part, labour to open and confirm these five things,

1. What the mortification or crucifixion of sin imports.

2. Why this work of the Spirit is expressed by crucifying.

3. Why all that are in Christ must be so crucified or mortified unto sin.

4. What is the true evangelical principle of mortification.

5. How the mortification of sin evinces our interest in Christ.

And then apply the whole.

First, What the mortification or crucifixion of sin imports.

And, for clearness sake, I shall speak to it both *negatively* and *positively*, shewing you what is not intended, and what is principally aimed at by the Spirit of God in this expression.

First, " The * crucifying of the flesh doth not imply the total " abolition of sin in believers, or the destruction of its very being " and existence in them for the present ; sanctified souls so put off

---

* *Mortificari carnem non est eam ita perimi, ut aut prorsus non sit, aut nulla prava in homine desideria commoveant, quod in corpore mortis hujus non contingit, &c.* Estius in loc.

" their corruptions with their dead bodies at death:" This will
be the effect of our future glorification, not of our present sanctification.   Sin doth exist in the most mortified believer in the world,
Rom. vii. 17. it still acteth and lusteth in the regenerate soul,
Gal. v. 17. yea, notwithstanding its crucifixion in believers, it still
may, in respect of single acts, surprize and captivate them, Psal.
lxv. 3. Rom. vii. 23.   This, therefore, is not the intention of the
Spirit of God in this expression.

Secondly, Nor doth the crucifixion of sin consist in the suppression
of the external acts of sin only : for sin may reign over the souls
of men, whilst it doth not break forth into their lives in gross and
open actions, 2 Pet. iii. 20. Mat. xii. 43.   *Morality* in the Heathens (as Tertullian well observes) did *abscondere, sed non abscin-*
dere vitia, hide them, when it could not *kill* them : Many a man
shews a white, and fair hand, who yet hath a very foul and black
heart.

Thirdly, The crucifixion of the flesh doth not consist in the cessation of the external acts of sin; for, in that respect, the lusts of
men may die of their own accord, even a kind of natural death.
The members of the body are the weapons of unrighteousness, as
the apostle calls them; age or sickness may so blunt or break those
weapons, that the soul cannot use them to such sinful purposes and
services as it was wont to do in the vigorous and healthful seasons
of life ; not that there is less sin in the heart, but because there
are less strength and activity in the body.   Just as it is with an old
soldier, who hath as much skill, policy, and delight as ever in
military actions ; but age and hard services have so enfeebled him,
that he can no longer follow the camp.

Fourthly, The crucifixion of sin doth not consist in the severe
castigation of the body, and penancing it by stripes, fasting, and
tiresome pilgrimages.   This may pass for mortification among Papists, but never was any lust of the flesh destroyed by this rigour.
Christians, indeed, are bound not to indulge and pamper the body,
which is the instrument of sin ; nor yet must we think that the
spiritual corruptions of the soul feel those stripes which are inflicted
upon the body : See Col. ii. 23. it is not the vanity of superstition,
but the power of true religion, which crucifies and destroys corruption ; it is faith in Christ's blood, not the spilling of our own blood,
which gives sin the mortal wound.

Secondly, But if you enquire, what then is implied in the mortification or crucifixion of sin, and wherein it doth consist? I answer,

First, It necessarily implies the soul's implantation into Christ,
and union with him : without which it is impossible that any one corruption should be mortified ; *They that are* [*Christ's*] *have crucified*

the flesh: * The attempts and endeavours of all others are vain and ineffectual: " When we were in the flesh, (saith the apostle) the " motions of sin which were by the law did work in our members, " to bring forth fruit unto death,".Rom. vii. 5. sin was then in its full dominion, no abstinence, rigour, or outward severity ; no purposes, promises, or solemn vows could mortify or destroy it ; there must be an implantation into Christ before there can be any effectual crucifixion of sin : What believer almost hath not in the days of his first convictions, tried all external. methods and means of mortifying sin, and found all in experience to be to as little purpose as the binding of Samson with green withs or cords ? But when he hath once come to act faith upon the death of Christ, then the design of mortification hath prospered and succeeded to good purpose.

Secondly, Mortification of sin implies the *agency of the Spirit of God* in that work, without whose assistances and aids, all our endeavours must needs be fruitless : Of this work we may say as it was said in another case, Zech. iv. 6. " Not by might, nor by power, " but by my Spirit, saith the Lord." When the *apostle* therefore would shew by what hand this work of mortification is performed, he thus expresseth it, Rom. viii. 13. " If ye through the Spirit do " mortify the deeds of the body, ye shall live:" The duty is ours, but the power whereby we perform it is God's : The Spirit is the only successful combatant against the lusts that war in our members, Gal. v. 17. It is true, this excludes not, but implies our endeavours; for it is we through the Spirit who mortify the deeds of the body ; but yet all our endeavours without the Spirit's aid and influence avail nothing.

Thirdly, The crucifixion of sin necessarily implies *the subversion of its dominion* in the soul : A mortified sin cannot be a reigning sin, Rom. vi. 12, 13, 14. Two things constitute the dominion of sin, viz. the fulness of its power, and the soul's subjection to it. As to the fulness of its power, that rises from the suitableness it hath, and pleasure it gives to the corrupt heart of man : It seems to be as necessary as the right hand, as useful and pleasant as the right-eye, Mat. v. 29. but the mortified heart is dead to all pleasures and profits of sin ; it hath no delight or pleasure in it ; it becomes its burden and daily complaint. Mortification presupposes the illumination of the mind and conviction of the conscience ; by reason whereof sin cannot deceive and blind the mind, or bewitch

---

* They mistake the very nature of Christian mortification, who place it in afflicting and using violence to the body ; whereas true mortification refers not principally to the body or inferior part of the soul, but chiefly to the mind and will. *Dav. on Col.* p. 256.

and ensnare the will and affections as it was wont to do, and consequently its dominion over the soul is destroyed and lost.

Fourthly, The crucifying of the flesh implies a *gradual weakening of the power of sin* in the soul. The death of the cross was a slow and lingering death, and the crucified person grew weaker and weaker every hour; so it is in the mortification of sin: The soul is still " cleansing itself from all filthiness of the flesh and spirit, " and perfecting holiness in the fear of God," 2 Cor. vii. 1. And as the body of sin is weakened more and more; so the inward man, or the new creature, is " renewed day by day," 2 Cor. iv. 16. For sanctification is a progressive work of the Spirit: And as holiness increases and roots itself deeper and deeper in the soul; so the power and interest of sin proportionably abates and sinks lower and lower, until at length it be swallowed up in victory.

Fifthly, The crucifying of the flesh notes to us the believers' *designed application of all spiritual means* and sanctified instruments for the destruction of it: There is nothing in this world which a gracious heart more vehemently desires and longs for than the death of sin and perfect deliverance from it, Rom. vii. 24. the sincerity of which desires doth accordingly manifest itself in the daily application of all God's remedies: such are daily watching against the occasions of sin, Job xxxi. 1. " I have made a covenant with mine " eyes ;" more than ordinary vigilancy over their special or proper sin, Psal. xviii. 23. " I kept myself from mine iniquity :" Earnest cries to heaven for preventing grace. Psal. xix. 13. " Keep back " thy servant also from presumptuous sins, let them not have do- " minion over me :" Deep humblings of soul for sins past, which is an excellent preventive unto future sins, 2 Cor. ii. 11. " in that " ye sorrowed after a godly sort, what carefulness wrought it ?" Care to give no furtherance or advantage to the design of sin by making provision for the flesh to fulfil the lusts thereof, as others do, Rom. xiii. 13, 14. Willingness to bear due reproofs for sin, Psal. cxli. 5. " Let the righteous smite me, it shall be a kindness :" These, and such like means of mortification, regenerate souls are daily using and applying, in order to the death of sin. And so much of the first particular, what the mortification of sin, or crucifying of the flesh implies.

Secondly, In the next place we shall examine the reasons why this work of the Spirit is expressed under that *trope*, or figurative expression of *crucifying the flesh*. Now the ground and reason of the use of this expression, is the resemblance which the mortification of sin bears unto the death of the cross : And this appears in five particulars.

First, The death of the cross was a *painful death*, and the mortification of sin is a very painful work, Mat. xxv. 29. it is as the cutting off our right hands, and plucking out our right eyes; it will cost many thousand tears and groans, prayers, and strong cries to heaven, before one sin will be mortified. Upon the account of the difficulty of this work, and mainly upon this account, the scripture saith, " narrow is the way, and strait is the gate that " leadeth unto life, and few there be that find it," Mat. vii. 14. and that the righteous themselves are *scarcely saved.*

Secondly, The death of the cross was *universally painful;* every member, every sense, every sinew, every nerve, was the seat and subject of tormenting pain. So it is in the mortification of sin; it is not this or that particular member or act, but the whole body of sin that is to be destroyed, Rom. vi. 6. and accordingly the conflict is in every faculty of the soul; for the Spirit of God, by whose hand sin is mortified, doth not combat with this or that particular lust only, but with sin, as sin; and for that reason with every sin, in every faculty of the soul. So that there are conflicts and anguish in every part.

Thirdly, The death of the cross was a *slow, and lingering death;* denying unto them that suffered it the favour of a quick dispatch; just so it is in the death of sin: though the Spirit of God be mortifying it day by day, * yet this is a truth sealed by the sad experience of all believers in the world, *that sin is long a dying.* And if we ask a reason of this dispensation of God, among others, this seems to be one; corruptions in believers, like the Canaanites in the land of Israel, are left to prove and to exercise the people of God, to keep us watching and praying, mourning and believing; yea, wondering and admiring at the riches of pardoning and preserving mercy all our days.

Fourthly, The death of the cross was a very *opprobrious, or shameful death;* they that died upon the cross were loaded with ignominy; the crimes for which they died were exposed to the public view; after this manner dieth sin, a very shameful and ignominious death. Every true believer draws up a charge against it in every prayer, aggravates and condemns it in every confession, bewails the evil of it with multitudes of tears and groans; making sin as vile and odious as he can find words to express it, though not so vile as it is in its own nature. " O my God, (saith Ezra) I am ashamed, " and even blush to look up unto thee," Ezra ix. 6. So Daniel in his confession, Dan. ix. 7. " O Lord, righteousness belongeth " unto thee, but unto us confusion of faces, as at this day." Nor

---

* Mortification of sin is not completed in one moment, but is a daily conflict. Sin languishes as soon as the work of mortification is begun; in the progress of it sin wastes and pines away, and in the end, even at our death, it is destroyed. *Origen Ep. Rom.*

can it grieve any believer in the world, to accuse, condemn, and shame himself for sin, whilst he remembers and considers, that all that shame and confusion of face which he takes to himself goes to the vindication, glory and honour of his God.   As David was content to be more vile still for God, so it pleaseth the heart of a Christian to magnify and advance the name and glory of God, by exposing his own shame, in humble and broken hearted confessions of sin.

Fifthly, In a word, the death of the cross *was not a natural, but a violent death :* Such also is the death of sin : sin dies not of its own accord, as nature dieth in old men, in whom the *balsamum radicale,* or radical moisture is consumed : for if the Spirt of God did not kill it, it would live to eternity in the souls of men ; it is not the everlasting burnings, and all the wrath of God which lies upon the damned for ever, that can destroy sin.   Sin, like a *sala-mander,* can live to eternity in the fire of God's wrath ; so that either it must die a violent death by the hand of the Spirit, or it never dieth at all.   And thus you see, why the mortification of sin is *tropically* expressed by the crucifying of the flesh.

Thirdly, Why all that are in Christ must be so crucified, or mortified unto sin : And the necessity of this will appear divers ways.

First, From the inconsistency and contrariety that there is be-twixt Christ and unmortified lust, Gal. v. 17. " These are contrary " the one to the other."   There is a threefold inconsistency be-twixt Christ and such corruptions ; they are not only contrary to the *holiness of Christ,* 1 John iii. 6. " Whosoever abideth in him sin-" neth not ; whosoever sinneth hath not seen him, neither known " him ; i. e. whosoever is thus ingulphed and plunged into the lust of the flesh, can have no communion with the pure and holy Christ ; but there is also an inconsistency betwixt such sin and the *honour of Christ,* 2 Tim. ii. 19. " Let every one that nameth the " name of Christ, depart from iniquity."   As Alexander said to a soldier of his name, *recordare nominis Alexandri,* remember thy name is *Alexander,* and do nothing unworthy of that name.   And unmortified lusts are also contrary to the *dominion* and government of *Christ,* Luke ix. 23. " If any man will come after me, let him " deny himself, and take up his cross daily, and follow me :" These are the self-denying terms upon which all men are admitted into Christ's service : And without mortification and self-denial, he allows no man to call him Lord and Master.

Secondly, The necessity of mortification appears from the neces-sity of conformity betwixt Christ, the Head, and all the members of his mystical body ; for how incongruous and uncomely would it be to see a holy, heavenly Christ, leading a company of unclean, carnal, and sensual members? Mat. xi. 29. " Take my yoke " upon you, and learn of me, for I am meek and lowly," q. d. it would be monstrous to the world, to behold a company of *lions* and *wolves* following a meek and harmless *lamb :* Men of raging and unmortified lusts, professing and owning me for their head of government. And again, 1 John ii. 6. " He that saith he abideth " in him, ought himself also to walk, even as he walked," q. d. either imitate Christ in your *practice*, or never make pretensions to Christ in your *profession*. This was what the apostle complained of, Phil. iii. 18. for " many walk of whom I have told you often, " and now tell you, even weeping, that they are the enemies of " the cross of Christ. Men cannot study to put a greater dishonour and reproach upon Christ, than by making his name and profession a cloke and and cover to their filthy lusts.

Thirdly, The necessity of crucifying the flesh appears from the method of salvation, as it is stated in the gospel. God every where requires the practice of mortification, under pain of damnation. Mat. xviii. 8. " Wherefore if thy hand, or thy foot, offend thee, " cut them off, and cast them from thee : it is better for thee to " enter into life, halt or maimed, rather than having two hands, " or two feet, to be cast into everlasting fire." The gospel legitimates no hopes of salvation, but such as are accompanied with serious endeavours of mortification. 1 John iii. 3. " Every man " that hath this hope in him, purifieth himself, even as he is " pure." It was one special end of Christ's coming into the world, " to save his people from their sins," Mat. i. 21. nor will he be a saviour unto any who remain under the dominion of their own lusts.

Fourthly, The whole stream and current of the gospel, puts us under the necessity of mortification ; gospel-precepts have respect unto this, Col. iii. 5. " Mortify your members, therefore, which " are upon the earth." 1 Pet. i. 15. " Be ye holy, for I am holy." Gospel-precedents have respect unto this, Heb. xii. 1. " Where- " fore seeing we, also, are compassed about with so great a cloud " of witnesses, let us lay aside every weight, and the sin which " doth so easily beset us," &c. Gospel-threatenings are written for this end, and do all press mortification in a thundering dialect, Rom. viii. 13. " If ye live after the flesh, ye shall die." Rom. i. 18. " The wrath of God is revealed from heaven, against all un- " godliness, and unrighteousness of men." The *promises* of the gospel are written designedly to promote it, 2 Cor. vii. 1. " Having " therefore these promises, dearly beloved, let us cleanse our- " selves from all filthiness of flesh and spirit, perfecting holiness " in the fear of God." But in vain are all these precepts, precedents, threatenings, and promises written in the scriptures, except mortification be the daily study and practice of professors.

Fifthly, Mortification is the very scope and aim of our regeneration, and the infusion of the principles of grace. " If we live " in the spirit, let us walk in the spirit," Gal. v. 25. In vain were the habits of grace planted, if the fruits of holiness and mortification be not produced; yea, mortification is not only the design and aim, but it is a special part, even the one half of our sanctification.

Sixthly, If mortification be not the daily practice and endeavour of believers, then the way to heaven no way answers to Christ's description of it in the gospel. He tells us, Mat. vii. 13, 14. " Wide is the gate, and broad is the way that leadeth to destruc- " tion, and many there be that go in thereat : because strait is " the gate, and narrow is the way which leadeth unto life, and " few there be that find it." Well then, either Christ must be mistaken in the account he gave of the way to glory, or else all unmortified persons are out of the way; for what makes the way of salvation narrow, but the difficulties and severities of mortification?

Seventhly, In a word, he that denies the necessity of mortification, confounds all discriminating marks betwixt saints and sinners; pulls down the pale of distinction, and lets the world into the church, and the church into the world : It is a great design of the gospel to preserve the boundaries betwixt the one and the other, Rom. ii. 7, 8. Rom. viii. 1, 4, 5, 6, 13. But if men may be Christians without mortification, we may as well go into the *taverns, ale-houses,* or *brothel-houses,* among the roaring or sottish crew of sinners, and say, here are those that are redeemed by the blood of Christ; here are his disciples and followers; as to go to seek them in the purest churches, or most strictly religious families : by all which the necessity of mortification, unto all that are in Christ, is abundantly evidenced.

Fourthly, In the next place, we are to enquire into the true *principle* of mortification; it is true, there are many ways attempted by men for the mortification of sin, and many rules laid down, to guide men in that great work; some of which are very trifling and impertinent things: such are those prescribed by *Popish Votaries.* But I shall lay down this as a sure conclusion, that *the sanctifying Spirit is the only effectual principle of mortification;* and, without him, no resolutions, vows, abstinences, castigations of the body, or any other external endeavours, can ever avail to the mortification of one sin. The *moral Heathens* have prescribed many pretty rules and helps for the suppression of vice : Aristides, Seneca, and Cato, were renowned among them upon this account : formal

Christians have also gone far in the reformation of their lives, but could never attain true mortification; formality pares off the excrescences of vice, but never kills the root of it: it usually recovers itself again, and their souls, like a body not well purged, relapses into a worse condition than before, Mat. xii. 43, 44. 2 Pet. ii. 20.

This work of mortification is peculiar to the Spirit of God, Rom. viii. 13. Gal. v. 17. and the Spirit becomes a principle of mortification in believers two ways, namely,

1. By the implantation of contrary habits.

2. By assisting those implanted habits in all the times of need.

First, The Spirit of God implants habits of a contrary nature, which are destructive to sin, and are purgative of corruption, 1 John v. 4. Acts xv. 9. Grace is to corruption what water is to fire; betwixt which, there is both a *formal* and *effective opposition;* a contrariety both in nature and operation, Gal v. 17. There is a threefold remarkable advantage given us by grace, for the destruction and mortification of sin. For,

First, Grace gives the mind and heart of man a contrary bent and inclination; by reason whereof spiritual and heavenly things become connatural to the regenerate soul. Rom. vii. 22. " For I " delight in the law of God after the inner man." Sanctification is in the soul as a living spring running with a kind of *central force* heaven-ward, John iv. 14.

Secondly, Holy principles destroy the interest that sin once had in the love and delight of the soul; the sanctified soul cannot take pleasure in sin, or find delight in that which grieves God, as it was wont to do; but that which was the object of delight, hereby becomes the object of grief and hatred. Rom. vii. 15. *What I hate, that I do.*

Thirdly, From both these follow a third advantage for the mortification of sin, in as much as sin being contrary to the new nature, and the object of grief and hatred, cannot possibly be committed without reluctancy and very sensible regret of mind; and actions done with regret are neither done frequently nor easily. The case of a regenerate soul under the surprizals and particular victories of temptation, being like that of a captive in war, who marches not with delight, but by constraint among his enemies *. So the apostle expresseth himself, Rom. vii. 23. " But I see another law in " my members warring against the law of my mind; and bringing " me into captivity unto the law of sin which is in my members."

---

* Αιχμαλωτιζω, When one is so taken that he can neither struggle, nor resist him by whom he is taken captive.

Thus the Spirit of God promotes the design of mortification, by the implantation of contrary habits.

Secondly, By assisting those gracious habits in all the times of need, which he doth many ways; sometimes notably awakening and rousing grace out of the dull and sleepy habit, and drawing forth the activity and power of it into actual and successful resistances of temptations. As Gen. xxxix. 9. "How can I do this great "wickedness and sin against God?" Holy fear awakens first and raises all the powers of grace in the soul to make a vigorous resistance of temptation: the Spirit also strengthens weak grace in the soul. 2 Cor. xii. 9. "My grace is sufficient for thee, for my "strength is made perfect in weakness:" And, by reason of grace thus implanted and thus assisted, "he that is born of God keepeth "himself, and the wicked one toucheth him not."

Fifthly, The last query to be satisfied is, how mortification of sin solidly evinceth the soul's interest in Christ; and this it doth divers ways, affording the mortified soul many sound evidences thereof. As,

Evidence 1. Whatsoever evidences the indwelling of the Holy Spirit of God in us, must needs be evidential of a saving interest in Christ, as hath been fully proved before; but the mortification of sin doth plainly evidence the indwelling of the Spirit of God; for, as we proved but now, it can proceed from no other principle. There is as strong and inseparable a connection betwixt mortification and the Spirit, as betwixt the effect and its proper cause; and the self-same connection betwixt the inbeing of the Spirit and union with Christ: So that to reason from mortification to the inhabitation of the Spirit, and from the inhabitation of the Spirit to our union with Christ, is a strong scriptural way of reasoning.

Evidence 2. That which proves a soul to be under the *covenant of grace,* evidently proves its interest in Christ; for Christ is the head of that *covenant,* and none but sound believers are under the blessings and promises of it: but mortification of sin is a sound evidence of the soul's being under the covenant of grace, as is plain from those words of the apostle, Rom. vi. 12, 13, 14. "Let not "sin, therefore, reign in your mortal body, that ye should obey it "in the lust thereof; neither yield ye your members as instru-"ments of unrighteousness unto sin; but yield yourselves unto "God, as those that are alive from the dead, and your members "as instruments of righteousness unto God: for sin shall not have "dominion over you; for ye are not under the law, but under "grace." Where the apostle presseth believers unto mortification by this encouragement, that it will be a good evidence unto them of a new covenant interest; for all legal duties and endeavours can never mortify sin: it is the Spirit in the new covenant, which produces this. Whoever, therefore, hath his corruptions mortified, hath his interest in the covenant, and consequently in Christ, so far cleared unto him.

Evidence 3. That which is the fruit and evidence of saving faith, must needs be a good evidence of our interest in Christ ; but mortification of sin is the fruit and evidence of saving faith.   Acts xv. 9. " Purifying their hearts by faith."   1 John v. 4.   " This is the " victory whereby we overcome the world, even our faith."   Faith overcomes both the allurements of the world on the one hand, and the terrors of the world on the other hand, by mortifying the heart and affections to all earthly things : a mortified heart is not easily taken with the ensnaring pleasures of the world, or much moved with the disgraces, losses, and sufferings it meets with from the world ; and so the strength and force of its temptations are broken, and the mortified soul becomes victorious over it ; and all this by the instrumentality of faith.

Evidence 4. In a word, there is an intimate and indissoluble connexion betwixt the mortification of sin, and the life of grace. Rom. vi. 11. " Reckon yourselves to be dead indeed unto sin, but " alive unto God, through Jesus Christ :" and the life of Christ must needs involve a saving interest in Christ.   By all which is fully proved what was asserted in the observation from this text. The application follows in the next sermon.

SERMON XXVIII.

GAL. v. 24.

And they that are Christ's, have crucified the flesh, with the affections and lusts.

From hence our observation was,

*T*HAT *a saving interest in Christ, may be regularly and strongly inferred and concluded from the mortification of the flesh, with its affections and lusts.*

Having opened the nature and necessity of mortification in the former sermon, and shewn how regularly a saving interest in Christ may be concluded from it ; we now proceed to apply the whole, by way of

     1. Information.
     2. Exhortation.
     3. Direction.
     4. Examination.
     5. Consolation.

First use, for information.

Inference 1. If they that be Christ's have crucified the flesh, *Then the life of Christians is no idle or easy life:* the corruptions of his heart continually fill his hands with work, with work of the most difficult nature; sin-crucifying work, which the scripture calls the cutting off the right hand, and plucking out of the right eye: sin-crucifying work is hard work, and it is constant work throughout the life of a Christian; there is no time nor place freed from this conflict; every occasion stirs corruption, and every stirring of corruption calls for mortification: corruptions work in our very best duties, Rom. vii. 23. and put the Christian upon mortifying labours. The world and the devil are great enemies, and fountains of many temptations to believers, but not like the corruptions of their own hearts; they only tempt objectively and externally, but these tempt internally, and therefore are much more dangerous; they only tempt at times and seasons; these continually, at all times and seasons: besides, whatever Satan or the world attempts upon us, would be altogether ineffectual were it not for our own corruptions, John xiv. 30. So that the corruptions of our own hearts, as they create us most danger, so they must give us more labour; our life and this labour must end together; for sin is long a dying in the best heart: those that have been many years exercised in the study of mortification, may haply feel the same corruption tempting and troubling them now, which put them into tears, and many times brought them to their knees twenty or forty years ago. It may be said of sin as it was said of Hannibal, that active enemy, that it will never be quiet, whether conquering or conquered: and until sin cease working, the Christian must not cease mortifying.

Inf. 2. If mortification be the great work of a Christian, *then certainly those that give the corruptions of Christians an occasion to revive, must needs do them a very ill office;* they are not our best friends that stir the pride of our hearts by the flattery of their lips. The graces of God in others, I confess, are thankfully to be owned, and under discouragements, and contrary temptations, to be wisely and modestly spoken of; but the strongest Christians do scarcely shew their own weakness in any one thing more than they do in hearing their own praises. Christian, thou knowest thou carriest gun-powder about thee, desire those that carry fire to keep at a distance from thee; it is a dangerous crisis when a proud heart meets with flattering lips; *auferte ignem, &c.* take away the fire, (said a holy divine of Germany, when his friend commended him upon his death-bed) for I have yet combustible matter about me; faithful, seasonable, discreet reproofs are much more safe to us, and advantageous to our mortifying work: but alas, how few have the boldness or wisdom duly to administer them? It is said of Alexander, that he bid a philosopher (who had been long with him) to be gone; for, said he, so long thou hast been with me, and never reproved me; which must needs be thy fault; for either thou sawest nothing in me worthy of reproof which argues thy ignorance; or else thou durst not reprove me, which argues thy unfaithfulness. A wise and faithful reprover is of singular use to him that is heartily engaged in the design of mortification; such a faithful friend, or some malicious enemy, must be helpful to us in that work.

Inf. 3. Hence it follows, *that manifold and successive afflictions are no more than what is necessary for the best of Christians :* the mortification of our lusts require them all, be they never so many, 1 Pet. i. 5. "If need be, ye are in heaviness:" it is no more than need, that one loss should follow another, to mortify an earthly heart; for so intensely are our affections set upon the world, that it is not one, or two, or many checks of providence, that will suffice to wean and alienate them. Alas, the earthliness of our hearts will take all this, it may be much more than this, to purge them: the wise God sees it but necessary to permit frequent discoveries of our own weakness, and to let loose the tongues of many enemies upon us, and all little enough to pull down our pride, and the vanity that is in our hearts. Christian, how difficult soever it be for thee to bear it; yet the pride of thy heart requires all the scoffs and jeers, all the calumnies and reproaches, that ever the tongues or pens of thy bitterest enemies, or mistaken friends, have at any time thrown upon thee. Such rank weeds as grow in our hearts, will require hard frosts and very sharp weather to rot them; the straying bullock needs a heavy clog, and so doth a Christian whom God will keep within the bounds and limits of his commandments, Psal. cxix. 67. Dan. xi. 35.

Inf. 4. If they that be Christ's have crucified the flesh *, *then the number of real Christians is very small.* It is true, if all that seem to be meek, humble, and heavenly, might pass for Christians, the number would be great; but if no more must be accounted Christians, than those who crucify the flesh, with its affections and lusts, O, how small is the number! For, O, how many be there under the Christian name, that pamper and indulge their lusts, that secretly hate all who faithfully reprove them, and really affect none but such as feed their lusts, by praising and admiring them? How many that make provision for the flesh to fulfil its lusts, who cannot endure to have their corruptions crossed?

---

* He who is not crucified with Christ, and who is not a member of Christ, is not saved by his cross. *Prosper.*

How many are there that seem very meek and humble, until an occasion be given them to stir up their passion, and then you shall see in what degree they are mortified: the flint is a cold stone, till it be struck, and then it is all fiery. I know the best of Christians are mortified but in part; and strong corruptions are oftentimes found in very eminent Christians; but they love them not so well as to purvey for them; to protect, defend, and countenance them; nor dare they secretly hate such as faithfully reprove them; as many thousands that go under the name of Christians do. Upon the account of mortification it is said, Mat. vii. 13. " Narrow is the way, and strait is the gate that leadeth unto life, and few there be " that find it."

Inf. 5. If they that be Christ's have crucified the flesh, i. e. if mortification is their daily work and study; *then how falsely are Christians charged as troublers of the world, and disturbers of the civil peace and tranquillity of the times and places they live in;* Justly may they retort the charge, as Elijah did to Ahab, " It is " not I that trouble Israel, but thou and thy father's house:" It is not holy, meek, and humble Christians that put the world into confusion; this is done by the profane and atheistical; or by the designing and hypocritical world, and laid at the door of innocent Christians: as all the public calamities which from the immediate hand of God, or by foreign or domestic enemies befel Rome, were constantly charged upon Christians; and they condemned and punished, for what the righteous hand of God inflicted on the working heads of the enemies of that state without their privity contrived. The apostle James propounds and answers a question very pertinent to this discourse, James iv. 1. " From whence come wars " and fightings among you? Come they not hence, even of your " lusts that war in your members?" O, if men did but study mortification and self-denial, and live as much at home in the constant work of their own hearts as some men do; what tranquillity and peace, what blessed halcyon-days should we quickly see! It is true, Christians are always fighting and quarrelling, but it is with themselves and their own corrupt hearts and affections; they hate no enemy but sin; they thirst for the blood and ruin of none but of that enemy; they are ambitious of no victory, but what is over the corruptions of their own hearts; they carry no grudge except it be against this enemy, sin; and yet these are the men who are the most suspected and charged with disturbing the times they live in; just as the wolf accused the lamb, which was below him, for puddling and defiling the stream. But there will be a day when God will clear up the innocency and integrity of his mistaken and abused servants; and the world shall see, it was not preaching and praying, but drinking, swearing, profaneness, and enmity unto true godliness, which disturbed and broke the tranquillity and quietness of the times: mean time let innocency commit itself unto God, who will protect, and in due time vindicate the same.

Inf. 6. If they that be Christ's have crucified the flesh, *then whatsoever religion, opinion, or doctrine doth in its own nature countenance and encourage sin, is not of Christ.* The doctrine of Christ every where teacheth mortification: the whole stream of the gospel runs against sin; the doctrine it teacheth is holy, pure, and heavenly; it hath no tendency to extol corrupt nature, and feed its pride, by magnifying its freedom and power, or by stamping the merit and dignity of the blood of Christ upon its works and performances; it never makes the death of Christ a *cloke* to cover sin, but an *instrument* to destroy it. And whatsoever doctrine it is which nourishes the pride of nature, to the disparagement of grace, or encourages licentiousness and fleshly lust, is not the doctrine of Christ, but a spurious offspring begotten by Satan upon the corrupt nature of man.

Inf. 7. If mortification be the great business and character of a Christian, *Then that condition is most eligible and desirable by Christians, which is least of all exposed to temptation,* Prov. xxx. 8. " Give me neither poverty nor riches, but feed me with food convenient." That holy judicious man was well aware of the danger lurking in both extremes, and how near they border upon deadly temptations, and approach the very precipice of ruin that stand upon either ground: few Christians have an head strong and steady enough to stand upon the pinnacle of wealth and honour; nor is it every one that can grapple with poverty and contempt. A mediocrity is the Christian's best external security, and therefore most desirable: and yet how do the corruption, the pride and ignorance of our hearts grasp and covet that condition which only serves to warm and nourish our lusts, and make the work of mortification much more difficult? It is well for us that our wise Father leaves us not to our own choice, that he frequently dashes our earthly projects, and disappoints our fond expectations. If children were left to carve for themselves, how often would they cut their own fingers?

Inf. 8. If mortification be the great business of a Christian, *then Christian fellowship and society duly managed and improved, must needs be of singular use and special advantage to the people of God.* For thereby we have the friendly help and assistance of many other hands to carry on our great design, and help us in our most difficult business; if corruption be too hard for us, others this way come in to our assistance, Gal. vi. 1. " Brethren, if a man be overtaken in a " fault, ye which are spiritual restore such an one in the spirit of

" meekness." If temptations prevail, and overbear us that we fall under sin, it is a special mercy to have the reproofs and counsels of our brethren, who will not suffer sin to rest upon us, Lev. xix. 17. Whilst we are sluggish and sleepy, others are vigilant and careful for our safety : The humility of another reproves and mortifies my pride : The activity and liveliness of another awakens and quickens my deadness : The prudence and gravity of another detects and cures my levity and vanity : The heavenliness and spirituality of another may be exceeding useful, both to reprove and heal the earthliness and sensuality of my heart. Two are better than one, but wo unto him that is alone. The devil is well aware of this great advantage, and therefore strikes with special malice against embodied Christians, who are as a well disciplined army, whom he therefore more especially endeavours to rout and scatter by persecutions, that thereby particular Christians may be deprived of the sweet advantages of mutual society.

Inf. 9. *How deeply hath sin fixed its roots in our corrupt nature, that it should be the constant work of a Christian's whole life, to mortify and destroy it ?* God hath given us many excellent helps, his Spirit within us, variety of ordinances and duties are also appointed as instruments of mortification : And from the very day of regeneration unto the last moment of dissolution, the Christian is daily at work in the use of all sanctified means, external and internal, yet can never dig up and destroy corruption at the root all his life long. The most eminent Christians of longest standing in religion, who have shed millions of tears for sin, and poured out many thousand prayers for the mortification of it, do, after all, find the remains of their old disease, that there is still life and strength in those corruptions which they have given so many wounds unto in duty. O the depth and strength of sin ! which nothing can separate from us, but that which separates our souls and bodies. And upon that account, the day of a believer's death is better than the day of his birth. Never till then do we put off our armour, sheath our sword, and cry, victory, victory.

Second use, for exhortation.

If they who are Christ's have crucified the flesh, &c. Then as ever we hope to make good our claim to Christ, let us give all diligence to mortify sin ; in vain else are all our pretences unto union with him. This is the great work and discriminating character of a believer. And seeing it is the main business of life, and great evidence for heaven, I shall therefore press you to it by the following motives and considerations.

1 *Motive.* And first, methinks the comfort and sweetness resulting from mortification should effectually persuade every believer to more diligence about it. There is a double sweetness in mortifi-

cation, one in the nature of the work, as it is a duty, a sweet Christian duty ; another as it hath respect to Christ, and is evidential of our union with him.   In the first consideration there is a wonderful sweetness in mortification, for dost thou not feel a blessed calmness, cheeriness, and tranquillity in thy conscience, when thou hast faithfully repelled temptations, successfully resisted and overcome thy corruptions ? Doth not God smile upon thee ; conscience encourage and approve thee ? Hast thou not an heaven within thee ? whilst others feel a kind of hell in the deadly gripes and bitter accusations of their own consciences, are covered with shame, and filled with horrors.   But then consider it also as an evidence of the soul's interest in Christ, as my text considers it ; and what an heaven upon earth must then be found in mortification ! These endeavours of mine to subdue and mortify my corruptions, plainly speak the Spirit of God in me, and my being in Christ ! and O what is this ! What heart hath largeness and strength enough to receive and contain the joy and comfort which flow from a cleared interest in Jesus Christ ! Certainly, Christians, the tranquillity and comfort of your whole life depend upon it ; and what is life without the comfort of life ? Rom. viii. 13. " If ye through the Spirit " do mortify the deeds of the body, ye shall live," i. e. you shall live a serene, placid, comfortable life ; for it is corruption unmortified which clouds the face of God, and breaks the peace of his people, and consequently imbitters the life of a Christian.

2 *Motive.*   As the comfort of your own lives, which is much, so your instrumental fitness for the service of God, which is much more, depends upon the mortification of your sins, 2 Tim. ii. 21. " If a man therefore purge himself from these, he shall be a ves- " sel unto honour ; sanctified and meet for the Master's use, and " prepared unto every good work." Where is the mercy of life but in the usefulness and serviceableness of it unto God ? It is not worth while to live sixty or seventy years in the world to eat and drink, to buy and sell, to laugh and cry, and then go down to the place of silence.   So far as any man lives to God an useful, ser. viceable life to his praise and honour ; so far only, and no farther, doth he answer the end of his being.   But it is the purged, mortified soul which is the vessel of honour, prepared, and meet for the Master's use.   Let a proud, or an earthly heart be employed in any service for God, and you shall find that such an heart will both spoil the work, by managing it for a self-end as Jehu did ; and then devour the praise of it by a proud boast : *Come see my zeal.*   When the Lord would employ the prophet Isaiah in his work and service, his iniquity was first purged : and after that he was employed, Isa. vi. 6, 7, 8.   Sin is the soul's sickness, a consumption upon the inner man ; and we know that languishing consumptive per-

sons are very unfit to be employed in difficult and strenuous labours. Mortification, so far as it prevails, cures the disease, recovers our strength, and enables us for service to God in our generations.

3 *Motive.* Your stability and safety in the hour of temptation, depend upon the success of your mortifying endeavours. Is it then a valuable mercy in your eyes to be kept upright and stedfast in the critical season of temptation, when Satan shall be wrestling with you for the crown, and the prize of eternal life! Then give diligence to mortify your corruptions. Temptation is a siege, Satan is the enemy without the walls, labouring to force an entrance; natural corruptions are the traitors within, that hold correspondence with the enemy without, and open the gate of the soul to receive him. It was the covetousness of Judas' heart which overthrew him in the hour of temptation. They are our fleshly lusts which go over unto Satan in the day of battle, and *fight against our souls,* 1 Pet. ii. 11. the corruptions (or infectious atoms which fly up and down the world in times of temptation, as that word μιασματα, 2 Pet. ii. 20. imports) are through lusts, 2 Pet. i. 4. It is the lust within, which gives a lustre to the vanities of the world without, and thereby makes them strong temptations to us, 1 John ii. 16. Mortify therefore your corruptions, as ever you expect to maintain your station in the day of trial: cut off those advantages of your enemy, lest by them he cut off your souls, and all your hopes from God.

4 *Motive.* As temptations will be irresistible, so afflictions will be unsupportable to you without mortification. My friends, you live in a mutable world, providence daily rings the changes in all the kingdoms, cities, and towns, all the world over. You that have husbands or wives to-day, may be left desolate to-morrow: You that have estates and children now, may be bereaved of both before you are aware. Sickness will tread upon the heel of health, and death will assuredly follow life as the night doth the day. Consider with yourselves; are you able to bear the loss of your sweet enjoyments with patience? Can you think upon the parting hour without some tremblings? O get a heart mortified to all these things, and you will bless a taking as well as a giving God. It is the living world, not the crucified world, that raises such tumults in our souls in the day of affliction. How cheerful was holy Paul under all his sufferings! and what think you gave him that peace and cheerfulness, but his mortification to the world? Phil. iv. 12. " I know both how to be abased, and I know how to abound; " every where, and in all things I am instructed, both to be full, " and to be hungry, both to abound and suffer need." Job was the mirror of patience, in the greatest shock of calamity, and what

made him so, but the mortifiedness of his heart, in the fullest enjoyment of all earthly things? Job xxxi. 25.

5 *Motive.* The reputation and honour of religion are deeply concerned in the mortification of the professors of it: For unmortified
professors will, first or last, be the scandals and reproaches of it.
The profession of religion may give credit to you, but to be sure
you will never bring credit to it. All the scandals and reproaches
that fall upon the name of Christ in this world, flow from the fountain of unmortified corruption. Judas and Demas, Hymeneus, and
Philetus, Ananias and Sapphira ruined themselves, and became rocks
of offence to others by this means. If ever you will keep religion
sweet, labour to keep your hearts mortified and pure.

6 *Motive.* To conclude, what hard work will you have in your
dying hour, except you get a heart mortified to this world, and
all that is in it? Your parting hour is like to be a dreadful hour,
without the help of mortification. Your corruptions, like glue,
fasten your affections to the world, and how hard will it be for such
a man to be separated by death? O what a bitter and doleful parting
have carnal hearts from carnal things! whereas the mortified soul
can receive the messengers of death without trouble, and as cheerfully put off the body at death, as a man doth his clothes at night:
Death need not pull and hale; such a man goes half way to meet
it, Phil. i. 23. " I desire to be dissolved, and to be with Christ, which
" is far better." Christian, wouldst thou have thy death-bed soft
and easy; wouldst thou have an ευθανασια, as the *philosopher* desired
for himself, an easy death, without pain or terror; then get a mortified heart: the *Surgeon's* knife is scarce felt when it cuts off a
mortified member.

Third use, for direction.

Are you convinced, and fully satisfied of the excellency and
necessity of mortification, and inquisitive after the means, in the use
whereof it may be attained; then, for your help and encouragement, I will in the next place, offer my best assistance in laying
down the rules for this work.

Rule 1. If ever you will succeed and prosper in the work of
mortification, then get, and daily exercise more faith. Faith is
the great instrument of mortification; " This is the victory, (or
" sword by which the victory is won, the instrument) by which
" you overcome the world, even your faith," 1 John v. 4. By
faith alone eternal things are discovered to your souls, in their
reality and excelling glory, and these are the preponderating things,
for the sake whereof, self-denial and mortification become easy
to believers; by opposing things eternal to things temporal, we

resist Satan, 1 Pet. v. 8.   This is the shield by which we quench the fiery darts of the wicked one, Eph. vi. 16.

Rule 2. Walk in daily communion with God, if ever you will mortify the corruptions of nature ; that is the apostle's own pre-scription, Gal. i. 17. " This I say then, walk in the Spirit, and " ye shall not fulfil the lusts of the flesh." Spiritual and frequent communion with God, gives manifold advantages for the mortifi-cation of sin, as it is a bright glass wherein the holiness of God and the exceeding sinfulness of sin, as it is opposite thereunto, are most clearly and sensibly discovered, than which, scarce any thing can set a keener edge of indignation upon the spirit of a man against sin. Besides, all communion with God is assimilating and transformative of the soul into his image ; it leaves also a heavenly relish and savour upon the soul; it darkens the lustre and glory of all earthly things, by presenting to the soul a glory which excelleth : it marvellously improves, and more deeply radicates sanctification in the soul; by all which means it becomes singularly useful and successful in the work of mortification.

Rule 3. Keep your consciences under the awe and in the fear of God continually, as ever you hope to be successful in the mortifi-cation of sin. The fear of God is the great preservative from sin, without which all the external rules and helps in the world signify nothing : " By the fear of the Lord, men depart from evil," Prov. xvi. 6. Not only from external and more open evils, which the fear of men, as well as the fear of God, may prevent, but from the most secret and inward evils, which is a special part of mortifi-cation, Lev. xix. 14. It keeps men from those evils which no eye nor ear of man can possibly discover. The fear of the Lord breaks temptations, baited with pleasure, with profit, and with secresy. In a word, if ever you be cleansed from all filthiness of flesh and spirit, it must be by the fear of God, 2 Cor. vii. 1.

* *Rule* 4. Study the vanity of the creature, and labour to get true notions of the emptiness and transitoriness thereof, if ever you will attain to the mortification of your affections towards it.

It is the false picture and image of the world, in our fancy, that crucifies us with so many cares, fears, and solicitudes about it : and it is the true picture and image of the world, represented to us in the glass of the word, which greatly helps to crucify our affections to the world. O, if we did but know and believe three things about the world, we should never be so fond of it as we are,

---

* Readers, if ever you would have a true sight of the emptiness and vanity of the creature, and get a mortified heart to the world, now is the time ; for at this day the providence of God hath withered all the fading flowers of earthly delights, and shewed you the world's back parts, as it is departing from you.

viz. the fading, defiling, and destroying nature of it. The best and sweetest enjoyments in the world,. are but fading flowers and withered grass, Isa. xiv. 6. James i. 10, 11. yea, it is of a defiling, as well as a fading nature, 1 John v. 19. it lies in wickedness, it spreads universal infection among all mankind, 2 Pet. i. 4. yea, it destroys as well as defiles multitudes of souls, *drowning men in perdition*, 1 Tim. vi. 9. Millions of souls will wish, to eternity, they had never known the riches, pleasures, or honours of it. Were this believed, how would men slacken their pace, and cool themselves in the violent and eager pursuit of the world? This greatly tends to promote mortification.

Rule 5. Be careful to cut off all the occasions of sin, and keep at the greatest distance from temptations, if ever you would mortify the deeds of the body. The success and prevalency of sin, mainly depend upon the wiles and stratagems it makes use of to ensnare the incautious soul; therefore the apostle bids us keep off, at the greatest distance. 1 Thes. v. 22. " Abstain from all appearance of evil." Prov. v. 8. " Come not nigh unto the door of her house." He that dares venture to the very brink of sin, discovers but little light in his understanding, and less tenderness in his conscience, he neither knows sin nor fears it as he ought to do: And it is usual with God to chastise self-confidence by shameful lapses into sin.

Rule 6. If you will successfully mortify the corruptions of your nature, never engage against them in your own single strength, Eph. vi. 10. When the apostle draws forth Christians into the field, against sin, he bids them " be strong in the Lord, and in " the power of his might." O remember what a mere feather thou art in the gusts of temptation; call to mind the height of Peter's confidence, " though all men forsake thee, yet will not " I ;" and the depth of his fall, shame and sorrow. A weak Christian, trembling in himself, depending by faith upon God, and graciously assisted by him, shall be able to stand against the shock of temptation, when the bold and confident resolutions of others (like Pendleton in our English story) shall melt away as wax before the flames.

Rule 7. Set in with the mortifying design of God, in the day of thine affliction; sanctified afflictions are ordered and prescribed in heaven for the purging of our corruptions, Isa. xxvii. 9. " By this, therefore, shall the iniquity of Jacob be purged, and " this is all the fruit to take away his sin." It is a fair glass to represent the evil of sin, and the vanity of the creature, to imbitter the world, and disgust thy affections towards it: Fall in, therefore, with the gracious design of God; follow every affliction with prayer, that God would follow it with his blessing. God kills thy comforts, out of no other design but to kill thy corruptions with

them: wants are ordained to kill wantonness, poverty is appointed to kill pride, reproaches are permitted to pull down ambition:
Happy is the man who understands, approves, and heartily sets in
with the design of God, in such afflicting providences.

Rule 8. Bend the strength of your duties and endeavours against
your proper and special sin; it is in vain to lop off branches,
whilst this root of bitterness remains untouched: This was David's
practice, Psal. xviii. 23. " I was also upright before him, and I
" kept myself from mine iniquity." We observe, in natural men,
that one faculty is more vigorous than another; we find in nature,
that one soil suits with some sorts of seeds rather than another: And
every believer may find his nature and constitution inclining him
to one sin rather than another. As graces, so corruptions exceed
one another, even in the regenerate. The power of special corruption arises from our constitutions, education, company, custom,
callings, and such like occasions; but from whensoever it comes,
this is the sin that most endangers us, most easily besets us; and,
according to the progress of mortification in that sin, we may safely
estimate the degrees of mortification in other sins; Strike, therefore,
at the life and root of your own iniquity.

Rule 9. Study the nature and great importance of those things
which are to be won or lost, according to the success and issue of
this conflict. Your life is a race, eternal glory is the prize, grace
and corruption are the antagonists, and accordingly as either finally
prevails, eternal life is won or lost. 1 Cor. ix. 24. " Know ye
" not that they which run a race, run all, but one receiveth
" the prize? So run that ye may obtain." This condition will
make mortification appear the most rational and necessary thing
to you in the whole world. Shall I lose heaven for indulging the
flesh, and humouring a wanton appetite! God forbid. " I keep
" under my body, (saith Paul) and bring it into subjection; lest
" that by any means, when I have preached to others, I myself
" should be a cast away," 1 Cor. ix. 28.

Rule 10. Accustom your thoughts to such meditations as are
proper to mortify sin in your affections, else all endeavours to mortify it will be but faint and languid: To this purpose, I shall re-
commend the following meditations, as proper means to destroy the
interest of sin.

Meditation 1. Consider the evil that is in sin, and how terrible
the appearances of God will one day be against those that obey it,
in the lusts thereof. Rom. i. 18. " The wrath of God is revealed
" from heaven against all ungodliness and unrighteousness of men,"
1 Thes. i. 7, 8, 9. " The Lord Jesus shall be revealed from hea-
" ven, with his mighty angels, in flaming fire, taking vengeance

" on them that know not God, and that obey not the gospel of
" our Lord Jesus Christ: who shall be punished with everlasting
" destruction from the presence of the Lord, and from the glory
" of his power." Let your thoughts dwell much upon the consideration of the fruits and consequences of sin; it shews its fairest
side to you in the hour of temptation. O but consider how it will
look upon you in the day of affliction, Numb. xxii. 23. in that day
your sin will find you out: Think what its aspect will be in a dying
hour. 1 Cor. xv. 56. " The sting of death is sin." Think what
the frightful remembrances of it will be at the bar of judgment,
when Satan shall accuse, conscience shall upbraid, God shall condemn, and everlasting burnings shall avenge the evil of it: such
thoughts as these are mortifying thoughts.

Meditation 2. Think what it cost the Lord Jesus to expiate the
guilt of sin by suffering the wrath of the great and terrible God for
it in our room: the meditations of a crucified Christ are very crucifying meditations unto sin, Gal. vi. 14. he suffered unspeakable
things for sin; it was a divine wrath which lay upon his soul
for it; that wrath of which the prophet saith, Nahum i. 5, 6.
" The mountains quake at him, and the hills melt. Who can
" stand before his indignation? And who can abide in the fierce-
" ness of his anger? his fury is poured out like fire, and the rocks
" are thrown down by him." It was unmixed and unallayed
wrath, poured out in the fulness of it, even to the last drop: and
shall we be so easily drawn to the commission of those sins which
put Christ under such sufferings? O do but read such scriptures as
these, Luke xxii. 44. Matth. xxvi. 36, 37. Mark xiv. 33. and see
what a plight sin put the Lord of glory into; how the wrath of
God put him into a sore amazement, a bloody sweat, and made his
soul heavy unto death.

Meditation 3. Consider what a grief and wound the sins of believers are to the Spirit of God, Eph. iv. 30. Ezek. xvi. 43. Isa.
lxiii. 10. O how it grieves the Holy Spirit of God! Nothing is
more contrary to his nature. " O do not that abominable thing
" which I hate," saith the Lord, Jer. xliv. 4. Nothing obstructs
and crosses the sanctifying design of the Spirit, as sin doth; defacing and spoiling the most rare and admirable workmanship that
ever God wrought in this world; violating all the engagements
laid upon us by the love of the Father, by the death of his Son, by
the operations of his Spirit in all his illuminations, convictions,
compunctions, renovation, preservation, obsignation, and manifold
consolations. Lay this meditation upon thy heart, believer, and
say, *Sicne rependis?* dost thou thus requite the Lord, O my ungrateful heart, for all his goodness? Is this the fruit of his tem-

poral, spiritual, common, and peculiar mercies, which are without number ?

Meditation 4. Consider with yourselves, that no real good, either of profit or pleasure can result from sin ; you can have no pleasure in it, whatever others may have, it being against your new nature ; and as for that brutish pleasure and evanid joy which others have in sin, it can be but for a moment ; for either they must repent or not repent : if they do repent, the pleasure of sin will be turned into the gall of asps here ; if they do not repent, it will terminate in everlasting howlings hereafter. That is a smart question, Rom. vi. 21. " What fruit had ye in those things where-" of ye are now ashamed ? For the end of those things is death." You that are believers must never expect any pleasure in sin ; for you can neither commit it without regret, nor reflect upon it with-out shame and confusion : expect no better consequents of sin than the woundings of conscience and the dismal cloudings of the face of God ; that is all the profit of sin. O let these things sink into your heart.

Meditation 5. Consider what the damned suffer for those sins which the devil now tempteth you to commit ; it hath deprived them of all good, all outward good, Luke xvi. 25. all spiritual good, Mat. xxv. 41. and of all hope of enjoying any good for ever : and as it hath deprived them of all good, so it hath remedilessly plunged them into all positive misery : misery from without, the wrath of God being come upon them to the uttermost ; and misery from within, for *their worm dieth not*, Mark ix. 44. The memory of things past, the sense of things present, and the fearful expecta-tions of things to come, are the gnawings and bitings of the worm of conscience, at every bite whereof damned souls give a dreadful shriek ; crying out, O the worm ! the worm ! Would any man that is not forsaken by reason, run the hazard of those eternal miseries for the brutish pleasures of a moment ?

Meditation 6. Bethink yourselves what inexcusable hypocrisy it will be in you to indulge yourselves in the private satisfaction of your lusts, under a contrary profession of religion : you are a peo-ple that profess holiness, and professedly own yourselves to be under the government and dominion of Christ : and must the worthy name of Christ be only used to cloak and cover your lusts and corruptions, which are so hateful to him ? God forbid. You daily pray against sin, you confess it to God, you bewail it, you pour out supplications for pardoning and preventing grace ; are you in jest or earnest in these solemn duties of religion ? Certainly, if all those duties produce no mortification, you do but flatter God with your lips, and put a dreadful cheat upon your own souls. Nay, do you not frequently censure and condemn those things in others, and dare you allow them in yourselves? What horrid hypocrisy is this? Christians are dead to sin, Rom. vi. 2. dead to it by profession, dead to it by obligation, dead to it by relation to Christ, who died for them; and how shall they that are so many ways dead to sin, live any longer therein? O think not that God hates sin the less in you because you are his people *, nay, that very consideration aggravates it the more, Amos iii. 2.

Meditation 7. Consider with yourselves what hard things some Christians have chosen to endure and suffer rather than they would defile themselves with guilt; and shall every small temptation ensnare and take your souls? Read over the xi. chapter to the Hebrews, and see what the saints have endured to escape sin; no torments were so terrible to them as the displeasure of God, and woundings of conscience; and did God oblige them more by his grace and favour than he hath obliged you? O Christians, how can you that have found such mercies, mercies as free, and pardons as full as ever any souls found, shew less care, less fear, less tenderness of grieving the Spirit of God than others have done; certainly, if you did see sin with the same eyes they saw it, you would hate it as deeply, watch against it as carefully, and resist it as vigorously as any of the saints have done before you.

Meditation 8. Consider with yourselves what sweet pleasure, rational and solid comfort is to be found in the mortification of sin: It is not the fulfilling of your lusts can give you the thousandth part of that comfort and contentment that the resistance of them, and victory over them will give you. Who can express the comfort that is to be found in the cheering testimony of an acquitting and absolving conscience? 2 Cor. i. 12. Remember what satisfaction and peace it was to Hezekiah upon his supposed death-bed, when he turned to the wall, and said, " Remember now, O Lord, I be- " seech thee, how I have walked before thee in truth, and with a " perfect heart; and have done that which is good in thy sight," Isa. xxxviii. 3.

Fourth use, for examination.

In the next place, this point naturally puts us upon the examination and trial of our own hearts, whether we, who so confidently claim a special interest in Christ, have crucified the flesh with its affections and lusts. And because two sorts of persons will be concerned in this trial, viz. the weaker and the stronger Christians; I shall therefore lay down two sorts of evidences of mortification, one respecting the sincerity and truth, the other respecting the strength

---

* The very faults and sins of the faithful are the objects of God's hatred and displeasure, but this is merely a hatred of their sin, not of their persons. *Daven. on Col.* i. 10.

and progress of that work in confirmed and grown Christians, and both excluding false pretenders.

First, There are some things that are evidential of the truth and sincerity of mortification, even in the weakest Christians: as,

First, True tenderness of conscience as to all known sins, one as well as another, is a good sign sin hath lost its dominion in the soul. O it is a special mercy to have a heart that shall smite and reprove us for those things that others make nothing of: To check and admonish us for our secret sins, which can never turn to our reproach among men: this is a good sign that we hate sin, however, through the weakness of the flesh we may be ensnared by it. Rom. vii. 15. " What I hate, that I do."

Secondly, The sincere and earnest desires of our souls to God in prayer for heart-purging and sin-mortifying grace, is a good sign our souls have no love for sin. Canst thou say, poor believer, in the truth of thy heart, that if God would give thee thy choice, it would please thee better to have sin cast out, than to have the world cast in: that thy heart is not so earnest with God for daily bread, as it is for heart-purging grace? This is a comfortable evidence that sin is nailed to the cross of Christ.

Thirdly, Do you make conscience of guarding against the occasions of sin? Do you keep a daily watch over your hearts and senses, according to 1 John v. 18. Job xxxi. 1. This speaks a true design and purpose of mortification also.

Fourthly, Do you rejoice and bless God from your hearts, when the Providence of God orders any means for the prevention of sin? Thus did David, 1 Sam. xxv. 33. " And David said to Abigail, " Blessed be the Lord God of Israel which sent thee this day to " meet me, and blessed be thy advice, and blessed be thou which " hast kept me this day from coming to shed blood, and from " avenging myself with my own hand."

Fifthly, In a word, though the thoughts of death may be terrible in themselves, yet if the expectation and hope of your deliverance from sin thereby, do sweeten the thoughts of it to your souls, it will turn unto you for a testimony, that you are not the servants and friends of sin. And so much briefly of the first sort of evidences.

Secondly, There are other signs of a more deep and thorough mortification of sin, in more grown and confirmed believers, and such are these.

First, The more submissive and quiet any man is under the will of God, in smart and afflicting providences, the more that man's heart is mortified unto sin, Psal. cxix. 67, 71. Col. i. 11.

Secondly, The more able any one is to bear reproaches and

rebukes for his sin, the more mortification there is in that man, Psal. cxli. 5.

Thirdly, The more easily any man can resign and give up his dearest earthly comforts at the call and command of God, the more progress that man hath made in the work of mortification, Heb. xi. 17. 2 Sam. xv. 25.

Fourthly, The more power any man hath to resist sin in the first motions of it, and stifle it in the birth ; the greater degree of mortification that man hath attained, Rom. vii. 23, 24.

Fifthly, If great changes, upon our outward condition, make no change for the worse upon our spirits, but we can bear prosperous and adverse providences with an equal mind ; then mortification is advanced far in our souls, Phil. iv. 11, 12.

Sixthly, The more fixed and steady our hearts are with God in duty, and the less they are infested with wandering thoughts, and earthly interpositions ; the more mortification there is in that soul. And so much briefly of the evidences of mortification.

Fifth use, for consolation.

It only remains, that I shut up all with a few words of consolation unto all that are under the mortifying influence of the Spirit. Much might be said for the comfort of such.   In brief,

First, Mortified sin shall never be your ruin : It is only *reigning* sin that is *ruining* sin, Rom. viii. 13.   Mortified sins and pardoned sins shall never lie down with us in the dust.

Secondly, If sin be *dying,* your souls are *living;* for dying unto sin, and living unto God, are inseparably connected, Rom. vi. 11.

Thirdly, If sin be dying in you, it is certain that Christ died for you, and you cannot desire a better evidence of it, Rom. vi. 5, 6.

Fourthly, If sin be dying under the mortifying influences of the Spirit, and it be your daily labour to resist and overcome it, you are then in the direct way to heaven, and eternal salvation ; which few, very few in the world shall find, Luke xiii. 24.

Fifthly, To shut up all, if you, through the Spirit, be daily mortifying the deeds of the body, then the death of Christ is effectually applied by the Spirit unto your souls, and your interest in him is unquestionable : For they that are Christ's have crucified the flesh, with the affections and lusts ; and they that have so crucified the flesh with its affections and lusts are Christ's.

Blessed be God for a crucified Christ.

SERMON XXIX.

Of the Imitation of CHRIST in holiness of Life, and the necessity of it in Believers.

1 JOHN ii. 6.

He that saith he abideth in him, ought himself also to walk, even as he walked.

THE express and principal design of the apostle, in this chapter, is to propound marks and signs, both *negative* and *positive*, for the trial and examination of men's claims to Christ; amongst which (not to spend time about the coherence) my text is a principal one; a trial of men's interest in Christ, by their imitation of Christ. It is supposed by some expositors, that the apostle, in laying down this mark, had a special design to overthrow the wicked doctrine of the Carpocratians, who taught (as Epiphanius relates it) that men might have as much communion with God in sin as in duty. In full opposition to which the apostle lays down this proposition, wherein he asserts the necessity of a Christ-like conversation in all that claim union with him, or interest with him. The words resolve themselves into two parts, viz.

1. A claim to Christ supposed.

2. The only way to have our claim warranted.

First, We have here a claim to Christ supposed; " if any man " say he abideth in him." Abiding in Christ is an expression denoting proper and real interest in Christ, and communion with him; for it is put in opposition to those temporary, light, and transient effects of the gospel, which are called a morning dew, or an early cloud; such a receiving of Christ as that, Mat. xiii. 21. which is but a present flash, sudden and vanishing; abiding in Christ notes a solid, durable, and effectual work of the Spirit, thoroughly and everlastingly joining the soul to Christ. Now, if any man, whosoever he be (for this indefinite is equivalent to an universal term) let him never think his claim to be good and valid, except he take this course to adjust it.

(2.) *Secondly*, The only way to have this claim warranted, and that must be by *so walking even as he walked;* which words carry in them the necessity of our imitation of Christ. But it is not to be understood indefinitely and universally of all the works or actions of Christ, some of which were extraordinary and miraculous; some purely mediatory, and not imitable by us: In these paths no Christian can follow Christ; nor may so much as attempt to walk as he walked. But the words point at the ordinary and imitable ways and works of Christ; therein it must be the care of all to follow him, that profess and claim interest in him; they must so walk as he walked, this [so] is a very bearing word in this place; the emphasis of the text seems to lie in it; however, certain it is that this *so walking*, doth not imply an equality with Christ in holiness and obedience; for as he was filled with the Spirit without measure, and anointed with that oil of gladness above his fellows; so the purity, holiness, and obedience of his life are never to be matched, or equalized by any of the saints. But this *so walking*, only notes a sincere intention, design, and endeavour to imitate and follow him in all the paths of holiness and obedience, according to the different measures of grace received. The life of Christ is the believer's copy, and though the believer cannot draw one line or letter exact as his copy is, yet his eye is still upon it, he is looking unto Jesus, Heb. xii. 2. and labouring to draw all the lines of his life, as agreeably as he is able, unto Christ his pattern.

Hence the observation is,

Doct. *That every man is bound to the imitation of Christ, under penalty of forfeiting his claim to Christ.*

The saints imitation of Christ is solemnly enjoined by many great and express commands of the gospel; so you find it, 1 Pet. i. 15. " But as he that hath called you is holy, so be ye holy in all man- " ner of conversation:" So Eph. v. 1, 2. " Be ye therefore follow- " ers of God as dear children, and walk in love, as Christ also hath " loved us." " Christians (saith * Bernard) receive this name from " Christ; and it is very meet that as they inherit his name, so they " should also imitate his holiness." Now to state the method of this discourse, it will be needful to discuss and open three things in the doctrinal part.

1. What the saints imitation of Christ supposes and comprizes.

2. In what particulars they are especially bound to imitate Christ.

3. Why no claim to Christ is valid without this imitation of him.

And then apply the whole in divers uses.

(1.) *First*, What the saints imitation of Christ supposeth and compriseth. Now there are divers great and weighty truths supposed and implied in this imitation of Christ, or walking as he walked, viz.

---

* *Christiani a Christo nomen acceperunt, et operæ pretium est, ut sicut sunt hæredes nominis, ita sint imitatores sanctitatis.* Bern. sent. lib. p. 436.

First, It supposes, that no Christian is, or may pretend to be a rule to himself, to act according to the dictates of his own will and pleasure; for as no man hath wisdom enough to direct and govern himself, so if his own will were made the rule of his own actions, it would be the highest invasion of the divine prerogative that could be imagined: " I know, O Lord, (saith Jeremiah) that the " way of man is not in himself, it is not in him that walketh to " direct his own steps, Jer. x. 23. We may as well pretend to be our own makers as our own guides. It is a pretty observation of Aquinas, that if the workman's hand were the rule of his work, it were impossible he should ever err in working: And if the will of man were the only law and guide of his way, we might then say no man would sin in his walking. The apostle, indeed, saith of the Heathens, Rom. ii. 14. " That they are a law to themselves;" but it is not his meaning, that their will is their law, but the law of God engraven upon their hearts; the light and dictates of their own consciences did oblige and bind them as a law.

Secondly, This imitation of Christ implies, that as no man is, or may pretend to be his own guide, so no mere man, how wise or holy soever he be, may pretend to be a rule to other men; but Christ is the rule of every man's way and walking. It is true indeed, the apostle saith, " We should be followers of them, who " through faith and patience, inherit the promises," Heb. vi. 12. And again, James v. 10. " Take, my brethren, the prophets, " who have spoken in the name of the Lord, for an example of " suffering affliction, and of patience." But you must always remember, that there is a two-fold rule;

1. *Regula regulans*, the rule ruling.
2. *Regula regulata*, the rule ruled.

The wisest and holiest among men, may pretend no higher than *a ruled rule*. The great apostle, though filled with as great a measure of the Spirit of wisdom and holiness, as ever was possessed by any mere man, yet goes no higher than this, 1 Cor. xi. 1. " Be ye followers of me, as I also am of Christ." The best of men are but men at best; they have their errors and defects, which they freely acknowledge; and where they differ from Christ, it is our duty to differ from them. We may not pin our faith to any man's sleeve, for we know not where he will carry it. It was the commendation which Paul gave of the Thessalonians, 1 Thes. i. 6. " And you became followers of us and of the Lord." The noble Bereans were also commended for searching the scriptures, and examining the apostles' doctrine by it; and it was a good reply of the *father* to a clamorous disputant, crying, Hear me, hear me; " * I

---

* *Nec ego te, nec tu me, sed ambo audiamus Christum.* Aug.

" will neither hear thee, nor do thou hear me; but let us both
" hear Christ."

Thirdly, The imitation of Christ implies the necessity of sanctification in all his followers; forasmuch as it is impossible there
should be a practical conformity in point of obedience, where there
is not a conformity in spirit and in principle; all external conformity to Christ's practice, depends upon an internal conformity to
Christ in the principle and Spirit of holiness. It is very plain, from
Ezek. xi. 19, 20. that a new heart must be given us, and a new
spirit put into us, before we can walk in God's statutes; we
must first live in the Spirit, before we can walk in the Spirit, Gal.
v. 25.

Fourthly, The imitation of Christ plainly holds forth this, that
the Christian religion is a very precise and strict religion; no way
countenancing licentiousness, or indulging men in their lusts: it allows no man to walk loosely and inordinately, but rejects every
man's claim to Christ, who studies and labours not to tread exactly
in the footsteps of his holy and heavenly example. Profaneness
and licentiousness, therefore, can find no shelter or protection
under the wing of the gospel; this is the universal rule laid upon all
the professors of the Christian religion, " Let every one that
" nameth the name of Christ, depart from iniquity," 2 Tim. ii. 19.
i. e. let him either put on the life of Christ, or put off the name
of Christ; let him shew the hand of a Christian, in works of holiness and obedience, or else the tongue and language of a Christian
must gain no belief or credit.

Fifthly, The imitation of Christ necessarily implies the defectiveness and imperfection of the best of men in this life; for if the life
of Christ be our pattern, the best and holiest of men must confess
they come short in every thing of the rule of their duty. Our
pattern is still above us, the best of men are ashamed when they
compare their lives with the life of Christ: It is true, a vain heart
may swell with pride, when a man compares himself with other
men: thus measuring ourselves by ourselves, and comparing ourselves among ourselves, we shew our folly and nourish our pride;
but if any man will compare his own life with Christ's, he will find
abundant cause at every time and in every thing to be humbled.
Paul was a great proficient in holiness and obedience, he had been
long striving to come up to the top of holiness, yet when he looks
up and sees the life of Christ, and rule of duty, so far above him,
he reckons himself still but at the foot of the hill. Phil. iii. 12.
" Not as though I had already attained, either were already per-
" fect, but I follow after, if that I may apprehend that for which
" also I am apprehended of Christ Jesus." q. d. Alas! I am not
come up to my duty, I am a great way behind; but I am following

after, if at last I may attain it: Perfection is in my expectation and hope, at last, not in my attainment here.

Sixthly, The imitation of Christ, as our general rule or pattern, necessarily implies the transcending holiness of the Lord Jesus; his holiness is greater than the holiness of all creatures "For only " that which is first and best in every kind, is the rule and mea-" sure of all the rest *." It is the height of saints' ambition to be made conformable to Christ, Phil. iii. 10. Christ hath a double perfection, a perfection of *being*, and a perfection of *working*. His life was a perfect rule, no blot or error could be found therein; for he was "holy, harmless, undefiled, separate from sinners:" And such an high-priest becomes us, as the apostle speaks, Heb. vii. 26. The conformity of professors to Christ's example, is the test and measure of all their graces; the nearer any man comes to this pattern, the nearer he approaches towards perfection.

Seventhly, The Christian's imitation of Christ, under penalty of losing his claim to Christ, necessarily implies sanctification and obedience to be the evidences of our justification and interest in Christ: Assurance is unattainable without obedience; we can never be comfortable Christians except we be strict and regular Christians. Gal. vi. 16. "As many as walk according to this rule, peace be " unto them, and mercy; and upon the Israel of God." A loose and careless conversation can never be productive of true peace and consolation, 2 Cor. i. 12. "This is our rejoicing, the testimony " of our conscience, that in simplicity and godly sincerity, not " with fleshly wisdom, but by the grace of God, we have had our " conversation in the world." Let men talk what they will of the immediate sealings and comforts of the Spirit, without any regard to holiness, or respect to obedience; sure I am, whatever delusion they meet with in that way, true peace, and consolation is only to be expected and found here: "The fruit of righteousness shall " be peace, and the effect of righteousness quietness, and assurance " for ever." We have it not for our holiness, but we always have it in the way of holiness. And so much of the first particular, namely, what the imitation of Christ implies and comprizes in it.

Secondly, In the next place we are to enquire, in what things all who profess Christ are obliged to the imitation of him; or what those excellent graces in the life of Christ were, which are propounded as patterns to the saints.

The life of Christ was a living law; all the graces and virtues of the Spirit were represented in their glory, and brightest lustre in his conversation upon earth †: Never man spake as he spake;

---

* *Primum et optimum in unoquoque genere est regula et mensura cæterorum.*
† What have you to do with virtues, who are ignorant of Christ's virtue?

never any lived as he lived. " We beheld his glory (saith the evan-
" gelist) as the glory of the only begotten of the Father, full of
" grace and truth," John i. 14. But to descend to the particular,
imitable excellencies in the life of Christ, which are high patterns
and excellent rules for the conversation of his people, we shall,
from among many others, single out the ten following particulars,
which we are obliged to imitate.

Pattern 1. And first of all, the purity and holiness of the life of
Christ is proposed as a glorious pattern for the saint's imitation.
1 Pet. i. 15. " As he which hath called you is holy, so be ye holy
" in all manner of conversation ;" εν παση αναςροφη, in every point
and turning of yourselves. There is a two-fold holiness in Christ,
the holiness of his nature, and the holiness of his practice ; his holy
being and his holy working: This obligeth all that profess interest
in him to a two-fold holiness, viz. holiness *in actu primo*, in the
principles of it in their hearts, and holiness *in actu secundo*, in the
practice and exercise of it in their conversations. It is very true
we cannot in all respects imitate the holiness of Christ, for he is *essentially* holy ; proceeding, by nature, as a pure beam of holiness
from the Father ; and when he was incarnate, he came into the
world immaculate, and pure from the least stain of pollution : There
it was said, Luke i. 25. " That holy thing which shall be born of
" thee shall be called the Son of God." In this we can never be
like Christ, in the way of our production ; for " who can bring a
" clean thing out of that which is unclean ? Not one." The
Lord Jesus was also *efficiently* holy, i. e. he makes others holy ;
therefore his sufferings and blood are called a fountain opened
" for sin and for uncleanness," i. e. to cleanse other men's souls,
Zech. xiii. 1. In this Christ also is inimitable ; no man can make
himself or others holy. That is a great truth, though it will hardly
go down with proud nature, *Minus est te fecisse hominem, quam
sanctum ;* we may sooner make ourselves to be men, than to be
saints. Beside Christ is infinitely holy, as he is *God ;* and there
are no measures set to his holiness, as *Mediator.* John iii. 34. " For
" God giveth not the Spirit by measure unto him." But notwithstanding these excepted respects, the holiness of Christ is propounded as a pattern for our imitation six ways.

First, He was *truly* and *sincerely holy,* without fiction or simula-
tion ; and this appeared in the greatest trial of the truth of holiness that ever was made in this world. John xiv. 30. " The prince
" of this world cometh, and hath nothing in me :" When he was
agitated and shaken with the greatest temptations, no dregs ap-

---

Where, pray you, is true prudence, but in Christ's doctrine ? Or true temperance,
but in Christ's life ? Or true fortitude, but in Christ's passion ?

peared; he was like pure fountain-water in a chrystal glass. The hypocrite makes shew of more holiness than he hath, but there was more holiness in Christ than ever appeared to the view of men. We may say of the way of Christ what the* *philosopher* saith of the *milky way* in the heavens; and those faint streams of light which we see there, are nothing else but the reflection of innumerable stars which shine there, though they are invisible to us. There was much inward beauty in him, and so there ought to be in all his followers; our holiness, like Christ's, must be sincere and real, Eph. iv. 24. shining with inward beauty towards God rather than towards men.

Secondly, Christ was *uniformly* holy at one time as well as another; in one place and company as well as another: He was still like himself, an holy Christ; one and the same tenor of holiness ran throughout his whole life from first to last: So must it be with all his people, holy in all manner of conversation. Christians, look to your copy, and be sure to imitate Christ in this; write fair after your copy; let there not be here a word and there a blot: one part of your life heavenly and pure, and another earthly and dreggy; or (as one expresses it) now an heavenly rapture, and by and by a fleshly frolic.

Thirdly, Christ was *exemplarily* holy; a pattern of holiness to all that came nigh him and conversed with him: O imitate Christ in this. It was the commendation of the Thessalonians, that they " were ensamples to all that believed in Macedonia and Achaia; " and that in every place their faith to God-ward was spread " abroad," 1 Thes. i. 7, 8. Let no man go out of your company without conviction or edification. So exemplary were the primitive Christians, Phil. iii. 17.

Fourthly, Christ was *strictly* and *precisely* holy: " Which of you " convinceth me of sin?" The most envious and observing eyes of his greatest enemies could not pick a hole, or find a flaw in any of his words or actions: It is our duty to imitate Christ in this. Phil. ii. 15. " That ye may be blameless and harmless, the sons of " God, without rebuke, in the midst of a crooked and perverse " nation, among whom ye shine (or, as the word may be rendered imperatively, φαινεσθε ως φωστηρες, among whom shine ye) as lights " in the world." Thus it becomes the followers of Christ to walk circumspectly, or precisely; " for so is the will of God that with " well-doing ye may put to silence the ignorance of foolish men," 1 Pet. ii. 15.

---

* The Galaxy is a very great multitude of stars of the smallest size, whose smallness hinders their being perceived by us distinctly like the other stars, and their beams are mutually intermingled and confounded. *Conimh. de Meteor. cap.* 2.

Fifthly, Christ was perseveringly holy, holy to the last breath; as he began, so he finished his whole life in a constant course of holiness: in this also he is our great pattern. It becomes not any of his people to begin in the Spirit and end in the flesh; but on the contrary, their last works should be more than their first: " Let him that is holy, be holy still," Rev. xxii. 11.

Sixthly, In a word, the delight of Christ was only in holy things and holy persons: they were his chosen companions; even so it becometh his people to have all their delights in the saints, and in the excellent of the earth, Psal. xvi. 3. Thus, Christians, be ye followers of Christ in his holiness; God hath decreed this conformity to Christ in all that shall be saved, Rom. viii. 29. he banished all unholy ones from his gracious presence for ever, 1 Cor. vi. 9. Heb. xii. 14. The design of Christ in dying for you was to make you pure and holy, Eph. v. 25, 26. O then, study holiness, eye your pattern, and as dear children, be ye followers of your most holy Lord Jesus Christ.

Pattern 2. The obedience of Christ to his Father's will, is a pattern for the imitation of all Christians: it is said of Christ, Heb. v. 8. that he " learned obedience by the things which he suffered ;" a text which labours under some difficulties; Christ learned obedience, and yet was not ignorant before of what he learned afterward; he was perfect in knowledge, and yet the apostle speaks of him as a proficient in the school of wisdom. But we must consider there are two ways of learning, viz. by

1. The comprehension of the mind.

2. By the experience of the sense.

Christ, as God, was perfect in knowledge; nothing could be added to him: but when he became man, then he came to understand, or learn by sufferings, as the apostle here speaks; which, though it added nothing to his knowledge, yet it was a new method and way of knowing. Now the obedience of Christ is our pattern whereunto we are obliged (as ever we will warrant our claim of interest in him) to conform ourselves in the following properties of it.

First, Christ's obedience was free and voluntary, not forced or compulsory; it was so from the very first undertaking of the work of our redemption, Prov. viii. 30, 31. " Then was I by him as " one brought up with him; and I was daily his delight, rejoicing " always before him : Rejoicing in the habitable part of his earth ; " and my delights were with the sons of men." And when the fulness of time was come for executing that blessed design, which had been in prospect from all eternity, how cheerfully did the will of Christ echo to his Father's call, Psal. xl. 7. " Then said I, lo I " come, in the volume of thy book it· is written of me, I delight

" to do thy will, O my God, yea, thy law is within my heart."
Nor was this a flourish before he came into the field and saw the
enemy, for he laid down his life with the greatest cheerfulness and
spontaneity that could be, John x. 17, 18. " Therefore doth my
" Father love me, because I lay down my life that I may take it
" again; no man taketh it from me, but I lay it down of myself :"
and indeed the voluntariness of Christ, in his obedience unto
death, gave his death the nature and formality of a sacrifice; for
so all sacrifices ought to be offered, Lev. i. 3. and so Christ's sacrifice was offered unto God, Eph. v. 2. It was as grateful a work
to Christ to die for us, as it was to Moses' mother to take him to
nurse from the hand of Pharaoh's daughter. O Christians, tread
in the steps of Christ's example, do nothing grudgingly for God,
let not his commands be grievous, 1 John v. 3. If you do any
thing for God willingly, you have a reward; if otherwise, a dispensation only is committed to you, 1 Cor. ix. 7. Obedience in
Christ was an abasement to him, but in you a very great honour
and advancement : you have reason therefore to obey with cheerfulness.

Secondly, The obedience of Christ was universal and complete,
he was obedient to all the will of God, making no *demur* to the
hardest service imposed by the will of God upon him, Phil. ii. 8.
" He became obedient unto death, even the death of the cross;"
and though it is true, the humanity of Christ recoiled and stagger-
ed when that bitter cup of the wrath of God was given him to
drink; yet how soon was that innocent aversion overcome in him
by a perfect submission ? Nevertheless, not my will, but thine be
" done," Matt. xxvi. 39. Christians, here is your pattern : happy
art thou, reader, if thou canst say, when God calls thee to suffering
and self-denying work, I am filled with the will of God. Such
was Paul's obedience, Acts xxi. 13. " I am ready not only to be
" bound, but to die at Jerusalem for the name of the Lord
" Jesus."

Thirdly, The obedience of Christ was sincere and pure, without any base or by-end, purely aiming at the glory of God, John
xvii. 4. " I have glorified thee on earth, I have finished the work
" thou gavest me to do." He sought not honour of men. This
was the great desire of his soul, John xii. 28. " Father glorify thy
name :" And truly the choicest part of your obedience consists in
the purity of your ends, and in this Christ is propounded as your
pattern, Phil. ii. 3, 4, 5.

Fourthly, The streams of Christ's obedience flowed from the
spring and fountain of ardent love to God, John xiv. 31. " But
" that the world may know that I love the Father, and as the
" Father gave me commandment, even so I do ;" Thus let all

your obedience to God turn upon the hinge of love; for "love is "the fulfilling of the law," Rom. xiii. 10. Not as if no other duty but love were required in the law, but because no act of obedience is acceptable to God, but that which is performed in love.

Fifthly, In a word, The obedience of Christ was constant; he was obedient unto death, he was not weary of his work to the last. Such a patient continuance in well-doing is one part of your conformity to Christ, Rom. ii. 7. it is laid upon you by his own express command, and a command backed with the most encouraging promise, Rev. ii. 10. "Be thou faithful unto the death, and I "will give thee the crown of life."

Pattern 3. The *self-denial* of Christ is the pattern of believers, and their conformity unto it is their indispensible duty, Phil. ii. 4, 5, 6. 2 Cor. viii. 9. "For ye know the grace of our Lord Jesus "Christ, that though he was rich, yet for our sakes he became "poor, that ye through his poverty might be rich." Jesus Christ, for the glory of God, and the love he bare to the elect, denied himself all the delights and pleasures of this world, Matt. xx. 28. "The Son of man came not to be ministered unto, but to minis- "ter, and to give his life a ransom for many;" he was all his life- time in the world, "a man of sorrows and acquainted with grief," Isa. liii. 5. more unprovided of comfortable accommodations than the birds of the air, or beasts of the earth, Luke ix. 58. "The "foxes have holes, and the birds of the air have nests, but the "Son of man hath not where to lay his head *." Yet this was the least part of Christ's self-denial : What did he not deny when he left the bosom of his Father, with the ineffable delights and pleasures he there enjoyed from eternity, and instead thereof to drink the cup, the bitter cup of his Father's wrath, for our sakes? O Christians, look to your pattern, and imitate your self-denying Saviour. There is a threefold self you are to deny for Christ.

First, Deny your *natural self,* for him, Luke xiv. 26. Hate your own life, in competition with his glory, as well as your natural lusts, Tit. ii. 12.

Secondly, Deny your *civil self* for Christ; whether they be gifts of the mind, Phil. iii. 8. or your dearest relations in the world, Luke xiv. 26.

---

* *Vulpibus in saltu rupes exisa latebras*
Præbet, et aereis avibus dat silva quietem :
Ast hominis Nato nullis succedere tectis
Est licitum.————   Heins. in loc.
The craggy rock to foxes holes affords,
The pleasant woods a resting-place to birds ;
For Christ no fixed habitation's found.
But what was borrow'd, or the naked ground.

Thirdly, Deny your *moral* and *religious self* for Christ; your own righteousness, Phil. iii. 10.   Deny sinful self absolutely, Col. iii. 4, 5.   Deny natural self conditionally, i. e. be ready to forsake its interests at the call of God.   Deny your religious self, even your own graces, comparatively, not in the notion of duties, but in the notion of righteousness : and to encourage you in this difficult work, consider,

First, What great things Christ denied for you, and what small matters you have to deny for him.

Secondly, How readily he denied all for your sakes, making no objections against the difficultest commands.

Thirdly, How incapable you are to put any obligation upon Christ, to deny himself in the least for you, and what strong obligations Christ hath put you under, to deny yourselves in your greatest interests upon earth for him.

Fourthly, Remember that your self-denial is a condition consented to, and subscribed by yourselves, if ever you received Christ aright.

Fifthly, In a word, consider how much your self-denial for Christ, makes for your advantage in both worlds, Luke xviii. 29. O therefore, look not every man upon his own things, but upon the things that are of Christ ; let not that be justly charged upon you, which was charged upon them, Phil. ii. 21.   "All seek their " own, not the things which are Christ's."

Pattern 4. The activity and diligence of Christ in finishing the work of God which was committed to him, was a pattern for all believers to imitate.   It is said of him, Acts x. 38.   "He went about doing good."   O what a great and glorious work did Christ finish in a little time !   A work to be celebrated to all eternity by the praises of the redeemed.   Six things were very remarkable in the diligence of Christ about his Father's work.

First, That his heart was intently set upon it, Psal. iv. 8. " Thy law is in the midst of my heart," or bowels.

Secondly, That he never fainted under the many great discouragements he frequently met withal in that work, Isa. xliii. 4. " He shall not fail, nor be discouraged."

Thirdly, That the shortness of his time provoked him to the greatest diligence, John ix. 4.   " I must work the work of him that " sent me, while it is day, for the night cometh, when no man " can work."

Fourthly, That he improved all opportunities, companies, and occurrences to further the great work which was under his hand, John iv. 6, 10.

Fifthly, Nothing more displeased him than when he met with dissuasions and discouragements in his work ; upon that account it was that he gave Peter so sharp a check, Mat. viii. 33. " Get thee behind me, Satan."

Sixthly, Nothing rejoiced his soul more, than the prosperity and success of his work, Luke x. 20, 21. When the disciples made the report of the success of their ministry, it is said, " In that hour " Jesus rejoiced in Spirit." And O what a triumphant shout was that upon the cross at the accomplishment of his work, John xix. 30. *It is finished !*

Now, Christians, eye your parent, look unto Jesus ; trifle not away your lives in vanity. Christ was diligent, be not you slothful. And to encourage you in your imitation of Christ in labour and diligence, consider,

First, How great an honour God puts upon you in employing you for his service : every vessel of service is a vessel of honour, 2 Tim. ii. 21. The apostle was very ambitious * of that honour, Rom. xv. 20. It was the glory of Eliakim to be fastened as a nail in a sure place, and to have many people hang upon him, Isa. xxii. 33.

Secondly, Your diligence in the work of God will be your great security in the hour of temptation ; for " the Lord is with you " while you are with him," 2 Chron. xv. 2. The *schoolmen* put the question, How the saints in heaven became impeccable ? and resolve it thus, that they are therefore freed from sin, because they are continually employed and swallowed up in the blessed visions of God.

Thirdly, Diligence in the work of God is an excellent help to the improvement of grace. For, though gracious habits are not acquired, yet they are greatly improved by frequent acts ; " To " him that hath shall be given," Mat. xxv. 29. It is a good note of *Luther, Fides pinguescit operibus,* Faith improves by obedience.

Fourthly, Diligence in the work of God is the direct way to the assurance of the love of God, 2 Pet. xv. 10. This path leads you into a heaven upon earth.

Fifthly, Diligence in obedience is a great security against backsliding : small remissions in duty, and little neglects, increase by degrees unto great apostasies, you may see how that disease is bred by the method prscribed for its cure, Rev. ii. 5. *Do thy first works.*

Sixthly, In a word, laborious diligence, in the day of life, will be your singular comfort when the night of death overtakes you, 2 Pet. i. 11. 2 Kings xx. 3.

Pattern 5. Delight in God, and in his service, was eminently con-

---

* Φιλοτιμεμαι, ambio, dictum verbum ab amore honoris.   Zanch.

spicuous in the life of Christ, and is a rare pattern for believers
imitation, John iv. 32, 34. " But he said unto them, I have meat
" to eat that ye know not of, my meat is to do the will of him that
" sent me, and to finish his work." The delights of Christ were
all in heaven. The Son of man was in heaven, in respect of delight in God, while he conversed here among men. And if you
be Christ's, heavenly things will be the delight of your souls also.
Now spiritual delight is nothing else but the complacency and well-
pleasedness of a renewed heart, in conversing with God, and the
things of God, resulting from the agreeableness of them to the spiritual temper of his mind. Four things are considerable about
spiritual delight.

First, The nature of it, which consisteth in the complacency,
rest, and satisfaction of the mind in God and spiritual things.
The heart of a Christian is centered, it is where it would be; it is
gratified in the highest, in the actings forth of faith and love upon
God ; as the taste is gratified with a suitable delicious relish, Psal.
lxiii. 5, 6. Psal. cxix. 14, 24. Psal. xvii. 18.

Secondly, The object of spiritual delight, which is God himself,
and the things which relate to him. He is the blessed ocean into
which all the streams of spiritual delight do pour themselves, Psal.
lxxiii. 25. " Whom have I in heaven but thee, and on earth there
" is none that I desire in comparison of thee."

Thirdly, The subject of spiritual delight, which is a renewed
heart, and that only so far as it is renewed, Rom. vii. 22. " I de-
" light in the law of God after the inward man."

Fourthly, The principle and spring of this delight, which is the
agreeableness of spiritual things to the temper and frame of a renewed mind. A sensitive pleasure arises from the suitableness of
the faculty and object. So it is here, no delicious sweetness can be
so pleasant to the taste, or beautiful colours to the eye, or melodious sounds to the ear, as spiritual things to renewed souls, because spiritual senses are delicate, and the objects more excellent.

But my business here is not so much to open its nature, as to
press you to the practice thereof in conformity to your great pattern,
whose life was a life of delight in God, and whose work was performed with the greatest delight in God. " I delight to do thy
" will, O my God." O Christians, strive to imitate your pattern
in this. And to encourage you, I will briefly hint a few things.

First, Scarce any thing can be more evidential of sincerity than
a heart delighting in God, and the will of God. Hypocrites go as
far as others in the material parts of duties, but here they are defective ; they have no delight in God and things spiritual ; but do
whatsoever they do in religion, from the compulsions of conscience,
or accommodations of self-ends.

Secondly, An heart delighting in God will be a choice help and means to perseverance. The reason why many so easily part with religion is, because their souls never tasted the sweetness of it; they never delighted in it; but the Christian who delights in the law of God will be meditating on it day and night, and shall be like a tree planted by a river of water, whose leaf fadeth not, Psal. i. 2, 3.

Thirdly,. This will represent religion very beautifully to such as are yet strangers to it; you will then be able to invite them to Christ by your example, the language whereof will be like that, Psal. xxxiv. 8. " O taste and see that God is good."

Fourthly, This will make all your services to God very pleasing and acceptable through Christ; you will now begin to do the will of God on earth, as it is done in heaven; your duties are so far *angelical* as they are performed in the strength of delight in God.

Object. But may not a sincere Christian act in duty without delight? Yea, may he not feel some kind of weariness in duties?

Solut. Yes, doubtless he may; but then we must distinguish betwixt the *temper* and *distemper* of a renewed heart; the best hearts are not always in the right frame.

Pattern 6. The *inoffensiveness* of the life of Christ upon earth is an excellent pattern to all his people; he injured none, offended none, but was holy and harmless, as the apostle speaks, Heb. vii. 26. He denied his own liberty to avoid occasion of offence; as in the case of the tribute-money, Mat. xix. 27. " The children are " free, notwithstanding, lest we should offend them, go," &c. So circumspect was Christ, and inoffensive among all men, that though his enemies sought occasion against him, yet could they find none, Luke vi. 7. Look unto Jesus, O ye professors of religion; imitate him in this gracious excellency of his life, according to his command, Phil. ii. 15. " That ye may be harmless and blameless, the " sons of God, without rebuke, in the midst of a crooked and per- " verse nation." You are indeed allowed the exercise of your prudence, but not a jot farther than will consist with your innocence. " Be ye wise as serpents, and harmless as doves." It is the rule of Christ that you offend none, 1 Cor. x. 32. 2 Cor. vi. 3. And to engage you to the imitation of Christ in this, I must briefly press it with a few encouragements, which methinks should prevail with any heart that is truly gracious.

First, For the honour of Jesus Christ, be you inoffensive, his name is called upon you, his honour is concerned in your deportment; if your carriage in the world give just matter of offence, Christ's worthy name will be blasphemed thereby, Jam. ii. 7. Your inoffensive carriage is the only means to stop the mouths of detractors, 1 Pet. ii. 15.

Secondly, For the sake of souls, the precious and immortal souls of others, be wary that you give no offence: " Wo to the world, (saith Christ,) because of offence," Matth. xiii. 7. Nothing was more commonly objected against Christ and religion by the Heathens in Cyprian's time, than the loose and scandalous lives of professors: * " Behold, say they, these are the men who boast them-
" selves to be redeemed from the tyranny of Satan, to be dead to
" the world; nevertheless, see how they are overcome by their
" own lusts." And much after the same rate Salvian brings in the wicked of his time, stumbling at the looseness of professors, and saying, Where is that catholic law which they believe? Where are the examples of piety and chastity which they have learned? &c. O Christians, draw not the guilt of other men's eternal ruin upon your souls.

Thirdly, In a word, answer the ends of God in your sanctification and providential dispose in the world this way; by the holiness and harmlessness of your lives, many may be won to Christ, 1 Pet. iii. 1. What the Heathens said of moral virtue, (which they called *verticordia,* turn-heart) that if it were but visible to mortal eyes, all men would be enamoured with it, will be much more true of religion when you shall represent the beauty of it in your conversation.

Pattern 7. The humility and lowliness of Christ is propounded by himself as a pattern for his people's imitation. Mat. xi. 29. " Learn of me, for I am meek and lowly." He could abase and empty himself of all his glory, Phil. ii. 5, 6, 7. He could stoop to the meanest office, even to wash the disciples feet. We read but of one triumph in all the life of Christ upon earth, when he rode to Jerusalem, the people strewing branches in the way, and the very children in the streets of Jerusalem, crying, " Hosanna to the son of David, Ho-
" sanna in the highest;" and yet with what lowliness and humility was it performed by Christ, Matth. xxi. 5. " Behold thy King
" cometh unto thee meek and lowly." The humility of Christ appeared in every thing he spake or did. Humility discovered itself in his language, Psal. xxii. 6. " I am a worm, and no man." In his actions, not refusing the meanest office, John iii. 14. In his condescensions to the worst of men, upon which ground they called him " a friend to publicans and sinners," Matth. xi. 19. But especially, and above all, in stooping down from all his glory to a state of the deepest contempt, for the glory of God and our salvation. Christians! here is your pattern; look to your meek and humble Saviour, and tread in his steps; be you " clothed with

---

* *Ecce qui jactant se redemptos a tyrannide Satanæ, qui prædicant se mortuos esse mundo, nihilominus vineuntur cupiditatibus suis.* Cyprian.

" humility," 1 Pet. v. 5. Whoever are ambitious to be the world's *great ones*, let it be enough for you to be Christ's *little ones*. Convince the world, that since you knew God and yourselves, your pride hath been dying from that day. Shew your humility in your *habits*, 1 Pet. iii. 3. 1 Tim. ii. 9, 10. In your *company*, not contemning the meanest and poorest that fear the Lord, Psal. xv. 4, Rom. xii. 16. In your *language*; that *dialect* befits your 'lips, Eph. iii. 8. *Less than the least of all saints*; but especially in the low value and humble thoughts you have of yourselves, 1 Tim i. 15. And to press this, I beseech you to consider,

First, From how vile a root pride springs. Ignorance of God, and of yourselves, gives rise and being to this sin : They that know God will be humble, Isa. vi. 5. And they that know themselves cannot be proud, Rom. vii. 9.

Secondly, Consider the mischievous effects it produces; it estrangeth the soul from God, Psal. cxxxviii. 6. It provokes God to lay you low, Job xl. 11, 12. It goes before destruction and a dreadful fall, Prov. x. 18.

Thirdly, As it is a great *sin*, so it is a bad *sign*, Hab. ii. 4. " Behold his heart which is lifted up, is not upright in him."

Fourthly, How unsuitable it is to the sense you have, and the complaints you make of your own corruptions and spiritual wants; and above all, how contrary it is to your pattern and example : Did Christ speak, act, or think as you do ! O, learn humility from Jesus Christ, it will make you precious in the eyes of God, Isa. lvii. 15.

Pattern 8. The contentation of Christ in a low and mean condition in the world, is an excellent pattern for his people's imitation. His lot in this world fell upon a condition of deepest poverty and contempt : Yet how well was he satisfied and contented with it ! hear him expressing himself about it, Psal. xvi. 6. " The lines " are fallen unto me in pleasant places : yea, I have a goodly heri- " tage." The contentation of his heart with a suffering condition, evidenced itself in his silence under the greatest sufferings, Isa. liii. 7. " He was oppressed, and he was afflicted ; yet he opened not " his mouth : He is brought as a lamb to the slaughter, and as a " sheep before the shearers is dumb, so he opened not his mouth." O that in this also the poorest Christians would imitate their Saviour, and learn to manage an afflicted condition with a contented spirit : Let there be no murmurs, complaints, or foolish charges of God heard from you, whatever straits or troubles he brings you into : For,

First, The meanest and most afflicted Christian is owner of many rich, invaluable mercies, Eph. i. 3. 1 Cor. iii. 33. Is sin pardoned and God reconciled? then never open your mouths any more, Ezek. xvi. 63.

Secondly, You have many precious promises that God will not forsake you in your straits, Heb. xiii. 5. Isa. xli. 17.   And your whole life hath been a life of experiences of the faithfulness of God in his promises.   Which of you cannot say with the church, Lam. iii. 23. " His mercies are new every morning, and great is his " faithfulness."

Thirdly, How useful and beneficial are all your afflictions to you! they purge your sins, prevent your temptations, wean you from the world, and turn to your salvation : and how unreasonable then must your discontentedness at them be?

Fourthly, The time of your relief and full deliverance from all your troubles is at hand; the time is but short that you shall have any concernment about these things, 1 Cor. vii. 26.   If the candle of your earthly comfort be blown out, yet remember it is but a little while to the break of day, and then there will be no need of candles.   Besides,

Fifthly, Your lot falls by divine direction upon you, and as bad as it is, it is much easier and sweeter than the condition of Christ in this world was: Yet he was contented, and why not you? O that we could learn contentment from Christ in every condition.   And thus I have laid before you some excellent patterns in the life of Christ for your imitation.

———◄◄◄◄◎►►►►———

SERMON XXX.

1 John ii. 6.

He that saith he abideth in him, ought himself also so to walk, even as he walked.

THESE words have been resolved into their parts, and their sense opened in the former sermon: The observation was this:

That every man is bound to the imitation of Christ, under penalty of forfeiting his claim to Christ.

In prosecution of this point, we have already shewn what the imitation of Christ imports, and what the imitable excellencies in the life of Christ are : It now remains that I shew you in the next place, why all that profess Christ are bound to imitate his example, and then apply the whole.   Now the necessity of this imitation of Christ will convincingly appear divers ways.

First, From the established order of salvation, which is fixed

and unalterable: God that hath appointed the end, hath also
established the means and order by which men shall attain the ultimate end.   Now conformity to Christ is the established method
in which God will bring souls to glory, Rom. viii. 29. " For whom
" he did foreknow, he also did predestinate, to be conformed to the
" image of his Son; that he might be the first born among many
" brethren."   The same God who hath predestinated men to salvation, hath in order thereunto, predestinated them unto conformity
to Christ, and this order of heaven is never to be reversed; we may
as well hope to be saved without Christ, as to be saved without conformity to Christ.

Secondly, The nature of Christ-mystical requires this conformity,
and renders it indispensably necessary.   Otherwise, the body of
Christ must be *heterogeneous;* of a nature different from the head,
and how monstrous and uncomely would this be? This would represent Christ to the world in an image, or idea, much like that,
Dan. ii. 32, 33. " The head of fine gold, the breasts and arms of
" silver, the thighs of brass, the legs of iron, the feet part of iron
" and part of clay."   Christ, the head, is pure and holy, and
therefore very unsuitable to sensual and earthly members.   And
therefore the apostle in his description of Christ-mystical, describes
the members of Christ (as they ought to be) of the same nature and
quality with the head, 2 Cor. xv. 48, 49. " As is the heavenly,
" such are they also that are heavenly; and as we have borne the
" image of the earthy, so we shall also bear the image of the hea-
" venly."   That image or resemblance of Christ, which shall be
complete and perfect after the resurrection, must be begun in its
first draught here by the work of regeneration.

Thirdly, This resemblance and conformity to Christ appears
necessary from the communion which all believers have with Christ
in the same spirit of grace and holiness.   Believers are called
Christ's *fellows,* or co-partners, Psal. xlv. 7. from their participation with him of the same spirit; as it is 1 Thes. iv. 8.   God giveth
the same Spirit unto us, which he more plentifully poured out
upon Christ.   Now where the same Spirit and principle is, there
the same fruits and operations must be produced, according to the
proportions and measures of the Spirit of grace communicated; and
this reason is farther enforced by the very design and end of God,
in the infusion of the Spirit of grace: For it is plain, from Ezek.
xxxvi. 27. that practical holiness and obedience is the scope and
design of that infusion of the Spirit.   The very innate property of
the Spirit of God in men, is to elevate their minds, and set their
affections upon heavenly things, to purge their hearts from earthly
dross, and fit them for a life of holiness and obedience.   Its
nature also is assimilating, and changeth them in whom it is, into

the same image with Jesus Christ their heavenly head, 2 Cor.
iii. 18.

Fourthly, The necessity of this imitation of Christ may be ar-
gued, from the design and end of Christ's exhibition to the world
in a body of flesh.   For though we detest that doctrine of the So-
cinians, which makes the exemplary life of Christ to be the whole
end of his incarnation; yet we must not run so far from an error,
as to lose a precious truth.   We say, the satisfaction of his blood
was a main and principal end of his incarnation, according to Mat.
xx. 28.   We affirm also, that it was a great design and end of the
incarnation of Christ to set before us a pattern of holiness for our
imitation; for so speaks the apostle, 1 Pet. ii. 21.   " He hath left
" us an example that we should follow his steps."   And this example of Christ greatly obliges believers to his imitation, Phil. ii. 5.
" Let this mind be in you, which also was in Christ Jesus."

Fifthly, Our imitation of Christ, is one of those great articles
which every man is to subscribe, whom Christ will admit into the
number of his disciples, Luke xiv. 27.   " Whosoever doth not come
" after me, cannot be my disciple."   And again, John xii. 26.   " If
" any man serve me, let him follow me."   To this condition we
have submitted, if we be sincere believers; and therefore are strictly
bound to the imitation of Christ, not only by God's *command*, but
by our own *consent*.   But if we profess interest in Christ, when our
hearts never consented to follow, and imitate his example, then are
we self-deceiving hypocrites, wholly disagreeing from the scripture
character of believers, Rom. viii. 1.   They that are Christ's being
here described to be such as walk not after the flesh, but after the
Spirit.   And Gal. v. 25.   " If we live in the Spirit, let us walk in
" the Spirit."

Sixthly, The honour of Christ necessitates the conformity of
Christians to his example, else what way is there left to stop
detracting mouths, and vindicate the name of Christ from the
reproaches of the world?   How can wisdom be justified of her
children, except it be this way?   By what means shall we cut off
occasion from such as desire occasion, but by regulating our lives by
Christ's example?   The world hath eyes to see what we *practise*, as
well as ears to hear what we *profess*.   Therefore either shew the
consistency between your profession and practice, or you can never
hope to vindicate the name and honour of the Lord Jesus.   The
uses follow; for

   1. Information.
   2. Exhortation.
   3. Consolation.

First use, for information.

Inference 1. *If all that profess interest in Christ, be strictly bound to imitate his holy example; then it follows, that religion is very unjustly charged by the world, with the scandals and evils of them that profess it.* Nothing can be more unjust and irrational, if we consider,

First, That the Christian religion severely censures loose and scandalous actions in all professors, and therefore is not to be censured for them. It is absurd to condemn religion for what itself condemns: looseness no way flows from the principles of Christianity, but is most opposite and contrary to it, Tit. ii. 11, 12. " For " the grace of God that brings salvation, hath appeared unto all " men; teaching us, that denying all ungodliness and worldly " lusts, we should live soberly, righteously, and godly, in this pre- " sent world."

Secondly, It is an argument of the excellency of the Christian religion, and that even wicked men themselves covet the name and profession of it, though they only cloak and cover their evils under it. I confess it is a great abuse of such an excellent thing as religion is; but yet, if it had not an awful reverence paid it by the consciences of all men, it would never be abused to this purpose, by hypocrites, as it is.

Thirdly, According to this reasoning, there can be no religion in the world; for name me that religion which is not scandalized by the practices of some that profess it. So that this practice hath a natural tendency to Atheism; and is, no doubt, encouraged by the devil for that end.

Inf. 2. *If all men forfeit their claim to Christ, who endeavour not to imitate him in the holiness of his life, then how small a number of real Christians are there in the world?* Indeed, if liberal talking, without accurate walking: if common profession without holy practices, were enough to constitute a Christian; then this quarter of the world would abound with Christians: But if Christ owns none for such but those that tread in the steps of his example; then the number of real Christians is very small. The generality of men that live under the Christian name, are such as walk after the flesh, Rom. viii. 2. according to the course of this world, they yield their members as instruments of unrighteousness unto sin, Rom. vi. 13. Strict godliness is a mere bondage to them; narrow is the way, and few there be that walk therein.

Inf. 3. *What blessed times should we all see, if true religion did once generally obtain, and prevail in the world!* How would it humble the proud, meeken the passionate, and spiritualize those that are carnal! The perverse world charges religion with all the tumults and disturbances that are in it; whereas nothing in the world but religion, advanced in the power of it, can heal and cure these *epidemical* evils.   O if men were once brought under the power of religion indeed, to walk after Christ in holiness, obedience, meekness, and self-denial; no such miseries as these would be heard of among us, Isa. xi. 8, 9. " The sucking child shall play upon the " hole of the asp, and a weaned child shall put his hand on the " cockatrice den; they shall not hurt nor destroy in all my holy " mountain: For the earth shall be full of the knowledge of the " Lord, as the waters cover the sea."

Inf. 4. *Hence it also follows, that real Christians are the sweetest companions.* It is a comfortable thing to walk with them that walk after the example of Christ; the holiness, heavenliness, humility, self-denial, and diligence in obedience, which was in Christ, are, in some measure, to be found in all sincere Christians: They shew forth the virtues of him that calleth them; the graces of the Spirit do more or less shine forth in them: And O how endearing, sweet, and engaging are these things! Upon this very account the apostle invited others into the fellowship of the saints, 1 John i. 3. " That " ye might have fellowship with us, and truly our fellowship is with " the Father, and with his Son Christ Jesus."   And is it not sweet to have fellowship with them who have fellowship with Christ? O let all your delights be in the saints, and in the excellent of the earth, who excel in virtue, Psal. xvi. 3.   Yet, mistake not, there is a great deal of difference betwixt one Christian and another, and even the best of Christians are sanctified but in part. If there be something sweet and engaging, there is also something bitter and distasteful in the best of men. If there be something to draw forth your delight and love, there is also something to exercise your pity and patience. Yet this is most certain, that notwithstanding all their infirmities and corruptions, they are the best and sweetest company this world affords.

Inf. 5. *In a word, if no men's claim to Christ be warranted but theirs that walk as he walked; how vain and groundless then are the hopes and expectations of all unsanctified men, who walk after their own lusts?* None are more forward to claim the privileges of religion than those that reject the duties of it; multitudes hope to be saved by Christ, who yet refuse to be governed by him: But such hopes have no scripture warrant to support them; yea, they have many scripture testimonies against them, 1 Cor. vi. 9. " Know ye " not that the unrighteous shall not inherit the kingdom of God? " Be not deceived, neither fornicators, nor idolaters, nor adul- " terers, nor effeminate, nor abusers of themselves with mankind; " nor thieves, nor covetous, nor drunkards, nor revilers, nor ex- " tortioners, shall inherit the kingdom of God."   O how many

thousand vain hopes are laid in the dust, and how many thousand
souls are sentenced to hell by this one scripture!

Second use, for exhortation.

If this be so, it naturally presses all the professors of Christianity
to strict godliness in their conversations, as ever they expect benefit
by Christ. O professors, be ye not conformed unto this world, but
be ye transformed by the renewing of your minds: Set the example
of Christ before you, and labour to tread in his steps. This is the
great business of religion, the main scope of the gospel. Give me
leave, therefore, closely to press it upon your hearts, by the following motives.

Motive 1. Christ hath conformed himself to you by his abasing
incarnation; how reasonable therefore is it that you conform yourselves to him in the way of obedience and sanctification? He came
as near to you as it was possible for him to do, strive you therefore
to come as near to Christ as it is possible for you to do: he hath
taken your nature upon him, Heb. ii. 14. yea, and with your nature
he hath taken your weaknesses and infirmities, Rom. viii. 3. and not
only your natures and your infirmities, but your condition also, for
he came under the law for your sakes, Gal. iv. 4. He conformed
himself to you, though he was infinitely above you; that was his
abasement: do you conform yourselves to him who are infinitely
beneath him: that will be your advancement: his conformity to you
emptied him of his glory, your conformity to him will fill you with
glory: he conformed himself to you, though you had no obligation
upon him; will you not conform yourselves to him, who lie under
infinite obligations so to do?

Motive 2. You shall be conformed to Christ in glory; how reasonable therefore is it you should now conform yourselves to him in
holiness? The apostle saith, 1 John iii. 2. "We shall be like unto
"him, for we shall see him as he is:" Yea, not only your souls shall
be like him, but your very bodies, even those vile bodies of yours
"shall be changed, that they may be fashioned like unto his glorious
"body." How forcible a motive is this to bring men into conformity with Christ here! especially, seeing our conformity to him in
holiness, is the evidence of our conformity to him in glory, Rom.
vi. 5. 2 Pet. iii. 11. O professors, as ever you look to be with
Christ in glory hereafter, see that ye walk after Christ's example in
holiness and obedience here.

Motive 3. The conformity of your lives to Christ, your pattern, is
your highest excellency in this world: The measure of your grace
is to be estimated by this rule. The excellency of every creature
rises higher and higher, according as it approaches still nearer and
nearer to its original; the more you resemble Christ in grace, the

more illustrious and resplendent will your conversations be in true spiritual glory.

Motive 4. So far as you imitate Christ in your lives, and no farther, you will be beneficial in the world in which you live: so far as God helps you to follow Christ, you will be helpful to bring others to Christ, or build them up in Christ; for all men are forbidden by the gospel to follow you one step farther than you follow Christ, 1 Cor. xi. 1. and when you have finished your course in this world, the remembrance of your ways will be no further sweet to others, than they are ways of holiness and obedience to Christ, 1 Cor. iv. 17. If you walk according to the course of this world, the world will not be the better for your walking.

Motive 5. To walk as Christ walked, is a walk only worthy of a Christian; this is to " walk worthy of the Lord," 1 Thess. ii. 12. Col. i. 10. By worthiness * the apostle doth not mean meritoriousness, but comeliness, or that decorum which befits a Christian: as, when a man walks suitably to his place and calling in the world, we say he acts like himself; so, when you walk after Christ's pattern, you then act like yourselves, like men of your character and profession; this is consonant to your vocation, Eph. iv. 1. " I beseech you, that you walk worthy of the vocation where-" with you are called." This walking suits with your obligation, 2 Cor. v. 15. for it is to live unto him who died for us. This walking only suits with your designation, Eph. ii. 10. " For you " are created in Christ Jesus unto good works, which God hath " before ordained we should walk in them." In a word, such walking as this, and such only becomes your expectation, 2 Pet. iii. 14. " Wherefore [beloved] seeing that you look for such things, " be diligent, that ye may be found of him in peace, without spot, " and blameless."

Motive 6. How comfortable will the close of your life be at death, if you have walked after Christ's pattern and example in this world: A comfortable death is ordinarily the close of a holy life, Psal. xxxvii. 37. " Mark the perfect man, and behold the up-" right; for the end of that man is peace." A loose, careless life puts many terrible stings into death. As worms in the body are bred of the putrefaction there, so the worm of conscience is bred of the moral putrefaction or corruption that is in our natures and conversations. O then be prevailed with by all these considerations to imitate Christ in the whole course and compass of your conversations.

---

* The word worthiness, as used in scripture, does not always denote an exact proportion of equality between one thing and another, but a certain suitableness and fitness which excludes inconsistency. *Davenant on Coloss. p.* 25.

Third use, for consolation.

Lastly, I would leave a few words of support and comfort to snch as sincerely study and endeavour, according to the tendency of their new nature to follow Christ's example, but being weak in grace, and meeting with strong temptations, are frequently carried aside from the holy purposes and designs of their honest, well-meaning hearts, to the great grief and discouragement of their souls.   They heartily wish and aim at holiness, and say with David, Psal. cxix. 5. " O that my ways were directed to keep thy sta- " tutes." They follow after exactness in holiness as Paul did, Phil. iii. 12. " If by any means they might attain it."   But find-ing how short they come in all things of the rule and pattern, they mourn as he did, Rom. vii. 24. " O wretched man that I am, who " shall deliver me from the body of this death?" Well, if this be thy case, be not discouraged, but hearken to a few words of support and comfort, with which I shall close this point.

SUPPORT I.

Such defects in obedience make no flaw in your justification : for your justification is not built upon your obedience, but upon Christ's, Rom. iii. 24. and how complete and defective soever you be in yourselves, yet at the same instant, " you are complete in him " which is the head of all principality and power," Col. ii. 10. Wo to Abraham, Moses, David, Paul, and the most eminent saints that ever lived, if their justification and acceptation with God had depended upon the perfection and completeness of their own obedience.

SUPPORT II.

Your deep troubles for the defectiveness of your obedience, do not argue you to be less, but more sanctified than those who make no such complaints ; for these prove you to be better acquainted with your own hearts than others are; to have a deeper hatred of sin than others have ; and to love God with a more fervent love than others do ; the most eminent saints have made the bitterest complaints upon this account, Psal. lxv. 3. Rom. vii. 23, 24.

SUPPORT III.

The Lord makes excellent uses even of your infirmities and failings to do you good, and makes them turn to your unexpected advantage : for, by these defects he hides pride from your eyes ; he beats you off from self-dependence ; he makes you to admire the riches of free grace : he makes you to long more ardently for heaven, and entertain the sweeter thoughts of death ; and doth not the Lord then make blessed fruits to spring up to you from such a bitter root ? O the blessed chymistry of heaven, to extract such mercies out of such miseries !

Support IV.

Your bewailed infirmities do not break the bond of the ever-lasting covenant. The bond of the covenant holds firm, notwith-standing your defects and weaknesses, Jer. xxxii. 40. " Iniquities " prevail against me," saith David, yet in the same breath he adds, " as for our transgressions thou shalt purge them away," Psal. lxv. 3. He is still thy God, thy Father for all this.

Support V.

Though the defects of your obedience are grievous to God, yet your deep sorrows for them are well-pleasing in his eyes, Psal. li. 17. " The sacrifices of God are a broken spirit, a broken and a " contrite heart, O God, thou wilt not despise." Ephraim was never a more pleasant child to his father, than when he bemoaned himself, and smote upon his thigh, as thou dost, Jer. xxxi. 20. Your sins grieve him, but your sorrows please him.

Support VI.

Though God have left many defects to humble you, yet he hath given many things to comfort you. This is a comfort that the desire of thy soul is to God, and to the remembrance of his name. This is a comfort, that thy sins are not thy delight as once they were; but thy shame and sorrow. This is a comfort, that thy case is not singular; but more or less, the same complaints and sorrows are found in all gracious souls through the world; and to say all in one word, this is the comfort above all comforts, that the time is at hand, in which all these defects, infirmities, and fail-ings shall be done away, 1 Cor. xiii. 10. " When that which is " perfect is come, then that which is in part shall be done " away."

For ever blessed be God for Jesus Christ.

And thus I have finished the third general use of examination, whereby every man is to try his interest in Christ, and discern whether ever Christ hath been effectually applied to his soul. That which remains is

An use of Lamentation.

Wherein the miserable and most wretched state of all those to whom Jesus Christ is not effectually applied, will be yet more par-ticularly discovered and bewailed.

SERMON XXXI.

Of the State of Spiritual Death, and the Misery thereof.

EPH. v. 14.

Wherefore he saith, Awake thou that sleepest, and arise from the dead, and Christ shall give thee light.

THIS scripture represents unto us the miserable and lamentable state of the unregenerate, as being under the power of spiritual death, which is the cause and inlet of all other miseries. From hence, therefore, I shall make the first discovery of the woful and wretched state of them that apply not Jesus Christ to their own souls.

The scope of the apostle in this *context*, is to press believers to a circumspect and holy life; to "walk as children of light." This exhortation is laid down in ver. 8. and pressed by divers arguments in the following verses.

First, From the tendency of holy principles, unto holy fruits and practice, ver. 9, 10.

Secondly, From the convincing efficacy of practical godliness, upon the consciences of the wicked, ver. 11, 12, 13. It awes and convinces their consciences.

Thirdly, From the co-incidence of such a conversation with the great design and drift of the scriptures, which is to awaken men by regeneration, out of that spiritual sleep, or rather death, which sin hath cast them into; and this is the argument of the text, *Wherefore he saith, Awake thou that sleepest, &c.* There is some difficulty in the reference of these words. Some think it is to Isa. xxvi. 19. "Awake and sing ye that dwell in the dust." Others to Isa. lx. i. "Arise, shine, for thy light is come," &c. But most probably, the words neither refer to this or that particularly, but to the drift and scope of the whole scriptures, which were inspired and written upon this great design, to awaken and quicken souls out of the state of spiritual death. And in them we are to consider these three things more distinctly and particularly.

1. The miserable state of the unregenerate; they are *asleep and dead.*

2. Their duty; which is to "awake, and stand up from the "dead."

3. The power enabling them thereunto; "Christ shall give "thee light."

First, The miserable state of the unregenerate, represented under the motions of *sleep* and *death:* both expressions intending one and the same thing, though with some variety of notion. The Christless and unregenerate world is in a deep sleep; a spirit of slumber, senselessness and security is fallen upon them, though they lie exposed immediately to eternal wrath and misery, ready to drop into hell every moment. Just as a man that is fast asleep in a house on fire, and whilst the consuming flames are round about him, his fancy is sporting itself in some pleasant dream; this is a very lively resemblance of the unregenerate soul. But yet he that sleeps hath the principle of life entire in him, though his senses be bound, and the actions of life suspended by sleep. Lest therefore we should think it is only so with the unregenerate, the expression is designedly varied, and those that were said to be *asleep*, are positively affirmed to be *dead;* on purpose to inform us that it is not a simple *suspension* of the acts and exercise, but a total *privation* of the principle of spiritual life, which is the misery of the unregenerate.

Secondly, We have here the duty of the unregenerate, which is to "awake out of sleep, and arise from the dead." This is their great concernment; no duty in the world is of greater necessity and importance to them. "Strive (saith Christ) to enter in at the "strait gate," Luke xiii. 24. And the order of these duties is very natural. First awake, then arise. Startling and rousing convictions make way for spiritual life; till God awake us by convictions of our misery, we will never be persuaded to arise and move towards Christ for remedy and safety.

Thirdly, But you will say, if unregenerate men be dead men, to what purpose is it to persuade them to arise and stand up: The very exhortation supposes some powers or ability in the unregenerate; else in vain are they commanded to arise *. This difficulty is solved in this very text, though the duty is ours, yet the power is God's. God commands that in his word, which only his grace can perform. "Christ shall give thee light." Popish commentators would build the tower of free-will upon this scripture, by a very weak argument, drawn from the order wherein these things are here expressed; which is but a very weak foundation to build upon, for it is very usual in scripture to put the effect before, and the cause after, as it is here, so in Isa. xxvi. 19. "Awake and sing, "ye that dwell in the dust." But I will not here intangle my discourse with that controversy; that which I aim at is plain in the words, viz.

---

* Though the words seem to import a willingness first to awake and rise, and then to be enlightened, yet we are to understand, that it is by the efficacy of Christ's light that the sinner is made to awake and rise. *Roll. on the place.*

Doct. *That all Christless souls are under the power of spiritual
death; they are in the state of the dead.*

Multitudes of testimonies are given in scripture to this truth;
Eph. ii. 1, 5. "You hath he quickened who were dead in tres-
"passes and sins." Col. ii. 13. "And you being dead in your
"sins, and the uncircumcision of your flesh, hath he quickened
"together with him;" with many other places of the same importance. But the method in which I shall discourse this point
will be this;

First, I will shew you in what sense Christless and unregene-
rated men are said to be dead.

Secondly, What the state of spiritual death is.

Thirdly, How it appears that all unregenerate men are in this
sad state. And then apply it.

First, In what sense are Christless and unregenerate men said to
be dead men.

To open this, we must know there is a three-fold death, viz.

1. Natural.
2. Spiritual.
3. Eternal.

Natural death is nothing else but the privation of the principle
of natural life, or the separation of the soul from the body, James
ii. 26. "The body without the spirit is dead." Spiritual death is
the privation of the principle of spiritual life, or the want and absence of the quickening Spirit of God in the soul; the soul is the
life of the body, and Christ is the life of the soul; the absence of
the soul is death to the body, and the absence or want of Christ is
death to the soul. Eternal death is the separation both of body
and soul from God, which is the misery of the damned. Now
christless and unregenerate men are not dead in the first sense;
they are naturally alive though they are dead while they live; nor
are they yet dead in the last sense, eternally separated from God
by an irrevocable sentence as the damned are; but they are dead
in the second sense; they are spiritually dead, whilst they are naturally alive; and this spiritual death is the fore-runner of eternal
death. Now spiritual death is put in scripture in opposition to a
two-fold spiritual life, viz.

1. The life of justification.
2. The life of sanctification.

Spiritual death in opposition to the life of justification, is nothing else but the guilt of sin bringing us under the sentence of
death. Spiritual death, in opposition to the life of sanctification,
is the pollution or dominion of sin. In both these senses, unrege-

nerate men are dead men ; but it is the last which I am properly
concerned to speak to in this place, and therefore,

Secondly, Let us briefly consider what this spiritual death is,
which, as before was hinted, is the absence of the quickening
Spirit of Christ from the soul of any man. That soul is a dead
soul, into which the Spirit of Christ is not infused in the work of
regeneration ; and all its works are dead works, as they are called,
Heb. ix. 14. For, look how it is with the damned, they live, they
have sense and motion, and an immortality in all these ; yet because they are eternally separated from God, the life which they
live, deserves not the name of life, but it is every where in scripture stiled death : so the unregenerate, they are naturally alive ;
they eat and drink, they buy and sell, they talk and laugh, they
rejoice in the creatures ; and many of them spend their days in
pleasures, and then go down to the grave. This is the life they
live, but yet the scripture rather calls it death than life ; because
though they live, yet it is without God in the world, Eph. ii. 12.
though they live, yet it is a life alienated from the life of God,
Eph. iv. 18. And therefore while they remain naturally alive, they
are in scripture said " to remain in death," 1 John iii. 14. and to
be " dead while they live," 1 Tim. v. 6. And there is great reason
why a christless, an unregenerate state, should be represented in
scripture, under the notion of death ; for there is nothing in nature which more aptly represents that miserable state of the soul,
than natural death doth. The dead see and discern nothing, and
the natural man perceiveth not the things that are of God. The
dead have no beauty or desirableness in them ; " Bury my dead
(saith Abraham) out of my sight ;" neither is there any spiritual
loveliness in the unregenerate. True it is, some of them have
sweet natural qualities and moral excellencies, which are engaging
things, but these are so many flowers, decking and adorning a
dead corpse. The dead are objects of pity and great lamentation :
men used to mourn for the dead, Eccl. xii. 5. " Man goeth to his
" long home, and the mourners go about the streets." But unregenerate, and christless souls, are much more the objects of pity
and lamentation. How are all the people of God (especially those
that are naturally related to them) concerned to mourn over them
and for them, as Abraham did for Ishmael, Gen. xvii. 18. " O that
" Ishmael might live before thee." Upon these, and many other
accounts, the state of unregeneracy is represented to us in the
notion of death.

Thirdly, And that this is the state of all Christless and unsanctified persons, will, undeniably, appear two ways.

1. The causes of spiritual life have not wrought upon them.

2. The effects and signs of spiritual life do not appear in them,

and therefore they are in the state, and under the power of spiritual death.

First, The causes of spiritual life have not wrought upon them. There are two causes of spiritual life,

1. Principal, and internal.
2. Subordinate and external.

The principal internal cause of spiritual life is the regenerating Spirit of Christ, Rom. viii. 2. "The law of the Spirit of life in "Christ Jesus hath made me free from the law of sin and death." It is the Spirit, as a regenerating Spirit, that unites us with Christ, in whom all spiritual life originally is, John v. 25, 26. "Verily I "say unto you, that the hour is coming, and now is, when the "dead shall hear the voice of the Son of God; and they that hear "shall live: For as the Father hath life in himself, so hath he "given to the Son to have life in himself." As all the members of the natural body receive animation, sense, and motion, by their union with their natural head; so all believers, the members of Christ, receive spiritual life and animation by their union with their natural head; so all believers, the members of Christ, receive spiritual life and animation by their union with Christ their mystical head, Eph. iv. 15, 16. Except we come to him, and be united with him in the way of faith, we can have no life in us, John v. 40. "Ye will not come unto me that ye may have life." Now the Spirit of God hath yet exerted no regenerating, quickening influences, nor begotten any special saving faith in natural, unsanctified men; whatever he hath done for them in the way of natural, or spiritual common gifts, yet he hath not quickened them with the life of Christ. And as for the subordinate external means of life, viz. the preaching of the gospel, which is the instrument of the Spirit in this glorious work, and is therefore called, *The word of life*, Phil. ii. 16. This word hath not yet been made a regenerating, quickening word to their souls. Possibly it hath enlightened them, and convinced them: it hath wrought upon their minds in the way of common illumination, and upon their consciences in the way of conviction, but not upon their hearts and wills, by way of effectual conversion. To this day the Lord hath not given them an heart opening itself, in the way of faith, to receive Jesus Christ.

Secondly, The effects and signs of spiritual life do not appear in them: For,

First, They have no feeling, or sense of misery and danger. I mean no such sense as thoroughly awakens them to apply Christ their remedy. That spiritual judgment lies upon them, Isa. vi. 9, 10. "And he said, Go and tell this people, Hear ye indeed, but "understand not; and see ye indeed, but perceive not; make the

" heart of this people fat, and their ears heavy, and shut their
" eyes."

Secondly, They have no spiritual motions towards Christ, or after
things that are spiritual; all the arguments in the world cannot
persuade their wills to move one step towards Christ in the way of
faith, John v. 30. *Ye will not come unto me:* Were there a principle of spiritual life in their souls, they would move Christ-ward
and heaven-ward, John iv. 14. It would be in them a well of
water springing up into eternal life. The natural tendency of the
spiritual life is upward.

Thirdly, The unregenerate have no appetite unto spiritual food;
they savour not things that are spiritual; they can go from week
to week, and from year to year, all their life-time, without any
communion betwixt God and their souls, and feel no need of it, nor
any hungerings or thirstings after it; which could never be, if a
principle of spiritual life were in them; for then they would
" esteem the words of God's mouth more than their necessary
" food," Job xxx. 12.

Fourthly, They have no heat or spiritual warmth in their affections to God, and things above; their hearts are as cold as a stone
to spiritual objects. They are heated, indeed, by their lusts and
affections to the world, and the things of the world: but O how
cold and dead are they towards Jesus Christ, and spiritual excellencies.

Fifthly, They breathe not spiritually, therefore they live not
spiritually: were there a spiritual principle of life in them, their
souls would breathe after God in spiritual prayer, Acts ix. 11.
" Behold he prayeth." The lips of the unregenerate may move
in prayer, but their hearts and desires do not breathe and pant
after God.

Sixthly, They have no cares or fears for self-preservation, which
is always the effect of life; the poorest fly, or silliest worm will shun
danger. The wrath of God hangs over them in the threatenings,
but they tremble not at it: hell is but a little before them; they
are upon the very precipice of eternal ruin, yet will use no means
to avoid it. How plain, therefore, is this sad case which I have un-
dertaken here to demonstrate, viz. that christless and unregenerate
souls are dead souls? The uses follow.

Inf. 1. *If all Christless and unregenerate souls be dead souls, then
how little pleasure can Christians take in the society of the unregenerate?*

Certainly, it is no pleasure for the living to converse among the
dead. It was a cruel torment invented by Mezentius the tyrant,
to tie a dead and living man together. The pleasure of society
arises from the harmony of spirits, and the hopes of mutual en-

joyment in the world to come; neither of which can sweeten the society of the godly with the wicked in this world *. It is true, there is a necessary civil converse which we must have with the ungodly here; or else, (as the apostle speaks) we must go out of the world. There are also duties of relation which must be faithfully and tenderly paid, even to the unregenerate: but certainly, where we have our free election, we shall be much wanting both to our duty and comfort, if we make not the people of God our chosen companions. Excellently to this purpose speaks a modern author†, "Art thou a godly master? when thou takest a servant
" into thine house, chuse for God as well as thyself.—A godly ser-
" vant is a greater blessing than we think on: he can work, and
" set God on work also. for his master's good, Gen. xxiv. 12.
" O Lord God of my master Abraham, I pray thee send me good
" speed this day, and shew kindness unto my master." And surely
" he did his master as much service by his prayer, as by his pru-
" dence in that journey.—Holy David observed, while he was at
" Saul's court, the mischief of having wicked and ungodly ser-
" vants, (for with such was that unhappy king so compassed, that
" David compares his court to the profane and barbarous Hea-
" thens, among whom there was scarce more wickedness to be
" found, Psal. cxx. 6. "Wo is me, that I sojourn in Meshech,
" that I dwell in the tents of Kedar;" i. e. among those who
" were as prodigiously wicked as any there); and no doubt, but
" this made this gracious man, in his banishment, before he came
" to the crown, (having seen the evil of a disordered house) to
" resolve what he would do when God should make him the head
" of such a royal family, Psal. ci. 7. " He that worketh deceit,
" shall not dwell within my house; he that telleth lies shall not
" tarry in my sight."
  " Art thou godly? shew thyself so in the choice of husband or
" wife. I am sure, if some, (and those godly ones) could bring
" no other testimonials for their godliness than the care they have
" taken in this particular, it might justly be called into question
" both by themselves and others. There is no one thing that
" gracious persons, (even those recorded in scripture as well as
" others, have shewn their weakness, yea, given offence and
" scandal more in, than in this particular, "The sons of God saw
" that the daughters of men were fair," Gen. vi. 2. One would
" have thought that the sons of God should have looked for grace
" in the heart, rather than beauty in the face; but we see, even

---

* As diseases bred in one part of the body use to spread their pernicious influence to the other members which are near to that part; so the vices of the wicked use to infect those that have intercourse with them. *Tertullian against Valentine.*

† Gurnal's Christian Armour, part 2. p. 256, 257.

" they sometimes turn in at the fairest sign, without much enquir-
" ing what grace is to be found dwelling within." Look to the
rule, O Christian, if thou wilt keep the power of holiness, that is
clear as the sun-beam written in the scripture, " Be not unequally
" yoked together with unbelievers," 2 Cor. vi. 14.

*Inf. 2. How great and wholly supernatural, marvellous, and won-
derful is that change which regeneration makes upon the soul of men!*
It is a change from death to life, Luke xv. 24. " This my son was
" dead and is alive again." Regeneration is life from the dead;
the most excellent life from the most terrible death: it is the life of
God re-inspired into a soul alienated from it by the power of sin,
Eph. iv. 11. There are two stupendous changes made upon the
souls of men, which justly challenge the highest admiration, viz.

    1. That from sin to grace.

    2. From grace to glory.

The change from grace to glory is acknowledged by all, and
that justly, to be a wonderful change for God to take a poor creature out of the society of sinful men; yea, from under the burden
of many sinful infirmities, which made him groan from day to day
in this world; and in a moment to make him a complete and perfect soul, shining in the beauties of holiness, and filling him as a
vessel of glory, with the unspeakable and inconceivable joys of his
presence; to turn his groanings into triumphs, his fightings into
songs of praise; this, I say, is marvellous, and yet the former
change from sin to grace is no way inferior to it, nay, in some
respect, beyond it; for the change which glory makes upon the
regenerate is but a gradual change, but the change which regeneration makes upon the ungodly is a specifical change. Great and
admirable is this work of God; and let it for ever be marvellous in
our eyes.

*Inf. 3. If unregenerate souls be dead souls, what a fatal stroke
doth death give to the bodies of all unregenerate men?* A soul dead
in sin, and a body dead by virtue of the curse for sin, and both soul
and body remaining for ever under the power of eternal death, is so
full and perfect a misery, as that nothing can be added to make it
more miserable: It is the comfort of a Christian that he can say
when death comes, *Non omnis moriar*, I shall not wholly die; there
is a life I live which death cannot touch, Rom. viii. 13. " The
" body is dead, because of sin; but the spirit is life because of
" righteousness." Blessed and holy is he that hath part in the first
resurrection: on such the second death hath no power. As death
takes the believer from amidst many sorrows and troubles, and
brings him to the vision of God, to the general assembly of all the
perfected saints, to a state of complete freedom and full satisfaction; so it drags the unregenerate from all his sensitive delights,

and comforts, to the place of torment: it buries the dead soul out of the presence of God for ever: it is the king of terrors, a serpent with a deadly sting to every man that is out of Christ.

Inf. 4. *If every unregenerate soul be a dead soul, how sad is the case of hypocrites and temporary believers, who are twice dead?* These are those cursed trees, of which the apostle Jude speaks, Jude ver: 12. " Trees whose fruit withereth, without fruit, twice " dead, plucked up by the roots." The apostle alludes unto dying trees, trees that are dying the first time in the spring, then they fade, decay, and cast off their leaves, when other trees are fragrant and flourishing: but from this first death they are sometimes recovered, by pruning, dressing, or watering the roots; but if in autumn, they decay again, which is the critical and *climacterical* times of trees, to discover whether their disease be mortal or not; if then they wither and decay the second time, the fault is *ab intra,* the root is rotten, there is no hope of it; the husbandmen bestows no more labour about it, except it be to root it up for fuel to the fire. Just thus stands the case with false and hypocritical professors, who though they were still under the power of spiritual death, yet in the beginning of their profession, they seemed to be alive; they shewed the world the fragrant leaves of a fair profession, many hopeful buddings of affection towards spiritual things were seen in them, but wanting a root of regeneration, they quickly began to wither and cast their untimely fruit. However, by the help of or-dinances, or some rousing and awakening providences, they seem to recover themselves again; but all will not do, the fault is *ab in-tra,* from the want of a good root, and therefore, at last, they who were always *once dead,* for want of a principle of regeneration, are now become *twice dead,* by the withering and decay of their vain profession. Such trees are prepared for the severest flames in hell, Matth. xxiv. 51. their portion is the saddest portion allotted for any of the sons of death. Therefore the apostle Peter tells us, 2 Pet. ii. 20, 21. " For if, after they have escaped the pollutions " of the world, through the knowledge of the Lord and Saviour " Jesus Christ, they are again entangled therein, and overcome; " the latter end is worse with them than the beginning. For it " had been better for them not to have known the way of righte- " ousness, than after they have known it, to turn from the holy " commandment delivered unto them." Double measures of wrath seem to be prepared for them that die this double death.

Inf. 5. *If this be so, then unregenerate persons deserve the greatest lamentations.* And were this truth heartily believed, we could not but mourn over them, with the most tender compassion and hearty sorrow. If our husbands, wives, or children are dying a natural death, how are our hearts rent in pieces with pity and sorrow for them? What cries, tears, and wringing of hands, discover the deep sense we have of their misery! O Christians, is all the love you have for your relations spent upon their bodies? Are their souls of no value in your eyes? Is spiritual death no misery? Doth it not deserve a tear? The Lord open your eyes, and duly affect your hearts with spiritual death and soul miseries.

Consider, my friends, and let it move your bowels, (if there be bowels of affection in you,) whilst they remain spiritually dead, they are useless and wholly unserviceable unto God in the world, as to any special and acceptable service unto him, 2 Tim. ii. 21. they are incapable of all spiritual comforts from God; they cannot taste the least sweetness in Christ, in duties, or in promises, Rom. viii. 6. they have no beauty in their souls, how comely soever their bodies are; it is grace, and nothing but grace that beautifies the inner man, Ezek. xvi. 6, 7. The dead have neither comfort nor beauty in them: they have no hope to be with God in glory; for the life of glory is begun in grace, Phil. i. 6. their graves must be shortly made, to be buried out of the sight of God for ever in the lowest hell, the pit digged by justice for all that are spiritually dead: the dead must be buried.. Can such considerations as these draw no pity from your souls, nor excite your endeavours for their regeneration? then it is to be feared your souls are dead as well as theirs. O pity them, pity them, and pray for them; in this case only, prayers for the dead are our duty: who knows but at the last, God may hear your cries, and you may say with comfort, as he did, " This " my son was dead, but is alive; was lost, but is found; and they " began to be merry," Luke xv. 24.

SERMON XXXII.

The Condemnation of Unbelievers, illustrated and applied.

JOHN iii. 18.

——*But he that believeth not is condemned already, because he hath not believed in the name of the only begotten Son of God.*

CHRIST having discoursed with Nicodemus in the beginning of this chapter, about the necessity of regeneration, proceeds to shew in this following discourse, the reason and ground why regeneration and faith are so indispensably necessary, viz. because

there is no other way to set men free from the curse and condemnation of the law. The curse of the law, like the fiery serpents
in the wilderness, hath smitten every sinner with a deadly stroke
and sting, for which there is no cure but Christ lifted up in the gospel, " as Moses lifted up the serpent in the wilderness," ver. 14.
Neither doth Christ cure any but those that, believingly, apply
him to their own souls. The result and conclusion of all you have
in my text; " He that believeth in him is not condemned; but
" he that believeth not is condemned already," &c. In this clause
which I have pitched upon we find these three parts;

1. The sin threatened, viz. Unbelief.
2. The punishment inflicted, viz. Condemnation.
3. The immediate relation of the one to the other; " he is con-
" demned already."

First, Let us take into consideration the sin which is here threatened, viz. *unbelief*; the neglecting or refusing of an exalted and
offered Jesus. Unbelief is two-fold, viz. *negative* or *positive*. *Negative* unbelief is the sin of the Heathens, who never had the gospel among them, nor the offers of Christ made to them; these cannot believe on him of whom they have not heard. *Positive* unbelief is the sin of men and women under the gospel, to whom Christ
is actually opened and offered by the preaching of the gospel; but
they make light of it, and neglect the great salvation: Receive not
Christ into their hearts, nor consent to the severe and self-denying
terms upon which he is offered. This is the sin threatened.

Secondly, The punishment inflicted, and that is *condemnation*: a
word of deep and dreadful signification; appearing, in this text as
the hand-writing upon the plaister of the wall unto Belteshazzar,
Dan. v. 5. a word whose deep sense and emphasis are fully understood in hell. *Condemnation* is the judgment, or sentence of God,
condemning a man to bear the punishment of his eternal wrath for
sin; the most terrible of all sentences.

Thirdly, The immediate relation or respect this punishment
hath to that sin of unbelief. The unbeliever is condemned already,
i. e. he is virtually condemned by the law of God; his *mittimus*
is already made for hell; he is condemned, as *a sinner*, by the
breach of the first covenant; but that condemnation had never
been his ruin except it had been ratified by the sentence of God,
condemning him, as an *unbeliever*, for slighting and rejecting the
grace offered in the second covenant. So that the believer is already virtually condemned by both, as he is a sinner, and as he is
an unbeliever; as he hath transgressed the law, and as he hath refused the gospel; as he hath contracted sin the moral disease, and
refused Christ the only effectual remedy. He is virtually condemned, and will be, sententially, condemned in the judgment of the

great day.   Unbelief is his great sin, and condemnation is his great
misery.   Hence the observation will be this:

Doct. *That all unbelievers are presently, and immediately under
the just and dreadful sentence of God's condemnation.* John
xii. 48. " He that rejecteth me, and receiveth not my words,
" hath one that judgeth him.   The word that I have spoken,
" the same shall judge him in the last day." John iii. 36.
" He that believeth not the Son shall not see life, but the
" wrath of God abideth on him."

Three things are to be opened in the doctrinal part of this
point:
1. What unbelief, or the not receiving of Jesus Christ is.
2. What condemnation, the punishment of this sin, is.
3. Why this punishment unavoidably follows that sin.

First, What the sin of unbelief, or not receiving Christ, is.   By
unbelief, we are not here to understand the relics or remains
of that sin in the people of God, which is mixed with their imperfect faith; for there is some unbelief still mingled with faith,
in the best of hearts: He that can say, *Lord, I believe,* hath
cause enough to cry out with tears, *help thou my unbelief.*
However, this doth not bring the soul under condemnation, or
into the state of wrath; the word condemns this unbelief in them,
but doth not condemn their persons for this unbelief: But the unbelief here spoken of, is the neglecting or refusing to take Christ
as he is offered in the gospel, and so is exclusive of the saving act
and effects of faith.

First, It is exclusive of the saving act of faith, which (as hath
been already declared) is the due receiving of Christ offered in the
gospel, consenting to take him upon his own terms.   This, the
unbeliever will by no means be persuaded to do; he will be persuaded to accept the promises of Christ, but not to accept the person of Christ: He is willing to accept Christ in part, a divided
Christ, but not to accept Christ entirely, in all his offices.   He
will accept the righteousness of Christ in conjunction with his own
righteousness; but he will not accept the righteousness of Christ as
the sole matter of his justification, exclusive of his own righteousness: he is willing to wear the crown of Christ, but cannot be persuaded to bear the cross of Christ.   Thus Christ and unbelievers
part upon terms; God will come down no lower, and the unbeliever will come up no higher; God will not alter his terms, and
the unbeliever will not alter his resolution; and so Christ is refused, salvation neglected, and in effect the unbeliever chuseth
rather to be damned, than to comply with the severe terms of self-

denial, mortification, and bearing the cross of Christ. Thus it excludes the saving act of faith.

Seconaly, It is exclusive of the saving fruits and effects of faith. Faith produces love to God, but the unbeliever doth not truly love him; " But I know you (saith Christ to unbelievers) that the love " of God is not in you," John v. 42. Faith purifies the heart of a believer, but the hearts of unbelievers are full of all impurity. The believer overcomes the world, the world overcomes the unbeliever: Faith makes the cross of Christ sweet and easy to the believer, unbelief makes Christ, because of the cross, bitter and distasteful to the unbeliever. Thus unbelief excludes both the saving act and fruits of faith, and consequently bars the soul from the saving benefits and privileges of faith, viz. justification and peace with God.

Secondly, Next let us consider the punishment of this sin, which is condemnation. Condemnation, in the general, is the sentence of a judge awarding a mulct, or penalty to be inflicted upon the guilty person. There is a twofold condemnation.

1. *Respectu culpæ,* In respect of the fault.

2. *Respectu pœnæ,.* In respect of the punishment.

First, Condemnation, with respect to the fault, is the casting of the person as guilty of the crime charged upon him; condemnation, with respect to the punishment, is the sentencing of the convicted offender to undergo such a punishment for such a fault; to bear a penal for a moral evil. This *forensic* word, *condemnation,* is here applied unto the case of a guilty sinner cast at the bar of God, where the fact is clearly proved, and the punishment righteously awarded. Thou art an unbeliever, for this sin thou shalt die eternally. Condemnation with respect to the fault, stands opposed to justification, Rom. v. 16. Condemnation with respect to the punishment, stands opposed to salvation, Mark xvi. 16. More particularly,

First, Condemnation is the sentence of God, the great and terrible God, the omniscient, omnipotent, supreme, and impartial Judge, at whose bar the guilty sinner stands. It is the law of God that condemns him now: he hath one that judgeth him, a great and terrible one too. It is a dreadful thing to be condemned at man's bar; but the courts of human judicature, how awful and solemn soever they are, are but trifles to this court of heaven, and conscience, wherein the unbeliever is arraigned and condemned.

Secondly, It is the sentence of God adjudging the unbeliever to eternal death, than which, nothing is more terrible. What is a prison to hell? What is a scaffold and an ax, to " go ye cursed into " everlasting fire?" What is a gallows and a halter, to everlasting burnings?

Thirdly, Condemnation is the final sentence of God, the supreme judge, from whose bar and judgment there lies no appeal for the unbeliever, but execution certainly follows condemnation, Luke xix. 27. If man condemn, God may justify and save; but if God condemn, no man can save or deliver. If the law cast a man, as a sinner, the gospel may save him as a believer: but if the gospel cast him as an unbeliever, a man that finally rejects Jesus Christ, whom it offers to him, all the world cannot save that man. O then what a dreadful word is condemnation! All the evils and miseries of this life are nothing to it. Put all afflictions, calamities, sufferings, and miseries of this world into one scale, and this sentence of God into the other, and they will be all lighter than a feather.

Thirdly, In the next place, I shall shew you that this punishment, viz. condemnation, must unavoidably follow that sin of unbelief. So many unbelieving persons as be in the world, so many condemned persons there are in the world; and this will appear two ways.

1. By considering what unbelief excludes a man from.

2. By considering what unbelief includes a man under.

First, Let us consider what unbelief excludes a man from; and it will be found, that it excludes him from all that may help and save him. For,

First, It excludes him from the pardon of sin, John viii. 24. " If ye believe not that I am he, ye shall die in your sins." Now he that dies under the guilt of all his sins, must needs die in a state of wrath and condemnation for ever. " For the wages of sin is " death," Rom. vi. 23. If a man be saved without a pardon, then may the unbeliever hope to be saved.

Secondly, Unbelief excludes a man from all the saving benefits that come by the sacrifice or death of Christ. For if faith be the only instrument that applies and brings home to the soul the benefits of the blood of Christ, as unquestionably it is, then unbelief must of necessity exclude a man from all those benefits, and consequently leave him in the state of death and condemnation. Faith is the applying cause, the instrument by which we receive the special saving benefit of the blood of Christ, Rom. v. 25. " Whom God " hath set forth to be a propitiation through faith in his blood." Eph. ii. 8. " By grace are ye saved through faith." So then if the unbeliever be acquitted and saved, it must be without the benefit of Christ's death and sacrifice, which is utterly impossible.

Thirdly, Unbelief excludes a man from the saving efficacy and operation of the gospel, by shutting up the heart against it, and crossing the main scope and drift of it, which is to bring up men

to the terms * of salvation. To persuade them to believe, this is
its great design, the scope of all its commands, 1 John iii. 23.
Mark i. 14, 15. John xii. 36. It is the scope of all its promises;
they are written to encourage men to believe, John vi. 35, 37.
So then if the unbeliever escape condemnation, it must be in a way
unknown to us by the gospel; yea, contrary to the established order
therein. For the unbeliever obeyeth not the great command of the
gospel, 1 John iii. 23. Nor is he under any one saving promise of
it, Gal. iii. 14, 22.

Fourthly, Unbelief excludes a man from union with Christ, faith
being the bond of that union, Eph. iii. 17. The unbeliever therefore may as reasonably expect to be saved without Christ, as to be
saved without faith. Thus you see what unbelief excludes a man
from.

Secondly, Let us next see what guilt and misery unbelief includes
men under, and certainly it will be found to be the greatest guilt
and misery in the world. For,

First, It is a sin which reflects the greatest dishonour upon God,
1 John vi. 10. " He that believeth on the Son of God, hath
" the witness in himself. He that believeth not God, hath made
" him a liar; because he believeth not the record that God gave
" of his Son."

Secondly, Unbelief makes a man guilty of the vilest contempt of
Christ, and the whole design of redemption managed by him. All
the glorious attributes of God were finally manifested in the work of
redemption by Christ; therefore the apostle calls him " the wisdom
" of God, and the power of God," 1 Cor. i. 23, 24. But what doth
the careless neglect, and wilful rejection of Christ speak, but the
weakness and folly of that design of redemption by him.

Thirdly, Unbelief includes in it the sorest spiritual judgment that
is or can be inflicted in this world upon the soul of man; even
spiritual blindness, and the fatal darkening of the understanding by
Satan, 2 Cor. iv. 4. of which more hereafter.

Fourthly, Unbelief includes a man under the curse, and shuts
him up under all the threatenings that are written in the book of
God; amongst which, that is an express and terrible one, Mark
xvi. 10. " He that believes not, shall be damned." So that nothing
can be more evident than this, that condemnation necessarily follows
unbelief. This sin and that punishment are fastened together with
chains of adamant. The uses follow:

Inf. 1. If this be so, then how great a number of persons are
visibly in the state of condemnation ! So many unbelievers, so many

---

* i. e. Those things which accompany salvation. *Editor.*

condemned men and women.   That is a sad complaint of the prophet, Isa. liii. i. " Who hath believed our report, and to whom is
" the arm of the Lord revealed ?"   Many there be that talk of faith,
and many that profess faith ; but they only talk of and profess it :
There are but few in the world unto whom the arm of the Lord
hath been revealed, in the work of faith with power.   It is put
among the great mysteries and wonders of the world, 1 Tim. iii. 16.
That Christ is believed on in the world.   O what a great and terrible day will the day of Christ's coming to judgment be, when so
many millions of unbelievers shall be brought to his tribunal to be
solemnly sentenced !   They are (as my text speaks) *condemned already* ; but then that dreadful sentence will be solemnly pronoun-
ced by Jesus Christ, whom they have despised and rejected : Then
shall that scripture be fulfilled, Luke xix. 27. " These mine ene-
" mies that would not that I should reign over them, bring them
" hither, and slay them before me."

   Inf. 2.   Hence be informed how great a mercy the least measure
of saving faith is : for the least measure of true faith unites the soul
to Jesus Christ ; and then " there is no condemnation to them that
" are in Christ Jesus," Rom. viii. 1.   Not one sentence of God
against them.   So Acts xiii. 39. " By him all that believe are jus-
" tified from all things."   The weakest believer is as free from condemnation as the strongest ; the righteousness of Christ comes upon
all believers without any difference.   Rom. iii. 22. " Even the
" righteousness of God, which is by faith of Christ Jesus unto all,
" and upon all them that believe ; for there is no difference."   It
is not imputed, as it is in inherent righteousness ; one man hath
more holiness than another : The faith that receives the righteousness of Christ may be different in degrees of strength ; but the received righteousnes is equal upon all believers : A piece of gold is
as much worth in the hand of a child, as it is in the hand of a man.
O the exceeding preciousness of saving faith !

   Inf. 3.   How dreadful a sin is the sin of unbelief, which brings
men under the condemnation of the great God.   No sin startles
less, or damns surer : It is a sin that doth not affright the conscience as some other sins do, but it kills the soul more certainly than
any of those sins could do : For, indeed, other sins could not damn
us, were it not for unbelief, which fixes the guilt of them all upon
our persons.   This is the condemnation.   Unbelief is the sin of
sins ; and when the Spirit comes to convince men of sin, he begins
with this as the capital sin, John xvi. 9.   But more particularly,

   First, Estimate the evil of unbelief from its object.   It is the slighting and refusing of the most excellent and wonderful person in heaven or earth : the vision of Christ by faith is the joy of saints upon

earth: the vision of Christ above is the happiness of saints in heaven.   It is a despising of him who is altogether lovely in himself,
who hath loved us and given himself for us.

It is a rejecting of the only Mediator betwixt God and man;
after the rejecting of whom there remains no sacrifice for sin.

Secondly, Let the evil of unbelief be valued by the offer of Christ
to our souls in the gospel: It is one part of the great mystery of
godliness that Christ should be preached to the Gentiles, 1 Tim.
iii. 16.   That the word of this salvation should be sent to us, Acts
xiii. 26.   A mercy denied to the fallen angels, and the greatest
part of mankind, which aggravates the evil of this sin beyond all
imagination.   So that in refusing or neglecting Jesus Christ are
found vile ingratitude, highest contempt of the grace and wisdom
of God; and in the event, the loss of the only season and opportunity of salvation, which is never more to be recovered to all eternity.

Inf. 4. If this be the case of all unbelievers, it is not to be admired, that souls under the first convictions of their miserable condition, are plunged into such deep distresses of spirit.   It is said of
them, Acts ii. 27. " That they were pricked at the heart, and
" cried out, men and brethren, what shall we do?" And so the
jailor, " He came in trembling and astonished, and said, Sirs, what
" must I do to be saved?" Certainly, if souls apprehend themselves
under the condemnation and sentence of the great God in all tears
and trembling, their weary days and restless nights are not without
just cause and reason.   Those that never saw their own miserable
condition by the light of a clear and full conviction, may wonder to
see others so deeply distressed in spirit.   They may mis-judge the
case, and call it melancholy or madness: but spiritual troubles do
not exceed the cause and ground of them, let them be as deep and
as great as they will: And, indeed, it is one of the great mysteries of grace and providence; a thing much unknown to men,
how such poor souls are supported from day to day under such fears
and sorrows as are able, in a few hours, to break the stoutest spirit
in the world.   Luther was a man of great natural courage; and
yet, when God let in spiritual troubles upon his soul, it is noted of
him, *ut nec vox, nec calor, nec sanguis superesset;* he had neither
voice, nor heat, nor blood appearing in him.

Inf. 5. How groundless and irrational is the mirth and jollity of
all carnal and unregenerate men? They feast in their prison, and
dance in their fetters.   O the madness that is in the hearts of men!
If men did but see their *mittimus* made for hell, or believe they are
condemned already, it were impossible for them to live at that rate
of vanity they do: And is their condition less dangerous because it
is not understood? Surely no; but much more dangerous for that,

O poor sinners, you have found out an effectual way to prevent your present troubles; it were well if you could find out a way to prevent your eternal misery: But it is easier for a man to stifle conviction, than prevent damnation. Your mirth hath a two-fold mischief in it; it prevents repentance, and increases your future torment. O what a hell will your hell be, who drop into it, out of all the sensitive and sinful pleasures of this world! If ever man may say of mirth, that it is mad; and of laughter, what doth it! He may say so in this case.

Inf. 6. Lastly, what cause have they to rejoice, admire, and praise the Lord to eternity, who have a well-grounded confidence that they are freed from God's condemnation? " O give thanks " to the Father, who hath delivered you from the power of dark- " ness, and translated you into the kingdom of his dear Son," Col. i. 13. Rejoice, and be exceeding glad; for if you be freed from condemnation, you are out of Satan's power, he hath no more any dominion over you. The power of Satan over men comes in by virtue of their condemnation, as the power of the *jailor*, or *executioner*, over the bodies of condemned prisoners doth, Heb. ii. 14. If you be freed from condemnation, the sting of death shall never touch you; for the sting of death smites the souls of men with a deadly stroke, only by virtue of God's condemnatory sentence, 1 Cor. xv. 55, 56. " The sting of death is sin, and the " strength of sin is the law." If you be freed from condemnation now, you shall stand with comfort and boldness at the judgment-seat of Christ in the great-day; and verily in this thing is the love of God perfected, 1 John iv. 17. O it is a privilege in which the grace, mercy, and love of God shine forth as clearly as the sun when it shineth in its full strength. And certainly you will find cause to lie at the feet of God, astonished and overwhelmed with the sense of this mercy, when you shall find yourselves free from the condemnation of God, whilst many others, as good as you were, are still under condemnation. Yea, yourselves freed, and many of your superiors in the world still under the curse, 1 Cor. i. 26. Yea, yourselves freed, and others that sat under the same means of grace, and had the same external advantages as you had, still in chains, 2 Cor. ii. 16. O brethren! This is a marvellous deliverance; look on it which way you will, your ransom is paid, and not a penny of it by you; it cost you nothing to procure your pardon; your pardon is full, and not one sin excepted out of it that you ever committed. You are freed, and Jesus Christ condemned in your stead to procure your discharge; your pardon is sealed in his blood, and that for ever; so that you shall never any more come into condemnation. " He that heareth my word, and

" believeth on him that sent me, hath everlasting life, and shall
" not come into condemnation, but is passed from death to life,"
John v. 24.

Let them that are so delivered, spend their days on earth in
praise and cheerful obedience ; and, when they die, let them not
shrink away from death, nor be afraid to take it by the cold hand,
it can do them no harm. Yea, let them close their dying lips
with—*Thanks be to God for Jesus Christ.*

SERMON XXXIII.

Of the Aggravation of the Sin, and Punishment of Unbelief under the light of the Gospel.

JOHN iii. 19.

*And this is the condemnation, that light is come into the world, and
men loved darkness rather than light, because their deeds were evil.*

OUT of the foregoing verse it was fully proved in our last sermon, that all christless and unregenerate men are no better than
dead men, being *condemned already.* Our Saviour proceeds in this
verse to aggravate the misery of those that refuse and despise him ;
yet farther, and to let them know, that those who remain in unbelief
and the state of unregeneracy, must expect some greater and sorer
wrath than other men ; not only a simple condemnation, but an aggravated and peculiar condemnation, " This is the condemnation,
" that light is come," &c.

In the words we find these three parts.

1. The aggravation of sin by the abuse of gospel-light, " Light
" is come," &c.

2. The aggravation of misery, in proportion to that abuse of light,
" This is the condemnation."

3. The cause and occasion, drawing men into this sin and misery,
" Because their deeds were evil."

First, We have here the aggravation of sin by the abuse of gospel-light, " Light is come." By light we are to understand the
knowledge, discovery, and manifestation of Christ, and redemption by him in the gospel. He is the Sun of righteousness that
arises in the gospel upon the nations, Mal. iv. 1. When he came
in the flesh, then did " the day spring from on high visit us,"
Luke i. 78. And the light may be said to come two ways ; either,

First, In the means by which it is conveyed to us ; or, *Secondly,* in the efficacy of it upon our minds, when it actually shines in our souls. Light may come among a people in the means, and yet they actually remain in darkness all the while. As it is in nature; the sun may be up and a very glorious morning far advanced, whilst many thousands are drowning upon their beds with their curtains drawn about them. Light in the *means*, we may call *potential light*. Light in the *mind*, we may call *actual light*. It is but seldom that light comes in the means, and continues long among men, but some light must needs actually shine into their souls also; but this actual light is twofold.

1. Common, and intellectual only, to *conviction;* or,

2. Special and efficacious light, bringing the soul to Christ by real *conversion*, called, in 1 Cor. iv. 6.——God " shining into the " heart."

Wherever light comes, in this last sense, it is impossible that such men should prefer darkness before it: But it may come in the means, yea, it may actually shine into the consciences of men by those means, and convince them of their sins, and yet men may hate it, and chuse darkness rather than light. And this is the sense of this place, light was come in the gospel-dispensation among them, yea, it had shined into many of their consciences, galled and reproved them for sin, but they hated it, and had rather be without such a troublesome inmate. In a word,.by the coming of light, we are here to understand a more clear and open manifestation of Christ by the gospel than ever was made to the world before: For we are not to think that there was no light in the world till Christ came, and the gospel was published in the world by the apostles' ministry. For Abraham saw Christ's day, John viii. 56. and all the faithful before Christ saw the promises, i. e. their accomplishment in Christ, afar off, Heb. xi. 13. For it was with Christ, the Sun of righteousness, as it is with the natural sun, " which illuminates the hemisphere before it actually rises or " shews its body above the horizon * ;" but when it rises and shews itself, the light is much clearer; so it was in this case. The greater therefore was their sin that rebelled against it, and preferred darkness to light; this was their sin, with its fearful aggravation.

Secondly, In a most just proportion to this sin, we have here the aggravated condemnation of them who sinned against such clear gospel-light: " This is the condemnation," this is the judgment of all judgments, the greatest and most intolerable judgment; a severer sentence of condemnation than ever did pass against any others that sinned in the times of ignorance and darkness: they

---

* *Sol nondum conspectus, illuminat orbem.*

that live and die impenitent and unregenerate, how few soever the means of salvation have been which they have enjoyed, must be condemned: yea, the Pagan world, who have no more but natural light to help them, will be condemned by that light; but " this is the condemnation," i. e. such sinning as this is the cause of the greatest condemnation and sorest punishment, as it is called, Heb. x. 19.

Thirdly, The cause and occasion, drawing men into this sin and misery, " because their deeds are evil," i. e. the convincing light of truth put a great deal of vigour and activity into their consciences, which they could not endure. The accusations and condemnations of conscience are very irksome and troublesome things to men: To avoid this, they are willing to be ignorant. An enlightened conscience gives an interruption also unto men in their sinful courses and pleasures; they cannot sin at so easy a rate in the light as they did in darkness; and this made them hate the light as a very troublesome thing to them. Thus you see what was the sin, what the punishment, and what the cause of both.

Hence the Observation is,

Doct. *That the greater and clearer the light is, under which the impenitent and unregenerate do live in this world, by so much greater and heavier will their condemnation and misery be in the world to come.*

Mat. xi. 21, 22. " Wo unto thee Chorazin, wo unto thee " Bethsaida; for. if the mighty works which were done in you, " had been done in Tyre and Sidon, they would have repented " long ago in sackcloth and ashes: But I say unto you, it shall be " more tolerable for Tyre and Sidon at the day of judgment than " for you." Two things require explication in the doctrinal part of this point, viz.

1. How light puts a deeper guilt and aggravation into sin.

2. Why sin so aggravated, makes men liable to greater condemnation.

First, We will enquire into the grounds and reasons why greater light, greatens and aggravates, proportionably, the sins that are committed under it, and it will appear that it doth so, upon divers accounts.

First, All light (especially evangelical light) is a great preservative from sin, and an excellent means to prevent it: It is the property of light to inform the judgment, and rectify the mistakes and errors of it; and thereby to give check to the affections in the pursuit of sinful designs and courses: It is a plain case, that many men

would never do as they do, if their understandings were better informed. 1 Cor. ii. 8. " Which none of the princes of the world
" knew; for had they known it, they would not have crucified
" the Lord of glory." It was want of light and better information which drew them under that horrid and unparalleled guilt.
Our Saviour also supposes, in the place before cited, that if Tyre
and Sidon had enjoyed the same light and means of grace that
Chorazin and Bethsaida did, they would never have been so sinful as they were: light discovers danger, and thereby overawes
and stops men from proceeding farther in those parts and courses
that will run them into it.

Secondly, Sinning under and against the light, supposes and involves in it a greater contempt and despite of God's authority, than
sinning in ignorance and darkness doth. Every man that breaks
the law of God, doth not in the same degree, despise and slight the
authority of the law-maker: But when a man hath light to discover the evil and danger of what he doth, and yet will dare to do it,
what is this but the treading of God's authority under foot? The
casting of his word behind our backs? Wilful sinning is a despite-
ful sinning against God, Heb. x. 26. it argues a low and vile esteem
of the law of God, which is reverend and holy; and by so much
the more it maketh sin to be exceeding sinful.

Thirdly, Sinning under and against the light, admits not of those
excuses and pleas to extenuate the offence, which sins of pure ignorance do. Those that live without the sound of the gospel may
say, Lord, we never heard of Christ, and the great redemption
wrought by him; if we had, we would never have lived and acted
as we did: and therefore Christ saith, John xv. 22. " If I had
" not come and spoken unto them, they had not had sin, but now
" they have no cloak for their sin."
The meaning is, that if the gospel-light had not shined among
them, their sin had not been of that deep guilt that now it is:
For now it is foul and heinous, by reason of the light under and
against which it is committed, that they have no pretence or excuse to extenuate or mitigate it.

Fourthly, Evanglical light is a very rich favour and mercy of
God to men; one of the choicest gifts bestowed upon the nations
of the world; and therefore it is said, Psal. cxlvii. 19, 20. " He
" sheweth his word unto Jacob, and his statutes and his judgments
" unto Israel: He hath not dealt so with any nation; and as for
" his judgments they have not known them." Other nations have
corn and wine, gold and silver, abundance of earthly delights and
pleasures; but they have not a beam of heavenly light shining
upon them. We may account this mercy small; but God who is
best able to value the worth of it, accounts it great, Hos. viii. 12.

" I have written unto them the great things of my law." Christ reckoned Capernaum to be exalted unto heaven by the ministry of the gospel in that place. Now the greater the mercy is which the light of truth brings with it, by so much the more horrid and heinous must the abusing and despising of it be.

Fifthly, Sinning against the light, argues a love to sin, as sin; to naked sin, without any disguise or cover. It is nothing near so bad for a man through a mistake of judgment, when he thinks that to be lawful, which is indeed sinful; he doth not now close with sin, as sin, but he either closes with it as his duty, or at least his liberty. It is hard for Satan to persuade many men to embrace a naked sin; and therefore he clothes it in the habit of a duty, or liberty, and thereby deceives and draws men to the commission of it. But if a man have light shining into his conscience, and convincing him that the way he is in, is the way of sin, quite contrary to the revealed will of God, stripping the sin naked before the eye of his conscience, so that he hath no cover or excuse, and yet will persist in it; this, I say, argues a soul to be in love with sin, as sin. Now, as for a man to love grace as grace is a solid argument to prove the truth of his grace; so on the contrary for a man to love sin as sin, doth not only argue him to be in the state of sin, but to be in the fore-front, and amongst the highest rank of sinners.

Sixthly, The greater and clearer the light is, under and against which men continue in sin, the more must the consciences of such sinners be supposed to be wasted and violated by such a way of sinning: For this is a sure rule, * that " the greatest violation of " conscience, is the greatest sin." Conscience is a noble and tender part of the soul of man: it is in the soul, as the eye in the body, very sensible of the least injury; and a wound in the conscience is like a blow in the eye: But nothing gives a greater blow to conscience, nothing so much wastes it and destroys it as sins against the light do. This puts a plain force upon the conscience, and gives a dreadful stab to that noble power, God's vicegerent in the soul. And thus you see the first thing made good, that light puts deep guilt and aggravation into sin.

Secondly, In the next place, let us examine why sin, so aggravated by the light, makes men liable to the greater condemnation: For that it doth so, is beyond all debate or question; else the apostle Peter would not have said of those sinners against light, as he doth, 2 Pet. ii. 21. "that it had been better for them not to have known " the way of righteousness." Nor would Christ have told the inhabitants of Chorazin or Bethsaida, that it should be more tolera-

---

* *Maxima violatio conscientiæ est maximum peccatum.*

ble for Tyre and Sidon at the day of judgment than for them. There is a twofold reason of this.

1. *Ex parte Dei*, on God's part.

2. *Ex parte peccatoris*, on the sinner's part.

First, Ex parte Dei, on God's part, who is the righteous Judge of the whole earth; and will therefore render unto every man according as his work shall be; For shall not the Judge of the whole earth do right? He will judge the world in righteousness, and righteousness requires that difference be made in the punishment of sinners, according to the different degrees of their sins. Now that there are different degrees of sin, is abundantly clear from what we have lately discoursed under the former head; where we have shewed, that the light under which men sin, puts extraordinary aggravations upon their sins, answerable whereunto will the degrees of punishment be awarded by the righteous Judge of heaven and earth. The Gentiles who had no other light but that dim light of nature, will be condemned for disobeying the law of God written upon their hearts: but yet, the greater wrath is reserved for them who sin both against the light of nature, and the light of the gospel also: And therefore it is said, Rom. ii. 9. " Tribulation and anguish upon every soul of man that doth evil; " of the Jew first, and also of the Gentile." Impenitent Jews and Gentiles will all be condemned at the bar of God; but with this difference, to the Jew first, i. e. principally and especially, because the light and mercies which he abused and violated were far greater than those bestowed upon the Gentiles, " because unto " them were committed the oracles of God:" And God hath not dealt with any nation as with that nation. Indeed, in the rewards of obedience, the same reason doth not hold; he that came into the vineyard the last hour of the day, may be equal in reward with him that bare the heat and burthen of the whole day; because the reward is of grace and bounty, not of debt and merit: But it is not so here, justice observes an exact proportion in distributing punishments, according to the degrees, deserts, and measures of sin: And therefore it is said concerning Babylon, Rev. xviii. 7. " How much she hath glorified herself, and lived deliciously; so " much torment and sorrow give her."

Secondly, Ex parte peccatoris, upon the account of sinners; it must needs be, that the heaviest wrath and most intolerable torments should be the portion of them who have sinned against the clearest light and means of grace: For we find, in the scripture account, that a principal and special part of the torment of the damned, will arise from their own consciences. Mark ix. 44. " Where " their worm dieth not, and the fire is not quenched." And nothing is more manifest than this, that if conscience be the tormentor of the damned, then sinners against light must needs have the greatest torment. For,

First, The more knowledge any man had in this world, the more was his conscience violated and abused here by sinning against it: And O what work will these violations and abuses make for a *tormenting conscience* in hell ! With what rage and fury will it then avenge itself upon the most stout, daring, and impudent sinner ! The more guilt now, the more rage and fury then.

Secondly, The more knowledge, or means of knowledge any man hath enjoyed in this world, so much the more matter is prepared and laid up for conscience to upbraid him with in the place of torment ? And the upbraidings of conscience are a special part of the torments of the damned. O what a peal will conscience ring in the ears of such sinners ! " Did not I warn thee of the issue of such " sins, undone wretch ? How often did I strive with thee, if it " had been possible to take thee off from thy course of sinning, " and to escape this wrath ? Did not I often cry out in thy bosom, " Stop thy course, sinner ? Hearken to my counsel, turn and live ; " but thou wouldst not hearken to my voice ! I forewarned thee of " this danger, but thou slightest all my warnings ; thy lusts were " too strong for my light, and now thou seest whither thy way " tended, but, alas, too late !"

Thirdly, The more knowledge, or means of knowledge any man hath abused and neglected in this world, so many fair opportunities and great advantages he hath lost for heaven ; and the more opportunities and advantages he hath had for heaven, the more intolerable will hell be to that man ; as the mercy was great which was offered by them, so the torment will be unspeakable that will arise from the loss of them. Sinners, you have now a wide and open door, many blessed opportunities of salvation under the gospel ; it hath put you in a fair way for everlasting happiness : Many of you are not far from the kingdom of God : there will be time enough in hell to reflect upon this loss. What think you, will it not be sad to think there : O how fair was I once for heaven, to have been with God, and among yonder saints ! My conscience was once convinced, and my affections melted under the gospel. I was almost persuaded to be a Christian, indeed the treaty was almost concluded betwixt Christ and my soul ; there were but a few points in difference betwixt us ; but wretch that I was, at those points I stuck, and there the treaty ended to my eternal ruin : I could not deny my lusts, I could not live under the strict yoke of Christ's government ; but now I must live under the insupportable wrath of the righteous and terrible God for ever : and this torment will be peculiar to such as perish under the gospel. The Heathen, who enjoyed no such means, can therefore have no such reflections; nay, the very devils themselves, who never had such a plank after their shipwreck, I mean, a mediator in their nature, or such terms of reconciliation, offered them, will not reflect upon their lost opportunities of recovery, as such sinners must and will. This, therefore, "is the condemnation, that light is come " into the world; but men loved darkness rather than light."

Inf. 1. Hence it follows, that neither knowledge, nor the best means of knowledge, are in themselves sufficient to secure men from wrath to come.   Light in itself is a choice mercy, and therefore the means that begat and increased it must be so too; but yet is a mercy liable to the greatest abuse, and the abuse of the best mercies brings forth the greatest miseries. Alas! Christians, your duty is but half learnt when you know it; obedience to light makes light a blessing indeed. John xiii. 17. "If ye know these things, happy " are ye if ye do them." Happiness is not intailed upon simple knowing, but upon doing; upon obedience to our knowledge; otherwise he that increaseth knowledge, doth but increase sorrow : " For that servant which knew his Lord's will, and prepared not " himself, nor did according to his will, shall be beaten with " many stripes," Luke xiii. 47. "And to him that knoweth to do " good, and doth it not, to him it is sin," James iv. 17. We are bound with all thankfulness to acknowledge the bounty of heaven to this sinful generation, in furnishing us with so many excellent means of light, beyond many other nations and generations that are past, but yet we ought to rejoice with trembling when we consider the abuses of light in this wanton age, and what a dismal event is like to happen unto many thousands among us. I fear the time is coming when many among us will wish they had never set foot on English ground. God hath blessed this nation with many famous, burning and shining lights. It was once said to the honour of this nation *, *that the English ministry was the world's wonder;* and when a man of another nation began to preach methodically and convincingly, they were wont to say †, *We perceive this man hath been in England:* The greater will our account be for abusing such light and rebelling against it. The clearer our light is now, the thicker will the mists of darkness be hereafter, if we are thus wanton under it. The devils have more light than we, and therefore the more torment: Of them it is said, James ii. 19. "The " devils also believe, and tremble;" the horror of their consciences is answerable to their illumination, *they tremble;* "the ‡ word sig-

---

* *Clerus Anglicanus stupor mundi.*
† *Percipimus hunc hominem fuisse in Anglia.*
‡ Φρισσσι ; φρίξ, *est maris agitatio.* Eust.

" nifies the roar of the sea," or such a murmuring, dreadful noise
as the tempestuous seas use to make when they break themselves
against the rocks.

*Inf. 2. If the abuse of light thus aggravate sin and misery, then
times of great temptations are like to be times of great guilt.*   Wo
to an enlightened, knowing generation, when strong temptations
befal them.   How do many, in such times, imprison the known
truth to keep themselves out of prison ? offer violence to their own
consciences, to avoid violence from other hands ?

Plato * was convinced of the unity of God, but durst not own
his convictions ; but said, " It was a truth neither easy to find, nor
" safe to own."   And even Seneca †, the renowned moralist, was
" forced by temptation to dissemble his convictions ;" of whom
Augustine saith, " ‡ He worshipped what himself reprehended,
" and did what himself reproved."   And even a great Papist of
later times was heard to say, as he was going to mass, *Eamus ad
communem errorem*, Let us go to the common error.   O how hard
is it to keep conscience pure and peaceable in days of temptation !
Doubtless, it is a mercy to many weak and timorous Christians to
be removed by a seasonable death out of harm's way ; to be dis-
banded by a merciful providence before the heat of the battle.
Christ and Antichrist seem at this day to be drawing into the field;
a fiery trial threatens the professors of this age : but when it comes
to a close engagement, indeed we may justly tremble, to think how
many thousands will break their way through the convictions of
their own consciences, to save their flesh.   Believe it, sirs, if Christ
hold you to himself by no other tie than the slender thread of a
single conviction ; if he have not interest in your hearts and affections, as well as in your understandings and consciences; if you be
men of great light and strong unmortified lusts ; if you profess
Christ with your tongues, and worship the world with your hearts ;
a man may say of you, without the gift of prophecy, what the
prophet said of Hazael, I know what you will do in the day of
temptation.

*Inf. 3. If this be so, what a strong engagement lieth upon all en-
lightened persons to turn heartily to God, and reduce their knowledge
into practice and obedience?* The more men know, the more violence
they do their own consciences in rebelling against the light, this is
to sin with an high hand, Numb. xv. 30.   Believe it, sirs, you
cannot sin at so cheap a rate as others do ; knowledge in a wicked
man, like high metal in a blind horse, doth but the sooner precipi-

---

* *Opificem aniversi neque invenire facile, neque inventum in vulgus promulgare tutum.*
† *In animo religionem habeat, sed in actibus fingat.*
‡ *Colebat quod reprehendebat, agebat quod arguebat, quod culpabat adorabat.*

tate him into ruin. You may know much more than others, but if ever you come to heaven, it must be in the same way of faith and obedience, mortification, and self-denial, in which the weakest Christian comes thither; whatever knowledge you have, to be sure you have no wisdom, if you expect salvation upon any other, or easier terms than the most illiterate Christian finds it. It was a sad observation of the father, *Surgunt indocti, et rapiunt cœlum;* the unlearned rise, and take heaven. What a pity is it that men of such excellent parts should be enslaved to their lusts! that ever it should be said, *Sapientis sapienter descendunt in Gehennam;* their learning doth but hang in their light, it doth but blind them in spiritual things, and prepareth them for greater misery.

Inf. 4. Hence also it follows, that the work of conversion is a very difficult work; the soul is scarcely half won to Christ, when Satan is cast out of the understanding by illumination. The devil hath deeply intrenched himself, and strongly fortified every faculty of the soul against Christ; the understanding, indeed, is the first entrance into the soul, and out of that faculty he is oftentimes cast by light and conviction, which seems to make a great change upon a man: now he becomes a professor, now he takes up the duties of religion, and passes up and down the world for a convert; but, alas, alas! all the while Satan keeps the fort-royal, the heart and will are in his own possession; and this is a work of more difficulty: the weapons of that warfare must indeed be mighty through God, which do not only cast down imaginations, but bring every thought of the heart into captivity to the obedience of Christ, 2 Cor. x. 4, 5. While the heart stands out, though the understanding be taken in, the soul remains in Satan's possession; it is a greater work, (and we daily find it so,) to win one heart than to convince twenty understandings.

Inf. 5. Hence also we may learn what strength and power there is in the lusts of men's hearts, which are able to bear down so strong convictions of the conscience before them. That is a great truth, though a very sad one, Eccl. viii. 11. "The heart of the sons of " men is fully set in them to do evil." O how common is it every day, and in every place to see men hazarding their souls to satisfy their lusts! Every man, saith the prophet, "turneth to his course, " as the horse rusheth into the battle." The horse is a very fierce and warlike creature; and when his courage is roused by the sounds of drums and trumpets and shouts of armies, he breaks headlong into the ranks of armed men, though death is before him. Such boisterous and headlong lusts are found in many enlightened persons, though their consciences represent damnation before them; onward they will rush, though God be lost, and a precious soul undone for ever.

Inf. 6. To conclude, *As ever you will avoid the deepest guilt, and escape the heaviest condemnation, open your hearts to obey and practise whatsoever God hath opened your understandings and consciences to receive of his revealed will*; obey the light of the gospel, while you have opportunity to enjoy it : this was the great counsel given by Christ, John xii. 35, 36. " Yet a little while the light is " with you, walk while you have the light, lest darkness come upon you." The manifestation of Christ in the gospel, is the light of the world; all the nations of the earth that want this light are benighted; and those upon whom this light is risen, have but a short time under it ; " Yet a little while the light is with you :" and whatever patience God may exercise towards poor ignorant souls, yet commonly he makes short work with the despisers of this light. The light of the gospel is a shining lamp, fed with golden oil; God will not be at the expence for such a light for them that do but trifle with it. The night is coming when no man can work. There are many sad signs upon us of a setting sun, a night of darkness approaching ; many burning and shining lights are extinguished, and many *put under a bushel ;* your work is great, your time short, this is the only space you have for repentance, Rev. ii. 21. If this opportunity of salvation be lost it will never come again, Ezek. xxiv. 13. How pathetical was that lamentation which Christ made over Jerusalem, Luke xix. 41, 42. " And when he was come near, " he beheld the city, and wept over it, saying, If thou hadst known, " even thou, at least in this thy day, the things which belong unto " thy peace, but now they are hid from thine eyes." Christ is threatening those nations with the removal of his gospel presence ; he hath found but cold entertainment among us : England hath been unkind to Christ ; many thousands there are that rebel against the light, that say unto God, " Depart from us, we desire not the " knowledge of thy ways." Christ will not tarry where he is not welcome ; who would, that hath any where else to go ? Obey the light therefore, lest God put it out in obscure darkness.

SERMON XXXIV.

The blinding Policies of Satan opened, as the cause of Unbelief, and Forerunner of Destruction.

2 Cor. iv. 3, 4.

But if our gospel be hid, it is hid to them that are lost; in whom the god of this world hath blinded the minds of them which believe not, lest the light of the glorious gospel of Christ, who is the image of God, should shine unto them.

THE aversions of men from Jesus Christ, their only remedy, is as much to be admired as lamented; one would think the news of deliverance should make the hearts of captives leap for joy, the tidings of a Saviour should transport the heart of a lost sinner. A man would think a little rhetoric might persuade the naked soul of a sinner to put on the rich robes of Christ's righteousness, which will cost him nothing but acceptance; or the perishing, starving sinner to accept the bread of God which cometh down from heaven, and giveth life unto the world. This is the great design I have managed in this whole discourse; the centre to which all these lines are drawn; many arguments have been used, and many ways attempted to prevail with men to apply and put on Christ, and I am afraid, all too little. I have but laboured in vain, and spent my strength for nought; all these discourses are but the beating of the air, and few, if any, will be persuaded to come unto Christ, who is clearly opened, and freely offered in the gospel to them. For alas! while I am reasoning, Satan is blinding their minds with false reasonings and contrary persuasions; the god of this world turns away the ears, and draws away the hearts of almost the whole world from Christ; " The god of this world " hath blinded the minds of them which believe not, lest the light " of the glorious gospel of Christ, who is the image of God, " should shine unto them." Satan is a great and jealous prince, and is well aware, that so many of his subjects as shall be brought to see the misery of their condition, will never endure to abide any longer in subjection to him: it is therefore his great policy to put out their eyes, that he may secure their souls; to darken their understandings, that he may keep his interest firm and entire in their wills and affections: and this makes the effectual application of Christ so great a difficulty, that, on the contrary, it is just matter of admiration that any soul is persuaded and prevailed with to quit the service of Satan, and come to Christ. And therefore, in the last place, to discover the great difficulty of conversion, and shew you where it is that all our endeavours are obstructed, so that we can move the design no further, with all our labouring and striving, reasoning and persuading; as also to mourn over and bewail the misery of christless and unregenerate souls, with whom we must part, upon the saddest terms; I have chosen this scripture, which is of a most awakening nature, if haply the Lord, at last, may persuade any soul to come over to Christ thereby.

These words come into the apostle's discourse, by way of *prolepsis;* he had been speaking in the former chapter, of the transcendent excellency of the gospel above the law, and, among other respects, he prefers it to the law in point of clearness. The law was an obscure and cloudy dispensation; there was a vail upon the face of Moses, and the hearts of the people, that they could not see to the end of that which is abolished; but under the gospel we all, with open face, behold, as in a glass, the glory of the Lord. Against this discourse, the apostle foresaw, and obviated this objection; If your gospel be so clear, what is the reason that many, who live under the ministration of it, (and they none of the meanest, neither for wisdom nor understanding) do yet see no glory, nor excellency in it? To this he returns in the words I have read, " If our gospel be hid, it is hid from them that are lost, whose eyes " the god of this world hath blinded," &c. q. d. It is true, multitudes there are, who see no glory in Christ or the gospel, but the fault is not in either; but in the minds of them that believe not. The sun shines forth in its glory, but the blind see no glory in it; the fault is not in the sun, but in the eye.   In the words themselves we have three parts to consider:

1. A dreadful, spiritual judgment inflicted.
2. The wicked instrument by whom it is inflicted.
3. The politic manner in which he doth it.

First, We have here a very dreadful, spiritual judgment inflicted upon the souls of men, viz. the hiding of the gospel from them: if our gospel be hid; for these words, Ει·δε και εςι, are a concession, that so it is; a very sad, but undeniable truth.   Many are there who see no beauty in Christ, nor necessity of him; though both are so plainly and evidently revealed in our gospel, " if our " gospel be hid."   It is called our gospel, not as if St. Paul and other preachers of it, were the authors and inventors of it; but our gospel, because we are the preachers and dispensers of it.   We are put in trust with the gospel, and though we preach it, in the demonstration of the Spirit, and of power, using all plainness of speech to make men understand it, yet it is hid from many under our ministry: it is hid from their understandings, they see no glory in it; and hid from their hearts, they see no power in it.   Our gospel, notwithstanding all our endeavours, is a hidden gospel unto some; this is the sorest, and most dreadful judgment.

Secondly, We have here an account of that wicked instrument by whom this judgment is inflicted, viz. Satan, called here (by a *mimesis) the god of this world;* not simply and properly, but because he challenges to himself the honour of a god, rules over a vast empire, and hath multitudes of souls, even the greater part of the world, in subjection and blind obedience to his government.

Thirdly, Here, also, we have an account of the politic manner of this government, how he maintains his dominion among men, and keeps the world in quiet subjection to him; namely, by blinding the minds of all them that believe not; putting out the eyes of all his subjects, darkening that noble faculty, the mind, or understanding; the thinking, considering, and reasoning power of the soul, which the philosophers truly call το ηγεμονικον, the leading and directing faculty; for it is to the soul, what eyes are to the body, and it is therefore called, " the eyes of the understanding," Eph. i. 18. These eyes Satan blinds, i. e. he darkens the mind and understanding with ignorance and error; so that when men come to see and consider spiritual things, " they see indeed, but perceive " not," Isa. vi. 9, 10. They have some general, confused notions, but no distinct, powerful, and effectual apprehensions of those things: and this is the way, indeed, none like it, to bar men effectually from Jesus Christ, and hinder the *application of the benefits of redemption* to their souls. It is true, the righteous God permits all this to be done by Satan, upon the souls of men; but wheresoever he finally prevails thus to blind them, it is as the text speaks, εν τοις απογγυμενοις, *in them that are lost,* or appointed of God unto perdition. The elect of God are all blinded for a time, but Christ applieth unto them his eye-salve, effectually opens the eyes of their understandings, and recovers them thereby, out of Satan's power and dominion; but as for those who still continue thus blinded, the symptoms and characters of eternal death appear upon their souls; they are a company of lost men.

Doct. That the understandings of all unbelievers are blinded by Satan's policies, in order to their everlasting perdition.

Four things must be opened in the doctrinal part of this point.

First, What the blinding of the understanding, or hiding of the gospel from the understanding, is.

Secondly, I shall demonstrate, that the understandings of many are thus blinded, and the gospel hidden from them.

Thirdly, I shall shew what policies Satan uses to blind the minds of men.

Fourthly, That this blindness is the sorest judgment, and in order to men's everlasting perdition.

Fifthly, And then apply the whole.

First, We shall enquire what the blinding of the mind, or hiding the gospel from it, is. Two sorts of men are thus blinded in the world.

1. Those that want the means of illumination.

2. Those that have the means, but are denied the blessing and efficacy of them.

The former is the case of the Pagan world, who are in midnight darkness for want of the gospel. The latter is the case of the Christian world. The greatest part of them that live within the sound of the gospel, being blinded by the god of this world, Isa. vii. 9, 10. " And he said, Go, and tell this people; hear ye in- " deed, but understand not; and, see ye indeed, but perceive not: " Make the heart of this people fat, and make their ears heavy; " and shut their eyes, lest they see with their eyes, and hear with " their ears, and understand with their heart, and convert, and be " healed." Thus, when the Sun of righteousness actually arose on the world, it is said, John i. 5. " The light shined in darkness, but " the darkness comprehended it not." So we may say of all that light which is in the understanding of all unbelievers, what Job speaks of the grave, Job x. 22. " That the light there is as dark- " ness." But more particularly, to open the nature of this spiritual blindness, I will shew you,

1. What it is not opposed unto.

2. What it is opposed unto.

1. Let us examine what spiritual blindness, or the hiding the gospel from the minds of men is not opposed unto: and we shall find,

First, That it is not opposed unto natural wisdom; a man may be of an acute and clear understanding; eagle-eyed, to discern the mysteries of nature, and yet the gospel may be hidden from him. Who were more sagacious and quick-sighted in natural things than the Heathen Philosophers, renowned for wisdom in their generations; yet unto them the gospel was but *foolishness,* 1 Cor. i. 20, 21. St. Augustin confesseth, that before his conversion he was filled with offence and contempt of the simplicity of the gospel. *Dedignabur esse parvulus,* saith he, I scorned to become a child again. And that great Bradwardine, the profound doctor, who was learned, *usque ad stuporem,* even to a wonder, profes- sed, that when he first read Paul's epistles, he despised them, be- cause he found not in them, *metaphysicum ingenium,* those metaphy- sical notions which he expected. Upon this account it was, that Christ brake forth into the pathetical gratulation of his Father's

love to the elect, Mat. xi. 25. " At that time Jesus answered and
" said, I thank thee, O Father, Lord of heaven and earth; be-
" cause thou hast hid these things from the wise and prudent, and
" hast revealed them unto babes."

Secondly, It is not opposed to all light and knowledge in spiritual
truths.   A man may have a true understanding of the scriptures,
give an orthodox exposition of them, and enlighten the minds of
others by them; and yet the gospel may be hidden from himself,
Mat. vii. 22. " Many will say unto me in that day, Lord, Lord,
" have we not prophesied in thy name!" So Rom. ii. 19. " And
" art confident that thou thyself art a guide of the blind, a light
" to them that sit in darkness," &c.   A man may shew others the
way to Christ and salvation, whilst both are hid from himself.

Thirdly, It is not opposed to all kind of influences upon the affections; for, it is possible, the gospel may touch the affections
themselves, and cause some sweet motions and raptures in them;
and yet be an hidden gospel to the soul, Heb. vi. 5, 9.

But if these three things may consist with spiritual blindness unto
what then is it opposed?   To which I answer, that spiritual blindness stands only opposed to that saving manifestation of Jesus
Christ in the gospel by the Spirit, whereby the soul is regenerated,
and effectually changed by a real conversion unto God: Where-
ever the gospel thus comes in the demonstration of the Spirit, and
of power, producing such an effect as this in the soul, it is no
longer an hidden gospel to that soul, though such persons do not
see clearly all that glory which is revealed by the gospel; though
they know but in part, and see darkly as through a glass; yet the
eyes of their understandings are opened, and the things which belong
to their peace are not hidden from them.

Secondly, But though this be the happiness of some men, yet it
is demonstrable that the eyes of many are blinded by the god of
this world, and the gospel is an hidden gospel from them; for,

First, Many that live under the gospel are so entirely swallowed up in the affairs of this world, that they allow themselves no
time to ponder the great concernment of their souls in the world to
come; and judge you, whatever the gifts and knowledge of these
men are, whether the god of this world hath not blinded their eyes.
If it were not so, it were impossible that ever they should thus waste
the most precious opportunities of salvation upon which their everlasting well-being depends, and spend time at the door of eternity
about trifles which so little concern them.   Yet this is the case of
the greatest number that go under the Christian name.   The earth
hath opened her mouth and swallowed up their time, thoughts,
studies, and strength, as it did the bodies of Corah and his *accom-*

plices. The first, the freest, yea, the whole of their time, is devoted to the service of the world; for even at that very time when they present their bodies before the Lord, in the duties of his worship, their hearts are wandering after vanities, and "going after "their covetousness," Ezek. xliii. 31. Judge whether the god of this world hath blinded these men or no, who can see so much beauty in the world, but none in Christ, and put an absolute necessity upon the vanities of this world, but none upon their own salvation. If this be not spiritual blindness, what is?

Secondly, The great stillness and quietness of men's consciences, under the most rousing and awakening truths of the gospel, plainly prove that the god of this world hath blinded their eyes. For did men see and apprehend the dangerous condition they are in as the word represents it; nothing in the world would quiet them but Christ. As soon as men's eyes come to be opened, the next enquiry they come to make is, "What shall we do to be saved?" It is not impossible that a man should hang over hell, see Christ and the hopes of salvation going, and the day of patience ending, and yet be quiet. O! it cannot be, that conscience should let them be quiet in such a case, if it were not blinded and stupified; but whilst the god of this world, "that strong man armed keepeth "the house, all his goods are in peace," Luke xi. 21. If once your eyes were opened by conviction, a man may then say, be quiet if you can; sit still, and let the hopes and seasons of salvation pass quietly away if you can. Suppose one should come into the congregation, and whisper but such a word as this in your ears, your child is fallen into the fire, and is a dying, since you came from home; will it be in the power of all friends you have to quiet you, and make you sit still after such an information? much less when a man apprehends his own soul in immediate danger of everlasting burnings.

Thirdly, The strong confidences and presumptuous hopes men have of salvation, whilst they remain in the state of nature and unregeneracy, plainly shew their minds to be blinded by the policy of Satan. This presumption is one of those παραλογισμοι, false reasonings, by which Satan deludes the understanding, as the apostle calls them, James i. 22. It is the cunning sophistry of the devil, fathered by self-love, Prov. xxi. 2. "Every way of a man is right "in their own eyes," and partly by self-ignorance, Rev. iii. 17. "Thou saidst I am rich, and have need of nothing, and knowest "not that thou art poor." You have no fears, no doubts, no ease to propound that concerns your future state; and why so? but because you have no sight; your consciences are quieted, because your eyes are blinded.

Fourthly, The trifling of men with the duties of religion plainly

discovers the blinding power of Satan upon their minds and understandings, else they would never play and dally with the serious
and solemn ordinances of God at that rate they do; if their eyes
were once opened, they would be in earnest in prayer, and apply
themselves with the closest attention of mind to hearing the
gospel.   There are two sorts of thoughts about any subject of
meditation.   Some think at a distance, and others think close to
the subject.   Never do thoughts of men come so close to Christ, to
heaven, and to hell, as they do immediately upon their illumination.   When John's ministry enlightened the people's minds, it is
said, Matth. xi. 12.   "From the days of John the Baptist until
" now, the kingdom of heaven suffereth violence, and the vio-
" lent take it by force."   Surely these men were more in good
earnest who would receive no repulse, take no denial, but even
force themselves through all difficulties into heaven; and so would
it be with you.   If the god of this world had not blinded your
minds you would never pray with so much unconcernedness, nor
hear with so much negligence and carelessness ; pray as if you prayed not, and hear as if you heard not.   It is with many of your
hearts as it was with Aristotle, who after a quaint oration made before him, was asked how he liked it ; truly, said he, I did not hear
it ; for I was thinking all the while of another matter.

Fifthly, This also is a plain evidence that the god of this world
hath blinded many men's eyes among us, for that they fear not
to commit great sins to avoid small hazards and troubles, which all
the world could never persuade them to do, if they were not hoodwinked by the god of this world.   Those that have seen sin as sin,
in the glass of God's law, " will chuse as Moses did, to suffer any
" affliction with the people of God, rather than enjoy the plea-
" sures of sin, which are but for a season," Heb. xi. 25.   Those
that have seen and felt the evil of sin in the deep troubles of their
spirits for it, will account all reproaches, all losses, all sufferings
from men, to be but as nothing to the burthen of sin.

Sixthly, The pride and self-conceitedness of many thousands
who profess Christianity, plainly shew their minds to be blinded by
the *sophistry of Satan,* and that they do not understand themselves,
and the woful state of their own souls.   Those that see God in the
clearest light, abhor themselves in the deepest humility, Isa. vi. 5.
John xliii. 5.   If ever the Lord had effectually opened your eyes
by a clear discovery of your state by nature, and the course of your
life, under the efficacy and influence of continual temptations and
corruptions, how would your plumes fall ?   None in the world
would rate you lower than you yourselves would.   By all which it
appears that multitudes are blinded by the god of this world,

Thirdly, In the third place we are to consider what policies Satan useth to blind the minds of them that believe not, and we shall find there are three sorts of policies practised by the god of this world upon the minds and understandings of men, which he darkens, by

1. Hindering the reception of gospel-light.
2. Obstructing the efficacy of it when received.
3. Making misapplication of it to other purposes.

First, It is a great policy in Satan, to blind the understandings of men, by hindering and preventing the reception of gospel-light, which he doth especially these five ways;

First, By tempting the dispensers of the gospel to darken the truths thereof, in the delivering of them, to shoot over the heads of their hearers, in lofty language and terms of art, so that common understandings can give no account, when the sermon is done, what the preacher would have; but, however, commend him for a good scholar, and an excellent orator. I make no doubt but the devil is very busy with ministers in their studies, tempting them, by the pride of their own hearts, to gratify his designs herein; he teaches them how to paint the glass, that he might keep out the light.

I acknowledge, a proper, grave, and comely stile, befits the lips of *Christ's ambassadors;* they should not be rude and careless in their language, or method. But this affectation of great swelling words of vanity, is but too like the proud Gnostics, whom the apostle is supposed to tax for this evil, Jude ver. 16. " This is to " darken counsel by words without knowledge," Job xxxi. 2. To amuse and bemist poor ignorant souls, and nullify the design of preaching: for every thing is accounted so far good, as it is good to the end it is ordained for. A sword that hath an hilt of gold, set thick with diamonds, is no good sword, if it hath no edge to cut, or want a good back to follow home the stroke. O that the ministers of Christ would chuse rather * sound, than great words, such as are apt to pierce the heart, rather than such as tickle the fancy; and let people beware of furthering the design of Satan against their own souls, in putting a temptation upon their ministers, by despising plain preaching. The more popular, plain, and intelligible our discourses are, so much the more probable they are to be successful; that is the most excellent oratory, that persuades men to Christ.

Secondly, Satan hinders the access of light to the understandings of men, by employing their minds about impertinent things, while

---

* They who speak in a popular, plain, and simple manner, are the best instructors of the people. *Bucholtz.*

they are attending upon the ordinances of God; thus he tempted them, in Ezek. xxxiii. 31, 32. "And they come unto thee as the "people cometh, and they sit before thee, as my people; and "they hear thy words, but they will not do them; for with their "mouth they shew much love, but their heart goeth after their "covetousness. And lo! thou art unto them as a very lovely song "of one that hath a pleasant voice." The modulation of the prophet's voice was very pleasing to their ears, but mean while their fancies and thoughts were wandering after their lusts; their hearts were full of earthly projects.

Thirdly, Satan hinders the access of light to the understandings of men, by raising objections, and picking quarrels with the word, on purpose to shake its authority, and hinder the assent of the understanding to it, and so the word makes no more impression than a fable, or a romance would do. And never did this design of Satan obtain more than in this atheistical age, wherein the main pillars and foundation of religion are shaken in the minds of multitudes. The devil hath persuaded many, that the gospel is but a cunningly-devised fable; *fabula Christi,* as that blaspheming pope called it; that ministers must say something to get a living. That heaven and hell are but fancies, or at most things of great uncertainty, and doubtful credit. This being once obtained, the door of the soul is shut against truth. And this design of Satan hath prospered the more in this generation, by the corrupt doctrines of seducing spirits, "Which have overthrown the faith of some," 2 Tim. ii. 18. And partly from the scandalous lives of loose and vain professors, the gospel hath been brought into contempt; but especially by Satan's artificial improvement of the corrupt natures of men in an age wherein conscience hath been so much debauched, and Atheism thereby spread as a gangrene in the body politic.

Fourthly, Satan hinders the access of light, by helping erroneous minds to draw false conclusions and perverse inferences from the great and precious truths of the gospel; and thereby bringing them under prejudice and contempt: Thus he assists the errors of men's minds about the doctrine of *election:* when he either persuades them, that it is an unreasonable doctrine, and not worthy of credit, that God should chuse some, and refuse others every way as good as those he hath chosen; or, if there be any certainty in that doctrine, then men may throw the reins upon the neck of their lusts, and live at what rate they list; for if God hath chosen them to salvation, their wickedness shall not hinder it; and if he have appointed them unto wrath, their diligence and self-denial cannot prevent it.

Thus the doctrine of free grace is by the like sophistry of Satan turned into lasciviousness. If grace abound, men may sin the more freely; and the shortness of our time upon earth, which in its own nature awakens all men to diligence, is, by the subtilty of Satan, turned to a quite contrary purpose, " Let us eat and drink, for to-" morrow we die."

Fifthly, Satan darkens the minds of men, and shuts them up against the light, by blowing them up with pride and self-conceit-edness, persuading them that they know all these things already, and causing them to contemn the most weighty and precious truths of God, as trite and vulgar notions. The word cannot be received without meekness and humility of mind, James i. 21. Psal. xxv. 8, 9. and pride is the nurse of ignorance, 1 Tim. vi. 4. 1 Cor. viii. 7. The devil is aware of this, and therefore blows up the pride and conceitedness of men's hearts all that he can: And this temp-tation of his generally prevails wherever it meets with a knowing head, matched with a graceless and unsanctified heart. And thus we see by what wiles and policies Satan keeps out the light, and prevents the access of it to the minds of men.

But if he miss his design here, and truth gets into the mind, Then

Secondly, He labours to obstruct the efficacy and operation of the light; and though it do shine into the understanding, yet it shall be imprisoned there, and send down no converting influences upon the will and affections: And this design he promotes and manages divers ways.

First, By hastening to quench convictions betimes, and nip them in the bud. Satan knows how dangerous a thing it is, and de-structive to his interest, to suffer convictions to continue long; and therefore it is said of him, Matth. xiii. 19. When any " one " heareth the word of the kingdom, and understandeth it not, then " cometh the wicked one, and catcheth away that which was sown " in his heart." Satan is compared in this scripture to the fowls in the air, which pick up the seed before it take any root in the earth. The devil is very jealous of this, and therefore labours all he can to destroy the word before it comes to operate upon the heart; which he doth sometimes by the cares of the world, and sometimes by vain companions, who prove mere quench coals unto the beginning con-victions. One sinner destroyeth much good.

Secondly, No sooner doth the god of this world observe the light of truth begin to operate upon the heart, but he obstructeth that design by *procrastinations* and delays, which delude and baffle con-vinced souls; he persuades them if they will alter their course, it will be time enough hereafter, when such encumbrances and trou-bles in the world are over; if he prevail here, it is a thousand to one but the work miscarries. James i. 13, 14. If the hearer of the

word be not a doer, i. e. a present doer, while the impressions of
it are fresh upon the soul, *he doth but deceive himself.* For it is
with the heart, as it is with melted wax; if the seal be clapped to
it presently, it will receive a fair impression; but if it be let alone,
but for a little while, you can make none at all; it was therefore
David's great care and wisdom to set about the work of religion
under the first *impetus,* or vigorous motion of his heart and affections. Psal. cxix. 60. " I made haste, and delayed not to keep
" thy commandments." Multitudes of souls have perished by these
delays. It is a temptation incident to all that are under beginning
convictions, especially young persons, whom the devil persuades that
it were no better than madness in them to abridge and deny themselves so much delight and pleasure, and steep their youthful
thoughts in such a melancholy subject as religion is.

Thirdly, If all this will not do, but convictions still continue to
get ground in the conscience, then he endeavours to scare and
fright them out of their convictions, by representing to them the
inward terrors, troubles, and despairs into which they are about
to plunge themselves, and that henceforth they must never expect
a pleasant day, or comfortable hour. Thus doth the god of this
world blind the minds of them that believe not, both by hindering
the access of light to the mind, and the influence of it upon the
heart.

Thirdly, There is yet one policy of Satan to keep souls in darkness, and that is, by the misapplication of truth; persuading them,
that whatsoever they read or hear of the misery and danger of christless and unregenerate persons, doth not in the least touch or concern
them, but the more notorious and profane part of the world; and
by this policy he blinds the minds of all civil and moral persons.
Thus the " Pharisees trusted in themselves that they were righteous,
" and despised others." And so the Laodiceans thought themselves
rich, and increased with goods; that is, in a very safe and good
condition *. Now there are divers things notably improved by
Satan's policy, in order to these misapplications of truth. As,

First, The freedom of their lives from the most gross pollutions
of the world, Mat. xix. 20. " All these things have I kept from my
" youth up." A civil, sober course of life is a most effectual blind
before the eyes of many a man's conscience.

Secondly, It is the policy of Satan to prevent convictions by conviction; I mean effectual convictions, by convictions that have
been ineffectual, and are now vanished away. Thus the troubles
that some persons have been under, must pass for their conversion,

---

* See my Touchstone of Sincerity upon *Rev.* iii. 17, 18.

though the temper of their heart be the same it was: Their ineffectual troubles are made use of by the devil to blind them in the true knowledge and apprehension of their condition. For these men and women can speak of the troubles they have had for sin, and the many tears they have shed for it; whereby thorough conviction is effectually prevented.

Thirdly, Gifts and knowledge are improved by the policy of Satan against the true knowledge of Jesus Christ, and our own estate by nature. As conviction is improved by Satan's policy against conviction, so is knowledge against knowledge. This was the case of them in Rom. ii. 17, 18. " Thou art called a Jew, and restest " in the law, and makest thy boast of God, and knowest his will, " and approvest the things that are excellent; being instructed out " of the law, and art confident that thou thyself art a guide to the " blind," &c. And this is the temptation and delusion of knowing persons, who are so far from being blind in their own account, that they account themselves the guides of the blind: Yet who blinder than such men?

Fourthly, External reformation is improved by the policy of Satan against true spiritual reformation, and passes current up and down the world for conversion; though it serve only to strengthen Satan's interest in the soul, Matth. xii. 44. and for want of a real change of heart, doth but increase their sin and misery, 2 Pet. ii. 20. This is the generation that is pure in their own eyes, and yet are not washed from their filthiness. The *cleanness* of their hands blinds them in discovering the *foulness* of their hearts.

Fifthly, The policy of Satan improves diligence in some duties, against the convictions of neglect in other duties. The external duties of religion, as hearing, praying, fasting, against the great duties of repenting and believing. This was their case, Isa. lviii. 2, 3. " Yet they seek me daily, and delight to know my ways, as a " nation that did righteousness, and forsook not the ordinances of " their God. They ask of me the ordinances of justice, they take " delight in approaching to God. Wherefore have we fasted, say " they, and thou seest not? Wherefore have we afflicted our souls, " and thou takest no knowledge?" Thus duty is improved against duty, the externals against the internals of religion, and multitudes are blinded this way.

Sixthly, The policy of Satan improves zeal against zeal; and thereby blinds a great part of the world: he allows men to be zealous against a false religion, if thereby he may prevent them from being zealous in the true religion. He diverts their zeal against their own sins, by spending it against other men's. Thus Paul was once blinded by his own zeal for the law, Acts xxii. 3. And many men, at this day, satisfy themselves in their own zeal against the corruptions of God's worship, and the superstitions of others, who never felt the power of true religion upon their own hearts; a dangerous blind of Satan.

Seventhly, The policy of Satan improves the esteem and respect men have for the people of God against their great duty and interest to become such themselves, Rev. iii. 1. " Thou hast a name " that thou livest, but thou art dead." It is enough to many men that they obtain acceptation among the saints, though they be none of that number; the good opinion of others begets and confirms their good opinion of themselves.

Eighthly, The policy of Satan improves soundness of judgment, against soundness of heart. An orthodox head against an orthodox heart and life; dogmatical faith, against justifying faith. This was the case of them before-mentioned, Rom. ii. 18, 19. Men satisfy themselves, that they have a sound understanding, though, at the same time, they have a very rotten heart. It is enough for them that their heads are regular, though their hearts and lives be very irregular.

Ninthly, The policy of Satan improves the blessings of God against the blessings of God, blinding us by the blessings of providence, so as not to discern the want of spiritual blessings: persuading men that the smiles of providence in their prosperity, success, and thriving designs in the world, are good evidences of the love of God to their souls, not at all discerning how the prosperity of fools deceives them, and that riches are given often to the hurt of the owners thereof.

Tenthly, The policy of Satan improves comfort against comfort, false and ungrounded comforts under the word, against the real grounds of comfort lying in the soul's interest in Christ. Thus many men finding a great deal of comfort in the promises, are so blinded thereby, as never to look after union with Christ, the only solid ground of all true comfort, Heb. vi. 5, 9.

And thus you see how the god of this world blindeth the minds of them that believe not, and how the gospel is hid to them that are lost.

SERMON XXXV.

2 Cor. iv. 3, 4.

But if our gospel be hid, it is hid to them that are lost; in whom the god of this world hath blinded the minds of them which believe not, lest the light of the glorious gospel of Christ, who is the image of God, should shine unto them.

THE words have been opened, and this point observed:—

Doct. *That the understandings of all unbelievers are blinded by Satan's policies, in order to their everlasting perdition.*

We have shewn already what the blinding the mind, or hiding of the gospel from it is; it hath also been demonstrated that the gospel is hid, and the minds of many blinded under it; you have also seen what policies Satan uses to blind the minds of men, even in the clearest light of the gospel. It remains now that I open to you the dreadful nature of this judgment of God upon the souls of men, and then make application of the whole.

There are many judgments of God inflicted upon the souls and bodies of men in this world; but none of them are so dreadful as those spiritual judgments are which God inflicts immediately upon the soul; and among spiritual judgments few or none are of a more dreadful nature and consequence than this of spiritual blindness; which will appear by considering,

First, The subject of this judgment, which is the soul, and the principal power of the soul, which is the mind and understanding faculty; the soul is the most precious and invaluable part of man, and the mind is the superior and most noble power of the soul; it is to the soul what the eye is to the body, the directive faculty. The bodily eye is a curious, tender, and most precious part of the body. When we would express the value of a thing, we say, we prize it as our eyes. The loss of the eyes is a sore loss, we lose a great part of the comfort of our souls by it. Yet such an affliction (speaking comparatively) is but a trifle to this. If our bodily eyes be blinded, we cannot see the sun, but if our spiritual eye be blinded, we cannot see God, we wander in the paths of sin, 1 John ii. 11. We are led blindfold to hell by Satan, as the Syrians were in Samaria, 2 Kings vi. 19, 20. And then our eyes like theirs will be opened to see our misery when it is too late. " The light of the body is the eye, (saith Christ). If therefore " thine eye be single, thy whole body shall be full of light; but " if thine eye be evil, thy whole body shall be full of darkness.

" If therefore the light that is in thee be darkness, how great is
" that darkness?" Mat. vi. 22, 23.   By the eye he means the
practical judgment, the understanding faculty, which is the seat for
principles, the common treasury of the rules of practice, according
unto which a man's life is formed, and his way directed.   If therefore that power of the soul be darkened, how great must that
darkness be; for now the blind lead the blind, and both fall into
the ditch.   The blind judgment misguides the blind-affections,
and both fall into hell.   O what a sad thing is it, that the devil
should lead that that leads thee! That he should sit at the helm,
and steer thy course to damnation! The blinding of this noble faculty precipitates the soul into the most dangerous courses; persecution, by this means, seems to be true zeal for God, John xvi. 2.
" They that persecute you shall think that they do God service.
" Paul once thought verily with himself, that he ought to do many
" things contrary to the name of Jesus of Nazareth, Acts xxvi. 9.
i. e. He thought he had pleased God, when he was imprisoning
and persecuting his people, as many do at this day; it will make a
man to sin conscientiously, which is a very dangerous way of sinning, and difficult to be reclaimed.

Secondly, It is a dreadful judgment, if we consider the object
about which the understanding is blinded, which is Jesus Christ,
and union with him; regeneration, and the nature and necessity
thereof.   For this blindness is not universal, but respective and
particular.   A man may have abundance of light and knowledge
in things natural and moral; but spiritual things are hidden from
his eyes.   Yea, a man may know spiritual things in a natural way,
which increaseth his blindness; but he cannot discern them spiritually; this is a sore judgment, and greatly to be bewailed.
" Thou hast hid these things (said Christ) from the wise and pru-
" dent, and hast revealed them unto babes," Mat. xi. 25.   Learned
and knowing men are ignorant of those things, which very babes
in Christ understand.   They are prudent in the management of
earthly affairs; but to save their own souls they have no knowledge.
They are able, with Berengarius, to dispute *de omni scibili*, of
every thing investigable by the light of nature; yea, to open the
scripture solidly, and defend the doctrines and truths of Christ
against his adversaries successfully; and yet blinded in the great
mystery of regeneration, *Blindness in part*, (saith the apostle) *is
happened unto Israel?* and that indeed was the principal part of
knowledge, viz. the knowledge of Jesus Christ, and him crucified,
we see farther than they.   The literal knowledge of Jesus Christ
shines clearly in our understanding.   We are only blinded about
those things which should give us saving interest in him, about the
effectual application of Christ to our own souls.

Thirdly, The dreadful nature of this spiritual blindness farther appears from the consideration of the season in which it befals men, which is the very time of God's patience, and the only opportunity they have for salvation; after these opportunities are over, their eyes will be opened to see their misery, but alas, too late. Upon this account, Christ shed those tears over Jerusalem, Luke xix. 42. " O that thou hadst known, at least in this thy day, the " things that belong to thy peace; but now they are hid from " thine eyes." Now the season of grace is past and gone; opportunities are the golden spots of time, and there is much time in a short opportunity, as there are many pieces of silver in one piece of gold. Time signifies nothing when opportunities are gone; to be blinded in the very season of salvation, is the judgment of all judgments, the greatest misery incident to man; to have our eyes opened when the seasons of salvation are past, is but an aggravation of misery: there is a twofold opening of men's eyes to see their danger, viz.

1. Graciously to prevent danger.
2. Judicially to aggravate misery.

They whose eyes are not opened graciously in this world, to see their disease and remedy in Christ, shall have their eyes opened judicially in the world to come, to see their disease without any remedy. If God open them now, it is by way of prevention; if they be not opened till then, it will produce desperation.

Fourthly, The horrible nature of this judgment farther appears from the exceeding difficulty of curing it, especially in men of excellent natural endowments and accomplishments, John ix. 40, 41. " And some of the Pharisees which were with him, heard these " words, and said unto him, Are we blind also? Jesus said unto " them, If ye were blind, ye should have no sin: but now ye say, " We see: therefore your sin remaineth," q. d. the pride and conceitedness of your heart and obstinacy and incurableness to your blindness; these are " the blind people that have eyes;" Isa. lxiii. 8. *In seeing they see not.* The conviction of such men is next to an impossibility.

Fifthly, The design and end of this blindness under the gospel is most dreadful *; so saith my text, " The god of this world hath " blinded the minds of them which believe not, lest the light " of the glorious gospel of Christ, who is the image of God, " should shine unto them." Answerable whereunto are those words, Isa. vi. 10. " Make the heart of this people fat, and make

---

* It is a sign of God's displeasure, when men understand not their faults lest repentance follow. *Cypr. Ep.* 2. But to be smitten with blindness of mind, so as neither to know nor lament their faults, is a higher evidence of the displeasure of an angry God, *Cypr. de Lapsis.*

" make their ears heavy, and shut their eyes; lest they see with
" their eyes, and hear with their ears, and understand with their
" hearts, and convert, and be healed." So that it is plain, this
blinding is a *præludium* to damnation, as the covering of Haman's
face was to his destruction. When the Lord hath no purpose of
grace and mercy to a man's soul, then, to bring about the damnation of that man by a righteous permission, many occasions of
blindness befal him, which Satan improves effectually unto his
eternal ruin; among which fatal occasions, blind guides and scandalous professors are none of the least; they shall be fitted with
ministers suitably to their humours, which shall speak smooth
things: *If a man walk in the spirit and falsehood,* (i. e. by an
εν δια δυοιν,— the spirit of falsehood) *do lie, saying, I will prophesy
to thee of wine and strong drink, he shall even be the prophet of
this people:* and the slips and falls of professors shall do the devil
not a little service in this his fatal design; Mat. xviii. 7. " Wo to
" the world because of offences." This shall blind them, and harden them to purpose. Thus you see what a dreadful judgment this
is, a stroke of God upon the soul, which cuts off all the present comforts of Christ and religion from it, takes away the bridle of restraint from sin, and makes way for the final ruin of the soul. A
far greater judgment it is than the greatest calamity or affliction
which can befal us in this world. If our names suffer by the greatest reproaches, our bodies by the most painful diseases, our estates
by the greatest losses; if God strike every comfort we have in this
world dead by affliction; all this is nothing, compared with this
blinding judgment of God upon the soul; for they may come
from the tender love of God to us, Heb. xii. 6. but this is the
effect of his wrath; they may cleanse sin, Isa. xxvii. 9. but this
increases it; they often prove occasions of conversion, Job xxxvi.
8, 9. but this is the great obstruction to it. In a word, they only
wound the flesh, and that with a curable wound; but this stabs
the soul, and that with a mortal wound.

First use, of information.

Inference 1. If this be the case of the unbelieving world, to be so
blinded by the god of this world; *How little should we value the
censures and slanders of this blind world?* Certainly they should
move no other affection but pity in our soul: if their eyes were
opened, their mouths would be shut; they would never traduce
religion, and the sincere profession of it as they do, if Satan had
not blinded their minds: they speak evil of the things they know
not; their reproaches, which they let fly so freely, are but so
many arrows shot by the blind man's bow, which only stick in our
clothes, and can do us no hurt, except we thrust them onward by

our own discontent to the wounding of our spirits. " * I could al-
" most be proud upon it, said Luther, that I have got an ill name
" among the worst of men." Beware, Christians that you give
them no occasion to blaspheme the name of your God, and then
never trouble yourselves, however they use your names. If they
tread it in the dirt now, God (as one speaks) will take it up, wash
off all the dirt, and deliver it to you again clear and shining.
Should such men speak well of us, we might justly suspect ourselves of some iniquity which administers to them the occasions
of it.

   Inf. 2. *How absurd and dangerous must it be for Christians to
follow the examples of the blind world?* Let the blind follow the
blind, but let not those whom God hath enlightened do so. Christians, never let those lead you, who are led blindfold by the devil
themselves. The holiness and heavenliness of Christians was wont
to set the world a wondering that they would not run with them
into the same excess of riot, 1 Pet. iv. 4. But sure, since God hath
opened your eyes, and shewed you the dangereous courses they
walk in, it would be the greatest wonder of all, if you should be the
companions of such men, and tread in the steps of their examples.
Christian, as humble and lowly thoughts as thou hast of thyself,
yet I would have thee understand thyself to be too good to be the
associate of such men. *Discamus sanctam superbiam, et sciamus
nos esse illis meliores.* If they will walk with you in the way of
duty and holiness, let them come and welcome; receive them with
both arms, and be glad of their company; but beware you walk
not in their paths, lest they be a snare unto you. Did they see the
end of their way, they would never walk in it themselves; why
then will you walk with them who do see it?

   Inf 3. If this be so, *Let Christians be exact and circumspect in
their walking, lest they lay a stumbling-block before the blind.* It
is a great sin to do so in a proper sense, Lev. xix. 14. " Thou shalt
" not put a stumbling-block before the blind." And a far greater
to do it in a metaphorical sense, Rom. xiv. 13. It is the express
will of God, " that no man put a stumbling-block, or an occasion to
" fall in his brother's way." It is an argument of little regard to
the honour of Christ, or the souls of men, so to do. O professors,
look to your steps; the devil desires to make use of you for such
purposes. The sins of thousands of others, who make no profession
of godliness, will never so fit his purpose for the blinding of those
men's eyes, as the least slip or failing of yours will do. It is the
living bird that makes the best stale to draw others into the net:

---

* *Superbus fio, quod video nomen pessimum mihi crescere.* Luther. *Gratias ago Deo
meo, quod dignus sum quem mundus oderit.* Hieron.

the grossest wickedness of profane sinners passeth away in silence, but all the neighbourhood shall ring with your miscarriages. " A " righteous man falling down before the wicked, is as a troubled " fountain and a corrupt spring," Prov. xxv. 26. The scandalous falls of good men are like a bag of poison cast by Satan into the spring from whence the whole town is supplied with water. You little know what mischief you do, and how many blind sinners may fall into hell by your occasion.

Inf. 4. How dangerous a thing is zeal in a wicked man? It is like a sharp sword in a blind man's hand, or like a high mettle in a blind horse. How much hath the church of God suffered upon this account, and doth suffer at this day: The world hath ever been full of such blind and blustering zeal, which, like a hurricane, over-turns all that stands in its way : yea, as we noted before, it makes a man a kind of conscientious persecutor. I confess it is better for the persecutor himself to do it ignorantly, because ignorance leaves him in a capacity for mercy, and sets him a degree lower than the malicious, enlightened persecutor, 1 Tim. i. 13. else it were the dreadful case described in Heb. x. But yet, as it is, John xvi. 2 these are the fierce and dreadful enemies of the church of God. Such a man was Paul, a devout persecutor, and such persecution God afterward suffered to befal himself, Acts xiii. 50. " But the " Jews stirred up the devout and honourable women, and the chief " men of that city; and raised persecution agsinst Paul and Bar- " nabas, and expelled them out of their coasts." An erroneous conscience binds, as well as an informed conscience ; and wherever God gives such men opportunity to vent the spleen and rage of their hearts upon his people, they will be sure to do it to purpose. With other men Gamaliel's counsel may have some influence, and they may be afraid lest they be found fighters against God; but blind zeal spurs on, and saith, as Jehu did, " Come, see my zeal " for the Lord of Hosts." O blind sinners, be sure of your mark before you discharge your arrows. If you shoot at a wicked man, as you suppose him, and God finds one of his dear children wounded or destroyed, what account will you give of that fact to God when you shall come before his judgment-seat?

Second use, of exhortation.

This point is very improveable by way of exhortation. Both,

1. Unto those who are blinded by the god of this world.

2. To those that are enlightened in the knowledge of Christ, by the true God.

First, To those who are still blinded by the god of this world, to whom the Lord hath not given unto this day eyes to see their misery in themselves, or their remedy in Christ, so as to make an

effectual application of him to their own souls. To all such my
counsel is,

To get a sense of your own blindness.

2. To seek out for a cure, whilst yet it may be had.

First, Labour to get a deep sense of the misery of such a
condition; for till you be awakened by conviction, you can never
be healed. O that you did but know the true difference betwixt
common and saving light; the want of this keeps you in darkness:
you think because you know the same things that the most unsanctified men doth, that therefore there is no difference betwixt his knowledge and yours; and are therefore ready to say to them, as Job to
his friends; " Lo, mine eye hath seen all this, mine ear hath
" heard and understood it: what ye know, the same do I know
" also; I am not inferior unto you," Job xiii. 1, 2. But O that
you would be convinced that your knowledge vastly differs from the
knowledge of believers. Though you know the same things that
they do, it is a knowledge of another kind and nature. You know
spiritual things in another way, merely by the light of reason, assisted and improved by the common light of the gospel; they know
the same things by spiritual illumination, and in an experimental
way. 1 John ii. 20. " Ye have an unction from the holy One,
" and ye know all things." Their knowledge is practical, yours
is idle. They are working out their salvation, by that light which
God hath given them, Psal. cxi. 10. Their knowledge of God
and Christ produces the fruits of faith, obedience, and mortification, and heavenly-mindedness in them: it hath no such fruits in
you; whatever light there be in your understandings, it makes no
alteration at all upon your hearts. The light brings them to heaven,
John xvii. 3. Yours shall be blown out by death, 1 Cor. xiii. 8.
and yourselves left in the mists of eternal darkness, except your
eyes be opened seasonably by the anointing of the Holy Ghost.
Conviction is a great part of your cure.

Secondly, Labour to get a remedy for this dangerous disease of
your minds: " Awake to righteousness, and sin not, for some have
" not the knowledge of God: I speak this to your shame," 1 Cor.
xv. 34. These things speak encouragement to you, though it be a
sore judgment that lies upon you, and very difficult to be removed:
yet remember Jesus Christ is commissioned by God the Father to
open the blind eyes, Isa. xlii. 6, 7. and this excellent physician bespeaks you for his patients, Rev. iii. 18. " Anoint thine eyes,
" (saith he) with eye-salve that thou mayest see." Yea, the most
enlightened Christians were once as dark and blind in spiritual
things as you are, and Christ hath cured them, Eph. v. 8. " Once
" were you darkness, now are ye light in the Lord." Attend
therefore upon the ordinances of the gospel diligently; that is God's

enlightening instrument by which he couches those cataracts which blind the eyes of men's understandings, Acts xxvi. 28. And if ever you will have your eyes opened, allow yourselves time to ponder and consider what you hear. The duty of meditation is a very enlightening duty: above all, cry to the Lord Jesus Christ, as that poor man did, " Lord, that mine eyes may be opened, that " I may receive my sight." Say, Lord, this is my disease and danger, that in seeing I see not. Others see natural things in a spiritual way, whilst I see spiritual things only in a natural way. Their light is operative upon their hearts, mine is but an idle impractical notion of religion, which brings forth no fruit of holiness. Their knowledge sets their hands a work in duties of obedience; mine only sets my tongue a work in discourses of those things which my heart never felt. Lord, open mine eyes, and make me to see out of this obscurity : All the light that is in me is but darkness. O Lord, enlighten my darkness, enlighten mine eyes, lest I sleep the sleep of death.

Secondly, Let it be a word of counsel and exhortation to such as once were blind, but do now see.

First, I beseech you, bless God for the least degree of spiritual illumination. " Truly light is sweet, and it is a pleasant thing for " the eyes to behold the sun," Eccles. xi. 7. But O how sweet is spiritual light ! and what a pleasant thing to behold the Sun of righteousness ! Blessed are your eyes, for they see God hath brought you out of darkness into marvellous light. And marvellous indeed it must needs be, when you consider how many wise and prudent men are under the power of spiritual darkness, whilst such babes as you are enlightened, Mat. xi. 25. It greatly affected the heart of Christ ; O let it affect yours also.

Secondly, Labour to get a clearer sight of spiritual things every day. For all spiritual light is increasing light, " which shineth " more and more unto the perfect day," Prov. iv. 18. O ! if a little spiritual light be so comfortable, what would more be ? The wisdom of God is *a manifold wisdom,* Eph. iii. 10. The best of us see but little of it. Labour therefore to know spiritual things more *extensively,* and more experimentally, Phil. ii. 8, 9. Be still increasing in the knowledge of God.

Thirdly, Walk as men whose eyes are opened. " Once ye were " in darkness, now are ye light in the Lord ; walk as children of " the light, Eph. v. 8. else your light will but aggravate your sin. Remember how it displeased God, that Solomon's heart was turned from the Lord God of *Israel who appeared to him twice,* 1 Kings xi. 9. Remember how angry God was with the Heathens for abusing the dim common light of nature, Rom. i. 21.

How much more evil is it in you to abuse the most precious light that shineth in this world? and what mischievous effects the abuse of your light will have upon this blind world? It was a smart rebuke given once by an Atheist to a good man, who being asked by him how he could satisfy his conscience to live as he did? Nay rather, said the Atheist, I wonder how you can satisfy yourself to live as you do; for did I believe as you do, that there is such a Christ, and such a glory as you believe there are, I would pray and live at another rate than you do.

THE CONCLUSION.

And now, reader, if all my discourses of the method of Christ in purchasing the great salvation for us, and the way of the Spirit in applying it, and making it effectual to God's elect; thou hast two wonders before thine eyes, either of which may astonish thy soul, in the consideration of them, viz.

1. This admirable grace of God in preparing   } this great
2. The desperate wickedness of man in rejecting } Salvation.

First, Behold the riches of the goodness and mercy of God in preparing such a remedy as this for lost man. This is that which is justly called "The great mystery of godliness," 1 Tim. iii. 16. that mystery which the *prophets* enquired diligently after, yea, which the " angels desired to look into," 1 Pet. i. 10, 12. In this glorious mystery of redemption, that πολυποικιλος σοφια, manifold wisdom of God, or that wisdom which hath such curious and admirable variety in it, is illustriously displayed, Eph. iv. 10. Yea, the contrivance of our redemption, this way, is the most glorious display of divine *love* that ever was made, or can be made, in this world to the children of men; for so the apostle will be understood, when he saith, Rom. v. 8. Συνιϛησι την εαυϸ αγαπην,———God hath set forth, or presented his love to man in the most engaging manner, in a way that commends it beyond all compare to the acceptation of men. " This is a faithful saying, and worthy of all ac- " ceptation, that Jesus Christ came into the world to save sinners," 1 Tim. i. 15. It might be justly expected, that when this glorious mystery should come to be published by the gospel in the ears of sinners, all eyes should be withdrawn from all other objects, and fixed with admiration upon Christ, all hearts should be ravished with these glad tidings; and every man pressing to Christ with the greatest zeal and diligence. But behold, instead thereof,

Secondly, The desperate wickedness of the world, in rejecting the only remedy prepared for them. This was long since foretold by the prophet, Isa. liii. 3. " He is despised and rejected of men,

" * a man of sorrows, and acquainted with grief; and we hid
" our faces from him; he was despised, and we esteemed him
" not." His poor and mean appearance, which should endear
him beyond all considerations to the souls of men, (since it was for
their sakes, that he emptied himself of all his glory) yet this lays
him under contempt, he is looked on as the very off-cast of men †,
when his own love to man had emptied him of all his riches, the
wickedness of men loaded him with contempt, and as it was prophesied of him, so it was, and at this day is sadly verified all the
world over; for,

First, The Pagan world hath no knowledge of him, they are
lost in darkness. " God hath suffered them to walk in their own
" ways," Acts xiv. 16.

Secondly, The Mahometans which overspread so great a part of
the world reject him, and instead of the blessed gospel, which they
hiss at with abhorrence, embrace the blasphemous and ridiculous
Alcoran, which they confidently affirm came down from God
immediately in that *Laylatto Hanzili* (as they call it) the night of
demission, calling all Christians, *Cafirouna,* i. e. Infidels.

Thirdly, The Jews reject him with abhorrence, and spit at his
very name, and being blind-folded by the devil, they call Jesus
Anathema, 1 Cor. xii. 3. And in a blind zeal for Moses, blaspheme
him as an impostor. " He came to his own, and his own received
" him not," John i. 11.

Fourthly, The far greater part of the Christianized world reject
him ‡; those that are called after his name, will not submit to his
government. The *nobles* of the world think themselves dishonoured by submitting their necks to his yoke. The *sensualists* of the
world will not deny their lusts, or forsake their pleasures, for all
the treasures of righteousness, life and peace, which his blood hath
purchased. *Worldlings* of the earth prefer the dirt and dung of
the world before him; and few there be among them that profess
Christianity, who love the Lord Jesus in sincerity. The only reason why they are called Christians is, because, by the advantageous
cast of providence, they were born and educated in a nation where
Christianity is professed and established by the laws of the coun-

---

* חדל אישים *Cessans virorum :* i. e. *Infimus hominum, qui citius desinit quam
ullus virorum.*

† *Nil habet infelix paupertas durius in se,*
Quam quod ridiculos homines sacit :——
                              Juvenal. Sat. III. v. 152.
Want is the scorn of ev'ry wealthy fool,
And wit in rags is turn'd to ridicule.

‡ To put on the profession of Christ's name, and not to walk in Christ's way, what
is it but prevaricating with that divine name? *Cyp. de Zelo.*

try; and if the wind should turn, and the public authority think fit to establish another religion, they can shift their sail, and steer a contrary course.

But now, reader, let me tell thee, that if ever God send forth these two grim *serjeants*, his law, and thine own conscience, to arrest thee for thy sins, if thou find thyself dragged away by them towards that prison from whence none return, that are once clapt up therein, and that in this unspeakable distress Jesus Christ manifest himself to thy soul, and open thy heart to receive him, and become thy surety with God, pay all thy debts, and cancel all thy obligations, thou wilt love him at another rate than others do; his blood will run deeper in thine eyes than it doth in the shallow apprehensions of the world; he will be *altogether lovely*, and thou wilt account all things but dung and dross in comparison of the excellency of Jesus Christ thy Lord.   To work thy heart to this frame, these things are written, which the Lord prosper upon thy soul, by the blessing of his good Spirit upon thee.

Blessed be God for Jesus Christ!

PNEUMATOLOGIA.

A TREATISE

OF THE

SOUL OF MAN.

————⟐✕⟐————

THE EPISTLE DEDICATORY.

To the much honoured, his dear kinsman, Mr. JOHN FLAVEL, and
Mr. EDWARD CRISPE, of London, Merchants; and the rest of
my worthy friends in London, RATCLIFFE, SHADWELL, and
LYMEHOUSE, grace, mercy, and peace.

DEAR FRIENDS,

"AMONG all the creatures in this lower world, none deserves to
" be stiled *great*, but *man ;* and in *man* nothing is found worthy of
that epithet, but his *soul* *.

The study, and knowledge of his *soul* was, therefore, always
reckoned a rich and necessary improvement of time.   All ages have
magnified these two words, " *Know thyself,* as an *oracle* descending
" from heaven †."

" No knowledge, saith Bernard ‡, is better than that whereby
" we know ourselves; leave other matters therefore, and search
" thyself; run through thyself, make a stand in thyself; let thy
" thoughts, as it were, circulate, begin and end in thyself."
Strain not thy thoughts in vain about other things, thyself being
neglected.

---

* *Nihil in terra magnum præter hominem, nihil in homine præter mentem.*   Favorin.
† ——*E cælo descendit,* γιωθι σεαυτον.   Juvenal. Sat. 11. v. 27.
‡ *Nulla scientia melior illa, qua homo novit seipsum; relinque ergo cætera, et teipsum
discute: per te curre, in te consiste; a te ncipiat cogitatio tua, et in te finiatur.*

The study and knowledge of *Jesus Christ* must still be allowed to be the most excellent and necessary : But yet the worth and necessity of *Christ* is unknown to men, till the value, wants, and dangers of their own *souls* be first discovered to them.

The disaffectedness, and aversion of men to the study of their own souls, are the more to be admired ; not only because of the weight and necessity of it, but the alluring pleasure, and sweetness that are found therein.   What * Cardan speaks, is experimentally felt by many, " That scarce any thing is more pleasant and " delectable to the soul of man, than to know what he is, what " he may and shall be ; and what those divine and supreme " things are, which he is to enjoy after death, and the vicissitudes " of this present world."   For we are creatures conscious to ourselves of an immortal nature, and that we have something about us which must overlive this mortal flesh, and therefore it is ever and anon some way or other hinting and intimating to us its expectations of, and designation for a better life than that it now lives in the body, and that we shall not cease to *be*, when we cease to *breathe*.

And certainly, my friends, discourses of the soul, and its immortality ; of *heaven* and of *hell*, the next, and only receptacles of unbodied spirits, were never more seasonable and necessary than in this atheistical age of the world, wherein all serious piety and thoughts of immortality are ridiculed, and hissed out of the company of many : As if those old condemned Heretics, the Θνητοψυχιται, who asserted the corruptibility and mortality of the soul as well as the body, had been again revived in our days.

And as the *Atheism* of some, so the *tepidity*, and unconcerned carelessness of the most, need and call for such potent remedies, as discourses of this kind do plentifully afford.   I dare appeal to your charitable judgments, whether the conversations and discourses of the *many*, do indeed look like a serious *pursuit* of heaven, and a *flight* from hell ?

Long have my thoughts bended towards this great and excellent *subject*, and many earnest desires I have had, (as I believe all thinking persons must needs have) to know what I shall be when I breathe not.   But when I had engaged my meditations about it, two great rubs opposed the farther progress of my thoughts therein : Namely,

I. The difficulty of the subject I had chosen : And,

II. The distractions of the times in which I was to write upon it.

---

* *Quid jucundius quam scire quid simus, quid fuerimus, quid erimus, et cum his etiam divina atque suprema illa post obitum mundique vicissitudines.*

I. As for the subject, such is the subtilty and sublimity of its nature, and such the knotty controversies in which it is involved, that it much better deserves that *inscription*, than *Minerva's* temple at *Saum* did, * " *Never did any mortal reveal me plainly.*

" It is but little that the most clear and sharp-sighted do discern " of their own souls, now in the state of *composition;* and what can " we positively and distinctly know of the life they live in the state " of separation ? The darkness in which these things are involved " doth greatly exercise, even the greatest wits, and frequently " elude and frustrate the most generous attempts †." Many great *scholars* whose natural and acquired abilities singularly furnished and qualified them to make a clearer discovery, have laboured in this field, *usque ad sudorem et pallorem*, even to sweat and paleness, and done little more but entangle themselves, and the subject more than before; this cannot but discourage new attempts.

And yet, without some knowledge of the *hability*, and subjective capacity of our souls to enjoy the good of the world to come, even in a state of absence from the body, a principal relief must be cut off from them, under the great and manifold trials they are to encounter in this evil world.

As for myself, I assure you, I am deeply sensible of the inequality of my shoulders to this burden ; and have often thought (since I undertook it) of that grave and necessary caution of the poet‡, to wield and poise the burden as *porters* use to do, before I undertook it. Zuinglius blamed Carolostadius (as some may do me) for undertaking the controversy of that age; because, saith he, *Non habet satis humerorum ;* his shoulders are too weak for it.

And yet I know men's labours prosper not according to the art and elegancy of the composure, but according to the divine blessing which pleaseth to accompany them. Ruffinus tells us of a learned *philosopher* at the *Council of Nice*, who stoutly defended his *thesis* against the greatest wits and scholars there, and yet was at last fairly vanquished by a man of no extraordinary parts: of which conquest the *philosopher* gave this candid and ingenuous account ;— *Against words* (said he) *I opposed words ; and what was spoken I over-*

---

* Τον εμον πεπλον ȣδεις πωθνητος απεκαλυψεν.

† *Animam præsentem mentis acie vix, aut ne vix quidem assequimur ; sed qualis sit futura, quomodo indagabimus ? Laborant hic maxima ingenia, et caligo conatus etiam generosos non raro eludit.* Jos. Stern. de morte, cap. 20.

‡ *Sumite materiam vestris, qui scribitis, æquam,*
Viribus : et versate diu, quid ferre recusent,
Quid valeant humeri—— Horat. de arte poet. I. 37.
Examine well, ye writers, weigh with care
What suits your genius, what your strength can bear ;
For when a well-proportion'd theme you chuse,
Nor words nor method will their aid refuse.

*threw by the art of speaking: But when, instead of words, power
came out of the mouth of the speaker, words could no longer with-
stand truth ; nor man oppose the power of God.*

O that my weak endeavours might prosper under the influence
of the like Spirit, upon the hearts of them that shall read this in-
artificial, but well-meant discourse.

I am little concerned about the contempts and censures of fas-
tidious readers. I have resolved to say nothing that exceeds sobriety, nor to provoke any man, except my dissent from his unproved
dictates must be his provocation.

Perhaps there are some doubts and difficulties relating to this
subject which will never fully be solved till we come to heaven.
For man, by the fall, being less than himself, doth not understand
himself, nor will ever perfectly do so until he be fully restored to
himself ; which will not be whilst he dwells in a body of sin and
death. And yet it is to me past doubt, that this, as well as other
subjects, might have been much more cleared than it is, if instead
of the proud contendings of masterly wits for victory, all had humbly fand peaceably applied themselves to the impartial search of
truth.

Truth, like an orient pearl in the bottom of a river, would have
discovered itself by its native lustre and radiancy, had not the feet
of Heathen *philosophers,* cunning Atheists, and daring school *divines*
disturbed and fouled the stream.

II. And as the difficulties of the subject are many, so many have
been the interruptions and avocations I have met with, whilst it
was under my hand : Which I mention for no other end but to
procure a more favourable censure from you, if it appear less exact than you expected to find. Such as it is, I do with much
respect and affection tender to your hands, humbly requesting the
blessing of the Spirit may accompany it to your hearts. If you will
but allow yourselves to think close to the matter before you, I
doubt not but you may find somewhat in it apt both to inform
your minds and quicken your affections. I know you have a mul-
tiplicity of business under your hands, but yet I hope your great concern makes all others daily to give place ; and that how clamorous
and importunate soever the affairs of the world be, you both can
and do find time to sit alone, and bethink yourselves of a much more
important business you have to do.

My friends, we are borderers upon eternity, we live upon the
confines of the spiritual and immaterial world : we must shortly be
associated with bodiless beings, and shall have, after a few days are
past, no more concerns for meat, drink, and sleep, buying and sel-
ling, habitations and relations, than the angels of God now have.
Besides, we live here in a state of trial : Man, (as Scaliger fitly calls

him,) is *utriusque mendi nexus*, One in whom both worlds do meet; his body participates of the lower, his soul of the upper world; hence it is that he finds such tugging and pulling this way and that way, upward and downward; both worlds, as it were, contending for this invaluable prize, the precious soul. All Christ's ordinances are instituted, and his officers ordained for no other use or end but the salvation of souls. Books are valuable according to their conducibility to this end: how rich a reward of my labours shall I account it, if this treatise of the soul may but promote the sanctification and salvation of any reader's soul.

To your hands I first tender it: it becomes your property, not only as a debt of justice, the fulfilling of a promise made you long since, upon your joint and earnest desires for the publication of it; but, as an acknowledgment of the many favours I have received from you: To one of you I stand obliged in the bond of relation, and under the sense of many kindnesses, beyond whatever such a degree of relation can be supposed to exact.

You have here a succinct account of the nature, faculties and original of the soul of man, as also of its infusion into the body by God, without intitling himself to the guilt and sin resulting from that their union.

You will also find the breath of your nostrils to be the *nexus*, tie, or bond, which holds our souls and bodies in personal union; and that, whilst the due crasis and temperament of the body remains, and breath continues, your souls hang, as by a weak and slender thread, over the state of a vast eternity in heaven or in hell; which will inform you both of the value of your breath, and the best way of improving it, whilst you enjoy it.

The immortality of the soul is here asserted, proved, and vindicated from the most considerable objections; so that it will evidently appear to you, by this discourse, you do not cease to *be*, when you cease to *breathe:* and, seeing they will overlive all temporal enjoyments, they must necessarily perish as to all their joys, comforts, and hopes, (which is all the death that can be incident to an immortal spirit,) if they be not in the proper season secured and provided of that never-perishing food of souls, God in Christ, their portion for ever.

Here you will find the grounds and reasons of that strong inclination, which you all feel them to have to your bodies, and the necessity notwithstanding that, of their divorce, and separation from their beloved bodies; and that it would manifestly be to their prejudice, if it should be otherwise: and to overcome the unreasonable aversations of believers, and to bring them to a more becoming cheerful submission to the laws of death, whensoever the writ of ejection shall be served upon them ; you will here find a representation of that blessed life, comely order, and most delightful employment of the incorporeal people inhabiting the city of God ; wherein, beside those sweet meditations which are proper to feast your hungry affections, you will meet with divers unusual, though not vain or unuseful, questions stated and resolved, which will be a grateful entertainment to your inquisitive and searching minds.

It is possible they may be censured by some as underminable and unprofitable curiosities ; but as I hate a presumptuous intrusion into unrevealed secrets, so I think it is a weakness to be discouraged in the search of truth, so far as it is fit to trace it, by such damping and causeless censures. Nor am I sensible I have in any thing transgressed the bounds of Christian sobriety, to gratify the palate of a nice and delicate reader.

I have also here set before the reader an idea or representation of the state and case of damned souls, that, if it be the will of God, a seasonable discovery of hell may be the means of some men's recovery out of the danger of it ; and close up the whole with a demonstration of the invaluable preciousness of souls, and the several dangerous snares and artifices of Satan, their professed enemy, to destroy and cast them away for ever.

This is the design and general scope of the whole, and of the principal parts of this treatise. And, O that God would grant me my heart's desire on your behalf, in the perusal of it ! Even that it may prove a sanctified instrument in his hand both to prepare you for, and bring you in love with the unbodied life, to make you look with pleasure into your graves, and die by consent of will, as well as necessity of nature. I remember Dr. Stoughton, in a sermon preached before king James, relates a strange story of a little child in a shipwreck, fast asleep upon its mother's lap, as she sat upon a piece of the wreck amidst the waves ; the child being awaked with the noise, asked the mother what those things were? She told it, They were drowning waves to swallow them up. The child, with a pretty smiling countenance, begged a stroke from its mother to beat away those naughty waves, and chide them as if they had been its play-mates. Death will shortly shipwreck your bodies ; your souls will sit upon your lips ready to expire, as they upon the wreck ready to go down. Would it not be a comfortable and most becoming frame of mind, to sit there with as little dread, as this little one did among the terrible waves? Surely, if our faith hath but first united us with Christ, and then loosed our hearts off from this enchanting and ensnaring world, we might make a fair step towards this most desirable temper ; but unbelief and earthly-mindedness make us loth to venture.

I blush to think, what bold adventures those men made, who,

upon the contemplation of the properties of a despicable stone first adventured quite out of sight of land, under its conduct and direction, and securely trusted both their lives and estates to it, when all the eyes of heaven were veiled from them, amidst the dark waters, and thick clouds of the sky, when I either start, or at least give an unwilling shrug, when I think of adventuring out of the sight of this world, under the more sure and steady direction and conduct of faith and the promises. To cure these evils, in my own and the reader's heart these things are written, and in much respect and love tendered to your hands, as a testimony of my gratitude, and deep sense of the many obligations you have put me under. That the blessing of the Spirit may accompany these discourses to your souls, afford you some assistance in your last and difficult work, of putting them off at death with a becoming cheerfulness, saying in that hour, Can I not see God till this flesh be laid aside in the grave? must I die before I can live like myself? then die my body, and go to thy dust, that I may be with Christ. With this design, and with these hearty wishes, dear and honoured cousin, and worthy friends, I put these discourses into your hands, and remain,

Your most obliged

kinsman and servant,

JOHN FLAVEL.

THE PREFACE.

———⟨◦⟩———

AMONG many other largesses and rich endowments, bestowed by the Creator's bounty upon the *soul of man*, the * *sentiments* and impressions of the world to come, and the ability of *reflection and self-intuition*, are peculiar, invaluable, and heavenly gifts. By the former, we have a very great evidence of our own immortality, and designation for nobler employments and enjoyments than this embodied state admits. And by the latter we may discern the agreeableness of our hearts, and therein the validity of our title to that expected blessedness.

But these heavenly gifts are neglected and abused all the world over. Degenerate souls are every where fallen into so deep an oblivion of their excellent original, spiritual and immortal nature, and alliance to the Father of spirits; that (to use the upbraiding expression of a great † philosopher) " they seem to be buried in their " bodies, as so many silly worms that lurk in their holes, are loth " to peep forth, and look abroad."

So powerfully do the cares and pleasures of this world charm all, (except a small remnant of regenerate souls) that nothing but some smart stroke of calamity, or terrible messengers of death can startle them ; (and even those are not always able to do it,) and when they do, all the effect is but a transient glance at another, and an unwilling shrug to leave this world, and so to sleep again. And thus the impressions and sentiments of the world to come (which are the natural growth and offspring of the soul) are either stifled and suppressed, as in Atheists; or borne down by impetuous masterly lusts, as in Sensualists.

And for its self-reflecting and considering power, it seems in many to be a power received in vain. It is with most souls as it is with the eye, which sees not itself, though it sees all other objects. There be those that have almost finished the course of a long life, (wherein a great part of their time hath lain upon their hands, as

---

* We have demonstrated from the common consent of all nations and people since the creation of the world, especially from the consent of the good and learned, that the human soul is incorruptible and immortal ; and that therefore it survives the corrupted body, that it may be for ever either rewarded for good actions, or punished for bad actions. *Zanch. on the immortality of the soul.*

* H δε δειλη ψυχη καλορωρυγμενη εν σωμαλι ως ερπελον νηθει εις Φωλεον, φιλει τ' φωλεον, &c. Max. Tyr. Diss. 41.

a cheap and useless commodity, which they knew not what to do with) who never yet spent one solemn entire hour in discourse with their own souls *. What serious heart doth not melt into compassion over the deluded multitude, who are mocked with dreams, and perpetually busied about trifles? Who are, (after so many frustrated attempts both of their own, and all past ages) eagerly pursuing the fleeting shadows, who torture and rack their brains to find out the natures and qualities of birds, beasts, and plants; indeed any thing rather than their own souls, which are certainly the most excellent creatures that inhabit this world. They know the true value and worth of other things, but are not able to estimate the dignity of that high-born spirit that is within them. A spirit which (without the addition of any more natural faculties or powers, if those it hath be but sanctified and devoted to God) is capable of the highest perfections and fruitions, even complete conformity to God, and the satisfying visions of God throughout eternity. They herd themselves with beasts, who are capable of an equality with angels. O what compassionate tears must such a consideration as this draw from the eyes of all that understand the worth of souls!

As for me it hath been my sin, and is now the matter of my sorrow, that whilst myriads of souls, (of no higher original than mine) are some of them beholding the highest Majesty in heaven, and others giving all diligence to make sure their salvation on earth, I was carried away so many years in the course of this world, (like a drop with the current of the tide) wholly forgetting my best self, my invaluable soul; whilst I prodigally wasted the stores of my time and thoughts upon vanities, that long since passed away as the waters which are remembered no more †. It shall be no shame to me to confess this folly, since the matter of my confession shall go to the glory of my God. I studied to know many other things, but I knew not myself. It was with me as with a servant to whom the master committed two things, viz. the *child*, and the *child's clothes*; the servant is very careful of the clothes, brushes and washes, starches and irons them, and keeps them safe and clean, but the child is forgotten and lost. My body which is but the garment of my soul, I kept and nourished with excessive care, but my soul was long forgotten, and had been lost for ever, as others

---

* *Ita est ista vita mortalis, ubi homo vanitati similis factus est: dies ejus velut umbra præterunt.* Aug. de Civ. lib. 21. c. 24.

† Saints after their hearts are renewed by repentance, are not ashamed to acknowledge their ignominious faults, to the glory of God. For nothing is lost to us that redounds to his praise, who, pardoning our sins, transfers us from misery to happiness. *Brightman on Cant. p.* 12.

daily are, had not God roused it, by the convictions of his Spirit, out of that deep oblivion and deadly slumber.

When the God that formed it, out of free grace to the work of his own hands, had thus recovered it to a sense of its own worth and danger, my next work was to get it united with Christ, and thereby secured from the wrath to come ; which I found to be a work difficult to effect, if it be yet effected) and a work of time to clear, though but to the degree of good hope through grace.

And since the hopes and evidences of salvation began to spring up in my soul, and settle the state thereof, I found these three great words, viz. *Christ, soul,* and *eternity,* to have a far different and more awful sound in my ear, than ever they used to have. I looked on them from that time, as things of the greatest certainty and most awful solemnity. These things have laid some weight upon my thoughts, and I felt, at certain seasons, a strong inclination to sequester myself from all other studies, and spend my last days, and most fixed meditations upon these three great and weighty subjects.

I know the subject matter of my studies and enquiries (be it never so weighty) doth not therefore make my meditations and discourse upon it great and weighty ; nor am I such a vain *opinionator,* as to imagine my discourses every way suitable to the dignity of such subjects ; no, no, the more I think and study about them, the more I discern the indistinctness, darkness, crudity, and confusion of my own conceptions, and expression of such great and transcendent things as those ; but *In magnis voluisse sat est,* I resolved to do what I could ; and accordingly some years past I finished and published, in two parts, the *Doctrine of Christ ;* and by the acceptation and success the Lord gave that, he hath encouraged me to go on in this second part of my work, how unequal soever my shoulders are to the burden of it.

The *nature, original, immortality,* and *capacity,* of mine own soul, for the present lodged in and related to this vile body, destined to corruption ; together with its *existence, employment, perfection, converse with God,* and other *spirits,* both of its own, and of a superior rank and order : when it shall (as I know it shortly must) *put off this its tabernacle ;* these things have a long time been the matters of my limited desires to understand, so far as I could see the pillar of fire (God in his word) enlightening my way to the knowledge of them. Yea, such is the value I have for them, that I have given them the next place in my esteem, to the knowledge of Jesus Christ, and my interest in him.

God hath formed me, as he hath other men, a *prospecting creature.* I feel myself yet uncentered, and short of that state of rest and satisfaction to which my soul, in its natural and spiritual capacity, hath a designation. I find that I am in a continual motion towards my everlasting abode, and the expence of my time; and many infirmities tell me that I am not far from it: by all which I am strongly prompted to look forward, and acquaint myself as much as I can, with my next place and employment. I look with a greedy and inquisitive eye that way.

Yet would I not be guilty of an unwarrantable curiosity in searching into revealed things; how willing soever I am to put my head by faith into the world above, and to know the things which Jesus Christ hath purchased and prepared for me, and all the rest that are waiting for his appearance and kingdom, I feel my curiosity checked and repressed by shat elegant *paronomasia,* Rom. xii, 3. Μη υπερφρονειν πα, ο δει φρονειν, αλλα φρονειν εις το σωφρονειν, In all things I would be wise unto sobriety. I groan under the effects of Adam's itching ambition to *know,* and would not by repeating his sin, increase my own misery; nor yet would I be scared, by his example, into the contrary evil of neglecting the means God hath afforded me, to know all that I can of his revealed will.

* The helps philosophy affords in some parts of this discourse are too great to be despised, and too small to be admired. I confess I read the definitions of the soul given by the ancient philosophers with a compassionate smile. When Thales calls it *a nature without repose;* Asclepiades, *an exercitation of sense!* Hesiod, *a thing composed of earth and water:* Parmenides, *a thing composed of earth and fire;* Galen saith it is *heat;* Hippocrates, *a spirit diffused through the body;* Plato, *a self-moving substance;* Aristotle calls it *Entelechia, that by which the body is moved:* If my opinion should be asked which of all these definitions I like best, I should give the same answer which Theocritus gave an ill poet, repeating many of his verses, and asked which he liked best; *Those* (said he) *which you have omitted.* Or if they must have the garland as the prize they have shot for, let them have it upon the some reason that was once given to him that shot wide.—*Difficilius est toties non attingere,*—Because it was the greatest difficulty to aim so often at the mark, and never come near it. One word of God gives me more light than a thousand such laborious trifles. As Cæsar was best able to write his own *commentaries,* so God only can give the best account of his own creature, on which he hath impressed his own image.

Modern philosophers, assisted by the divine oracles, must needs come closer to the mark, and give us a far better account of the

<hr>

* For to whom is the truth known with certainty without God? or God without Christ? or Christ explorated without the Spirit? or the Spirit vouchsafed without faith?—*Tertullian on the soul.*

nature of the soul.   Yet I have endeavoured not to cloud this subject with their controversies, or abstruse notions ; remembering
what a smart but deserved check, Tertullian gives those, *Qui Pla-
tonicum et Aristotelicum Christianismum producunt Christianis.*
Words are but the servants of matter, I value them as merchants
do their ships, not by the gilded head and stern, the neatness of
their mould, or curious flags and streamers, but by the soundness
of their bottom, largeness of their capacity, and richness of their
cargo and loading.   The quality of the subject necessitates, in many
places, the use of scholastic terms, which will be obscure to the
vulgar reader : but apt and proper words must not be rejected for
their obscurity, except plainer words could be found that fit the
subject as well, and are as fully expressive of the matter.   The unnecessary I have avoided, and the rest explained as I could.

The principal fruits I especially aim at, both to my own and the
reader's soul, are, That whilst we contemplate the freedom, pleasure, and satisfaction of that spiritual, incorporeal people, who
dwell in the region of light and joy, and are hereby forming to
ourselves a true scriptural idea of the blessed state of those disem-
bodied spirits, with whom we are to serve and converse in the tem-
ple-worship in heaven ; and come more explicitly and distinctly to
understand the constitution, order, and delightful employments of
those our everlasting associates ; we may answerably feel the sound
and inordinate love of this animal life sub-acted and wrought down ;
the frightful vizard of death drop off, nd a more pleasing aspect
appear ; that no upright soul that shall read these discourses may
henceforth be convulsed at the name of death, but cheerfully aspire,
and with a pleasant expectation wait for the blessed season of its
transportation to that blessed assembly.   It is certainly our ignorance of the life of heaven, that makes us dote as we do upon the
present life.   There is a gloom, a thick mist overspreading the next
life, and hiding, even from the eyes of believers, the glory that is
there.   We send forth our thoughts to penetrate this cloud, but
they return to us without the desired success.   We reinforce them
with a sally of new and more vigorous thoughts, but still they come
back in confusion and disappointment, as to any perfect account
they can bring us from thence ; though the oftener and closer we
think, still the more we grow up into acquaintance with these
excellent things.

Another benefit I pray for, and expect from these labours, is,
that by describing the horrid estate of those souls which go the
other way, and shewing to the living the dismal condition of souls
departed in their unregenerate state, some may be awakened to a
seasonable and effectual consideration of their wretched condi-

tion, whilst they yet continue under the means and among the instruments of their salvation.

Whatever the fruit of this discourse shall be to others, I have cause to bless God for the advantage it hath already given me. I begin to find more than ever I have done, in the separate state of sanctified souls, all that is capable of attracting an intellectual nature; and if God will but fix my mind upon this state, and cause my pleased thoughts about it to settle into a steady frame and temper, I hope I shall daily more and more depreciate and despise this common way of existence in a corporeal prison; and when the blessed season of my departure is at hand, I shall take a cheerful farewell of the greater and lesser elementary world, to which my soul hath been confined, and have an abundant entrance through the broad gate of assurance, unto the blessed, unembodied inhabitants of the world to come.

A

TREATISE

OF THE

SOUL OF MAN.

━━━━➲◉✕◉⋐━━━

Gen. ii. 7.

*And the Lord God formed man out of the dust of the ground, and
breathed into his nostrils the breath of life ; and man became a
living soul.*

"THREE things (saith * Athanasius) are unknown to men
" according to their essence, viz. *God, angels*, and the *souls* of
" men." Of the *nature* of the divine and high-born soul, we may
say, as the learned † Whitaker doth of the way of its infection by
original sin, " it is easier sought than understood, and better under-
" stood than explicated." And for its *original*, the most sagacious
and renowned for wisdom amongst the ‡ ancient *philosophers* understood nothing of it. It is said of § Democritus, that " there is
" nothing in the whole workmanship of nature of which he did
" not write ;" and in a more lofty and swelling *hyperbole*, they stile
their eagle-eyed Aristotle, " the rule, yea, and miracle of nature ;
" learning itself, the very son of knowledge :" yet both these are
not only said, but proved by Lactantius to be learned ideots.
How have the schools of Epicurus, and Aristotle, the Cartesians,
and other sects of *philosophers* abused and troubled the world with
a kind of *philosophical enthusiasm*, and a great many ridiculous
fancies about the original of the soul of man ! and when all is done

---

* *Tria sunt quæ secundum essentiam hominibus sunt* αγνωςα, και αοριςα, *Deus, angelus, anima hominis.* Ath. in Tract. de defin.

† *Quæri facilius est quam intelligi, et melius intelligitur quam explicatur.*

‡ Plato doubted, Aristotle denied, and Galen derided the doctrine of the world's
creation.

§ *Nihil est in toto opificio naturæ, de quo non scripsit Democritus.* And for Aristotle,
they stiled him, *Regula naturæ, Naturæ miraculum, ipsa eruditio, sol scientiarum, An-
tistes literarum et sapientiæ.* Lactantius, lib. iii. cap. 17, 18.

three words of God, by the pen of his inspired Moses *, enlightens us more than all the subtle notions of the accidental concretion of atoms, their *materia subtilis*, and *anima mundi*, and the rest of their unintelligible fancies could ever do.

The account Moses gives us in this context, of the origin of the world, and of man the epitome of it, is full of sense, reason, congruity, and clearness ; and such as renders all the essays of all the Heathen philosophers to be vain, inevident, self-repugnant, and inexplicable theories.

The inspired penman gives us, in this context, a compendious narrative of the world's creation, relating more generally the rude, inform, and indigested chaos ; and then more particularly the specificating, and diversifying of the various beautiful beings, thence educed by the motion of the Spirit of God upon the face of the waters.

When the first matter was strictly created out of nothing, " the " Spirit (as Moses excellently expresseth it, chap. i. 2.) † hovered, " or moved over it as a bird over her eggs, and, as it were, by " way of incubation, cherishing and influencing it," did thereby draw forth all the creatures into their several forms, and distinct particular natures, wherein we now, with delight and admiration, behold them.

In this manner and order was the stately fabric of the world produced and erected ; but as yet, it remained as a fair and well-furnished house without an inhabitant. God had employed infinite wisdom and power about it, and engraven his name upon the meanest creature in it ; but there was no creature yet made (except angels, the inhabitants of another city) to read the name and celebrate the praises of the Almighty Creator.

He therefore thought the world imperfect till there was a creature made that could contemplate, praise, and worship the Maker of it ; for this very use and purpose was man created, that he might not only see, but consider the things he saw ; discourse, and rationally collect out of them the things he saw not ; and both praise, and love the Maker for, and in them all.

The palaces of princes are not beautified and adorned, to the intent men should pay their respects and honours to the walls, but to shew the grandeur and magnificence of the king, to whose per-

---

* Philosophy seeks or searches after truth, but theology finds it. *Jo. Picus Miran.*

† רחף *Motus est.* He moved ; a metaphor taken from the action of the eagle, when she provokes her brood to the action of flying ; and is applied by some to the communication of motion to the several parts of the planetary system. Vid. *Stokius on the word, and a Dissertation of Dr. Jennings on the place.* *Editor.*

son their honour is due, as * Athenagoras in his excellent apology for the Christians, speaks. The world is a glorious and magnificent pile, raised designedly to exhibit the wisdom and power of its Creator to the reasonable creature man, that from him God might receive the glory of all his other works. Of this creature man, the master-piece of all the visible world, (and therefore crowned king over it the first moment he was made, Psal. viii. 5.) Moses in the next place, gives us the account, both of his original, whence he came, and of his dignity, what he is. " The Lord God formed " man out of the dust of the ground, and breathed into his nos- " trils the breath of life; and man became a living soul." Where we find,

$$\text{The original} \left\{ \begin{array}{l} \text{I. Of the body} \\ \text{II. of the soul} \end{array} \right\} \text{of man.}$$

I. The original of the body of man : " Formed out of the dust " of the ground." " Dust was its original matter; of dust was it " made, and into dust it must be resolved, Gen. iii. 19. The con- " sideration is humbling, and serves to tame the pride of man †," who is apt to dote upon his own beauty. Man's body was not made of heavenly matter, as the radiant sun, and sparkling stars: no, nor yet of the most precious and orient earthly matter: God did not melt down the pure and splendid gold and silver, or powder the precious pearls and sparkling diamonds, but he formed it of the vile and despicable dust.

We find that the sprinkling of dust upon new writing prevents many a foul blot: I am sure, the sprinkling of our original dust upon our minds by serious consideration, is the way to prevent many a proud boast.

However, the baseness of the matter, and coarseness of the stuff, serves to set off the admirable skill of the most wise and powerful Architect, who out of such mean, despicable materials, has fashioned so exact and elegant a piece. " The Lord God formed " man out of the dust."

" *The Lord God.*] The name of God is here set down at full ‡,

---

* This world is indeed most beautiful, yet it is not the world itself that is to be adored, but that great Artificer, its Creator: even as your subjects, when applying to you for what they need, do not act so foolish a part as to overlook you their lords and princes, omitting all the honour due to you, and confining their regards to the magnificence of your palaces: but, on the contrary, viewing the fine structure of your palaces only by the by, they revere and honour yourselves before and above all things else. *Athen. Apol.*

† עָפָר מִן הָאֲדָמָה *Pulverem tenuissimam ad domandam superbiam.* **Fagius.**

‡ יהוה אלהים *Dominus Deus. Nomen Dei hic plenum est, propter hominis dignitatem.* **Nachm.**

to set forth the dignity of man," the subject matter wrought upon, as some conceive.

Formed.] Fashioned, or curiously moulded, and figured it *. The *Hebrew verb*, primarily signifies " to press, compress, or " squeeze together ; and by a *metalepsis*, by pressing or compres- " sing, to mould or fashion, as the potter doth his clay." The Psalmist useth another word to express the artificial elegancy of the body of man, Psal. cxxxix. 15, 16. רקמתי *acupictus sum*, I am embroidered, painted, or flourished as with a needle. We ren- der it *curiously wrought.* Whatsoever beauty and comely propor- tion God hath bestowed by creation upon it, "it is all answerable " to that excellent *idea*, or model † before conceived in his mind " and purpose." All this care and cost was bestowed upon the body of man, which, when all is done, is but the case in which that inestimable jewel, the soul, was to be lodged. This therefore I must lay aside, and come to the more noble subject,

II. *The soul of man :* about which we have before us four things to ponder in this text, viz.

(1.) The nature and property,
(2.) The descent, and original, ⎫
(3.) The manner of infusion,   ⎬ the soul of man.
(4.) The *nexus*, or bond that unites ⎭

(1.) The nature and property of it, a *living soul.* The word נפש as also the Chaldee *Naphsha ;* and the Greek ψυχη, have one and the same *etymology*, all signifying to breathe, or respire ; not that the breath is the soul, but denoting the manner of its infu- sion by the breath of God, and the means of its continuation in the body, by the breath of our nostrils. God's breath infused it, and our breath continues it in union with the body. It signifies here the rational soul ; and the *Hebrew* נפש, a soul, hath a very near affinity with the word שמים the heavens ; and indeed there is a nearer affinity betwixt the things, viz. soul and heaven, than there is betwixt the names.

The epithet חיה which we translate *living*, the *Arabic* renders a *rational soul*, and indeed, none but a rational deserves the name of a living soul; for all other forms or souls, which are of an earthly extract, do both depend on, and die with the matter out of which they were educed; but this being of another nature, a spiritual and substantial being, is therefore rightly stiled, *a living soul*.

The *Chaldee* renders it, *a speaking soul.* And indeed, it de- serves a remark, that the ability of speech is conferred on no other

---

* Pressit עיר Compressit, et per Metalepsin, premendo et comprimendo formavit.
† Imaginem mente divina conceptam, quasi manu format. Fagius.

soul but man's.   Other creatures have apt and elegant organs ;
birds can modulate the air, and form it into sweet delicious notes,
and charming sounds ; but no creature, except man, whose soul
is of an heavenly nature and extraction, can articulate the sound,
and form it into words, by which the notions and sentiments of
one soul are in a noble, apt, and expeditious manner conveyed to
the understanding of another soul.   And indeed, what should any
other creature do with the faculty or power of speech, without a
principle of reason to guide and govern it ? It is sufficient to them
that they discern each others meaning by dumb signs, much after
the manner that we traded at first with the Indians ; but speech is
proper only to a rational, or living soul, however, we render it a
living, a rational, or a speaking soul, it distinguishes the soul of
man from all other souls.

(2.) We find here the best account that ever was given of the
origin of the soul of man, or whence it came, and from whom it
derives its being.   O, what a dust and pother have the disputes
and contests of philosophers raised about this matter ! which is
cleared in a few words in this scripture ; * " God breathed into
" his nostrils the breath of life, and man became a living soul :"
which plainly speaks it to be the immediate effect of God's creating
power.   Not a result from matter ; no, results flow *e sinu materiæ*, out of the bosom of matter ; but this comes *ex halitu divino*,
from the inspiration of God.   That which is born of the flesh, is
flesh ; but this is a spirit descending from the Father of spirits.
God formed it, but not out of any pre-existent matter, whether
celestial or terrestrial ; much less out of himself, as the † Stoicks
speak ; but out of nothing.   An high-born creature it is, but no
particle of the Deity.   The indivisible and immutable essence of
God is utterly repugnant to such notions ; and therefore they speak
not strictly and warily enough, that are bold to call it a ray or
emanation from God.

A spirit it is, and flows by way of creation, immediately from the
Father of spirits ; but yet is a spirit of another inferior rank and
order.

(3.) We have also the account of the way and manner of its infusion into the body, viz. by the same breath of God which gave it

---

* He breathed the breath of life into man, to shew that man's soul is from an external cause by creation, and that at the same time, in being created, it is infused into
the body. *Pol. Synops. on the place.*

† The Stoicks, saith Simplicius, called the soul Μερος η μελος τȣ Θεȣ, i. e. a
particle or member of the Deity ; and Seneca calls it, God dwelling in the human
body, which comes near to Θεος νε σαρχι φανερωθεις, i. e. God manifested in the
flesh.

its being. It is therefore a rational, scriptural, and justifiable expression of St. Augustine, *Creando infunditur, et infundendo crea-
tur ;* it is infused in creating, and created in infusing; though Dr.
Brown * too slightingly calls it a mere *rhetorical antimetathesis.*
Some of the fathers, as Justin, Ireneus, and Tertullian, were of
opinion, That the Son of God assumed a human shape at this time,
in which afterwards he often appeared to the fathers, as a prelude
to his true and real incarnation; and took dust or clay in his hands,
out of which he formed the body of man, according to the pattern
of that body in which he appeared: and that being done, he afterwards, by breathing, infused the soul into it.   But I rather think it
is an *anthropopathia,* or usual figure in speech, by which the Spirit
of God stoops to the imbecility of our understandings, " He breathed
" into his nostrils the breath of life;" Hebrew, *lifes.*   But this plural
word חיים notes rather the twofold life of man, in this world, and
in that to come; or, " the several faculties and powers belonging
" to one and the same soul, viz. the intellective, sensitive, and vege-
" tative offices thereof; than that there are more souls than one,
" essentially differing, in one and the same man; for that, (as
" † Aquinas truly saith,) is impossible."   We cannot trace the way of
the Spirit, or tell in what manner it was united with this clod of
earth.   But it is enough, that he who formed it, did also unite, or
marry it to the body.   This is clear, not by way of natural resultancy from the body, but by way of inspiration from the Lord; not
from the warm bosom of matter, but from the breath of its Maker.

4. *Lastly,* We have here the *nexus, copula,* the tie or band by
which it is united with the body of man, viz. *The breath of his* (i. e.
of man's) *nostrils.*   It is a most astonishing mystery to see heaven
and earth married together in one person ; the dust of the ground,
and an immortal spirit clasping each other with such dear embraces
and tender love; such a noble and divine guest to take up its residence within the mean walls of flesh and blood.   Alas, how little
affinity, and yet what dear affection is found betwixt them !

Now, that which so sweetly links these two different natures together, and holds them in union, is nothing else but the breath of
our nostrils, as the text speaks: it came in with the breath; whilst
breath stays with us, it cannot go from us; and as soon as the
breath departs, it departs also.   All the rich elixirs and cordials in
the world cannot persuade it to stay one minute after the breath is
gone.   One puff of breath will carry away the wisest, holiest, and

---

* *Religio Medici,* Sect. 36.
† *Impossibile est in uno homine esse plures animas per essentiam differentes ; sed una
tantum est anima ; quæ vegetativæ, et sensitivæ, et intellectivæ officiis fungitur.* Aquin.
12, Q. 26. art. 2.

most desirable soul that ever dwelt in flesh and blood. When our breath is corrupt, our days are extinct, Job xvii. 1. "Thou takest "away their breath, they die, and return to their dust," Psal. cxiv. 19.

Out of the text thus opened, arise two doctrinal propositions, which I shall insist upon, viz.

Doct. 1. *That the soul of man is of a divine original, created and inspired immediately by the Lord.*

Doct. 2. *That the souls and bodies of men are linked, or knit together, by the feeble band of the breath of their nostrils.*

In the prosecution of these two propositions, many things will come to our hands, of great use in religion; which I shall labour to lay as clearly and orderly to the reader's understanding, and press as warmly upon his heart as I can. And first,

Doct. 1. *That the soul of man is of a divine original, created and inspired immediately by the Lord.*

In this first proposition, two things are to be distinctly pondered, viz.

$$\left.\begin{array}{l}\text{1. The nature}\\\text{2. The original}\end{array}\right\}\text{ of the soul.}$$

Or, what it is, and from whence it came.

I. The first thing which arrests our thoughts, and requires their attention and exercise, is the *nature of the soul*, or what kind of being it is.

Those that are most curiously inquisitive into all other beings, and put nature upon the rack to make her confess her secrets, are in the mean time found shamefully slight and negligent in the study of themselves. Few there are that can prevail with themselves to sit down and think close to such questions as these. *What manner of being is this soul of mine? whence came it? why was it infused into this body? and where must it abide, when death has dislodged it out of this frail tabernacle?* There is a natural aversation in man to such exercises of thought as these, although in the whole universe of beings in this lower world, a more noble creature is not to be found *.

The soul is the most wonderful and astonishing piece of divine

---

* Therefore they who at any time have disputed concerning the soul, must be reckoned to have disputed not of a vain thing, that has nothing but a name, but about a very weighty subject, of the greatest moment, than which nothing under heaven is more excellent. *Zanch. on the soul.*

workmanship; it is no *hyperbole* to call it the breath of God, the beauty of men, the wonder of angels, and the envy of devils. One soul is of more value than all the bodies in the world.

The nature of it is so spiritual and sublime, that it cannot be perfectly known by the most acute and penetrating understanding, assisted in the search by all the aid philosophy can contribute.

It is not my design in this discourse to treat of the several faculties and powers of the soul, or to give you the rise, natures, or numbers of its affections and passions: but I shall confine my discourse to its general nature and original. And seeing " none can so well discover " the nature of it, as he who is the author of it," as Tertullian * speaks, I therefore justly expect the best light from his words, though I will not neglect any other aid he is pleased elsewhere to afford.

† The soul is variously denominated from its several powers and offices, as the sea from the several shores it washes. I will not spend time about the several names by which it is known to us in scripture, but give you that description of it, with which my understanding is most satisfied, which take thus:

The soul of man is a vital, spiritual, and immortal substance, endowed with an understanding, will, The description *and various affections ; created with an inclination* of the soul. *to the body, and infused thereinto by the Lord.*

In this description we have the two general parts into which I distributed this discourse: viz. its general nature, and divine original. The nature of the soul is expressed to us in these following terms.

I. *It is a substance.*

That is to say, not a *quality*, nor an *accident* inhering in another being, or subject; as whiteness doth in the snow: but a being by ‡ itself. Qualities and accidents have no existence of their own, but require another being, or subject to their existence; but the soul of man is a substantial being of itself, which will evidently appear upon the following grounds.

(1.) Because it is, in a strict and proper sense, created by God, " He formeth, or createth the spirit in man," Zech. xii. 1. To

---

* *Si quid de anima certandum est, ad Dei regulas dirigat : certe nullum alium potiorem animæ demonstrationem, quam Auctorem.* Tertul. de anima, &c.

† As it quickens the body, it is called *anima*, i. e. the life ; as it exerts acts of the will, it is called *animus*, i. e. power of volition ; as it is the subject of knowledge, it is called the mind ; when it recollects, it is called the memory ; when it judges right, it is called reason ; as it produces breathing, it is called spirit. *Isidor. Etym. v. 5.*

‡ The soul is a being by itself, i. e. it does not exist in any object as a part or form of it, depending on it, as to its being. *Colleg. Conimb. in lib.* 11.

him we are advised to "commit it, as to a faithful Creator," 1 Pet. iv. 19. The substantial nature of the soul is implied in the very notion of its creation; "for whatsoever is created, is a *substance*, an " *ens par se* *. Accidents are not said to be created, but con- " created;" the crasis of humours and results of matter are not sub- stances created, but things rising in a natural way from created substances. They flow from, and as to their essence, depend upon pre-existent matter; but the soul was created out of nothing, and infused into the body after it was formed and organized; which evidenceth its substantial nature.

(2.) This evidenceth the soul to be a substance; that it can, and doth exist, and subsist by itself alone, when separated from the body by death, Luke xxiii. 43. " To-day shalt thou, (i. e. thy soul) be " with me in paradise," and Mat. x. 20. " Fear not them that kill " the body, but cannot kill the soul." Were the soul but an acci- dent, a quality, or a result, he that kills the body must needs kill the soul too; as he that casts a snowball into the fire, must needs destroy the whiteness with the snow. Accidents fail and perish with their subjects: but seeing it is plain in these and many other scriptures, the soul doth not fail with the body; nothing can be more plain and evident, than that it is of a substantial nature.

When the Spaniards came first among the poor Indians, they thought the horse and his rider to be one creature; as many ig- norant ones think the soul and body of man to be nothing but breath and body: whereas indeed, they are two distinct creatures, as vastly different in their natures as the rider and his horse, or the bird and his cage. While the man is on horseback, he moves according to the motion of the horse; and while the bird is in- caged, he eats and drinks, and sleeps, and hops and sings in his cage. But if the horse fail and die under his rider, or the cage be broken, the man can go on his own feet, and the bird enjoy itself as well, yea, better in the open fields and woods, than in the cage; neither depend, as to being, or action, on the horse or cage.

(3.) Both scripture and philosophy consent in this, that the soul is the chief, most noble, and principal part of man, from which the whole man is, and ought to be denominated. So Gen. xlvi. 26. " All the souls that came with Jacob into Egypt," i. e. all the persons; as the Latins say, *tot capita*, so many heads or persons. The apostle, in 2 Cor. v. 8. seems to exclude the body from the notion of personality, when he saith, *We are willing rather to be absent*

---

* *Quicquid a Deo proprie creatum est; accidentia enim non dicuntur creari, sed con- creari.* Polani Synt. p. 319.

from the body, and to be present with the Lord: That *we*, a term of personality is there given to the soul, exclusively of the body, for the body cannot be absent from itself: But *we*, that is, the souls of believers, may be both absent from it, and present with Christ.

To this we may add, 2 Cor. iv. 16. where the soul is called the *man*, and the *inner man* too, the body being but the external face, or shadow of the man. And to this *philosophers* agree. The best *philosophers* are so far from thinking that the body is the substantial part of man, and the soul a thing dependent on it, that contrarily they affirm, that the body depends upon the soul *, and that it is the soul that conserves and sustains it; and that the body s in the soul, rather than the soul in the body, and that which is seen not the man, but that is the man which is invisible, that the body might be killed and the man not hurt; meaning the soul, which only deserves the name of man. Now if it be the chief part of man, and that which is only worthy the name of man, and from which therefore the whole is and ought to be denominated a man; if it be so far from depending on the body, or being contained within the body, that the body rather depends upon it, and is in it, then surely the soul must be, what we describe it to be, a substantial *being*.

(4.) It is past all controversy, that the soul is a *substance*, because it is the subject of properties, affections and habits; which is the very strict and formal notion of a substance. All the affections and passions of hope, desire, love, delight, fear, sorrow, and the rest, are all rooted in it, and springing out of it; and for habits, arts and sciences †, it is the soul in which they are lodged and seated. Having once gotten a promptitude to act, either by some strong, or by some frequently repeated acting, they abide in the soul, even when the acts are intromitted, as in sleep, a navigator, scribe, or musician, are really artists, when they are neither sailing, or writing, or playing; because the habits still remain in their minds, as is evident in this, that when they awake, they can

---

* The soul preserves and sustains the animated body, but when it leaves the body, the nature of an animated body subsists no more: the soul exists not in the body, as in a place, seeing it cannot be circumscribed by place. The whole soul pervades the whole body; nor is there any part of it, in which it is not present: for it is not contained in the body, but rather itself contains the body; neither is it in the body, as in a vessel or bottle, but rather the body is in it. *Nys. on the soul, b.* 2. *c.* 11. 8κ εϛιν Ανθρωπος το ορωμενον, i. e. That which is seen is not the man, but every man's soul is himself.

† The soul is the subject and seat of all the virtues and vices, arts and sciences. *Buchan. loc. com. p.* 86.

perform their several works, without learning the rules of their art
anew.

II. *The soul is a vital substance,* i. e.

A substance which hath an essential principle of life in itself; a
living, active being.   A *living* soul, saith Moses in the text; and
hereby it is distinguished from, and opposed to matter or body.
The soul moves itself and the body too; it hath a self-moving
virtue or power in itself; whereas the matter, or body is wholly
passive, and is moved and acted, not by itself, but by this vital
spirit, James ii. 26. " The body without the spirit is dead." It
acts not at all, but as it is acted by this invisible spirit.   This is so
plain, that it admits of sensible proof and demonstration.   Take
mere matter, and compound or divide it, alter it, and change it
how you will, you can never make it see, feel, hear, or act vitally
without a quickening and actuating soul.   Yet we must still remember, that this active principle, the soul, though it hath this
vital power in itself, it hath it not from itself, but in a constant
receptive dependence upon God, the first cause, both of its being
and power.

III. *It is a spiritual substance.*

All substances are not gross, material, visible and palpable substances; but there are spiritual and immaterial, as well as corporeal substances, discernable by sight or touch.   To deny this were
to turn a downright Sadducee, and to deny the existence of angels
and spirits, Acts xxiii. 8.   The word *substance,* as it is applied to
the soul of man, puzzles and confounds the dark understandings
of some, that know not what to make of an immaterial substance,
whereas in this place it is no more than *substare accidentibus* *, i. e.
to be a subject in which properties, affections, and habits are seated and subjected.   This is a spiritual substance, and is frequently in
scripture called a spirit; " Into thy hands I commit my spirit,"
Luke xxiii. 46.   " Lord Jesus receive my spirit," Acts vii. 59. and
so frequently all over the scriptures.   And the spirituality of its
nature appears, (1.) By its descent, in a peculiar way, from the
Father of spirits.   (2.) In that it rejoiceth in the essential properties
of a spirit.   (3.) That at death it returns to that great Spirit who
was its efficient and former.

(1.) It descends, in a peculiar way, from the Father of spirits,
as hath been shewn in the opening of this text.   God stiles himself
its Father, Heb. xii. 9. its former, Zech. xii. 1.   It is true, he

---

* A substance in this use of the word, is that which depends not, in respect of its
being, upon any fellow-creature as accidents and qualities do, whose being is by having
their in-being in another fellow-creature as their subject; but this being, *the soul,* exists in itself.

giveth to all living things ζωην μαι πνοην, life and breath, Acts xvii.
25. Other souls are from him, as well as the rational soul; but
in a far different way and manner. They flow not immediately
from him by creation, as this doth. It is said, Gen. i. 24, 27. " Let
" the earth bring forth the living creature after its kind ;" but " God
" created man in his own image." Which seems plainly to make a
specified difference betwixt the reasonable, and all other souls.

(2.) It rejoiceth in the essential properties of a spirit : For it is
an incorporeal substance, as spirits are. It hath not *partes extra
partes*, extension of parts ; nor is it divisible, as the body is. It
hath no dimensions and figures as matter hath ; but is a most
pure, invisible, and (as the acute Dr. Moore expresseth it) indis-
cernable substance. It hath the principle of life and motion in itself, or rather, it is such a principle itself, and is not moved as
dull and sluggish matter is, *peraliud*, by another. Its efficacy is
great, though it be unseen, and not liable to the test of our touch,
as no spiritual substances are. " A spirit (saith Christ) hath not
" flesh and bones," Luke xxiv. 39. We both grant and feel, that
the soul hath a love and inclination to the body, (which indeed is
no more than it is necessary it should have) yet can we no more
infer its corporiety from that love to the body, than we can infer
the corporiety of angels from their affection and benevolent love to
men. It is a spirit of a nature vastly different from the body in
which it is immersed. *There is* (saith a learned author *) *no
greater mystery in nature, than the union betwixt soul and body :
That a mind and spirit should be so tied and linked to a clod of
clay, that while that remains in a due temper, it cannot by any art
or power free itself !—What so much a-kin are a mind and a piece
of earth, a clod and a thought, that they shall be thus affixed to
one another ?*
Certainly, the heavenly pure bodies do not differ so much from
a dunghill, as the soul and body differ. They differ but as more
pure and less pure matter ; but these, as material, and immaterial. If we consider wherein consists the being of a body, and
wherein that of a soul, and then compare them, the matter will
be clear.
We cannot come to an apprehension of their beings, but by considering their primary passions and properties, whereby they make
discovery of themselves. The first and primary affection of a
body † (as is rightly observed) is that extension of parts whereof it
is compounded, and a capacity of division, upon which, as upon the

* Mr. How's Fun. Serm. p. 9, 10.
+ Philosophical Essay, p. 2, § 2. p. 39.

fundamental mode, the particular dimensions (that is, the figures) and the local motion do depend.

Again, for the being of our souls, if we reflect upon ourselves, we shall find that all our knowledge of them resolves into this, that we are beings conscious to ourselves of several kinds of cogitations; that by our outward senses we apprehend bodily things present; and by our imagination we apprehend things absent; and that we oft recover into our apprehension things past and gone, and, upon our perception of things, we find ourselves variously affected.

Let these two properties of a soul and body be compared, and upon the first view of a considering mind it will appear, that divisibility is not apprehension, or judgment, or desire, or discourse: That to cut a body into several parts, or put it into several shapes, or bring it to several motions, or mix it after several ways, will never bring it to apprehend, or desire. No man can think the combining of fire, and air, and water, and earth, should make the lump of it to know and comprehend, what is done to it, or by it. We see manifestly, that upon the division of the body, the soul remains entire and undivided. It is not the loss of a leg or arm, or eye, that can maim the understanding, or the will, or cut off the affections.

Nay, it pervades the body it dwells in, and is whole in the whole *, and in every part, which it could never do if it were material. Yea, it comprehends, in its understanding, the body or matter in which it is lodged; and more than that, it can, and doth form conceptions of pure spiritual and immaterial beings, which have no dimensions or figures; all which shew it to be no corporeal, but a spiritual and immaterial substance.

(3.) As it derives its being from *the Father of spirits*, in a peculiar way, and rejoiceth, in its spiritual properties: So at death it returns to *that great Spirit* from whence it came. It is not annihilated, or resolved into soft air, or sucked up again by the element of fire, or catched back again into the soul of the world, as some have dreamed; but it returns to God who gave it, to give an account of itself to him, and receive its judgment from him. " Then shall " the dust return to the earth as it was, and the spirit shall return " to God who gave it," Eccl. xii. 7. Each part of man to its like, dust to dust, and spirit to spirit. Not that the soul is resolved into God, as the body is into earth: but as God created it a rational spirit, conscious to itself of moral good and evil, so when it

---

* Understand it negatively, that the soul is not in the parts of the body *per partes*, part in one part, and part in another, seeing it is indivisible, and hath no parts.

hath finished its time in the body, it must appear before the God of the spirits of all flesh, its Arbiter and final Judge.

By all which we see, that as it is elevated too high on the one hand, when it is made a *particle of God himself*; not only the creature, but a part of God, as * Plutarch and Philo Judeus †, and others have termed it ; (spirit it is, but of another and inferior kind :) So it is degraded too low, when it is affirmed to be matter, though the purest, finest, and most subtle in nature ; which approacheth nearest to the nature of spirit.   A spirit it is, as much as an angel is a spirit, though it be a spirit of another *species*. This is the name it is known by throughout the scriptures.   In a word, it is void of mixture and composition ; there are no jarring qualities, compound elements, or divisible parts in the soul, as there are in bodies ; but it is a pure, simple, invisible, and indivisible substance, which proves its spirituality, and brings us to the fourth particular, viz.

IV. *It is an immortal substance.*

The simplicity and spirituality of its nature, of which I spake before, plainly shews us, that it is in its very nature designed for immortality ; for such a being or substance as this hath none of the seeds of corruption and death in its nature, as all material and compounded beings have.   It hath nothing within it tending to dissolution : No jarring elements, no contrary qualities are found in spirits as there are in other creatures of a mixed nature.   Physicians and Philosophers have disputed and contended eagerly about the true causes of natural death ; "‡ and whilst they have been con-" tending about the way, they have come to the end."   The ingress of the soul is obscure, and its egress not clear.   But this seems to be the thing in which they generally centre, that the expence and destruction of the § natural moisture, or radical balsam, as others call it, which is the oil that maintains natural heat, or the bridle that restrains that flame of life from departing, as others express it : this is the cause of natural death : Others ‖

---

* *Anima autem mentis particeps facto, non solum Dei opus est, verum etiam pars : neque ab eo, sed de eo, et ex eo facta.* Plut. de Qu. Platon.

† *Quomodo credibile videtur tam exiguum mentem humanam membranula cerebri, aut cordi, haud amplis spaciis inclusam ; totam cœli mundique magnitudinem capire, nisi illius divinæ fœlicisque animæ particula esset indivisibilis ?* Philo.

‡ *Litiganius de via, interiam ad-terminum rapimur.*

§ Δει γαρ λαϐειν οτι το ζωον εϛι φυσει υγρον και θερμον και το ζην τοιϛτον. Το δε γηρας ψαχρον, και ξηρον και το τεθνηκος φαινεται γαρ ϛτος. *i. e.* For we must understand, that the animal hath a natural moisture and heat, which makes it to live.   But old age drying up that moisture, and changing that heat into coldness, occasions death. *Aristotle, on long and short life.*

‖ *Tum flammat et micat calidum nativum corporis nostri in humido primigenio, ejus humi-*

assign the unequal reparation of the parts of the body as the cause of death. But be it one or another, it is evident the soul, which consists neither of contrary qualities, nor of dissimilar parts, must be above the reach and stroke of death. For if the soul die, it must be either from some seeds, and principles of death and corruption within itself, or by some destructive power without itself. In itself you see there is no seed or principle of death ; and if it be destroyed by a power without itself, it must be either by the stroke of some creature, or from the hand of God that first formed and created it : But the hand and power of no creature can destroy it ; the creature's power reaches no farther than the body, Mat. x. 28. " They cannot kill the soul." And though the Almighty power of God, that created it out of nothing, can as easily reduce it to nothing ; yet he will never do so. For besides the designation for eternity, which is discernible in its very nature, (as before was observed) and which speaks the intention of God to perpetuate the threatenings of eternal wrath, and promises of everlasting life, respectively made to the souls of men, as they shall be found in Christ, or out of Christ, puts it beyond all doubt that they shall never die ; as will be more fully evidenced in the following discourse.

Well then, I hope so far our way is clear, in the search of the nature of the soul, that it is a *substance*, a *spiritual* substance, and being so, it is also an *immortal substance*. No doubt remains with me as to either of these. Let us then proceed to the consideration of its faculties and powers by which it may be yet more fully known, and we shall find that,

It is a vital, spiritual, and immortal substance, endued with an understanding.

This is the noble leading faculty of the soul : We are not distinguished from *brutes* by our senses, but by our *understanding*. As grace sets one man above another, so understanding sets the meanest man above the best of brutes. Strange and wonderful things are performed by the natural instinct and sagacity of beasts ; but yet what is said of one, is true of them all, " God hath not imparted understanding to them," Job xxxix. 17. This is a jewel which adorns none but rational creatures, men and angels.

---

di substantia consumitur, non aliter quam in lampade oleum a flamma exhauritur. Heornius Aphor. 1. *Tam diu durat vigor vitæ, quam diu stat calidum nativum, donec ad mortem fuerit deventum. Et quantum a calido et humido receditur, tantus ad mortem sit accessus.* J. Bapt. Montan. *Ortus nostri primordio, caloris es humoris nativi habent summum complementum, &c.* Fernelius liber de spir. et. cal. *Vergente ætate, inæqualis admodum sit reparatio, aliæ partes reparantur satis fœlicitur, sed aliæ ægre, et in pejus. Ut ab eo tempore corpora humana subiri incipiunt tormentum illud* Mezentii, *ut viva in amplexu mortuorum immoriantur.* Verulam. in additu Hist. vit. et. mort.

The understanding is a faculty of the reasonable soul by which a man apprehends and judges all intelligible things.

The *object* of it is *every being*, so far as it is true in itself, and apprehensible by man. It hath a two-fold use in the life of man, viz.

(1.) To distinguish truth from error and falsehood. By this candle of the Lord, lighted up in the soul of man, he may discern betwixt duty and sin, good and evil: It is the eye of the soul, by which it seeth the way in which we should go, and the dangerous precipices that are on either side. It is the soul's *taster*, and discerns wholesome food from baneful poison, Job xii. 11. "Doth not "the ear (i. e. the understanding by the *ear*) try words, as the "mouth tasteth meat?" It brings all things as it were in the lump before it, and then sorts them, and orderly ranks them into their proper *classes* of *lawful* and *unlawful*, necessary and indifferent, *expedient* and *inexpedient*, that the soul may not be damnified by mistaking one for another. And this judgment of discretion every man must be allowed for himself. No man is obliged to shut the eyes of his own understanding, and follow another man blindfold.

(2.) *To direct* and guide us in our practice. This faculty is by *philosophers* rightly called το ηγεμονικον, *the leading faculty ;* because the will follows its practical dictates. It sits at the helm, and guides the course of the soul; not impelling, or rigorously enforcing its dictates upon the will; for the will cannot be so imposed upon; but by giving it a directive light, or pointing, as it were, with its finger, what it ought to chuse, and what to refuse.

To this faculty belong two other excellent and wonderful powers of the soul, viz.

1. Thoughts. | 2. Conscience.

1. The power or ability of cogitation; " * *Thoughts* are properly "the actings and agitations of the mind, or any actual operation "of the understanding." They are the musings of the mind, which are acted in the speculative part of the understanding. It is observable that the † Hebrew word שׂיח *suach,* which is used for meditation, or thinking, signifies both to think and to speak in the mind. When the understanding, or mind resolves, and meditates the things that come into it, that very meditation is an inward speaking, or hidden word in the heart, Deut. xv. 9. "Beware, lest there be a thought in thy wicked heart," as some ren-

---

* Διανοια, *cogitatio est mentis agitatio* Pas. *vel actio mentis.* Zanch.

† שׂיח *cum puncto sinistro, locutus est ore, aut corde : et* διαλογιζομαι *est sermocinari intra se,* i. e. *apud se in animis suis.* Mat. xxi. 25.

der it: In the Hebrew it is דכר עם לכבך "a word in thy heart."
So Mat. ix. 3, 4. ειπον ει αυτοις, " they spake within themselves,"
i. e. "they thought in their hearts." The objects presented to the
mind are the companions with whom our hearts talk and converse.

Thoughts are the figments and creatures of the mind: They are
formed within it, in multitudes innumerable. The power of cogitation is in the mind, yea, in the spirit of the mind.

" * The fancy indeed, whilst the soul is embodied, ordinarily,
" and for the most part presents the appearances and likenesses of
" things to the mind;" but yet it can form thoughts of things
which the fancy can present no image of, as when the † soul thinks
of God, or of itself. This power of cogitation goes with the soul,
and is rooted in it when it is separated from the body; and by it
we speak to God, and converse with *angels*, and other spirits in the
unbodied state, as will be more fully opened in the process of this
discourse.

2. The *conscience* belongs also to this faculty; for it being the
judgment of a man upon himself, with respect or relation to the
judgment of God, it must needs belong to the understanding part
or faculty. " *Thoughts* are formed in the *speculative*, but ‡ con-
" conscience belongs to the practical understanding." It is a very
high and awful power; it is *solo Deo mi nor*, and rides (as Joseph
did) in the second chariot; the next and immediate officer under
God. He saith of conscience with respect to every man, as he once
said of Moses with respect to Pharaoh. " See I have made thee a
" god to Pharaoh," Exod. vii. 1. The voice of conscience is the voice
of God; for it is his vicegerent and representative. *What it binds
on earth, is bound in heaven: and what it looseth on earth is loosed
in heaven.* It observes records, and bears witness of all our actions; and acquits and condemns, as in the name of God, for them.
Its consolations are most sweet, and its condemnations most terrible:
so terrible, that some have chosen death, which is the king of terrors, rather than to endure the scorching heat of their own consciences. The greatest deference and obedience is due to its command, and a man had better § endure any rack or torture in the
world, than incur the torments of it. It accompanies us as our

---

* *Phantasia menti offert phantasmata.* Picol.

† When we think of God, saith *Max. Tyr. Diss.* I. we must think of nothing material, μητε μεγεθος, μητε χρωμα, μητε αλλο τι υλης παθος, i. e. Neither magni-
tude nor colour, nor any other property of matter.

‡ *Judicium appello conscientiam, ut ad intellectum eam pertinere ostendam.* Ames.

§ What deaths would I not chuse? What punishment would I not undergo? Yea,
into what vault of hell would I not rather chuse to be thrown, than to witness against
my conscience?

shadow wherever we go : and when all others forsake us, (as at death they will) conscience is then with us, and is then never more active and vigorous than at that time.   Nor doth it forsake us after death ; but where the soul goes, it goes, and will be its companion in the other world for ever.   How glad would the damned be if they might but have left their consciences behind them, when they went hence !   But as * Bernard rightly says, " It is both witness, " judge, tormentor, and prison ;" it accuseth, judgeth, punisheth, and condemneth.

And thus briefly of the understanding, which hath many offices, and as many names from those offices.

It is sometimes called *wit, reason, understanding, opinion, wisdom, judgment.*   And why we bestow so many names upon one and the same faculty, the learned *author* of that small, but excellent † tract *de anima,* gives this true and ingenious account.

The wit, *the pupil of the soul's clear eye,*
And in man's world the only shining star,
Looks in the mirror of the fantasy,
Where all the gatherings of the senses are ;
And after by discoursing to and fro,
Anticipating and comparing things,
She doth all universal natures know,
And all effects into their causes brings.

When she rates things, and moves from ground to ground,
The name of reason *she obtains by this :*
But when by reason she the truth hath found,
And standeth fix'd, she understanding is.
When her assent she lightly doth incline
To either part, she is opinion *light :*
But when she doth by principles define
A certain truth, she hath true judgment's *sight.*

And as from senses, reason's work doth spring :
So many reasons understanding gain ;
And many understandings knowledge bring,
And by much knowledge wisdom we obtain.

VI.   God hath endued the soul of man not only with an *understanding* to discern, and direct, but also a *will* to govern, moderate, and over-rule the actions of life.

---

* *Ipsa judicat, ipsa imperat, ipsa observat, ipsa torter, ipsa carcer.*   Bern. lib. de Consc. cap. 9.

† *Nosce teipsum,* p. 48, 49.

The will is a faculty of the rational soul, whereby a man either chuseth or refuseth the things which the understanding discerns and knows.

This is a very high and noble power of the soul. The understanding seems to bear the same relation to the will, as a grave counsellor doth to a great *prince*. It glories in two excellencies, viz.

1. Liberty.
2. Dominion.

1. It hath a freedom and liberty; it cannot be compelled and forced: Coaction is repugnant to its very nature *. In this it differs from the understanding, that the understanding is wrought upon *necessarily*, but the will acts *spontaneously*. This liberty of the will respects the choice, or refusal of the means for attaining those ends it prosecutes, according as it finds them more or less conducible thereunto. The liberty of the will must be understood to be in things natural, which are within its own proper sphere, not in things *supernatural*. It can move, or not move the *body*, as it pleases, but it cannot move towards *Christ*, in the way of faith, as it pleaseth; it can open or shut the hand or eye at its pleasure, but not the heart. True, indeed, it is not compelled, or forced to turn to God by supernatural grace, but in a way suitable to its nature, it is determined and drawn to Christ, Psal. cx. 3. It is drawn by a mighty power, and yet runs freely; Cant. i. 4. " Draw me, and " I will run after thee."

Efficacious grace, and victorious delight, is a thing very different from compulsive force. " Pelagius (as a late † author speaks) " at first gave all to nature, acknowledged no necessity of divine " grace; but when this proud doctrine found little countenance, " he called nature by the name of grace; and when that deceit " was discovered, he acknowledged no other grace but outward " instruction, or the benefit of external revelation, to discourse, " and put men in mind of their duty. Being yet driven farther, " he acknowledged the grace of pardon; and before a man could " do any thing acceptably, there was a necessity of the remission of " sin, and then he might obey God perfectly. But that not suf- " ficing, he acknowledged another grace, viz. the example of " Christ, which doth both secure our rule and encourage our " practice. And last of all, his followers owned some kind of in- " ternal grace, but they made that to consist in some illumination " of the understanding, or moral persuasion, by probable argu- " ments, to excite the will, and this not absolutely necessary, but

---

* Ελευθερα εξυσια αυτο πραγιας. *i. e.* It hath a free liberty of action. *Zeno.*
† .Dr. Manton in Psal. cxix. v. 36.

" only for facilitation, as a horse to a journey, which otherwise a
" man might go on foot. Others grant the secret influences of
" God's grace, but make the will of man a co-ordinate cause with
" God, namely, that God doth propound the object, hold forth in-
" ducing considerations; give some remote power and assistance;
" but still there is an indifferency in the will of man, to accept or
" refuse, as liketh him best." Thus have they been forced to quit
and change their ground; but still the pride of nature will not let
men see the necessity of divine efficacious influences upon the will,
and the consistency thereof with natural liberty.

(2.) Its dignity in its *dominion*, as well as in its liberty. The will
hath an *empire*, and sceptre belonging to it; yea, a double empire,
for it rules,

Imperium
{
1. Despo-
   ticum.
2. Politi-
   cum.
}
{
1. Over the body, *imperio despotico*, by way of absolute command.
2. Over the other powers and passions of the soul,
   imperio politico, by way of *suasion*.
}

(1.) The will, like an absolute sovereign*, reigns over the
body, i. e. its external members by way of absolute command. It
saith, as the *centurion* did, I am in authority, and God hath put
the many members of the body in subjection to me; I say to one,
move, and it moves; to another, stop, and it stops; and to a
third, do this, and it doth it. The obsequious members of the
body, like so many servants, have their eyes waiting on the impe-
rial commands of the will, and it is admirable to behold with what
dispatch and speed they execute its commands, as if their obedient
motions were rather concomitant than subsequent acts to the will's
mandates. Let it but command to have the windows of the body,
open or shut, and it is done in a moment, in the twink of an eye;
and so for the rest of the external senses and members, they pay it
most ready obedience. Yet when I say, the will hath a *despotical*,
and absolute sovereignty over the members, it must be understood
with a double limitation. *First*, They are only at its beck for use
and service; it can use them whilst well and rightly disposed; but
it cannot perpetuate them, or restore them when indisposed. If
the soul will the health and life of the body never so intensely and
vehemently, it cannot keep off death one moment the longer from
it. And, *Secondly*, Its sovereignty no way intrenches upon, nor
interferes with the dominion of providence over the members of

---

* Man acts not by necessity of nature, but freely, namely in a rational way, that is
by way of command; this command requires the final determination of the practical
understanding, and while the efficacy of the command stands, the will is moved freely.
Camel. de volun. p. 50.

the body, and the various motions of them.   God hath reserved a sovereign, *negative voice* to himself, whatever decrees the will passes. Jeroboam stretches out his hand against the man of God to smite him; but God puts a *remora* in the very instant to the loco-motive faculty, that though he would never so fain, he could not pull in his hand again to him, 1 Kings xiii. 4.   The will commands the service of the tongue, and charges it to deliver faithfully such or such words, in which, it may be, the ruin of good men may be imported; and when it comes to do its office, the tongue faulters; and contrary to the command of the will, drops some word that discovers and defeats the design of the will, according to that in Job xii. 20. " He removeth away the speech of the trusty."   This is its despotical and sovereign power over the external members of the body.

(2.) It hath a *political* power over the faculties and passions of the soul, not by way of absolute command, but by way of *suasion* and *insinuation.*   Thus it can oft times persuade the understanding and thoughts to lay by this or that subject, and apply themselves to the study of another.   It can bridle and restrain the affections and passions, but yet it hath no absolute command over the inner, as it hath over the outward man.   Its weakness and inability to govern the inner man appears in two things, more especially remarkable, viz. 1. It cannot, with all its power and skill command and fetch off the thoughts from some subjects, which are set on, at some times, with extraordinary weight upon the soul.   However, the thoughts may obsequiously follow its beck at some times, yea, for the most part; yet there are cases and seasons, in which its authority and persuasions cannot disengage one thought.

As (1.) When God hath to do with the soul, in the work of conversion, when he convinceth of sin and danger, and sets a man's evils in order before his eyes: These are terrible representations, and fain would the carnal will disengage the thoughts from such sad subjects, and strives by all manner of persuasions and diversions so to do, but all to no purpose, Psal. li. 3. " My sin is ever before " me."   The thoughts are fixed, and there is no removing of them.   It may give them a little interruption, but they return with the more impetuous violence.   And instead of gaining them off, they at last, or rather God by them gains over the will also.

(2.) When Satan hath to do with the soul, in the way of *temptation* and hellish *suggestion:* Look, as the carnal will opposes itself to the thoughts in the former case to no purpose; so that the sanctified will opposes itself to them in this case, oft-times with as little effect or success, as he that opposeth his weak breath to the strong current of a mighty river.   Well were it, if the sanctified will were now the master of the fantasy, and could controul the thoughts of the heart ; but, like a mad horse, the *fancy* takes the bit in its teeth, and runs whither it pleaseth ; the will cannot govern it. Think quite another way saith the *will*, turn thy thoughts to other things ; but notwithstanding, the soul turneth a deaf ear to its counsels. 2. It cannot quiet and compose a raging conscience, and reduce it at its pleasure to rest and peace. This is the peculiar work of God. He only that stills the stormy seas, can quiet the distressed and tempestuous soul. The impotence of the will, in this case, is known to all that have been in those deeps of trouble. And this is the misery of the *devil* and the *damned*, that though they would never so fain, yet they cannot get rid of those tormenting impressions made upon them by their own trembling and condemning consciences. There would not be so many pale, sweating, affrighted consciencies on earth, and in hell, if the will had any command or power over them.

> *Tam frigida mens est.*
> *Criminibus ; tacita sudant præcordia culpa.*

It is an horrible sight to see such a trembling upon all the members, such a cold sweat upon the panting bosom of a self-condemned, and wrath-presaging soul, in which it can, by no means relieve or help itself. These things are exempt from the liberty and dominion of the will of man ; but notwithstanding these exemptions, it is a noble faculty, and hath a vastly extended empire in the soul of man ; it is the door of the soul, at which the Spirit of God knocks for entrance. When this is won, the soul is won to Christ ; and if this stand out in rebellion against him, he is barred out of the soul, and can have no saving union with it. The truth of grace is to be judged and discerned by its compliance with his call, and the measure of grace to be estimated by the degree of its subjection to his will.

VII. The soul of man is not only endued with an *understanding* and *will*, but also with *various affections* and *passions*, which are of great use and service to it, and speak the excellency of its nature. They are originally designed and appointed for the happiness of man, in the promoting and securing its chiefest good, to which purpose they have a natural aptitude : for the true happiness and rest of the soul not being in itself, nor in any other creature, but in God, the soul must necessarily move out of itself, and beyond all other created beings, to find and enjoy its true felicity in him. The soul considered at a distance from God, its true rest and happiness, is furnished and provided with *desire* and *hope* to carry it on, and quicken its motion towards him. These are the arms it is to stretch out towards him, in a state of absence from him. And seeing it is to meet with many obstacles, enemies, and difficulties,

in its course, which hinder its motion, and hazard its fruition of him,
God hath planted in it, fear, grief, indignation, jealousy, anger, &c.
to grapple with, and break through those intercurrent difficulties
and hazards *.   By these weapons in the hands of grace, it conflicts
with that which opposes its passages to God, as the apostle expresseth
that holy fret and passion of the Corinthians, and what a fume
their souls were in by the gracious motion of the irrascible appetite;
2 Cor. vii. 11.   " For behold this self-same thing, that ye sorrowed
" after a godly sort; what carefulness it wrought in you, yea, what
" clearing yourselves, yea, what indignation, yea, what fear, yea,
" what vehement desire, yea, what zeal, yea, what revenge ?" Much
like the raging and struggling of waters, which are interrupted in
their course by some dam or obstacle which they strive to bear down,
and sweep away before them.

But the soul considered in full union with and fruition of God, its
supreme happiness, is accordingly furnished with affections of love,
delight, and joy, whereby it rests in him and enjoys its proper
blessedness in his presence for ever.   Yea, even in this life, these
affections are in an imperfect degree exercised upon God, according
to the prelibations and enjoyments it hath of him by faith, in its
way to heaven.   In a word,

The true uses, and most excellent ends for which these affections
and passions are bestowed upon the soul of man, are to qualify it,
and make it a fit subject to be wrought upon in a moral way of persuasions and allurements, in order to its union with Christ, (for by
the affections, as Mr. Fenner rightly observes, the soul becomes
marriageable, or capable of being espoused to him) and being so,
then to assist it in the prosecution of its full enjoyment in heaven,
as we heard but now.

But, alas, how are they corrupted and inverted by sin ! The
concupiscible appetite greedily fastens upon the creature, not upon
God; and the irrascible appetite is turned against holiness, not sin.
But I must insist no farther on this subject here, it deserves an entire treatise by itself.

VIII. The soul of man hath, in the very frame and nature of
it, an inclination to the body.   There is in it a certain *pondus,* or
inclination which naturally bends or sways it towards matter, or a
body.   There are three different natures found in living creatures,
viz.

　　1. The brutal.
　　2. The angelical.

---

* *Passio animæ nihil aliud est quam motus appetitivæ virtutis prosecutione boni, vel
fuga mali,* i. e. A passion of the soul is nothing else but the motion of desire in seeking
good, and shunning evil.

3. The human.

(1.) The soul of a *brute* is wholly confined to, and dependent on the matter or body with which it is united. It is dedendent on it, both *in esse et in operari*, in its being and working; it is but a material form, which arises from, and perisheth with the body. " The " soul of a brute, (saith a great person *) is no other than a fluid " bodily substance, the more lively and refined part of the blood " (called spirit) quick in motion, and from the arteries by the " branches of the *carotides* carried to the brain; and from thence " conveyed to the nerves and muscles, move the whole frame and " mass of the body; and receiving only certain weak impressions " from the senses, and of short continuance, hindered and ob- " structed of its work and motion, vanishes into the soft air."

(2.) An angel is a spirit free from a body, and created without an appetite or inclination to be embodied. The Stoicks call the angels ხიας ψυχικας, souly substances; and the *Peripatetics, formas abstractas*, abstract forms. They are spirits free from the fetters and clogs of the body.

" † An angel is a perfect soul, and an human soul is an imper- " fect angel." Yet angels have no such rooted disaffection to, and abhorrence of a body, but they have assumed, and can, in a ready obedience to their Lord's commands, and delight to serve him, assume bodies, for a time, to converse with men in them, i. e. ærial bodies in the figure and shape of human bodies. So we read, Gen. xviii. 2. *three men*, i. e. angels in human shape and appearance, stood by Abraham, and talked with him; and at Christ's sepulchre, Luke xxiv. " There appeared two men in shining gar- " ments." But they abide in these bodies, as we do in an inn, for a night, or short season; they dwell not in them as our souls in those houses of flesh, which we cannot put on and off at pleasure as they do; but as we walk in our garments, which we can put off without pain.

(3.) The human soul is neither wholly tied to the body, as the brutal soul is; nor created without inclination to a body, as angels are; but loves and inclines to it, though it can both live and act without it, when it is parted from it at death. The proof of this assertion, and the reasons why God created it with such an inclination, will, in their proper place, be more fully spoken to, in the following discourse. All that I shall add is, that in this, as well

---

* Lord Chief Justice Hale, in his treatise *de anima*, p. 56.

† *Angelus est anima perfecta, et anima est angelus imperfectus.* Bell. de ascen. mentis.

as in some other respects, our souls are made *a little lower than the angels*; but when they are unclothed of the body, and have received it again, in a new edition, a spiritual body, then they shall be *ισαγγελοι*, equal unto angels, in the way and manner of life and action.

Thus I have, as briefly as I could, dispatched the first thing propounded, viz. the nature of the soul, in the explication of these seven particulars: it is a substance, a vital, spiritual, and immortal substance, a substance endued with understanding, will, affections, and an inclination to the body. And now we are come to the

II. Branch, viz. *Its original and infusion.*

I. As to its original, I have described it to be immediately from God, in the way of creation: an honour done to no other living creature except angels. The world hath been troubled with a great many extravagant and wild notions about the original of the soul of man; a certain mark and argument of its apostasy from God. * " Solinus writes of one, who by a wound in the hinder " part of his head, fell into such a degree of ignorance and obli- " vion, that he forgot his own name, and could not tell whether " he had any name at all." But oh! what a stunning blow did man receive by the fall, that he should forget the very Author of his being, and rather claim alliance, and derive the being of his soul from any thing than God; though it bears the very marks and characters of its divine Author and Father upon it! The principal errors about the origin of the soul (for that wild notion of Epicurus hath been laid so flat by the pens of many learned men, that it is a vanity to strike one blow more at it) may be reduced to these three heads.

(1.) Some affirm it to be by way of † *traduction*, or natural generation from the parents to the child. This opinion is very ancient; Tertullian, and divers of the Western Fathers, closed with it, as judging it the best expedient to solve the difficulties of the soul's taint and defilement with original sin. But antiquity is no passport for errors. The grey hairs of opinion, as one well notes, are then honourable, when they are found in the way of truth. Doctor Brown ‡ tells us, " He should rather incline to the crea- " tion, than the traduction of the soul, though either opinion,

---

* *Solinus refert de quodam, quod accepto vulnere in occipitio, ad tantam devenit ignoran-tiam, ut nesciret se habuisse nomen.* Augustodun. de Philosoph. Mundi, lib iv. c. 24.

† *Datur agens physicum quod aliud esse non potest quam parens; qui ei seminis animam e materiæ sinu eliciat. i. e.* There is a physical agent which can be no other than the parent, who produces the soul of the seed from the bosom of matter.

‡ *Religio Medici,* Sect. 36.

" (saith he) will consist well enough with religion, did not one ob-
" jection haunt him, and this is a conclusion from the equivocal
" and monstrous productions by unnatural copulation, as of a man
" and beast: for, if the soul of man, saith he, be not transmitted
" and transfused in the seed, why are not these productions mere-
" ly beasts, but have also an impression and tincture of reason in
" as high a measure as it can evidence itself in those improper or-
" gans?"

Which way the doctor's judgment had inclined in this controversy, had been of no great consideration to the determination of
it; though it is a pity we should lose his consent and company, for
the sake of such a beastly objection as this, which haunts his mind:
for if there be any such creatures that seem to have a tincture of
reason, it is but a tincture, and a seeming, not a real tincture neither, which many other brutes have.

The doctor is too well acquainted with philosophy, and a man
of too much reason to allow himself to think that such a production as he speaks of hath two natures and essential forms in one
body, as of a man and a horse. He knows that every entity hath
but one special essence, and can have no more, except he will place
one and the same thing under divers species in the predicament of
substance. And as there cannot be two distinct forms, so neither
can there be a mixture of them in the *Centaur* or monstrous birth:
for, *ex duobus entibus per se, non fit unum ens per se.* But he confesseth this *objection* was bred among the weeds and tares of his own
brain, (a rank soil no doubt) and I am pretty confident he had
weeded it out in his latter years; for I find this notion of the *Cen-
taurs*, (that is, half horse, half man), put into its proper place among
his vulgar errors, B. 1. chap. 4. And so I suppose that rub being
out of the way, he returned again to us.

(2.) A second opinion was, That they were procreated by angels: and that which gave the ground, such as it is, to this opinion
or fancy, is the similitude or resemblance which is found betwixt
angels and the souls of men. But this fancy needs not any industry
to overthrow it; for though it be certain there is a similitude
and resemblance * betwixt angels and souls, both being immaterial
and spiritual substances, yet angels neither propagate by generation,
nor is it in their power to create the least fly or worm in the world,
much less the soul of man, the highest and noblest, and most excellent being. Great power they have, but no creating power, that

---

* That is perfect which produces some other thing like itself: but substances that
are immaterial, are far more perfect than those which are material; therefore, if these
last make others like in kind to themselves, much more must angels be able to procreate some other incorporeal substances of an inferior nature, namely, the human soul.
D. Dionys. c. 4. de divinis nominibus.

is God's incommunicable property; and procreate our souls they did not, for though they are spirits, yet spirits of another species.

(3.) A third sort there are, who deny that souls are created substances, and proceeded from God; but affirm withal, that he created them *simul, et semel,* together and at once, as the angels were, and not one by one, as men are born into the world. " Of this " opinion was Plato, who thought all human souls to be created " together before their bodies, and placed in some glorious and suit- " able mansions, as the stars; till, at last, growing weary of hea- " venly, and falling in love with earthly things, for a punishment of " that crime, they were cast into bodies, as into so many prisons *." Origen sucked in this notion of the pre-existence of souls: and upon this supposition it was that Porphyry tells us, in the life of Plotinus, he blushed as often as he thought of his being in a body, as a man that lived in reputation and honour, blushes when he is lodged in a prison. The ground on which the Stoics bottomed their opinion was, the great dignity and excellency of the soul, which inclined them to think they had never been degraded and abased, as they are by dwelling in such vile bodies, but for their faults; and that it was for some former sins of theirs, that they slid down into gross matter, and were caught into a vital union with it; whereas, had they not sinned, they had lived in celestial and splendid habitations, more suitable to their dignity.

But this is a pure creature of fancy; for, (1.) No soul in the world is conscious to itself, of such a pre-existence, nor can remember when it was owner of any other habitation than that it now dwells in. (2.) Nor doth the scripture give us the least hint of any such thing. Some indeed would catch hold of that expression, Gen. ii. 2. " God rested the seventh day from all the works " which he had made;" and it is true, he did so, the work of creation was finished and sealed up, as to any new species or kinds of creatures to be created; no other sort of souls will be created, than that which was at first: but yet God still creates individual souls, *(My Father worketh hitherto and I work)* of the same kind and nature with Adam's soul. And, (3.) For their detrusion into these bodies as a punishment of their sins in the former state; if we speak of sin in *individuals,* or particular persons, the scripture mentions none, either original or actual, defiling any soul in any other way but by its union with the body. Pre-existence therefore is but a dream.

But to me it is clear, that the soul receives not its beginning by

---

* *Plato in Timæo finxit Deum omnes animas humanas ante corpora simul creasse, et incomparibus stellis constituisse; tum eas cœlestium rerum tædio, et terrenarum amore captas, ut tanti sceleris pœnas luerent, in corpora tanquam in carcerem conjectas.*

traduction or generation; for that which is generable, is also corruptible; but the spiritual, immortal soul (as it hath been proved to be) is not subject to corruption. Nor is it imaginable how a soul should be produced out of matter, which is not endued with reason: or, how a bodily substance can impart that to another, which it hath not in-itself. If it be said, the soul of the child proceeds from the souls of the parents, that cannot be; for spiritual substances are impartible, and nothing can be discinded from them. " * And it is absurd to think the soul of Adam should spring from " one original, and the souls of his offspring from another, whilst " both his and theirs are of one and the same nature and species." To all which let me add, That as the assertion of their creation is most reasonable, so it is most scriptural. It is reasonable to think and say, " † That no active power can act beyond, or above the " proper sphere of its activity and ability." But if the soul be elicited out of the power of matter, here would be an effect produced abundantly more noble and excellent than its cause. And as it is most reasonable, so it is most scriptural. To this purpose diverse testimonies of scripture are cited and produced by our divines, among which we may single out these four, which are of special remark and use; Heb. xii. 9. " Furthermore, we had " fathers of our flesh which corrected us, and we gave them re- " verence; shall we not much rather be in subjection to [the Fa- " ther of spirits] and live?" Here God is called the Father of spirits, or of souls, and that in an emphatical *antithesis*, or contradistinction to our natural fathers, who are called the fathers of our flesh, or bodies only. The true scope and sense of this text, is, with great judgment and clearness, given us by that learned and judicious divine, Mr. Pemble ‡, in these words; " [Nothing " is more plain and emphatical than this antithesis; We receive " our flesh and body from our parents, but our souls from God: " if then we patiently bear the chastisements of our parents, who " are the authors of the vilest part, and have the least right or " power over us; with how much more equal a mind should we " bear his chastisements, who hath the supreme right to us, as he " is the Father and only giver of that which is most excellent in

---

* *Absurdum est aliunde esse animam nostram, aliunde animam Adæ : cum omnes sunt ejusdem speciei.* Zanch.

† *Nulla virtus activa agit ultra suum genus, sed anima intellectiva excedit totum genus, corporeæ naturæ, cum sit substantia spiritualis, &c.* Conimbr.

‡ Pemble de origine animæ, p. 56. *Nihil apertius et εμφατιχοτερον ista Antithesi, carnem corpusque a parentibus, animas a Deo accipimus ; quod si vilioris partis authores, et qui in nos minus juris habent, patienter castigantes ferimus ; quanto æquiore animo feremus eum qui supremum in nos jus obtinet, uptote partis, quæ in nobis est præstantissima, unicus Dator Conditorque.*

" us, viz. our souls or spirits ?"] Here it appears evident, that our souls flow not to us in the material channel of fleshly generation or descent, as our bodies do, but immediately from God, their proper Father, in the way of creation. Yet he begets them not out of his own essence or substance, as Christ, his natural Son, is begotten, but, εκ μη οντων, out of nothing that had been before, as Theodoret well expresseth it. Agreeable hereunto is that place also in Zech. xii. 1. " The Lord which stretcheth forth the hea-
" vens, and layeth the foundations of the earth, and formeth the
" spirit of man within him:" " * Where the forming of the
" spirit, or soul of man, is associated with these two other glori-
" ous effects of God's creating power, namely, the expansion of
" the heavens, and laying the foundations of the earth:" all three
are here equally assumed by the Lord, as his remarkable and glorious works of creation. He that created the one, did as much create the other.

Now the two former we find frequently instanced in scripture, as the effects of his creating power, or works implying the Almighty power of God; and therefore are presented as strong props to our faith, when it is weak and staggering for want of visible matter of encouragement, Isa. xl. 22. and xlii. 5. Jer. x. 12. Job ix. 8. Psal. civ. 2. q. d. Are my people in captivity, and their faith nonplussed and at a loss, because there is nothing in sight that hath a tendency to their deliverance, no prepared matter for their salvation? Why, let them consider who it was that created the heavens and the earth, yea, and their souls also, which are so perplexed with doubts, out of nothing; the same God that did this, can also create deliverance for his people, though there be no pre-existent matter to work it out of.

Add to this that excellent place of † Solomon, in Eccl. xii. 7. " Then shall the dust return to the earth, as it was; and the spi-
" rit to God who gave it." Where he shews us what becomes of man, and how each part, of which he consists, is bestowed, and disposed of after his dissolution by death, and thus he states it: The two constitutive parts of man are a soul and a body: these two parts have two distinct originals: the body, as to its material cause, is dust; the soul, in its nature, is a spirit, and as to its origin, it

---

* *Testimonium satis clarum, quo docemur, pari passu hæc tria ambulare; expansionem cœli, fundationem cerræ, et formotionem animæ rationalis.*

† Solomon resolves both the parts of man into their first principles; as therefore he resolves the body into the dust, whence it was taken; so also, if the soul had been made of an heavenly substance, or, (as Plato says) of the soul of the world, Solomon would have resolved the soul into it; but when he says simply of the soul, that it returns to God who gave it, he teaches us, That it was created of nothing, into which it could not be resolved. *Zanch.*

proceed from the Father of spirits; it is his own creature, in an immediate way. *He gave it :* he gave it the being it hath by creation, and gave it to us, i. e. to our bodies by inspiration. Now *qualis Genesis, talis Analysis.* When death dissolves the union which is betwixt them, each part returns to that from whence it came, dust to dust, and the spirit to God that gave it. The body is expressed by its material cause, dust; the soul only by its efficient cause, as the gift of God ; because it had no material cause at all, nor was made out of any pre-existent matter, as the body was. And therefore Solomon here speaks of God, as if he had only to do with the soul, leaving the body to its material and instrumental causes, with which he concurs by a general influence. It is God, not man alone, or God by man, that hath given us these bodies; but it is not man, but God alone, who hath given us these souls. He therefore passeth by the body, and speaks of the soul as the gift of God ; because that part of man, and that only, flows immediately from God, and at death, returns to him that gave it. All these expressions, *The Father of spirits,* the *former of the spirit of man,* the *giver of the spirit:* how agreeable are they to each other, and all of them to the point under hand, that the soul flows from God by immediate creation ? You see it hath no principle out of which, according to the order of nature, it did arise, as the body had, and therefore it hath no principle into which, according to the order of nature, it can be returned, as the body hath; but returns to God, its efficient cause: if reconciled, to a Father, not only by creation, but adoption ; if unreconciled, as a creature guilty of unnatural rebellion against the God that formed it, to be judged.

II. God created and infused it into the body, with an inherent inclination and affection to it. The * nature of the soul and body is vastly different, there is no affinity or similitude betwixt them; but it is in this case as in that of marriage. Two persons of vastly different educations, constitutions, and inclinations, coming under God's ordinance, into the nearest relation to each other, find their affections knit and endeared by their relation to a degree beyond that which results from the union of blood: So it is here. Whence this affection arises, in what acts it is discovered, and for what reason implanted, will be at large discovered in a distinct branch of the following discourse, to which it is assigned. Mean while, I find myself concerned to vindicate what hath been here asserted

---

* The body is necessary to the soul, which is the perfection of the organical body, for it is not a separate form, i. e. a form properly so called, therefore it requires matter, in so much that the soul, when separate from the body, still retains its relation and inclination to it, which is followed with the resurrection of the body. *Cameron prælect. in Mat. p.* 124.

from the arguments which are urged against the immediate creation
and infusion of the soul, and in the defence of the opinion of its
traduction from the parents. To conceal, or dissemble these arguments and objections, would be but a betraying of the truth I have
here asserted, and give occasion for some jealousy, that they are
unanswerable. To come then to an issue ; and first,

Objec. 1. It is urged, that it is manifest in itself, and generally
yielded, that the souls of all other creatures come by generation,
and therefore it is probable the human souls flow in the same
channel also.

Solut. There is a specific difference betwixt rational souls, and
the souls of all other creatures, and therefore no force at all in the
consequence. A material form may rise out of matter ; but a
spiritual, rational being (as the soul of man is) cannot so rise, being
much more noble and excellent than matter is.

What animal is there in the world, out of whose soul the acts
of reason spring and flow, as they do out of human souls ? Are
they capable of inventing, (or which is much less) of learning the
arts and sciences ? Can they correct their senses, and demonstrate
a star to be far greater than the whole earth, which to the eye
seems no bigger than the rowel of a spur ? Do they foreknow the
positions and combination of the planets, and the eclipses of the
sun and moon many years before they suffer them ? And if they
cannot perform these acts of reason, as it is sure they cannot, how
much less can they know, fear, love, or delight in God, and long
for the enjoyments of him ! These things do plainly evince human
souls to be of another *species*, and therefore of a higher original
than the souls of brutes. If all have one common nature and
original, why are they not all capable of performing the same
rational and religious acts ?

Obj. 2. But though it should be granted, that the soul of the
first man was by immediate creation and inspiration of God ; yet
it follows not, that the souls of all his posterity must be so too. God
might create him with a power of begetting other souls after his
own image. The first tree was created with its seed in itself to propagate its kind, and so might the first man.

Sol. 1. Trees, animals, and such-like, were not created immediately out of nothing, as the soul of man was ; but the earth
was the pre-existent matter out of which they were produced by
the word of God's blessing and power ; but man's soul was immediately breathed into him by God, and had no pre-existent
matter at all : And besides, all human souls being of one *species*,
have therefore one and the same original : The soul of the poorest
child is of equal dignity with the soul of Adam. And if we consult Job xxxiii. 4. we shall find Elihu giving us there the same

account, and almost in the same words, of the original of his soul that Moses in my text gives us of the original of Adam's soul : "The Spirit of God hath formed me, and the breath of the Al- "mighty hath given me life."

Sol. 2. But it is evident, souls spring not from the parent, as one plant, or an animal doth from another; for they have their seed in themselves, apt and proper to produce their kind; but the seed of souls is not to be found in man : It is not to be found in his body; for then (as was said before) a spiritual and nobler essence must be produced out of a material and baser matter, (*i. e.*) the matter must give to the soul that which it hath not in itself; nor is it to be found in his soul; for the soul being a pure, simple, and invisible being, can suffer nothing to be descinded from it, towards the production of another soul. A spirit, as the soul is, is *substantia, simplex et impartibilis;* an uncompounded, and indiscernible, or im-partible being. Nor can it spring partly from the body, and partly from the soul, as from con-causes; for then it should be partly corporeal, and partly incorporeal, as its causes are. "So that "there is no matter, seed, or principles of souls found in man; and "to be sure (as * Baronius strongly argues) he cannot produce a "soul without pre-existent matter; for that were to make him "omnipotent, and assign a creating power to a creature." Besides, that which is generable, is also corruptible, as we see trees animals, &c. which are produced that way, to be; but the soul is not corruptible, as hath in part been already proved, and more fully, in the following discourse. So that Adam's soul, and the souls of his posterity spring not from each other, but all from God by creation.

Obj. 3. If the soul be created and infused immediately by God, either it comes out of his hands pure, or impure; if pure, how comes it to be defiled and tainted with sin? If impure, how do we free God from being the author of sin?

Sol. If the question be, whether souls be pure or impure, as soon as they are united with their bodies? The answer is, they are impure, and tainted as soon as united : For the union constitutes a child of Adam, and consequently a sinful impure creature. But if it respect the condition and state in which God created them, I answer with Baronius †. "They are created neither morally pure,

---

* *Pater neque producit animam filii ex aliqua re prœ-existente; neque producit cam ex nulla re prœ existente : hoc enim est creare; ergo nullo modo eam producit.* Baronii dis-sert, secunda de Origine Animæ, p. 120.

† *Animæ nostræ a Deo creante neque accipiunt puritatem, seu justitiam; neq; impurita-tem et propensionem ad malum : Sed tantum essentiam spiritualim, et proprietates ab essentia dimanantes.* Baroni exercit. p. 103.

" nor impure; they receive neither purity nor impurity from him,
" but only their naked essence, and the natural powers and pro-
" perties flowing therefrom." He inspires not any impurity into
them; for he cannot be the author of sin, who is the revenger of
it.   Nor doth he create them in their original purity and rectitude;
for the sin of Adam lost that, and God justly withholds it from his
posterity.   Who wonders (saith ‡ one) to see the children, the
palaces and gardens of a traitor to droop and decay, and the arms
of his house, and the badge of his nobility, to be defaced and reversed? That which is abused by man to the dishonour of God,
may justly be destroyed (I add in this case, or *with-held*) by God to
the detriment of man.   Adam voluntarily and actually deprived
himself, and meritoriously deprived all his posterity of that original
righteousness and purity in which he was created. As an holy God,
he cannot inspire any impurity, and as a just and righteous God, he
may, and doth with-hold, or create them void and destitute of that
holiness, and righteousness which was once their yea, of happiness
and glory.

Obj. 4. But how come they then to be defiled and tainted with
original sin? It is confessed God did not make them impure, and
the body cannot; for being matter, it cannot act upon a spirit;
itself it is a dead lump, and cannot act at all.

Sol. What if this be one of those mysteries reserved for the world
to come, about which we cannot in this state solve every difficulty
that may be moved? Must we therefore deny its divine original?
What if I cannot understand some mysteries, or answer some
questions about the *hypostatical union* of the two natures, in the
wonderful person of our *Emmanuel?* Must I therefore question
whether he be Θεανθρωπος, God-man? We must remain ignorant of
some things about our souls, till we come into the condition of the
spirits of just men made perfect ‖. Mean time, I think it much
more our concernment to study how we may get sin out of our souls,
than to puzzle our brains to find how it came into them.

But that the *objector* may not take this for an handsome slide, or
go-by to this great objection, I return to it, in a few particulars.

(1.) That I think not original sin follows either part singly; it
comes in neither by the soul alone, nor by the body alone, apart
from the soul; but upon the union and conjunction of both in one
person.   It is the union of these two which constitutes a child of
Adam, and as such only we are capable of being infected with his
sin.

---

‡ Jenkins on Jude, Vol. i. p. 5, 9.
‖ Man since the fall, being less than himself, understands not himself; nor will he
fully, till he be fully restored to himself in glory. *Norton's Orth. Evang. p.* 237.

(2.) * And whereas it is so confidently asserted in the objection, that sin cannot come into the soul by, or from the body, because it being matter, cannot act upon a spirit; I say, this is *gratis dictum*, easily spoken, but difficultly proved. Cannot the body act upon, or influence the soul? Pray then, how comes it to pass that so many souls become foolish, forgetful, injudicious, &c. by their union with ill-disposed bodies? Nothing is more sensible, plain, and evident, than that there is a reciprocal communication betwixt the soul and body. The body doth as really (though we know not how) affect the soul with its dispositions, as the soul influences it with life and motion. The more excellent any form is, the more intimate is its union and conjunction with the matter. The soul of man hath therefore a more intimate and perfect union with the body, than light hath with the air, which is made, by some, to be the emblem and similitude to shadow forth this union. But the union betwixt them is too intimate to be conceived by the help of any such similitudes. That this infection is by way of *physical agency*, as a rusty scabbard infects and defiles a bright sword when sheathed therein, I will not confidently affirm as some do. It may be by way of *natural concomitancy*, as Estius will have it; or to speak, as Dr. Reynolds (modestly, and as becomes men that are conscious of darkness and weakness) by way of ineffable resultancy and emanation.

(3.) Upon the whole, original sin consists in two things, *viz.*

1. In the privation of that original rectitude which ought to be in us.

2. In that habitual concupiscence which carrieth nature to inordinate motions.

This privation and inordinate inclination, make up that original corruption, the rise whereof we are searching for: And to bring us as near as we can come, without a daring intrusion into unrevealed secrets, our solid *divines* proceed by these steps, in answering this objection.

(1.) If it be demanded how it comes to pass that an *infant* becomes guilty of Adam's sin; The answer is, because he is a child of Adam by natural generation.

(2.) But why is he deprived of that original rectitude in which Adam was created? They answer, because Adam lost it by his sin,

---

* The soul (say some) in the moment of its creation and infusion by God, being united with the body by the plastic and formative virtue of the parental seed: the parent may be truly said to generate the man, though he do not produce the form: Because proper generation consists in the union, and not in the production of parts So that original sin is not propagated from body to body, nor yet from soul to soul but from man to man.

and therefore could not transmit what he had lost to his posterity.

(3.) But how comes he to be inclined to that which is evil? Their answer is, because he wants that original rectitude: For whosoever wants original rectitude, naturally inclines to that which is evil. And so the propension of nature to that which is evil, seems to be by way of concomitancy with the defect or want of original righteousness.

And thus I have given some account of the nature and original of the soul of man: though alas! my dim eyes see but little of its excellency and glory. Yet, by what hath been said, it appears the master-piece of all God's work of creation, in this lower world.

But because I suspect the description I have given of it will be obscure and cloudy to vulgar readers, of a plain and low capacity, by reason of divers *philosophical* terms which I have been forced to make use of; and reckoning myself a debtor to the weak and unlearned, as well as others, I will endeavour to strip this description of the soul, for their sakes, out of those artificial terms which darken it to them, and present it once more in the most plain and intelligible *epitome* I am capable to give it in; that so the weaker understanding may be able to form a true notion of the nature and original of the soul, in this manner.

The soul of mine is a true and real being; not a fancy, conceit, a very nothing. It hath a proper and true being in itself, whether I conceit it or not. Nor indeed can I conceive of it, but by it. It is not such a thing as whiteness is in snow, a mere accident, which depends upon the snow in which it is for the being it hath, and must perish as soon as the snow is dissolved: My soul doth not so much depend upon my body, or any other fellow-creature for its being; but is as truly a substance as my body is, though not of so gross and material a kind and nature. My soul can, and will subsist and remain what it is, when my body is separated from it; but my body cannot subsist and remain what it now is, when my soul is separated from it: So that I find my soul to be the most substantial and noble part of me; it is not my body, but my soul which makes me a man. And if this depart, all the rest of me is but a dead log, a lump of inanimate clay, a heap of vile dust and corruption. From this independent substance it hath in itself, and the dependence its properties and affections have upon it, I truly apprehend and call it a *substance*.

But yet, when I call it a substance, I must not conceive of it as a gross material, palpable substance, such as my body is, which I can see and feel: No, there are *spiritual substances*, as well as gross, visible, *material substances*. An angel is a spiritual *substance*, a real creature, and yet imperceptible by my sight or touch, such a substance is my soul. Spiritual substances are as real, and much more excellent than bodily substances are. I can neither see, hear, nor feel it, but I both see, hear, and feel by it.

My soul is also a vital substance. It is a principle of life to my body: It hath a life in itself, and quickens my body therewith. My soul is the spring of all the actions and motions of life which I perform. It hath been an error taken in from my childhood, that sense is performed in the outward organ, or members of my body ; as touching in the hand, seeing in the eye, hearing in the ear, &c. in them, I say, and not only by them, as if nothing were required to make sense, but an *object* and an *organ*. No, no, it is not my eye that seeth, nor my ear that heareth, nor my hand that toucheth, but my soul, in and by them, performs all this. Let but an *apoplex* hinder the operations of my soul in the brain, and of how little use are my eyes, ears, hands, or feet to me? My life is originally in my soul, and secondarily by way of communication in my body. So that I find my soul to be a *vital*, as well as a *spiritual substance*.

And being both a vital and spiritual substance, I must needs conclude it to be an immortal substance. For in such a pure, spiritual nature as my soul is, there can be found no seeds or principles of death. Where there is no composition, there will be no dissolution. My body indeed having so many jarring humours, mixed elements, and contrary qualities in it, must needs fall and die at last : but my soul was formed for immortality, by the simplicity and spirituality of its nature. No sword can pierce it from without, nor opposition can destroy it from within; man cannot, and God will not.

And being an immortal spirit, fitted and framed to live for ever, I find that God hath, answerably, endued and furnished it with an *understanding*, *will*, and *affections*, whereby it is capable of being wrought upon by the Spirit in the way of grace and sanctification in this world in order to the enjoyment of God, its chief happiness in the world to come.

By this its *understanding*, I am distinguished from, and advanced above all other creatures in this world. I can apprehend, distinguish, and judge of all other intelligible beings. By my *understanding* I discern truth from falsehood, good from evil ; it shews me what is fit for me to chuse, and what to refuse.

To this faculty or power of *understanding*, my thoughts and conscience do belong; the former to my *speculative*, the latter to my *practical understanding*. My thoughts are all formed in my mind or understanding in innumerable multitudes and variety. By it I can think of things present, or absent; visible, or invisible ; of God, or myself ; of this world, or the world to come.

To my *understanding* also belongs by *conscience*, a noble, divine, and awful power: By which I summon and judge myself, as at a solemn *tribunal;* bind and lose, condemn and acquit myself and actions, but still with an eye and respect to the judgment of God. Hence are my best comforts, and worst terrors.

This *understanding* of mine is the director and guide of my *will*, as the *counsellor;* and my will is as the *prince:* It freely chuseth and refuseth, as my understanding directs and suggests to it. The members of my body, and the passions of my soul, are under its dominion: The former are under its absolute command, the latter under its suasions and insinuations, though not absolutely, yet always with effect and success.

And both my *understanding* and *will* I find to have great influence upon my *affections.*

These passions and *affections* of my soul are of great use and dignity. I find them as manifold as there are considerations of good and evil. They are the strong and sensible motions of my soul, according to my apprehensions of good and evil. By them by soul is capable of union with the highest good. By love and delight I am capable of enjoying God, and resting in him as the centre of my soul. This noble *understanding, thoughts, conscience, will, passions,* and *affections,* are the principal faculties, acts, and powers of this my high and heaven-born soul. And being thus richly endowed and furnished,

I find it could never rise out of matter, or come into my body by way of generation; the souls of brutes, that rise that way, are destitute of understanding, reason, conscience, and such other excellent faculties and powers as I find in my own soul. They cannot know, or love, or delight in God, or set their affections on things spiritual, invisible, and eternal as my soul is capable to do; it was therefore created and infused immediately into this body of mine by the Father of spirits, and that with a strong inclination, and tender affection to my flesh, without which it would be remiss and careless in performing its several duties and offices to it, during the time of its abode therein.

Fearfully and wonderfully, therefore, am I made, and designed for nobler ends and uses, than for a few days to eat, and drink, and sleep, and talk, and die. My soul is of more value than ten thousand worlds. *What shall a man give in exchange for his soul?*

USE.

From the several parts and branches of this description of the soul, we may gather the choice fruits which naturally grow upon them, in the following *inferences* and deduction of truth and duty. For we may say of them all what the *historian* doth of Palestine, that there is *nihil infructuosum, nihil sterile,* no branch or shrub is barren, or unfruitful. Let us then search it branch by branch: and,

Inf. 1. From the substantial nature of the soul, which we have proved to be a being distinct from the body, and subsisting by itself, we are informed, *That great is the difference betwixt the death of a man, and the death of all other creatures in the world.* Their souls depend on, and perish with their bodies; but ours neither result from them, nor perish with them *. My body is not a body, when my soul hath forsaken it; but my soul will remain a soul when this body is crumbled into dust. Men may live like beasts, a mere sensual life; yea, in some sense, they may die like beasts, a stupid death; but in this there will be found a vast difference: Death kills both parts of the beasts, destroys the matter and form; it toucheth only one part of man; it destroyeth the body, and only *dislodgeth* the soul, but cannot *destroy* it.

In some things Solomon shews the agreement betwixt our death and theirs, Eccl. iii. 19, 20, 21. " That which befalleth the sons " of men, befalleth the beasts; even one thing befalleth them: " as the one dieth, so dieth the other; all go to one place; all " are of the dust, and all turn to dust again." We breathe the same common air they breathe; we feel the same pains of death they feel; our bodies are resolved into the same earth theirs are. Oh! but in this is the difference, *The spirit of man goeth upward, and the spirit of a beast goeth downward to the earth.* Their spirits go two ways at their dissolution; the one to the earth, and the other to God that gave it; as he speaks, chap. xii. 7. Though our dissolution and expiration have some agreement, yet great is the odds in the consequences of death to the one and the other. They have no pleasures nor pains besides those they enjoy or feel now; but so have we, and those eternal, or unspeakable too. The soul of man, like the bird in the shell, is still growing or ripening in sin or grace, till at last the shell breaks by death, and the soul flies away to the place it is prepared for, and where it must abide for ever. The body, which is but its shell, perisheth; but the soul lives when it is fallen away †.

How doth this consideration expose and aggravate the folly and madness of this sensual world, who herd themselves with beasts, though they have souls so near akin to angels! The princes and nobles of the world abhor to associate themselves with *mechanics*

---

* So great a prerogative manifestly proves that the soul, which is the governing part, is not material and mortal, but of a superior and more excellent nature, greatly different from the condition of other souls. *Conimb. Disp. on separate souls, p.* 584. .

† They grow up together, and are again separated, and both return to whence they came; the earth downward, and the spirit upward. *Epicha.*

in their shops, or take a place among the sottish rabble upon an ale-bench; they know and keep their distance and *decorum*, as still carrying with them a sense of honour, and abhorring to act beneath it: But we equalize our high and noble souls in the manner of life with the beasts that perish. Our tables differ little from the *crib* at which they feed; or our houses from the *stalls* and *stables* in which they lie down to rest, in respect of any divine worship or heavenly communication that is to be heard there. Happy had it been for such men (if so they live and die) that their souls had been of no higher extraction, or larger capacity, or longer duration than that of a beast: for then, as their comforts, so also their miseries had ended at death. And such they will one day wish they had been.

A separate soul immediately capable of blessedness.

Inf. 2. The soul of man being substance, and not depending in its being on the body or any other fellow-creature, *There can be no reason, on the soul's account, why its blessedness should be delayed till the resurrection of the body.*

It is a great mistake (and it is well it is so) that the soul is capable only of social glory, or a blessedness in partnership with the body: and that it can neither exert its own powers, nor enjoy its own happiness in the absence of the body. The opinion of a sleeping interval took its rise from this error (as it is usual for one mistake to beget another;) they conceived the soul to be so dependent on the body, at least in all its operations, that when death rends it from the body, it must needs be left in a swoon or sleep, unable to exert its proper powers, or enjoy that felicity which we ascribe to it in its state of separation.

But certainly its substantial nature being considered, it will be found, that what perfection soever the body receives from the soul, and how necessary soever its dependence upon it is *, the soul receives not its perfection from the body, nor doth it necessarily depend on it, in its principal operations; but it can live and act out of a body as well as in it. Yea, I doubt not but it enjoys itself in a much more sweet and perfect liberty than ever it did, or could, whilst it was clogged and fettered with a body of flesh. " Doubtless, (saith † Tertullian) when it is separated, and as it " were strained by death, it comes out of darkness into its own

---

* The rational soul receives no perfection from matter, which it could not receive without it. *Conimbr. disp.* 2. *art* 3.

† *Procul dubio cum vi mortis exprimitur de concretione carnis, et ipsa expressione colatur, certo de oppanso corpore erumpit in aportum, ad meram et puram, et suam lucem, statim semetipsam in expeditione substantiæ recognoscit, ut de somno emergens ab imaginibus ad veritates.* Tertul. in lib. de Anima.

" pure, perfect light, and quickly finds itself a substantial being,
" able to act freely in that light." Before the eyes of the dead
body are closed, I doubt not, but the believing soul, with open
eyes, beholdeth the face of Jesus Christ, Luke xxiii. 43. Phil. i.
23. But this will also be further spoken to hereafter.

Inf. 3. The souls of men being created immediately out of nothing, and not seminally traduced; it follows, *That all souls by
nature are of equal value and dignity ; one soul is not more excellent, honourable, or precious than another : but all by nature equally
precious.*

The soul of the poorest beggar that cries at the door for a crust,
is, in its own nature, of equal dignity and value with the soul of
the most glorious monarch that sits upon the throne. And this appears to be so,

1. Because all souls flow out of one and the same fountain, viz.
the creating power of God. They were not made of better or
worse, finer or coarser matter, but εκ μη οντων, out of nothing at
all. The same Almighty Power was put forth to the forming of
one, as of another. *All souls are mine*, saith he that created them,
Ezek. xviii. 4. the soul of the child as well as of the father, the
soul of the beggar as well as of the king; those that had no pre-
existent matter, but received their beings from the same efficient
cause, must needs be equal in their orignal nature and value. The
bodies of men, which are formed out of matter, do greatly differ
from one another; some are moulded (as we say) *e meliori luto*, out
of better and finer clay ; some are more exact, elegant, vigorous,
and beautiful than others; but souls, having no matter of which
they consist, are not so differenced.

2. All souls are created with a capacity of enjoying the infinite
and blessed God. They need no other powers, faculties, or capacities than they are by nature endued with (if these be sanctified
and devoted to God) to make them equally happy and blessed with
them that are now before the throne of God in heaven, and with
unspeakable delight and joy behold his blessed face. We pass
through the fields, and take up an egg which lies under a clod,
and see nothing in it but a little squalid matter ; yea, but in that
egg is seminally and potentially contained such a melodious lark as,
it may be, at the same time we see mounting heavenward, and
singing delicious notes above. So it is here, these poor despised
souls, that are now lodged in crazy, despicable bodies on the earth,
have, in their natures, a capacity for the same employments and
enjoyments with those in heaven. They have no higher original
than these have, and these have the same capacity and ability with
them. They are beings improveable by grace, to the highest per-

fections attainable by any creature. If thou be never so mean, base, and despicable a creature in other respects, yet thou hast a soul, which hath the same alliance to the Father of spirits, the same capacity to enjoy him in glory, that the most excellent and renowned saints ever had.

3. All souls are rated and valued in God's book, and account, at one and the same price; and therefore by nature are of equal worth and dignity. Under the law, the rich and the poor were to give the same ransom, Exod. xxx. 15. " The rich shall not give " more, and the poor shall not give less than half a shekel." The redemption of souls, by the blood of Christ, costs one and the same price. The poorest and the most despised soul that believes in Jesus, is as much indebted to him for the ransom of his soul, as the greatest and most illustrious person in the world. Moses, Abraham, Paul, &c. did not cost Christ any thing more than poor Lazarus, or the meanest among all the saints did. " The righte- " ousness of Christ is unto all, and upon all that believe, for there " is no difference," Rom. iii. 22.

But yet we must not understand this *parity* of human souls universally, or in all respects. Though being of one *species* or common nature, they are all equal, and those of them that are purchased by the blood of Christ are all purchased at one rate; yet there are divers other respects and considerations, wherein there are remarkable differences betwixt soul and soul. As, (1.) Some souls are much better lodged and accommodated in their bodies than others are, though none dwell at perfect rest and ease. God hath lodged some souls in strong, vigorous, comely bodies; others in feeble, crazy, deformed, and uncomfortable ones. The historian saith of Galba, *Anima Galæ male habitat;* the soul of Galba dwelt in an ill body. And a much better man than Galba was as ill accommodated. John wishes in behalf of his beloved Gaius, that his body might but prosper as his soul did, Epistle iii. ver. 2. Timothy had his often infirmities. Indeed the world is full of instances and examples of this kind. * If some souls had the advantages of such bodies as others have, who make little or very bad use of them; oh, what service would they do for God! (2.) There is a remarkable difference also betwixt soul, and soul, in respect of natural gifts and abilities of mind. Some have great advantages above others in this respect. The natural spirits and organs of the body being more brisk and apt, the soul is more vegete, vigorous, and able to exert itself in its functions and operations. How clear, nimble, and firm, are the apprehensions, fancies, and

---

* Tostatus, bishop of Abulam, had so strong and firm a constitution to endure severe studies, that he is said *ænea intestina habuisse,* to have had a body of brass.

memories of some souls beyond others! What a prodigy of memory, fancy, and judgment, was father Paul the Venetian! and Suarez, of whom Strada saith, "Such was the strength of his parts, that he "had all St. Augustine's works (the most copious and various of all "the fathers) as it were by heart, *so that I have seen him*, saith he "*, *readily pointing with the finger to any place or page he disputed "of.*" Our Dr. Reynolds excelled this way, to the astonishment of all that knew him, so that he was a *living library*, a third *university*. But above all, the character given by Vives of Budaeus is amazing, *That there was nothing written in* Greek *or* Latin, *which he had not turned over and examined ; that both languages were alike to him, speaking either with more facility than he did the* French, *his mother tongue ; and all by the penetrating force of his own natural parts, without a tutor ; "so that* † France *never brought forth a man of* "*sharper wit, more piercing judgment, exact diligence, and greater* "*learning, nor, in his time,* Italy *itself.*" Fœlix et fœcundum ingenium, quod in se uno invenit, et doctorem, et discipulum! *A happy and fruitful wit, which in itself found both a master and a scholar!* And yet Pasquier relates what is much more admirable of a young man, who came to *Paris*, in the 20th year of his age, and in the year 1445, shewed himself so excellent and exact in all the arts, sciences, and languages, that if a man of an ordinary good wit, and sound constitution, should live an hundred years, and during that time study incessantly, without eating, drinking, sleeping, or any recreation, he could hardly attain to that perfection. (3.) And yet a far greater difference is made betwixt one soul and another, by the sanctifying work of the Spirit of God. This makes yet a greater disparity; for it alters and new-moulds the frame and temper of the soul, and restores the lost image of God to it; by reason whereof the *righteous* is truly said to be "more excellent "than his neighbour," Prov. xii. 26. This ennobles the soul, and stamps the highest dignity and glory upon it, that it is capable of in this world. It is true, it hath naturally an excellency and perpetuity in it above other beings; as *cedar* hath not only a beauty and fragrancy, but a soundness and durability far beyond other trees of the wood: but when it comes under the sanctification of the Spirit, then it is as *cedar* over-laid with gold. (4.) Lastly, a wonderful difference will be made betwixt one soul and another, by the judgment of God in the great day. Some will be blessed, and others cursed souls, Mat. xxv. 46. some received into glory,

---

* *Statim quo loco quaque pagina disseruerit, ea super re expedite docentem, ab digito commonstrantem sæpe vidimus.*

† *Quo viro Gallia, auctiore ingenio, acriore judicio, exactiore diligentia, majore eruditione, nullum unquam produxit : hac vero ætate nec Italia quidem.* Lud. Viv. in 17. cap. de Civ. Dei.

others shut out into everlasting misery; Mat. viii. 11, 12. "Many
"shall come from the East, and West, and shall sit down with
"Abraham, and Isaac, and Jacob, in the kingdom of heaven;
"but the children of the kingdom shall be cast out into outer
"darkness, there shall be weeping and gnashing of teeth." And
that which will be the sting and aggravation of the difference
which will. then be made, will be this parity and equality in the
nature and capacity of every soul; by reason whereof they that
perish will find they were as naturally capable of blessedness, as
those that enjoy it; and that it was their own inexcusable *negligence* and *obstinacy* that were there their ruin.

Inf. 4. If God be the immediate Creator, and former of the soul
of man, *Then sin must needs involve the most unnatural evil in it,
as it is an horrid violation of the very law of nature.* No title can
be so full, so absolute, as that which creation gives. How clear is
this in the light of reason? If God created my soul, then my soul
had once no being at all: that it had still remained nothing, had not
the pleasure of its Creator chosen and called it into the being it
hath, out of the millions of mere possible beings: for as there are
millions of possible beings, which yet are nothing; so there are
millions of possible beings, which never shall be at all. So that
since the pleasure and power of God were the only fountain of my
being, he must needs be the rightful owner of it. What can be
more his own, than that whose very being flowed merely from
him, and which had never been at all, had he not called it out of
nothing?

And seeing the same pleasure of God, which gave it a being,
gave it also a reasonable being, capable of, and fitted for moral
government, by laws, which other inferior natures are incapable of;
it must needs follow that he is the supreme Governor, as well as the
rightful owner of this soul.

Moreover, it is plain that he who gave my soul its being, and
such a being, gave it also all the good it ever had, hath, or shall
have: and that it neither is, nor hath any thing but what is purely
from him: and therefore he must needs be my most bountiful
Benefactor, as well as absolute Owner, and supreme Governor.
There is not a soul which he hath created but stands bound
to him, in all these ties and titles. Now for such a creature to
turn rebelliously upon its absolute Owner, whose only, and wholly
it is; upon its supreme Governor, to whom it owes entire and
absolute obedience; upon its bountiful Benefactor, from whom it
hath received all, and every mercy it ever had, or hath; to violate
his laws, slight his sovereignty, despise his goodness, contemn his
threatenings, pierce his very heart with grief, darken the glory of
all his attributes, confederate with Satan his malicious enemy; and

strike, as far as a creature can strike, at his very being (for in a sense, *Omne peccatum est Deicidium*, every sin strikes at the life and very existence of God): Blush, O heavens, at this, and be ye horribly afraid! O cursed sin, the evil of all evils, which no epithet can match; no name worse than its own can be invented, *sinful sin*. This is as if some venomous branch should drop poison upon the root that bears it. Love and gratitude to benefactors, is an indelible principle engraven by nature upon the hearts of all men. It teacheth children to love and honour their parents, who yet are but mere instruments of their being. O how just must their perdition be, who casting off the very bonds of nature, turn again with enmity against that God, in whom they both live, and move, and have their being! O think, and think again, on what an * holy man once said; What a sad charge will this be against many a man at the great day, when God shall say, Hadst thou been made a dog, I never had had so much dishonour as I have had? It is pity God should not have honour from the meanest creature that ever he made, from every pile of grass in the field, or stone in the street; much more that he should not have glory from a soul more precious and excellent than all the other works of his hands. Surely it is better for us, our souls had still remained only in the number of possible beings, and had never had an actual existence in the second rank of beings, but a very little lower than the angels; than that we should be still dishonouring God by them. O that he should be put to levy his glory from us passively; that it should be with us as it was with Nebuchadnezzar, from whom God had more glory when he was driven out amongst the beasts of the field, than when he sat on the throne. In like manner, his glory will rise passively from us, when driven out among devils, and not actively and voluntarily, as from the saints.

Infer. 5. If God create and inspire the reasonable soul immediately, *This should instruct and incite all Christian parents to pray earnestly for their children, not only when they are born into the world, but when they are at first conceived in the womb.*

It is of great concernment both to us and our children, not only to receive them from the womb, with bodies perfectly and comely fashioned; but also with such souls inspired into them, whereby they may glorify God to all eternity. It is natural to parents to desire to have their children full and perfect in all their bodily members; and it would be a grievous affliction to see them come into the world defective, monstrous, and misshapen births; should a leg, an arm, an eye be wanting, such a defect would make their lives miserable, and the parents uncomfortable. But how few are

---

* Mr. Burrough's Excellency of the soul of man, p. 232.

concerned with what soul they are born into the world? " Good
" God, (saith * Musculus,) how few shall we find, who are equally
" solicitous to have such children as may live piously and honestly,
" as they are to leave them inheritances upon which they may live
" splendidly and bravely?" It pleaseth us to see our own image
stamped upon their bodies; but, O! how few pray, even whilst
they are in the womb, that their souls may, in due time, bear the
image of the heavenly, and not animate and use the members of
their bodies, as weapons of unrighteousness against the God that
formed them?

Certainly, except they be quickened with such souls, as may in
this world be united with Christ, better had it been for them that
they had perished in the womb, whilst they were pure *embryo's* and
had never come into the number and account of men and women;
for such *embryo's* go for nothing in the world, having only rudi-
ments and rough draughts of bodies, never animated and informed
by a reasonable soul, Job iii. 11, 12. But as soon as such a soul
enters into them, though for never so little a time, it entails eternity
upon them. We also know that as soon as ever God breathes, or
infuses their souls into them, sin presently enters, and death by sin,
and that by us, as the instruments of conveying it to them: which
should have the efficacy of a mighty argument with us to lay our
prayers and tears for mercy in the very foundation of that union.

Think on this particularly, you that are mothers of children,
when you find the fruit of the womb quickened within you, that
you then bear a creature within you of more value than all this
visible world; a creature, upon whom, from that very moment, an
eternity of happiness or misery is entailed; and therefore it concerns
you to travail as in pain for their souls, before you feel the sorrows
and pangs of travail for their bodies. O what a pity is it, that a
part of yourselves should eternally perish! that so rare and excellent
a creature as that you bear, should be cast away for ever, for want
of a new creation super-added to that it hath already! O let your
cries and prayers for them anticipate your kisses and embraces of
them. If you be faithful and successful herein, then happy is the
womb that bears them; if not, happy had it been for them, that the
knees had prevented them, and the breasts they have sucked. O!
ye cannot begin your suits for mercy too early for them, nor continue them too long, though your prayers measure all the time
betwixt their conception and their death.

---

* *Bone Deus! quam paucos reperias qui tam soliciti quomodo pie et honeste vivant filii,
quam curant ut amplam relinquant illis hæreditatem qua post obitum illorum splendide et
otiose declientur?* Musculus in 8 Gen.

Inf. 6. Moreover, if God hath created our souls vital substances to animate and act those bodies, *How indispensably necessary is it that such a principle of spiritual life do quicken and govern that soul which quickens and governs our bodies and all the members of them ?* Otherwise, *though in a natural sense, we have living souls, yet they are dead whilst they live.*

The apostle, in 1 Cor. xv. 45, 46. compares the animal life we live, by the union of our souls and bodies, with the spiritual life we live, by the union of our souls with Jesus Christ. And so it is written, (viz. in my text " The first man Adam was made a living " soul, the last Adam was made a quickening Spirit." He opposes the animal to the spiritual life, and the two Adams, from whom they come ; and shews, in both respects, the excellency of the spiritual above the animal life; not in point of *priority,* for that which is natural is before that which is spiritual, (and it must be so, because the natural soul is the recipient subject of the Spirit's quickening and sanctifying operations;) but in point of dignity and real excellency. To how little purpose, or rather to what a dismal and miserable purpose are we made living souls, except the Lord from heaven by his quickening power, make us spiritual and holy souls? The natural soul rules and uses the body as an * artificer doth his tools : and except the Lord renew it by grace, Satan will rule that which rules thee, and so all thy members will be instruments of iniquity to fight against God. " The actions performed by our bodies, are justly " reputed and reckoned by God to the soul †," because the soul is the spring of all its motions, the fountain of its life and operations. What it doth by the body, its instrument, is as if it were done immediately by itself; for without the soul it can do nothing.

Inf. 7. Moreover, from the immaterial and spiritual nature of the soul, we are informed, *That communion with God, and the enjoyment of him, are the true and proper intentions and purposes for which the soul of man was created.*

Such a nature as this is not fitted to live upon gross, material, and perishing things as the body doth. The food of every creature is agreeable to its nature ; one cannot subsist upon that which another doth : as we see among the several sorts of animals, what is food to one, is none to another. In the same plant is found a root which is food for swine, a stalk which is food for sheep, a flower which feeds the bee, a seed on which the bird lives : the sheep cannot live upon the root, as the swine do ; nor the bird upon the flower as the bee doth : but every one feeds upon the

---

* The body bears resemblance to an organ, the soul to an artist. *Iren. b.* 2.

† *Omnia quæcunque secerit, corpus sive bonum, sive malum, animæ reputantur.* Origen in Job.

different parts of the plant which are agreeable to its nature. So
it is here, our bodies being of an earthly, material nature, can live
upon things earthly and material, as most agreeable to them; they
can relish and suck out the sweetness of these things; but the soul
can find nothing in them suitable to its nature and appetite;
it must have spiritual food, or perish. It were therefore two brutish and unworthy of a man that understood the nature of his own
soul, to cheer it up with the stores of earthly provision made for it,
as he did, Luke xii. 20. " I will say to my soul, Soul, thou hast
" much goods laid up for many years, take thine ease, eat, drink,
" and be merry." Alas! the soul can no more eat, drink, and be
merry with carnal things, than the body can with spiritual and immaterial things: it cannot feed upon bread that perisheth, it can
relish no more the best and daintiest fair of an earthly growth,
than the white of an egg: but bring it to a reconciled God in
Christ, to the covenant of grace, and the sweet promises of the
gospel: set before it the joys, comforts, and earnests of the Spirit;
and if it be a sanctified renewed soul, it can make a rich feast upon
these. These make it a feast of fat things, full of marrow, as it is
expressed, Isa. xxv. 6. Spiritual things are proper food for spiritual and immaterial souls.

Inf. 8. The spiritual nature of the soul farther informs us, *That
no acceptable service can be performed to God, except the soul be
employed and engaged therein.*

The body hath its part and share in God's worship as well as
the soul; but its part is inconsiderable, in comparison; Prov.
xxiii. 26. " My son give me thy heart;" i. e. thy soul, thy spirit.
The holy and religious acts of the soul are suitable to the nature of
the object of worship: John iv. 24. " God is a Spirit, and they
" that worship him, must worship him in spirit and in truth."
Spirits only can have communion with that great Spirit. They
were made spirits for that very end, that they might be capable of
converse with the Father of spirits, " They that worship him must
" worship him in spirit and in truth;" that is, with inward love,
fear, delight, and desires of soul, that is, to worship him in our
spirits; and *in truth*, i. e. according to the rule of his word which
prescribes our duty. *Spirit* respects the inward power; *truth* the
outward form. The former strikes at hypocrisy, the latter at superstition and idolatry: the one opposes the inventions of our heads,
the other the looseness and formality of our hearts.

No doubt but the service of the body is due to God, and expected by him: for both the souls and bodies of his people are bought
with a price, and therefore he expects we glorify him with our souls
and bodies which are his: but the service of the body is not accepted of him otherwise than it is animated and enlivened by an

obedient soul, and both sprinkled with the blood of Christ. Separate from these, bodily exercise profits nothing, 1 Tim. iv. 8. What pleasure can God take in the fruits and evidences of men's hypocrisy? Exek. xxxiii. 31.

Holy Paul appeals to God in this matter; Rom. i. 9. " God is " my witness (saith he) whom I serve with my spirit ;" q. d. I serve God in my spirit, and he knows that I do so. I dare appeal to him who searches my heart, that it is not idle and unconcerned in his service. The Lord humble us, the best of us, for our careless, dead, gadding, and vain spirits, even when we are engaged in his solemn services. O that we were once so spiritual, to follow every excursion from his service with a groan, and retract every wandering thought with a deep sigh ! Alas, a cold and wandering spirit in duty is the disease of most men, and the very temper and constitution of unsanctified ones. It is a weighty and excellent expression of the Jews, in their Euchologium or prayer-book, " * Where- " withal shall I come before his face, unless it be with my spirit ? " For man hath nothing more precious to present to God than his " soul." Indeed it is the best man hath : thy heart is thy *totum posse :* it is all that thou art able to present to him. If thou cast thy soul into thy duty, thou dost as the poor widow did, cast in all that thou hast : and in such an offering the great God takes more pleasure than in all the external, costly, pompous ceremonies, adorned temples, and external devotions in the world. It is a remarkable and astonishing expression of his own in this case, Isa. lxvi. 1, 2. " Thus saith the Lord, The heaven is my throne, and " the earth is my footstool : Where is the house that ye built me ? " and where is the place of my rest ? For all these things have " mine hands made, and all these things have been, saith the " Lord; but unto this man will I look, even to him that is poor, " and of a contrite spirit, and trembleth at my word ;" q. d. Think not to please me with magnificent temples, and adorned altars ; if I had pleasure in such things, heaven is a more glorious throne than any you can build me ; and yet I have more delight in a poor contrite spirit, that trembles with an holy awe and reverence at my word, than I have in heaven or earth, or all the works of my hands in either. Oh! if there had been more trembling at his word, there had not been such trembling as now there is, under fears of the loss and removal of it. Some can superstitiously reverence and kiss the sacred dust of the sanctuary, as they call it, and express a great deal of zeal for the externals of religion, but

---

* *Qua re potius prœveniam faciem ejus, nisi spiritu meo ? nihil enim est homini preciosious anima sua.*

little consider how small the interest of these things is in religion, and how little God looks at, or regards them.

Inf. 9. *How much are the spirits of men sunk by sin, below the dignity and excellency of their nature?*

Our souls are spirits by nature, yet have they naturally no delight in things spiritual: they decline that which is homogeneal and suitable to spirits, and relish nothing but what is carnal and unsuitable to them. How are its affections inverted and misplaced by sin! That noble, spiritual, heaven-born creature the soul, whose element and centre God alone should be, is now fallen into a deep oblivion both of God and itself, and wholly spends its strength in the pursuit of sensual and earthly enjoyments, and becomes a mere drudge and slave to the body. Carnal things now measure out and govern its delights and hopes, its fears and sorrows. O! how unseemly is it to behold such a high-born spirit lacqueying up and down the world in the service of the perishing flesh. "Their heart (saith the prophet) goeth after their covet-"ousness, Ezek. xxxiii. 31. as a servant at the beck or nod of his master.

O how many are there to be found in every place who melt down the precious affections and strength of their souls, in sensitive brutish pleasures and delights? Jam. v. 5. "Ye have lived in plea-"sures upon earth," as the fish in the waters, or rather as the eel in the mud; never once lifting up a thought or desire to the spiritual and eternal pleasures that are at God's right hand.

Our creation did not set us so low; we are made capable of better and higher things.

God did not inspire such a noble, excellent, spiritual soul into us, merely to salt our bodies, or carry them up and down this world for a few years, to gaze at the vanities of it. It was a great saying of an Heathen, I am greater, and born to greater things, "than that I should be a slave to my body*." We have a spirit about us, that might better understand its original, and know it is not so base a being, as its daily employments speak it to be. The Lord raise our apprehensions to a due value of the dignity of our own souls, that we may turn from these sordid employments with a generous disdain, and set our affections on what is agreeable to, and worthy of an high-born spirit.

Inf. 10. Is the soul of man a vital, spiritual, and *immortal substance? Then it is no wonder, that we find the resentments and impressions of the world to come, naturally engraven upon the souls of men all the world over.* These impressions and sentiments of another life after this, do as naturally and necessarily spring out of an

---

* *Major sum, et ad majora natus, quam ut corporis mei sim mancipium.* Seneca.

immortal nature, as branches spring out of the body of a tree, or feathers out of the body of a bird.   So fairly and firmly are the characters and impresions of the life to come sealed upon the immortal spirits of all men, that no man can offer violence to this truth, but he must also do violence to his own soul, and unman himself by the denial of it.   Who feels not a cheeriness to spring from his absolving, and an horror from his accusing conscience? neither of which could arise from any other principle than this.   We are beings conscious to ourselves of a future state, and that our souls do not vanish when our breath doth: that we cease not to be when we cease to breathe.

And this is common to the most barbarous and savage Heathens: " They shew (saith the apostle) the work of the law written in " their hearts, their consciences also bearing them witness, and " their thoughts in the mean time accusing, or else excusing one " another." By the work of the law, understand the sum and substance of the ten commandments, comprising the duties to be done, and the sins to be avoided.   This work of the law is said to be written upon the hearts of the Gentiles, who had no external written law; upon their hearts it was written, though many of them gave themselves over to all uncleanness ; and they shewed or gave evidence and proof, that there was such a law written upon their hearts.   They shewed it two ways : (1.) Some of them shewed it in their temperance, righteousness, and moral honesty, wherein they excelled many of us, who have far greater advantages and obligations.   (2.) In the efficacy of their consciences; which, as it cleared and comforted them for things well done : so it witnessed against them, yea, judged and condemned them for things ill done.   And these evidences of a law written on the heart are to be found, wherever men are to be found.   Their ignorance and barbarity cannot stifle these sentiments and impressions of a future state, and a just tribunal to which all must come.   And the universality of it plainly evinces, that it springs not out of education, but the very nature of an immortal soul.

Let none say that these universal impressions are but the effects of an universal *tradition,* which have been, time out of mind, spread among the nations of the world : for as no such universal tradition can be proved ; so if it could, the very propension that is found in the minds of all men living, to embrace and close with the proposals of a life to come, will evince the agreeableness of them to the nature of an immortal soul.   Yea, the natural closing of the soul with these proposals, will amount to an evidence of the reality and existence of those invisible things.   For as the natural senses and their organs prove that there are colours, sounds, savours, and juices; as well as, or rather because there are eyes, ears, &c. naturally fitted to close with; and receive them; so it is here, if the soul naturally looks beyond the line of time, to things eternal, and cannot bound and confine its thoughts and expectations within the too narrow limits of present things, surely there is such a future state, as well as souls made apprehensive of it, and propense to close with the discoveries thereof. So natural are the notions of a future state to the souls of men, that those who have set themselves designedly to banish them, and struggled hard to suppress them, as things irksome and grievous to them, giving interruption to their sensual lusts and pleasures; yet still these apprehensions have returned upon them, and gotten a just victory over all their objections and prejudices; they follow them wheresoever they go; they can no more flee from them than from themselves; whereby they evidence themselves to be natural and indelible things.

Inf. 11. Hath God endued the soul of man with understanding, will, and affections, whereby it is made capable of knowing, loving, and enjoying God? *It is then no wonder to find the malice and envy of Satan engaged against man more than any other creature, and against the soul of man, rather than any thing else in man.*

It grates that Spirit of envy to see the soul of man adorning and preparing, by sanctification, to fill that place in glory from which he fell irrecoverably. It cut Haman to the very heart, to see the honour that was done to Mordecai; much more doth it grate and gall Satan, to see what Jesus Christ hath purchased and designed for the souls of men. Other creatures being naturally incapable of this happiness, do therefore escape his fury; but men shall be sure to feel it as far as he can reach them; 1 Pet. v. 8. "Your ad-"versary the devil goeth about like a roaring lion, seeking whom "he may devour." *He walks to and fro;* that speaks his diligence; *seeking whom he may devour;* that speaks his design; his restlessness in doing mischief is all the rest and relief he hath in his own torments. It is a mark of pure and perfect malice to endeavour to destroy, though he knows he shall never be successful in his attempts. We read of many bodies possessed by him; but he never takes up his quarters in the body of any but with design to do mischief to the soul. No room but the best in the house will satisfy him; no blood so sweet to him as soul-blood. If he raise prosecution against the bodies of men, it is to destroy their souls: holiness is what he hates, and happiness is the object of his envy: the soul being the subject of both, is therefore pursued by him as his prey.

Inf. 12. Upon the consideration both of its excellent nature and divine original, it follows, *That the corruption and defacing of such an excellent creature by sin deserves to be lamented and greatly be-*

wailed; and the recovery of it by sanctification to be studied and diligently prosecuted, as the great concern of all men.

What a beautiful and blessed creature was the soul of man at first, whilst it stood in its integrity? His mind was bright, clear, and apprehensive of the law and will of God; his will cheerfully complied therewith; his sensitive appetite and inferior powers stood in an obedient subordination. God made man upright, Eccles. vii. 29. ישר straight, and equal, bending to neither extreme. The law of God was fairly engraven upon the table of his heart. Principles of holiness and righteousness were inlaid in the frame of his mind, fitting him for an exact and punctual discharge of his duties both to God and man. This was the soundness of his constitution, the healthful temper of his inner-man, whereby it became the very region of light, peace, purity, and pleasure. For think how serene, lightsome, and placid the state of the soul must be, in which there was no obliquity, not a jar with the Divine will; but joy and peace continually transfused through all its faculties!

But sin hath defaced its beauty, razed out the Divine image which was its glory, and stamped the image of Satan upon it; turned all its noble powers and faculties against the author and fountain of its being. Surely if all the posterity of Adam, from the beginning to the end of the world, should do nothing else but weep and sigh for the sin and misery of the fall, it could not be sufficiently deplored: Other sins, like single bullets, kill particular persons: but Adam's sin, like a chain-shot, mowed down all mankind at once. It murdered himself *actually*, all his posterity *virtually*, and Christ himself *occasionally*. Oh! what a black train of doleful consequents attend this sin! It hath darkened the bright eye of the soul's understanding, 1 Cor. ii. 14. made its complying and obedient will stubborn and rebellious, Job v. 40. rendered his tender heart obdurate and senseless, Ezek. xxxvi. 26. filled its serene and peaceful conscience with guilt and terror, Tit. i. 15. The considerations of these things is very humbling, and should cause those that glory in their high and illustrious descents, to wrap their silver star in cypress, and cover all their glory with a mourning veil. But this is but one part of their duty.

How should this consideration provoke us to apply ourselves with the most serious diligence to recover our lost beauty and dignity in the way of sanctification! This is the great and most proper use of the fall, as Musculus excellently speaks;—*ut gratiam Christi eo subnixiusa ambimus*,—to inflame our desires the more vehemently after grace.

Sanctification restores the beauty of the soul, which sin defaced, Eph. iv. 25. Col. iii. 10. Yea, it restores it with this advantage, that it shall never be lost again; holiness is the beauty of God im-pressed upon the soul, and the impression is everlasting. Other beauty is but a fading flower: Time will plough deep furrows upon the fairest faces, but this will be fresh to eternity.

All moral virtues, homilitical qualities, which adorn and beautify nature, and make it attractive and lovely in the eyes of men, are but separable accidents, which death discinds and crops off like a sweet flower from the stalk, Job iv. 21. " Doth not their excellency that " is in them go away?" But sanctification is inseparable, and will ascend with the soul into heaven. Oh! that God would set the glass of the law before us, that we may see what defiled souls we have by nature, that we might come by faith to Jesus Christ, who cometh to us by water and by blood, 1 John v. 6.

Inf. 13. To conclude. Upon the consideration of the whole matter before us, if this excellent creature, the soul, receive both its being and excellencies from God; *Then he that formed it must needs have the full, and only right to possess and use it, and is therefore most injuriously kept out of the possession of it by un-sanctified and disobedient persons.*

The soul of man is a building of God; he hath laid out the treasures of his wisdom, power, and goodness in this noble struc-ture; he built it for an habitation for himself to dwell in; and in-deed such noble rooms as the understanding, will, and affections, are too good for any other to inhabit. But sin hath set open the gates of this hallowed temple, and let in the abomination which maketh desolate. All the doors of the soul are barred and chained up against Christ, by ignorance and infidelity; he seeks for admis-sion into the soul which he made, but findeth none. A forcible entry he will not make; but expects when the will shall bring him the keys of the soul, as to its rightful owner. So he expresseth himself to us in Rev. iii. 20. " Behold I stand at the door and " knock: If any man hear my voice, and open the door, I will " come in to him, and sup with him, and he with me." His *standing at the door,* denotes his earnest desire and patient waiting, in the use of all those means that are introductive of Jesus Christ into the souls of men. His *knocking,* signifies the various essays he makes by his ordinances and providences externally, and the con-victions and persuasions of his Spirit, and the consciences of sinners internally: Every call of the word, and every conviction of con-science is a call, a knock from heaven, at the door of the soul, for the admission of Christ into it. By *the soul's hearing his voice, and opening the door,* understand its approbation, and consent to the motion and offer of God. By Christ's *coming in,* is meant his uniting that soul unto himself that opens to him. And as his *coming in* denotes union, so his supping with the soul, and the soul with nim denotes his sweet communion; imperfect here, complete and full in heaven.

O the admirable condescension of God to poor sinners! The God that formed you with a word, and can as easily ruin you with a frown, yet waits at the gates of your souls for admission into them. There be many souls within the sound of this complaint, that have kept God out of his own right all their days. They have shut out Jesus Christ, and delivered up their souls to Satan: If he but knock by a slight temptation, the door is presently opened; but Jesus Christ may wait in vain upon them from sabbath to sabbath, and from year to year: But the longest day of his patience hath an end; and there is a refusal of grace, after which no more tenders of mercy shall ever be made.

What say you, Souls? Will you at last open the door to Jesus Christ, or will you still exclude him? If you will open to him, he will not come empty-handed, he will bring a feast with him, such a feast as you never tasted any thing like it in your lives: But, if you will not open to him, then I call heaven and earth to witness against you this day, that you have once barred the doors of your soul against him, whose pleasure and power gave them their very beings; against him who is their sovereign Lord, and rightful Owner. And consequently this act of yours must stop your mouths, and deprive you of all pleas and apologies when you shall knock hereafter at the door of mercy, and God shall ever shut it up against you, according to his just, but dreadful threatenings, Mat. vii. 22. Prov. i. 24, 25. And thus much of the divine original, and excellent nature of the soul of man.

Having taken a view of this excellent creature, the soul, in opening the former proposition: we come next to the consideration of its union with the body, in this second proposition.

Doct. II. *That the souls and bodies of men are knit together, by the feeble band of the breath in their nostrils.*

" There is (saith a learned * man) no greater mystery in nature,
" than the union betwixt the soul and body; that a mind and spi-
" rit should be so tied and linked with a clod of clay, that while
" that remains in a due temper, it cannot by any art or power free
" itself. It can by an act of the will move an hand, or a foot, or
" the whole body, but cannot move from it one inch. If it move
" hither, or thither, or by a leap upward do ascend a little, the
" body still follows it; it cannot shake or throw it off. We can-

---

* *Mr. How* in a funeral Sermon, p. 9, 10.

" not take ourselves out; by any allowable means we cannot; nor
" by any at all (that are at least, within mere human power) as long
" as the temperament lasts.   While that remains, we cannot go;
" if that fail, we cannot stay; though there be so many open
" avenues, (could we suppose any material bounds to hem in, or
" exclude a spirit) we cannot go out or in at pleasure.   A wonder-
" ful thing! and I wonder we no more wonder at our own make
" and frames in this respect.————What, so much a-kin are a
" mind and a piece of earth, a clod and a thought, that they should
" be thus affixed to one another?"

My design here is to shew by what ligament, tie, or bond, it
hath pleased the great and wise Creator, to affix and link these so
different parts of man together: And this Moses in the text tells
us, is no other but the breath of his nostrils.

The breath and soul of man are two distinct things.   His breath
is not his soul, nor his soul his breath, but the *nexus* or bond that
couples and unites his soul and body in a personal union.   The
body hath no life in itself, but its life results from its union with
the soul, James ii. 26.   This union is maintained by the breath of
our nostrils, which upon that account is here called the *breath of
life*.   *Breath is an act of life, proceeding from the soul's union with
its body, and ending with the dissolution of it*.   Life is continued
by its *respiration*, and ended by its *expiration*.   Whilst we live,
and whilst breath is in our bodies, are terms *synonymous*.

That little quantity of air, which we thus breathe in and out at
our nostrils, is more to us, than all the three regions of air, which
fill up the vast space between earth and heaven.   It is, in a sense,
our life.

For this use and office of respiration, the *lungs* were formed and
placed where they are, not without the most wise counsel and direction of God.   They are that organ in the * body, which, by
the help of that *artery* called *arteria trachea*, leading to them as a
channel, for the passage of air from the mouth and nostrils, the air
is transmitted to, and ventilated by them for the refreshment of the
† heart, and exhaling the fumes thereof.

The heart hath continual need of such a vent and refreshment;
and therefore the lungs, like a pair of bellows, must be kept continually going.   No longer than breath is going, is the heart a
dying; that which stops the one, suffocates the other.

---

* The lungs are the instrument of breathing and respiration; to the lungs there
leads a pipe, which is called the wind-pipe, formed for two uses, &c.

† The heart is moved by a twofold motion, namely, that of its contraction, and dila-
tation, whereby its innate heat is mitigated and cooled by means of the air sucked in.
Alsted. Theol. Nat. p. 614.

And here we may, with admiration, contemplate the wonders by which our lives are continued. These lungs are the most frail and tender part of the body, and kept in continual motion and agitation; yet are made serviceable for seventy or eighty years together, which is the wonder of Providence. Were a piece of brass, or iron or steel kept in continual and incessant use, it would not endure half the time. In a word, the * heart, that noble part of the body, is the *shop* wherein the *spirits* are laboured and prepared, which therefore is in continual motion and heat; and so needs continual cooling and refreshing. We can live no longer than it labours, it can labour no longer than it is refreshed and cooled by respiration.

God hath therefore prepared the lungs for this service; which being of a thin, porous, and spungy substance, can easily be dilated and contracted. By dilating themselves, they attract and suck in the air into themselves; first duly to prepare and temper it, and then communicate it to the heart for its refreshment; which being quickly heated in the heart, is again breathed out by the lungs, by contracting themselves again. This double motion of inspiration and expiration, we call respiration; and this respiration is the bond that holds our souls and bodies together.

And indeed, this is but a feeble bond, a very slender and weak thread, which holds our souls and bodies in union. What more *volatile, evanid* and *uncertain* than a puff of breath? The nostrils are the outer door of the body, our breath is continually in our nostrils; and how soon may that depart, which is day and night at the door, as if it were still taking leave of us? Our breath is always going; and what is still going, will be gone at last. How small a difference is there betwixt respiration and expiration, a breathing and a breathless lump of clay? Breath cannot continue long, and life cannot stay a moment behind it, Psal. civ. 29. " Thou takest " away their breath, they die, and return to their dust." Life is breath given, and death is breath taken away. The breath of man is like a written sentence, in which there are divers commas, or

---

* Because the heart is the fountain of life, and the laborious forge where the animal spirits are framed ; so that being in the posture of a pendulum, it is agitated by a perpetual motion; by which means it is vehemently heated, even to so great a degree, that, unless that heat was moderated by respiration, of necessity it would happen, that both the natural heat and moisture would be destroyed by the excessive heat of the heart. The lungs are nothing else but a certain kind of natural bellows, which by being dilated, draw in the air and transmit it to the heart, so that the heart, though always hot, is cooled by the air; which air, after being warmed within the recesses of the heart, is again sent out from the heart into the lungs, which by contracting themselves, emit it again by expiration. *Keckern, Phys. p.* 560-70.

short pauses, after which speedily follows a full stop, and there is an end of it.

Some conceive Solomon points at the continual motion of the lungs, in that figurative and elegant description of the death of man, * Eccles. xii. 6. " Or ever the silver cord be loosed, or the " golden bowl be broken, or the pitcher be broken at the fountain, " or the wheel be broken at the cistern." The double motion of the lungs he seems here to compare to the double motion of the buckets in a well; the turn of the wheel sends one down, and draws the other up. But as we use to say proverbially, The bucket or pitcher that goes so often to the cistern or well, is broken at last: So we must say of these, they will fail at last. One sitting by the bed-side of a dying person, sighed out this compassionate expression, *Ah! quid sumus?* His sick friend hearing it, replied *Pulvis umbra, fumus,* dust, a shadow, a puff of wind. The wind without us is fickle and inconstant to a proverb, and so is that within us too. Many grudge at the shortness of life; but considering the feebleness of this bond, we have more cause to wonder at the slowness of death. For let us seriously consider the frailty of our breath, on a double account, *viz.*

1. In respect of our breathing instruments.
2. Or of breath-stopping accidents.

1. Great is the frailty of our breathing instruments. What is flesh but weakness? even the most solid and substantial; it is as fading grass, Isa. xl. 6 " But our † lungs are the most lax, spungy, " and tender of all flesh, if that which is so airy, light, and spu- " mous, deserves the name of flesh." And as it is the most frail of all flesh, so it is in continual motion, labouring night and day without rest or intermission; and that which wants alternate rest cannot be durable. We see motion wears out the wheels of the watch, though made of brass; but our *strength* (as Job speaks) *is not the strength* of stones; *nor our bones* (the most solid, much less our lungs the most frail and feeble parts) *of brass.* Beside,

2. There are a multitude of breath-stopping accidents, which may, and daily do beat the last breath out of men's nostrils, before any decay of nature cause it to expire.

Many mortal diseases are incident to these frail and tender parts. Phtysics, interneations, ulcers, easily bar the passage of our breath

---

* The lungs are like the pulleys of a cistern, for the pulley first lets down the bucket into the well, then raises it again ; in like manner, the lungs by a perpetual motion admit and expel the air. *Alsted. Theol. nat. p.* 623.

† The substance of the lungs is a lax, spungy, airy kind of flesh, replete with innumerable air-bladders, which alternately admit and repel the external air. *Alsted Theol. nat. p.* 623.

there; yea, and slighter accidents, which immediately touch not that part, are sufficient to stop our breath, and dislodge our souls. A *fly*, a *gnat*, the stone of a *raisin*, a *crumb* of bread, have often done it. There is not a *pore* in the body but is a door large enough to let in death, nor a creature so despicably small but is strong enough (if God commission it) to serve a writ of ejection upon the soul: The multitudes of diseases are so many lighted candles put to this slender thread of our breath, besides the infinite diversity of external accidents by which multitudes daily perish. So that there are as great and astonishing wonders in our preservation as in our creation.

Inf. 1. *How admirable then is the mystery of providence in the daily continuation of the breath of our nostrils ?*

That our breath is yet in our nostrils, is only from hence, that he who breathed it into them at first is our life, and the length of our days, as it is Deut. xxx. 20. It is because our breath is in his hand, Dan. v. 23. not in our own, nor in our enemies' hands. Till he take it away, none shall be able to do it; Psal. civ. 29. " Thou takest away their breath, they die, and return to their " dust."

It is neither food nor physic, but God in and by them, that "·holdeth our souls in life," Psal. lxvi. 9. We hang every moment of our life over the grave and the gulph of eternity, by this slender thread of our breath : But it cannot break, how feeble soever it be, till the time appointed be fully come. If it be not extinguished and suffocated, as others daily are, it is because he puts none of these diseases upon us, as it is Exod. xv. 26. or if he do, yet he is *Jehovah Rophe*, the Lord that healeth us, as it follows in that text.

We live in the midst of cruel enemies, yea, " among them that " breathe out cruelty," as the psalmist complaineth, Psal. xxvii. 12. Such breath would quickly suffocate ours, did not he, in whose hand ours is, wonderfully prevent it. O what cause have we to employ and spend that breath in his praise, who works so many daily wonders to secure it !

Inf. 2. Is it but a puff of feeble breath which holds our souls and bodies in union ? *Then every man is deeply concerned to make all haste, to take all possible care and pains to secure a better and more durable habitation for his soul in heaven, whilst yet it sojourns in this frail tabernacle of the body.*

The time is at hand, when all these comely and active bodies shall be so many breathless carcases, no more capable of any use or service for our souls than the seats you sit on, or the dead bodies that lie under your feet. Your breath is yet in your nostrils, and all the means and seasons of salvation will expire with it ; and then it will be as impossible for the best minister in the world to help your souls, as for the ablest Physician to recover your bodies. As physic comes too late for the one, so counsels and persuasions for the other.

Three things are worth thinking on this matter.

1. That you are not without the hopes and possibilities of salvation, whilst the breath of life is in your nostrils. A mercy, (how lightly soever you value it) that would ravish with joy those miserable souls that have already shot the gulf of eternity, and turn the shrieks and groans of the damned unto joyful shouts and acclamations of praise. Poor wretch, consider what thou readest; that thy soul is not yet in Christ, is thy greatest misery; but that yet it may be in Christ, is an unspeakable mercy; though thy salvation be not yet secured, yet what a mercy is it that it is not desperate?

2. When this uncertain breath is once expired, the last hope of every unregenerate person is gone for ever: It is as impossible to recover hope as it is to recover your departed breath, or recal the day that is past. When the breath is gone, the *compositum* is dissolved; we cease to be what we now are, and our life is as water spilt on the ground which shall not be gathered up till the resurrection. Our life is carried like a precious liquor in a brittle glass, which death breaks to pieces. The spirit is immediately presented to God, and fixed in its unalterable state, Heb. ix. 27. All means of salvation now cease for ever; no *ambassadors* of peace are sent to the dead; no more calls or strivings of the spirit: no more space for repentance. O! what an inconceivable weight hath God hanged on a puff of breath!

3. And since matters stand thus, it is to be admired what shift men make to quiet themselves in so dangerous a state as most souls live in; quiet and unconcerned, and yet but one puff of breath betwixt them and hell! O the stupifying and besotting nature of sin! O the efficacy and power of spiritual delusions! Are our lives such a throng and hurry of business that we have no time to go alone and think where we are, and where we shortly must be? What shall I say? If bodily concerns be so weighty, and the matters of eternity such trifles; if meat and drink, and trade and children be such great things, and Christ, and the soul, and heaven, hell, and the world to come such little things in your eyes, you will not be long in that opinion I dare assure you.

Inf. 3. Is the tie so weak betwixt our souls and bodies? How close and near then do all our souls confine and border upon eternity?

There is no more than a puff of breath, a blast of wind betwixt this world and that to come. A very short step betwixt time and eternity: There is a breath which will be our last breath: respiration must, and will terminate in expiration: The dead are the *inha-*

bitants, and the living are *borderers* upon the invisible world. This consideration deserves a dwelling place in the hearts of all men whether,

 I. Regenerate, or

 II. Unregenerate.

 I. Regenerate souls should ponder this with pleasure. O it is transporting to think how small a matter is betwixt them and their complete salvation. No sooner is your breath gone, but the full desire of your hearts is come ; every breath you draw, draws you a degree nearer to your perfect happiness; Rom. xiii. 11. " Now " is your salvation nearer than when ye believed;" therefore, both your cheerfulness and diligence should be greater than when you were * in the infancy of your faith. You have run through a considerable part of your Christian course and race, and are now come nearer the goal and prize of eternal life. O despond not, loiter not now at last, who were so fervent and zealous in the beginning.

 It is transporting to think how near you approach the region of light and joy. O that you would distinctly consider,

 1. Where you lately were.

 2. Where now you are.

 3. Where shortly you shall be.

 1. You that are now so near salvation, were lately very near unto damnation, there was but a puff of breath betwixt you and hell. How many nights did you sleep securely in the state of nature and unregeneracy? How quietly did you rest upon the brink of hell, not once imagining the danger you were in? Had any of those sicknesses you then suffered, been suffered by God, like a candle, to burn asunder this slender thread of life which was so near them, you had been as miserable, and as hopeless as those that now are roaring in the lowest hell. I have heard of one that rid over a dangerous bridge in the night, who, upon the review of that place, fell into a swoon, when he was sensible of that danger which the darkness of the night hid from him. O reader, shall not an escape from hell affect thee as much as such an escape would do?

 2. It is no less marvellous to consider where you now are; you that were afar off are now made nigh, Eph. ii. 13. You that were not beloved, are now beloved, Rom. ix. 25. You were in the state of death and condemnation. You are now passed from death to life by your free justification, 1 John iii. 14. Your union with Christ hath set you free from condemnation, Rom. viii. 1. Die

---

 * He says this, because the faithful had been, when they first believed, more diligent and cheerful in good works, but afterwards grew cold, or turned lukewarm. *Estius on the place.*

you must though Christ be in you, but there is no hazard or hurt in your death. The stopping of your breath can put no stop to your happiness, it will hasten not hinder it: If the pale horse come for you, heaven, not hell, will now follow him; your sins are pardoned, the covenant of your salvation sealed. Death is disarmed of its fatal sting; and what then should hinder you from a like triumph, even upon your death-bed with that, 1 Cor. xv. 55. " O death, where is thy sting? O grave, where is thy victory?

3. And yet you have more room for joy, whilst you consider where you must, and shall shortly be. You are now *in Christ,* but in a few days you shall be *with Christ* as well as in him; it is well now, but it will be better ere long. Your sin is now fully *pardoned,* but not fully *purged* out of your souls. Your *persons* are freed from guilt, but your *hearts* are not either freed from filth or grief: But in a little time you shall be absolutely and eternally freed from both. Your present condition is in heaven, compared with your former, and your future state will be in heaven indeed, compared with your present. " The path of the just is as the shining light, " which shineth more and more unto the perfect day," Prov. iv. 18.

II. But on the other side, what meditation can be more startling and amazing to all the unregenerate and christless world? Ponder it, thou poor christless and unsanctified soul. Get thee out of the noise and clamour of this world, which make such a continual din in thine ears, and consider how thou hangest over the mouth of hell itself, by the feeble thread which is spun every moment out of thy nostrils; as soon as that gives way, thou art gone for ever. What shift do you make to quiet your fears, and eat, drink, and labour with any pleasure? It is storied of Dionysius the tyrant, that when Damocles would have flattered him into a conceit of the perfection of his happiness, as he was an absolute sovereign prince, and could do what he pleased with others, as his vassals; Dionysius, to confute his fancy, caused him to be placed at a table richly furnished, and attended with the most curious music, but just over his head hanged a sharp and heavy sword by one single hair; which when Damocles saw, no meat would go down with him, but he earnestly begged for a discharge from that place. This is the lively emblem of thy condition, thou unregenerate man.

There are *three* things in thy state, sadly opposed to the former state last described.

    1. The state you were born in, was bad.

    2. The state you are now in, is worse.

    3. The state you shall shortly be in, if you thus continue, will be unspeakably the worst of all.

1. The state you were born in was a sad state; you were born in sin, Psal. li. 5. and under wrath, Eph. ii. 3. The womb of nature cast you forth into this world, defiled and condemned creatures.

2. The state you are in now is much worse than that you were born in; for what have you been doing ever since you were born, but treasuring up wrath against the day of wrath? Rom. ii. 5. For every sand of time which runs out of the glass of God's patience towards you, a drop of wrath hath been running into the vials of his indignation against you. Oh! what a treasure of sin and wrath then, is laid up in so many years as you have lived in sin! Every sin committed, every mercy abused, every call of God neglected and slighted, adds still more and more to this treasure.

3. It will be much worse shortly than it is now, except preventing, renewing grace step in betwixt you and that wrath, into which you are hastening so fast. It is sad to be under the *sentence* of condemnation, but unspeakably worse to be under the *execution* of that sentence. To be a *christless* man is lamentable, but to be a *hopeless* man is more lamentable. For though you be now without Christ, yet whilst the breath of life is in your nostrils, you are not absolutely without hope. But when once that breath is gone, all the world cannot save or help you. Your last breath and your last hope expire together. Though you be under God's damning sentence, yet that sentence, through the riches of forbearance, is not executed; but as soon as you die, all that wrath which hanged over your heads so many years, in the black clouds of God's threatenings, will pour down in a furious storm upon you, which will never break up whilst God is God. O! think, and think again, and let your thoughts think close to this sad and solemn subject, there is but a breath betwixt you and hell.

Inf. 4. *Doth God maintain your life by breath? Let not that breath destroy your life, which God gave to preserve it.*

No man can live without breath; and yet some might live longer than they do, if their breath were better employed. " Some " men's throats have been cut by their own tongues," as the * Arabian proverb intimates. Life and death (saith Solomon) are in the power of the tongue. Critics observe, that a *word* and a *plague* grow upon the same root in the Hebrew tongue. It is certain, that some men's breath hath been baneful poison both to themselves and others. It was a word that cut off the life of Adonijah, 1 Kings ii. 23. and thousands since his day have died upon the point of the same weapon. It is therefore wholesome advice that is given us, Psal. xxxiv. 12. " What man is he that desireth

---

* *Cave, ne feriat lingua tua collum tuum.* Scal. Arab. Prov. Cent. i.

" life, and loveth many days, that he may see good; keep thy
" tongue from evil, and thy lips from speaking guile."

And the more evil the times are, the stricter guard we should keep
upon our lips. "It is an evil time, the prudent will keep silence,"
Amos v. 13. When wicked men watch to make a man an *offender
for a word*, as it is, Isa. xxix. 20, 21. it behoves us to be upon our
watch, that we offend not with our lips. It is good to keep, what
is not safe to trust. David was a deaf and dumb man, when in
the company of wicked men, Psal. xxxviii. 13. he thought silence
to be his prudence. It is better they should *call* you fools, than
find you so.

*Inf. 5. Employ not that breath to the dishonour of God, which
was first given, and is still graciously maintained by him for your
comfort and good.*

It were better you had never breathed at all, than to spend your
breath in profane oaths, or foolish and idle chat, whereby at once,
you wound the name of God, draw guilt upon your own souls, and
help on the ruin of others. That is a startling text, Matt. xii. 36.
" But I say unto you, that every idle word that men shall speak,
" they shall give an account thereof in the day of judgment."

To give an account, is here, by a *metalepsis* of the antecedent for
the consequent, put for punishment in hell-fire, without an inter-
vening change of heart, and sprinkling of the blood of Jesus.

And there is more evil in this abuse of our breath, than we can
easily discern, especially upon two accounts; (1.) Because it is a
sin most frequently committed, and seldom repented of. The intercourse betwixt the heart and tongue is quick, and the sense of
the evil as easily and quickly passeth away. (2.) Because the poisonous and malignant influence thereof abides and continues long
after: our words may do mischief to others, not only a long time
after they are spoken, but a long time after the tongue that spake
them is turned to dust. How many years may a foolish or filthy
word, a profane scoff, an atheistical expression, stick in the minds of
them that heard them, after the speaker's death. A word spoken
is *physically* transient, and passed away with the breath that delivered it; but *morally*, it is permanent: For as to its moral efficacy,
no more is required, but its objective existence in the minds and
thoughts of them that once heard it: And, upon that very ground,
Suarez argues for a general judgment, after men at death have
passed their particular judgment; because (saith he) long after
that, abundance of good and evil will be done in this world by
the dead, in the persons of others that over-live them. For look,
as it was said of Abel, that being dead, he yet speaketh; so it may
be said of Julian, Porphyry, and multitudes of scoffing Atheists,
that being dead, they yet speak. Oh, therefore, get a sanctifi-

ed heart to season your breath, that it may minister grace to the
hearers.

*Inf. 6. Let your breath promote the spiritual life of others, as
well as maintain the natural life in yourselves.*

Though the maintaining of your natural life be one end why
God gave you breath, yet it is not the only, or principal end of it.
Your breath must be food to others, as well as life to you; Prov.
x. 21. " The lips of the righteous feed many." It will be comfortable to resign that breath to God at death, which hath been instrumental to his glory in this life. It was no low encomium Christ
gave of the church, when he said, Cant. iv. 11. " Thy lips, O my
" spouse, drop as the honey-comb, honey and milk are under thy
" tongue." Sweet, wholesome, and pleasant words drop from her
lips. They drop (saith Christ) *as the honey-comb.* Some drops
ever and anon fall actually, and others hang, at the same time,
prepared and ready to fall. Such a prepared and habitual disposition should every Christian continually have. Your words may
stick upon men's hearts to their edification and salvation, when you
are in your graves. Your tongues may now sow that precious
seed, which may spring up to the praise of God, though you may
not live to reap the comfort of it in this world, John iv. 36, 37.
It is a rich expence of your breath, to bring but one soul to God,
and yet God hath used the breath of one, as his instrument, to
save, edify, and comfort the souls of thousands, Prov. xi. 30.
" The fruit of the righteous is a tree of life, and he that winneth
" souls is wise." The good Lord make all his people wise in this.

Surely, whether we consider the invaluable worth and preciousness of souls, the benefits you have had from the breath of others
yourselves, the innate property of grace, wherever it is, to diffuse
and communicate itself, how short a time you have to breathe, and
how comfortable it will be, when you breathe your last, to remember how it hath been employed for God; all this should open your
lips to counsel, reprove, and comfort others, as often as opportunity is ministered.

Did Christ spend his blood for our souls, and shall not we spend
our breath for them! Oh! let our lips dispense knowledge. If
you will not spend your breath for God, how will you spend your
blood for him? If you will not speak for him, I doubt you will not
die for him. Away with a sullen reservedness, away with unprofitable chat; all subjects of discourse are not fit for a Christian's
lips. It is a grave admonition God once gave his people by the
pen of a faithful * minister. " You may rue (saith he) the oppor-

---

* Mr. West.

" tunities you have lost.   Here lay a poor wretch with one foot in
" hell; would he not have started back, if he had had light to dis-
" cover his danger? Well, you are now together, something you
" must say; the same breath would serve for a compassionate ad-
" monition, as for a complacent impertinency, which will redound
" to the advantage of neither.   You part, the man dies, and in the
" midst of hell cries out against you, one word of yours might have
" saved me; you had me in your reach, you might have told me
" my danger; you forebore, I hardened; the Lord reward your
" negligence."

Inf. 7. If breath be the tie betwixt soul and body, *How are we
concerned to improve, and draw forth the precious breath of ministers and Christians, whilst it is yet in their nostrils.*

The breath of many ministers is judicially stopt already, their
breath serves to little other use than to preserve their own lives;
it will be stopt ere long by death, and then those excellent treasures
of gifts and graces, wherewith they are richly furnished, will be
gone out of your reach, never to be further useful to your souls.
You should do by them therefore (as one aptly speaks) as scholars
do by some choice book they have borrowed, and must return in a
few days to the owner: They diligently read it night and day, and
carefully transcribe the most useful and excellent notes they can
find in it, that they may make them their own, when the book is
called out of their hands.

But alas! we rather divert, than draw forth these excellencies
that are in them. You may yet converse with them, and greatly
benefit yourselves by these converses; but (as one speaks) by the
stream of your impertinent talk, that season is neglected.   Afterwards you see your lack of knowledge, but then the instrument is
removed.   How must it gall an awakened Jew, to think what discourse he had with Jesus Christ! *Is it lawful to give tribute to
Cæsar? Why do not thy disciples fast?* Oh! had I nothing else to
enquire of the Lord Jesus? Would it not have been here pertinent
to have asked, What shall I do to be saved? But he is gone, and
I dead in my sins.   How many persons have we sent away, that
had a word of wisdom in their hearts, having only learnt from them
what a clock it is, what weather, or what news; forgetting to ask
our own hearts, what is all this to us? and to enquire of them
things worthy of their wisdom and experience.   " Wherefore is
" there a price in the hand of a fool, seeing he hath no heart to it?"
Prov. xvii. 16.   The expence of one minute's breath in season,
may, if God concur with it, be to you the ground of breathing forth
praises to God to all eternity.

Inf. 8. Are soul and body tacked together by so frail a thing as a puff of breath? *How vain and groundless then are all those plea-sures men take in their carnal projects and designs in this world?*

We lay the plot and design of our future earthly felicity in our own thoughts; we mould and contrive a design for a long and pleasant life. The model for raising an estate is already formed in our thoughts, and we have not patience to defer our pleasure till the accomplishment of it, but presently draw a train of pleasing consequents from this *chimera*, and our thoughts can stoop to no-thing less than sitting down all the remainder of our days in the very lap of delight and pleasure; forgetting that our breath is all the while in our nostrils, and may expire the next moment: and if it do, the structure of all our expectations and projects comes to nothing in the same moment. " His breath goeth forth, he re-" turneth to his dust: And in that very day his thoughts perish," Psal. cxlvi. 4. The whole frame of his thoughts fall instantly abroad, by drawing out this one pin, his breath. It is good with all our earthly designs to mingle the serious thoughts of the domi-nion of providence, and our own frailty; James iv. 15. " If the Lord will, and we live."

It is become a common observation, that as soon as men have ac-complished their earthly designs, and begin to hug and bless them-selves in their own acquisitions, a sudden and unexpected period is put to their lives and pleasures, as you may see Luke xii. 19, 20. Dan. iv. 30.

Oh then drive moderately; you will be at the end of all these things sooner than you imagine. We need not victual a ship to cross the channel, as they do that are bound to the Indies. " What " is your life? It is even a vapour which appeareth for a little " while, and then vanisheth away," James iv. 14. " In one mo-" ment the projects of many years are overturned for ever.

Inf. 9. Is it but a puff of breath that holds men in life? *Then build not too much hope and confidence upon any man.*

Build not too high upon so feeble a foundation. " Cease ye " from man (saith the prophet) whose breath is in his nostrils; for " wherein is he to be accounted of?" Isa. ii. 22. There are two things that should deter us from dependence upon any man, viz. his falseness and his frailty. Grace in a great measure may cure the first, but not the last. The best of men must die, as well as the worst, Rom. viii. 10. it is a vanity therefore to rely upon any man. It was the saying of a philosopher when he heard how mer-chants lost great estates at sea in a moment,—*Non amo felicita-tem e funibus pendentem;*—I love not that happiness (saith he) which hangs upon a rope. But all the happiness of many men hangs upon a far weaker thing than a rope, even the perishing breath of a creature.

Let not parents raise their hopes too high, or lean too hard upon their children. Say not of thy child, as Lamech did of Noah, " This son shall comfort us," Gen. v. 29. The world is full of the lamentings and bitter cries of disappointed parents. Let not the wife depend too much on her husband, as if her earthly comforts were secured in him against all danger. God is often provoked to stop our friend's breath, that thereby he may stop our way to sin, 1 Tim. v. 5. The trust and dependence of a soul are too weighty to be hanged upon such a weak and rotten pin as the breath of a creature.

Inf. 10. To conclude; if this frail breath be all that differenceth the living from the dead, *then fear not man whose breath is in his nostrils.* There is as little ground for our fear of man, as there is for our trust in man. As death, in a moment, can make the best man useless, and put him out of a capacity to do us any good; so it can in a moment make the worst man harmless, and put him out of capacity to do us any injury. Indeed, if the breath of our enemies were in their power, and ours at their mercy, there would be just cause to tremble at them; but they are neither masters of their own, nor ours. " Who art thou that thou shouldest be afraid of a " man that shall die ?" said God to Jacob, Isa. li. 12. The breath of the mightiest is no better secured than of the meanest, nor never in more danger to be stopt than when they breathe out threatenings against the upright.

Julian's breath was soon stopt after he threatened to root out the Galileans. Queen Mary resigned her breath at the very time when she had filled the prisons with many of Christ's sheep, and designed them for the slaughter. Read Isa. xvii. 12. and see what mushrooms we are afraid of. The best way to continue your relations and friends to your comfort, is to give God and not them your dependence; and the best way to secure yourselves against the rage of enemies, is to give God your fear, and not them. And thus much of the nature of the soul, and its tie with the body.

Rev. vi. 9, 10, 11.

And when he had opened the fifth seal, I saw under the altar the souls of them that were slain for the word of God, and for the testimony which they held.

And they cried with a loud voice, saying, How long, O Lord, holy and true, dost thou not judge and avenge our blood on them that dwell on the earth?

And white robes were given unto every one of them, and it was said unto them, that they should rest yet for a little season, until their fellow servants also, and their brethren, that should be killed as they were, should be fulfilled.

HAVING, from the former text, spoken of the nature of the soul, and the tie betwixt it and the body; I shall, from this scripture, evince the *immortality of the soul*, which is a chief part of its excellency and glory; and in this scripture it hath a firm foundation.

This book of the *Revelation* completes and seals up the whole sacred canon, Rev. xxii. 18. It also comprehends all the great and signal events of providence, relating either to the Christian church, or to its antichristian enemies in the several periods of time, to the end of the world; chap. i. 19. All which the Spirit of God discovers to us in the opening of the seven seals, the sounding of the seven trumpets, and the pouring out of the seven vials.

The first *five seals* express the state of the church under the bloody, persecuting, Heathen emperors.

Seal I.

The first seal opened, ver. 2. gives the church a very encouraging and comfortable prospect of the victories, successes, and triumphs of Christ, notwithstanding the rage, subtlety, and power of all its enemies. He shall ride on conquering, and to conquer, and his arrows shall be sharp in the hearts of his enemies, whereby the people shall fall under him. And this cheering prospect was no more than was needful: For,

Seal II.

The second seal opened, ver. 3, 4. represents the first bloody persecution of the church under Nero, whom Tertullian calls * *Dedicator damnationis nostræ :* he that first condemned Christians to the slaughter. And the persecution under him is set forth by the type of a *red horse*, and a great sword in the hand of him that rode thereon. His cruelty is by Paul compared to the *mouth of a lion*, 2 Tim. iv. 17. Paul, Peter, Bartholomew, Barnabas, Mark,

---

* Tertul. Apol. c. 5.

are all said to die by his cruel hand; and so fierce was his rage
against the Christians, that at that time, as * Eusebius saith, " a
" man might see cities lie full of dead bodies, the old and young,
" men and women, cast out naked, without any reverence of per-
" sons or sex, in the open street." And when the day failed,
Christians (saith † Tacitus) were burnt in the night, instead of
torches, to give them light in the streets.

SEAL III.

The third seal opened, ver. 5, 6. sets forth the calamities which
should befal the church by famine; yet not so much a literal as a
figurative famine, as a grave and learned commentator ‡ expounds
it, like that mentioned, Amos viii. 11, 12. which fell out under
Maximinus and Trajan; the former directing the persecution, especially against ministers, in which many bright lamps were extinguished; the latter expressly condemning all Christian meetings
and assemblies by a law. The type by which this persecution was
set forth, is a *black horse.* A gloomy and dismal day it was indeed
to the poor saints, when they eat the bread of their souls, as it
were, by weight; for he that sat on him had a pair of balances in
his hand. Then did John hear this sad voice, " A measure of
" wheat for a penny, and three measures of barley for a penny."
The quantity was but the ordinary allowance to keep a man alive
for a day, and a Roman penny was the ordinary wages given for a
day's work to a labourer. The meaning is, that in those days,
all the spiritual food men should get to keep their souls alive from
day to day, with all their travail and labour, should be but sufficient
for that end.

SEAL IV.

The fourth seal opened, ver. 7, 8. represents a much more sad
and doleful state of the church; for under it are found all the former sufferings, with some new kinds of trouble super-added.
Under this seal, Death rides upon the *pale horse,* and Hell, or the
Grave, follows him. It is conceived to point at the persecution
under Dioclesian, when the church was mowed down as a
meadow.

SEAL V.

The fifth seal is opened in my text, under which the Lord Jesus
represents to his servant John, the state and condition of those
precious souls which had been torn and separated from their bodies,
by the bloody hands of tyrants, for his name's sake, under all the
former persecutions. The design whereof is, to support and en-

---

* *Adeo ut viderit repletas humanis corporibus civitatès, jacentes mortuos, simul cum par-*
vulis senes, fœminarumque absque ulla sexus reverentia, in publico rejecta cadavera.

† Taciti l. xv. Annal.

‡ Durham on the place.

courage all that were to come in the same bloody path. *I saw under the altar, &c.* In which we have an account,

    1. Of what John saw.
    2. Of what he heard.

1. We have an account of what he saw; "I saw the souls of " them that were slain for the word of God, and for the testimony " which they held."

Souls, in this place, are not put for blood, or the dead carcases of the saints who were slain, as some have groundlessly imagined; but are to be understood properly and strictly, for those * spiritual and immortal substances, which once had a vital union with their bodies, but were now separated from them by a violent death; yet still retained a love and inclination to them, even in a state of separation; and therefore here brought in complaining of the shedding of their blood, and destruction of their bodies.

These souls (even of all that died for Christ, from Abel to that time) John saw, that is, † *in spirit;* for these immaterial substances are not perceptible by the gross external senses. He had the privilege and favour of a spiritual representation of them, being therein extraordinarily assisted, as Paul was when his soul was wrapt into the third heaven, and heard things unutterable, 2 Cor. xii. 2. God gave him a transient visible representation of those holy souls, and that *under the altar:* he means not any material *altar,* as that at *Jerusalem* was; but as the holy place figured heaven, so the *altar* figured Jesus Christ, Heb. xiii. 10. And most aptly Christ is represented to John in this figure, and souls of the martyrs at the foot or basis of this altar; thereby to inform us,

(1.) That however men look upon the death of those persons, and though they kill their names by slanders, as well as their persons by the sword; yet, in God's account, they die as sacrifices, and their blood is no other than a drink-offering poured out to God, which he highly prizeth, and graciously accepteth. Suitable whereunto Paul's expression is, Phil. ii. 17.

(2.) That the value and acceptation their death and blood-shed have with God, are through Christ, and upon his account; for it is the altar which sanctifieth the gift, Mat. xxiii. 19. And,

(3.) It informs us, that these holy souls, now in a state of separation from their bodies, were very near to Jesus Christ in heaven. They lay, as it were, at his foot.

Once more, they are here described to us by the cause of their

---

* Ειδον τας ψυχας. i. e. *I saw the souls;* here the word *soul* is taken for the immortal spirit of man, as in Mat. x. 28. in which sense John here says, that he saw the souls, &c. *Marlorat on the place.*

† Souls divested of bodies are invisible to corporeal eyes; therefore John saw them in the Spirit. *Pareus on the place.*

sufferings and death in this world; and that was, " for the word
" of God, and for the testimony which they held;" i. e. They
died in defence of the truths, or will of God revealed in his word,
against the corruptions, oppositions, and innovations of men.   As
one of the Martyrs, that held up the Bible at the stake, said, This
is it that brought me hither.   They died not as malefactors, but as
witnesses.   They gave a threefold testimony to the truth ; a lip-
testimony, a life-testimony, and a blood-testimony ; whilst the
hypocrite gives but one, and many Christians but two.   Thus we
have an account what John saw.

2. Next he tells us what he heard : and that was,

(1.) A vehement cry from those souls to God.

(2.) A gracious answer from God to them.

(1.) The cry which they uttered with a loud voice was this,
" How long, O Lord, holy and true, dost thou not avenge our
" blood on them that dwell on the earth ?"   A cry like that from
the blood of Abel.   Yet let it be remembered,

1. This cry doth not imply these holy souls to be in a restless
state, or to want true satisfaction and repose out of the body ;
nor yet,

2. That they carried with them to heaven any malevolent or
revengeful disposition : that which is principally signified by this
cry, is their vehement desire after the abolition of the kingdom of
Satan, and the completion and consummation of Christ's kingdom
in this world ; that those his enemies, which oppose his kingdom,
by slaying his saints, may be made his footstool : which is the same
thing Christ waits for in glory, Heb. x. 13.

(2.) Here we find God's gracious answer to the cry of these
souls, in which he speaks satisfaction to them two ways :

1. By somewhat given them for present.

2. By somewhat promised them hereafter.

1. That which he gives them in hand ; " White robes were
" given to every one of them."   It is generally agreed, that these
white robes given them, denote heavenly glory, the same which is
promised to all sincere and faithful ones, who preserve themselves
pure from the corruptions and defilements of the world, Rev. iii.
4. And it is as much as if God should have said to them, Although
the time be not come to satisfy your desires, in the final ruin and
overthrow of Satan's tyrannical kingdom in the world, and Christ's
consummate conquest of all his enemies, yet it shall be well with
you in the mean time : you shall *walk with me in white, and enjoy
your glory in heaven.*

2. And this is not all ; but the very things they cry for shall be
given them also after a little season ; q. d. wait but a little while,
till the rest that are to follow, in the same suffering path, be got

through the red-sea of martyrdom, as you are, and then you shall see the foot of Christ upon the necks of all his enemies, and justice shall fully avenge the precious, innocent blood of all the saints which in all ages hath been shed for my sake; from the blood of Abel, to the last that shall ever suffer for righteousness sake in the world. From all which, this conclusion is most fair and obvious.

> Doct. *That the souls of men perish not with their bodies, but do certainly over-live them, and subsist in a state of separation from them.* Mat. x. 28. " Fear not them that kill the body, " but are not able to kill the soul,"

The bodies of these Martyrs of Jesus were destroyed by divers sorts of torments, but their souls were out of the reach of all these cruel engines; they were in safety under the altar, and in glory clothed with their white robes, when their bodies they lately inhabited on earth, were turned to ashes, or torn to pieces by wild beasts.

The point I am to discourse from this scripture, is the immortality of the soul. For the better understanding whereof, let it be noted that there is a twofold immortality.

I. Simple, and absolute in its own nature.

II. Derived, dependent, and from the pleasure of God.

In the former sense, God only hath immortality, as the apostle speaks, 1 Tim. vi. 16. Our souls have it as a gift from him. He that created our souls out of nothing, can, if he please, reduce them to nothing again; but he hath bestowed immortality upon them, and produced them in a nature suitable to that his appointment, fitted for an everlasting life. So that though God by his absolute power can, yet he never will annihilate them, but they shall, and must live for ever in endless blessedness or misery; death may destroy these mortal bodies, but it cannot destroy our souls. And the certainty of this assertion is grounded upon these reasons, and will be cleared by these following arguments.

ARGUMENT I.

The first argument for proof of the soul's immortality, may be taken from the simplicity, spirituality, and uncompoundedness of its nature; it is a pure, simple, unmixed being. * Death is the dissolution of things compounded; where therefore no composition or mixture is found, no death or dissolution can follow.

Death is the great divider, but it is of things that are divisible. The more simple, pure, and refined any material thing is, by so

---

* Death is a separation, dissolving, or tearing asunder of parts that had been joined by some union. *Tullius.*

much the more permanent and durable it is found to be. The nearer it approaches to the nature of spirits, the farther it is removed from the power of death: but that which is not material, or mixed at all, is wholly exempt from the stroke and power of death. It is from the contrarient qualities, and jarring humours, in mixed bodies, that they come under the law and power of dissolution. Matter and mixture, are the doors at which death enters naturally upon the creatures.

But the soul of man is a simple, spiritual, immaterial, and unmixed being, not compounded of matter and form, as other creatures are, but void of matter, and altogether spiritual, as may appear in the vast capacity of its understanding faculty, which cannot be straitened by receiving multitudes of truths into it. It need not empty itself of what it had received before, to make way for more truth; nor doth it find itself clogged or burdened by the greatest multitudes or varieties of truths; but the more it knows, the more it still desires to know. Its capacity and appetite are found to enlarge themselves according to the increase of knowledge. So that to speak, as the matter is, If the knowledge of all arts, sciences, and mysteries of nature, could be gathered into the mind of one man, yet that mind would thirst, and even burn with desire after more knowledge, and find more room for it than it did when it first sipt, and relished the sweetness of truth. Knowledge, as knowledge, never burdens or cloys the mind; but like fire increases and enlarges, as it finds more matter to work upon. Now this could never be, if the soul were a material being. Take the largest vessel, and you shall find the more you pour into it, the less room is still left for more; and when it is full, you cannot pour in one drop more, except you let out what was in it before *. But the soul is no such vessel, it can retain all it had, and be still receptive of more; so that nothing can fill it, and satisfy it, but that which is infinite and perfect.

The natural appetite after food is sometimes sharp and eager, but then there is a stint and measure beyond which it craves not; but the appetite of the mind is more eager and unlimited; it never saith till it come to rest in God, it is enough †, because the faculty which produceth it, is more active, spiritual, and immaterial. All matter has its limits, bounds, and just measures, beyond which it cannot be extended. But the soul is boundless, and its appetition infinite; it rests not, but in the spiritual and infinite

---

* *Intus existens prohibet alienum.* i. e. What is already within, refuses access to what is without.

† *Appetitus finis est infinitus.* There is no end of desiring, till we come at the desired end, which is God.

Being, God alone being its adequated object, and able to satisfy its desires; which plainly proves it to be a spiritual, immaterial, and simple being. And being so, two things necessarily follow therefrom.

1. That it is void of any principle of corruption in itself.

2. That it is not liable to any stroke of death, by any adverse power without itself.

1. It cannot be liable to death, from any seeds or principles of corruption within itself; for where there is no composition, there is no dissolution: the spirituality and simplicity of the soul admit of no corruption.

2. Nor is it liable to death by any adverse power without itself; no sword can touch it, no instrument of death can reach it: it is above the reach of all adversaries, Mat. x. 28. " Fear not them " that kill the body, but cannot kill the soul." The bounds and limits of creature-power are here fixed by Jesus Christ, beyond which they cannot go. They can wound, torment, and destroy the body, when God permits them : but the soul is out of their reach. A sword can no more hurt or wound it, than it can wound or hurt the light; and consequently it is, and must needs be of an immortal nature.

Object. But there seems to be a decay upon our souls in our old age, and decays argue and imply corruption, and are so many steps and tendencies towards the death and dissolution thereof. The experience of the whole world shews us how the apprehensions, judgments, wit, and memory of old men fail, even to that degree that they become children again in respect of the abilities of their minds: their souls only serving, as it were, to salt their bodies, and keep them from putrefaction for a few days longer.

Sol. It is a great mistake; there is not the least decay upon the soul; no time makes any change upon the essence of the soul: all the alteration that is made, is upon the organs and instruments of the body, which decay in time, and become unapt and unserviceable to the soul.

The soul, like an expert, skilful musician, is as able as ever it was, but the body, its instrument, is out of tune: and the ablest artist can make no pleasing melody upon an instrument whose strings are broken, or so relaxed that they cannot be screwed up to their due height.

Let Hippocrates, the prince of physicians, decide this matter for us. " The soul (saith he) cannot be changed or altered as to its " essence, by the access of meat or drink, or any other thing what- " soever; but all the alterations that are made, must be referred " either to the spirits with which it mixeth itself, or to the vessels

" and organs through which it streameth *." So that this proves not its corruptibility : and being neither corruptible in itself, nor vulnerable by any creature without itself; seeing man cannot, and God will not destroy it, the conclusion is strongly inferred, *That therefore it is immortal.*

ARGUMENT II.

The immortality of the souls of men may be concluded from the promises of everlasting blessedness, and the threatenings of everlasting miseries, respectively made in the scriptures of truth, to the godly and ungodly after this life; which promises and threatenings had been altogether vain and delusory, if our souls perish with our bodies.

1. God has made many everlasting promises of blessedness, yea, he hath established an everlasting covenant betwixt himself and the souls of the righteous, promising to be their God for ever, and to bestow endless blessedness upon them in the world to come. Such a promise is that, John viii. 28. " I give unto them eternal life, and " they shall never perish." And John iv. 14. " Whosoever " drinketh of the water that I shall give him shall never thirst; " but the water that I shall give him, shall be in him a well of " water springing up into everlasting life." And again, John xi. 26. " Whosoever liveth and believeth in me, shall never die." And once more, Rom. ii. 7. " To them who by patient continu- " ance in well-doing, seek for glory and honour, and immortality, " eternal life;" with multitudes more of like nature.

Now if these be no vain and delusory promises, (as to be sure they are not, being the words of a true and faithful God) then those souls to whom they are made, must live for ever; for if the subject of the promises fail, consequently the performance of the promises must fail too. For how shall they be made good, when those to whom they are made, are perished?

Let it not be objected here, That the bodies of believers are concerned in the promises as well as their souls, and yet their bodies perish notwithstanding.

For we say, though their bodies die, yet they shall live again, and enjoy the fruit of the promises in eternal glory; and whilst their bodies lie in the grave, their souls are with God, enjoying the covenanted blessedness in heaven, Rom. viii. 10, 11. and so the covenant-bond is not loosed betwixt them and God by death, which it must needs be, in case the soul perish when the body doth. And upon this hypothesis, that argument of Christ is built, Mat. xxii.

---

* *Anima nostra quoad essentiam mutari non potest, aut alterari, sive cibi, sive potus, cujuscunque rei alterius accessu : referenda est enim omnium alterationum causa, aut ad Spiritus, quibus see immiscet, aut ad vasa, sive organa quæ permeat.* Hippocrat. lib. de diaeta,

32. proving the resurrection from the covenant God made with Abraham, Isaac, and Jacob; " I am the God of Abraham, and the " God of Isaac, and the God of Jacob: God is not the God of " the dead, but of the living," q. d. If Abraham, Isaac, and Jacob be perished in soul as well as in body, how then is God their God; what is become of the promise and covenant-relation? for if one correlate fail, the relation necessarily fails with it. If God be their God, then certainly they are in being; " for God is not the God " of the dead," i. e. of those that are utterly perished. Therefore it must needs be, that though their bodies be naturally dead, yet their souls still live; and their bodies must live again at the resurrection by virtue of the same promise.

On the contrary, many threatenings of eternal misery, after this life, are found in the scriptures of truth, against ungodly and wicked persons. Such is that in 2 Thess. i. 7, 8, 9. " The Lord Jesus " shall be revealed from heaven in flaming fire, to render vengeance " on them that know not God, and that obey not the gospel of our " Lord Jesus Christ, who shall be punished with everlasting de- " struction, from the presence of the Lord, and the glory of his " power." And speaking of the torments of the damned, Christ thus expresseth the misery of such wretched souls in hell, Mark ix. 44. " Where their worm dieth not, and the fire is not quenched." But how shall the wicked be punished with everlasting destruction, if their souls have not an everlasting duration? or how can it be said, *Their worm* (viz. the remorse and anguish of their conscience) *dieth not*, if their souls die? Punishment can endure no longer than its subject endureth. If the being of the soul cease, its pains and punishments must have an end.

You see then, there are everlasting promises and threatenings to be fulfilled, both upon the godly and ungodly, " He that believeth " on the Son hath everlasting life, and he that believeth not the " Son, shall not see life, but the wrath of God abideth on him," John iii. 16. The believer shall never see spiritual death, viz. the separation of his soul from God; and the unbeliever shall never see life, viz. the blessed fruition of God; but the wrath of God shall abide on him. If wrath must abide on him, he must abide also as the wretched subject thereof, which is another argument of the immortality of souls.

ARGUMENT III.

The immortality of the soul is a truth asserted and attested by the universal consent of all nations and ages of the world. " We " give much (said * Seneca) to the presumption of all men," and

---

*. *Multum dare solemus præsumptioni omnium hominum: cum de animæ æternitate disserimus, nonc leve momentem apud nos habet, consensus hominum aut timentium inferos, aut colentium.* Senec. Ep. 17.

that justly; for it would be hard to think that an error should obtain the general consent of mankind, or that God would suffer all the world, in all ages of it, to bow down under an universal deception.

This doctrine sticks close to the nature of man; it springs up easily, and without force from his conscience. It hath been allowed as an unquestionable thing, not only among Christians who have the oracles of God to teach and confirm this doctrine, but among Heathens also, who had no other light but that of nature to guide them into the knowledge and belief of it. Learned Zanchius * cites out of Cicero an excellent passage to this purpose. " *In every thing* saith he, *the consent of all nations is to be accounted* " *the law of nature;* and therefore, with all good men, it should " be instead of a thousand demonstrations; and to resist it, (as he " there adds) what is it, but to resist the voice of God?" and how much more, when, with his consent, the word of God doth also consent? As for the consent of nations, in this point, the learned author last mentioned, hath industriously gathered many great and famous testimonies from the ancient Chaldeans, Grecians, Pythagoreans, Stoics, Platonists, &c. which evidently shew they made no doubt of the immortality of their souls. How plain is that of Phocylides? ψαχη δε αθαιατος και αγηρος ζη δια παντος. Speaking of the soul, in opposition to the body, which must be resolved into dust, he saith, " But for the soul, that is immortal, and never " grows old, but lives for ever." And Tresmegistus, the famous and celebrated Philosopher†, gives this account of man, " That " he consists of two parts, being mortal in respect of his body, " but immortal in respect of his soul, which is the best and principal part." Plato ‡ not only asserts the immortality of the souls of men, but disputes for it: and among other arguments, he urges this; " That if it were not so, wicked men would certainly have " the advantage of righteous and good men, who, after they have " committed all manner of evils, should suffer none." But what speak I of philosophers? the most barbarous nations in the world constantly believe it §. The Turks acknowledge it in their Alcoran; and though they grossly mistake the nature of heaven, in

---

* *In omni re consensio ommium gentium lex naturæ putanda est: coque instar mille demonstrationum talis consensio apud bonos esse debet.* Zanchius de immortalitate animarum. p. 644.

† Ανθρωπος δυπλες, δια το σωμα θνητος, αθανατος κ δια ψυχην, τον εσιωδη ανθρωςον.

‡ E μεν γαρ, &c. *Si enim mors dissolutio esset utriusque (corporis sc. et anima) lucrum foret malis cum moriantur.* Plato in Epist.

§ Why do I speak of the Turks, Tartars, Muscovites, Indians, Persians, and all other nations which are at this day barbarous? None is so barbarous and

fancying it to be a paradise of sensual pleasures, as well as the way thither, by their impostor Mahomet; yet it is plain they believe the soul's immortality, and that it lives in pain or pleasure after this life.

The very savage and illiterate Indians are so fully persuaded of the soul's immortality, that wives cast themselves cheerfully into the flames to attend the souls of their husbands; and subjects, to attend the souls of their kings into the other world.

Two things are objected against this argument.

1. That some particular persons have denied this doctrine, as Epicurus, &c. and by argument maintained the contrary.

To which I answer, That though they have done so, yet (1.) This no way shakes the argument from the consent of nations, because some few persons have denied it: we truly say, the earth is spherical, though there be many hills and risings in it. If Democritus put out his own eyes, must we therefore say all the world is blind?

(2.) It is worth thinking on, whether they that have questioned the immortality of the soul, have not rather made it the matter of their option and desire, than of their faith and persuasion. We distinguish Atheists into three classes, such as are so in *practice*, in *desire*, or in *judgment*; but of the former sorts there may be found multitudes, to one that is so in his settled judgment. If you think it strange that any man should wish his soul to be mortal, Hierocles * gives us the reason of it: " A wicked man (saith he) " is afraid of his Judge; and therefore wishes his soul and body " may perish together by death, rather than it should come to God's " tribunal."

Object. 2. Nor can the strength of the argument be eluded, by saying, " All this may be but an universal tradition," one nation receiving it from another.

Sol. For as this is neither true in itself, nor possible to be made good; so if it were, it would not invalidate the argument: for if it were not a truth agreeable to the light of nature, and so easily received by all men upon the proposal of it, it were impossible that all the nations in the world should embrace it so readily, and hold it so tenaciously as they do.

ARGUMENT IV.

The immortality of the soul may be evinced from the everlasting

---

wicked, but he is convinced, that, after death, there are places in which souls are either punished for their bad actions, or rewarded and blest with delights for their good actions. *Zanch.*

* Ο κακος αθανατον ειναι την αυτε ψυχην να μη υπομενη τιμωρεμενος και φθανετον εχει δικαεην. Hieroc.

habits which are subjected, and inherent in it. If these habits abide for ever, certainly so must the souls in which they are planted.

The souls of good men are the good ground, in which the seed of grace is sown by the Spirit, Mat. xiii. 23. i. e. the subjects in which gracious properties and affections do inhere and dwell, (which is the formal notion of a substance) and these implanted graces are everlasting things. So John iv. 14. "It shall be in him a well of " water, springing up into everlasting life," i. e. the graces of the Spirit shall be in believers, permanent habits, fixed principles, which shall never decay. And therefore that seed of grace, which is cast into their souls at their regeneration, is in 1 Pet. i. 23. called "incorruptible seed, which liveth and abideth for ever:" and it is incorruptible, not only considered abstractly, in its own simple nature, but concretely, as it is in the sanctified soul, its subject: for it is said, 1 John iii. 9. "The seed of God remaineth in " him." It abideth for ever in the soul. If then these two things be clear unto us, viz.

1. That the habits of grace be everlasting;

2. That they are inseparable from sanctified souls;

It must needs follow, That the soul, their subject, is so too, an everlasting and immortal soul. And how plainly do both these propositions lie before us in the scriptures? As for the immortal and indeterminable nature of saving grace, it is plain to him that considers, not only what the forecited scriptures speak about it, calling it *incorruptible seed, a well of water springing up into everlasting life*; but add to these, what is said of these divine qualities in 2 Pet. i. 4. where they are called the *divine nature*; and Eph. iv. 18. *the life of God*, noting the perpetuity of these principles in believers, as well as their resemblance of God in holiness, who are endowed with them.

I know it is a great question among divines, *An gratia in renatis sit natura et essentia sua interminabilis?* Whether these principles of grace in the regenerate be everlasting and interminable in their own nature and essence? For my own part, I think that God only is naturally, essentially, and absolutely interminable and immortal. But these gracious habits, planted by him in the soul, are so by virtue of God's appointment, promise, and covenant. And sure it is, that by reason hereof they are interminate, which is enough for my purpose, if they be not essentially interminable. Though grace be but a creature, and therefore hath a *posse mori*, yet it is a creature begotten by the Word and Spirit of God, which live and abide for ever, and a creature within the promise and covenant of God, by reason whereof it can never actually die.

And then as for the inseparableness of these graces from the souls in whom they are planted, how clear is this from John ii. 27. where sanctifying grace is compared to an unction, and this unction is said to abide in them? And 1 John iii. 9. it is called the seed of God, which remaineth in the soul. All our natural and moral excellencies and endowments go away when we die; Job iv. 21. " Doth not their excellency that is in them go away?" Men may outlive their acquired gifts, but not their supernatural graces. These stick by the soul, as Ruth to Naomi, and where it goes they go too: so that when the soul is dislodged by death, all its graces ascend up with it into glory; it carries away all its faith, love, delight in God, all its comfortable experiences, and fruits of communion with God, along with it to heaven. For death is so far from divesting the soul of its graces, that it perfects in a moment all that was defective in them; 1 Cor. xiii. 10. " When " that which is perfect shall come, then that which is in part " shall be done away," as the twilight is done away when the sun is up, and at its zenith. So then, grace never dieth, and this never-dying grace is inseparable from its subject; by which it is plain to him that considers, that as graces, so souls, abide for ever.

Object. But this only proves the immortality of regenerate souls.

Sol. It doth so. But then consider, as there be gracious habits in the regenerate that never die, so there are vicious habits in the unregenerate that can never be separated from them in the world to come. Hence, John viii. 24. they are said to " die in their sins;" and Job xx. 11. " Their iniquities lie down with them in the dust;" and Ezek. xxiv. 13. " They shall never be purged." Remarkable is that place, Rev. xxii. 11. " Let him that is filthy be filthy still." And if guilt sticks so fast, and sin be so deeply engraven in impenitent souls, they also must remain for ever, to bear the punishment of them.

ARGUMENT V.

The immortality of the soul of man may be evinced from the dignity of man above all other creatures, (angels only excepted) and his dominion over them all.

In this, the scriptures are clear, that man is the master-piece of all God's other works; Psal. viii. 5, 6. " For thou hast made " him a little lower than the angels, and hast crowned him with " glory and honour. Thou hast made him to have dominion over " the works of thy hand, thou hast put all things under his feet." Other creatures were made for his service, and he is crowned king over them all. One man is of more worth than all the inferior creatures.

But wherein is his dignity and excellency above all other creatures, if not in respect of the capacity and immortality of his soul? Sure it can be found no where else; for as to the body, many of the creatures excel man in the perfections of sense, greatness of strength, agility of members, &c.

> *Nos aper auditu praecellit, aranea tactu,*
> *Vultur odoratu, lynx visu, simia gustu**.

And for beauty, *Solomon in all his glory was not arrayed like one of the lilies of the field.* The beasts and fowls enjoy more pleasure, and live divested of all those cares and cumbers which perplex and wear out the lives of men. It cannot be in respect of bodily perfections and pleasures, that man excels other creatures.

If you say, He excels them all in respect of that noble endowment of reason, which is peculiar to man, and his singular excellency above them all.

It is true, this is his glory: but if you deprive the reasonable soul of immortality, you despoil it of all, both of its glory and comfort, and put the reasonable into a worse condition than the unreasonable and brutish creatures. For if the soul may die with the body, and man perish as the beast, happier is the life of the beast, which is perplexed with no cares nor fears about futurities: our reason serves to little other purpose but to be an engine of torture, a mere rack to our souls.

Certainly, the privilege of man doth not consist in reason, as abstracted from immortality. But in this, it properly consists, that he enjoys not only a reasonable, but also rejoiceth in an immortal soul, which shall over-live the world, and subsist separate from the body, and abide for ever, when all other souls, being but a material form, perish with that matter on which they depend. This is the proper dignity of man, above the beast that perisheth; and to deprive him of immortality, and leave him his reason, is but to leave him a more miserable and wretched creature than any that God hath put under his feet. For man is a prospecting creature, and raiseth up to himself vast hopes and fears from the world to come: by these he is restrained from the sensual pleasures, which other creatures freely enjoy, and exercised with ten thousand cares, which they are unacquainted with; and to fail at last of all his hopes and expectations of happiness, in the world to come, is to fall many degrees lower than the lowest creature shall fall; even so much lower as his expectations and hopes had lifted him higher.

ARGUMENT VI.

The souls of men must be immortal, or else the desires of immortality are planted in their souls in vain.

---

* The bear excels man in hearing, the spider in feeling, the vulture in smelling, the lynx in seeing, and the ape in tasting.

That there are desires of immortality found in the hearts of all men, is a truth too evident to be denied or doubted *. Man cannot bound and terminate his desires within the narrow limits of this world, and the time that measures it. Nothing that can be measured by time is commensurate to the desires of man's soul. No motto better suits it than this, *Non est mortale quod opto;* I seek for that which will not die, Rom. ii. 7. And his great relief against death lies in this, *Non omnis moriar:* That he shall not totally perish. Yea, we find in all men, even in those that seem to be most drowned and lost in the love and delights of this present world, a natural desire to continue their names and memories to posterity after death. Hence it is said, Psal. xlix. 11. "Their in-"ward thought is, that their houses shall continue for ever, and "their dwelling places to all generations; they call their lands after "their own names."

And hence is the desire of children, which is, as one saith, *nodosa æternitas,* a knotty eternity; when our thread is spun out and cut off, their thread is knit to it; and so we dream of a continued succession in our name and family.

Absalom had no children to continue his memory; to supply which defect, he reared up a pillar, 2 Sam. xviii. 18. Now it cannot be imagined that God should plant the desire of immortality in those souls, that are incapable of it; nor yet can we give a rational account how these apprehensions of immortality should come into the souls of men, except they themselves be of an immortal nature. For, either these notions and apprehensions of immortality are impressed upon our souls by God, or do naturally spring out of the souls of men: If God impress them, those impressions are made in vain, if there be no such thing as immortality to be enjoyed; and if they spring and rise naturally out of our souls, that is a sufficient evidence of their immortality. For we can no more conceive, and form to ourselves, ideas and notions of immortality, if our souls be mortal, than the brutes which are void of reason, can form to themselves notions and conceptions of rationality. So then the very apprehensions and desires that are found in men's hearts of immortality, do plainly speak them to be of an immortal nature †.

---

* I beseech men, for God's sake, that if any time there arise in them a desire, or a wish that others should speak well of them rather than evil after their death, then at that time they would seriously consider whether these motions are not from some spirit, to continue a spirit after it leaves its earthly habitation, rather than from an earthly spirit, a vapour, which cannot act, or imagine, or desire, or fear things beyond its continuance. *Hale de anima, p.* 72.

† It forms conceptions of things spiritual and abstract from matter, and discerns objects which have no dimensions, figure, colour, or affection of matter. If the soul itself is the fountain or idea of immortality, it must be immortal; because what is

ARGUMENT VII.

Moreover, the account given us in the scripture of the return of several souls into their own bodies again after death, and real separation from them, shews us that the soul subsists and lives in a separate state after death, and perisheth not by the stroke of death: For if it were annihilated or destroyed by death, the same soul could never be restored again to the same body. A dead body may indeed be acted by an assisting form, which may move and carry it from place to place; so the devil hath acted the dead bodies of many; but they cannot be said to live again by their own souls, after a real separation by death, unless those souls over-lived the bodies they forsook at death, and had their abode in another place and state. You have divers unquestionable examples of the soul's return into the body recorded in scripture: As that of the Shunamite's son, 2 Kings iv. 18, 19, 20, 32, 33, 34, 35, 36, 37. That of the ruler's daughter, Mat. ix. 18, 23, 24, 25. That of the widow's son, Luke vii. 12, 13, 14, 15. And that of Lazarus, John xi. 39, 40, 41, 42, 43, 44, 45. " These are no other * but the very same " souls, their own souls which returned to them again; which, as " Chrysostom well observes, is a great proof of their immortality " against them that think the soul is annihilated after the death of " the body."

It is true, the scripture gives us no account of any sense or apprehension they retained after their re-union of the place or state they were in during their separation. There seemed to be a perfect αμνησια, forgetfulness of all that they saw or felt in the state of separation. And indeed it was necessary it should be so, that our faith might be built rather upon the sure promises of God, than such reports and narratives of them that come to us from the dead, Luke xvi. 31. And if we believe not the word, neither would we believe *if one came from the dead.*

ARGUMENT VIII.

Moreover, *Eighthly,* The supposition of the soul's perishing with the body, is subversive of the Christian religion in the principal doctrines and duties thereof: take away the immortality of the soul, and all religion falls to the ground. I will instance in

1. The doctrines }
2. The duties } of religion.

First, It overthrows the main principles and doctrines of the

---

momentary, cannot form an idea of an immortal nature, for the soul which is void of reason cannot form a conception of rationality. *Stern on death, p.* 198.

* *Non aliam, sed ipsam priorem animam corpori mortuo restitutam esse, contra eos qui putaverunt et hodie putant animam post mortem corporis nihil esse.*

Christian religion, upon which both our faith and comfort is founded; and consequently it undoes and ruins us as to all solid hope
and true joy. The doctrines or principles it overthrows, are, among
many other, such as follow.

1. It nullifies and makes void the great design and end of God's
eternal election. The scriptures tells us, That from all eternity God
hath chosen a certain number in Christ Jesus, to eternal life, and
to the means by which they shall attain it, out of his mere good
pleasure, and for the praise of his grace. This was (1.) An eternal act of God, Eph. i. 4. long before we had our being, Rom. ix.
11. (2.) This choice of God, or his purpose to save some, is immutable, 2 Tim. ii. 19. James i. 17. (3.) This choice he made in
Christ, Eph. i. 4. Not that Christ is the cause of God's choosing
us: For we were not elected because we were, but that we might be
in Christ. Christ was ordained to be the *Medium* of the execution
of this decree. And all the mercies which were purposed and ordained for us, were to be purchased by the blood of Christ. He was
not the *cause* of the decree, but the purchaser of the mercies decreed for us. (4.) This choice was of a certain number of persons
who are all known to God, 2 Tim. ii. 19. and all given to Christ
in the covenant of redemption, John xvii. 2, 6. So that no elect
person can be a reprobate, no reprobate an elect person. (5.) This
number was chosen to salvation, 1 Thess. v. 9. No less did God
design for them that glory and happiness, and that for ever. (6.)
The same persons that are appointed to salvation as the end, are
also appointed to sanctification as the way and means by which they
shall attain that end, 1 Pet. i. 1, 2. 2 Thess. ii. 13, 14. (7.) The
impulsive cause of this choice was the mere good pleasure of his will,
2 Tim. i. 9. Rom. ix. 15, 16. Eph. i. 9. (8.) The end of all this
is the praise of his glorious grace, Eph. i. 5, 6. to make a glorious
manifestation of the riches of his grace for ever. This is the account the scripture gives us of God's eternal choice.

But if our souls be mortal, and perish with our bodies, all this is
a mistake, and, we are imposed upon, and our understandings are
abused by this doctrine: For to what purpose are all these decrees
and contrivances of God from everlasting, if our souls perish with
our bodies? Certainly, if it be so, he loses all the thoughts and
counsels of his heart about us; and that counsel of his will, which
is so much celebrated in the scriptures, and admired by his people,
comes to nought. For this is evident to every man's consideration,
that if the soul (which is the object about which all those counsels
and thoughts of God were employed and laid out) fail in its being,
all those thoughts and counsels that have been employed about it,
and spent on it, must necessarily fail and come to nothing with it.
The thoughts of his heart cannot stand fast, as it is said, Psal. xxxiii.

11. if the soul slide, about which they are conversant. In that day the elect soul perisheth, the eternal consultations and purposes of God's heart perish with it. Keckerman tells us, that " * Albertus " Magnus, with abundance of art, and the study of thirty years, " made a vocal statue in the form of a man. It was a rare con- " trivance, and much admired; the cunning Artist had so framed " it, that by wheels and other *machines* placed within it, it could " pronounce words articulately." Aquinas being surprized to hear the statue speak, was affrighted at it, and brake it all to pieces; upon which Albertus told him he had at one blow destroyed the work of thirty years. Such a blow would the death of the soul give to the counsels and thoughts, not of man, but of God, not of thirty years, but from everlasting.

If the souls of men perish at death, either God never did appoint any souls to salvation, as the scriptures testify he did, 1 Thess. v. 9. or else the foundation of God stands not sure, as his word tells us it doth, 2 Tim. ii. 19. So then this supposition overturns the eternal decrees and counsels of God, which is the first thing.

2. It overthrows the covenant of redemption betwixt the Father and the Son before this world was made. There was a federal transaction betwixt the Father and the Son from eternity, about our salvation, 2 Tim. i. 9. Zech. vi. 13. In that covenant Christ engaged to redeem the elect by his blood; and the Father promised him a reward of those his sufferings, Isa. liii. 12. Accordingly he hath poured out his soul to death for them, finished the work, John xvii. 4. and is now in heaven, expecting the full reward and fruits of his sufferings, which consist not in his own personal glory, which he there enjoys, but in the completeness and fulness of his mystical body, John xvii. 24.

But certainly, if our souls perish with our bodies, Christ would be greatly disappointed: Nor can that promise be ever made good to him; Isa. liii. 11. " He shall see of the travail of his soul and " be satisfied." He hath done his work, but where is his reward? See how this supposition strikes at the justice of God, and wounds his faithfulness in his covenant with his Son. He hath as much comfort and reward from the travail of his soul, as a mother that is delivered after many sharp pangs of a child that dies almost as soon as born.

3. It overthrows the doctrines of *Christ's incarnation, death, resurrection, ascension,* and *intercession* in heaven for us. And these are the main pillars both of our faith and comfort. Take away

---

* *Albertus Magnus statuam hominis construxit, quæ cum libramentis quibusdam, rotis atque aliis machinis intra latentibus peritissime compositis, linguam quadam ratione et- disciplina moventibus, articulata verba pronunciaret.*

these, and take away our lives too, for these are the springs of all joy and comfort to the people of God, Rom. viii. 34.

His *incarnation* was necessary to capacitate him for his mediatorial work : It was not only a part of it, but such a part, without which he could discharge no other part of it.   This was the wonder of men and angels, 1 Tim. iii. 16.   A God incarnate is the world's wonder; no condescension like this, Phil. ii. 6, 7.

The *death* of Christ hath the nature and respect of a ransom, or equivalent price laid down to the justice of God for our redemption, Matth. xx. 28. Acts xx. 28.   It brought our souls from under the curse, and purchased for them everlasting blessedness, Gal. iv. 4, 5.

The *resurrection* of Christ from the dead hath the nature both of a testimony of his finishing the work of our redemption, and the Father's full satisfaction therein, John vi. 10. and of a principle of our resurrection to eternal life, 1 Cor. xv. 20.

The *ascension* of Christ into heaven was in the capacity and relation of a forerunner, Heb. vi. 20. it was to prepare places for the redeemed, who were to come after him to glory in their several generations, John xiv. 2, 3.

The *intercession* of Christ in heaven, is for the security of our purchased inheritance to us, and to prevent any new breaches which might be made by our sins, whereby it might be forfeited, and we divested of it again, 1 John ii. 1, 2.

All these jointly make up the foundation of our faith and hope of glory : But if our souls perish, or be annihilated at death, our faith, hope, and comforts, are all delusions, vain dreams, which do but amuse our fond imaginations.   For,

(1.) It was not worth so great a stoop and abasement of the blessed God, as he submitted to in his incarnation, when he appeared in flesh, yea, in the likeness of sinful flesh, Rom. viii. 3. and made himself of no reputation, Phil. ii. 7.   An act that is, and ever will be admired by men and angels: I say, it was not worth so great a miracle as this, to procure for us the vanishing comfort of a few years, and that short-lived comfort no other than a deluding dream, or mocking phantasm : For seeing it consists in hope and expectation from the world to come, as the scriptures every where speak, 1 Thess. v. 8. and 2 Cor. iii. 12. Rom. v. 3, 4, 5. if there be no such enjoyments for us there (as most certainly there are not, if our souls perish) it is but a vanity, a thing of nought, that was the errand upon which the Son of God came from the Father's bosom, to procure for us.

(2.) And for what, think you, was the blood of God upon the cross ? What was so vast and inconceivable a treasure expended to purchase ? What ! the flattering and vain hopes of a few years, of which we may say, as it was said of the Roman consulship, *unius anni volaticum gaudium;* the fugitive joy of a year: Yea, not only short-lived and vain hopes in themselves, but such for the sake whereof we abridge ourselves of the pleasures and desires of the flesh, 1 John iii. 3. and submit ourselves to the greatest sufferings in the world, Rom. viii. 18. For the hope of Israel am I bound with this chain, *&c.* Acts xxviii. 20. Was this the purchase of his blood? Was this it for which he sweat, and groaned, and bled, and died? Was that precious blood no more worth than such a trifle as this?

(3.) To what purpose did Christ rise again from the dead? Was it not to be the *first-fruits of them that sleep?* Did he not rise as the common head of believers, to give us assurance we shall not perish, and be utterly lost in the grave? Col. i. 18. But if our souls perish at death, there can be no resurrection; and if none, then Christ died and rose in vain, *we are yet in our sins,* and all those absurdities are unavoidable, with which the apostle loads this supposition, 1 Cor. xv. 13, *&c.*

(4.) And to as little purpose was his triumphant ascension into heaven, if we can have no benefit by it. The professed end of his ascension was " to prepare a place for us," John xiv. 2. But to what purpose are those mansions in the heavens prepared, if the inhabitants for whom they are prepared be utterly lost? And why is he called the *forerunner*, if there be none to follow him? as surely there are not, if our souls perish with our bodies. Those heavenly mansions, that city prepared by God, must stand void for ever if this be so.

(5.) To conclude; in vain is the intercession of Christ in heaven for us, if this be so. They that shall never come thither, have no business there to be transacted by their advocate for them. So that the whole *doctrine of redemption by Christ* is utterly subverted by this one supposition.

4. As it subverts the *doctrine of redemption by Christ*, and all the hopes and comforts we build thereon, so it utterly destroys all the works of the spirit, upon the hearts of believers, and makes them vanish into nothing.

There are divers acts and offices of the Spirit of God about, and upon our souls; I will only single out three, *viz.* his *sanctifying, sealing* and *comforting work:* all things of great weight with believers.

(1.) His *sanctifying work*, whereby he alters the frames and tempers of our souls, 2 Cor. v. 17. " Old things are passed away, " behold all things are become new."

The declared and direct end of this work of the Spirit upon our souls, is to attemper and dispose them for heaven, Col. i. 12. For seeing " nothing that is unclean can enter into the holy place,"

Rev. xxi. 27. " and without holiness no man shall see the Lord,"
Heb. xii. 14. it is necessary that all those that have this hope in
them, should expect to be partakers of their hopes in the way of
purification, 1 John iii. 3.   And this is the ground upon which the
people of God do mortify their lusts, and take so much pains with
their own hearts, Mat. xviii. 8. counting it better (as their Lord tells
them) " to enter into life halt and maimed, than having two eyes or
" hands to be cast into hell."   But to what purpose is all this self-
denial, all these heart-searchings, heart-humblings, cries, and tears,
upon the account of sin, and for an heart suited to the will of God,
if there be no such life to be enjoyed *with God, after this animal
life is finished ;*
    Object. If you say there is a present advantage resulting to us in
this world, from our abstinence and self-denial; we have the truer
and longer enjoyment of our comforts on earth by it; debauchery
and licentiousness do not only flatten the appetite, and debase and
alloy the comforts of this world, but cut short our lives by the exor-
bitances and abuses of them.
    Solut. Though there be a truth in this worth our noting, yet (1.)
morality could have done all this without sanctification; there was
no need for the pouring out of the Spirit, for so low an use and
purpose as this.   (2.) And therefore as the wisdom of God would
be censured and impeached, in sending his Spirit for an end which
could as well be attained without it; so the veracity of God must
needs be affronted by it, who, as you heard before, hath declared
our salvation to be the end of our sanctification.
    (2.) His *sealing, witnessing,* and *assuring* work. We have a full
account in the scriptures, of these offices and works of the Spirit,
and some spiritual sense and feeling of them upon our own hearts,
which are two good assurances that there are such things as his
bearing witness with our spirit, Rom. viii. 16. " his sealing us to
" the day of redemption," Eph. iv. 30. " his earnest given into
" our hearts," 2 Cor. i. 22. All which acts and works of the Spirit
have a direct and clear aspect upon the life to come, and the happiness of our souls in the full enjoyment of God to eternity; for it is
to that life we are now sealed; and of the full sum of that glory,
that these are the pledges and earnests. But if our souls perish by
death, these witnesses of the Spirit are delusions, and his earnests are
given us but in jest.
    (3.) His *comforting work* is a sweet fruit and effect sensibly felt
and tasted by believers in this world. He is from this office stiled the
Comforter, John xvi. 7. *signanter, et eminenter.* He so comforts
as none other doth, or can. And what is the matter of his com-

forts, but the blessedness to come, the joys of the coming world?
John xvi. 13. *Eye hath not seen*, &c.

Upon the account of these unseen things, he enableth believers
to glory in tribulation, Rom. v. 4. to despise present things,
whether the smiles or the frowns of the world, Heb. xi. 24. and
ver. 26. But if the being of our souls fail at death, these are
but the fantastic joys of men in a dream, and the experiences of
all God's people are found but so many fond conceits, and gross
mistakes.

5. This supposition overthrows the doctrine of the resurrection,
which is the consolation of Christians. We believe, according to
the scripture, that after death hath divorced our souls and bodies
for a time, they shall meet again, and be re-united, and that the
joy at their re-union will be to all that are in Christ, greater than
the sorrows they felt at parting. This seems not incredible to us,
whatever natural improbabilities and carnal reasons may be against
it, Acts xxvi. 8. and that because the Almighty Power, which is
able to subdue all things to himself, undertakes this task, Phil. iii.
21.

We believe this very same numerical body shall rise again, Job
xxi. 27. by the return of the same soul into it, which now dwelleth
in it; and that we shall be the same persons that now we are: the
remunerative justice of God requiring it to be so.

We believe the souls of the righteous shall be much better accommodated, and have a more comfortable habitation in their bodies than
now they have, 1 Cor. xv. 42, 43. seeing they shall be made like
unto Christ's glorious body, Phil. iii. 22. and that then we shall live
after the manner of angels, Luke xx. 36. without the necessities of
this animal life. These are the things we look for according to promise; and this expectation is our great relief against (1.) The fears
of death, 1 Cor. xv. 55. (2.) Against the death of our friends and
relations, 1 Thes. iv. 14. (3.) Against all the pressures and afflictions
of this life, Job xix. 25, 26, 27.

But if the being of our souls fall at death, all hopes and comforts
from the resurrection fail with it; for it is not imaginable that the
body should rise till it be revived, nor how it should be revived, but
by the re-union of the soul with it: and if it be not the same soul
that now inhabits it, we cannot be the same persons in the resurrection
we are now; and consequently, this supposition subverts not only
the doctrine of the resurrection, but,

6. It overthrows also the faith of the judgment to come. For
if the soul perish, the body cannot rise; or if it rise by a new-
created soul, the person raised is another, and not the same that
lived and died in this world; and consequently the rewards and
punishments to be bestowed and awarded to all men in that day

cannot be just and equal: for we believe, according to the scriptures, that,

(1.) The actions which men perform in this life, are not transient, but are filed to their account in the world to come: Gal. vi. 7. *here we sow, and there we reap.* Actions done in this world are two ways considerable, viz. physically, or morally; in the first consideration they are transient, in the last permanent and everlasting. A word is spoken, or an act done in a moment, but though it be past and gone, and perhaps by us quite forgotten, God registers it in his book, in order to the day of account.

(2.) We believe that God hath appointed a day in which all men shall appear before his judgment-seat, to give an account of all they have done in the body, whether it be good or evil, 2 Cor. v. 10.

(3.) And that in order hereunto, the very same persons shall be restored by the resurrection, and appear before God, the very same bodies and souls, which did good or evil in this world: Shall not the Judge of all the earth do right? Justice requires that the rewards and punishments be then distributed to the same persons that did good or evil in this world: which strongly infers the immortality of the soul, and that it certainly overlives the body, and must come back from the respective places of their abode, to be again united to them, in order to their great account.

By all which you see the clearest proof of the soul's immortality, and how the contrary supposition overthrows our faith, duties, and comforts. Yet notwithstanding all this, how apt are we to suspect this doctrine, and remain still dissatisfied and doubting about it, when all is said? Which comes to pass partly from the subtlety of Satan, who knows he can never persuade men to live the life of beasts, till he first persuade them to think they shall die as the beasts do. (2.) And partly from the influence of sense and reason upon us, whereby we do too much suffer ourselves to be swayed and imposed upon in matters of the greatest moment in religion. For these being proper arbiters and judges in other matters within their sphere, they are arrogant, and we easy enough to admit them to be arbiters also in things that are quite above them. Hence come such plausible objections as these:

Object. 1. The soul seems to vanish and die, when it leaves the body: for when it hath struggled as long as it can to keep its possession in the body, and, at last, is forced to depart, we can perceive nothing but a puff of breath, which immediately vanishes into air, and is lost.

Solut. We cannot perceive, therefore it is nothing but what we do and can perceive, viz. a puff of vanishing breath. By this argument the being of the soul in the body is as questionable as after its departure out of the body; for we cannot discern it by sight in the body: yea, by this argument we may as well deny the existence of God and angels as of the soul; for it is a spiritual and invisible being as they are; our gross senses are incapable of discerning spirits, which are immaterial and invisible substances.

Object. 2. But you allow the soul to have a rise and beginning, it is not eternal *a parte ante;* and it is certain, whatever had a beginning, must have an end.

Solut. Every thing which had a beginning may have an end, and what once was nothing, may by the power that created it, be reduced to nothing again. But though we allow it may be so, by the absolute power of God, we deny the consequence, that therefore it shall, and must be so. Angels had a beginning, but shall never have an end. And indeed, their immortality, as well as ours, flows not so much from the nature of either as from the will and pleasure of God, who hath appointed them to be so. He can, but never will, annihilate them.

Object. 3. But the soul depends upon matter in all its operations, nothing is in the understanding which was not first in the senses; it useth the natural spirits, as its servants and tools in all its operations, and therefore how can it either subsist or act in a state of separation?

Sol. 1. The hypothesis is not only uncertain, but certainly false. There are acts performed by the soul, even whilst it is in the body, wherein it makes no use at all of the body. Such are the acts of self-intuition and self-reflection: and what will you say of its acts, in raptures and extasies, such as that of Paul, 2 Cor. xii. 2. and John, Rev. xxi. 10. what use did their souls make of the bodily senses or natural spirits then?

Solut. 2. And though in its ordinary actions in this life, it doth use the body as its tool or instrument in working, doth it thence follow that it can neither subsist or act separate from them in the other world? Whilst a man is on horseback in his journey, he useth the help and service of his horse, and is moved according to the motion of his horse; but doth it thence follow, he cannot stand nor walk alone, when dismounted at his journey's end? We know angels both live and act, without the ministry of bodies, and our souls are spiritual substances as well as they.

Object. 4. But many scriptures seem to favour the total cessation of the soul's actions, if not of its being also, after separation, as that in 2 Sam. xiv. 14. We must needs die, and are as water spilt upon the ground which cannot be gathered up; and Psal. lxxxviii. 10, 11, 12. with Isa. xxxviii. 18, 19. The dead cannot praise thee.

Solut. These words of the woman of Tekoah, are not to be understood absolutely, but respectively : and the meaning is, that the soul is in the body as some precious liquor in a brittle glass, which being broken by death, the soul is irrecoverably gone, as the water spilt on the ground, which by no human power or art of man can be recovered again. All the means in the world cannot fetch it back into the body again. She speaks not of the resurrection, or what shall be done in the world to come, by the Almighty power of God, but of what is impossible to be done in this world by all the skill and power of man.

And for the expressions of Heman and Hezekiah, they only respect and relate unto those services their souls were now employed about for the praise of God, with respect to the conversion or edification of others, as Psal. xxx. 8, 9. or at most, to that mediate service and worship which they give God, in and by their attendance upon his ordinances in this world, and not of that immediate service and praise that is performed and given him in heaven by the spirits of just men made perfect ; such was the sweetness they had found in these ordinances and duties, that they express themselves as loth to leave them.

The same answer solves also the objections grounded upon other mistaken scriptures, as that of Psal. lxxviii. 39. where man is called a wind that passeth away and cometh not again. It is only expressive of the frailty and vanity of the present animal life we live in this world, to which we shall return no more after death ; it denies not life to departed souls, but affirms the end of this animal life at death : the life we live in the other world is of a different nature.

Inf. 1. Is the soul immortal? Then *it is impossible for souls to find full rest and contentment in any enjoyments on this side heaven.* All temporary things are inadequate, and therefore unsatisfying to our souls. What gives the soul rest and satisfaction, must be as durable as the soul is ; for if we could possibly find in this world a condition and state of things most agreeable in all other respects to our desires and wishes, yet if the soul be conscious to itself, that it shall, and must overlive and leave them all behind it, it can never reach true contentment in the greatest affluence and confluence of them. Man being an immortal, is therefore a prospecting creature, and can never be satisfied with this, that it is well with him at present, except he can be satisfied that it shall be so for ever. The thoughts of leaving our delightful and pleasant enjoyments embitters them all to us whilst we have them. All outward things are *fluxu continuo,* passing away as the waters, 1 Cor. vii. 31. Riches are uncertain, 1 Tim. vi. 17. " They fly away as an eagle " towards heaven, and with wings of their own making," Prov. xxiii. 5. i. e. As the feathers that enable a bird to fly from us, grow out of its own substance, so doth that vanity that carries away all earthly enjoyments. This alone will spoil all contentment.

Inf. 2. *Then see the ground and reason of Satan's envy and enmity against the soul, and his restless designs and endeavours to destroy it.* It grates that spirit of envy, to find himself, who is by nature immortal, sunk everlastingly and irrecoverably into misery, and the souls of men appointed to fill up those vacant places in heaven from which the angels fell. No creature but man is envied by Satan, and the soul of man much more than his body : it is true, he afflicts the bodies of men when God permits him, but he ever aims at the soul when he wounds the body, Heb. x. 37. This roaring lion is continually going about, " seeking whom he may devour," 1 Pet. v. 8. It is the precious soul he hunts after; that is the *Morsus diaboli*, the bit he gapes for, as the wolf tears the fleece to come at the flesh. All the pleasure those miserable creatures find, is from the success of their temptations upon the souls of men. It is a kind of delight to them to plunge souls into the same condemnation and misery with themselves. This is the trade they have been driving ever since their fall. By destroying souls he at once exercises his revenge against God, and his envy against man, which is all the relief his miserable condition allows him.

Inf. 3. Do the souls of men out-live their bodies ? *Then it is the height of madness and spiritual infatuation, to destroy the soul for the body's sake ;* to cast away an immortal soul for the gratification of perishing flesh ; to ruin the precious soul for ever, for the pleasures of sin which are but for a moment ; yet this is the madness of millions of men. They will drown their own souls in everlasting perdition, to procure necessary things for the body, 1 Tim. vi. 9. " They that will be rich," &c. Every cheat and circumvention in dealing, every lie, every act of oppression, is a wound given the immortal soul, for the procuring some accommodations to the body.

O what soul-undoing bargains do some make with the devil! Some sell their souls out-right for the gratification of their lusts, 1 Kings xxi. 20. Many pawn their souls to Satan in a conditional bargain ; so do all that venture upon sin, upon a presumption of pardon and repentance. The devil is a great trader for souls, he hath all sorts of commodities to suit all men's humours that will deal with him. He hath profits for the covetous, honours for the ambitious, pleasures for the voluptuous : but a soul is the price at which he sells them ; only he will be content to sell at a day, and not require present pay : so that it be paid on a death-bed, in a dying hour, he is satisfied. But oh ! what an undoing bargain do sinners make, to part with a treasure for a trifle ! Matt. xvi. 26. the precious soul for ever, " for the pleasures of sin, which are but

Prov. xx. 17. for a season! Heb. xi. 25. We are charmed with
Prov. xxiii. 31, the present pleasure and sweetness there is in sin;
32. Job xx. 12, but how bitter will the after-fruits thereof be!—See
13. James i. 15. the texts in the margin. You will say hereafter as
Jonathan did, 1 Sam. xiv. 31. " I tasted but a little honey, and I
" must die,"

Inf. 4. *Then the exposing of the body to danger, yea, to certain
destruction, for the preservation of the soul, is the dictate of spiritual
wisdom, and that which every Christian is bound to chuse and practise, when both interests come in full opposition,* Heb. xi. 35. Dan.
iii. 28. Rev. xii. 11. No promises of preferment, no threats of torments, have been able to prevail with the people of God to give the
least wound, or do the least wrong to their own souls. When Se-
cundus was commanded to deliver his bible, he answered, *Christianus sum, non traditor:* I am a Christian, I will not deliver it:
then they desired him to deliver *aliquam ecvolam,* a chip, a straw,
any thing that came to his hand in lieu of it: he refused to redeem
his life by delivering the least trifle on that account to save it.

That is a great word of our Lord's, Luke ix. 24. " He that will
" save his life, shall lose it: and he that loseth it for my sake
" shall find it." Christians, this is your duty and wisdom, and
must be your resolution and practice in the day of temptation, to
yield your bodies to preserve your souls, as we offer our arm to defend the head. Oh! better thy body had never been given thee,
than that it should be a snare to thy soul, and the instrument of
casting it away for ever. Oh! how dear are some persons like to
pay for their tenderness and indulgence to the flesh, when the
hour of temptation shall come! mortify your irregular affections to
the body, and never hazard your precious immortal souls for their
sakes. It is the character of an hypocrite to chuse sin rather than
affliction, Job xxxvi. 21. But if ever thou hast been in the deeps
of spiritual troubles for sin, if God have opened thine eyes to see
the evil of sin, the immense weight and value of thy soul, and of
eternity, " Thou wilt not count thy life dear to thee, to finish thy
" course with joy," Acts xx. 24.

Inf. 5. If the soul be an immortal being, that shall have no end,
*Then it is the great concern of all men to strive to the utmost for the
salvation of their souls, whatever become of all lesser temporary interests in this world,* Luke xiii. 24. There is a gate, i. e. an introductive means of life and salvation; This gate is strait, i. e. there
are a world of difficulties to be encountered in the way of salvation:
but he that values and loves his never-dying soul, must, and will
be diligent and constant in the use of all those means that have a
tendency to salvation, be they never so difficult or unpleasant to
flesh and blood. There be difficulties from within ourselves, such

as mortification, self-denial, contempt of the world, parting with all at the call of Christ; and difficulties from without, the reproaches, persecutions, and sufferings for Christ, which would not be so great as they are, were it not for our unmortified lusts within; but be they what they will, we are bound to strive through them all, for the salvation of our precious and immortal souls.

(1.) For it is the greatest concernment of the soul, yea, of our own souls; we are bound to do much for the saving of another's soul, 2 Tim. ii. 10. much more for our own; this is our darling, Psal. xxii. our only one.

(2.) Others have done and suffered much for the saving of their souls; and are not ours, or ought they not to be, as dear to us, as the souls of any others have been to them? Mat. xxi. 32.

(3.) The utmost diligence is little enough to save them. Do all that you can do, and suffer all that you can suffer, and deny yourselves as deeply as ever any did, yet you shall find all this little enough to secure them, 1 Pet. iv. 18. The righteous themselves are scarcely saved, 1 Cor. ix. 24.

(4.) The time to strive for salvation is very short and uncertain, Luke xiii. 25. John xii. 35. It will be to no purpose, when the seasons and opportunities of salvation are once over. There is no striving in hell, a death-pang of despair hath seized them, hope is extinguished, and endeavours fail.

(5.) Doth not reason dictate and direct you to do now, whilst you are in the way, as you will wish you had done, and repent with rage, and self-indignation, because you did it not, when you come to the end, and behold the final issues of things? Suppose but thyself now either, (1.) Upon a death-bed launching into eternity; (2.) Or at the bar of Christ; (3.) Or in view of heaven; (4.) Or in the sight and hearing of the damned: what think you? will not you then wish, Oh! that I had spent every moment in the world that could possibly be redeemed from the pure necessities of life, in prayer, in hearing, in striving for salvation? From a prospect of this it was, that one spent many hours daily on his knees to the macerating of his body; and being admonished of the danger of health, and advised to relax, he answered, *I must die, I must die.*

Objection 1. Do not say, you have many incumbrances, and other employments in the world: for (1.) "One thing is necessary," Luke x. 42. Those are conveniences, but this is of absolute necessity. (2.) They will strive the better for this, Mat. vi. 33. "Seek "this, and they shall be added." (3.) Do but *redeem the time* that can be redeemed to this purpose; let not so much precious time run waste as daily doth.

Objection 2. Say not, no man can save his soul by his own striving, and therefore it is to little purpose; for "it is not of him that

" willeth, nor of him that runneth, but of God that sheweth
" mercy," Rom. ix. 16.

True, this in itself cannot save you; but what then? must we
oppose those things which God hath subordinated? Bring this
home to your natural or civil actions, eating, drinking, ploughing,
or sowing, and see how the consequence will look.

Objection 3. Say not, it is a mercenary doctrine, and disparages
free grace; for, are not all the enjoyments and comforts of this
life confessedly from free frace, though God hath dispensed them
to you in the way of your diligence and industry.

Objection 4. To conclude; Say not, the difficulties of salvation
are insuperable; it is so hard to watch every motion of the heart,
to deny every lust, to resist a suitable temptation, to suffer the *loss
of all for Christ*, that there is no hope of over-coming them.

For (1.) God can, and doth make difficult things easy to his
people, who work in the strength of Christ, Phil. iv. 13.   (2.)
These same difficulties are before all others that are before you, yet
it discourageth not them, Phil. iii. 11.   Others strive to the uttermost.   There are extremes found in this matter: some work for
salvation, as an hireling for his wages, so the Papists; these dis-
parage grace, and cry up works.   Others cry down obedience as
legal, as the Antinomians, and cry up grace to the disparagement
of duties.   Avoid both these, and see that you strive: But (1.)
Think not heaven to be the price of your striving, Rom. iv. 3.
(2.) Strive, but not for a spurt; let this care and diligence run
throughout your lives; whilst you are living, be you still striving:
your souls are worth it, and infinitely more than all this amounts
to.

Inf. 6. Doth the soul out-live the body, and abide for ever?
*Then it is a great evil and folly to be excessively careful for the
mortal body, and neglective of the mortal inhabitant.*   In a too much
indulged body, there ever dwells a too much neglected soul.

The body is but a *vile thing*, Phil. iii. 21. the soul *more valuable
than the whole world*, Matth. xvi. 26.   To spend time, care, and
pains for a vile body, whilst little or no regard is had to the precious
immortal soul, is an unwarrantable folly and madness.   *To have a
clear and washed body, and a soul all filth,* (as one speaks) *a body
neatly clothed and dressed, with a soul all naked and unready: a
body fed, and a soul starved; a body full of the creature, and a soul
empty of Christ; these are poor souls indeed.*   We smile at little
children, who in a kind of laborious idleness take a great deal of pains
to make and trim their babies, or build their little houses of sticks
and straws: And what are they but children of a bigger size, that
keep such ado about the body, a house of clay, a weak pile, that
must perish in a few days.   It is admirable, and very convictive of

most Christians, what we read in a Heathen. " I confess (saith *
" Seneca) there is a love to the body implanted in us all ; we have
" the tutelage and charge of it ; we may be kind and indulgent to
" it, but must not serve it ; but he that serves it, is a servant to
" many cares, fears, and passions. Let us have a diligent care of
" it, yet so as when reason requires, when our dignity or faith re-
" quire it, we commit it to the fire."

It is true, the body is beloved of the soul, and God requires
that it moderately care for the necessities and conveniences of it ;
but to be fond, indulgent, and constantly solicitous about it, is both
the sin and snare of the soul. One of the fathers being invited to
dine with a lady, and waiting some hours till she was dressed, and
fit to come down ; when he saw her, he fell a weeping ; and being
demanded why he wept, *Oh !* said he, *I am troubled that you should
spend so many hours this morning in pinning and trimming your
body when I have not spent half the time in praying, repenting and
caring for my own soul.* Two things a master commits to his
servant's care, (saith one) the child, and the child's clothes : It will
be but a poor excuse for the servant to say, at his master's return,
Sir, here are all the child's clothes neat and clean, but the child is
lost. Much so will be the account that many will give to God of
their souls and bodies, at the great day, *Lord, here is my body, I
was very careful for it, I neglected nothing that belonged to its
content and welfare : But for my soul, that is lost and cast away
for ever, I took little care and thought about it.* It is remarkable
what the apostle saith, Rom. viii. 12. We owe nothing to the
flesh, we are not in its debt, we have given it all, more than all that
belongs to it : But we owe many an hour, many a care, many a
deep thought to our souls, which we have defrauded it of for the
vile body's sake. You have robbed your souls to pay your flesh.
This is madness.

*Inf. 7. How great a blessing is the gospel which brings life and
immortality to light, the most desirable mercies to immortal souls !*
This is the great benefit we receive by it, as the apostle speaks, 2
Tim. i. 10. " Christ hath abolished death, and brought life and
immortality to light by the gospel." Life and immortality by a
εν δια δυοιν, is put for immortal life, the thing which all immortal
souls desire and long for. These desires are found in souls that
enjoy not the gospel light ; for, as I said before, they naturally
spring out of the very nature of all immortal souls : But how and

---

* *Fateor insitam esse nobis corporis nostri charitatem. Fateor nos hujus gerere tutelam,
nes ego indulgendum illi, serviendum nego. Multis enim serviet qui corpori servit, qui pro
illo nimium timet, qui ad illud omnia refert ; hujus nos nimius amor timoribus inquietat,
solicitudinibus onerat, contumeliis objicit : honestum ei vile est cui corpus nimis charum est :
agatur ejus diligentissima cura ; ita tamen ut cum exiget ratio, cum dignitas, cum fides,
mittendum in ignem sit. Senec. Ep. 14. p. 545.*

where it is to be obtained, that is a secret for which we are entirely beholden to the gospel-discovery. It lay hid in the womb of God's purpose, till by the light of gospel-revelation it was made manifest. But now all men may see what are the gracious thoughts and purposes of God concerning men, and what that is he hath designed for their immortal souls, even an immortal life; and this life is to be obtained by Christ, than which no tidings can be more welcome, sweet, or acceptable to us.

O therefore study the gospel. " This is life eternal, to know Thee " the only true God, and Jesus Christ whom thou hast sent," John xvii. 3. And see that you prize the gospel above all earthly treasure. *It is a faithful saying, and worthy of all acceptation.* You have two inestimable benefits and blessings by it. (1.) It manifests and reveals eternal life to you, which you could never have come to the knowledge of any other way; those that are without it are groping or feeling after God in the dark, Acts xvii. 27. Poor souls are conscious to themselves, that there is a just and terrible God, and that their sins offend and provoke him; but how to atone the offended Deity they know not, Micah vi. 6, 7. But the way of reconciliation and life is clearly discovered to us by the gospel. (2.) As it manifests and reveals eternal life to us, so it frames and moulds our hearts, as God's sanctifying instrument for the enjoyment of it. It is not only the instrument of revelation, but of salvation; the word of life, as well as the word of light, Phil. ii. 16. It can open your hearts, as well as your eyes, and is therefore to be entertained as that which is in the first rank of blessings, a peerless and inestimable blessing.

Inf. 8. If our souls be immortal, *certainly our enemies are not so formidable as we are apt, by our sinful fears, to represent them.* They may, when God permits them, destroy your bodies, they cannot touch or destroy your souls, Mat. x. 28. As to your bodies, no enemy can touch them till there be leave and permission given them by God, Job i. 10. The bodies of the saints, as well as their souls, are within the line or hedge of Divine Providence : They are securely fenced, sometimes mediately by the ministry of angels, Psal. xxxiv. 7. and sometimes immediately by his own hand and power, Zech. ii. 5. As to their souls, whatever power enemies may have upon them, (when Divine permission opens a gap in the hedge of providence for them) yet they cannot reach their souls to hurt them, or destroy them, but by their own consent. They can destroy our perishing flesh, it is obnoxious to their malice and rage ; they cannot reach home to the soul: No sword can cut asunder the band of union between them and Christ : they would be dreadful enemies indeed if they could do so. Why then do we tremble and fear at this rate, as if soul and body were at their mercy, and in their power and hand? The souls of those *martyrs* were in safety under the *altar* in heaven, they were clothed with *white robes*, when their bodies were given to be meat to the fowls of heaven, and the beasts of the earth. The devil drives but a poor trade by the persecution of the saints; he tears the *nest*, but the *bird* escapes; he cracks the *shell*, but loseth the *kernal*. Two things make a powerful defensative against our fears: (1.) That all our enemies are in the hand of Providence. (2.) That all providences are steered by that promise, Rom. viii. 28.

Inf. 9. If souls be immortal, *Then there must needs be a vast difference beewixt the aspects and influences of death upon the godly and ungodly.*

Oh! if souls would but seriously consider what an alteration death will make upon their condition, for evil or for good, how useful would such meditations be to them! (1.) They must be disseized and turned out of these houses of clay, and live in a state of separation from them; of this there is an inevitable necessity, Eccl. viii. 8. It is in vain to say, I am not ready; ready or unready, they must depart when their lease is out. It is as vain to say, I am not willing; for willing or unwilling, they must be gone; there is no hanging back, and begging, *Lord, let death take another at this time, and spare me;* for no man dies by a proxy. (2.) The time of our soul's departure is at hand, 2 Pet. 1, 13, 14. Job xvi. 22. The most firm and well-built body can stand but a few days; but our ruinous tabernacles give our souls warning, that the days of their departure is at hand. The lamp of life is almost burnt down, the glass of time is almost run; yet a few, a very few days and nights more, and then time, nights and days shall be no more. (3.) When that most certain and near-approaching time is come, wonderful alterations will be made on the state of all souls, godly, and ungodly.

(1.) A marvellous alteration will then be made on the souls of the godly. For, (1.) No sooner is the dividing stroke given by death, and the parting pull over, but they shall find themselves in the arms of angels, mounting them through the upper regions in a few moments, far above all the aspectable heavens, Luke xvi. 22. The airy region is, indeed, the place where devils inhabit, and have their haunts and walks; but angels are the saints convoy through Satan's territories. They pass from the arms of mourning friends, into the welcome arms of officious and benevolent angels. (2.) From the sight and converses of men, to the sight of God, Christ, and the general assembly of blessed and sinless spirits. The soul takes its leave of all men at death, Isa. xxxviii. 11. Farewell vain world, with all the mixed and imperfect comforts of it, and welcome the more sweet, suitable, and satisfying company of Father,

Son, and Spirit, holy angels, and perfected saints, Heb. xii. 23. " The " spirits of just men made perfect." (3.) From the bondage of corruption to perfect liberty and everlasting freedom; so much is implied, Heb. xii. 23. " The spirits of just men made perfect." (4.) From all fears, doubtings, and questionings of our conditions, and anxious debates of our title to Christ, to the clearest, fullest, and most satisfying assurance; for what a man sees, how can he doubt of it? (5.) From all burdens of affliction, inward and outward, under which we have groaned all our days, to everlasting rest and ease, 2 Cor. v. 1, 2, 3. Oh what a blessed change to the righteous must this be!

(2.) A marvellous change will also be then made upon the souls of the ungodly, who shall then part from (1.) All their comforts and pleasant enjoyments in the world; for here they had their consolation; Luke xvi. 25. here was all their portion, Psal. xvii. 14. and, in a moment, find themselves arrested and seized by Satan, as God's gaoler, hurrying them away to the prison of hell, 1 Pet. iii. 19. " there to be reserved to the judgment of the great day," Jude 6. (2.) From under the means of grace, life, and salvation, to a state perfectly void of all means, instruments, and opportunities of salvation, John ix. 4. Eccl. ix. 10. never to hear the joyful sound of preaching or praying any more; never to hear the wooing voice of the blessed bridegroom, saying, Come unto me, come unto me, any more. (3.) From all their vain, ungrounded, presumptuous hopes of heaven, into absolute and final desperation of mercy. The very sinews and nerves of hope are cut by death, Prov. xiv. 32. " The wicked is " driven away in his wickedness, but the righteous hath hope in his " death." These are the great and astonishing alterations that will be made upon our souls, after they part with the bodies which they now inhabit. Oh that we, who cannot but be conscious to ourselves that we must over-live our bodies, were more thoughtful of the condition they must enter into, after that separation which is at hand.

Inf. 10. If our souls be immortal, *then death is neither to be feared by them in heaven, nor hoped for them in hell.* The being of souls never fails, whether they be in a state of blessedness or of misery. " In glory they are ever with the Lord," 1 Thes. iv. 17. There shall be no death there, Rev. xxi. 4. And in hell, though they shall wish for death, yet death shall flee from them *. Though there be no fears of annihilation in heaven, yet there be many wishes for it in hell, but to no purpose; there never will be an end put, either to their being, or to their torments. In this respect no other creatures are capable of the misery that wicked men

---

* O death thou art sweet to those to whom thou wast formerly bitter: They desire thee alone, who did hate thee alone. *August.*

are capable of: When they die, there is the end of all their misery; but it is not so with men. Better therefore had it been for them, if God had created them in the basest and lowest order and rank of creatures; a dog, a toad, a worm, is better than a man in endless misery, ever dying, and never dead. *And so much of the soul's immortality.*

EPH. v. 29.

For no man ever yet hated his own flesh; but nourisheth and cherisheth it, even as the Lord the church.

HAVING given some account of the nature and immortality of the soul, we next come, from this text, to discourse of its *love and inclination to the body*, with which it is united. The scope of the apostle is, to press Christians to the exact discharge of those relative duties they owe to each other; particularly, he here urgeth the mutual duties of husbands and wives, ver. 22. wives to an obedient subjection, husbands to a tender love of their wives. This exhortation he enforceth from the intimate union, which, by the ordinance of God, is betwixt them, they being now one flesh. And this union he illustrates by comparing it with,

1. The mystical union of Christ and the church.
2. The natural union of the soul and body.

And from both these, as excellent examples and patterns, he, with great strength of argument, urgeth the duty of love: ver. 28. " So ought men to love their wives as their own bodies; he that " loveth his wife, loveth himself." Self-love is naturally implanted in all men, and it is the rule by which we measure out and dispense our love to others.——" Thou shalt love thy neighbour as thyself."

This self-love he opens in this place, by,

(1.) The universality of it.
(2.) The effects that evidence it.

1. The universality of it. *No man ever yet hated his own flesh.* By *flesh*, understand the body by an usual *metonymy* of a part for the whole, called flesh. By *hating* it, understand a simple hatred, or hatred itself. It is usual for men to hate the deformities and diseases of their own bodies, and upon that account to deal with the members of their own bodies as if they hated them; hence it is, they willingly stretch forth a gangrened leg or arm to be cut off for the preservation of the rest: but this is not a simple hatred of a man's self, but rather an argument of the strength of the soul's love to the body, that it will be content to endure so much pain and anguish for its sake. And if the soul be at any time weary of,

and willing to part, not with a single member only, but with the whole body, and loaths its union with it any longer, yet it hates it and loaths it not simply in, and for itself, but because it is so filled with diseases all over, and loads the soul daily with so much grief, that how well soever the soul loves it in itself, yet upon such sad terms and conditions it would not be tied to it. This was Job's case, Job x. 1. " My soul is weary of my life;" yet not simply of his life, but of such a life of pain and trouble. Except it be in such respects and cases, *no man*, saith he, *ever yet hated his own flesh*, i. e. no man in his right mind, and in the exercise of his reason and sense; for we must expect distracted and delirious men, who know not what they do, as also men under the terrors of conscience, when God suffers it to rage in extremity, as Spira and others, who would have been glad with their own hands to have cut the thread that tied their miserable souls to their bodies, supposing that way, and by that change, to find some relief. Either of these cases forces men to act beside the stated rule of nature and reason.

2. This love of the soul to the body is further discovered by the effects which evidence it, *viz.* its nourishing and cherishing the body, εκτρεφει και θαλπει. These two comprize the necessaries for the body, *viz.* food and raiment. The first signifies to nourish with proper food; the latter to warm by clothing, as the word θαλπειν is rendered, James ii. 16. to which the Hebrew word יחממם answers, Job xxxi. 20. The care and provision of these things for the body evidences the soul's love to it.

Doct. *That the souls of men are strongly inclined, and tenderly affected towards the bodies in which they now dwell.*

The soul's love to the body, is so strong, natural, and insepa-rable, that it is made the rule and measure by which we dispense and proportion our love to others, Mat. xix. 19. *Thou shalt love thy neighbour as thyself.* And the apostle, Gal. v. 14. tells us, That the whole law, i. e. the second table of the law, is fulfilled, or summoned up in this precept, *Thou shalt love thy neighbour as thyself.* The meaning is not, that all and every one who is our neighbour, must be equally near to us as our own bodies; but it intends, (1.) The sincerity of our love to others, which must be without dissimulation, for we dissemble not in self-love. (2.) That we be as careful to avoid injuring others, as we would ourselves, Mat. vii. 12. To do by others, or measure to them, as we would have done or measured unto us: for which rule, Severus, the Heathen emperor, honoured Christ and Chris-tianity, and caused it to be written in capital letters of gold. (3.) That we take direction from this principle of self-love, to measure out our care, love, and respect to others, according to the different degrees of nearness in which we stand to them.   As, (1.) The wife of our bosom, to whom, by this rule, is due our first care and love as in the text.   (2.) Our children and family, 1 Tim. v. 8.   (3.) To all in general, whether we have any bond of natural relation upon them or no; but especially those to whom we are spiritually related, as Gal. vi. 10.   And indeed, as every Christian hath a right to our love and care above other men, so in some cases, we are to exceed this rule of self-love, by a transcendent act of self-denial for them, 1 John iii. 16.   And Paul went higher than that, in a glorious excess of charity to the community or body of God's people, preferring their salvation not only to his own body, but to his soul also, Rom. ix. 3.   But to these extraordinary cases we are seldom called; and if we be, the gospel furnisheth us with an higher rule than self-love, John xiii. 34.   But by this principle of self-love, in all ordinary cases, we must proportion and dispense our love to all others; by which you see what a deep-rooted and fixed principle in nature self-love is, how universal and permanent alone this is, which else were not fit to be made the measure of our love to all others.

Two things well deserve our consideration in the doctrinal part of this point.

First, Wherein the soul evidenceth its love to the body.

Secondly, What are the grounds and fundamental causes or reasons of its love to it; and then apply it.

First, Wherein the soul evidenceth its love to the body, and that it doth in divers respects.

1. In its cares for the things needful to the body, as the text speaks, in nourishing and cherishing it, i. e. taking care for food and raiment for it.   This care is universal, it is implanted in the most savage and barbarous people; and is generally so excessive and exorbitant, that though it never needs a spur, yet most times, and with most men, it doth need a curb; and therefore Christ, in Matth. vi. 32. shews how those cares torture and distract the nations of the world, warns them against the like excesses, and propounds a rule to them for the allay and mitigation of them, ver. 25, 26, 27.   So doth the apostle also, 1 Cor. vii. 29, 30, 31.   To speak as the matter is, most souls are over-heated with their cares, and eager pursuits after the concerns of the body.   They pant after the dust of the earth.   They pierce themselves through with many sorrows, 1 Tim. vi. 10.   They are cumbered like Martha with much serving.   It is a perfect drudge and slave to the body, bestowing all its time, strength, and studies about the body; for one soul that puts the question to itself, " What shall I do to be saved ?" a thousand are to be found that mind nothing more but " What shall

" I eat, what shall I drink, and wherewithal shall I and mine be
" clothed?" I do not say, that these are proofs of the soul's regular love to the body; no, they differ from it, as a fever does from
natural heat. This is a doating fondness upon the body. He
truly loves his body, that moderately and ordinately cares for what
is necessary for it, and can keep it under, 1 Cor. ix. 27. and deny
its whining appetite, when indulgence is prejudicial to the soul, or
warm its lusts. Believers themselves find it hard to keep the golden
bridle of moderation upon their affections in this matter. It is not
every man that hath attained Agur's cool temper, Prov. xxx. 8.
that can slack his pace and drive moderately where the interests of
the body are concerned: the best souls are too warm, the generality in raging heats, which distract their minds, as that word, Mat.
vi. 25. μη μεριμνατε, signifies. If the body were not exceeding dear
to the soul, it would never torture itself, day and night, with such
anxious cares about it.

2. The soul discovers its esteem and value for the body in all
the fears it hath about it. Did not the soul love it exceedingly, it
would never be affrighted for it, and on its account, so much and
so often as it is. What a panic fear do the dangers of the body cast
the soul into? Isa. vii. 2. When the body is in danger, the soul
is in distraction, the soul is in fears and tremblings about it: these
fears flow from the souls tender love and affection to the body; if
it did not love it so intensely, it would never afflict and torment
itself at that rate it doth about it: Satan, the professed enemy of
our souls, being thoroughly acquainted with those fears which flow
from the fountain of love to the body, politicly improves them in
the way of temptation to the utter ruin of some, and the great hazard of other's souls; he edges and sharpens his temptations upon
us this way; he puts our bodies into danger, that he may thereby
endanger our souls; he reckons, if he can but draw the body into
danger, fear will quickly drive the soul into temptation; it is not
so much from Satan's malice or hatred of our bodies, that he stirs
up persecutions against us: but he knows the tie of affection is so
strong betwixt these friends, that love will draw, and fear will drive
the soul into many and great hazards of its own happiness, to free
the body out of those dangers. Prov. xxix. 25. " The fear of man
" brings a snare:" and Heb. xi. 37. " Tortured and tempted."

Upon this ground also it is, that this life becomes a life of temptation to all men, and there is no freedom from that danger, till we
be freed from the body, and set at liberty by death. Separated
souls are the only free souls. They that carry no flesh about them,
need carry no fears of temptation within them. It is the body
which catches the sparks of temptation.

3. The soul manifests its dear love and affection to the body, by its sympathy, and compassionate feeling of all its burdens: whatever touches the body, by way of injury, affects the soul also by way of sympathy. The soul and body are as strings of two musical instruments set exactly at one height; if one be touched, the other trembles. They laugh and cry, are sick and well together. This is a wonderful mystery, and a rare secret (as a learned man observes) how the soul comes to sympathize with the body, and to have not only a knowledge, but as it were a feeling of its necessities and infirmities; how this fleshly lump comes to affect, and make its deep impressions upon a creature of so different a nature from it, as the soul or spirit is. But that it doth so, though we know not how, is plain and sensible to any man. If any member of the body, though but the lowest and meanest, be in pain and misery, the soul is presently affected with it, and commands the eyes to watch, yea, to weep, the hands to bind it up with all tenderness, and defend it from the least injurious touch; the lips to complain of its misery, and beg pity and help from others for it. If the body be in danger, how are the faculties of the soul, understanding, memory, invention, &c. employed with utmost strength and concernment for its deliverance! This is a real and unexceptionable evidence of its dear and tender love to the body. As those that belong to one mystical body shew their sincere love this way, 1 Cor. xii. 25, 26. so the soul.

4. The soul manifesteth its love to the body, by its fears of death, and extreme aversion to a separation from it. On this account death is called in Job xviii. 14. " The king of terrors," or the black prince, or the prince of clouds and darkness, as some translate that place: We read it, " The king of terrors," meaning, that the terrors at death are such terrors as subdue and keep down all other terrors under them, as a prince doth his subjects. Other terrors compared with those that the soul conceives and conflicts with at parting, are no more than a cut finger, to the laying one's head on the block. Oh! the soul and body are strongly twisted and knit together in dear bands of intimate union and affection, and these bands cannot be broken without much struggling: Oh! it is a hard thing for the soul to bid the body farewell, it is a bitter parting, a doleful separation: Nothing is heard in that hour but the most deep and emphatical groans; I say *emphatical groans*, the deep sense and meaning of which the living are but little acquainted with: For no man living hath yet felt the sorrows of a parting pull; whatsoever other sorrows he hath felt in the body, yet they must be supposed to be far short of these.

The sorrows of death are in scripture set forth unto us, by the bearing throes of a travailing woman, Acts ii. 24. ωδινας τȣ θανατȣ, and what those mean, many can tell. The soul is in labour, it will not let go its hold of the body, but by constraint: Death is a close siege, and when the soul is beaten out of its body, it disputes the passage with death, as soldiers use to do with an enemy that enters by storm, and fights and strives to the last. It is also compared to a *battle* or *sharp fight*, Eccl. viii. 8. *that war.* That war with an emphasis. No conflict so sharp, each labour to the utmost to drive the other from the ground they stand on, and win the field. And though grace much over-powers nature in this matter, and reconciles it to death, and makes it desire to be dissolved, yet saints wholly put not off this reluctation of nature, 2 Cor. v. 2. Not that we would be unclothed; as it is with one willing to wade over a brook to his father's house, puts his foot into the water, and feels it cold, starts back, and is loth to venture in; *Not that we would be unclothed.* And if it be so with sanctified souls, how is it, think you, with others? Mark the scripture language, Job xxvii. 8. God taketh away their souls, saith our translation; but the root is, כשל *extrahere*, and signifies to pull out by plain force and violence. A graceless soul dieth not by consent, but force. Thus Adrian bewailed his departure, *O Animula, vagula, blandula, heu quo vadis !** Yea, though the soul have never so long a time been in the body, though it should live as long as the *Antediluvian fathers* did, for many hundred years, yet still it would be loth to part; yea, though it endure abundance of misery in the body, and have little rest or comfort, but time spent in griefs and fears, yet for all that it is loth to part with it. All this shews a strong inclination and affection to it.

5. Its desire of re-union continuing still with it, in its state of separation, speaks its love to the body. As the soul parted with it in grief and sorrow, so it still retains, even in glory, an inclination to re-union, and waits for a day of re-espousals: and to that sense some searching and judicious men understand those words of Job, chap. xiv. 14. " If a man die, shall he live again?" viz. by a resurrection: if so, then all the days of my appointed separation, my soul in heaven shall wait till that change come. And to the same sense is that cry of separated souls, Rev. vi. 9, 10, 11. " How " long, O Lord, how long?" i. e. to the consummation of all things, when judgment shall be executed on them that killed our bodies, and our bodies so long absent restored to us again? In that day of resurrection, the souls of the saints come willingly from heaven itself, to repossess their bodies, and bring them to a partnership with them in their glory: for it is with the soul in heaven as it is with an husband who is richly entertained, feasted, and lodg-

---

* O my little soul, my dear, endeared wanderer, whither goest thou ?

ed abroad, but his dear wife is solitary and comfortless; it abates the completeness of his joy. Therefore we say, the saints joy is not consummate till that day.

There is an exercise for faith, hope, and desire, on this account in heaven.

The union of soul and body is natural, their separation is not so: many benefits will redound to both by a re-union, and the resurrection of the body is provided by God, as the grand relief against those prejudices and losses the bodies of the saints sustain by separation. I say not that the propension or inclination of the soul to re-union with its body, is accompanied with any perturbation or anxiety, in its state of separation; for it enjoys God, and in him a placid rest; and as the body, so the soul rests in hope; it is such a hope as disturbs not the rest of either; yet when the time is come for the soul to be re-espoused, it is highly gratified by that second marriage, glad it is to see its old dear companion, as two friends after a long separation. And so much of the evidence of the soul's love to the body.

Secondly, Next we are to enquire into the grounds and reasons of its love and inclination to the body. And,

1. The fundamental ground and reason thereof will be found in their natural union with each other. There my text lays it: " No " man ever yet hated his [own] flesh." Mark, the body is the soul's own; they are strictly married and related to each other: the soul hath a property in its body, these two make up, or constitute one person. True, they are not essentially one, they have far different natures, but they are personally one *; and though the soul be what it was, after its separation, yet to make a man the *who* he was, i. e. the same complete and perfect person, they must be re-united. Hence springs its love to the body. Every man loves his own, John xvii. 19. All the world is in love with its own, and hence it cares to provide for its welfare; 1 Tim. v. 8. " If any man provide not for his own, he is worse than an infidel." For nature teacheth all men to do so. Why are children dearer to parents than to all others, but because they are their own? Job xix. 17. But our wives, our children, our goods are not so much our own as our bodies are; this is the nearest of all natural unions.

In this propriety and relation are involved the reasons and motives of our love to, and care over the body, which is no more than what is necessary to their preservation. For, were it not for

---

* And this is no more than necessary for the conservation of the species, else the body would be neglected, exposed, and quickly perish, being had in no more regard than any other body.

this propriety and relation, no man would be at any more cost or pains for his own body, than for that of a stranger. It is propriety which naturally draws love, care, and tenderness along with it; and these are ordered by the wisdom of providence, for the conservation of the body, which would quickly perish without it.

2. The body is the soul's ancient acquaintance and intimate friend, with whom it hath assiduously and familiarly conversed from its beginning. They have been partners in each others comforts and sorrows. They may say to each other, as Miconius did to his colleague, with whom he had spent twenty years in the government of the *Thuringian church: Currimus, certavimus, laboravimus, pugnavimus, vicimus, et viximus conjunctissime.* We have run, striven, laboured, fought, overcome, and lived most intimately and lovingly together. Consuetude, and daily conversation, begets and conciliates friendship and love betwixt creatures of contrary natures: Let a lamb be brought up with a lion, and the lion will express a tenderness towards it, much more the soul to its own body.

3. The body is the soul's house and beloved habitation, where it was born, and hath lived ever since it had a being, and in which it hath enjoyed all its comforts, natural and supernatural, which cannot but strengthen the soul's engagement to it. Upon this account the apostle calls it the soul's home, 2 Cor. v. 6. " Whilst we are " at home in the body." It is true, this house is not so comfortable an habitation, that it should be much desired by many souls; we may say of many gracious souls, that they pay a dear rent for the house they dwell in: or as it was said of Galba, *Anima Galbæ male habitat,* their souls are but ill accommodated; but yet it is their home, and therefore beloved by them.

4. The body is the soul's instrument by which it doth its work and business in the world, both natural and religious, Rom. vi. 13. Through the bodily senses it takes in all the natural comforts of this world, and by the bodily members it performs all its duties and services. When these are broken and laid aside by death, the soul knows it can work no more in that way it now doth, John ix. 4. Eccl. ix. 10. Natural men love their bodies for the natural pleasures they are instrumental to convey to their souls; and spiritual men, for the use and service they are of to their own and other souls, Phil. i. 23.

5. The body is the soul's partner in the benefit of Christ's purchase. It was bought with the same price, 1 Cor. vi. 20. sanctified by the same Spirit, 1 Thess. v. 23. interested in the same promise, Mat. xxii. 32. and designed for the same glory, 1 Thess. iv. 16, 17. So that we may say of it as it was said of Augustine and his friend Alippius, they are *sanguine Christi conglutinati,* glued

together by the blood of Christ. And thus of the grounds and reasons of its love.

Inf. 1. Is it so? *Learn hence the mighty strength and prevalence of divine love, which, overpowering all natural affections, doth not only enable the souls of men to take their separation from the body patiently, but to long for it ardently,* Phil. i. 23. While some need patience to die, others need it as much to live, 2 Thes. iii. 5. It is said, Rev. xii. 11. " They loved not their lives." And, indeed, on these terms they first closed with Christ, Luke xii. 26. " to hate their lives for his sake," (i. e.) to love them in so remiss a degree, that whenever they shall come in competition with Christ, to regard them no more than the things we hate.

The love of Christ is to be the supreme love, and all others to be subordinate to it, or quenched by it. It is not its own comfort in the body, it principally and ultimately designs and aims at, but Christ's glory; and if this may be furthered by the death of the body, its death thereupon becomes as eligible to the soul as its life, Phil. i. 20. Oh! this is an high pitch of grace, a great attainment to say as one did, *vivere renuo, ut Christo vivam;* I refuse life, to be with Christ: Or another, when he was asked whether he was willing to die? answered, *illius est nolle mori, qui nolit ire ad Christum;* let him be loth to die, that is loth to go to Christ. So 2 Cor. v. 8. " We are willing rather to be absent from the body, " and present with the Lord."

It is not every Christian that can arrive to this degree of love, though they love Christ sincerely, yet they shrink from death cowardly, and are loth to be gone. There are two sorts of grounds upon which Christians may be loth to be unbodied;

1. Sinful.   2. Allowable.

1. The sinful and unjustifiable grounds are such as these, viz. (1.) Guilt upon the conscience, which will damp and discourage the soul, and make it loth to die. It arms death with terror, " the sting of death is sin." (2.) Unmortified affections to the world, I mean in such a degree as is necessary to sweeten death, and make a man a volunteer in that sharp engagement with that last and dreadful enemy. It is with our hearts as with fuel; if green, and full of sap, it will not burn; but if that be dried up, it catches presently. Mortification is the drying up of carnal affections to the creature, which is that which resists death, as green wood doth the fire. (3.) The weakness and cloudiness of faith. You need faith to die by, as well as live by. Heb. xi. 13. *All these died in faith.* The less strength there is in faith, the more in death. A strong believer welcomes the messengers of death, when a weak one, unless extraordinarily assisted, trembles at them.

2. There are grounds on which we may desire a longer conti-

nuance in the body, warrantably and allowably: As (1.) to do him yet more service in our bodies, before we lay them down. Thus the saints have pleaded for longer life, Psal. xxx. 9. Psal. lxxxviii. 11, 12, 13. and Isa. xxxviii. 18, 19. (2.) To see the clouds of God's anger dispelled, whether public or personal, and a clear light break out e'er we die; Psal. xxvii. 13. (3.) They may desire, with submission, to out-live the days of persecution, and not to be delivered into the hands of cruel men, but come to their graves in peace, Psal. xxxi. 15. and 2 Thess. iii. 2. that they may be delivered from absurd men.

3. But though some Christians shun death upon a sinful account, and others upon a justifiable one; yet others there be, who seeing their title clear, their work done, and relishing the joys of heaven, in the prelibations of faith, are willing to be unclothed, and to be with Christ. Their love to Christ hath extinguished in them the love of life; and they can say with Paul, Acts xxi. 13. *I am ready.* Ignatius longed to come to those beasts that were to devour him; and so many of the primitive Christians: Christ was so dear, that their lives were cheap, and low-prized things for this enjoyment. And here indeed is the glory and triumph of a Christian's faith and love to Christ: For (1.) it enables him to part cheerfully with what he sees and feels, for what his eyes never yet saw, 1 Pet. i. 8. " Whom having not seen, ye love." (2.) To part with what is dearest on earth, and lies nearest the heart of all he enjoys for Christ's sake. (3.) To reconcile his heart to what is most abhorrent and formidable to nature. (4.) To endure the greatest of pains and torments to be with him. (5.) To cast himself into the vast ocean of eternity, the most amazing change, to be with Christ, O the glorious conquests of love !

Inf. 2. *Then the apostasy of unregenerate professors in times of imminent danger, is not to be wondered at.* They will, and must warp from Christ, when their lives are in hazard for him. The love of the body will certainly prevail over their love to Christ and religion. *Amor meus pondus meum.* Self-love will now draw. Love is the weight of the soul, which inclines and determines it, in the competition of interests, and the predominant interest always carries it. Every unregenerate professor loves his own life more than Christ, prefers his body before his soul; such an one may, upon divers accounts, as education, example, slight convictions of conscience, or ostentation of gifts, fall into a profession of religion, and continue a long time in that profession, before he visibly recede from Christ; *hope* of the resurrection of the interest of religion in the world; *shame* of retracting his profession; *applause* of his zeal and constancy in higher trials, the peace of his own conscience, and many such motives, may prevail with a carnal professor to endure a while: but, when dangers of life come to an height, they are gone, Matth. xxiv. 8, 9, 10. And therefore, our Lord tells us, that they " who hate not their lives, cannot be his disciples," Luke xii. 26. Now will they lose their lives by saving them, Matth. xvi. 25. and the reasons are plain and forcible: For,

1. Now is the proper season for the predominant love to be discovered, it can be hid no longer: and the love of life is the predominant love in all such persons; for do but compare it with their love to Christ, and it will easily be found so. They love their lives truly and really, they love Christ but feignedly and pretendedly; and the real will, and must prevail over the feigned love. They love their lives fervently and intensely, they love Christ but coldly and remissly: And the fervent love will prevail over the remiss love. Their love to their bodies hath a root in themselves, their love to Christ hath no root in themselves, Matth. xiii. 21. And that which hath a root must needs out-last and out-live that which hath none.

2. Because when life is in hazard, conscience will work in them by way of discouragement; it will hint the danger of their eternal state to them, and tell them they may cast away their souls for ever in a bravado; for though the cause they are called to suffer for be good, yet their condition is bad; and if the condition be not good as well as the cause, a man is lost for ever, though he suffer for it, 1 Cor. xiii. 3. Conscience, which encourages and supports the upright, will discourage and daunt the hypocrite, and tell him, he is not on the same terms in sufferings that other men are.

3. Because then all the springs by which their profession was fed and maintained, fail and dry up. Now the wind that was in their backs is come about, and blows a storm in their faces; there are no preferments nor honours now to be had from religion. These men's sufferings are a perfect surprize to them, for they never counted the cost, Luke xiv. 28. Now they must stand alone, and resist unto blood, and sacrifice all visibles for invisibles; and this they can never do.

O therefore, professors, look to your hearts, try their predominant love; compare your love to Christ with that to your lives. Now the like question will be put to you, that once was put to Peter, John xxi. 15. " Lovest thou me more than these?" What say you to this? You think now you do, but alas your love is not yet brought to the fire to be tried: you think you hate sin, but will you be able to strive unto blood against sin? Heb. xii. 4. Will you choose suffering rather than sin? Job xxvi. 21. O try your love to Christ, before God bring it to the trial. Sure I am, the love of life will make you warp in the hour of temptation; except,

1. You sat down and counted the cost of religion before-hand: if you set out in procession only for a walk, not for a journey? If you go to sea for recreation, not for a voyage; if you be mounted among other processors, only to take the air, and not to engage an enemy in sharp and bloody encounters, you are gone.

2. Except you live by faith, and not by sense, 2 Cor. iv. 18. " Whilst we look not at the things that are seen." You must balance present sufferings with future glory. You must go by that account and reckoning, Rom. viii. 18. or you are gone. " Now " the just shall live by faith;" and if faith do not support, your fears will certainly sink you.

3. Except you be sincere and plain-hearted in religion, driving no design in it but to save your souls; you may see your lot in that example, 2 Tim. iv. 10. " Demas hath forsaken me." O take heed of a cunning, deceitful, double heart in religion; be plain, be open, care not if your ends lie open to the eyes of all the world.

4. Except you experience the power of religion in your own souls, as well as wear the name of it. O my brethren, it is not a name to live that will do you service now. Many ships are gone down to the bottom, for all the brave names of the *Success*, the *Prosperous*, the *Happy Return*, and so will you. There is a knowing of ourselves by taste and real experience, Heb. x. 34. which doth a soul more service in a suffering hour, than all the splendid names and titles in the world.

5. Except you make it your daily work to crucify the flesh, deny self for Christ, in all the forms and interests of it. He that cannot deny himself, will deny Jesus Christ, Matth. xvi. 24. " Let him deny himself, take up his cross, and follow me," else he cannot be my disciple. Ponder these things in your hearts, whilst yet God delays the trial.

Inf. 3. If the souls of men be naturally so strongly inclined and affected towards the body; *Then hence you may plainly see the wisdom of God in all the afflictions and burdens he lays upon his people in this world, and find that all is but enough to wean off their souls from their bodies, and make them willing to part with them.*

The life of the saints in this world, is generally a burdened and a groaning life; 2 Cor. v. 2. " In this tabernacle we groan, being " burdened." Here the saints feel, (1.) A burden of sin, Rom. vii. 24. this is a dead and a sinking weight. (2.) A burden of affliction; of this all are partakers, Heb. xii. though not all in an equal degree, or in the same kind, yet all have their burdens equal to, and even beyond their own strength to support it; 2 Cor. i 8. " pressed above measure." (3.) A burden of inward troubles

for sin, and outward troubles in the flesh both together, so had Job,
Heman, David, and many of the saints.

Certainly this befals them not, (1.) Casually, Job v. 6. " It
" rises not out of the dust :" (2.) Nor because God loves and
regards them not, for they are fruits of his love; Heb. xii. 6.
" Whom he loveth he correcteth :" (3.) Nor because he takes
pleasure in their groans; Lam. iii. 34. " To tread under his feet
" the prisoners of the earth,—the Lord hath no pleasure :" it
is not for his own pleasure, but his children's profit, Heb. xii. 10.
And among the profits that result from these burdens, this is not
the least, to make you less fond of the body than you would else
be, and more willing to be gone to your everlasting rest. And certainly all the diseases and pains we endure in the body, whether
they be upon inward or outward accounts, by passion or compassion from God or men, will be found but enough to wean us,
and loose off our hearts from the fond love of life. Afflictions are
bitter things to our taste, Ruth i. 20. so bitter, that Naomi thought
a name of a contrary signification fitter for her afflicted condition:
call me *Marah*, i. e. bitter, not *Naomi*, pleasant, beautiful. And
the church, Lam. iii. 9. calls them wormwood and gall.

The great design of God in afflicting them, is the same that a
tender mother projects in putting wormwood to her breast when
she would wean the child.

It hath been observed by some discreet and grave ministers, that
before their removal from one place to another, God hath permitted and ordered some weaning providence to befal them; either
denying wonted success to their labour, or alienating and cooling
the affections of their people towards them, which not only makes
the manner of their departure more easy, but the grounds of it
more clear. Much so it falls out in our natural death, the comfort of the world is imbittered to us before we leave it; the longer
we live in it, the less we shall like it. We over-live most of our
comforts which engaged our hearts to it, that we may more freely
take our leave of it. It were good for Christians to observe the
voice of such providences as these, and answer the designs of them
in a greater willingness to die.

1. Is thy body which was once hale and vigorous, now become
a crazy, sickly, pained body to thee, neither useful to God, nor
comfortable to thee ? a tabernacle to groan and sigh in ; and little
hopes it will be recovered to a better temper; God hath ordained
this to make thee willing to be divorced from it: the less desirable
life is, the less formidable death will be.

2. Is thy estate decayed and blasted by providence, so that thy
life which was once full of creature-comforts, is now filled with
cares and anxieties ? O it is a weaning providence to thee, and

bespeaks thee the more cheerfully to bid the world farewell. The less comfort it gives you, the less it shall entangle and engage you. We little know with what aching hearts, and pensive breasts, many of God's people walk up and down, though for religion, or reputation sake, they put a good face upon it; but by these things, God is bespeaking and preparing them for a better state.

3. Is an husband, a wife, or dear children dead, and with them the comfort of life laid in the dust? why this the Lord sees necessary to do to persuade you to come after willingly? It is the cutting asunder thy roots in the earth, that thou mayest fall the more easily. O how many strokes must God give at our names, estates, relations, and health, before we will give way to the last stroke of death that fells us to the ground?

4. Do the times frown upon religion? Do all things seem to threaten stormy times at hand? Are desirable assemblies scattered? nothing but sorrows and sufferings to be expected in this world? by these things God will imbitter the earth, and sweeten heaven to his people.

5. Is the beauty and sweetness of Christian society defaced and decayed? Is that communion which was wont to be pithy, substantial, spiritual, and edifying, become either frothy or contentious, so that thy soul has no pleasure in it? this also is a weaning providence to our souls: Strigelius desired to die that he might be freed *ab implacabilibus theologorum odiis*, from the wranglings and contentions that were in his time. Our fond affection to the body requires all this and much more to wean and mortify them.

Inf. 4. *How comfortable is the doctrine of the resurrection to believers, which assures them of receiving their bodies again, though they part with them for a time!*

Believers must die as well as others; their union with Christ privileges them not from a separation from their bodies, Rom. viii. 10. Heb. ix. 27. But yet they have special grounds of consolation against this doleful separation above all others. For,

1. Though they part with them, yet they part in hopes of receiving them again, 1 Thes. iv. 13, 14. They take not a final leave of them when they die. Husbandmen cast their seed-corn into the earth cheerfully and willingly, because they part with it in hope; so should we, when we commit our bodies to the earth at death.

2. Though death separates these dear friends from each other, yet it cannot separate either the one or other from Christ, Luke xx. 37, 38. " I am the God of Abraham," &c. Your very dust is the Lord's, and the grave rots not the bond of the covenant.

3. The very same body we lay down at death, we shall assume again at the resurrection; not only the same specifical, but the

same numerical body; Job xix. 25, 26. "With these eyes shall I " see God."

4. The unbodied soul shall not find the want of its body, so as to afflict or disquiet it; nor the body the want of its soul; but the one shall be at rest in heaven, and the other sweetly asleep in the grave; and all that long interval shall slide away without any afflicting sense of each others absence. The time will be long, Job xiv. 12. but if it were longer, it cannot be afflicting, considering how the soul is clothed immediately, 2 Cor. v. 1, 2. and how the body sleeps sweetly in Jesus, 1 Thes. iv. 14.

5. When the day of their re-espousals is come, the soul will find the body so transformed and improved, that it shall never receive prejudice from it any more, but a singular addition to its happiness and glory. Now it clogs us: Matt. xxvi. 41. "The spirit indeed " is willing, but the flesh is weak." It encumbers us with cares to provide for it, and eats up time and thoughts; but then it will be a spiritual body, 1 Cor. xv. 43. like to the angels for manner of subsistence, Luke xx. 35, 36. 1 Cor. vi. 13. and, which is the highest step of glory, like unto Christ's glorious body, Phil. iii. 21. Well therefore might the father say, *Resurrectio mortuorem est consolatio Christianorum;* the resurrection of the dead is the consolation of Christians.

Use second, of reproof.

In the next place, let me press you to regulate your love to your bodies, by the rules of religion and right reason. I must press you to love them, though nature itself teacheth you so to do; but I press you to love them as Christians, as men that understand the right use and improvement of their bodies. There are two sorts of errors in our love to the body, one in defect, the other in excess; both come fitly here to be censured and healed.

First, Some offend in the defect of love to their own bodies, who use them as if they had no love for them, whose souls act as if they were enemies to their own bodies; they do not formally and directly hate them, but consequentially and eventually they may be said to hate them, and that,

(1.) By defiling them with filthy lusts; so the apostle speaks, 1 Cor. vi. 18. "Every sin that a man doth, is without the body, but " he that committeth adultery sinneth against his own body:" In other sins it is the instrument, but here it is both instrument and object; not only God, but your own bodies are abused and wronged by it. The body may be considered two ways, Either,

1. As our vessel; or
2. As the Spirit's temple.

1. As our vessel or instrument for natural and spiritual uses and services: and on that account we should not injure or defile it, 1

Thess. iv. 4, 5. but possess it in sanctification and honour. The lusts of uncleanness, gluttony, and drunkenness, quench the vigour, blast the beauty, and destroy the health and honour of the body; and so render it both naturally and morally unfit for the service and use of the soul.

2. And the injury is yet greater, if we consider it as the Spirit's temple. On this ground the apostle strongly convinceth and dissuadeth Christians from these abuses of the body, 1 Cor. vi. 15, 16. He argues from the dignity God will put upon our bodies by the resurrection, ver. 13, 14. They are to be transformed, and made like unto Christ's glorious body; and from the honour he has already put upon the bodies of the saints in their union with Christ, ver. 15, 16. They, as well as the soul, are ingrafted into him, and joined with him; they are his temples, to be dedicated, hallowed, and consecrated to his service. O let them not be made a sink for lusts, or mere strangers for meat and drink.

(2.) By macerating them with covetous lusts, denying them their due comforts and refreshments, and unmercifully burdening them with labours and sorrows about things that perish. (1.) Some deny their bodies due comforts and refreshments, which the natural and positive laws of God both allow and command. Their souls are cruel step-mothers to their bodies, and keep them too short; not out of a prudent and Christian design to starve their lusts, but to advance their estates. Of this Solomon speaks, Eccl. vi. 22. " There is an evil which I have seen under the sun, and " it is common among men; A man to whom God hath given " riches, wealth and honour, so that he wanteth nothing for his " soul of all that he desireth; yet God giveth him not power to " eat thereof, but a stranger eateth it. This is vanity, and it is " an evil disease." *Tenacity* is a disease of the soul, like that of a *dyscrasy* in the stomach, which so indisposeth it that it cannot receive with any appetite or delight the best refreshments at a plentiful table. (2.) And others there are that wrong and abuse their own bodies, by laying unreasonable and unmerciful loads upon them, especially loads of grief and sorrow, wasting and weakening them beyond all rules of reason or religion. If a friend or relation die, they have less mercy on their own bodies than a conscientious man hath on the horse he rides. Cares and sorrows are as deadly to the body as a sword, 1 Tim. vi. 10. Intense and immoderate griefs about worldly losses and crosses have slain their ten thousands; and, which is strange, the soul seems to take a certain kind of pleasure in loading and tormenting the body. There is a real truth in that strange expression of * Seneca, " Sorrow itself hath a " certain kind of pleasure attending it."

---

* *Inest quiddam dulce tristitiæ.* Eph. 806.

The souls of some mourners do willingly excite and provoke their own grief, when they begin to abate, which is like the whetting of the knife that grows dull, to make it cut the deeper into the body. Thus, as † Seneca observes, "some parents that have " lost their beloved children, willingly call to mind their pleasant " sayings, and pretty actions to find a kind of pleasure in a fresh " shower of tears for them;" when, poor hearts! sorrow hath so broken them already, that they need consolations under their pre‑ sent sorrows, rather than irritations of new ones. And the soul's unmercifulness to the body, is in such causes farther discovered by its obstinate refusal of all that is comforting and relieving. So it is said of Rachel, Jer. xxxi. 15. "Rachel weeping for her children, " would not be comforted, because they were not." So the Israelites hearkened not unto Moses, because of the anguish of spirit, and the cruel bondage, Exod. vi. 9. Thus we studiously rake together and exasperate whatsoever is piercing, wounding, and overwhelming; and shut our ears to all that is relieving and supporting, which is cruelty to our own bodies, and that which hath so far broken the health and strength of some bodies, that they are never like to be useful instruments to the soul any more in this world; such deep and desperate wounds have their own souls given them by immoderate grief, as will never be perfectly healed, but by the resurrection. Of those wounds the body may say, as it is Zech. xiii. 6. These are the wounds "with which I " was wounded in the house (or by the hand) of my friend;" thus my own soul hath dealt cruelly and unmercifully with me.

Secondly, Others offend in the excess and extravagancy of their love to the body, and these are a hundred to one in number com‑ pared with those that sin in defect of love. My friends, upon a due search, it will be found, that the love of our souls generally degene‑ rates into fondness and folly: there is but little well-tempered and ordinary love found among men. We make fondlings, yea, we make idols of our bodies; we rob God, yea, our own souls, to give to the body. It is not a natural and kindly heat of love, but a mere feverish heat, which preys upon the very spirits of religion, which is found with many of us. The feverish distemper may be discovered, by the beating of our pulse, in three or four particulars.

(1.) This appears by our sinful indulgence to our whining ap‑ petites. We give the flesh whatsoever it craves, and can deny it nothing it desires; pampering the body, to the great injury and hazard of the soul. Some have their conversation in the lusts of the flesh, as it is, Eph. ii. 3. trading only in those things that please

---

† *Cum occurrant sermones eorum jucundi, conversatio hilaris officiosa pietas : tunc oculi velut in gaudio relaxantur.* Id. ib.

and pamper the flesh; "They sow to the flesh," Gal. vi. 8. i. e. all their studies and labours are but the *sowing of the seeds of pleasure to the flesh*. Not a handful of spiritual seed sown in prayer for the soul all the day long: what the body craves, the obsequious soul like a slave, is at its beck to give it; Tit. iii. 3. "Serving divers lusts and pleasures;" attending to every knock and call, to fulfil the desires of the flesh. O how little do these men understand the life of religion, or the great design of Christianity! which consists in mortifying, and not pampering and gratifying the body, Rom. xiv. 13, 14. And according to that rule, all serious Christians order their bodies, giving them what is needful to keep them serviceable and useful to the soul, but not gratifying their irregular desires; giving what their wants, not what their wantonness calls for. So Paul, 1 Cor. ix. 27. "I beat it down, and keep it "under;" he understood it as his servant, not his master. He knew that Hagar would quickly perk up, and domineer over Sarah, expect more attendance than the soul, except it were kept under: these two verbs, υπωπιαζω and δελαγωγω, are very emphatical; the former signifies to make it black and blue with buffeting, the other to bring it under by checks and rebukes, as masters that understand their place and authority use to do with insolent and wanton servants.

It was a rare expression of a Heathen, *Major sum, et ad majora natus, quam ut corporis mei sim mancipium;* I am greater, and born to greater things, than that I should be a slave to my body. And it was the saying of a pious divine, when he felt the flesh rebellious and wanton, *Ego faciam, aselle, ut ne calcitres;* I will make thee, thou ass, that thou shalt not kick. I know the superstitious Papists place much of religion in these external things, but though they abuse them to an ill purpose, there is a necessary and lawful use of these abridgments and restraints upon the body; and it will be impossible to mortify and starve our lusts without a due rigour and severity to our flesh. But how little are many acquainted with these things? They deal with their bodies as David with Adonijah, of whom it is said, 1 Kings i. 6. His father had not displeased him at any time, in saying, Why hast thou done so? And just so our flesh requites us, by its rebellions and treasons against the soul; it seeks the life of the soul, which seeks nothing more than its content and pleasure; this is not ordinate love, but fondness and folly, and what we shall bitterly repent for at last.

(2.) It appears by our sparing and favouring of them, in the necessary uses and services we have for them in religion. Many will rather starve their souls, than work and exercise their bodies, or disturb their sluggish rest: thus the idle excuses and pretences of endangering our health, oftentimes put by the duties of religion,

or, at least, lose the fittest and properest seasons for them : we are
lazying upon our beds, when we should be wrestling upon our
knees : the world is suffered to get the start of religion in the
morning, and so religion is never able to overtake it all the day
long.   This was none of David's courses, he prevented the dawning of the morning, and cried, Psal. cxix. 147. and Psal. v. 3.
" My voice shalt thou hear in the morning, O Lord, in the morn-
" ing will I direct my prayers unto thee, and will look up."   And
indeed we should consecrate unto God the freshest and fittest parts
of our time, when our bodily senses are most vigorous ; and we
would do so, (except God by his providence disable us) were our
hearts fully set for God, and religion lay with weight upon our
spirits.

Some, I confess, cannot receive this injunction, being naturally
disabled by prevailing infirmities ; but those who can, ought to do
so.   But oh, how many slothful excuses doth the flesh invent to
put off duty ! We shall injure our health, &c.   O the hypocrisy of
such pleas ! If profit or pleasure calls us up, we have no shifts, but
can rise early and sit up late.

O, friends, why hath God given you bodies, if not to waste and
wear them out in his service, and the service of your own souls !
If your bodies must not be put to it, and exercised this way, where
is the mercy of having a body ? If a stately horse were given you
on this condition, that you must not ride or work him, what benefit would such a gift be to you ? Your bodies, must and will wear
out, and it is better to wear them with working, than with rusting :
we are generally more solicitous to live long than to live usefully
and serviceably ; and it may be our health had been more precious
in the eyes of God, if it had been less precious in our own eyes.
It is just with God to destroy that health with diseases, which he
sees we would cast away in sloth and idleness.   Think with thyself,
had such a soul as Timothy's or Gaius's been blest with such a body
as thine, so strong and vigorous, so apt and able for service, they
would have honoured God more in it in a day, than perhaps you do
in a year.   Certainly this is not love, but laziness ; not a due improvement, but a sinful neglect and abuse of the body, to let it rust
out into idleness, which might be employed so many ways for God,
for your own and others souls.   Well, remember death will
shortly dissolve them, and then they can be of no more use ; and
if you expect God should put glory and honour upon them at the
resurrection, use them for God now, with a faithful, self-denying
diligence.

(3.) It appears by our cowardly shrinking from dangers that
threaten them, when the glory of God, our own and others salvation, bid us expose and not regard them.   Some there are, that

rather than they will adventure their flesh to the rage of man, will hazard their souls to the wrath of God *. They are too tender to suffer pain or restraints for Christ, but consider not what sufferings are prepared for the fearful and unbelieving in the world to come, Rev. xxi. 8. How many sad examples do the church-histories of ancient and latter times afford us, of men, who, consulting with flesh and blood in time of danger, have, in pity to their bodies, ruined their souls!

There be but few like-minded with Paul, who set a low price upon his liberty or life for Christ, Acts xx. 24. or with those worthy Jews, Dan. iii. 28. who yielded their bodies to preserve their consciences. Few of Chrysostom's mind, who told the empress, *Nil nisi peccatum timeo,* I fear nothing but sin; or of Basil's, who told the emperor, God threatened hell, whereas he threatened but a prison. That is a remarkable rule that Christ gives us, Mat. x. 28. The sum of it is, to set God against man, the soul against the body, and hell against temporal sufferings; and so surmounting these low fleshly considerations, to cleave to our duty in the face of dangers. You read, Gal. i. 16. how in pursuit of duty, though surrounded with danger, Paul would not confer, or *consult with flesh and blood,* i. e. ask its opinion which were best, or stay for its consent, till it were willing to suffer; he understood not that the flesh had any voice at the council-table in his soul, but willing or unwilling, if duty call for it, he was resolved to hazard it for God.

We have a great many little politicians among us, who think to husband their lives and liberties a great deal better than other plain-hearted, and too forward Christians do: but these politics will be their perdition, and their craft will betray them to ruin. They will lose their lives by saving them, when others will save them by losing them, Mat. x. 39. For the interest of the body depends on, and follows the safety of the soul, as the cabin doth the ship.

O my friends, let me beg you not to love your bodies into hell, and your souls too for their sakes: be not so scared at the sufferings of the body, as, with poor Spira, to dash them both against the wrath of the great and terrible God. Most of those souls that are now in hell, are there upon the account of their indulgence to the flesh, they could not deny the flesh, and now are denied by God. They could not suffer from men, and now must suffer the vengeance of eternal fire.

---

* Here the soul receives a deadly wound upon itself, to ward it off from the body. So did Spira.

(4.) In a word; it appears we love them fondly and irregularly, in that we cannot with any patience think of death and separation from them. How do some men fright at the very name of death! And no arguments can persuade them seriously to think of an unbodied, and separated state. It is as death to them, to bring their thoughts close to that ungrateful subject. A Christian that loves his body regularly and moderately, can look into his own grave with a composed mind, and speak familiarly of it, as Job xvii. 14. And Peter speaks of the putting off of his body by death, as a man would of the putting off of his clothes at night, 2 Pet. i. 13, 14. And certainly such men have a great advantage above all others, both as to the tranquillity of their life and death. You know a parting time must come, and the more fond you are of them, the more bitter and doleful that time will be. Nothing, except the guilt and terrible charges of conscience, puts men into terrors at death, more than our fondness of the body. I do confess, christless persons have a great deal of reason to be shy of death; their dying day is their undoing day: but for Christians to startle and fright at it, is strange, considering how great a friend death will be to them that are in Christ. What are you afraid of? What, to go to Christ? to be freed of sin and affliction too soon? Certainly this hath not been so comfortable a habitation to you, that you should be loth to change it for a heavenly one.

Use third, of exhortation.

To conclude; Seeing there is so strict a friendship and tender affection betwixt soul and body, let me persuade every soul of you to express your love to the body, by labouring to get union with Jesus Christ, and thereby to prevent the utter ruin of both to all eternity.

Souls, if you love yourselves, or the bodies you dwell in, shew it by your preventing care in season, lest they be cast away for ever. How can you say you love them, when you daily expose them to the everlasting wrath of God, by employing them as weapons of unrighteousness, to fight against him that formed them? You feed and pamper them on earth, you give them all the delight and pleasure you can procure for them in this world; but you take no care what shall become of them, nor your souls neither, after death hath separated them. Oh cruel souls! cruel, not to others, but to yourselves, and to your own flesh, which you pretend so much love to! Is this your love to your bodies? What, to employ them in Satan's service on earth, and then to be cast as a prey to him for ever in hell? You think the rigour and mortification of the saints, their abstemiousness and self-denial, their cares, fears, and diligence, to be too great severity to their bodies: but they know these are the most real evidences of their true love to them;

they love them too well to cast them away as you do. Alas! your love to the body doth not consist in feeding, and clothing, and pleasing it; but in getting it united to Christ, and made the *temple of the Holy Ghost:* in using it for God, and dedicating it to God.

I beseech you, brethren, by the mercies of God, to present your bodies living sacrifices to God, which is your reasonable service, Rom. xii. 1. The soul should look upon the body as a wise parent upon a rebellious or wanton child, that would, if left to itself, quickly bring itself to the gallows; the father looks on him with compassion and melting bowels, and saith, with the rod in his hand, and tears in his eyes, " My child, my naughty, disobedient, " headstrong child, I resolve to chastise thee severely. I love thee " too well to suffer thee to be ruined, if my care or correction may " prevent it." So should our souls evidence their love to and care over their own rebellious flesh. · It is cruelty, not love or pity, to indulge them to their own destruction.

Except you have gracious souls, you shall never have glorified bodies: except your souls be united with Christ, the happiness of your bodies, as well as your souls is lost to all eternity. Know you not that the everlasting condition of your bodies follows and depends on the interest your souls now get in Christ? Oh that this sad truth might sink deep into all our considerations this day; that if your bodies be snares to your souls, and your souls be now regardless of the future state of themselves, and them; assuredly they will have a bitter parting at death, a terrible meeting again at the resurrection, and horrid reflections upon each other, naturally charging their ruin upon each other to all eternity. Whilst they that are in Christ, part in hope, meet with joy, and bless God for each other for evermore.

THE END OF THE SECOND VOLUME.